CICERO'S LETTERS TO HIS FRIENDS

AMERICAN PHILOLOGICAL ASSOCIATION

CLASSICAL RESOURCES SERIES

John T. Ramsey, Series Editor

NUMBER 1
CICERO'S LETTERS TO HIS FRIENDS

Translated by
D.R. Shackleton Bailey

CICERO'S LETTERS TO HIS FRIENDS

Translated by
D.R. Shackleton Bailey

Foreword by
James E.G. Zetzel

Scholars Press
Atlanta, Georgia

CICERO'S LETTERS TO HIS FRIENDS

Translated by
D.R. Shackleton Bailey

Reprinted with corrections and a new foreword by permission of Penguin Books, Ltd.

Scholars Press edition 1988

The cover shows folio 8 of Mediceus 49.9 (9th-10th cent.) containing the conclusion of *Ad Fam.* I.7 (= letter 18 in this translation) and the opening of I.8 (= letter 19); reproduced by permission of the Laurentian Library.

Library of Congress Cataloging in Publication Data
Cicero, Marcus Tullius.
Cicero's letters to his friends.

(Classical resources series / American Philological Association ; no. 1)
Reprint. Originally published: Harmondsworth, Eng. ; New York : Penguin Books, 1978.
1. Cicero, Marcus Tullius--Correspondence.
2. Authors, Latin--Correspondence. 3. Statesmen--Rome--Correspondence. I. Bailey, D.R. Shackleton (David Roy Shackleton), 1917- . II. Title.
III. Series: Classical resources series ; no. 1.
PA6308.E5B34 1988 937'.05'0924 [B] 88-38017
ISBN 978-1-55540-264-8 (pbk.)

CONTENTS

FOREWORD

Cicero's Letters to his Friends inaugurates a new series of publications sponsored by the American Philological Association under the rubric "Classical Resources" and supervised by the Editorial Board for Textbooks. Our goal in this series is to make available at a reasonable price works that will be of interest to a wider audience than we presently serve. It will include important translations, such as the present volume; it may also include books designed for use in courses in ancient literature, civilization, history, or law.

In 1978 D. R. Shackleton Bailey's translations of Cicero's letters were published by Penguin books under two titles. *Cicero's Letters to Atticus* incorporated in a single volume the translation which had previously appeared in Professor Shackleton Bailey's seven-volume edition of the Latin text with translation and commentary published by Cambridge University Press (1965–70). *Cicero's Letters to his Friends,* in two volumes, included not only the *Epistulae ad Familiares,* but also the *Epistulae ad Quintum Fratrem* and *Epistulae ad M. Brutum,* thus serving as a complement to the author's editions of the Latin text with commentary, but without translation, published by Cambridge University Press in 1977 and 1980, and still in print. These three volumes have now been replaced in the Penguin series by a single selection, *Cicero, Selected Letters* (1982). Both Professor Shackleton Bailey and Professor John Ramsey of the APA Editorial Board for Textbooks felt that it was particularly unfortunate to allow the complete translation of *Cicero's Letters to his Friends* to disappear; unlike the translation of *Letters to Atticus,* it is not otherwise available. We are grateful to Penguin Books for permission to reprint this work.

This translation is, of course, only one of Professor Shackleton Bailey's services to Latin literature and to Ciceronian studies in particular. His editions with commentary of the entire collection of Cicero's correspondence have been mentioned above: *Letters to Atticus* was followed by *Epistulae ad Familiares* (which received the Goodwin Award of Merit from the American Philological Association in 1978) and *Epistulae ad Quintum Fratrem et M. Brutum.* For this edition of Cicero's entire surviving correspondence he received the Kenyon Medal of the British Academy for 1985. He has since published an edition with commentary of *Select Letters* (Cambridge University Press, 1980), a new Teubner edition of Cicero's letters in four volumes (1987–88), and an edition with translation of the *Philippics* (University of North Carolina, 1986), as well as three volumes of textual and historical studies of Cicero: *Towards a Text of Cicero Ad Atticum* (Cambridge University Press, 1959), *Two Studies in Roman Nomenclature* (APA American Classical Studies, 1976), and *An Onomasticon to Cicero's Speeches* (University of Oklahoma Press, 1988), not to mention his biography of Cicero (Duckworth, 1971). This list does not even touch on his books and articles on other Latin authors. We are proud to have *Cicero's Letters to his Friends* inaugurate our new series.

The immense surviving corpus of Cicero's own writings, above all his correspondence, is of paramount importance for our knowledge of the last decades of the Roman republic in general, and of the character and actions of Cicero himself in particular. Two large collections of Cicero's letters survive, as well as two smaller ones. The sixteen books of letters to Atticus are not included in this volume, but the other three are: more than 400 letters to friends, including letters and documents sent to Cicero; 27 letters to Cicero's younger brother Quintus; and 26 letters to and from Marcus Brutus. The earliest letters in this volume were written in 62 B.C., shortly after the end of Cicero's consulate; the latest in the summer of 43, just a few months before Cicero's death in December.

Cicero's biography has often been written and need not be repeated here in any detail. Clear and brief accounts may be found in Shackleton Bailey's introductions to the Penguin *Selected Letters* and to the Cambridge University Press *Select Letters;* additional suggestions may be found in the Bibliographical Note following the introduction. The letters in this volume were all composed after the moment which Cicero himself considered the zenith of his career, his triumphant exposure and defeat, as consul in 63 B.C., of the conspiracy of Catiline. The Tullii Cicerones were one of the leading families of the town of Arpinum, about seventy miles southeast of Rome, and they had important associations with the nobility of Rome itself. Cicero came to Rome for his education, and rose rapidly as a result of his political connections and oratorical skill; he was the first "new man" in a generation to reach the consulate, and he reached it at the earliest possible age. Thereafter, however, his political career foundered. Exiled in 58 through the enmity of Publius Clodius and the acquiescence of Pompey for having put Catiline's fellow-conspirators to death without trial in 63, he was ineffective even after his triumphant recall in the following year. His attempt in 56 to reestablish political independence failed; he was compelled to deliver what he called a "palinode" at the insistence of Caesar, Pompey, and Crassus, the members of the so-called First Triumvirate.

But while the period after Cicero's recall from exile was one of political frustration, it was also the time of his greatest achievement as a writer. In these years he delivered a series of oratorical masterpieces including the *Pro Sestio, Pro Caelio,* and *In Pisonem;* he also wrote the dialogues *On the Orator* and *On the Commonwealth,* and his surviving correspondence is more prolific and elaborate. The most memorable and extensive parts of the *Letters to his Friends* come from the last decade of Cicero's life, beginning with the correspondence with Gaius Trebatius in 54 and 53 (letters 27–39). In the years from his reluctant departure for the governorship of Cilicia in 51 down to the assassination of Julius Caesar in 44, Cicero found little pleasure in either public life or in his own family. His brief and hesitant participation on the Pompeian side of the Civil War during 49–48, his enforced stay at Brundisium in 47, and his return to a Rome in which he had no political place at all were accompanied by bitter quarrels with his brother Quintus, two divorces in rapid succession, financial difficulties, and, above all, the death in 45 of his beloved daughter Tullia. Cicero took refuge from these personal and public disasters in writing, both philosophical treatises and letters, and the correspondence to and from his friends and political associates is both fascinating and moving.

The last stage of Cicero's life began with the assassination of Julius Caesar on the Ides of March, 44 B.C. Cicero played no part in this event, but was delighted by it; and although he hesitated for some months before re-entering active politics, he began in September the series of attacks on Antony known as the *Philippics,* and he took a leading role in directing senatorial policy in the hope of restoring the republican constitution. His correspondence in the *Letters to his Friends* with the leaders of the numerous factions is copious and of immense historical value; among the latest surviving letters are those to and from M. Brutus, in the spring and summer of 43. Cicero's policies in this period seem—at least through hindsight—to have been both naive and ill-conceived; his violent opposition to Antony was one of the reasons for the formation of the Second Triumvirate of Antony, Octavian, and Lepidus in November 43, and Cicero was himself one of the first to be proscribed by triumvirs. He was killed on December 7, 43, and his head and hands were placed on the rostra in Rome.

Cicero's reputation has varied greatly over the centuries; both his political career and his prose style have been praised and condemned with equal fervor. But whatever one's opinion of Cicero, his correspondence remains unique and invaluable. It not only reveals the complexity of Cicero's own character, but affords vivid glimpses of the leading political and intellectual figures of the late Republic and reveals the day-to-day concerns of public and private life. Shackleton Bailey's lucid and accurate translation makes the world of Cicero and his contemporaries accessible to the modern reader.

James E. G. Zetzel
Vice-President for Publications
American Philological Association

INTRODUCTION

THE collection of Cicero's 'Letters to Friends' (*Epistulae ad Familiares*) did not originally appear as such. Our manuscripts have it in sixteen 'Books'. Some of these consist entirely or mainly of letters to or from a single correspondent: Lentulus Spinther in 'Book' I, Appius Claudius Pulcher in 'Book' III, Caelius in 'Book' VIII, Terentia in 'Book' XIV, Tiro in 'Book' XVI. 'Book' XIII consists of letters of recommendation, 'Books' X–XII of correspondence relating to the struggle with Antony in 44–43. The other 'Books' show more or less of internal cohesion. The evidence suggests that they were arranged and published separately or in groups during the Augustan period by a single editor, who was in all probability Cicero's faithful secretary, Tiro; he is also likely to have produced the now lost collections of letters to individual correspondents other than Atticus known to have existed in antiquity, Caesar, Pompey, Octavian and others, as well as those surviving to Quintus Cicero and Marcus Brutus. At what time the collection of sixteen 'Books' came into being is unknown. The title 'Letters to Friends' seems to be no older than the Renaissance.

The 'friends' are a motley group. Some of them, as Trebatius Testa, Caelius, and Papirius Paetus, really were familiars, to whom Cicero could write as informally, though not as intimately, as to Atticus or to his brother. With powerful aristocrats like Cato, Lentulus Spinther, and Appius Pulcher he was on no such easy footing, and his letters to them are in as elaborate a style as his published works. The high sentiments, stately flatteries, and courteously veiled rebukes might have transposed naturally into eighteenth-century English, but put a modern translator at a disadvantage. In contrast with both types are a series of official or semi-official documents, including two dispatches from Cilicia, both models of elegant, straightforward language.

The letters are arranged and numbered as in my edition of the Latin texts (Cambridge, 1977), partly chronologically, partly by grouping according to correspondent or genre, and are translated from its text.

BIBLIOGRAPHICAL NOTE

THIS translation follows my recently published text and commentary, nos. 16–17 in the Cambridge Classical Texts and Commentaries series (Cambridge University Press, 1977). My *Cicero* (Gerald Duckworth, 1971) may be of use as a biographical and historical companion to the Correspondence. As a general history of the period T. Rice Holmes, *The Roman Republic* (3 vols., Oxford University Press, 1923), can still be recommended. Mommsen's *History of Rome*, however outmoded its ideological bias, keeps its fascination as a work of genius. Among contributions by living scholars R. Syme's *Roman Revolution* (Oxford University Press, 1939) is an established classic (largely, however, concerned with the period after Cicero's death). Anything by E. Badian and P. A. Brunt is worth reading. For penetrating analysis of the problems and determinants underlying late-republican politics I know nothing to equal the work of Christian Meier, especially *Res Publica Amissa* (Wiesbaden, Steiner, 1966) and *Caesars Bürgerkrieg* (1964; republished in *Entstehung des Begriffs Demokratie*, Frankfurt am Main, Suhrkamp Verlag, 1970); unfortunately it has not been translated.

Gaston Boissier's *Cicéron et ses amis* (1865; Engl. tr. 1897) can never be superseded as a delightful and sympathetic account of the man and his milieu. The straightforward biographies tend to be soporific. The only modern commentary on the whole Correspondence, that of Tyrrell and Purser (7 vols., 1904–33), is a mine of honest misinformation. On the other hand, J. Carcopino's *Les Secrets de la correspondance de Cicéron* (2 vols., 1947; Engl. tr. 1951), a farrago of garbled facts and false inferences, is more worthy of an unscrupulous prosecuting attorney than of a serious scholar.

CICERO'S LETTERS TO HIS FRIENDS

1 (V. 1)

METELLUS CELER TO CICERO

Cisalpine Gaul, c. 12 January 62

Q. Metellus Celer, son of Quintus, Proconsul, to M. Tullius Cicero greetings.

I hope you are well!

In view of our reciprocal sentiments and the restoration of our friendly relations I had not expected that I should ever be held up by you to offensive ridicule in my absence, or that my brother Metellus[1] would be attacked at your instance in person or estate because of a phrase.[2] If his own honourable character did not suffice for his protection, the dignity of our family and my zeal on behalf of you and your friends and the commonwealth should have been support enough. Now it seems that he has been beset, and I deserted, by those whom it least behoved.

So I wear the black of mourning[3] – I, in command of a province and an army conducting a war![4] Well, you and your friends have managed it so, without reason or forbearance. It was not like this in our forbears' time, and it will not be sur-

1. Q. Caecilius Metellus Nepos. Since entering office as Tribune on 10 December 63 he had demonstrated hostility to Cicero and his handling of the Catilinarian crisis. See next letter.

2. Probably the one reported in para. 7 of Cicero's reply ('that one who had punished others' etc.).

3. Customary when (e.g.) a close relative faced prosecution on a capital charge. Many Romans put on mourning for Cicero when threatened by Clodius in 58. Metellus Nepos had been suspended from office by the Senate.

4. Against Catiline.

prising if you all come to be sorry.[5] I did not think to find your own disposition so changeable towards me and mine. In the meantime neither domestic unhappiness nor any man's ill-usage shall turn me away from the commonwealth.

2 (V. 2)

CICERO TO METELLUS CELER

Rome, mid January 62

From M. Tullius Cicero, son of Marcus, to Q. Metellus Celer, son of Quintus, Proconsul, greetings.

I hope all is well with you and the army.[6]

You write that you had not expected ever to be held up to offensive ridicule by me, in view of our reciprocal sentiments and the restoration of friendly relations. What that means, I cannot precisely tell. But I suspect you have heard a report to the effect that, while arguing in the Senate that there were very many who regretted my saving of the commonwealth, I remarked that relatives of yours, to whom you could not say no, had prevailed upon you to suppress what you had decided you ought to say in the Senate in commendation of myself. In making this observation, I added that you and I had made a division of duty in the preservation of the commonwealth: my part was to guard Rome from domestic plots and the enemy within the gates, yours to protect Italy from armed force and underground conspiracy.[7] This partnership of ours in so vital

5. Perhaps a hint of what might happen when Pompey returned from the East.

6. It was usual to include the army in this formula when writing to a commanding general.

7. As Praetor in 63 Celer had raised troops in northern Italy and cut off Catiline's retreat to Gaul.

and splendid a task had been impaired by relatives of yours, who feared you might make me some gesture of mutual good-will in response to the ungrudging warmth of my tributes to yourself.

When in the course of my remarks I explained how eagerly I had been looking forward to your speech and how egregiously I had been astray, my speech caused some amusement and a moderate amount of laughter ensued – not directed at you, but rather at my mistake, and at the artless candour with which I admitted my desire to be praised by you. Really there could be nothing but compliment to you in my saying that at the very height of my glory I still hankered for some testimonial from *your* lips.

As for your reference to 'our reciprocal sentiments', I do not know how *you* define reciprocity in friendship. *I* conceive it to lie in good-will equally received and returned. If I were to say that I forwent a province[8] for your sake, you would think *me* less than sincere. It suited my purpose to do so, and I draw more pleasure and profit every day from my decision. What I do say is, that having announced the relinquishment of my province at a public meeting, I lost no time in planning how to transfer it to you. Of the lottery among the board of Praetors I say nothing. I only invite you to surmise that I was privy to all my colleague's actions in the matter. Be pleased to recall what followed, how promptly I called the Senate together on the day the lottery had taken place, and at what length I spoke about you. You said to me yourself that my speech was flattering to you to the point of being less than complimentary to your

8. Macedonia and Cisalpine Gaul had been assigned by the Senate as consular provinces for 62. Cicero enlisted support against Catiline from his unreliable colleague C. Antonius by letting him have Macedonia instead of drawing lots. Later he announced that he would not take a province at all, leaving Cisalpine Gaul to be allotted to one of the eight Praetors. He goes on to imply that Antonius, instigated by himself, had manipulated the lottery in Celer's favour.

colleagues. Moreover, the senatorial decree[9] passed that day contained a preamble which, as long as the document survives, will plainly testify to the friendly office I did you. Then, after you left Rome, I would ask you to recollect my speeches in the Senate with reference to yourself, my deliverances at public meetings, and the letters I sent you. When you have put all this together, I leave to your own judgement whether your conduct on the occasion of your recent visit[10] to Rome adequately 'reciprocated' mine at all these points.

You refer to 'the restoration of friendly relations'. I fail to understand why you should speak of a restoration of relations which have never been impaired.

You write that your brother Metellus should not have been attacked by me because of a phrase. Now in the first place I would ask you to believe that your sentiment here, your fraternal spirit redolent of good feeling and natural affection, has my warm approval. Secondly, if in any matter I have opposed your brother on public grounds, I ask you to forgive me – in public spirit I call no man my superior. But if I have defended my existence as a citizen in face of a savage onslaught on his part, you should be content that *I* do not protest to *you* about your brother's ill-usage. When I learned that he was planning and preparing his entire programme as Tribune with a view to my destruction, I addressed myself to your lady wife Claudia[11] and your sister Mucia[12] (her friendly disposition towards me as a friend of Cn. Pompeius had been plain to me in many connections) and asked them to persuade him to give up his injurious design. And yet, on the last day of the year, as I am

9. The decree (c. October 63) will have appointed Celer to a command in north Italy prior to his taking over the governorship of his province. Cicero's name would appear in the preamble with a complimentary reference to Celer's services as Praetor.

10. This visit must have taken place at the end of 63 while Celer was still Praetor.

11. See Glossary of Persons under 'Clodia'.

12. Actually half-sister, married to Pompey.

sure you have heard, he put upon me, Consul and saviour of the commonwealth, an insult which has never been put on any holder of any magistracy, no matter how disloyal: he deprived me of the power to address an assembly before retiring from office. This affront, however, redounded greatly to my honour. In face of his refusal to let me do more than take the oath,[13] I swore in loud tones the truest and finest oath that ever was, and the people likewise in loud tones swore that I had sworn the truth.

Even after receiving so signal an insult I sent common friends to Metellus that very same day to urge him to change his attitude. He replied that his hands were no longer free; and in fact he had declared at a public meeting a little while previously that one who had punished others without a hearing ought not to be given the right to speak himself. What sense of responsibility, what civic virtue! To judge the preserver of the Senate from massacre, of Rome from arson, of Italy from war, worthy of the same penalty as was inflicted by the Senate with the approbation of all honest men upon those who had designed to set fire to Rome, slaughter magistrates and Senate, and kindle a terrible conflict![14] Accordingly, I stood up to your brother Metellus face to face. On the Kalends of January we had a political disputation in the Senate which let him feel that he had to deal with a man of courage and resolution. In a speech on 3 January he named me in every sentence with threats; he had thoroughly made up his mind to bring me down by hook or by crook – not through due process of law, but by aggressive violence. If I had not offered a spirited and manly resistance to his indiscretions, nobody could have believed that my record

13. The usual oath taken by a retiring magistrate, that he had observed the laws during his term of office. Cicero neatly adapted it to the occasion by swearing that he alone had saved Rome and the Republic.

14. The Senate had decreed a public Thanksgiving in honour of Cicero's services almost in these terms.

as a courageous Consul was aught but a freak of chance.

If you were unaware of Metellus' intentions towards me, you must recognize that your brother has kept you in the dark about matters of the highest consequence. On the other hand, if he told you something of his plans, you ought to appreciate how mild and easy-going I show myself in not expostulating with you on this very subject. And if you recognize that I was not upset by a 'phrase' of Metellus but by the bitter hostility of his purpose and attitude towards me, I must ask you now to note my forbearance – if that is the right word for laxity and weakness in the face of the most severe provocation. I have never once spoken in the Senate for a motion against your brother; on all such occasions I have kept my seat and supported those who appeared to me to make the most lenient proposal. I will add something else: although I could not be expected, after what had passed, to be active in the matter, I was not sorry to see my enemy relieved[15] (because he was your brother) by a senatorial decree, and I even assisted, so far as in me lay, to bring this about.

Thus I made no attack upon your brother, but repelled *his* attack on me; and my disposition towards you, so far from being 'changeable', has been eminently stable, so much so that my feelings remained the same even when friendly actions on your part were no longer forthcoming. Even now, though you have written to me in almost menacing terms, this is the answer I have to make: I not only pardon your irritation, I highly commend it – my own experience of the power of a brother's affection is my monitor. In return, I ask you to be fair in your judgement of a similar feeling on my part, and to take the view that, if I have been the victim of a bitter, savage, and unprovoked attack by a member of your family, it was not incumbent on me to give way – that, on the contrary, I was entitled in such a situation to your support and that of the army you command.

15. Perhaps the decree allowed Nepos to leave Italy, as in fact he did.

I have ever wanted you to be my friend, and have tried to let you see that I am a very good friend of yours. My sentiments remain the same, and shall, as long as you so desire. I shall sooner give up my resentment against your brother out of affection for you than abate a jot of the good-will between us out of animosity towards him.

3 (V. 7)

CICERO TO POMPEY

Rome, April 62

From M. Tullius Cicero, son of Marcus, to Cn. Pompeius Magnus,[16] son of Gnaeus, Imperator, greetings.

I hope all is well with you and the army, as it is with me.

Like the rest of us I was immeasurably delighted with your dispatch,[17] in which you have held out the bright prospect of a peaceful future; such a prospect as I have ever been promising to all and sundry in reliance on your single self. I must tell you, however, that it came as a severe blow to your old enemies, nowadays your friends;[18] their high hopes dashed, they despond.

Your personal letter to me evinces but little of your friendly

16. Pompey's cognomen 'Magnus' ('the Great'), conferred by his victorious troops in 81 and confirmed by Sulla, was used officially, and in a formal address like this it would have been discourteous to omit it. Otherwise Cicero does not normally use it simply as a name, without further implications.

17. To the magistrates and Senate, no doubt announcing the writer's return to Italy in the near future. He actually arrived at the end of the year.

18. Who these were is disputed. Probably Caesar and perhaps Crassus were in mind, also subversives generally who hoped to see Pompey take their part against the senatorial establishment.

sentiments towards me, but you may be sure that it gave me pleasure all the same. My chief joy is apt to lie in the consciousness of my services to others. If these fail of a like response, I am perfectly content that the balance of good offices should rest on my side. I have no doubt that if my own hearty goodwill towards you does not suffice to win your attachment, the public interest will join us in confederacy.

Not to leave you in ignorance of the particular in which your letter has disappointed me, let me speak plainly, as becomes my character and our friendly relations. My achievements[19] have been such that I expected to find a word of congratulation upon them in your letter, both for friendship's sake and that of the commonwealth. I imagine you omitted anything of the sort for fear of giving offence in any quarter.[20] But I must tell you that what I have done for the safety of the country stands approved in the judgement and testimony of the whole world. When you return, you will find that I have acted with a measure of policy and a lack of self-regard which will make you well content to have me as your political ally and private friend – a not much lesser Laelius to a far greater Africanus.[21]

19. These had been described in a lengthy letter sent to Pompey the previous December.

20. i.e. to people like Caesar who condemned the execution of the Catilinarian conspirators.

21. Scipio Africanus the Younger, destroyer of Carthage in 146. His lifelong friend was C. Laelius, called Sapiens ('the Wise'). Both figure in Cicero's Dialogues.

4 (V. 6)

CICERO TO P. SESTIUS

Rome, mid or late December 62

From M. Cicero to P. Sestius, son of Lucius, Proquaestor, greetings.

When your secretary Decius called on me and asked me to do my best to ensure that no successor to you is appointed for the present, despite my estimation of his honesty and loyalty to yourself, I hardly believed him. I remembered how you had written to me earlier on, and here was this sensible fellow telling me that you had completely changed your mind! But after your Cornelia met Terentia and I had a word with Q. Cornelius,[22] I took care to attend whenever there was a meeting of the Senate; and I had a deal of trouble to make Tribune Q. Fufius and the others to whom you had written believe me rather than your letters. The whole question has been deferred till January, but we are carrying our point without difficulty.

You wrote to me some time ago about Crassus' house, wishing me luck in my bargain. Stimulated by your felicitations I actually bought the house some time after I received them, for HS3,500,000.[23] So take notice that I am so deeply in debt that I should be glad to join a plot, if anyone would have me. But some of them bar me out of prejudice – they hate me as a plot-breaker and make no bones about it. Others do not

22. Cornelia, daughter of L. Scipio Asiaticus, Consul in 83, was Sestius' wife. Q. Cornelius may have been a client of her family.

23. A very large sum, though there is evidence that much larger amounts were sometimes paid for houses in Rome. Cicero's purchase, situated on the Palatine above the Forum, was considered ostentatious (cf. *Letters to Atticus* 16 (I.16).8).

trust me. They fear a trap, and won't believe that the man who got the capitalists out of a tight corner can be short of cash! To be sure there's plenty of money to be had at ½%;[24] and my exploits have at least got me the reputation of being a good risk.

I have inspected your house and all the new building, and heartily approve.

The lack of friendship towards me on Antonius' part is universally remarked; notwithstanding which, I have defended him in the Senate in the most weighty and conscientious style. The House was strongly impressed by what I said and the fact that I said it.

Please write to me more often.

5 (V. 5)

CICERO TO C. ANTONIUS

Rome, c. 23 December 62

From M. Cicero to C. Antonius, son of Marcus, Imperator, greetings.

I had not intended to write you any letters except of recommendation – not that I had any reason to suppose they carry any particular weight with you, but because I did not wish to show the persons who asked for them that our connection was less close than formerly. However, T. Pomponius[25] knows my zeal and friendly offices on your behalf better than any man; he is a well-wisher of yours and a very devoted friend of mine. Since he is setting out to join you, I think I ought to write a few lines, especially as Pomponius himself would be disappointed if I did not.

24. Monthly.

25. Cf. *Letters to Atticus* 12 (I.12) and 13 (I.13). Atticus no doubt took the letter with him to Greece.

Nobody could fairly wonder if I were to expect great favours from you, for everything has been forthcoming on my side which might conduce to your interest, honour, and prestige. To the fact that I have received nothing from you in return you are the best witness; that in some measure you have even shown a disposition to the contrary I have heard from many sources – I dare not say 'learned' in case I might be using the very word which they tell me you often bring up against me (untruly).[26] But I had rather you heard of the stories which have reached me from Pomponius (he has been no less vexed by them than I) than from a letter of mine. The Senate and People of Rome stand witness to my conspicuously friendly disposition towards you. Of your gratitude yourself can judge, of your debt to me let the world judge.

What I have already done for you was done at first out of good-will and later for consistency's sake. But I assure you that the future will make far larger demands on my zeal, loyalty, and energy. I shall persevere with all my might, provided I do not seem to be throwing my trouble away. But if I find that it gets me no thanks, I shall not let myself be taken for an idiot – even by you. Pomponius will inform you of what I mean and explain its nature.[27] As for Pomponius himself, I recommend him to you, though I am confident that you will do all you can for his own sake. Still, I will ask you to show any regard for me that you may retain in Pomponius' affair.[28] You can do nothing that will oblige me more.

26. 'Learned' (*comperisse*) was the word used by Cicero when reporting to the Senate what he had discovered about Catiline's plot. His enemies took it up against him, no doubt with the implication that the 'intelligence' had been manufactured or doctored by Cicero himself. The word 'untruly' (*falso*) seems to be in denial of such an implication.

27. Antonius might, and in the event did, have to face charges when he returned to Rome, and Pompey was rumoured to intend getting him recalled.

28. The money owed to Atticus by the town of Sicyon (cf. *Letters to Atticus* 13 (I.13).1).

6 (XIV. 4)

CICERO TO HIS FAMILY

Brundisium, 29 April 58

From Tullius to his dear Terentia and Tullia and Marcus greetings.

I send you letters less often than I have opportunity, because, wretched as every hour is for me, when I write to you at home or read your letters I am so overcome with tears that I cannot bear it. If only I had been less anxious to save my life! Assuredly I should have seen no sorrow in my days, or not much. If fortune has spared me for some hope of one day recovering some measure of well-being, my error has not been so total. But if these present evils are to stay, then, yes, I want to see you, dear heart, as soon as I can, and to die in your arms, since neither the Gods whom you have worshipped so piously nor the men to whose service I have always devoted myself have made us any recompense.

I have stayed in Brundisium for thirteen days with M. Laenius Flaccus, a very worthy gentleman. He has disregarded the danger to his own property and status in his concern for my safety, and refused to be deterred by the penalties of a wicked law[29] from carrying out the established duties of hospitality and friendship. I pray that one day I may be able to show him my gratitude. Grateful I shall always be. I am leaving Brundisium on 29 April and making for Cyzicus by way of Macedonia.

Ah, what a desperate, pitiful case is mine! What now? Shall I ask you to come – a sick woman, physically and spiritually exhausted? Shall I *not* ask then? Am I to live without you? Perhaps I should put it like this: if there is any hope of my

29. See *Letters to Atticus* 49 (III.4).

return, you must build it up, and help in the campaign. On the other hand if all is over, as I fear, then come to me any way you can. Be sure of one thing: if I have you, I shall not feel that I am utterly lost. But what is to become of my Tulliola? You at home must take care of that – I have nothing to suggest. But assuredly, however matters turn out, the poor little girl's marriage and good name must be a primary consideration. Then there is my son. What will he do? I hope that *he* will always be with me, my darling child. I cannot write any more now. Grief clogs my pen.

How you have fared I do not know – whether you still have something left, or, as I fear, have been stripped of all. Yes, I trust that Piso[30] will always be faithful. You need not worry about the freeing of the household. In the first place, the promise made to your people was that you would treat each case on its merits (Orpheus, in fact, is loyal so far, none of the others very noticeably so). The position of the other slaves is that if it turned out that my property was no longer mine, they would be my freedmen, provided they could make good their claim to the status; whereas, if I still had a hold on them, they would remain my slaves except for just a few. But these are minor matters.

You urge me to hold my head high and hope for restoration. I wish the facts may give ground for reasonable hope. Meanwhile, as matters wretchedly stand, when am I going to get your next letter? Who will bring it to me? I should have waited for it at Brundisium if the sailors had let me, but they did not want to lose the fair weather.

For the rest, dearest Terentia, bear up with all the dignity you can muster. It has been a good life, a great career. The good in me, nothing bad, has brought me down. I have done nothing wrong, except that when I lost the good things of life I did not lose life itself. But if it was more for our children's happiness that I should live, let us bear what remains, intolerable though it be. And yet, while I tell you to be strong, I cannot tell myself.

30. Tullia's husband, C. Calpurnius Piso Frugi.

I am sending Clodius Philhetaerus back, because he is hampered by eye-trouble. He is a faithful fellow. Sallustius is the most forward of all. Pescennius is full of kindly feeling towards me; I think he will always be attentive to you. Sicca had told me that he would stay with me, but has left Brundisium.

Take care of your health as best you can, and believe that your unhappiness grieves me more than my own. My dear Terentia, loyalest and best of wives, my darling little daughter, and Marcus, our one remaining hope – goodbye.

29 April, from Brundisium.

7 (XIV. 2)

CICERO TO HIS FAMILY

Thessalonica, 5 October 58

From Tullius to his dear Terentia and his dear Tulliola and Marcus greetings.

You are not to suppose that I write letters of any length to anyone, unless somebody has written a lot to me and I feel I ought to reply. In fact I have nothing to write about, and at the present time I find it the most intractable of tasks. To you and our Tulliola I cannot write without many tears, for I see that you are very unhappy – you, for whom I wished all the happiness in the world. I ought to have given it to you, and should have done so if I had not been such a coward.

I have a great affection for Piso, as he deserves. I have written encouraging him as best I could and thanking him as was proper. I gather that you pin hopes on the new Tribunes. That will hold good, if Pompey is friendly; but I am still afraid of Crassus.

I see that courage and love shines in all you do, nor does that surprise me. But it is a heartbreaking situation when my distresses are relieved at the cost of so much distress to you. P. Valerius (he tries to help) has written to me an account, which I wept bitterly to read, of how you were taken from the Temple of Vesta to the Tabula Valeria.[31] Ah, my beloved, my heart's longing! To think that you, dearest Terentia, once everybody's refuge in trouble, should now be so tormented! There you are, plunged in tears and mourning, and it is my fault! In saving others, I ruined you and me.

As for what you say about the house, or rather the site on which it stood, indeed I shall not feel myself truly restored until that is restored to me. But these things are not in our hands. What grieves me is that in your unhappy and impoverished state you should be contributing to any necessary outlay. If the thing goes through, we shall win all. But if fortune stays my enemy, are you going to throw away what poor little you have left? My darling, I beg you, where expense is concerned, let others bear it who can, if only they will; and do not overstrain that frail health of yours, if you love me. For you are before my eyes night and day. I see you are shouldering every burden. I fear you may not have the strength. Yet clearly everything depends on you. So in order that we may win the prize of your hopes and efforts, take good care of your health.

I do not know whom I should write to, except those who write to me or who are mentioned in letters from home. Since it is your joint wish, I shall not go further away. But I hope you will send me letters as often as possible, especially if we have grounds for reasonable hope.

Goodbye, my absent loves, goodbye.

Dispatched 5 October, from Thessalonica.

31. In the Comitium, called after a painting set up by M. Valerius Messala (nothing to do with P. Valerius) to commemorate a victory in the first Punic War. The Tribunes met there officially and it seems that Terentia had been summoned before them in connection with a financial matter. Her half-sister Fabia was a Vestal Virgin.

8 (XIV, I)

CICERO TO TERENTIA

Dispatched from Dyrrachium, 25 November 58

From Tullius to his dear Terentia and to dear Tulliola and to dear Marcus greetings.

Many folk write to me and everybody talks to me about you, what amazing courage and fortitude you show, how no trials of body or spirit wear you out. Ah me, to think that my brave, loyal, true, gentle wife should have come by such misery because of me! And to think that our Tulliola should be suffering so much grief on account of her papa, who used to give her so much pleasure! As for Marcus, what can I say? Bitter sorrow and suffering has been his portion since the earliest dawn of intelligence. If I thought all this was the work of fate, as you say, I should find it a little easier to bear. But I am to blame for everything. I thought I was loved by people who were only jealous of my success, while I refused to follow those who sought my friendship. If only I had relied upon my own judgement instead of paying so much attention to the talk of friends, whether fools or knaves, how happy I might have been! As things are, since our friends tell us to hope, I shall take care not to let my health betray your efforts. I well understand the magnitude of the task, and how much easier it would have been to stay at home than it is to return. However, if we have all the Tribunes on our side, if Lentulus[32] is as zealous as he seems, and if we also have Pompey's and Caesar's good-will, we ought not to despair.

As to my household, I shall do as you tell me our friends think best. As to my place of residence, the epidemic has now dis-

32. P. Cornelius Lentulus Spinther.

appeared, but while it lasted it did not touch me. Plancius, who is untiring in his good offices, is anxious to have me with him, and keeps me here. I wanted to stay in some less frequented place in Epirus out of the way of Piso[33] and his soldiers, but Plancius still keeps me here. He hopes it may turn out that he leaves for Italy in my company. If I live to see that day, and return to my family's embraces, and get all of you and my own self back again, I shall feel that your devotion to me and mine to you have been sufficiently rewarded.

Piso's kindness, manliness, and affection for us all is quite superlative. I pray it may bring him happiness; certainly it will bring him honour. As regards my brother Quintus, I meant no criticism of yourself; but I wanted you all to be as close to one another as possible, especially as you are so few. I have thanked the persons you wished me to thank, and written that my information came from you.

Dearest, you tell me that you are going to sell a row of houses. This is dreadful. What in the name of heaven, *what* is to happen? And if no change of fortune comes to my relief, what is to become of our poor boy? I cannot go on, the tears overcome me, and I would not wish to draw yours. Just this I will say: if my friends are loyal, money will not be lacking; if not, you cannot achieve results with *your* money. For pity's sake, pitiable that we are, don't let our unfortunate boy be utterly ruined! If he has something to keep him above penury, he only needs a modicum of ability and a modicum of luck to gain the rest.

Take care of yourself and send me couriers, so that I know what is doing and what you and the children are doing. To be sure, I have not long to wait now. Give my love to Tulliola and Marcus. Goodbye to you all.

33. L. Calpurnius Piso Caesoninus, Consul in 58 and incoming governor of Macedonia. Distinguish from Cicero's son-in-law in the next paragraph.

I have come to Dyrrachium[34] because it is a Free City, and anxious to serve me, and the nearest point to Italy. But if I find there are too many people about for my liking, I shall go somewhere else and send you word.

Dispatched 25 November, Dyrrachium

9 (XIV. 3)

CICERO TO TERENTIA

Dyrrachium, 29 November 58

From Tullius to his dear Terentia and Tullia and Marcus greetings.

I have received three letters from Aristocritus, and almost blotted them out in tears. I am overwhelmed with grief, dearest Terentia; and my own distresses do not torture me more than yours and my family's. But my wretchedness is greater than yours (and yours is bitter enough) because, while we both share the disaster, the blame for it is mine and mine only. It was my duty either to avoid the impending danger by taking a Commissionership[35] or to oppose it by careful provision or to fall bravely. Nothing could have been more miserable, dishonourable, and unworthy of me than *this*. So I am overwhelmed by shame as well as grief. Yes, I am ashamed to have been found wanting in the courage and carefulness that the best of wives and most enchanting of children had the right to expect of me. Night and day I have before my eyes the sorry spectacle of my family in grief and mourning and the frailty

34. Para. 6 is a postscript added at Dyrrachium. The letter proper was written before Cicero left Thessalonica in mid November (cf. *Letters to Atticus* 67 (III.22)).

35. See Glossary of Terms under 'Legate'.

of your health. The hope of restoration held out to me is very slender. Many are hostile, almost all are jealous. To drive me out was a feat, but to keep me out is easy. However, as long as my family continues to hope, I shall do my part, for I would not wish to seem responsible for *every* fiasco.

You need not be concerned for my safety. That is no problem now, for even my enemies want me to stay alive in my present wretchedness. However, I shall do as you advise. I have thanked the friends you named and given the letters to Dexippus, and I have written that my information about their good offices came from you. Our dear Piso's extraordinary devotion and activity on my behalf is evident to me and everyone talks of it. The Gods grant that I may enjoy the blessing of such a son-in-law in person with you and our children! Our last hope now lies in the new Tribunes – and in the first few days; for if novelty is lost, we are finished. I am therefore sending Aristocritus to you straight away, so that you can write me an immediate account of the initial stage and a conspectus of the whole business. To be sure, Dexippus also has my orders to hurry back straight away, and I have written to my brother asking him to send couriers at short intervals. I am staying in Dyrrachium at the present time expressly so that I get the quickest possible news of what goes on. Also I am quite safe, having always been a patron of this town. When my enemies are reported to be on their way, it will be time to go to Epirus.

As regards your offer to join me if I wish, well, I know that a large share of this burden rests upon your shoulders, and so I want you to stay in Rome. If you and the others succeed in your efforts, it is for me to join you. If not – but there is no need to go on. I shall be able to decide what to do from your first letter, or at latest from your second. All I ask is that you write me the most comprehensive and detailed accounts – though it is results rather than letters I should be expecting now.

Take care of your health, and rest assured that nobody in the world is more precious to me than you, or ever has been.

Goodbye, dearest Terentia. I seem to see you, and my weeping exhausts me. Goodbye.

29 November.

10 (V. 4)

CICERO TO METELLUS NEPOS

Dyrrachium, mid January 57

From M. Cicero to Q. Metellus, Consul, greetings.

Letters from my brother Quintus and my friend and connection T. Pomponius had so raised my hopes that I counted on your assistance no less than on your colleague's.[36] Accordingly, I wrote to you at once in terms proper to my present position, both expressing my gratitude and soliciting your assistance in the future. Later it was conveyed to me, not so much by letters from home as by the talk of travellers passing this way, that your attitude had changed. That is why I did not venture to importune you with letters.

Now my brother has sent me the text of your speech in the Senate[37] in which you express yourself in the gentlest terms. It has emboldened me to write to you and to beg you, with whatever urgency your own sentiments make acceptable, to preserve those near to you[38] along with myself rather than attack me on account of *their* high-handed cruelty. In giving up a grudge of your own for the sake of the public interest you

36. Lentulus Spinther.

37. On 1 January 57. In his defence of Sestius (para. 75) in 56 Cicero says that Metellus declared himself as ready to give up his personal enmity (dating from 63–62) in deference to the Senate and in the public interest.

38. i.e. P. Clodius. It has recently been ascertained that he was half-brother to the Metelli, not cousin, as hitherto supposed.

have won a victory over yourself. Are you prevailed upon to support the grudges of others against that interest? If you will find it in your heart to help me, I give you my word that I shall be at your disposition in all things. If the violence which has overcome me and the commonwealth together shall prevent magistrates and Senate and People from assisting me, may I say a word of warning? When you would fain call back the time for saving *all*, you may call in vain, because there will be none to save.[39]

11 (V. 3)

METELLUS NEPOS TO CICERO

Hither Spain, latter half of 56

From Q. Metellus Nepos to M. Cicero, greetings.

The insults heaped upon my head by an unmannerly individual[40] in speech after speech are softened by your acts of friendship. From such a person they are of small account, and I despise them accordingly; and, welcoming the change of roles, I take *you* for my brother. Of him I do not even want to think, though I saved him twice over in spite of himself.[41]

As for my concerns, not wanting to trouble you and my other friends with a spate of letters, I have written in detail to

39. Cicero evidently did not care to put his meaning directly, but Metellus was to understand that (a) he, Cicero, could be saved without ruining Clodius, and (b) if rescue did not come soon it would be too late. The final words, though general in form, point to Cicero himself (not Clodius). His letters from exile hint more than once at suicide if hopes of return did not materialize.

40. Clodius.

41. During his Consulship the previous year, when he thwarted Milo's attempts to bring Clodius to trial.

Lollius,[42] telling him my wishes with regard to the administration of my province and asking him to inform and remind you all accordingly.

If you can, I hope you will keep your friendly sentiments towards me as in the past.

12 (I. 1)

CICERO TO LENTULUS SPINTHER

Rome, 13 January 56

From M. Cicero to P. Lentulus, Proconsul, greetings.

In all that is due to a friend, or rather a benefactor, my efforts on your behalf seem adequate to everyone except myself; for me they are never enough. Your services to me have been so great that my life turns sour when I think that I am failing to achieve in your case[43] what you achieved in mine, never relaxing short of complete success. The relevant facts are as follows: The king's representative, Hammonius, is openly working against us with money. His intermediaries are the creditors who played the same role when you were in Rome.

42. Probably L. Lollius, formerly fellow-Legate of Nepos under Pompey. They captured Damascus together in 65 or 64.

43. This refers to the affair of the exiled King of Egypt, Ptolemy XII, nicknamed 'the Piper', father of the famous Cleopatra. In September 57 the Senate had commissioned Lentulus, as proximate governor of Cilicia, to restore him to his throne. But in January the custodians of the Sibylline prophecies produced an oracle forbidding the employment of a 'host'. This was no doubt also a move against Pompey, who came more and more to be suspected of wanting to handle the restoration himself. The business dragged on until August (see Letter 18 (1.7)). In the end Lentulus did nothing, and Ptolemy was reinstated by the enterprising governor of Syria, A. Gabinius, in 55.

The king's well-wishers (there are not many of them) all want to see the business handed over to Pompey, whereas the Senate is approving the religious subterfuge;[44] not for religion's sake, but out of ill-will and the odium aroused by the royal largesse. I never stop urging and begging Pompey, even going so far as to take him pretty frankly to task and warning him to steer clear of a major scandal. But truth to tell, he leaves no opening for appeals or warnings on my part, since both in day-to-day conversation and publicly in the Senate he has pleaded your cause as eloquently, impressively, zealously, and vigorously as anybody could possibly have done, with the fullest acknowledgement of your services to himself and his affection for you. You write that Marcellinus is annoyed with you. He promises that he will be your most ardent champion in all respects, except this affair of the king. We take what he offers, but there is no diverting him from his determination to refer the religious point to the Senate, as he has already done on a number of occasions.

Up to the Ides this is the record (I am writing on the morning of the Ides): The resolution put forward by Hortensius, myself, and Lucullus[45] gives way to the religious objection as regards an army; we cannot gain our point in any other way. But in accordance with the decree which was passed on your own motion it gives you authority to restore the king, if you can do so without prejudice to the public interest. While an army is precluded by the religious obstacle, the Senate would thus retain you as the person responsible. Crassus proposes a Commission of Three, from which he does not exclude Pompey, since he provides that persons holding military command[46]

44. The aforesaid Sibylline oracle.

45. M. Terentius Varro Lucullus. His brother Lucius had died earlier in the year. He and the orator Hortensius, both senior Consulars, were Spinther's principal backers in the Senate along with Cicero.

46. Pompey at this time held proconsular *imperium* in virtue of his extraordinary office as controller of grain supplies.

shall be eligible. Bibulus[47] proposes a Commission of Three to be selected from those *not* holding command. He is supported by the other Consulars excepting Servilius,[48] who is against *any* restoration, Vulcatius,[49] who is for authorizing Pompey on Lupus'[50] motion, and Afranius, who supports Vulcatius. The last circumstance intensifies suspicion as to Pompey's wishes – support for Vulcatius by Pompey's intimates did not go unmarked. It is a hard struggle, and things are going against us. Energetic lobbying by Libo and Hypsaeus, which is no secret, and the interest shown by all Pompey's friends have led to the opinion that Pompey is anxious for the assignment. Those who are against him are no friends to you either, because of what you have done for him.

I carry less weight in the matter because of my obligations to you, and my private influence is nullified by the prevailing suspicion – they think they are obliging Pompey. We are dealing with a business that was inflamed in secret long before you left Rome by the king himself and by Pompey's close friends and familiars, and has subsequently been stirred up in public by the Consulars. It has now gained a highly invidious notoriety. My loyalty will be recognized by all, and my affection for you by your absent self and present friends. If others whose loyalty should have been beyond reproach were not falling short, we would not be in such difficulties.

47. Bitterly hostile to Pompey at this period.

48. P. Servilius Vatia Isauricus, Consul in 79.

49. Consul in 66. The contemporary spelling seems to have been 'Volcacius'.

50. The Tribune (see Glossary of Persons). On his motion see the next letter.

13 (I. 2)

CICERO TO LENTULUS SPINTHER

Rome, 15 January 56

From M. Cicero to P. Lentulus, Proconsul, greetings.

Nothing was settled in the Senate on the Ides of January because a large part of the day was taken up by an altercation between Consul Lentulus[51] and Tribune Caninius.[52] I spoke at length that day myself, and I think I made a very considerable impression on the Senate when I dwelt on your attachment to that Order. We therefore thought best to make only short speeches on the day following, feeling that we had regained the House's good-will – I had clear evidence of that both during my address and in approaches and appeals to individuals. Accordingly three proposals were put forward: first Bibulus', that the king be restored by a Commission of Three, second Hortensius', that he be restored by you without an army, and third Vulcatius', that he be restored by Pompey. There was a demand that Bibulus' motion should be split. So far as it concerned the religious issue it was agreed, opposition on this point being now out of the question, but on the Commission of Three it was heavily defeated. Hortensius' motion stood next, when Tribune Lupus began to insist that, having himself consulted the House earlier concerning Pompey, he had the right to take a vote before the Consuls. His speech was received with loud protests from all sides – it was unfair and without precedent. The Consuls did not give way, but neither did they put up much of a fight. They wanted the sitting talked out, which is what happened, because it was plain to them that Hortensius'

51. Marcellinus.
52. L. Caninius Gallus (see Glossary of Persons).

motion would get a thumping majority despite much open canvassing in support of Vulcatius – which again was not to the liking of the Consuls, who had wished Bibulus' motion to win the day. The argument was prolonged till nightfall, and the House rose.

I happened to be dining with Pompey that evening. It was a better moment than had ever come my way before, because we had just had our most successful day in the Senate since your departure. So I talked to him, and I could flatter myself that I led his mind away from all other notions and focused it upon upholding your position. When I listen to him talking, I quite acquit him of all suspicion of selfish aims. But when I look at his friends of all classes, I see what is now plain to everyone, that this whole business has for a long while past been bedevilled by certain individuals, not without the connivance of the king himself and his advisers.

I am writing this on 15 January before daybreak. The Senate is to meet today. At the meeting, as I hope, we shall maintain our position, so far as practicable in the general ambience of treachery and unfair play. As for the role of the People,[53] I think we have so managed that no proceedings in that quarter are possible without violation of the auspices and the laws, in fact without violence. Yesterday a senatorial resolution[54] in very impressive terms went through on these matters, and although Cato[55] and Caninius cast vetoes, it was placed on record. I think you have been sent a copy. On other matters I shall write to tell you whatever takes place, and shall use all my care, pains, diligence, and influence to ensure that things go as much as possible on the right lines.

53. i.e. the popular legislative assembly.
54. See Glossary of Terms.
55. C. Porcius Cato.

14 (I. 4)

CICERO TO LENTULUS SPINTHER

Rome, 17 (?) January 56

From M. Cicero to P. Lentulus, Proconsul, greetings.

We were holding up magnificently in the Senate on 15 January. Already on the previous day we had smashed that motion of Bibulus on the Commission of Three, and the only battle left to fight was Vulcatius' motion. However, our opponents dragged the proceedings out on various pretexts, because we were carrying our point in a full House, which showed little difference of opinion and no little irritation against those who were trying to put the king's affair out of your hands and into someone else's. We found Curio[56] bitterly hostile to us that day, Bibulus much fairer, almost friendly even. Caninius and Cato undertook not to bring forward any legislation before the elections. As you know, the Senate is debarred by the lex Pupia from meeting before the Kalends of February, and throughout February there can be no sitting until embassy business has been completed or deferred.[57] However, the belief of the Roman People is that the religious pretext was trumped up by your ill-wishers and detractors, and then adopted by others not so much to stand in *your* way as to stop anyone from wanting to go to Alexandria for the sake of a military command. Everyone judges that the Senate has taken proper account of your honour, since everybody knows that your opponents

56. The elder, Consul in 76.

57. All days in January after the 15th were 'comitial' days, on which it was illegal for the Senate to meet except by special dispensation. Another law (lex Gabinia) provided that during February the hearing of deputations from abroad should take precedence over other business.

prevented a decision. If they now make any move, nominally through the People but in reality by a criminal act of tribunician freebooting, sufficient means have now been taken to ensure that they can do nothing without violating the auspices and the laws, or indeed without the use of force.

I do not think it would be appropriate for me to describe my own zeal or the ill-usage of certain persons. There is no occasion for me to parade myself, for if I were to sacrifice my life in defence of your honour, I should not appear to have balanced a fraction of what I owe you; nor yet to complain of the wrongs done you by others, which I cannot do without heartfelt distress. I can offer you no guarantee against violence, especially in the present weakness of our officers of state, but, violence apart, I can say with confidence that you will maintain your high standing through the zealous good-will of the Senate and People of Rome.

15 (I. 5 a)

CICERO TO LENTULUS SPINTHER

Rome, c. 5 February 56

From M. Cicero to P. Lentulus, Proconsul, greetings.

It was my dearest wish that my gratitude to you should be abundantly demonstrated, first to yourself, and then to the world. But I am deeply sorry that conditions since your departure have been such as to give you in your absence a trial both of my loyalty and good-will towards you and of other people's. I see from your letter how keenly you are aware that the same brand of loyalty has been forthcoming on behalf of your honour as *I* experienced when my existence as a citizen was at stake. While I was striving my utmost in the king's matter, by dint of thought, zeal, hard work, and personal influence, Cato's abominable bill[58] suddenly made its appearance to hamper our efforts and divert our attention from the lesser concern to a grave alarm. However, although no unwelcome possibility can be ruled out in such an imbroglio as this, my main fear is treachery; as for Cato, we shall of course oppose him in any circumstances.

With regard to Alexandria and the king's business, I can promise you this much, that your absent self and your friends here present will be more than satisfied with my conduct. But I am afraid that the king's business will either be snatched out of our hands or let drop, and I find it hard to judge which of the two I like less. But if the worst comes to the worst, there is a third possibility, which neither Selicius nor I find inadmissible – namely not to let the matter go by the board, and at the same time not to let it be assigned *in the teeth of opposition from our side* to the person[59] to whom it has almost been assigned (so people think) already; throughout taking care on the one hand not to lose any possible success by default, and on the other to avoid the appearance of a rebuff in any failure.

As a wise and high-minded man, you must regard your status and honour as depending entirely upon your own qualities and achievements and your moral dignity. If any of the gifts which fortune has showered upon you is abstracted by the treachery of certain persons, you will judge that they more than yourself will be the sufferers. I am losing no opportunity of acting and planning in your interests. In all matters I am availing myself of Q. Selicius' services. None of your friends in my judgement surpasses him in shrewdness or loyalty or affection for you.

58. To deprive Lentulus of his province. It had been promulgated by C. Cato as Tribune.

59. Pompey.

16 (I. 5 b)

CICERO TO LENTULUS SPINTHER

Rome, shortly after 9 February 56

From M. Cicero to P. Lentulus, Proconsul, greetings.

I expect you have heard what is happening and has happened here from plenty of informants, both by letter and word of mouth. It is my business, I think, to write to you about matters of surmise and forecast.

Pompey appeared to me much shaken after his rough reception – noise and abuse – when he spoke for Milo[60] at the public meeting on 7 February, and Cato's bitter and vehement attack in the Senate, which was received by his enemies in portentous silence. He seems to me to have quite given up the Alexandrian business. Our position is intact, because the Senate has taken nothing from you except what cannot, on account of the same religious scruple, be given to anybody else.

What we are now hoping and working for is that when the king realizes that his plan of a restoration by Pompey is impracticable and that unless he is brought home by you he will be left totally in the lurch, he will go to you. Without the smallest doubt he *will* do this, if Pompey makes a sign, however slight, to show his approval. But you know how slow and uncommunicative Pompey is. However, I am letting nothing slip which might have a bearing on this question. As for the other outrages threatened in Cato's proposal, I hope we shall have no difficulty in resisting them. I do not find any of the Consulars to be your friend except Hortensius and Lucullus. The rest are either more or less overtly ill-disposed or undisguisedly in

60. Arraigned by Clodius before a popular assembly. Letter 7 (II.3). 2 of the letters to his brother Quintus gives a full account.

dudgeon. You must keep your courage and spirit high and be of good hope that, when we have crushed this irresponsible fellow's attack, you will flourish in your old dignity and repute.

17 (I. 6)

CICERO TO LENTULUS SPINTHER

Rome, March (?) 56

From M. Cicero to P. Lentulus, Proconsul, greetings.

You will learn what is toward from Pollio,[61] who has taken not only part but the leading part in every transaction. In the keen distress which I feel in your affairs hope is naturally my greatest comforter, since I have a strong inkling that the evil disposition now current will be worn down by the counter-measures of your friends and by mere lapse of time, which is weakening the devices of your enemies and betrayers.

I have a second comforter ready to hand in the recollection of my own experience, which I see mirrored in yours. True, your standing is injured in a smaller concern than that which brought mine so low. None the less, the similarity is so close that I hope you forgive me if I decline to fear contingencies which you never thought formidable. Only show yourself the man I have known you since your nails were tender,[62] as the Greeks say. Trust me, the wrong men do you will add lustre to your greatness. Expect from me at every turn the uttermost in zealous service; I shall not disappoint your good opinion.

61. Probably C. Asinius Pollio, though he was only about 21 at this time.

62. i.e. 'from childhood'. In Greek the expression can also mean 'from the finger-tips inward', i.e. 'all through'.

18 (I. 7)

CICERO TO LENTULUS SPINTHER

Rome, late June or July 56

From M. Cicero to P. Lentulus, Proconsul, greetings.

I have read your letter, in which you say you are glad to be kept informed through me on all points at such frequent intervals and to see such plain evidence of my good-will towards you. As for the latter, I must needs hold you in the highest regard, if I choose to be such as you have chosen to think me. As for the former, it is a pleasure to talk to you by letter as often as possible, separated as we are by distance of place and time. If I do so more rarely than you expect, the reason will be that my letters are such as I should not care to hand to the first comer. Whenever I find reliable persons, to whom I can safely entrust them, I shall not let the opportunity slip.

You wish to know how this person and that has behaved and felt towards you. It is difficult to speak of individuals. I only venture now to report in the light of ascertained fact what I have often intimated to you in the past, that certain persons, particularly those most bound in duty to help you and best able to do so, have been jealous of your standing, and that despite differences of circumstance there has been a remarkably close parallel between your present experience and mine in days gone by. Those whom you offended in the public interest have been your open adversaries, whereas those whose prestige, position, and purposes you supported have shown themselves less mindful of your manly conduct than hostile to your credit. In this crisis, as I have already informed you in detail, I have found Hortensius most anxious to serve you. Lucullus has shown good-will, and among those in office L. Racilius' loyalty and courage have been outstanding. My own role as champion and defender of your honour may perhaps with most minds count rather as a fulfilment of obligation than as an expression of opinion in view of the magnitude of your services to me. Aside from those mentioned, I cannot honestly report any good-will or service or friendly disposition on the part of any of the Consulars. You know, of course, that Pompey was not much in the Senate during the period in question. He talks to me about you very frequently, not only when I prompt him but of his own accord. I could easily see how much your latest letter pleased him. For my part, I was not only pleased but struck with admiration at your forbearance, or rather your excellent good sense. Bound to you as he was for your signally handsome behaviour to himself, he was inclined to suspect an estrangement on your side due to the notion some people entertained about his own aspirations. Now by that letter you have kept this eminent man's friendship. I always thought he wished you to emerge with credit, even during that highly suspicious episode of Caninius; and now that he has read your letter, I am clear that his one thought is for you and the honours and advantages to come to you.

So please regard what I am about to write as written with his approval and authority after frequent consultation between us. No decree of the Senate exists under which the restoration of the King of Egypt[63] is taken out of your hands. The recorded resolution, which as you know was vetoed, against the king's restoration by any person whomsoever, should be regarded as an ebullition of bias and spite rather than as the firm policy of the Senate, and its authority is to be measured accordingly. I therefore say that *you*, as governor of Cilicia and Cyprus, are in a position to judge what you can do and achieve. Should circumstances appear to furnish a fair prospect of your controlling Alexandria and Egypt, your honour and the Empire's will be

63. Literally 'the Alexandrian King', Cicero's usual way of referring to Ptolemy. So too Caelius at the end of Letter 81 (VIII. 4).

well served if you proceed to Alexandria with a naval and military force, after first settling the king at Ptolemais[64] or some other place in the vicinity; then, when you have established order in the city and stationed troops to secure it, let Ptolemy come back to his throne. In this way he will be restored by you, as the Senate originally resolved he should be, and he will be restored without a 'host', which according to our pious politicians is how the Sybil wants it done.

But both Pompey and I approve this view with the qualification that we realize your policy will be judged by results. If all turns out as we wish and pray, there will be universal praise for your good judgement and courage. If anything goes wrong, those same voices will say you acted ambitiously and rashly. That being so, it is not as easy for us as for you, almost within sight of Egypt as you are, to judge what you can accomplish. Our feeling is that if you are certain you can take over the kingdom, you should lose no time; but if this is doubtful, you ought not to make the attempt. I do guarantee that if you bring it off satisfactorily, many will applaud you in your absence, and everyone when you return. But I recognize that a setback would be dangerous because of the Senate's contrary resolution and the religious aspect. Well then, I am urging you forward to a certain success and at the same time I am warning you back from a doubtful conflict; and I return to my starting-point: your entire action will be judged by results, rather than by your own policy.

If the above way of proceeding seems to you too risky, we suggest the following: provided the king fulfils his engagements to your friends who have lent him money in your province and sphere of command, you should help him with auxiliary troops and supplies. The nature and situation of your province enable you either to support his restoration by lending

64. Cicero will have meant Ptolemais Hormos, an important Nile port at the southern entrance of the Fayum (not Ptolemais in Cyrenaica or Ptolemais in Phoenicia (Acre)).

him assistance or to hinder it by withholding the same. In this context nobody will perceive so readily and accurately as yourself just what is best in the particular circumstances of the case and time. I thought you ought to know *our* views from me rather than another.

You felicitate me on the state of my affairs, on Milo's friendship and Clodius' irresponsibility and impotence. Well, it does not at all surprise me to see a fine artist delighting in his own masterpieces. And yet the perverseness (I prefer not to use a stronger word) of folk is beyond belief. With good-will they could have kept me in the common cause; instead, their jealousy has estranged me. For I must tell you that their venomous backbiting has pretty well succeeded in turning me away from my old, long-established principles and brought me to the point, not indeed of forgetting my honour, but of paying some belated attention to my vital interest. The two could have run perfectly well in harness, if our Consulars had known the meaning of good faith and responsibility. But the majority are such fribbles that they are less pleased by my steadfastness in public affairs than irritated by my distinction. I write this to you the more frankly because you supported my public credit and standing almost from their earliest beginnings long ago as you do today – and that there *is* a today I owe to you. I can also write so because I find that it is not my birth, as I always used to think, that has aroused ill-will. For the evils of envy have been similarly manifest in your case, *crème de la crème* as you are. In your case, however, they were willing enough to see you figure among the leaders of the community, but as for any higher flight – no, no! I am glad that your lot has been different from mine; for it is one thing to lose some prestige and quite another to be left alone when one's existence is at stake. However, thanks to your noble self, I am not overmuch dissatisfied with *my* lot, for you saw to it that what I forfeited in worldly prosperity should appear more than made up to my future reputation and memory.

Your services to me and my affection for you alike prompt me to a word of admonition. Use all diligence and effort to win all the glory that has fired your imagination since you were a lad. Never let any man's injustice bend the greatness of spirit which I have always admired and loved in you. Yours is a great reputation, your liberality is loudly commended, your Consulship has left a fine memory. You cannot fail to see how much all this will gain in definition and brilliance by an access of credit from provincial office and command. All the same, while I want you to do what may properly be done by military means in the exercise of military authority, I also want you to plan well beforehand your future in Rome. Prepare for that, think of it, train for it. Realize – it is what you have always hoped for, so I do not doubt that you are aware now that you have achieved it – that without any difficulty you can hold the greatest and highest place in our society. I trust you will not think this exhortation on my part a piece of unnecessary verbiage. I offer it because I feel I should advise you in the light of our common experience to consider whom to trust, and of whom to beware, throughout the rest of your natural life.

You enquire as to the political situation. There is bitter conflict but the two sides are unequally matched. The party[65] superior in resources, armed force, and power has actually contrived, so it seems to me, to gain moral ascendancy as well, thanks to the stupidity and irresolution of their adversaries.[66] Accordingly they have secured from the Senate with very few opposing voices all that they did not expect to obtain even through the People without civil disorder. Caesar[67] has been voted a grant to pay his troops and ten Legates; and the ap-

65. i.e. the dominant coalition between Pompey, Caesar, and Crassus known as the 'First Triumvirate'.

66. M. Cato and his friends – the 'Optimates'.

67. Now in process of conquering Gaul north of the Roman provinces.

pointment of a successor under the lex Sempronia[68] has been blocked without difficulty. I tell you this rather briefly because the present political situation is little to my liking; but I tell it all the same, so that I can advise you to learn before you meet with any setback a lesson that I myself have learned from experience rather than books (devoted to every class of literature as I have been since childhood): we must not consider our security without regard to honour, nor honour without regard to security.

It is very kind of you to offer me your congratulations on my daughter's engagement to Crassipes. I hope and pray that the connection will bring us pleasure. Mind you instruct our dear Lentulus,[69] most promising and excellent young man that he is, in the accomplishments to which you have always applied yourself, but especially in the imitation of his father; he can have no finer education. I have a special regard and affection for him because he is your son and worthy to be yours, and because he is and has always been fond of me.

19 (I. 8)

CICERO TO LENTULUS SPINTHER

Rome, February (?) 55

From M. Cicero to P. Lentulus, Proconsul, greetings.

On all matters that concern you – proceedings, decisions,

68. Under this law of C. Sempronius Gracchus the Senate was bound to name two provinces for the Consuls of the following year (55) before their election. These they would take over in 54. Had one of the two Gauls been named, an extension of Caesar's command, which was due to expire that year, would have been precluded.

69. P. Lentulus Spinther the Younger. So Cicero regularly refers to his own son as 'Cicero' ('Marcus' in this translation).

Pompey's undertaking[70] – you will have an excellent informant in M. Plaetorius, who has taken, not only part, but the leading part in them. He has performed on your behalf every friendly service that affection, sagacity, and industry could render. You will likewise learn from him the whole state of public affairs, which are not easy to explain in writing. They are at all events in our friends'[71] control, so firmly that no change in the position seems likely for a generation to come.

For my part I follow my prescribed course, the course which you advised and which gratitude and expediency dictate; that is to say, I attach myself to the interests of the personage[72] whom you thought proper to attach to yourself where my interests were concerned. But you realize how hard it is to put aside one's political views, especially when they are well and firmly founded. However, as I cannot honourably oppose him, I adapt myself to his wishes. Nor in so doing am I belying my real feelings, as some may perhaps imagine. My inclination, indeed my affection for Pompey is strong enough to make me now feel that whatever is to his advantage and whatever he wants is right and proper. Even his opponents would in my opinion make no mistake if they gave up fighting, since they cannot be a match for him.

I have another consolation. Everyone agrees that I of all people am entitled either to support Pompey's every desire or to hold my peace or simply (and this is my chief wish) to return to my literary studies. That, you may be sure, is what I shall do, if the claims of Pompey's friendship allow me. As for what I had promised myself after attaining the highest state dignities and passing through the most severe ordeals – a lofty platform in the Senate, a position of independence in public life – there is an end to all that, not for me in particular, but for all and

70. Its nature is unknown. Pompey and Crassus were now Consuls.
71. The 'Triumvirs', or perhaps only Pompey and Caesar.
72. Pompey.

sundry. The choice lies between undignified support for a clique and fruitless opposition.

I am writing all this to you chiefly because I want you now to give thought to your own position. The whole face of things has changed – the Senate, the courts, the whole body politic. Tranquillity is what we have to pray for, and this the present holders of power seem likely to provide, if certain persons can submit with a modicum of patience to their domination. The old exalted notion of a Consular playing his firm and courageous part in the Senate must be dismissed from our minds. It has disappeared through the fault of those who lost the Senate the sympathies of a very friendly class and a very eminent individual.[73]

But to return to matters bearing more directly on your own position, I know that Pompey is very much your friend. While he is Consul, so far as I can judge, all you wish will be yours. In that connection he will have me close at his elbow, and I shall not neglect anything which may concern you. I have no fear of his finding me importunate – he will be glad even for his own sake to see that I know the meaning of gratitude.

I hope you will rest assured that the least of your concerns means more to me than all of mine put together. Such being my feelings, I could not be assiduous enough to satisfy my own mind; as for results, the reason why I fail to satisfy myself is that I cannot adequately repay, or even imagine myself repaying, any part of what I owe you.

There is a report that you have had a highly successful campaign.[74] We are waiting for a dispatch from you, as to which I have already had a talk with Pompey. Once it arrives, I shall be zealously to the fore in canvassing officers of state

73. i.e. the Knights (cf. *Letters to Atticus* 21 (II.1).5) and Pompey.

74. No doubt against the 'Free Cilicians' of the Taurus or Amanus mountains, at whose expense Cicero himself was to win laurels in 51. Lentulus seems to have mounted another campaign in 54 (see next letter, para. 1).

and members of the Senate;[75] and in other matters which concern you my efforts may go beyond my capacity, but they will fall short of my obligations.

20 (I. 9)

CICERO TO LENTULUS SPINTHER

Rome, December 54

From M. Cicero to Lentulus, Imperator, greetings.

I am glad to have your letter, which shows that you appreciate my *piety* towards you – I won't say my good-will, for even this solemn, sacred word 'piety' seems to me inadequate for what I owe you. When you write that you are grateful for my efforts on your behalf, it must be out of the overflowing affection of your heart. *Grateful*, because I do what it would be rank villainy to leave undone? But you would have a much better and clearer impression of my sentiments towards you, if we had been together and in Rome all this time we have been separated. Take what you say you have in view (nobody can do it better than you, and I am eagerly looking forward to the prospect) – speeches in the Senate and general activity and conduct of public affairs, as to which I shall tell you my opinion and position presently and answer your enquiries – well, at least I should have found in you the wisest and most affectionate of guides, while you would have found in me an adviser of experience perhaps not altogether negligible, and of undeniable loyalty and good-will. For your sake, it is true, I am duly delighted to think of you as Imperator, governing your province after a successful campaign at the head of a victorious

75. For a public Thanksgiving in honour of Lentulus' success. He finally celebrated his Triumph in 51.

army. But at least you could have enjoyed the due fruits of my gratitude fuller and fresher on the spot; and when it came to repaying certain people, some of them hostile to you, as you know, because you championed my restoration, others jealous of the grandeur and glory of the achievement – what a companion in arms I should have made you! To be sure, that inveterate enemy of his friends[76] who recompensed your signal favours by turning the feeble remnants of his violence against you[77] has done our work for us. The exposure of his recent operations[78] has robbed him of all independence in the future, let alone prestige. I could have wished that you had gained your experience in my case and not in your own as well, but I am glad in a bad business to think that you have not paid so very heavy a price for a lesson in the unreliability of mankind which *I* learned to my bitter sorrow.

This seems a good opportunity for me to give an exposition of the whole topic by way of a reply to your enquiries. You write that you have heard by letter that I am in good relations with Caesar and Appius, and you add that you have nothing to say against that. But you intimate that you would like to know my reasons for defending Vatinius and speaking to his character. To give you a clear explanation I must trace the principles of my political conduct a little further back.

To begin with, thanks to your public endeavours, dear sir, I conceived myself as restored, not only to my family and friends, but to my country. I owed *you* an affection wellnigh transcending reason and the most complete and signal personal devotion. To our country, which had lent you no slight assistance in your campaign for my restoration, I felt myself to owe

76. L. Domitius Ahenobarbus, now Consul along with Ap. Claudius Pulcher (see my commentary).

77. We do not know how Domitius had attacked Lentulus.

78. The scandalous electoral compact revealed by C. Memmius in September 54; see *Letters to Atticus* 91 (IV.17).2.

as a matter of gratitude at least the loyalty which I had formerly rendered only as the common duty of a Roman, and not as due in respect of any special favour to myself. The Senate heard these sentiments from my own lips during your Consulship, and you perceived them in the talks and discussions we had together. Yet even in those early days there was much to give me pause. I saw how your efforts to complete my rehabilitation met with covert ill-will in some quarters and doubtful support in others. In the matter of my memorials[79] those who ought to have helped you did not; similarly with respect to the criminal violence with which I and my brother were driven out of our homes.[80] I must add that even in those items to which, necessary as they were to me after the ruin of my private fortune, I attached minimal importance, I mean the indemnification of my losses by authority of the Senate, they showed a less forthcoming attitude than I had expected. I saw all this – it was plain enough; but any bitterness was outweighed by gratitude for what they had done.

And so, notwithstanding my regard for Pompey, to whom by your own declaration and testimony I owed a very great deal – a regard founded not only upon his goodness to me but on affection and what I might call life-long predilection – I made no account of his wishes and held firmly by all my old political sentiments. When Pompey came into town to speak to character on behalf of P. Sestius[81] and Vatinius said in evidence that I had made friends with C. Caesar because of his success and good fortune, I said in Pompey's presence that I thought M. Bibulus' sad plight (as Vatinius regarded it) preferable to any man's Triumphs and victories. At another point in Vatinius' evidence I said that the same people who had not allowed

79. No doubt including the one referred to on p. 48.

80. See *Letters to Atticus* 75 (IV.3).2.

81. Tried on charges of violence in February 56, Cicero defending. He was acquitted.

Bibulus to leave his home had forced me to leave mine.[82] My whole cross-examination was nothing but a condemnation of Vatinius' career as Tribune. On this topic I spoke throughout with the greatest frankness and spirit, dwelling on the use of violence, the auspices, and the grants of foreign kingdoms. And I did so not only at this trial but in the Senate, consistently and often. On the Nones of April in the Consulship of Marcellinus and Philippus the Senate actually adopted a proposal of mine that the question of the Campanian land should be referred to a full House on the Ides of May. Was not that invading the innermost citadel of the ruling clique? And could I have shown myself more oblivious of my past vicissitudes or more mindful of my political record?

That speech of mine caused a sensation, not only where I had intended but in quite unexpected quarters.[83] After the Senate had passed a decree in accordance with my motion, Pompey (without giving me any indication of displeasure) left for Sardinia and Africa, and joined Caesar at Luca on the way. Caesar there complained at length about my motion – he had been stirred up against me by Crassus, whom he had seen previously at Ravenna. Pompey by general admission was a good deal upset. I heard this from various sources, but my principal informant was my brother. Pompey met him in Sardinia a few days after leaving Luca. 'You're the very man I want,' he told him. 'Most lucky our meeting just now. Unless you talk seriously to your brother Marcus, you are going to have to pay up on the guarantee[84] you gave me on his behalf.' In short, he remonstrated in

82. As Consul in 59 Bibulus had spent most of the year shut up in his house. The remarks quoted here do not in fact occur in the extant speeches *pro Sestio* and *in Vatinium*.

83. Probably Caesar and Pompey are respectively indicated.

84. Pompey spoke metaphorically, Q. Cicero having in 57 made himself responsible for his brother's future political behaviour if restored from exile.

strong terms, mentioning his services to me, recalling the many discussions he had had with my brother himself about Caesar's legislation and the pledges my brother had given him concerning my future conduct, appealing to my brother's personal knowledge of the fact that his own support for my restoration had been given with Caesar's blessing. He asked him to commend to me Caesar's cause and prestige, with the request that I should refrain from attacking them if I would not or could not defend them.

Though my brother conveyed all this to me, Pompey also sent Vibullius with an oral message, asking me not to commit myself on the Campanian question till his return. Then I took stock. It was like a dialogue between me and my country. Would she not allow me, after all I had suffered and gone through for her sake, to behave with propriety and gratitude towards my benefactors and to honour my brother's pledge? Would she not let her loyal citizen, as I had always shown myself, be also a man of honour?

Now all the time I was acting and speaking in a manner liable to annoy Pompey, I received reports of how certain folk,[85] whose identity you should by now be able to guess, were talking. Fully as the course I was now following accorded with their past and present political sentiments, they were none the less expressing satisfaction at Pompey's disappointment with me and at the prospect that Caesar would be my sworn enemy in future. This was wounding enough; but much more so was their behaviour to my enemy[86] – the enemy, I should rather say, of law, justice, and tranquillity, of Rome and all honest men. This individual they chose to embrace and caress, petting and cosseting him before my very eyes. It was not enough to raise my spleen, because that organ has entirely disappeared, but enough at any rate to let them think they were raising it. At this point I surveyed the whole range of my

85. 'Optimates' like Hortensius, Bibulus, and Domitius.
86. Clodius.

affairs, so far as I could with only human wit to guide me, cast up my accounts in full, and arrived at the grand total of my cogitations. That is what I shall try to set out for you in brief.

If I had seen the state in the control of rascals and villains, as we know happened in Cinna's time and at some other periods of its history, no reward, or danger either (and while rewards count for little with me, even the bravest of us are influenced by dangers), would have driven me on to their side, no matter how much they might have done for me personally. But the leading man in Rome was Cn. Pompeius. The power and glory he enjoyed had been earned by state services of the highest importance and by the most signal military achievements. From early manhood I had rejoiced in his success, and as Praetor and Consul had come forward to promote it. On his side, he had individually helped me with his influence and voice in the Senate, and in conjunction with yourself by planned effort in my cause. His only enemy in Rome was also mine. All these points considered, I did not feel I need fear the reputation of inconsistency if in certain speeches I changed my tack a little and rallied in sentiment to the support of this great figure, my personal benefactor.

In this determination I could not but embrace Caesar, as you will recognize, for his interest and prestige were bound up with Pompey's. Here the old friendship which, as you are aware, existed between Caesar and myself and my brother Quintus counted for much, and no less Caesar's own gracious and generous attitude, which soon became plainly apparent to us in his letters and friendly acts.[87] Moreover, patriotic considerations had great weight with me. It was not, I felt, the will of our country that there should be a struggle with these men, especially after Caesar's great achievements; I felt she was keenly anxious to avoid such a struggle. But the weightiest element in thus persuading me was the pledge concerning

87. In the spring of 54 Q. Cicero left for Gaul to take up an appointment as Caesar's Legate.

myself which Pompey had given to Caesar and which my brother gave to Pompey.

I had besides to note in our community the phenomena which our favourite Plato has characterized so wonderfully – the tendency for the members of a political society to resemble its leaders.[88] I remembered that from the very first day of my Consulship sure foundations were laid for the strengthening of the Senate, so that no one ought to have been surprised either at the courage or the moral power of that Order as revealed on the Nones of December following.[89] Equally I remembered that after my retirement from office down to the Consulship of Caesar and Bibulus, so long as my views carried any considerable weight in the Senate, all honest men were pretty much of one mind. Later, while you were governor of Hither Spain and the state had no Consuls, only traffickers in provinces[90] and servile instruments of sedition, accident may be said to have flung my person as a bone of contention into the midst of civil conflict and strife. At that crisis the consensus in my defence of the Senate, of all Italy, of all honest men was truly remarkable, a thing transcending belief. I will not say what happened – the blame is complex and many shared in it – only this briefly, that it was generals, not an army, that I lacked. Granted that those who failed to defend me[91] were to blame, no less so were those who left me in the lurch;[92] and if those who were afraid should be in the dock, those who only pre-

88. Cf. *Laws*, 711 C. But Cicero's words are in fact an almost exact translation of a passage in Xenophon's *Education of Cyrus* (VIII.8.5).

89. The day on which the Senate voted for the execution of the Catilinarian conspirators.

90. According to Cicero's version of events the Consuls of 58, Piso and Gabinius, were bribed by Clodius with appointments to the provincial governorships of Macedonia and Syria respectively.

91. Not the mass of the 'honest men' but Pompey (cf. *Letters to Atticus* 171 (IX.5).2).

92. The 'optimate' leaders.

tended to be afraid are yet more deserving of censure.[93] At any rate there must be applause for my refusal to let my countrymen, whom I had preserved and who were desirous of saving me, be thrown leaderless against armed slaves – for my decision to let the potential power of honest[94] men united (had they been allowed to fight for me before I fell) be demonstrated rather when the opportunity came to raise me from the dust. You saw their spirit when you took action on my behalf; more, you confirmed and maintained it. In that campaign – so far from denying, I shall always remember and gladly proclaim it – you found certain very high-born personages more courageous in securing my reinstatement than they had shown themselves in preventing my exile. Had they chosen to hold to that policy, they would have recovered the respect of the community at the same time as they restored me to its membership. Your Consulship had put fresh heart into the honest men, roused from their apathy by your resolute and praiseworthy initiatives, especially when Cn. Pompeius joined the cause. Even Caesar, now that the Senate had recognized his splendid achievements by signal and unprecedented honours and marks of esteem, was moving towards a position of support for the authority of the House. No bad citizen would have had a loophole through which to injure his country.

Now pray mark the sequel. That embodiment of mischief, that pilferer of the secrets of women's worship, who treated the Good Goddess[95] with as little respect as his three sisters, escaped scot-free. A Tribune[96] was ready to bring the agitator to trial and punishment at the hands of honest men. He was saved by

93. In Cicero's obstinately held opinion the behaviour of certain of his friends (especially Hortensius) at the crisis of March 58 amounted to deliberate treachery (cf. *Letters to Atticus* 52 (III.7).2 etc.).

94. See Glossary of Terms.

95. See *Letters to Atticus* 12 (I.12).2.

96. Probably Racilius; cf. Letter 5 (II.1).3 of Cicero's letters to his brother Quintus.

the votes of those who thereby lost Rome what should have been a splendid example to posterity of the chastisement of sedition. Subsequently the same group allowed a memorial[97] – not my memorial, for the funds employed were not victory-spoils of mine, I merely signed the contract for the work – allowed the *Senate's* memorial to be inscribed with the name of a public enemy in letters of blood. These people desired my restoration, and for that I am deeply beholden. But I could have wished that they had not merely taken a doctor's interest in the life of the patient, but a trainer's in his strength and physical appearance. Certain persons in my case have followed the example of Apelles, who applied the utmost refinement of his art to perfecting the head and bust of his Venus, but left the rest of the body a mere sketch – they made a finished job of the *capital*[98] section only, leaving the rest unfinished and rough.

In this connection I disappointed the expectations of the jealous as well as the hostile. Once upon a time they were told, and believed, a false story about one of the boldest and most stout-hearted men who ever lived, whose equal in grandeur and resolution of spirit I do not know, Q. Metellus,[99] son of Lucius. He, so they like to say, was a broken man after his return from exile. A likely tale! Had he not gone quite readily into banishment, endured it with notable cheerfulness, and been at no great pains to return? Was he broken as the result of an episode in which he had emerged superior to all his contemporaries, even the eminent M. Scaurus, in resolution and integrity? Be that as it may, they formed the same notion about me as they had been given, or surmised for themselves,

97. Cf. p. 42. It may have been a building started at the end of Cicero's Consulship to commemorate the suppression of the Catilinarian conspiracy. Clodius seems to have effaced the inscription and substituted one bearing his own name.

98. Cicero plays on two meanings of *caput*, 'head' and 'status as a citizen'.

99. Numidicus (see Glossary of Persons).

about Metellus. They thought I should be a humbled man henceforth – whereas my country was making me actually prouder than I had ever been in my life! Had she not declared that she could not do without me – one single citizen? Metellus, after all, was brought back by the bill of a single Tribune, I by the whole state under the leadership of the Senate and with all Italy in attendance. The relevant law was promulgated by almost[100] the entire body of magistrates, moved by yourself as Consul at the Assembly of the Centuries with the enthusiastic support of all classes and individuals. In a word, all the forces of the commonwealth were mobilized to that one end.

Not that after this experience I made any pretensions, or make any today, to which the most jaundiced critic could fairly take exception. I merely endeavour to serve my friends, or even my acquaintances, with time and counsel and hard work. My way of life perhaps irritates those who look at its outward show and glitter, but cannot see the care and toil behind. One stricture, of which they make no secret, is that in my speeches in favour of Caesar I am more or less deserting the good old cause. Well, I have just advanced my reasons, but to these I would add another, not the least important, which I had begun to explain. Dear sir, you will not find again among our honest men that league of sentiment which you left behind you. Established in my Consulship, thereafter disturbed from time to time, shattered before you became Consul, and then restored by you in its entirety, it has now been forsaken by those who should have been its champions. Their faces, though faces can easily play the hypocrite, declare as much; more, they have shown it to be so by many a vote in Senate and courtroom – these men who in the world as we used to know it were called Optimates.

Accordingly, men of sense, of whom I hope I am and am considered to be one, have now completely to recast their views

100. See my edition. One Praetor (Clodius' brother Appius) and two Tribunes stayed out.

and sympathies. To cite Plato again, a very weighty authority with me; he tells us to push our political efforts as far as may be acceptable to our countrymen, but never to use force against parent or fatherland.[101] He gives his reason for keeping out of public affairs as follows: finding the people of Athens almost in its dotage, and seeing them without government either of persuasion or compulsion, he did not believe them amenable to persuasion and regarded compulsion as a sacrilege.[102] My situation was different. I was not dealing with a nation in its dotage, nor did I have a free choice whether or not to engage in public life, being inextricably involved. But I congratulated myself on having a cause to champion both expedient to myself personally and commendable to any honest man.[103] An added incentive was Caesar's quite remarkable, in fact amazing, generosity towards my brother and myself. He would have deserved my support however he was faring, but in so brilliant a career of success and victory I should think him worthy of homage even if he were not the good friend to us that he is. For I would have you believe that, apart from yourself and your fellow-architects of my restoration, there is no man to whose good offices I acknowledge myself so deeply beholden – and am glad to do so.

After this exposition your enquiries as to Vatinius and Crassus are easily answered – about Appius, as about Caesar, you say you have no criticism to offer, and I am glad my action has your approval. To take Vatinius then, Pompey originally arranged a reconciliation between us immediately after his election to the Praetorship,[104] although I had made some very

101. In *Crito*, 51c.

102. Cf. Plato, *Epist.* 5. 322a, b.

103. The maintenance of Caesar in his command, championed by Cicero in his speech 'On the Consular Provinces' (summer of 56; Caesar's personal generosity came later).

104. Early in 55. M. Cato's candidature was defeated by bribery and violence.

strong speeches in the Senate against his candidature – not so much to damage *him* as in support and compliment to Cato. Subsequently Caesar made a tremendous point of my undertaking his defence.[105] As for why I spoke for his character, I appeal to you not to ask me that question about Vatinius or any other defendant, otherwise I shall ask you a similar question when you come home. For that matter I can ask it while you are still abroad. Just call to mind the men for whom *you* have sent testimonials from the ends of the earth – don't be afraid, I do the same myself for the same people and shall so continue. To resume, I had another incentive to defend Vatinius, to which I referred in my speech at the trial. I said I was doing what the Parasite in the *Eunuch* recommends to the Captain:[106]

> When she says 'Phaedria', you must straight away
> Say 'Pamphila'. Should she want Phaedria in
> To dinner, you must counter 'Why not ask
> Pamphila for a song?' If she commends
> His handsome looks, you praise the girl's. In short,
> Give tit, my friend, for tat. The pin will prick.

So I drew the parallel. Certain high-born gentlemen, to whom I owed a debt of gratitude, were over-fond of an enemy of mine. In the Senate they would sometimes take him aside for a serious talk, sometimes salute him in hearty, hail-fellow-well-met style; this before my eyes. Well then, since they had *their* Publius, I hoped the gentlemen of the jury would allow *me* another Publius, with whom to sting those personages just a little in return for the mild provocation I had received! Nor did I merely *say* this; I often do it, Gods and men approving.

So much for Vatinius. Now as to Crassus: I was on very good terms with him, having in the interests of general harmony expunged by what I might call a deliberate act of oblivion all

105. In 54, when Vatinius was accused of bribery. Cicero's witness to character seems to have been given in a second trial.

106. Terence, *The Eunuch*, 440 ff. Phaedria is a male character, Pamphila female.

the grave wrongs he had done me. I should have stomached his sudden defence of Gabinius,[107] whom he had attacked on the days immediately preceding, if he had gone to work without abusing me. But when I argued with him politely, he insulted me. I flared up. It was not, I think, just the irritation of the moment, which might not have carried me so far, but my suppressed resentment at the many injuries he had done me. I thought I had dissipated all that, but a residue was still there without my being aware of it, and now it all suddenly came to the surface. Here again certain persons, the same whom I so often indicate without naming names, expressed the greatest satisfaction at my plain speaking, and told me that now at last they felt I was restored to Rome the man I used to be; and outside the House too this fracas brought me many congratulations. And yet they went around saying how pleased they were to think that Crassus would be my enemy henceforward, and that his associates would never be my friends. These backbitings were brought to my knowledge by very worthy folk; and when Pompey pressed me as strongly as I have ever known him do to make it up with Crassus and Caesar wrote a letter making it plain that this quarrel has greatly upset him, why, I took account of my circumstances and of my heart as well. And Crassus, as though to make all Rome witness of our reconciliation, set out for his province virtually from my doorstep. He offered to dine with me, and did so at my son-in-law Crassipes' place in the suburbs. Accordingly I took up his cause at his urgent request and defended it in the Senate,[108] as you say you have heard. Good faith required no less.

You now know my reasons for defending each particular

107. When Gabinius restored Ptolemy the Piper to his throne in 55 Cicero attacked him in the Senate. According to Dio Cassius (XXXIX. 60.1) the Consuls, Pompey and Crassus, came to his defence, calling Cicero 'exile', but no doubt the insult came from Crassus, not Pompey.

108. In January 54 (cf. letter 25.).

cause or case, and the general position from which I take such part in politics as I may. I should like it to be clear to you that my attitude would have been just the same if I had had a completely open and untrammelled choice. I should not be in favour of fighting such formidable power, nor of abolishing the pre-eminence of our greatest citizens, even if that were possible. Nor should I be for sticking fast to one set of opinions, when circumstances have changed and the sentiments of honest men are no longer the same. I believe in moving with the times. Unchanging consistency of standpoint has never been considered a virtue in great statesmen. At sea it is good sailing to run before the gale, even if the ship cannot make harbour; but if she *can* make harbour by changing tack, only a fool would risk shipwreck by holding to the original course rather than change and still reach his destination. Similarly, while all of us as statesmen should set before our eyes the goal of peace with honour to which I have so often pointed, it is our aim, not our language, which must always be the same.

Therefore, as I have just stated, my politics would be exactly what they now are, even if my hands were completely free. But since I am attracted to this standpoint by favours from some quarters and pushed to it by injuries from others, I am by no means loath to take and express the political views which I deem most conducive to the public welfare as well as my own. I take this line the more openly and frequently because my brother Quintus is Caesar's Legate, and because Caesar has always received my slightest intervention, even purely verbal, on his behalf with such display of gratitude as to make me feel that he is deeply obliged to me. I use all his influence, which is very powerful, and his resources, which you know to be very large, as though they were my own. In fact, I do not think I could have foiled the designs of evil men against me in any other way than by adding to the means of defence which have always been at my disposal the good-will of the powers that be.

Had I had you with me here, my belief is that I should have followed this same course. I know your natural temperance and moderation. I know that your warm friendship towards myself has no cast of malice towards others, that on the contrary you are as frank and straightforward as you are high-minded and unselfish. I have seen certain persons behave to you as you could once see them behaving to me. Surely my motives would have been yours. But when eventually I can avail myself of your presence, you will be my director in all things, with the same care for my standing as you had for my existence as a citizen. As for me, you may be sure of finding in me a partner and companion in all things, in your every act, opinion, and desire. No object in all my life will be so precious to me as to make you happier every day in the services you have rendered me.

You ask me to send you the products of my pen since you left Rome. There are some speeches, which I shall give to Menocritus – don't be alarmed, there are not very many of them! I have also composed – I am tending to get away from oratory and go back to the gentler Muses who please me best, as they always have from my youth – composed, as I was saying, three volumes in the form of an argument and dialogue *On the Orator*, in the manner (so at least I intended) of Aristotle. I think your son will find them of some use. They do not deal in the standard rules, but embrace the whole theory of oratory as the ancients knew it, both Aristotelian and Isocratic. I have also written a poem in three books *On my Vicissitudes*. I should have sent you this before, if I had thought right to publish it, for it is, and will be to all eternity, evidence of your services and of my gratitude. But I was inhibited by the thought, not so much of those who might feel themselves aspersed (*that* I have done sparingly and gently), but of my benefactors – if I had named them all, there would have been no end to it. All the same I shall see that you get these volumes too, if I can find a reliable bearer. All this part of my daily life I submit to you. Everything I may achieve in the way of literature and study, my old delights, I shall be most happy to bring to the bar of your judgement. You have always cared for these things.

What you say about your domestic concerns and the commissions you give me lie so close to my heart that I desire no reminder; a *request* I can scarcely take without real pain. You say you were unable to settle my brother Quintus' business, because sickness prevented you from crossing over to Cilicia[109] last summer, but that you will now use your best efforts to settle it. The fact is that my brother considers with good cause that once he has annexed this property his fortunes will have been placed on a firm foundation, thanks to you. I hope you will keep me abreast, as intimately and as often as you can, of your own affairs and of your (and my) dear boy's studies and exercises. And I would have you believe that you are to me the dearest and most valued friend that ever man had, and that I shall make it my business to prove this, not only to you, but to all mankind, indeed to all posterity.

Appius was in the habit of saying in private, and later said publicly in the Senate, that, if passage was given to a curiate law, he would draw lots for a province with his colleague; but if there was no curiate law, he would come to an arrangement with his colleague and supersede you. A curiate law, he contended, was something a Consul should have, but did not absolutely need. Since he had a province by decree of the Senate, he would hold military authority under the lex Cornelia until he re-entered the city boundary. What your various friends may write to you I do not know – I understand that opinions differ. Some think you have the right to stay in your province because you are being superseded without a curiate law; others that, if you go, you are entitled to leave a governor

109. i.e. Cilicia proper, as distinct from the whole Roman province so called. It has been suggested that Quintus wanted to buy a property adjoining one of his two estates near Arpinum, of which the owner was in Cilicia and so amenable to Lentulus' influence.

in charge. For my part, I am less certain of the legal position (though even that is not so very dubious) than of the advisability of your handing over the province to your successor without delay. Your high standing and prestige, your independence, in which I know you take especial satisfaction, are involved, particularly as you cannot rebuff Appius' exorbitance without incurring some suspicion of a similar fault. I regard myself as no less bound to tell you my sentiments than to defend whatever course you adopt.

After writing the foregoing I received your letter about the tax-farmers. I cannot but commend your sense of justice, but could have wished that you had had the good luck, as it were, to avoid offending the interests or sentiments of that class, which you have always favoured in the past. *I* shall steadily defend your rulings. But you know their way, you know how strongly hostile they were to the great Q. Scaevola himself. Despite what has happened, I hope you will do everything in your power to reconcile, or at any rate mollify, their feelings towards you. That is difficult I grant, but I think it is what a wise man like yourself ought to do.

21 (I. 10)

CICERO TO L. VALERIUS

Rome, 54 (?)

From M. Cicero to L. Valerius, Counsellor, greetings (I don't see why I should not make you a present of the title, especially in these days, when effrontery can stand substitute for good counsel).[110]

110. *sapientia*, 'wisdom' or 'good sense', has a special application to the science of the jurist with which Cicero likes to make play when writing to his legal friends Valerius and Trebatius.

I have written to thank our friend Lentulus on your behalf in suitable terms. But I wish you would stop using my letters and revisit us after all this while, and elect to spend your time here, where you will be a *kent* man,[111] rather than over yonder, where I suppose nobody *kens* but you. To be sure some travellers tell that you are grown arrogant, because you don't 'respond';[112] others complain of your incivility, because you 'respond' in bad form.[113] However, I hope I shall soon be cracking my joke with you face to face. So mind you come back as quickly as you can, and don't go to your beloved Apulia. We want some pleasure in your safe return.[114] If you go there after such an Odyssey, you won't recognize any of your folk.[115]

111. Literally 'where you will be in some number (account) ... where you seem to be the only man of sense' (legal learning; with a play on *sapere*). Robbed of *doubles entendres* the sense amounts to 'better be in Rome, where jurists have their place, than in Cilicia, where Roman law is unknown'. For 'ken' as a term in Scottish law (Valerius seems to have come from Apulia) see the *Oxford English Dictionary*.

112. *respondere* is technically used of a jurisconsult's 'opinions' – legal rulings given in response to questions. It is also used of answering a question or a greeting. Not to answer such would be the reverse of polite. Cicero is fond of playing on the various uses of this verb (see note in my C.U.P. edition of the *Letters to Atticus*, Vol. I, p. 222).

113. *male respondere* = 'reply insultingly' or alternatively 'give bad (mistaken) legal advice'. Cicero really seems to have had a poor opinion of Valerius professionally; see p. 116.

114. *salvum venisse gaudere*, 'to be glad you have arrived safely', is a polite formula (cf. *Letters to Atticus* 114 (v.21).1), to which Cicero here gives a special twist. Valerius' friends in Rome would *not* be glad if he buried himself down in Apulia.

115. In the *Odyssey* (as Cicero may not have precisely remembered) the returning hero recognizes his family and friends but they do not recognize him.

22 (V. 12)

CICERO TO LUCCEIUS

Cumae (?), c. 12 April 55

From M. Cicero to L. Lucceius, son of Quintus, greetings.

Although I have more than once attempted to take up my present topic with you face to face, a sort of shyness, almost awkwardness, has held me back. Away from your presence, I shall set it out with less trepidation. A letter has no blushes.

I have a burning desire, of a strength you will hardly credit but ought not, I think, to blame, that my name should gain lustre and celebrity through your works. You often promise me, it is true, that you will comply with my wish; but I ask you to forgive my impatience. The quality of your literary performances, eagerly as I have always awaited them, has surpassed my expectation. I am captivated and enkindled. I want to see my achievements enshrined in your compositions with the minimum of delay. The thought that posterity will talk of me and the hope, one might say, of immortality hurries me on, but so too does the desire to enjoy in my lifetime the support of your weighty testimony, the evidence of your goodwill, and the charm of your literary talent.

As I write these words, I am not unaware of the heavy burden weighing upon you of projects undertaken and already commenced. But seeing that you have almost finished your account of the Italian War and the Civil War,[116] and remembering that you told me you were embarking on subsequent events, I feel I should be failing myself if I did not suggest two alternatives for your consideration. Would you prefer to weave

116. i.e. from the beginning of the war between Rome and her Italian allies in 91 down to Sulla's final victory over the Marians in 81.

my affairs along with those of the rest of the period into a single narrative, or might you not rather follow many Greek precedents, as Callisthenes with the Phocian War, Timaeus with the War of Pyrrhus, and Polybius with that of Numantia, all of whom detached their accounts of these particular wars from their continuous histories? Just so, you might deal with the domestic conspiracy apart from wars against external enemies. From my point of view there seems little to choose, so far as my credit is concerned. But there is my impatience to be considered; and here it does make a difference, if, instead of waiting until you reach the place, you immediately seize upon that entire subject and period. Furthermore, if your whole mind is directed upon a single theme and a single figure, I can already envisage the great gain in general richness and splendour.

Not that I am unconscious of the effrontery of what I am about, first in laying such a burden upon you (pressure of work may refuse me), and secondly in asking you to write about me eulogistically. What if the record does not appear to you so eminently deserving of eulogy? But the bounds of delicacy once passed, it is best to be frankly and thoroughly brazen. Therefore I ask you again, not mincing my words, to write of this theme more enthusiastically than perhaps you feel. Waive the laws of history for this once. Do not scorn personal bias, if it urge you strongly in my favour – that sentiment of which you wrote very charmingly in one of your prefaces, declaring that you could no more be swayed thereby than Xenophon's Hercules by Pleasure.[117] Concede to the affection between us just a little more even than the truth will license.

117. Prodicus the Sophist's allegory of the Choice of Hercules is retailed by Xenophon in his *Memoirs of Socrates* (II.I.21). Cicero refers to it in his treatise *On Duties* (I.118). – This passage ought not to be taken too literally. It is an exhibition of false modesty – Cicero did not really believe that the wine of his achievements needed any bush – and a compliment to Lucceius, as showing how much store Cicero set upon his praise.

If I prevail upon you to undertake the task, I persuade myself that the material will be worthy of your ready and skilful pen. I fancy a work of moderate length could be made up, from the beginning of the plot down to my return from exile. In it you will also be able to make use of your special knowledge of political changes, in explaining the origins of the revolutionary movement and suggesting remedies for things awry. You will blame what you judge deserving of reproof and give reasons for commending what you approve; and if, according to your usual practice, you think proper to deal pretty freely, you will hold up to censure the perfidy, artifice, and betrayal of which many were guilty towards me. Moreover, my experiences will give plenty of variety to your narrative, full of a certain kind of delectation to enthrall the minds of those who read, when you are the writer. Nothing tends more to the reader's enjoyment than varieties of circumstance and vicissitudes of fortune. For myself, though far from desirable in the living, they will be pleasant in the reading; for there is something agreeable in the secure recollection of bygone unhappiness.[118] For others, who went through no personal distress and painlessly survey misfortunes not their own, even the emotion of pity is enjoyable. Which of us is not affected pleasurably, along with a sentiment of compassion, at the story of the dying Epaminondas on the field of Mantinea, ordering the javelin to be plucked from his body only after he had been told in answer to his question that his shield was safe, so that even in the agony of his wound he could meet an honourable death with mind at ease? Whose sympathies are not aroused and held as he reads of Themistocles' flight and death?[119] The actual chronological record of events exercises no very powerful fascination upon us; it is like the recital of an almanac. But in the doubtful and various fortunes of an outstanding individual we often find

118. Cf. Virgil's *forsan et haec olim meminisse iuvabit.*

119. The manuscripts say 'and return'. But Themistocles never returned from his exile.

surprise and suspense, joy and distress, hope and fear; and if they are rounded off by a notable conclusion, our minds as we read are filled with the liveliest gratification.

So I shall be especially delighted if you find it best to set my story apart from the main stream of your work, in which you embrace events in their historical sequence – this drama, one may call it, of what I did and experienced; for it contains various 'acts', and many changes of plan and circumstance. Nor am I apprehensive of appearing to angle for your favour with the bait of a little flattery when I declare that you of all others are the writer by whom I desire my praises to be sung. After all, you are not ignorant of your own worth; a man like you knows better than to see sycophancy in admiration rather than jealousy in its absence. Nor am I myself so foolish as to ask any author to immortalize my name but one who in so doing will gain glory for his own genius. Alexander the Great did not ask Apelles to paint his portrait and Lysippus to sculpt his statue in order to curry favour with these artists, but because he believed the work would redound to his own fame as well as theirs. Those artists, however, only made a physical likeness known to people unacquainted with the original; and even in default of such memorials famous men would lose none of their celebrity. Agesilaus of Sparta, who would not allow representations of himself in paintings or sculpture, is no less pertinent to my case than those who took pains over the matter. Xenophon's one little volume in eulogy of that king has achieved far more than all the portraits and statues under the sun.

There is a further reason why a place in your works as compared with those of other writers will bring my mind a more lively satisfaction and my memory more signal honour. You will confer upon me the benefit not only of your literary skill, as Timaeus did upon Timoleon or Herodotus upon Themistocles, but of your authority as a famed and admired public man, tried and notably approved in public affairs of the greatest moment. Not only shall I gain a herald, such as Alexander when he visited Sigeum said Homer was to Achilles, but a witness – the weighty testimony of a great and famous man. For I am of one mind with Naevius' Hector, who delights, not in praise merely, but, he adds, 'from one that praisèd is'.[120]

Suppose, however, I am refused; that is to say, suppose something hinders you (for I feel it would be against nature for you to *refuse* any request of mine), I shall perhaps be driven to a course often censured by some, namely to write about myself – and yet I shall have many illustrious precedents. But I need not point out to you that this *genre* has certain disadvantages. An autobiographer must needs write over-modestly where praise is due and pass over anything that calls for censure. Moreover, his credit and authority are less, and many will blame him and say that heralds at athletic contests show more delicacy, in that after placing garlands on the heads of the winners and loudly proclaiming their names, they call in another herald when it is *their* turn to be crowned at the end of the games, in order to avoid announcing their own victory with their own lips. I am anxious to escape these drawbacks, as I shall, if you take my case. I beg you so to do.

In case it may surprise you that I urge you so earnestly and at such length *now*, when you have repeatedly promised me that you will compose the record of my public career, its policies and events, and spare no pains, my motive is, as I wrote in the first place, impatience. I cannot wait to see the world learning about me in my lifetime from your books and to enjoy my modicum of glory myself before I die.

If it is not troubling you too much, please write back and tell me what you intend to do. If you undertake the case, I will prepare notes on all points.[121] If you put me off, I shall talk to

120. Cf. p. 217. The verse is from Naevius' (lost) play *Hector's Departure*.

121. i.e. factual statements for Lucceius to embellish.

you personally. Meanwhile, do not be idle. Give a thorough polish to the work you have in hand. And love me well.

23 (V. 17)

CICERO TO P. SITTIUS

Rome (?), 56 (?)

From M. Cicero to P. Sittius, son of Publius, greetings.

It is not from unmindfulness of our friendship, or any interruption in my normal habit, that I have not sent you a letter at an earlier time. A period of prostrating calamity for our country and for myself was followed by one in which your own misfortunes, as painful as they were undeserved, made me reluctant to write. But the interval has now grown long enough; and recalling more closely your manly and lofty spirit, I thought it would be consonant with my general practice to write you these lines.

My dear Sittius, in the days when you first became the object of a slanderous attack in your absence, I defended you; and when your closest friend[122] was brought to trial and his ordeal was conjoined with the charge against yourself, I championed you and your cause as diligently as I was able. Then latterly, shortly after my return to Rome, finding the matter had been handled otherwise than I should have wished if I had been on the spot, I none the less did everything I could to save you. But the public prejudice due to the grain shortage,[123] enemies –

122. P. Cornelius Sulla.

123. Evidently a reference to the grain crisis in September 57, just after Cicero's return from exile, when Pompey was given charge of supplies for five years. Why Sittius was blamed is unknown.

your friends' enemies as well as your own – the unfairness of the whole court proceedings, and many other disorders in the body politic proved more powerful than truth and the merits of the case. Then I did not fail your son Publius; my time, my advice, my trouble, my testimony were at his disposal.

Thus I may claim to have observed faithfully and strictly all the obligations of friendship; and these include another which I do not deem it right to leave unfulfilled, and that is to urge and beg you to remember that you are both a human being and a man: as the former, to bear with philosophy the working of chance, universal and unpredictable, which none of us can avoid and which none can by any means guarantee; and, as the latter, to offer stout resistance to pain and misfortune, and to bear in mind that such misadventures as a result of unjust trials have befallen many gallant and excellent men in our own and in other imperial states. I wish it were not true to add that you are deprived of a commonwealth in which no man of sense finds anything to give him pleasure.

As for your son, I am afraid that if I say nothing you may feel that I have withheld the tribute due to his merit; whereas if I write down all I feel, my letter may exacerbate the pain of your separation. Your wisest course, however, is to deem that wherever you may be, his filial affection, manliness, and diligence belong to you and are beside you. What we envisage in our minds is no less our own than what we see with our eyes. So his exemplary character and profound affection should be a great source of comfort to you; so too should be the thought of myself and those others who value you, and always shall, by your character, not your worldly fortune; and so above all should be your own conscience. You will reflect that you have deserved nothing of what has happened, and you will add the thought that wise men are troubled by dishonour, not by chance, and by their own fault, not by others' ill-usage.

Prompted by the memory of our old friendship and the

merit and attention of your son. I shall ever be ready both to comfort and to alleviate your plight. If you care to write me a few words, I shall not let you feel that you have written them for nothing.

24 (VII. 1)

CICERO TO M. MARIUS

Rome, late August 55

From M. Cicero to M. Marius greetings.

If some bodily distress or the frailty of your health has kept you from coming to the show,[124] I give credit to chance rather than to your own good sense. On the other hand, if you thought these objects of public wonderment unworthy of your notice, and chose not to come though your health would have permitted, why, I rejoice both at your freedom from physical distress and at your health of mind, in that you have disregarded these spectacles at which others idly marvel – always provided that you have reaped the fruits of your leisure. You have had a wonderful opportunity to enjoy it, left almost on your own in that delightful spot.[125] And after all, I don't doubt that throughout the period of the show you have spent the mornings browsing over your books in that bedroom of yours with its window that you let into the wall to overlook the bay of Stabiae. Meanwhile those who left you there were watching the public

124. Given by Pompey in his second Consulship to inaugurate his stone theatre (the first built in Rome) and the temple of Venus Victrix. Pliny the Elder and Cassius Dio write of their magnificence.

125. Elsewhere Cicero writes of Marius as his neighbour at Pompeii. But Marius' villa may have been two or three miles to the south above modern Castellammare di Stabia.

pantomimes half-asleep.[126] As for the rest of the day, you have been spending it in such diversions as you have provided to suit your own taste while we have had to endure what Sp. Maecius[127] presumably thought proper.

To be sure, the show (if you are interested) was on the most lavish scale; but it would have been little to your taste, to judge by my own. To begin with, certain performers honoured the occasion by returning to the boards, from which I thought they had honoured their reputation by retiring.[128] Your favourite, our friend Aesopus, gave a display which everyone was willing should be his finale. When he came to take an oath[129] and got as far as 'if I knowingly swear false', he lost his voice! I need not give you further details – you know the other shows.[130] They did not even have the sprightliness which one mostly finds in ordinary shows – one lost all sense of gaiety in watching the elaborate productions. These I don't doubt you are very well content to have missed. What pleasure is there in getting a *Clytemnestra* with six hundred mules or a *Trojan Horse* with three thousand mixing-bowls[131] or a variegated display of cavalry and infantry equipment in some battle or other? The public gaped at all this; it would not have amused you at all.

126. The weather in high summer was naturally oppressive. Valerius Maximus (II.6.4) says that streams of running water were channelled through the theatre to mitigate the heat.

127. Spurius Maecius Tarpa selected the plays to be produced at the show. He may have been Chairman (*magister*) of the Guild of Poets established in the third century: cf. Horace, *Satires*, I.10.38, *Art of Poetry*, 386.

128. The common phrase *honoris causa*, 'by way of compliment', is echoed in another sense, 'for the sake of (their) repute'.

129. Perhaps as part of his role. Others suppose that actors had to take an oath before starting their performance (but why?).

130. i.e. comedies and mimes.

131. The first of these two tragedies was by Accius. Grammarians ascribe a *Trojan Horse* both to Livius Andronicus and to Naevius. The bowls are thought to have figured as part of the spoils of Troy.

If you were listening to your man Protogenes[132] during those days (so long as he read you anything in the world except my speeches), you have certainly had a good deal better time of it than any of us. As for the Greek[133] and Oscan[134] shows, I don't imagine you were sorry to miss *them* – especially as you can see an Oscan turn on your town council,[135] and you care so little for Greeks that you don't even take Greek Street to get to your house! Or perhaps, having scorned gladiators,[136] you are sorry not to have seen the athletes! Pompey himself admits that they were a waste of time and midday oil![137] That leaves the hunts, two every day for five days, magnificent – nobody says otherwise. But what pleasure can a cultivated man get out of seeing a weak human being torn to pieces by a powerful animal or a splendid animal transfixed by a hunting spear? Anyhow, if these sights are worth seeing, you have seen them often; and we spectators saw nothing new. The last day was for the elephants. The groundlings showed much astonishment thereat, but no enjoyment. There was even an impulse of compassion, a feeling that the monsters had something human about them.[138]

As for me, these past days, during the plays (in case you

132. No doubt a reader (*anagnostes*).

133. Probably Greek plays performed in Greek, as distinct from Latin adaptations of Greek originals; cf. *Letters to Atticus* 410 (XVI.5).1.

134. i.e. *Fabulae Atellanae*, a type of coarse farce with stock characters, like a Punch and Judy show.

135. 'Oscan' standing for 'Campanian'. *Graffiti* found in Pompeii show that a M. Marius stood for election as Aedile.

136. i.e. some gladiatorial show (apparently a private allusion). The explanation that Marius had defied Clodius' gangs does not suit what is known of him.

137. *operam et oleum perdere* was a proverbial expression for a waste of time and money, *oleum* referring to 'midnight oil'. Here it is humorously applied to the oil used by athletes in anointing themselves.

138. Pliny's account (*Natural History*, VIII.21) that the whole crowd of spectators rose and cursed Pompey is evidently exaggerated.

picture me as a free man, if not a happy one), I pretty well ruptured my lungs defending your friend Caninius Gallus.[139] If only my public were as accommodating as Aesopus', upon my word I should be glad to give up my profession and spend my time with you and other congenial spirits. I was weary of it even in the days when youth and ambition spurred me forward, and when moreover I was at liberty to refuse a case I did not care for. But now life is simply not worth living. I have no reward to expect for my labours, and sometimes I am obliged to defend persons who have deserved none too well of me at the request of those who *have* deserved well.

Accordingly, I am looking out for any excuse to live as I please at long last; and you and your leisured manner of existence have my hearty commendation and approval. I resign myself to the rarity of your visits more easily than I otherwise should, because, even if you were in Rome, I am so confoundedly busy that I should not be able to enjoy the entertainment of your company, nor you of mine (if any entertainment it holds). When and if I slacken my chains (for to be loose of them entirely is more than I can ask), then, no question about it, I shall teach you the art of civilized living, to which you have been giving your undivided attention for years! Only you must go on propping up that frail health of yours and looking after yourself, so that you can visit my places[140] in the country and run around with me in my little litter.

I have written at unusual length, out of an abundance, not of spare time, but of affection for you, because in one of your letters you threw out a hint, if you remember, that I might

139. The charge may have referred to his activities as Tribune in 56 (cf. p. 25 etc.). As an adherent of Pompey's he will have been one of a number of defendants for whom Cicero appeared at this period at the behest of Pompey and Caesar, some of them old enemies of his own.

140. Possibly 'our places'; Marius too may have had more than one villa in the area. Cicero at this period had one at Pompeii and one at Cumae.

write something to prevent you feeling sorry to have missed the show. If I have succeeded in that, so much the better; but if not, I console myself with the thought that henceforth you will come to the shows and visit us, and that you won't forgo any prospect of pleasure to yourself on account of my letters.

25 (v. 8)

CICERO TO CRASSUS

Rome, January 54

From M. Cicero to M. Licinius Crassus, son of Publius, greetings.

I do not doubt that all your friends have apprised you in their letters of the zeal which I put forward on the Ides (?)[141] for the defence, or even enhancement, of your position. It was too ardent and too conspicuous to go unrecorded. Against the Consuls and many of the Consulars I joined issue with a vehemence which I have never before displayed in any cause, thus taking upon myself the standing role of protagonist on behalf of all that tends to your honour, and discharging more than amply the service which has long been owing to our old friendship, but which the many variations of circumstance had caused me to intermit.

But indeed I never lacked will to cultivate your friendship and contribute to your advancement. Only certain persistent fellows, whom it hurts to hear others well spoken of, estranged you from me more than once, and at times changed my attitude to you. But now the occasion has arisen which I prayed for,

141. Of January (but the reading is conjectural). The debate in the Senate concerned the allocation of funds etc. to Crassus as governor of Syria.

but scarcely hoped to see: in the full tide of your prosperity I have had the chance to show myself mindful of our mutual sentiments and loyal to our friendship. Yes, I have succeeded in making plain, not only to your entire domestic circle but to the community at large, that I am your very good friend. Your wife, the paragon of her sex, and your two sons, whose filial affection, high character, and popularity do them honour, rely on my counsels and promptings and my active support. And the Senate and People of Rome now know that in all matters affecting you during your absence my devoted and indefatigable service and the influence I command are absolutely and unreservedly at your disposal.

Day-to-day events, past and current, are presumably conveyed to you by your domestic correspondents. As for me personally, I very much hope you will thoroughly persuade yourself that I have not *happened* to embrace your cause and work for your greatness through any accident or sudden whim, but have always made it my aim ever since my entry into public life to be on the closest terms with you. Since those days I recall no failure of attention on my part or of good-will and generosity in the highest measure on yours. If in the meanwhile certain infringements, surmised rather than real, have affected our relations, these are mere figments of the imagination; let them be utterly eradicated from our memories and our lives. Between two men such as you are and I desire to be, whose lot has fallen on the same political ground, I would hope that alliance and friendship will conduce to the credit of both.

You yourself, therefore, will decide the place in your esteem which you think appropriate for me, and I trust your decision will take account of my standing in the world. On my side, I profess and promise you my signal and exemplary devotion in every kind of service tending to your dignity and glory. Many may be my rivals, but by the verdict of every beholder, and of your sons above all, I shall comfortably win the race. For both young men I have a particular regard, but, while both have my good-will equally, I am the more attached to Publius because ever since he was a boy, but especially at the present time, he pays me attention and regard as though to a second father.

Please believe that this is no ordinary letter; it will have the force of a covenant. Be sure that the promises and undertakings I give you will be religiously respected and carried out to the letter. Having taken up the defence of your position while you are abroad, I shall persevere therein, not only for our friendship's sake but to maintain my own reputation for consistency. Accordingly, I have thought it enough at present to assure you of my unsolicited activity wherever I myself see an opportunity to promote your wish, your interest, or your dignity; and to add that, should any suggestion reach me from you or yours, I shall take care you do not suppose any written word of your own or any representations from your folk to have been lost upon me. So please write to me yourself on all matters, large, small, or in between, as to a most sincere friend, and advise your people to make use of my service and counsel, my public and personal influence, in all concerns – no matter whether public or private, business or domestic, your own or your friends' or your guests' or your clients'. My labour shall go to fill, so far as may be, the void created by your absence.

26 (VII. 5)

CICERO TO CAESAR

Rome, April 54

From Cicero to Caesar, Imperator, greetings.

Please observe how fully I am persuaded that you are my *alter ego*, not only in my own concerns but in those of my friends also. I had intended to take C. Trebatius with me wherever I might go, in order to bring him home again the richer by any and every benefit and mark of good-will in my power to bestow. But Pompey has stayed on longer than I expected, and my own departure seems prevented, or at any rate delayed, by a certain hesitation on my part of which you are not uninformed.[142] So observe my presumption: I now want Trebatius to look to you for everything he would have hoped for from me, and I have assured him of your friendly disposition in terms really no less ample than I had previously been wont to use respecting my own.

But a remarkable coincidence has supervened, as though in evidence of the correctness of my opinion and in guarantee of your kindness. Just as I was talking rather seriously to our friend Balbus at my house on the subject of this very Trebatius, a letter comes in from you concluding as follows: 'I shall make M. Curtius' son[143] king of Gaul. Or, if you please, make him over to Lepta,[144] and send me somebody else on whom to bestow my favours.' Balbus and I both raised our hands to heaven. It came so pat as to seem no accident, but divine intervention.

I send you Trebatius accordingly. I thought it right to do so of my own accord in the first instance, but at your invitation in the second. In embracing his acquaintance with all your usual courtesy, my dear Caesar, I should wish you to confer upon his single person all the kindnesses which I could induce you to wish to confer upon my friends. As for him, I will answer that

142. In 55 Pompey received a five-year command in Spain and in the autumn of 54 he appointed Cicero as his Legate (cf. *Letters to his Brother Quintus* 21 (III.1).22, *Letters to Atticus* 93 (IV.19).2). But neither he nor Cicero went there. The 'hesitation' is generally referred to apprehensions about Clodius' designs.

143. *M. Curti filium*, conjectured for *M. itfiuium* in the manuscripts. The person referred to is clearly the M. Curtius whom Cicero had asked Caesar to appoint Military Tribune in the following year (*Letters to his Brother Quintus* 18 (II.14).3).

144. See Glossary of Persons. This is his first appearance in the Letters and Caesar's reason for mentioning him is unknown.

you will find him – I won't use that old-fashioned expression[145] of which you rightly made fun when I wrote to you about Milo, I'll say it in plain Latin, in the language of sensible men: there is no better fellow, no more honest and honourable gentleman alive. Add to which, he is a leading light in Civil Law; his memory is extraordinary, his learning profound.

I do not ask on his behalf for a Tribunate or Prefecture or any other specific favour. It is your good-will and generosity I bespeak; though if in addition you have a mind to decorate him with suchlike ambitious trinkets, I say nothing to deter you. In fine, I put him altogether, as the phrase goes, out of my hand into yours – the hand of a great conqueror and a great gentleman,[146] if I may become a trifle fulsome, though that's hardly permissible with you. But you will let it pass, I see you will.[147]

Take care of your health and keep that warm corner in your heart for me.

27 (VII. 6)

CICERO TO TREBATIUS

Cumae or Pompeii, latter May 54

From Cicero to Trebatius greetings.

Every letter I write to Caesar or to Balbus carries as a kind of statutory bonus a recommendation of yourself, and not the standard sort but phrased with some special indication of my

145. Or 'old saw'. What this was, or why Cicero wrote to Caesar about Milo, we do not know.

146. Literally 'pre-eminent both in victory' (i.e. with the sword) 'and loyalty' (to its pledges).

147. The good nature apparent in Caesar's letter will tolerate even flattery of himself.

regard for you. Now what you have to do is to put aside this foolish hankering after Rome and city ways, and by dint of perseverance and energy achieve the purpose with which you set out. I and your other friends will excuse you, as the 'rich and noble dames that dwelt in Corinth, lofty citadel'[148] excused Medea. She persuaded them 'hands thick in plaster' not to censure her for living abroad:

Helping self and helping country many a rover wide doth roam.
Naught accounted in his staying sitteth many a stay-at-home.

Which latter case would certainly have been yours, if I had not thrust you forth.

But I shall be writing more anon. Now you, who have learned how to enter caveats[149] for others, enter one for yourself against the tricks of those charioteers in Britain.[150] And since I have started to play Medea, always remember what she says: 'He who cannot help his own case, be he *wise*, his *wisdom's* vain.'[151]

Take care of your health.

148. The quotations are from a Latin version by Ennius of Euripides' *Medea*.

149. *cavere* ('beware,' 'look out for') was also used in a legal sense, of a jurisconsult advising a client or prescribing a form of procedure. I have had to resort to paraphrase.

150. Caesar's second expedition to Britain was now in preparation. He describes how the Britons used their war-chariots in *Bell. Gall.* IV.33.

151. The Euripidean original may be the line quoted in letter 317, which is not in our text of the Greek play. On 'wisdom' see n.110.

28 (VII. 7)

CICERO TO TREBATIUS

Rome, end of June (?) 54

From Cicero to Trebatius.

I am continually putting in a word for you, but with what effect I am anxious to hear from yourself. My greatest hope is in Balbus, to whom I write about you very earnestly and often. What surprises me is that I don't get a letter from you whenever one comes in from my brother Quintus. I hear there is not an ounce of either gold or silver in Britain. If that is true, my advice is to lay hold of a chariot and hurry back to us at full speed! But if we can gain our end even without Britain, contrive to make yourself one of Caesar's intimates. My brother will give you valuable assistance, and so will Balbus; but your greatest asset, believe me, is your own honourable character and hard work. You are serving under a very generous chief, your age is just right, your recommendation is certainly out of the ordinary. So the one thing you have to be afraid of is seeming to do yourself less than justice.

29 (VII. 8)

CICERO TO TREBATIUS

Rome, August (middle or late) 54

From Cicero to Trebatius.

Caesar has written to me very civilly, regretting that he has so far been too busy to get to know you very well, but assuring me that this will come. I told him in my reply how greatly he would oblige me by conferring upon you all he could in the way of good-will, friendly offices, and liberality. But your letter gave me an impression of undue impatience; also it surprised me that you make so little account of the advantages of a Tribunate, especially one involving no military service. I shall complain to Vacerra and Manilius.[152] I dare not say a word to Cornelius.[153] He is responsible if you play the fool, since you give out that it was from him you learned your *wisdom*. Now why don't you press this opportunity, this chance? – you'll never find a better.

As for what you say about that Counsellor Precianus,[154] I go on commending you to him, for he writes himself that he has given you reason to be grateful. Let me know how that matter stands. I am looking forward to Britannic letters from you all.

30 (VII. 9)

CICERO TO TREBATIUS

Rome, middle or late October 54

From Cicero to Trebatius.

It's a long time since I had news of you. You don't write, and the last two months I have not written to you myself. As you were not with my brother Quintus, I could not tell where to send a letter or whom to give it to. I am anxious to know what you are doing and where you will be spending the winter – with Caesar, I hope; but I have not ventured to write any-

152. Two of Trebatius' fellow-jurisconsults.

153. Q. Cornelius Maximus is mentioned in the *Digest* as Trebatius' teacher in law.

154. Unknown. Possibly *Preciano* means 'in the Precius business'.

thing to him on account of his recent loss.[155] I did write to Balbus though. Mind you don't let yourself down. Better later back to us, so you come fatter! There is no occasion for you to hurry, especially now that Battara[156] is no more. But you are well able to make your own plans. I am anxious to know what you have decided.

There is a certain friend of yours called Cn. Octavius (or is it Cn. Cornelius?), 'mother Earth's son, a fine old family'.[157] Knowing me to be a friend of yours, he showers me with invitations to dinner. So far he has not succeeded in getting me all the way, but I am obliged just the same.

31 (VII. 17)

CICERO TO TREBATIUS

Rome, October or November 54

From Cicero to Trebatius greetings.

On the strength of your letter I gave thanks to my brother Quintus, and can at last commend yourself in that you now seem to have fairly made up your mind. Your letters in the first few months disturbed me not a little, for they gave me an impression (if you will forgive me for saying so) at times of irresponsibility in your hankering for Rome and city ways, at times of indolence, at times of timidity in face of the labours of

155. Julia, Caesar's only child and Pompey's wife, died in September 54.

156. Who he was and what Cicero means is unknown. The suggestion that 'Battara' was a nickname for Vacerra (see previous letter) does not seem very likely.

157. Perhaps quoted from a play, though this is not certain. 'Son of Earth' (*terrae filius*) = 'a nobody'. The name which Cicero was, or pretended to be, unable to remember was in fact 'Octavius'; cf. p. 79.

army life, and often too, most uncharacteristically, of something not unlike presumption. You seemed to think you had brought a note of hand to the Commander-in-Chief instead of a letter – such a hurry you were in to take your money and get back home! It did not seem to occur to you that people who *did* go with notes of hand to Alexandria have thus far been unable to get a penny![158]

Were I thinking in terms of my own convenience, I should wish you to be with me of all things, for I gained no small pleasure from our intercourse and no small profit from your advice and services. But since from youth upwards you have confided yourself to my friendship and patronage, I have always felt a responsibility not only for your protection but for your promotion and betterment. Accordingly, as long as I expected to go myself on a provincial assignment, I made you certain unsolicited offers, which you doubtless remember. When that plan changed, I hit on another. Observing that Caesar extended to me the most flattering courtesies and held me in particular regard, knowing too his extraordinary generosity and punctilious loyalty to his engagements, I commended you to his care in the fullest and most emphatic terms I could find. He took my words in the same spirit, and has often intimated to me by letter and made clear to you by word of mouth and by act that he has been greatly impressed by my recommendation. Now that you have come by such a patron, if you credit me with any good sense or good-will towards you, don't let him go. Should anything occur to ruffle you, should you find him less prompt than you expected through pressure of affairs or some untoward circumstance, be patient and wait for the final outcome. That it will be agreeable to yourself I will guarantee.

158. Ptolemy the Piper had borrowed large sums with which to bribe Roman politicians to further his restoration to his throne; that achieved, he was in no hurry to pay his debts. Cicero's defence of C. Rabirius Postumus in the following winter had to do with this matter.

I must not urge you at greater length. I will only point out that if you let slip this opportunity of securing the friendship of a most eminent and generous personage in a wealthy province at just the right time of your life, you will never find a better. In this opinion, as you jurists say in your books, Q. Cornelius concurs.

I am glad that you have not gone to Britain. You are quit of the fatigues, and I shall not be listening to your accounts of it all! Please send me full details as to where you will be spending the winter, in what expectations or under what conditions.

32 (VII. 16)

CICERO TO TREBATIUS

Rome, late November 54

From M. Cicero to Trebatius greetings.

You remember the words at the end of the *Trojan Horse*:[159] 'Their wisdom comes too late.' But yours, you old fox, does not come too late. First you sent those snappish letters, which were silly enough. Then you showed yourself none too keen a sight-seer in the matter of Britain, for which I frankly don't blame you. *Now* you seem to be snug in winter quarters, and so you have no mind to stir. '*Wisdom* everywhere befitteth; that shall be thy sharpest arm.'[160]

If I were by way of dining out, I should not have disappointed your friend Cn. Octavius; though I did say to him after several invitations 'Do please tell me, who *are* you?' But really, in all seriousness, he is a pretty fellow. A pity you did not take him with you!

Let me know plainly what all of you are about and whether

159. Cf. n. 131.
160. From an unknown play.

you will be coming to Italy this winter. Balbus has assured me that you are going to be a rich man. Whether he uses the word in plain Roman style, meaning that you will have plenty of cash, or after the manner of the Stoics when they say that all are rich who can enjoy the sky and the earth, remains to be seen. Travellers from Gaul complain of your arrogance – they say you don't *respond*[161] to enquiries. Still you have one satisfaction; everybody agrees that there is no greater legal pundit than yourself in all Samarobriva.[162]

33 (VII. 10)

CICERO TO TREBATIUS

Rome, December 54

From M. Cicero to Trebatius greetings.

I have read your letter, from which I understand that our friend Caesar is impressed with you as a jurist. You may congratulate yourself on having got to your present part of the world, where you can pass for a man of some *wisdom*! Had you gone to Britain as well, I daresay there would have been no greater expert than you in the whole vast island. But really (you won't mind my jokes – after all, you challenged me), I am half inclined to be jealous of you, actually sent for by a personage whom affairs, not arrogance, make inaccessible to the rest of mankind.

But you say nothing in your letter about *your* activities, which I assure you interest me no less than my own. I am terribly afraid you may have a chilly time of it[163] in winter

161. Cf. n. 113.

162. Caesar's winter headquarters.

163. With innuendo. *frigere*, 'to be cold,' often = 'have nothing to do' or 'be coldly received' ('a frost').

quarters. So I advise you to install a good stove. Mucius and Manilius[164] concur. After all, you are not too well supplied with army greatcoats![165] To be sure, I hear that things are warm enough for you all out there just now,[166] and truly that intelligence made me very nervous about you. However, you are a much safer campaigner than counsel. Keen swimmer[167] as you are, you had no mind for a dip in the Ocean and you didn't care to watch those charioteers,[168] though in the old days we could never do you out of a blindfold gladiator. But enough of badinage.

How pressingly I have written to Caesar on your behalf, you know; how often, I know. But to tell the truth, I had temporarily given it up, because in dealing with so generous a man and so warm a friend of mine I did not want to risk appearing to lack confidence in his good-will. All the same, in my last letter I thought it time for a reminder, and wrote accordingly. Please let me know the result, and inform me at the same time of your whole situation and all your plans. I am anxious to learn of your present doings and future prospects. How long do you think this absence of yours will continue? For I do assure you that the only thing that consoles me and makes our

164. Famous lawyers of the past bore these names, M'. Manilius (Consul in 149) and (along with other members of his family) Q. Mucius Scaevola the Pontifex. Trebatius of course would catch the echo. But primarily Cicero must be referring to contemporaries (cf. p. 79 'Q. Cornelius concurs'). Manilius is obviously the lawyer mentioned on p. 76. For a contemporary Mucius Scaevola see Glossary of Persons. If he was, as may be presumed, a friend of Trebatius, Cicero might bring him in for the sake of the legal associations of his name even though he was not himself a jurist.

165. *saga.* Cicero pretends to assume that the unsoldierly Trebatius would be short of them.

166. The tribe of the Eburones in north-east Gaul rose against the Romans and destroyed two legions in the winter of 54–53.

167. Horace in his *Satires* (II.1.8) alludes to Trebatius' partiality for swimming, as well as for wine.

168. See n. 150.

separation easier to bear is the knowledge (if it be so) that you are the gainer thereby. If that is *not* the case, we are arrant fools, both of us – I for not hauling you back to Rome, you for not hastening hither. I'll be bound that a single meeting of ours, serious or jocose, will be worth more than all our Aeduan brethren,[169] to say nothing of the enemy. So please inform me on all points as soon as possible.

> By comfort or by counsel or by act
> I'll help.[170]

34 (VII. 11)

CICERO TO TREBATIUS

Tusculum (?), January 53

From Cicero to Trebatius.

If you had not already left Rome, you would surely be leaving now. Who wants a lawyer with all these *interregna*?[171] The advice I should give to all defendants in civil suits is to ask every Interrex for two adjournments.[172] Aren't you proud of your pupil in Civil Law?

But look here, what are you up to? Is anything happening? I notice that you now crack jokes in your letters. That looks well,

169. As the first Gaulish tribe to form an alliance with Rome the Aedui had been addressed by the Senate as 'brothers and kinsmen' (Caesar, *Bell. Gall.* 1.33.2; cf. *Letters to Atticus* 19 (1.19).2).

170. From Terence's *Self-Tormentor* (86).

171. See Glossary of Terms. The year 53 opened with no curule magistrates, disorders in Rome having made it impossible to elect them. Consuls were finally elected in July.

172. This would mean that the hearing would be postponed until a new Interrex came into office, and the process could be repeated indefinitely.

better than the statues[173] in my place at Tusculum! But I want to know what it means. You say that Caesar is consulting you. I had rather he consulted your interests! If that is happening, or you think it is going to happen, put up with your soldiering and stay right on. While missing you, I shall comfort myself with the hope of your advancement. But if all that is in the nature of moonshine, then rejoin us. Something will turn up here one of these days, and even if it doesn't, I'll be bound that a single conversation of ours will be worth more than all the Samarobrivas in Gaul. Furthermore, if you come back soon, there won't be any talk; whereas if you are away for a long while to no purpose, I am afraid of Laberius, even of our friend Valerius.[174] A Britannic counsellor would make a marvellous figure of fun! I am not laughing at all this, though maybe you are, but cutting jokes with you in my usual style about an extremely serious matter. Joking aside, my advice to you as a most sincere well-wisher is this: if as a result of my recommendation you are likely to receive in Gaul the recognition that is your due, then bear your homesickness and advance your standing and means; but if the outlook there is bleak, come back to us. You will doubtless achieve all your aims even so by your own energies and my wholehearted zeal for your welfare.

35 (VII. 12)

CICERO TO TREBATIUS

Rome, February 53

From Cicero to Trebatius.

I was wondering why you had stopped sending me letters.

173. A play on two senses of *signum*, 'sign' and 'statue'.

174. See Glossary of Persons. Not impossibly this Valerius is to be identified with an author of mimes called Catullus, mentioned by Martial and others.

Now my friend Pansa intimates that you have turned Epicurean. A remarkable camp yours must be! What would you have done if I had sent you to Tarentum[175] instead of Samarobriva? I was uneasy about you even in the days when you were maintaining the same position as my crony Velleius (?).[176]

But how are you going to be a champion of Civil Law if everything you do is done for your own sweet sake and not for the community?[177] And what becomes of the trust formula 'in accordance with honest practice proper between honest men'? Who is honest that does nothing except for his own interest? What rule will you lay down for division of goods held jointly, seeing that nothing can be joint among people whose only yardstick is their own pleasure? How will you think it proper to swear by Jupiter Stone,[178] when you know that Jupiter can't get angry with anybody? And what is to become of the good folk of Ulubrae,[179] if you decide that it is wrong to take part in public affairs?[180]

Well, if you are really forsaking us, I'm put out. But if it suits your book to humour Pansa, you have my forgiveness. Only write me at long last, and tell me what you are doing and what you want me to do or see to on your behalf.

175. A notorious centre of luxury and pleasure.

176. C. Velleius is the Epicurean spokesman in Cicero's dialogue *On the Nature of the Gods*, but the reading is doubtful. There is probably an allusion to some litigation in which Trebatius had been involved as legal adviser.

177. In this passage Cicero facetiously sets out to prove that Epicurean dogmas are incompatible with the vocabulary of Roman Civil Law.

178. The man swearing this most solemn of Roman oaths flung a stone, praying that if guilty of deliberate perjury he should be cast out like the stone.

179. A small place near the Pontine Marshes (see p. 88 ;). Trebatius had become its patron, no doubt by legal services.

180. As held by Epicurus.

36 (VII. 13)

CICERO TO TREBATIUS

Rome, 4 March 53

From M. Cicero to Trebatius greetings.

Did you really suppose me so unreasonable as to be angry with you because I thought you lacking in perseverance and too eager to leave Gaul? And do you imagine that this was the reason why I have not sent you a letter for some considerable time? The agitation visible in your first letters caused me distress, not annoyance; and there was no reason whatsoever for the intermission of mine other than my complete ignorance of your whereabouts. And now do you still persist in making false charges against me and refuse to accept my explanation? Hark ye, my good Testa: is it money that is swelling your head or the fact that you are consulted by the Commander-in-Chief? Upon my soul, you are such a coxcomb that I believe you would rather be consulted by Caesar than covered in gold! But if it's both together, I wonder who is going to put up with you except myself, who can put up with anything.

But to come back to the point, I am heartily glad that you are tolerably content to be out there. That gives me as much pleasure as the other gave me distress. My only apprehension is that your professional skill may stand you in poor stead, for out there, as I hear,

> No claim in form of laws lay they; with steel
> Their due they seek.[181]

You yourself are used to being called in to 'a using of force'. But you don't have to worry about that limiting clause in the

181. From Ennius' *Annals* (Vahlen,[2] 272).

injunction, 'provided you have not been the first to enter by armed force' – I know you are no ruffling blade to start a quarrel![182] However, to give you a caveat from your own legal arsenal, I advise you to keep clear of the Treviri – I hear they are *capital* customers, like their Roman namesakes. If you want a Board of Three, better try the Masters of the Mint![183] But we'll have our joke some other time. Please write to me in full detail about everything over there.

Dispatched 4 March.

37 (VII. 18)

CICERO TO TREBATIUS

The Pomptine Marshes, 8 April 53

From Cicero to Trebatius greetings.

I have received several letters from you in a batch, dispatched at different times. In every respect but one they made pleasant reading. They show that you are now bearing your army life with a stout heart, and that you are a man of fortitude and resolution. For a little while I missed these qualities in you, not however putting down your restlessness to weakness of spirit but to your pain at being parted from us. So carry on as you have begun. Tolerate your service with a stout heart. Depend upon it, you will be well rewarded. I shall follow up my

182. The joke, implying that Trebatius was not a man to risk his skin if he could help it, is based on procedural technicalities arising under Roman law of property. I forbear to discuss its details here.

183. Another complex joke with a pun on 'Treviri', a Gaulish tribe, and *tres viri* (probably pronounced identically), 'Board of Three'. Two Roman Boards of Three are involved, *tres viri capitales*, who were police functionaries (but in general usage *capitalis* = 'dangerous', 'deadly'), and *tres viri monetales*, in charge of the Roman mint.

recommendation, but at the right time. Rest assured that I am as anxious as yourself for you to derive the maximum of advantage from this separation of ours. And since the caveats you legal gentlemen enter are none too dependable, I am sending you a little caveat in Greek under my own hand.[184] On your side, please give me an account of the war in Gaul – the less adventurous my informant, the more I trust the information.

However, to get back to your letters: all very nice, except for one feature, which surprises me. Is it not unusual to send several identical letters in one's own handwriting?[185] As for the palimpsest, I applaud your thrift. But I wonder what could have been on that scrap of paper which you thought proper to erase rather than not write these screeds. Your forms of procedure perhaps?[186] I scarcely suppose that you rub out my letters in order to substitute your own. Or do you mean to imply that nothing is happening, that you are neglected, without even a supply of paper? Well, that is your own fault for taking your modesty away with you instead of leaving it behind with us.

When Balbus sets out to join you, I shall commend you to him in plain Roman style. If you get no further letter from me for some time, don't be astonished. I am going to be away through April. I am writing this in the Pomptine country,

184. What this was is doubtful. Some think a letter of advice on how to behave to Caesar, written in Greek for greater security. Rather perhaps an epigram or other literary *jeu d'esprit*.

185. Important letters were sometimes dispatched in two or more copies by separate messengers to ensure delivery. The sender would naturally use an amanuensis for such copies, though otherwise it was considered polite to write in one's own hand. Cicero jestingly implies that Trebatius' letters were so similar to one another as to be virtually copies. The quaint notion that Roman etiquette required letters sent as aforesaid *not* to be verbally identical is baseless.

186. With the usual implication that Trebatius did not know his legal business. Forms of procedure (*formulae*) drawn up by him would be expendable.

having turned in for the night at M. Aemilius Philemo's[187] house, from which I have already heard the hubbub created by my clients, those, that is, whom you have procured for me – it is common knowledge that a vast crowd of frogs in Ulubrae[188] have bestirred themselves to pay me their respects.

Take care of your health.

8 April, Pomptine Marshes.

P.S. I have torn up a letter of yours received from L. Arruntius – which did not deserve it, for it contained nothing that could not safely have been read out at a public meeting. However, Arruntius said that you had so requested, and you had added a note to the same effect. Well, no matter. I am much surprised that you have not written since then, especially in view of the startling developments.[189]

38 (VII. 14)

CICERO TO TREBATIUS

Rome, May or June 53

Cicero to Trebatius.

Vettius Chrysippus, Cyrus the architect's freedman, has made me think that you have some recollection of my existence; he has given me your kind regards. Very grand we have become! Was it too much trouble to give him a letter for me, and him practically one of my own household? If, however, you have forgotten how to put pen to paper, you will have fewer clients in future to lose their cases! If *I* have slipped your mind, I'll make shift to come to Gaul myself before I fade out

187. A freedman of Lepidus', the future Triumvir.
188. See n. 179.
189. In Gaul (revolts in north and north-east).

of it completely. But if it is apprehension of the summer campaign that is sapping your energies, you must think up an excuse, as you did in the matter of Britain.

One thing I was greatly pleased to hear from the same Chrysippus, that you are on close terms with Caesar. But I must say, I would rather have learned how you are getting on from your own letters as often as possible; it would have been more fitting. No doubt that is the way it would be, if you had cared to study the rules of friendship as thoroughly as those of court procedure.

But all this is badinage in your own style – and a little in mine too. I am very fond of you, and not only want you to be fond of me but am confident that you are.

39 (VII. 15)

CICERO TO TREBATIUS

Rome, June (?) 53

From Cicero to Trebatius.

'Lovers are contrary folk.' How true that is may be seen from the fact that I used to be distressed because you were unhappy in Gaul, whereas now I feel a prick when you write that you are well-content with life there. I used to be vexed that you were not pleased with the result of my recommendation, and now it hurts me to find that you can enjoy anything without me. However, I prefer that we put up with your absence than that you miss the advantages which I hope for on your account.

I cannot tell you how pleased I am to hear that you have struck up a friendship with C. Matius. He is a very charming, cultivated person. Make him as fond of you as possible. Take my word for it, nothing you can bring back from this province of yours will give you more pleasure.

Take care of yourself.

40 (XVI. 13)

CICERO TO TIRO

Cumae, 10 April 53

From Tullius to Tiro greetings.

I shall feel you have given me all I could ask, once I see you fit and well. I am writing in great anxiety for Andricus, whom I sent to you, to arrive. If you care for me, see that you get well and join us when you are thoroughly strong again.

Goodbye.

10 April.

41 (XVI. 14)

CICERO TO TIRO

Cumae, 11 April 53

From Tullius to Tiro greetings.

Andricus arrived a day later than I expected him, so I had a miserable, apprehensive night. I am none the wiser from your letters as to how you are, but still it made me feel better. I have nothing to amuse me, no literary work – I cannot touch it before I see you.

Give orders for the doctor to be promised whatever fee he asks. I have written to Ummius to that effect. I hear you are in distress of mind, and that the doctor says your sickness is due to this. If you care for me, rouse your dormant love of literary work and the things of the spirit, which makes you very dear to me. Now you need health of mind to recover health of body, and I ask you to gain it for my sake as well as your own. Keep Acastus, so that you are better looked after. Preserve yourself for me. My promise[190] is almost due now. If you come, I will even settle up right away.

Again, goodbye.

11, noon.

42 (XVI. 15)

CICERO TO TIRO

Cumae, 12 April 53

From Tullius to Tiro greetings.

Aegypta arrived today, 12 April. He told me that you are quite free of fever and in pretty good shape, but said you had not been able to write to me. That made me anxious, all the more so because Hermia, who ought also to have arrived today, has not come. You cannot imagine how anxious I feel about your health. If you relieve my mind on this score, I shall relieve yours of every worry. I should write more if I thought you could read with any pleasure at the present time. Put your clever brain, which I value so highly, to the job of preserving yourself for us both. Look after yourself carefully, I repeat.

Goodbye.

P.S. Hermia has arrived and I have received your letter, shakily written, poor fellow – no wonder, when you are so seriously ill. I have sent you Aegypta to be with you. He is not

190. To give Tiro his freedom.

uncivilized and I think he is fond of you. Also a cook for your use.

Goodbye.

43 (XVI. 10)

CICERO TO TIRO

Cumae, 17 April 53

From Tullius to Tiro greetings.

Indeed I want you to join me, but I am afraid of the journey. You have been very seriously ill, you are worn out, what with lack of food and purges and the disease itself. Serious illnesses often have serious repercussions, if there is any imprudence. And then, right on top of the two days you will have on the road travelling to Cumae, there will be five days for the return journey. I want to be at Formiae on the 28th. Let me find you there, my dear Tiro, well and strong.

My (or *our*) literary brain-children have been drooping their heads missing you, but they looked up a little at the letter which Acastus brought. Pompey is staying with me as I write, enjoying himself in cheerful mood. He wanted to hear my compositions, but I told him that in your absence my tongue of authorship is tied completely. You must get ready to restore your services to my Muses. My promise will be performed on the appointed day (I have taught you the derivation of 'faith').[191] Now mind you get thoroughly well. I shall be with you soon.

Goodbye.

17th.

191. *fides*, supposed to be derived from *fit* ('is done').

44 (XVI. 16)

Q. CICERO TO M. CICERO

Transalpine Gaul, May (end) or June (beginning) 53

From Quintus to his brother Marcus greetings.

My dear Marcus, as I hope to see you again and my boy and my[192] Tulliola and your son, I am truly grateful at what you have done about Tiro, in judging his former condition to be below his deserts and preferring us to have him as a friend rather than a slave. Believe me, I jumped for joy when I read your letter and his. Thank you, and congratulations!

If Statius' loyalty gives me so much pleasure,[193] how highly you must value the same qualities in Tiro, with the addition of literary accomplishments and conversation and culture, gifts worth even more than they! I have all manner of great reasons to love you, but this is a reason – the very fact that you so properly announced the event to me is a reason. I saw all that is you in your letter.

I have promised Sabinus'[194] boys all assistance, and shall be as good as my word.

192. Perhaps a mistake for 'your'.

193. Quintus will not have forgotten his brother's annoyance when Statius was freed; cf. *Letters to Atticus* 38 (II.18).4, 39 (II.19).1.

194. Sabinus is very likely Titurius Sabinus, one of Caesar's Legates who had lost his life and his army in the revolt of the Eburones. 'Boys' could mean either 'children' or 'slaves'.

45 (II. I)

CICERO TO CURIO[195]

Rome, 53 (first half)

From M. Cicero to Curio greetings.

I am sorry to be under suspicion of neglecting a friendly duty, but I am not so much put out by your accusation as I am pleased by your exigency – especially as I am innocent of the offence alleged against me, whereas when you show that you miss my letters, you demonstrate your affection for me. I am well aware of it to be sure, but it is delightful and gratifying to me none the less. Now *I* have let nobody set out without a letter whom I thought likely to reach you. After all, I can challenge all comers as an active correspondent. From *you*, on the other hand, I have heard only two or three times at most, and very short letters at that. So if you are a stern judge to me, I shall convict you on the same charge. Unless you want that to happen, you should take a lenient view of my case.

But there's enough about letters; I don't doubt I can give you your fill of them, especially if you are going to appreciate my efforts in that direction. I have been sorry that you have been so long away from us, because I have missed your most delectable company; but at the same time I am glad, because in your absence you have attained all your objectives with the greatest *éclat* and because in all your affairs fortune has seconded my prayers. One short admonition, which my transcendent affection for you compels me to offer: your spirit and talents are so eagerly expected that I don't scruple to beg and adjure you to shape yourself, before you come back to us, into one capable of matching and living up to the expectation you have

195. In 53 the younger Curio was serving as Proquaestor under the governor of the province of Asia, C. Claudius Pulcher.

aroused. No forgetfulness will ever wipe out the memory of your services[196] to me, and so I ask you to remember, whatever further success and honour may come your way, that you would never have attained them, if in the days of your boyhood you had not listened to my sincere and affectionate advice. So your feelings towards me should be such that my declining years may rest happily upon your affection and your youth.

46 (II. 2)

CICERO TO CURIO

Rome, 53 (first half)

From M. Cicero to C. Curio greetings.

I have lost a weighty witness to the great affection I bear you in your illustrious father;[197] with his own fine record and with you for a son, he would have been the most fortunate of men had it been granted him to see you before he passed away. However, I hope our friendship needs no testimony. May the Gods prosper you in your inheritance! In me you may be sure of having one to whom you are as dear and as delightful as you were to your father.

196. Rendered no doubt during Cicero's exile; cf. p. 99 .

197. Curio the Elder, Consul in 76. Cicero's relations with him had been chequered and never warmly friendly.

47 (II. 3)

CICERO TO CURIO

Rome, 53 (first half)

From M. Cicero to C. Curio greetings.

Rupa[198] was ready and willing to announce a show in your name, but I and all your friends thought that no step should be taken in your absence by which you would be committed on your return. I shall write to you later at greater length to give my views, or else, since you might then think of arguments to counter them, I shall take you unprepared and advance my opinion against yours face to face. In that way, if I do not convert you, I shall at least leave my sentiments on record in your mind; so that if the time comes (as I hope it never will) when you begin to repent your own counsel, you may remember mine. All the same, to put it in a few words, do realize that you are returning at a juncture in which your gifts of nature, application, and fortune will count for more in winning you the highest political prizes than will shows. Nobody admires the capacity to give shows, which is a matter of means, not personal qualities; and everybody is sick and tired of them.[199]

But I am doing what I said I was not going to do, starting to explain my reasons. So I defer the whole argument till your return. Be sure that the highest anticipations have been formed – all is expected of you that may be expected of the highest qualities and talents. If you are prepared to meet those hopes worthily, and I am confident you are, you will give us, your

198. An agent (not necessarily freedman) of Curio's. When an eminent man died his son(s) sometimes gave a show in his honour.

199. Curio did not take this advice, but gave a show of memorable splendour.

friends, and all your countrymen, and your country, the greatest of shows[200] - and many of them. One thing you will surely find, that no one is dearer or more delightful to me than yourself.

48 (II. 4)

CICERO TO CURIO

Rome, 54 (middle)

From Cicero to C. Curio greetings.

That there are many different categories of letters you are aware. But the most authentic, the purpose in fact for which letter-writing was invented, is to inform the absent of what it is desirable for them to know, whether in our interest or their own. Letters of this kind I suppose you do not expect from me, since you have your domestic correspondents and messengers to tell you about your affairs, and there is nothing very new to report about mine. That leaves two categories which give me great pleasure; one familiar and jocular, the other serious and grave. Which would be the less fitting for me to use I don't know. How can I joke with you in these times, when upon my word I don't think a Roman who can laugh deserves the name? As for something in more serious vein, what is there for Cicero to write seriously about to Curio except public affairs? But on that subject my predicament is that I dare not write what I think and do not care to write what I don't think.

Well then, having no topic left, I shall resort to my usual conclusion and urge you to strive for glory. You have a formidable adversary ready and waiting – public expectation, which is really amazingly high. This you will easily overcome, but in one way only, and that is by determining to work hard at

200. The Latin word for 'show' also means 'gift'.

those pursuits which bring the kind of credit you have set your heart on. I should write more in this strain, if I were not sure that you are your own sufficient spur. Even this little I have said, not to kindle *your* enthusiasm, but to demonstrate *my* affection.

49 (II. 5)

CICERO TO CURIO

Rome, 53 (middle)

From Cicero to C. Curio greetings.

The state of things here I dare not tell even to you in a letter. As I wrote once before, wherever you are, you are in the same boat; but all the same I congratulate you on your absence. On the one hand, you do not see what we are seeing; on the other, you are in a place where your merit shines high before the eyes of a multitude, Roman citizens and natives. The report of it comes to us, not by doubtful and various gossip, but in a single loud, concerted voice.

On one point I hardly know whether to congratulate you or to take alarm – the extraordinary eagerness with which your return is awaited. It is not that I doubt your capacity to live up to public expectation, but I am seriously afraid that when you do come home, you may no longer have anything to work for. Such is the decay, almost to extinction, of all our institutions. But perhaps even such remarks as this ought not to be entrusted to a letter, so I leave others to tell you the rest. But whether you see any ray of hope for the commonwealth or none, you must prepare and train and plan as befits a man and a Roman whose mission it is in sad times and evil manners to raise his country from the depth of affliction to her ancient dignity and freedom.

50 (II. 6)

CICERO TO CURIO

Rome, July (?) 53

From M. Cicero to C. Curio greetings.

As I dispatch this letter by the hand of my dear Milo's friend, Sex. Villius,[201] no news has yet come in of your approaching Italy. But your arrival is thought not to be far off, and reports agree that you have set out from Asia on your way to Rome. So, considering the importance of the matter in hand, I feel no scruples on the score of undue haste, for I am very anxious that you should get this letter at the earliest possible moment.

If obligations between us were all on your side, and my services to you had been such as you are apt to proclaim them rather than as I myself appraise them, I should approach you with some diffidence when the time came for me to ask an important favour. It is not easy for a man of sensibility to ask a great deal of someone who he thinks has reason to be grateful to him. He will be afraid of presenting the appearance of a creditor demanding payment rather than of a petitioner seeking a kindness. But in fact your benefactions to me are great and notorious, rendered the more conspicuous by the strange turns of fortune through which I have passed. And it is the mark of a liberal spirit to wish to owe more where one already owes much. Therefore I do not hesitate to write to you with a request of the highest consequence, one that lies very near to my heart. After all, I am not afraid of succumbing under the load of your good offices, past number though they may be. Whatever

201. His full name seems to have been Sex. Villius Annalis and he can be identified with the Villius mentioned by Horace (*Sat.* I.2.64) as a lover of Milo's wife Fausta.

favour you may confer upon me, I feel confident that my mind has the capacity to accept it and the power to make a generous return, such as will add lustre to your gift.

Well then, I have firmly concentrated all my efforts, all my time, care, diligence, and thought, my whole mind in short, on winning the Consulship for Milo. In so doing, as I see it, I have to look not only for the reward of friendly service but for the credit of gratitude displayed to a benefactor. I do not believe any man's life and fortune ever meant as much to himself as Milo's success means to me. On this, I have decided, everything for me now depends. It is evident to me that your single self, if you will, can lend such effectual assistance to our campaign that we shall need nothing else. We have so much on our side – the good-will of the honest men, acquired from his Tribunate through his championship of my cause, as I expect you appreciate; that of the common people, through the magnificence of his shows and the generosity of his nature; that of the younger generation and the electorally influential, through his own outstanding influence and activity in that sphere; and my own interest on his behalf, which may not be powerful, but is at any rate approved and right and due, and therefore perhaps not without some influence. What we need is a leader and a counsellor, one to govern and harness, as it were, the favourable currents of which I have spoken; and if we could choose from all the world, we should find no one comparable to you.

You may judge from the very depth of my concern on Milo's behalf whether I am a man who does not forget, a man of gratitude and honour. If so, if in short you consider me worthy of your kindness, then I appeal to you to come to my help at this anxious time, and to dedicate your efforts to a cause in which my credit, indeed I might more properly say my virtual existence, is involved. As for T. Annius[202] himself, I promise you that if you will take him to your heart you will

202. Milo's full name was T. Annius Milo or T. Annius Milo Papianus.

have no bolder, steadier, more resolute, or more sincere friend. As for me, you will add lustre and prestige to my name; and I shall readily recognize the same concern for my credit as you once showed for my existence as a citizen.

I should continue further, if I did not know how well you see my mind as I write this letter, that you realize what a load of obligation I carry and how in this candidature of Milo's I must needs labour and strive, and even fight, my hardest. Knowing that, I put the whole matter in your hands; Milo's cause and I myself are all yours to do with as you will. Only understand that, if you do as I ask, I shall owe you more almost than I owe Milo himself; for my restoration, in which he was my chief helper, meant less to me than the satisfaction I shall take in repaying a sacred debt of gratitude. That I am sure your single support will enable me to attain.

51 (V. 18)

CICERO TO T. FADIUS

Rome (?), 52 (after end of March)

From M. Cicero to T. Fadius greetings.

I, your would-be comforter, stand in need of comfort myself; for nothing this long while past has distressed me so deeply as your mishap.[203] However, I not only urge but earnestly beg and entreat you in the name of our mutual affection to take a firm hold of yourself and play the man. Remember the lot of mankind in general and the times in which *we* have been born. Your merit has given you more than fortune has taken from you. Few self-made men have attained what you have attained, whereas many of the highest birth

203. Fadius had been found guilty on a bribery charge, probably in connection with his election to the Praetorship.

have lost what you have lost. Moreover, the future of our laws, law courts, and political conditions in general is likely to be such that whoever makes his exit from this commonwealth under the lightest penalty may be accounted highly fortunate. *You* have your property and your children. You also have me and others closely attached to you in friendship and good-will. You will have ample opportunity to spend your time with me and all those dear to you. Yours is the only trial out of so many in which the verdict is criticized, as depending on a single dubious vote[204] and given, it is thought, to please a powerful personage.[205] For all these reasons you should take this trouble as easily as may be. My disposition towards you and your children will ever remain what you wish and what is right and proper.

52 (VII. 2)

CICERO TO M. MARIUS

Rome, January (?) 51

From M. Cicero to M. Marius greetings.

I shall execute your commission[206] with care. But shrewd business man that you are, you have selected the very person whose interest it is that the article should sell for as high a price as possible! Very wise of you, though, to set a limit on what I am to pay! Now if you had left me a free hand, my regard for you being what it is, I should have come to an arrangement with my co-heirs. As matters stand, now that I know your

204. Or possibly 'wavering'. The circumstances of Fadius' conviction are known only from this letter.

205. Presumably Pompey.

206. Marius had asked Cicero to buy on his account something (perhaps an article of *virtu*) at the auction of an estate to which Cicero was one of the heirs.

price, I'll put up a dummy bidder rather than see the thing go for less! But joking apart, I'll do your business with all proper care.

I am sure you are pleased about Bursa,[207] but you need not have been so diffident in your congratulations. You say you suppose I don't rate the triumph very high, because he's such a low creature. Well, I ask you to believe that this trial gave me more satisfaction than the death of my enemy.[208] To begin with, I prefer to get my revenge in a court of law than at sword-point. Secondly, I prefer my friend to come out of it with credit than with ruin.[209] I was especially pleased at the display of good-will towards me on the part of the honest men in the face of an astonishing amount of pressure from a very grand and powerful personage.[210] Lastly, and this may seem hard to credit, I detested this fellow far more than Clodius himself. I had been Clodius' adversary, whereas I had defended the other in court.[211] Clodius had a great object in view – he knew that the entire state would be jeopardized in my person; and he acted, not all on his own, but with the assistance of those whose power depended on my downfall.[212] Whereas this little ape selected me for attack just because he felt like it, giving certain ill-wishers of mine to understand that he was ready to be set on me at any time. Therefore I tell you to rejoice and be glad. It is a great victory. No braver Romans ever lived than those jurymen who dared to find him guilty in spite of all the power of the very personage who had empanelled them. They would

207. i.e. his condemnation on a charge of violence brought by Cicero himself (whose role as prosecutor in this case was for him most unusual).

208. Clodius, of whom Bursa had been a leading supporter. He was killed by Milo on 18 January 52.

209. Apparently the meaning is that Milo, who was in banishment for Clodius' murder, had been vindicated by Bursa's conviction.

210. Pompey.

211. Nothing more is known about this.

212. The 'Triumvirs'. It suits Cicero's argument here to ignore Clodius' personal reasons for attacking him in 58.

never have done that if they had not felt my grievance as their own.

What with the multitude of *causes célèbres* and the new legislation I am kept so busy here that I offer up a prayer against intercalation every day, so that I may be able to see you as soon as possible.

53 (XIII. 42)

CICERO TO CULLEOLUS

Rome (?), 61 or 60

From M. Cicero to L. Culleolus, Proconsul, greetings.

My friend L. Lucceius, who is the last man in the world to fail in appreciation of a kindness, has expressed to me the most profuse gratitude to yourself for your most handsome and liberal promises to his agents. Since your words have so deeply obliged him, you can imagine how beholden he will feel when you have actually performed what you have promised, as I look forward to your doing. To be sure the people of Byllis have expressed their readiness to meet Lucceius' claims at Pompey's discretion. But we urgently need your good-will, influence, and official authority in addition. Let me again request of you that they be forthcoming. I am particularly gratified that Lucceius' agents are aware, and Lucceius himself has gathered from the letter you sent him, that no man's word and influence counts for more with you than mine. Allow me to beg you yet again to let him find by experience that this is really so.

54 (XIII. 41)

CICERO TO CULLEOLUS

Rome (?), 61 or 60

Cicero to Culleolus greetings.

I want you to feel thoroughly assured that in doing what you have for L. Lucceius you have accommodated one who never forgets a favour. He is very much beholden to you for it, and Pompey expresses his gratitude in the warmest terms whenever we meet, as we often do. I will add what I feel sure will be highly agreeable to you, that I have personally been deeply gratified by your kindness to Lucceius. As for the future, I have no doubt that you will continue in your generosity, your earlier concern for our sakes being now supported by regard for your own consistency. However, let me again entreat you to be so good as to add at the conclusion some enhancing, crowning touches to your original promise and subsequent performance. You have my solemn guarantee that both Lucceius and Pompey will be deeply obliged and that your favour will be excellently placed.

I wrote to you a few days ago at some length about the political situation and about what is afoot here and my thoughts thereupon. I gave the letter to your boys.

Goodbye.

55 (XIII. 60)

CICERO TO C. MUNATIUS[213]

Rome (?), after 57

From Cicero to C. Munatius, son of Gaius, greetings.

213. Nothing known.

L. Livincius Trypho is to be sure a freedman of my close friend L. Regulus, whose misfortune[214] has made me even more anxious to serve him – *feel* more kindly than I always did I cannot. But I am fond of his freedman for his own sake. He rendered me great service at that crisis of my life in which it was easiest for me to discern the good-will and loyalty of my fellows.[215] I recommend him to you as men who gratefully remember what is done for them ought to recommend their benefactors. You will oblige me greatly if Trypho finds that, when he exposed himself to many dangers in the cause of my restoration (frequently taking ship in the depth of winter), he earned *your* gratitude as well as mine in virtue of your kindly disposition towards me.

56 (I. 3)

CICERO TO LENTULUS SPINTHER

Rome, January (?) 56

From M. Cicero to P. Lentulus, Proconsul, greetings.

For many years I have been on friendly terms with A. Trebonius,[216] who has important business concerns, both extensive and in good order, in your province.[217] In the past he has always been very well regarded in the province on account of his personal distinction and of recommendations from myself and his other friends; and he now trusts that this letter from me will put him in your good graces in view of your affection for me and the close relations between us. May I

214. Exile.
215. Cf. *Letters to Atticus* 62 (III.17).1.
216. Distinguish from Caesar's assassin, C. Trebonius.
217. Cilicia.

earnestly request you not to disappoint him, and commend to you all his business affairs, his freedmen, agents, and household? May I ask you in particular to confirm T. Ampius'[218] decisions with respect to his property, and to treat him in all matters in such a way as to let him understand that my recommendation has been more than formal?

57 (XIII. 6)

CICERO TO VALERIUS ORCA[219]

Rome (?), late 56 or 55

From M. Cicero to Q. Valerius Orca, son of Quintus, Proconsul, greetings.

I trust you are well, as I am.

I expect you have not forgotten that I spoke to you in P. Cuspius' presence when I accompanied you as you were leaving Rome for your province, and likewise that I subsequently asked you at considerable length to regard any friends of his whom I recommended to you as friends of mine. With the great friendship and courtesy you always show me, you gave me your promise in the kindest and most handsome fashion.

Cuspius, who makes a point of serving all his friends, takes a remarkably close and benevolent interest in certain individuals from your province – the reason being that he was twice in Africa in charge of important company business. It is my habit to second his friendly endeavours on their behalf with such means and influence as I can command. I have therefore deemed it proper in this letter to set before you the general position as regards my recommendation of Cuspius' people. In

218. Lentulus' predecessor.

219. Governor of the province of Africa.

future letters I shall simply affix the symbol on which you and I agreed, along with an intimation that the person concerned is one of Cuspius' friends.

Let me, however, assure you that the recommendation which I desire to put on record in this letter is of the most serious character. P. Cuspius has been extraordinarily urgent to have me give L. Julius[220] a most particular recommendation to you. He is so earnest in the matter that I hardly think it will be enough for me to use the phrases which we normally employ when we are making a very pressing request. He demands novelties, and supposes me to possess a special skill in this *genre*. I have promised him to produce from the secret stores of my art something quite amazing in the way of a recommendation. As I am unable to keep my word, I hope that *you* will use practical means to make him think that the style of my letter has worked wonders. To effect this you have only to bring out for the occasion all the manifold generosity that it lies within your good nature and your present power to provide, not only in a practical way but in words and even in looks. How much these things can do in a province I can guess, though unfortunately without experience.[221]

That the person whom I am recommending is very worthy to be your friend I believe not only because Cuspius tells me so, though that ought to be enough, but because I know his good judgement in choosing men and friends.

I shall soon be assessing the efficacy of this letter and, I feel sure, expressing my thanks to you. On my side I shall zealously and conscientiously attend to whatever I suppose to be relevant to your wishes and interests.

Take care of your health.

220. Perhaps L. Julius Calidus, a friend of Atticus and in his day a celebrated poet.

221. At this time Cicero's experience of provincial government was confined to the subordinate office of Quaestor, which he had held in Sicily in 75.

58 (XIII. 6 a)

CICERO TO VALERIUS ORCA

Rome (?), some time after the preceding

From M. Cicero to Q. Valerius, son of Quintus, Proconsul, greetings.

P. Cornelius, the bearer of this letter, has been recommended to me by P. Cuspius. Doubtless you have readily gathered from what I have told you how anxious I am, and ought to be, to serve Cuspius. Let me particularly ask you to ensure that as a result of this recommendation he thanks me as warmly, as soon, and as often as circumstances admit.

Goodbye.

59 (XIII. 40)

CICERO TO Q. ANCHARIUS[222]

Rome (?), 55 (late) or 54

From M. Cicero to Q. Ancharius, son of Quintus, Proconsul, greetings.

Let me warmly recommend to you L. and C. Aurelius, sons of Lucius, with whom and with that very worthy gentleman their father I am on the most familiar terms. They are highly accomplished young men, very close to me, and thoroughly deserving of your friendship. If any recommendation of mine has carried weight with you (and I know that many have carried a great deal), please accord it to this. If you deal with them in

222. L. Piso's successor as governor of Macedonia.

handsome and complimentary style, you will attach two excellent and most appreciative young men to yourself and greatly oblige me.

60 (XIII. 75)

CICERO TO T. TITIUS

Rome (?), 52 (end) or 51 (beginning)

From M. Cicero to T. Titius, son of Titus, Legate,[223] greetings.

Although I do not doubt that my original recommendation carries sufficient weight with you, I am none the less complying with the request of my very good friend C. Avianius Flaccus, whose well-wisher in all things I not only am but assuredly ought to be. I spoke of him to you in person at some length, and you answered me in the kindest way; also I have already written to you about him in detail. However, he thinks it is to his advantage that I should write to you as often as I can. So please forgive me if, in deferring to his wishes, I may seem less mindful than I should be of your dependability.

My request is the same as ever. I want you to accommodate Avianius with regard to his shipments of grain, both as to place and time of disembarcation. In both respects his wishes were met, likewise at my intercession, for the three years during which Pompey presided over the business.[224] The long and short of it is that you have the opportunity to oblige me greatly, if you will let Avianius, since he thinks that I am his good friend, know that you are mine. That will oblige me very much indeed.

223. Evidently serving in a grain-exporting province, probably Sicily, and perhaps identical with the recipient of Letter 187 (V.16).

224. Pompey's five-year term as High Commissioner for grain supplies expired in the autumn of 52. The concessions to Avianius appear to have come into operation in 55.

61 (XIII. 51)

CICERO TO P. CAESIUS[225]

Date uncertain

From Cicero to P. Caesius greetings.

May I most particularly recommend to you a Roman Knight, a man of quality in every sense of the word, and a very good friend of mine, P. Messienus, and request you in the name of my friendship with yourself and your father to take him under your patronage and protect his interests and reputation? You will attach to yourself an honourable man, worthy to be your friend, and you will greatly oblige me.

62 (XIII. 76)

CICERO TO THE MAGISTRATES AND TOWN COUNCIL OF FABRATERIA VETUS (?)

Date uncertain

From M. Cicero to the Board of Four and Councillors greetings.

I am attached to Q. Hippius by so many bonds that no relationship could be closer than ours. Otherwise I should not be departing from my practice of never troubling your worships. You yourselves can best testify that, although persuaded of your readiness to grant any request I might make, I have never cared to impose upon you. Therefore let me beg

225. Nothing is known about him or Messienus. There may be a connection with the Caesii of Arpinum (see Glossary of Persons).

of you most earnestly, as a compliment to myself, to give C. Valgius Hippianus the handsomest of treatment, and to come to a settlement with him so that he can hold his property purchased from your corporation in the district of Fregellae[226] free of all dues and charges. If you grant me this request, I shall feel myself beholden to your worships for a most important favour.

63 (XIII. 1)

CICERO TO C. MEMMIUS

Athens, June (end) or July (beginning) 51

From M. Cicero to C. Memmius greetings.

I was not quite sure whether it would have been in a way distressing to me to see you in Athens[227] or a pleasure. I should have felt pain in the injustice[228] of which you are the victim, but happiness in the philosophy with which you bear it. However, I would rather I *had* seen you. The measure of distress is not very much diminished when you are out of my sight, and, had I seen you, the pleasure I might have had would assuredly have been greater. So I shall not hesitate to try to see you as soon as I can fairly conveniently do so. In the mean-

226. The town of Fregellae, not far from Arpinum, was destroyed after its revolt in 125 and Fabrateria Nova founded in its place. But the latter was governed by two magistrates (*duoviri*). This letter may therefore have been addressed to the governing body of the old town, Fabrateria Vetus, which had four magistrates and may have been granted some of the Fregellane territory.

227. On his way to his province of Cilicia in 51 Cicero stopped in Athens from 24 June to 6 July. With this letter cf. *Letters to Atticus* 104 (v.11).6.

228. Condemnation for electoral bribery in 52.

while, allow me to raise with you now a matter which can be raised, and I imagine, settled, in correspondence. And first I would ask you not to do anything on my account which you would rather not. I hope you will grant me a favour which, as you will see, matters a good deal to me and not at all to you, but only if you are satisfied beforehand that you will do it gladly.

I have all manner of ties with Patro the Epicurean, except that in philosophy I strongly disagree with him. But in the early days in Rome I was one of those whose acquaintance he particularly cultivated (that was when he was also paying attentions to you and all connected with you). Recently too he gained all he wanted in the way of personal advantages and honoraria with myself as pretty well the chief among his protectors and friends. He was originally recommended to my care and regard by Phaedrus, of whom as a philosopher I had a great opinion when I was a boy, before I knew Philo, and whom ever afterwards I respected as a man, honourable, amiable, and obliging.

Well, Patro wrote to me in Rome, asking me to make his peace with you and to beg you to let him have those ruins (or whatever they are) of Epicurus' house. I did not write to you, not wanting your building plans to be interfered with by a vicarious request of mine. When I arrived in Athens he again asked me to write to you to the same effect. This time I consented, because all your friends were agreed that you had given up your building. If that is so, and your interests are now quite unaffected, I hope you will take a lenient view of any little vexation which the untowardness of certain people may have caused you (I know the breed!), out of the great goodness of your heart or even by way of compliment to me. For my part, if you wish to know my personal sentiments, I don't see why he should make such a point of it nor why you should object – except that, after all, it is much less allowable in *you* to make a fuss about nothing than in him. However, I am sure you know

Patro's case and how he puts it. He pleads that he owes a responsibility to his office and duty, to the sanctity of testaments, to the prestige of Epicurus' name, to Phaedrus' adjuration, to the abode, domicile, and memorials of great men. If we wish to find fault with his insistence in this matter, we are at liberty to deride his whole life and philosophical principles. But really, since we have no deadly enmity towards him and others who find these doctrines to their taste, perhaps we ought not to be hard on him for taking it so much to heart. Even if he is wrong, it is silliness rather than wickedness that is leading him astray.

However, to make an end (I must come to it some time), I love Pomponius Atticus like a second brother. Nothing is more precious and delightful to me than to have him as a friend. Nobody is less of a busybody, less inclined to importune, but I have never known him request anything of me so pressingly as this – not that he is one of the sect,[229] for he is a person of the most comprehensive and refined culture,[230] but he has a great regard for Patro, and had a deep affection for Phaedrus. He is confident that I should only have to signify a wish for you to grant the point, even if you intended to build. But now, if he hears that you have put aside your building project and that I have still not obtained the favour, he is going to think, not that you have been disobliging to me, but that I have not troubled to oblige *him*. May I therefore ask you to write to your people and tell them that the relevant decree of the Areopagus[231] (*hypomnematismos* as they call it) may be rescinded with your blessing?

However, I go back to where I started. Before you decide to comply with my request I want you to be satisfied that you will

229. A notable statement. Atticus' Epicurean leanings were not taken very seriously by those who knew him.

230. The Epicureans by their own profession were not, and Cicero often jeers at their supposed ignorance and stupidity.

231. The ancient Athenian court and council.

do so gladly for my sake. None the less, you may be sure that I shall be extremely grateful if you do what I ask.

Goodbye.

64 (III. 1)

CICERO TO APPIUS PULCHER

Rome, 53 (end) or 52 (beginning)

From Cicero to Appius, Imperator,[232] greetings.

If our country could tell you for herself how she does, you would find her no better a source of information than your freedman Phanias. He is so sensible and, what is more, so inquisitive, in a good sense of the word. So he will make all plain to you. That will help me to be brief, and will be wiser from other standpoints. As to my good-will towards you, there too Phanias can be your informant, but I think that I also have a word to say. Please assure yourself that you are very dear to me. Your natural gifts, your obliging and kindly disposition, attract me in many ways; furthermore, from what you write and others say, I know that you are very appreciative of anything I have been able to do for you. Since that is so, I must evidently contrive to make up for what has been sacrificed in the long period of suspension of our intercourse by the acceptability, the frequency, and the magnitude of the services I render you; and since you so wish, I flatter myself that I shall succeed – by grace of Minerva.[233] If by any chance I

232. As governor of Cilicia Appius had concluded a successful campaign.

233. More literally 'with Minerva's good-will' (*non invita Minerva*), i.e. 'not against the grain'. Minerva (Athene) represents intellect and natural aptitude. But Cicero uses the expression here for the sake of the following allusion to a statue of the goddess which he was apparently hoping to acquire from Appius (a famous art-collector). Cf. Letter 373 (XII.25).I.

obtain the Goddess from your collection,[234] I shall style her not Polias only, but Appias.[235]

I was not previously very well acquainted with your freedman Cilix, but after handing me your affectionate and friendly letter, he followed up its kind expressions with words of his own to quite remarkable effect. I enjoyed listening to his account of your disposition towards me and of what you say about me from day to day. In fact within a couple of days he has become my friend – but not so much so that I shall not miss Phanias sorely. When you send him back to Rome, as I imagine you will shortly be doing, please give him your commissions on all matters on which you would like action or attention from me.

Allow me to recommend to you warmly Counsellor L. Valerius,[236] but with the proviso that the quality of his counsel is not guaranteed – I want to make a better caveat[237] for him than he generally drafts for his clients. I have a strong regard for him; he is one of my inner circle of familiar friends. He expressed gratitude to you, it is true, but he also writes that a letter from me will carry great weight with you. May I particularly request that he be not disappointed therein?

Goodbye.

234. Or 'your people'.

235. 'Polias' ('of the city') and 'Poliouchos' ('guarding the city') were cult-titles of Athene; *Minerva custos urbis* is the Latin equivalent. The statue, whether or not the one dedicated by Cicero in the Capitol on the eve of his exile (see n. 930), represented the goddess in this guise (the vulgate 'Pallas' here is not supported by our only valid manuscript). 'Appias' is, of course, a title invented by Cicero on the spur of the moment to make a pleasantry.

236. See Letter 21 (I.10).

237. See n. 149.

65 (III. 2)

CICERO TO APPIUS PULCHER

Neighbourhood of Rome, February or March 51

From M. Cicero, Proconsul, to Appius Pulcher, Imperator, greetings.

Contrary to my own inclination and quite unexpectedly[238] I find myself under the necessity of setting out to govern a province. My only consolation in a multitude of various annoyances and preoccupations lies in the reflection that you could not have a more friendly successor than me, and that I could not take over the province from anyone more anxious to consign it to me in as orderly and unembarrassed a state as possible. If you on your side expect the same of my disposition towards yourself, you may be sure you will never be disappointed. Let me particularly pray and request you, bearing in mind the close bond between us and your characteristic consideration for others, to watch and provide for my interests in every way you can – and there will be many ways.

You see that I am obliged under a senatorial decree to take the province. If you hand it over to me free from all embarrassments, so far as you find that possible, I shall run my lap (so to speak) of tenure the more easily. It is for you to decide what you can do in this way, but you have my urgent request to take any steps which may occur to you as helpful.

238. A law passed during Pompey's third Consulship (52) enjoined a five-year interval between the holding of a Consulship or Praetorship and the consequent governorship of a province. To fill the resulting gap the Senate called upon former Consuls and Praetors who had not previously held provincial command, of whom Cicero was one. Cilicia was assigned to him for a term of one year. His reluctance seems to have been entirely sincere.

I will not use more words. Your kindness will not expect a lengthy discourse, our friendship does not permit it; nor does the case call for words, it speaks for itself. I should only like you to feel assured that, if I find you have been thoughtful for what concerns me, my gratitude will bring you deep and lasting satisfaction.

Goodbye.

66 (III. 3)

CICERO TO APPIUS PULCHER

Brundisium, shortly after 22 May 51

From Cicero to Appius Pulcher greetings.

On my arrival at Brundisium on 22 May your Legate Q. Fabius Vergilianus was there to meet me. He conveyed to me your admonition to the effect that a larger military force is needed for the defence of this province. The considerations you raise had occurred not only to me, whom they especially concern, but to the whole Senate, which declared almost without exception in favour of a levy in Italy to reinforce my troops and those of Bibulus.[239] However, Consul Sulpicius said he would not allow it. I protested at length, but in face of the Senate's unanimous desire for me to leave without delay I had no choice but to comply, as I have done.

Let me now repeat the request I made in the letter which I gave your couriers in Rome. I hope you will do whatever can be done by an outgoing governor to ease matters for a successor to whom he is bound by close ties of friendship. Bearing in mind the perfect harmony of sentiment which exists between us, employ your care and diligence in this regard, so that all may understand that I could have had no more benevolent

239. Consul in 59, now appointed governor of Syria.

predecessor and that you could not have handed over your province to a better friend.

I understood from the dispatch which you desired to be read aloud in the Senate, of which you sent me a copy, that you had given large numbers of soldiers their discharge. Fabius, however, has explained that you had proposed to do this, but that at the time he left you numbers were still up to complement. If that is so, I shall be very grateful if you make the minimum of reductions in the meagre forces under your command. I think the decrees passed by the Senate on this subject have been sent to you. For my part, my regard for you is such that whatever you do will have my approval, but I feel sure that you on your side will take such measures as you see to be most convenient for me.

I am waiting for my Legate C. Pomptinus at Brundisium, and expect him to arrive before the beginning of June. When he does, we shall sail at the first opportunity.

67 (III. 4)

CICERO TO APPIUS PULCHER

Brundisium, 4 (?) June 51

From Cicero to Appius Pulcher, greetings.

On 4 June I received a letter from you at Brundisium in which you write that you have commissioned L. Clodius[240] to discuss certain matters with me. I am eagerly expecting him, so as to learn as soon as possible what word he brings from you. You have, I hope, already had evidence in plenty of my good-will and desire to serve you, but I shall demonstrate it most conspicuously where I can most clearly show how precious to me are your good name and dignity. Your warm regard for myself

240. Appius' 'Prefect of Engineers' (see Glossary of Terms).

had been made plain to me by Q. Fabius Vergilianus, by C. Flaccus, son of Lucius, and especially by M. Octavius, son of Gnaeus.[241] I had previously deduced it from many indications, above all the charming gift of your volume on Augury[242] with its affectionate dedication to me.

All that I can do for you to the uttermost limits of friendly service shall be done. My esteem for you has increased from day to day ever since you began to have a regard for me. To that has accrued my associations with connections of yours, for two of whom, belonging to different generations, I have the greatest esteem, namely Cn. Pompeius, your daughter's father-in-law, and your son-in-law, M. Brutus; further our association in the same College, especially now that you have approved it in so flattering a fashion, has in my eyes added a tie of no small importance to the linking of our sentiments.

Well, when I have met Clodius, I shall write to you further in the light of what he has to say, and I shall do my best to see you as soon as possible. Your statement that you are staying on in order to meet me gives me pleasure, I won't deny it.

68 (III. 5)

CICERO TO APPIUS PULCHER

Tralles, 27 or 28 July 51

From Cicero to Appius Pulcher greetings.

I arrived at Tralles on 27 July. There to meet me was L. Lucilius with your letter and messages. You could not have sent me any friendlier or, as I suppose, better qualified or more

241. The first two certainly, and the third presumably, were on Appius' staff.

242. Cicero had been elected to the College of Augurs, of which Appius was a member, in 53.

sensible informant to tell me what I want to know. I was glad to read your letter, and I have listened carefully to Lucilius. Well, since you feel as you do (you write that, while the remarks in my letter about our services to one another gave you pleasure, you saw no need to go back so far into the past), and since reminders of services rendered are in truth superfluous between firm and tried friends, I shall leave that topic on one side. Nevertheless I shall thank you as I ought. From my own observation and from your letter I find that in all matters you have been studiously thoughtful of me, and that you have, as it were, predetermined and prepared everything so as to give me an easier and freer run. When I tell you that I am most grateful for this friendly behaviour on your part, it follows that I wish you to believe that I shall be, and now am, most sedulous for you yourself and all connected with you in the first place, and for the rest of the world in the second, to know how sincerely I am attached to you. Those who are still not altogether convinced on this point must, I think, be unwilling rather than unable to perceive our sentiments. But perceive them they surely will, for the persons involved are not obscure, nor are the issues trivial. But I want all this to come out better in the doing than in the saying or writing.

My itineraries seem to have raised some doubt in your mind as to whether you will be seeing me in the province. This is how the matter stands: When I spoke with your freedman Phanias at Brundisium, I told him in the course of conversation that I should be glad to go first to whatever part of the province I thought you preferred. Then he told me that you wished to leave by boat, and that it would therefore be very much to your convenience if I made my approach by sea and landed at Side. I said I would do so, and so I should have done, if our friend L. Clodius had not told me at Corcyra that this would not answer at all, and that you would be at Laodicea awaiting my arrival. That was a much shorter and more convenient route for me, especially as I supposed you preferred it. Later your plans changed. It will be easiest for you to decide what can be done now; I shall simply explain my own intentions. I expect to reach Laodicea on 31 July. I shall stay only a very few days, to collect the sum due on my Treasury draft. Then I shall proceed to join the army, so that I should expect to be in the neighbourhood of Iconium about the Ides of August. But if at such a distance from the places and circumstances I am at all out in what I write now, as soon as I start making progress I shall send you by letter, as quickly and as often as possible, full details of my dates and routes. I dare not and ought not to impose upon you, but I do think it important for both of us that we should meet before your departure, if you can conveniently manage it. If chance robs us of the opportunity, I shall still try to serve you in every way just as though I had seen you. On my own affairs I shall not send you any commissions by letter until I have given up hope of being able to discuss them with you personally.

You say you asked Scaevola[243] to take charge of the province in your absence pending my arrival. I saw him at Ephesus and he was on a familiar footing with me during the three days I spent in the city; but I heard nothing from him about any instructions from you. I certainly regret that he was unable to comply with your wish – for I do not believe him to have been unwilling.

69 (III. 6)

CICERO TO APPIUS PULCHER

Camp near Iconium, 29 August 51

From M. Cicero to Appius Pulcher greetings.

When I compare my conduct with yours, for all my desire

243. Probably another of Appius' Legates.

to give you no less credit than myself in the maintenance of our friendship, I feel much more satisfied with the former. At Brundisium I enquired of Phanias, of whose loyalty to you and place in your confidence I thought I had good evidence and knowledge, what part of the province he thought you would wish me to enter first as your successor. He replied that I could do nothing more agreeable to you than if I came by ship to Side. Although this mode of arrival was less dignified and in many ways less convenient to me, I promised so to do. Then, when I met L. Clodius in Corcyra, a person so close to you that in talking to him I felt I was talking to yourself, I told him that I should be sure to enter the province where Phanias had asked. He thanked me, but requested me emphatically to go straight to Laodicea, saying that you wanted to be on the borders of the province, so as to leave as quickly as possible; in fact, he said, if your successor were someone whom you were less desirous to see, you would have left before he arrived. That fitted in with the letter I had received in Rome, from which it seemed to me evident that you were in a hurry to leave. I replied to Clodius that I should do as he suggested, and should in fact be much better pleased than if I had had to do what I promised Phanias. Accordingly I altered my plan, and immediately dispatched a letter to you in my own hand. From your letter I see that it reached you in quite good time.

With my conduct, as described, I am well satisfied; nothing could have been more friendly. Now consider yours. Not only did you fail to be where you could see me soonest, you withdrew where I could not even follow you within thirty days, that being, I believe, the period prescribed for your departure by the lex Cornelia. Those who do not know our mutual sentiments might well regard your conduct as that of a person indifferent (to use no harsher word), avoiding his successor, whereas mine would appear that of the closest of friends. And yet before I entered the province a letter from you was delivered to me in which you held out assured hope of meeting me, although you intimated that you were leaving for Tarsus. Meanwhile malicious persons, as I believe (a widespread human failing, many have it), finding, however, a plausible theme for talk, tried to influence my mind in your disfavour, unaware how firmly it is anchored. They said you were holding assizes in Tarsus, making many decisions both administrative and judicial, although you already had reason to think that your successor had arrived – unusual procedure even when a governor expects to be superseded within a short time.

Their talk had no effect upon me. Indeed I can assure you that I considered any such action on your part as relieving me of trouble. My year of office seems all too long, and I am glad it has been reduced almost to eleven months, if a month's work has been taken off my hands in my absence. But I must candidly own that I am disturbed to find three cohorts missing from my exiguous force, and those the most nearly up to strength, and to be ignorant of their whereabouts. What vexes me most, however, is not to know where I shall see you. That is why I have been slow in writing, since I have been expecting you in person from day to day. Meanwhile I have not even had a letter to tell me what you are doing or where I am to see you. I am therefore sending to you Prefect of Reserves[244] D. Antonius, a gallant officer, one of the best I have, to take over the cohorts, if you have no objection, so that I can get something done before the season is over. Our friendship and your letter had led me to hope that I should have the benefit of your advice in that connection, nor have I given up hoping even now. But unless you write to me when and where I am to see you, I am quite unable even to make a guess.

I shall take good care to make it clear that I am your very good friend to well-wishers and ill-wishers alike. You appear to have given some handle to the latter for misconstruction of your attitude towards myself. I shall be grateful if you will put

244. *evocati*, an élite body of veterans, retained or re-enlisted after completing their service.

this straight. And to enable you to judge where you can meet me without breach of the lex Cornelia, I entered the province on 31 July, am travelling to Cilicia through Cappadocia, and am breaking camp near Iconium on 29 August. You will now decide on the basis of dates and route where and on what day you can most conveniently meet me, if you think a meeting with me is called for.

70 (III. 8)

CICERO TO APPIUS PULCHER

In camp near Mopsuhestia, 8 October 51

From Cicero to Appius Pulcher greetings.

So far as I can gather from your letter you will read this of mine after you get to Rome, when provincial tittle-tattle will have grown stale. None the less, as you have written to me at such length about what evil-minded folk have been saying, I feel I ought to reply briefly to your letter.

Its first two paragraphs, however, I must in a sense leave unanswered, since they contain nothing precise or positive, except that I am supposed to have indicated by looks and silences that I was no friend of yours, and that this was perceptible in proceedings before my Tribunal and at certain dinner-parties. That this is all nothing I can see; but since it *is* nothing, I cannot even make out what is being said. This I do know, that you might truthfully have been told of many notorious utterances of mine, both official and private, in which I praised you highly and implied the close relations between us in unmistakable terms.

As for the matter of delegates, how could I have acted with greater propriety or fairness than by reducing the outlays of penurious communes, at their own request moreover, without any derogation to your dignity? This whole matter of deputations travelling on your behalf lay outside my ken. When I was at Apamea, the leading men in a number of communes submitted to me that excessive sums were being voted for delegates, although the communes concerned were in a state of bankruptcy. I had many factors here to consider. First, I did not suppose that so intelligent and furthermore (to use the fashionable expression) so urbane a man as yourself would take any pleasure in such deputations. I made this point at considerable length from my Tribunal, at Synnada I think it was. I said that in the first place the Senate and People of Rome did not need a testimonial from the townsfolk of Midaium (the community concerned) in praise of Appius Claudius; his praises sang themselves. I further remarked that I had often seen deputations coming to Rome on this or that person's account, but did not remember them ever being given a time or place to deliver their encomia. While approving their zeal and gratitude to you for what you had done for them, I said that the whole plan seemed to me very far from necessary. If, however, they desired to manifest their loyalty in that way, those who travelled at their own expense would have my commendation, and those who claimed expenses authorized by law would have my permission; unlimited expenses I should not allow.

What is there to censure? To be sure, you add that certain persons thought my edict was framed as though on purpose to stop these deputations. At this point, I do not consider myself so much wronged by those who so contend as by those whose ears are open to such a contention. I drew up my edict in Rome, and made no addition except what the tax-farmers asked me to transfer *verbatim* from your edict into mine, when they waited upon me at Samos. The section directed to reducing the expenses of the communes was very carefully worded. It contains some novelties beneficial to the communes, in which I take much satisfaction, but the passage which has given rise to the suspicion that I went out of my way to cross you is common form. I was not so irrational as to suppose that these deputations were in a private interest, sent as they were to express gratitude to you, no private individual, for a matter not private to themselves but public, and in no private conclave but before the parliament of the world; that is to say, the Senate. And when I laid down that no one should leave without my authority, I did *not* eliminate persons unable to follow me to my camps or to the other side of the Taurus – this is the most ludicrous point in your letter. Why should they have to follow me to my camps or to cross the Taurus, when I so managed my journey from Laodicea to Iconium that the magistrates and deputations of all districts our side of the Taurus and of their appertaining communes could meet me? Or did they start appointing deputations after I had crossed the mountains? Certainly they did not. When I was at Laodicea, and at Apamea, and at Synnada, and at Philomelium, and at Iconium (I spent time in all these towns), all deputations of this sort had already been nominated. All the same, I wish you to know that I made no ruling for the reduction or cancellation of such expenditure on deputations except at the request of the leading men of the communes, to save charging expenditures of a far from necessary kind on the proceeds of the sale of taxes and those very harsh imposts (you will know to what I refer), the poll tax and the door tax.[245] As for me, having undertaken not only in justice but in mercy to relieve these wretched, ruined communes, ruined in the main by their own magistrates, I could not turn a blind eye to this unnecessary expenditure.

If such talk about me has been carried to you by others, you should not have believed them. If, on the other hand, you favour the practice of attributing to others the thoughts that enter your own mind, you introduce into friendship a far from gentlemanly mode of conversation. Had I ever had it in mind to derogate from your good name in the province, I should not * * * your son-in-law, nor should I have consulted your freed-

245. See *Letters to Atticus* 109 (v.16).2.

man at Brundisium or your Prefect of Engineers at Corcyra as to where you wished me to go. So, following the advice of learned men who have written excellent books on the conduct of friendship, you can dismiss this whole line of language – 'they contended . . . *I* argued to the contrary,' 'they said . . . *I* denied it.'

Perhaps you suppose that nothing has ever been said to *me* about *you*? For example, that after desiring me to go to Laodicea you yourself crossed the Taurus? That at one and the same time I held assizes at Apamea, Synnada, and Philomelium, and you at Tarsus? I will not continue, or I might seem to be following your example in the very point on which I am reproaching you. One thing I *will* say as I think: if the sayings you attribute to others are your own sentiments, you are very much to blame; but if others do talk to you in this strain, you are still in some degree to blame for listening. My attitude throughout our friendship will be found consistent and responsible. If I am credited with cunning, may I point out that I always upheld your interests in your absence, even though I had no thought that I should one day stand in need of your support in similar circumstances? Would I now give you an excellent justification for deserting my absent self? That would be artful dodging indeed!

One sort of talk, in which things are very frequently said which I imagine you would prefer unsaid, I put in a special category, I mean unfavourable comment on one or other of your Legates or Prefects or Military Tribunes. Even so, I can assure you that no such criticism has so far been uttered in my hearing in more severe terms or reflecting upon a larger number of persons than what Clodius said to me on the subject at Corcyra, when he spoke with especial emphasis of his regret that you should have been so unfortunate in the rascality of others. Since such talk is frequent and does not in my opinion damage *your* reputation, I have not repressed it very vigorously, though I have never encouraged it.

Anyone who believes that *bona fide* reconciliations are impossible does not convict my bad faith, but exposes his own; and he thinks as badly of you as of me. Whereas anyone who is dissatisfied with my administration here and considers himself injured by a certain dissimilarity between my administration and yours, the fact being that both of us have acted properly but on different principles, why, I do not care to have him as a friend. You, as a great nobleman, were more open-handed here than I have been. I may have kept a rather tight hand on the purse-strings – though your own bountiful and kindly instincts were a little cramped in your second year by something unpropitious in the times. I have always been naturally rather conservative in generosity at other people's expense and am influenced by the same temporary conditions as influence others. So folk ought not to be surprised that to be 'sweet to myself, I must be sour to them'.[246]

I am obliged for your information about affairs in Rome for its own sake, and also because you intimate that you will attend to all my commissions. On one of them I make a special request; please see that this charge of mine is not increased or its period extended, and please ask our friend and colleague[247] Hortensius, if he has ever voted or acted for my sake, to give up this two-year proposal. Nothing could be more hostile to me.

You ask my news. I left Tarsus for the Amanus on the Nones of October, and am writing this the following day from camp in the territory of Mopsuhestia. If I do anything, I shall write to you, and I shall never send a letter to my home without adding one to be forwarded to you. As for your question about the Parthians, I do not think there *were* any Parthians. There were Arabs,[248] some of them with Parthian equipment, and they are said to have all withdrawn. We are told that there is not a single enemy in Syria.

246. From an unknown Latin play.
247. As Augur.
248. See p. 171.

I hope you will write to me as often as you can about your affairs and my own and about the whole state of the commonwealth, as to which your information that our friend Pompey is to go to Spain has aggravated my concern.

71 (III. 7)

CICERO TO APPIUS PULCHER

Laodicea, soon after 11 February 50

From Cicero to Appius Pulcher greetings.

I shall be writing to you at greater length when I get more time. I am writing this in haste, Brutus' boys having met me at Laodicea and told me that they are in a hurry to get back to Rome. So I have given them no letters except this to you and one to Brutus.

Envoys from Appia have handed me a roll from you full of highly unreasonable complaints concerning their building, which is said to have been stopped by a letter of mine. In the same missive you ask me to set them free to proceed with the building as soon as possible before they run into winter, and at the same time you complain with much asperity of my having forbidden them to levy special taxes until I had examined the case and given permission. That, you say, was one way of stopping them, since I could not make any examination until I returned from Cilicia for the winter.

Allow me to answer all these points, and observe the justice of your expostulation. To start with, I had been approached by persons who claimed that they were being subjected to taxation on an intolerable scale. Was it so unfair that I should write instructing them not to proceed until I had investigated the facts of the case? Oh, but I could not do this before winter – that's what you say in your letter. As though it was for me to go to them to investigate, and not for them to come to me! 'At such a distance?' you ask. Come, when you gave them your letter asking me not to stop them building before winter, did you not suppose they would come to me? To be sure they managed this absurdly enough – they did not bring me the letter, which was meant to enable them to do the job during the summer, until after midwinter. But you must understand that the objectors to the taxes are in a large majority over those who want them levied – and that none the less I shall do what I think you wish. So much for the good folk of Appia.

I have heard from my marshal Pausanias, Lentulus' freedman, that you complained to him about my not having gone to meet you. I treated you with contempt, it seems, and my arrogance is quite monstrous! The facts are that your boy arrived about the second watch[249] with a message that you would join me before daybreak in Iconium. As there were two roads and he said it was uncertain which of them you were taking, I sent A. Varro, a close friend of yours, by one and my Prefect of Engineers, Q. Lepta, by the other to meet you, instructing both to hasten back from you to me so that I could go to meet you. Lepta came hurrying back to tell me that you had already passed the camp. I went to Iconium immediately. The rest you know.[250] Was it likely that I should not turn out to meet *you* – Appius Claudius, Commander-in-Chief, entitled by traditional practice to the courtesy, and, what is most to the purpose, my friend – I who am in the habit of carrying my desire to please in many such matters further than my own rank and dignity require? But I say no more. Pausanias also told me of the following remark of yours: 'Well, of course! Appius went to meet Lentulus, Lentulus went to meet Ampius;[251] but Cicero go to meet Appius, oh no!' Really! These absurdities from *you* – a man of excellent sound sense, as I judge, much

249. About 9 p.m.
250. We do not. But it seems unlikely that a meeting took place.
251. See n. 218.

learning also, great knowledge of the world, and, let me add, urbanity, which the Stoics very rightly rank as a virtue! Do you suppose that any Appiety or Lentulity[252] counts more with me than the ornaments of merit? Even before I gained the distinctions which the world holds highest, I was never dazzled by aristocratic names; it was the men who bequeathed them to you that I admired. But after I won and filled positions of the highest authority in such a fashion as to let me feel no need of additional rank or fame, I hoped to have become the equal (never the superior) of you and your peers. And I may add that I have never observed a different way of thinking in Cn. Pompeius or P. Lentulus, one of whom I judge the greatest man that ever lived, the other greater than myself. If *you* think otherwise, you might do worse than pay rather particular attention to what Athenodorus, son of Sandon, has to say on these points – in order to understand the true meaning of *noblesse*.

But to come back to the point. I want you to believe that I am not only your friend, but your very good friend. Naturally I shall do all I can in a practical way to enable you to decide that this is really so. As for yourself, if your object is not to appear bound to work for my interests while I am away as heartily as I worked for yours, why, I hereby relieve you of that preoccupation –

> Others stand by me
> to do me grace, and before all wise Zeus.[253]

But if you are a fault-finder by nature, you will not make me any the less your well-wisher; all you will achieve is to leave me less concerned about your reactions.

I have written rather frankly, in the consciousness of my own

252. i.e. nobility, as though Appius was the name of a family. In fact it was a personal name (*praenomen*), but one almost exclusive to the patrician Claudii. Both nouns are, of course, coined by Cicero.

253. *Iliad*, 1.174 f. 'Wise Zeus' seems to indicate Pompey.

friendliness and good-will, an attitude which, as I have adopted it of deliberate choice, I shall maintain so long as *you* wish.

72 (III. 9)

CICERO TO APPIUS PULCHER

Laodicea, shortly after 20 February 50

Cicero to Appius Pulcher greetings.

Well, at long last I have read a letter worthy of Appius Claudius, full of courtesy, friendliness, and consideration! It would seem that the sight of Rome has given you back your old urbanity.[254] For I was very sorry to read the letters you sent me *en route* before you left Asia, one concerning my alleged orders to stop deputations leaving, the other about my holding up the building in Appia; and so, in the consciousness of my unswerving good-will towards you, I wrote back in some irritation. But having read the letter you gave to my freedman[255] Philotimus, I find and understand that, whereas there are many in this province who would sooner we did not feel towards one another as we do, you had only to approach Rome, or rather to see your friends there, to learn from their lips how loyal I was to you during your absence, how attentive and steadfast in fulfilling all friendly offices towards you. So you can imagine how much I appreciate the promise you make in your letter to repay me in kind, should anything arise involving my own position – though you say such repayment is hardly possible. On the contrary, you will do it easily enough; for there is nothing beyond the power of zeal and good-will, or rather affection.

254. A sort of play on words: *urbis* (= Rome), *urbanitatem.*
255. In fact, Terentia's.

The confident, in fact assured, hope of a Triumph expressed in your letter, although it only conforms to my own judgement and the frequent intimations of my correspondents, has given me the greatest happiness. That was not because I may find it the easier to gain one myself (an Epicurean point of view!),[256] but because your dignity and greatness are, I do assure you, intrinsically dear to me. Now you are better placed than others to know of persons setting out for this province, because practically all of them call on you for your commissions; so I shall be deeply obliged if you will send me a letter as soon as you have won the prize which you expect and for which I pray. If the dilatory deliberations of the 'long bench',[257] to use Pompey's expression, cost you too a day or so (surely no more), your dignity will take no harm. But, if you care for me and wish me to care for you, send me a letter, so that I may rejoice at the earliest possible moment.

I hope too that you will discharge what remains of your promised gift[258] to me. I am anxious to instruct myself in augural law for its own sake, and am marvellously delighted, believe me, with your friendly gestures and gifts. I note that you would like something of the kind from me, and certainly must consider in what form I can best reciprocate your favour. It would hardly be in character in so industrious a writer as I am (to your amazement, as you often say) to let myself appear negligent through failure to write, especially where the charge of negligence would be aggravated by one of ingratitude.

But that we shall see. Now as to this other promise of yours, look to it, I beg you, as a man of your word and as our friendship (I won't say 'now established', for it is already inveterate) claims; do all you can to have me decreed a Supplication in

256. Friendship according to Epicurus (and Cicero himself in his younger days; cf. *Pro Roscio Amerino* 111) was founded on self-interest.

257. This probably means the Board of Tribunes.

258. The work on Augury. Evidently Cicero had received only the first section.

terms as complimentary, and with as little delay, as possible. I sent my dispatch later than I should have wished (there were tiresome difficulties of navigation, and I believe it will arrive just as the Senate goes into recess),[259] but I did so on your authority and advice. And after all, I think I was right not to send it as soon as I was saluted Imperator, but to wait for further achievements and the end of the season's campaigning. This then will be your concern, as you promise; and please regard me and all things and persons that are mine as entirely commended to your care.

73 (III. 10)

CICERO TO APPIUS PULCHER

Laodicea, April (first half) 50

Cicero to Appius Pulcher greetings.

The first news of the reckless behaviour of the trouble-makers[260] gave me a severe shock, for nothing could have happened more against my expectations. But having had time to take stock, I believe that, except in one respect, everything will be plain sailing. I set my hopes chiefly upon yourself, but in no small measure upon your family and friends; and many reasons occur to persuade me that this ordeal will actually enhance your reputation. But I certainly am disheartened to see that this piece of malice has robbed you of a perfectly secure and well-earned Triumph.[261] If you estimate that at what I have

259. The Senate often rose for a vacation in April.

260. A charge of lèse-majesté (see Glossary of Terms) had been laid against Appius by P. Cornelius Dolabella, of whose engagement to Tullia Cicero was informed three months later.

261. In order to answer the charge Appius had to cross the ancient city boundary and thereby give up his *imperium;* having given up his *imperium* he could not be decreed a Triumph.

always judged to be its proper importance, you will do wisely; and you will celebrate a well-earned Triumph in virtue of the chagrin of your defeated enemies. For it is abundantly clear to me that your energy, resources, and sagacity will give them good cause to repent their insolence. As for me, I call all the Gods to witness this my solemn pledge, that in this province of which you were governor I shall do what in me lies for your honour (I prefer to say 'honour' rather than 'safety'). On your behalf I shall solicit like an intercessor, and work like a blood-relation. My influence with the communes, which I flatter myself hold me in affection, and my authority as Commander-in-Chief shall be at your service. I want you to demand all things of me, and to expect no less. My good offices shall surpass anything you can imagine.

Q. Servilius gave me a very short letter from you. To me, however, it appeared too long, for I felt it an injury to be *asked*. Sorry I am that a time should have come in which you will be able to perceive the extent of my regard for yourself, and for Pompey (whom I esteem, as I ought, more than any man alive), and for Brutus – not that you would not have seen it in our day-to-day intercourse, as see it you will; but since such a time *has* come, I shall acknowledge any omission on my part as an offence against others and against my own honour.

Pomptinus, to whom you behaved with such truly remarkable loyalty and kindness,[262] as I myself am witness, does not fail to remember you with the regard that is your due. Important private business obliged him to leave me, greatly to my regret. He was at Ephesus, just taking ship, when he heard that your interests were at stake, and at once returned to Laodicea. Such is the zeal which you can command in countless quarters. With that before my eyes, I simply cannot doubt that your present anxiety will bring you greater honour. And if further you secure the appointment of Censor, and discharge that

262. Cf. *Letters to Atticus* 92 (IV.18).4..

office as you should and can,[263] you will clearly be a tower of enduring strength, not only to yourself, but to all connected with you. Only strive with might and main to prevent any extension of my tenure, so that, when I have done what is fitting for you here, I may have the opportunity to serve you as I wish in Rome.

What you write to me about the backing you get from all persons and classes gives me no surprise at all and a great deal of pleasure. My friends tell the same story in their letters. I am truly happy to see that one whose friendship is to me no less a pleasure than an honour should receive what is his due; happy also to find that brave and active men still inspire in our community that almost universal good-will which has always been vouchsafed to myself as the only reward of my toils and vigils.

I am, however, very much astonished to find a young man whom I have twice most strenuously defended on capital charges[264] so foolhardy and so wholly oblivious of his own fortunes and interests as to provoke your enmity. It is especially surprising when one considers the superabundance of assets and resources on your side and the many deficiencies (to put it mildly) on his. My friend M. Caelius had previously informed me of his silly, childish talk;[265] and you too wrote to me about it at some length. I should have been more likely to break off an old tie with a self-constituted enemy of yours than to form a new one. And indeed you ought not to have any doubts about my sentiments towards you; they are plain to everyone in the province, and were no less so in Rome.

And yet your letter *does* imply a certain suspicion, a doubt in

263. Cicero politely assumes that if Censors are elected Appius will be one of them (as in fact happened).

264. Their nature is unknown.

265. Clearly with reference to a marriage with Tullia. Caelius' letter has not survived.

your mind. Present circumstances make it inopportune for me to reproach you on that account, but necessary to exculpate myself. Now when did I ever stop the dispatch of a deputation to Rome to sing your praises? If I hated you openly, could I have taken any step which would have harmed you less? If secretly, could I have done anything to make hostility more obvious? Suppose I were as treacherous as those who tell such tales against me, I surely should not have been so stupid as to make a parade of enmity if I wished to hide my malice, or to show the utmost will to hurt you in a fashion which did not hurt you at all. I do remember being approached by certain folk, from the Annexed Territory[266] if I am not mistaken, who alleged that excessive sums were being voted for deputations. I did not so much order as advise them to vote such sums as far as possible in accordance with the lex Cornelia. But that I did not insist even on that point can be proved from the public accounts of the communes, in which each one entered whatever amount it desired as a grant to your delegates.

But what lies these irresponsibles have foisted upon you! Not only were these expenses ruled out for the future, they say, but refunds were demanded and exacted from the agents of those who had already left, and many did not go at all for this reason. I should complain and remonstrate with you, if I did not prefer and think more proper, as I have said above, to exculpate myself rather than to arraign you in your present circumstances. So of you and your belief in these tales I shall say nothing; but a little I *shall* say about myself, to show why you ought not to have believed them. If you know me as an honourable man, worthy of the studies and culture to which I have devoted myself since childhood, as one who in matters of great moment has shown no petty spirit and no contemptible intelligence, then you ought not to suppose me capable of meanness or paltriness in friendship, much less of treachery, guile, and

266. A district of Phrygia adjoining Bithynia, annexed by the king of Pergamum about 184. Hence the name Phrygia Epiktetos.

falsehood. But suppose you choose to think of me as a crafty dissembler, how do these allegations square with such a character? Would a person of this stamp spurn the good-will of one so prosperous? Would he attack in a province the reputation of a man whose credit he defended at home? Would he display hostility just where he could inflict no hurt? Would he elect to practise bad faith in a form at once blatantly declaratory of his spite and quite innocuous to its object? And then, why should I have borne you so implacable a grudge, knowing as I did from my brother that you were no enemy of mine even when circumstances almost compelled you to act like one?[267] After the reconciliation which we mutually sought, did you once during your Consulate solicit an action or a vote from me unsuccessfully? When I accompanied you on your outward journey as far as Puteoli, you gave me certain commissions. Was there one in which my assiduity did not surpass your expectation?

If it is especially characteristic of a crafty fellow to measure all things by the yardstick of his own interest, what, may I ask, could be more in mine, more advantageous and convenient to me than connection with a personage of the highest birth and rank, whose riches, talents, children, and relations by blood and marriage would be a source of pride and strength to me? Yet it was no craftiness which led me to seek those advantages in soliciting your friendship, rather I might call it sound judgement. And then there are other bonds whose constraint I am most happy to feel – similarity of pursuits, the charm of personal intercourse, the enjoyment of a way of life, the give-and-take of conversation, the more recondite studies we share. These are bonds! I speak of our private lives. But let us not forget that some things between us interest the world at large. Our reconciliation was so publicized that any slip, however accidental, cannot but create a suspicion of bad faith. We are

267. During the conflict between Cicero and Appius' brother P. Clodius.

colleagues in an exalted priestly office. Remember that any violation of friendship between such was held a sacrilege in the good old days; indeed no priest could be co-opted who was on terms of enmity with any member of the College.

Reasons in plenty, and of no light weight! But suppose I leave them aside, and only ask whether one man ever thought, ever could or should think, more of another than I think of your daughter's father-in-law, Cn. Pompeius? And well I may. If services count, it was through him that I consider I regained country, children, citizenship, rank, my very being; if the pleasures of private intercourse count, were two Roman Consulars ever faster friends? If the tokens of affection and regard count, has he not made me the confidant of all his secrets and projects? Has he not chosen me of all others to represent his interests in the Senate during his absences? Has he not desired for me all manner of high distinctions? Can I forget how readily and graciously he accepted my efforts on Milo's behalf, which sometimes ran counter to his own policies, how anxious he was to ensure that I was not touched by the public feeling aroused at that time? How he protected me by his dispositions, his authority, even his armed forces?[268] His firm and lofty mind in those days would not let him lend credence to ill-natured talk about me even from the highest quarters, let alone some denizen of Phrygia or Lycaonia, as you did in the matter of the delegates. Well, Pompey's son[269] is your son-in-law; and apart from that connection I am well aware how dear and delightful a friend you are to him. What then should be my feelings towards you? Add that he has sent me a letter, which, even if I had been your enemy, as I am so sincerely your friend, would have disarmed my resentment and rendered me

268. According to existing accounts Cicero was intimidated rather than protected by Pompey's troops at Milo's trial. But *Letters to Atticus* 174B (IX.7B).2 shows that he asked Pompey for a bodyguard and presumably obtained it.

269. Cn. Pompeius the Younger.

obedient to the wishes, the very nod, of the man to whom I owe so much.

But that will do. Perhaps I have already used more words than were needed. Now let me tell you what I have arranged and set in motion[270] * * *. All this I am doing and shall continue to do, more for your honour than for your protection. For shortly, I hope, we shall hear of you as Censor. I think the duties of that office, calling as they do for courage and policy of the highest order, more deserve your careful and diligent consideration than these steps I am taking on your behalf.

74 (III. 11)

CICERO TO APPIUS PULCHER

Camp on the Pyramus, 26 June (?) 50

From Cicero to Appius Pulcher, Censor (I hope), greetings.

Two letters from you were delivered to me in camp on the river Pyramus at the same time, sent on to me from Tarsus by Q. Servilius. One of them was dated the Nones of April; the other seemed to me more recent, but bore no date. I shall therefore reply first to the former, in which you write of your acquittal on the charge of lèse-majesté. I had been informed of this long before by letters and oral messages and general report – it was in all mouths; not that anyone expected a different result, but tidings concerning distinguished reputations seldom lack advertisement. Your letter, however, added to my pleasure in the event. It spoke more distinctly and fully than the common talk, and I had a more vivid sense of congratulating you as I heard your news from yourself. So in my mind I embraced you from afar and kissed the letter, congratulating myself as

270. The details which followed may have been omitted in the copy of the letter preserved by Cicero.

well as you. For I feel the tribute paid by the whole people and the Senate and the jury to talent, energy, and virtue as paid also to me, flattering myself perhaps in fancying that I possess these qualities.

What surprises me is not that your trial should have ended so gloriously, but that your enemies should have shown such perverseness.[271] You may ask what difference it makes – corruption or lèse-majesté. None at all, as to the substance. Corruption you have not touched, and as for the majesty of the state, you have enhanced it. Still there is something indeterminate about a lèse-majesté charge, in spite of Sulla's ordinance penalizing random declamation against individuals, whereas corruption is clearly defined – there must be rascality on one side of the case or on the other. For obviously the fact, whether improper disbursements have or have not taken place, cannot be unknown. And what suspicion has ever attached to *your* rise up the official ladder? How I regret that I was not there! The laughs I should have raised!

However, two points in your letter about the lèse-majesté proceedings have given me a great deal of pleasure. One is your remark that Rome herself was your advocate. To be sure, the country ought to protect men like yourself, no matter how plentiful the supply of brave and honest citizens. But as matters stand now, when at every grade of rank and age there is so sore a scarcity, our forlorn community could ill afford not to cling to such champions. The other point is your enthusiastic praise for the staunchness and good-will shown by Pompey and Brutus. I am delighted to learn of this sterling loyalty on their part – not only as they are connections of yours and very good friends of mine, but because one of them stands as the greatest

271. It is to be inferred from what follows that Dolabella had threatened to prosecute Appius for electoral corruption if he failed to get a conviction on the lèse-majesté charge; and he was as good as his word. The alleged corruption probably had to do with Appius' election as Censor.

man that any century or people has produced, while the other has for some time past been a leading figure among his contemporaries and is shortly, I hope, to become so in the community at large. As to the censures to be passed upon venal witnesses by the communities to which they belong, if steps have not already been taken through Flaccus, they will be taken by me on my way home through Asia.

Now I come to the other letter. Your detailed survey, marked by so much good sense, of the crisis which affects us all and the whole political situation is most welcome. The dangers, it appears, are less serious than I feared, and the resources to deal with them greater, since, as you tell me, the entire forces of the state have rallied to Pompey's leadership. At the same time I well see your ready and forward spirit in the defence of the constitution, and am most sincerely gratified by your attention, in that in the middle of such grave preoccupations of your own you wished me none the less to learn the state of the commonwealth from *your* pen. As for the work on Augury, keep it until both of us have time to spare – when I wrote demanding the fulfilment of your pledge, I imagined you at the capital without a care in the world. As it is, I shall none the less expect the edition of your complete speeches in lieu of the work on Augury, as you yourself promise.

D. Tullius, to whom you gave a message for me, has not come my way. In fact none of your people is with me at the moment – except for all *my* people, who are all yours! I am at a loss to know which letter of mine you have in mind when you refer to 'a rather irritable letter'. I wrote to you twice exculpating myself in detail and mildly reproaching you because you had been quick to believe what you heard about me – a friendly sort of expostulation, so *I* thought; but if it displeases you, I shall eschew it in future. But if the letter was, as you say, not well-expressed, you may be sure I did not write it. Just as Aristarchus denies the authenticity of any Homeric line which he does not like, so I would request you (being in jocular vein), if you find any piece of writing not well-expressed, not to believe I wrote it.

Goodbye – and in your Censorship, if Censor, as I hope, you now are, keep your ancestor[272] much in mind.

75 (III. 12)

CICERO TO APPIUS PULCHER

Side, 3 or 4 August 50

From Cicero to Appius Pulcher greetings.

I shall begin by offering you my congratulations, putting first things first, and then turn to myself.

Indeed I do congratulate you heartily on the corruption trial – not on your acquittal, which was a foregone conclusion, but on the circumstance that even behind the screen of a secret ballot no lurking malice dared to assail you. The better citizen you are, the greater public figure, the braver friend, the more distinguished for ability and energy, the more remarkable the fact. A thing quite out of tune with modern times and men and manners! Nothing for a long while past has so amazed me.

As for me, please for a moment put yourself in my shoes, imagine you are I; and if you have no difficulty in finding what to say, I won't ask you to forgive my embarrassment! I should indeed wish that the arrangement[273] made by my family without my knowledge may turn out well for my dear Tullia and myself, as you are charming and kind enough to desire. But that the thing should have come about just when it did – well, I hope and pray some happiness may come of it, but in so

272. Ap. Claudius Caecus ('The Blind'), whose famous Censorship beginning in 312 produced the Appian Way and the Claudian Aqueduct.

273. Tullia's engagement to Dolabella.

hoping I take more comfort in the thought of your good sense and kind heart than in the timeliness of the proceeding! And so how to get out of the wood and finish what I have begun to say I cannot tell. I must not take a gloomy tone about an event to which you yourself wish all good luck; but at the same time I can't but feel a rub. On one point, though, my mind is easy – you will not fail to realize that what has been done has been done by others. I had told them not to consult me since I should be so far away, but to act as they thought best. But as I write, the question obtrudes itself: What should I have done if I had been on the spot? Well, I should have approved in principle; but as for the timing, I should have taken no step against your wishes or without consulting you.

You perceive what a pother I am in all this while, at my wits' end to know how to defend what defend I must without offending you. Lift the load from my back. I don't think I have ever pleaded a more awkward case. But of this you may be sure: though my long-standing zeal to serve you appears to admit of no enhancement, yet, had I not already settled all matters with the utmost regard for your honour, I should have championed it after the announcement of this connection, not indeed more zealously, but more ardently, openly, and emphatically. Letters from my people reached me on my voyage home after the end of my year of office, on 3 August, when I put into Side. Q. Servilius was with me. I told him then and there (he seemed upset) that he might expect more from me on all fronts. In a phrase, I am no whit the friendlier disposed towards you than I was before, but I *am* much more anxious to show my friendly disposition to the world. Our old variance used to be a stimulus, leading me to guard against any suspicion that the reconciliation was not sincere on my side. Now my new connection makes me sedulous to avoid any semblance of a falling off in the profound regard I entertain for you.

76 (III. 13)

CICERO TO APPIUS PULCHER

Rhodes (?), August 50

From Cicero to Appius Pulcher greetings.

In the days when your achievements were under discussion I worked for your distinction[274] as though I had a presentiment that in time to come I should need your support in similar circumstances. But in all candour, you have more than repaid me. From every quarter letters have come telling me how you took upon yourself the load of service, leaving nothing for others to do. From a man like yourself I should have been well content with the support of your moral influence and speech and vote; but in addition to these you contributed your trouble and advice, visiting my house and meeting my domestic circle. To me these efforts mean far more than the prize for which they are undertaken. The badges of merit have often been obtained without the thing itself, but merit alone can enlist such zealous support from men like you.

The gain I promise myself from our friendship is – friendship itself. Nothing rewards more richly, especially in the context of those pursuits to which both of us are dedicated. For I profess myself both your ally in public affairs, on which our views are identical, and your comrade in daily life, which we live in these accomplishments and pursuits. I wish matters had so fallen out that you could feel as much regard for my connections as I feel for all of yours – and yet some presentiment tells me not to despair even of that. But this is no concern of yours, the onus lies on me. I should only like you to believe what you will find to be the fact, that this unexpected development has rather

274. A *supplicatio*, such as the Senate had just voted Cicero.

added something to the warmth of my sentiments towards you, which seemed to admit of no addition, than in any degree diminished it.

As I write these words I trust you are already Censor. My letter is the shorter on that account and the more sober, as addressed to a director of public morals.

77 (VIII. 1)

CAELIUS RUFUS TO CICERO[275]

Rome, c. 26 May 51

From Caelius to Cicero greetings.

Redeeming the promise I made as I took my leave of you to write you all the news of Rome in the fullest detail, I have been at pains to find a person to cover the whole ground so meticulously that I am afraid you may find the result too wordy. However, I know how curious you are and how much everybody abroad likes to be told of even the most trifling happenings at home. But I do hope you won't find me guilty of uppishness in my performance of this office because I have delegated the work to someone else. It is not that I shouldn't be charmed to give time to remembering you, busy though I am and, as you know, the laziest of letter-writers. But I imagine the volume[276] I am sending you makes my excuses easily enough. I don't know how anyone could have so much time on his hands as to observe all these items, let alone record them. It's all here – the Senate's decrees, the edicts, the gossip, the rumours. If this specimen does not happen to appeal to you,

275. The eighth Book of the *Letters to Friends* consists entirely of letters from M. Caelius Rufus. They abound in problems of reading and interpretation.

276. i.e. roll of papyrus.

please let me know, so that I don't spend money merely to bore you. If there is any major political event which these hirelings could not cover satisfactorily, I shall be careful to write you a full account of the manner of it and of consequent views and expectations.

At the moment we are not looking ahead to anything in particular. Those rumours about elections in Transpadane Gaul[277] were rife only as far as Cumae;[278] when I got back to Rome, I did not hear so much as a whisper on the subject. Moreover, Marcellus[279] has so far not referred the question of appointing new governors in the Gallic provinces to the Senate, and has put it off, so he told me himself, till the Kalends of June. That to be sure has elicited the same sort of talk as was going round about him when we were in Rome.[280]

If you found Pompey, as you wanted to do, be sure to write and tell me what you thought of him, how he talked to you, and what disposition he showed.[281] He is apt to say one thing and think another, but is usually not clever enough to keep his real aims out of view.

As regards Caesar,[282] rumours arrive in plenty about him and they are not pretty – but only of the whispering sort. One says he has lost his cavalry (which I think is certainly a fabrication), another that the Seventh Legion has taken a beating and that

277. Cf. *Letters to Atticus* 95 (v.2).4.

278. Caelius seems to have accompanied Cicero on his outward journey as far as Pompeii, and is referring to his own return journey to Rome.

279. M. Claudius Marcellus, Consul this year. The date on which Caesar should hand over his province was a main issue in Roman politics during the two years preceding the Civil War. After a vast amount of scholarly debate it is still doubtful when his command legally ended.

280. Perhaps that he was slow and inefficient; cf. p. 171.

281. Cf. *Letters to Atticus* 100 (v.7).

282. Now contending with the aftermath of the great Gallic revolt of 52.

Caesar himself is under siege in the country of the Bellovaci, cut off from the rest of his army. But nothing is confirmed as yet, and even these unconfirmed reports are not bandied about generally but retailed as an open secret among a small coterie – you know who. But Domitius claps hand to mouth before he speaks.

On 24 May our pavement gossips[283] had spread it around that you were dead (their funeral, I hope!). All over town and in the Forum there was a great rumour that Q. Pompeius had murdered you on your road. Knowing that Q. Pompeius is operating boats at Bauli with so little to eat that my heart bleeds for him, I was unperturbed, and prayed that if any dangers *are* hanging over you we may be quit of them for the price of this lie. Your friend Plancus[284] is at Ravenna. Despite a massive largesse from Caesar, he is the same dismal vulgarian.[285]

Your work on politics[286] is all the rage.

78 (VIII. 2)

CAELIUS RUFUS TO CICERO

June, early 51

From Caelius to Cicero greetings.

Yes, I tell you, it's true. He[287] has been acquitted (I was there

283. More literally 'loungers around the Rostra (in the Forum)'.

284. Bursa. Ravenna was in Caesar's province.

285. The word-play is untranslatable. After Caesar's liberality Plancus might be rich (*beatus*) and well provided (*bene instructus*); but he was not happy (*beatus*) and well educated (*bene instructus*). The latter deficiency is ridiculed in Letter 217 (IX.10).

286. The six Books *On the Republic*.

287. M. Valerius Messalla Rufus, Consul in 53, and a friend of Cicero. His uncle Hortensius had just successfully defended him on a charge of electoral malpractice; cf. *Letters to Atticus* 105 (V.12).2.

when the verdict was announced), and that by all three categories – but by one vote in each.[288] Just be thankful, sry you. No, really; nothing so contrary to expectation, no such universal scandal, has ever been seen. Even I, who as a friend was wholeheartedly on his side and had prepared myself for the sad event, was dumbfounded when this happened, and felt as though I had been cheated. You can imagine how others reacted. Naturally they howled abuse at the jury and made it plain that *this* was going beyond all patience. So now he's left in what looks like a more perilous predicament than ever, to face the lex Licinia.[289] On top of this, Hortensius walked into Curio's theatre[290] the day after the acquittal, presumably to let us share in his jubilation. You should have heard the 'din and hubbub, roar of thunder, tackle whistling in the gale'.[291] It was all the more noticed because Hortensius had come to old age without a single experience of the bird. But he had enough of it then to last anyone a lifetime, and rued his victory.

About politics I have nothing to tell you. Marcellus' initiatives have subsided, not from lack of energy, but, in my opinion, from policy. The consular elections are anybody's guess. *I* have got one nobleman to contend with and one acting-nobleman[292] – M. Octavius, son of Gnaeus, and C. Hirrus are standing with me. I am telling you this because I know how eagerly you will wait for the result of our elections on Hirrus'

288. At this period Roman juries were made up of equal numbers of Senators, Knights, and Paymaster Tribunes. The votes of each category were counted separately, but the verdict went by a majority of the whole jury.

289. A recently passed measure concerned with illegal associations. Messalla was in fact prosecuted and found guilty under it.

290. A wooden theatre of remarkable construction built by Curio in 53 for the show given in honour of his dead father.

291. From the *Teucer* of Pacuvius.

292. Literally 'playing the nobleman'. Hirrus' family was senatorial but not 'noble'.

account.[293] As soon as you hear I am designate, please see to the matter of the panthers.[294] I recommend Sittius' bond to your kind attention.[295] I gave my first Abstract of Affairs in Rome to L. Castrinius Paetus, my second to the bearer of this letter.

79 (VIII. 3)

CAELIUS RUFUS TO CICERO

Rome, mid June 51

From Caelius to Cicero greetings.

Well? Have I won? Am I sending you letters often, which as you were leaving you told me I should never bother to do for you? Yes – if those I dispatch get to their destination. I am all the more punctilious about it, because when I have no work on hand there is simply nowhere for me to amuse my leisure. When you were in Rome and I had any free time, I was sure of employment the most agreeable in the world – to pass it in your company. I miss that not a little. It is not merely that I feel lonely; Rome seems turned to desert now that you are gone. I am a careless dog, and when you were here I often used to let day after day go by without coming near you. Now it's a misery not to have you to run to all the time.

Above all else my fellow-candidate Hirrus sees to it that I miss you day and night. Just imagine his chagrin – this competitor of yours, this would-be Augur – at finding my prospects of election better than his own, imagine his efforts to pretend it's otherwise! Upon my word, it's for your sake rather than

293. Hirrus had earned Cicero's displeasure by standing against him for the Augurate.

294. For the 'games' which Caelius would have to give as Aedile.

295. Money was owing to Sittius (probably not the addressee of 23 (V.17)) in Cicero's province. Perhaps Caelius was his creditor.

my own that I want you to get the news you are praying for concerning him as soon as may be. As for *my* sake, if I do get elected, it might suit my book to be in company with the richer of the pair.[296] But *this* would be too delicious! If it happens, we shall never be short of a laugh for the rest of our days. Yes, it's worth a sacrifice. But it is a fact that the mislikes which a good many people feel for Hirrus keep him down without notably buoying M. Octavius up.[297]

With regard to the freedman Philotimus' duty and Milo's property,[298] I have been at pains to ensure that Philotimus behaves with complete propriety to the satisfaction of the absent Milo and of those close to him, and that with good faith and care on his part no harm comes to your reputation.

Now I have a favour to ask. If you are going to have time on your hands, as I expect you will, won't you write a tract on something or other and dedicate it to me, as a token of your regard? You may ask what put that into my tolerably sensible head. Well, I have a desire that among the many works that will keep your name alive there should be one which will hand down to posterity the memory of our friendship. I suppose you will want to know what sort of book I have in mind. With your command of the whole range of knowledge you will think out the most appropriate subject quicker than I; but in general terms, let it be something of relevance to me, with a didactic character so as to have a steady circulation.

296. Hirrus, a very wealthy man. A poor Aedile might draw credit from the outlay of a richer colleague, and Caelius had hoped to share expenses (cf. p. 158).

297. People could vote for as many candidates as there were places to fill (two in this instance) but were probably not obliged to vote for more than one. In that case a refusal to vote for Hirrus would not automatically be a vote for Octavius.

298. See *Letters to Atticus* 101 (v.8).2.

80 (II. 8)

CICERO TO CAELIUS

Athens, 6 July 51

From M. Cicero, Proconsul, to M. Caelius greetings.

Really! Is this what you think I asked you to do – to send me pairings of gladiators, court adjournments, Chrestus'[299] pilfering, all the trivia which nobody would dare tell me when I am in Rome? Let me show you how highly I value your judgement – and right I am, for I have never known a better *politique* than you! I do not even particularly want you to tell me day-to-day political developments in matters of major consequence, unless I am affected personally. Others will be writing, I shall have plenty of oral informants, even common report will transmit a good deal. So I do not expect things past or present from *your* pen. What I want from so far-sighted a fellow as yourself is the future. From your letters, having seen, as it were, an architect's drawing of the political situation, I shall hope to know what kind of building is to come. Not that I have any complaint so far. There has been nothing which you could foresee any better than the rest of us – myself especially, after spending several days with Pompey discussing nothing but public affairs. Of what passed between us I cannot and should not write, but of this much you may be sure: Pompey is a very good patriot, ready in spirit and plan for every contingency against which we have to provide. So court him; believe me, you will be welcomed. He now sees good citizens and bad exactly where we are wont to see them.

I have spent ten clear days in Athens, much in the company of our friend Caninius Gallus.[300] I leave today, 6 July, after

299. Unknown. 'Chrestus' is a common slave-name.
300. Perhaps in exile.

dispatching these few lines. I hope you will take all my interests under your special care, none more than the matter of my tenure here, which I do not want extended. This means everything to me. As to when, how, and through whom to proceed, you will be the best judge.

81 (VIII. 4)

CAELIUS RUFUS TO CICERO

Rome, 1 August 51

From Caelius to Cicero greetings.

I really envy you. So many surprises landing on your doorstep every day! First Messalla acquitted; then convicted. C. Marcellus elected Consul. M. Calidius defeated, and prosecuted by the two Gallii. P. Dolabella a Quindecimvir.[301] One thing I *don't* envy you – you missed a really beautiful sight, Lentulus Crus' face when he heard his defeat. He had gone down to the hustings in the highest fettle, thought to be a certainty. Even Dolabella had little opinion of his own chances. In fact I may say that but for the sharper eyes of your humble servant, Lentulus would have carried the day with his opponent practically conceding victory.

One thing I expect will *not* have surprised you, the conviction of Tribune-Elect Servaeus. C. Curio has announced himself as a candidate for the vacancy, much to the alarm of folk who don't know him and his easy ways. But as I expect and hope and as himself declares, he will be for the Senate and the honest men. At the moment he is absolutely frothing with this sentiment. Its origin and cause is that Caesar, who doesn't usually care how much money he spends to get the friendship

301. The Quindecimviri (Board of Fifteen) were official custodians of the Sibylline prophecies.

of any guttersnipe, has shown his indifference to Curio in no uncertain manner. À propos of which I feel this is a highly amusing coincidence, and others have noticed it – so much so that Curio, who does nothing except on impulse, is credited with deep cunning in evading the designs of certain persons who had set themselves to oppose him as Tribune, I mean Lollius (?), Antony, and other sturdy fellows of the same stamp.[302]

The interval between this letter and its predecessor has been the wider because the postponements of the elections kept me rather busy and made me wait for the outcome from day to day, in order to inform you when everything was over. I have waited until the Kalends of August. The Praetorian elections have been held up by various accidents. What is going to happen in my own I don't know. As regards Hirrus, the election of the Plebeian Aediles has produced an amazing current of opinion. M. Coelius Vinicianus was suddenly brought down (with loud shouts to follow as he lay) by that silly statement of his which we laughed at together at the time and the notice of legislation about a Dictator.[303] After that came a universal hue and cry that *now* Hirrus must not be elected. I trust that it won't be long before you hear the news you have been hoping for about me and the news for which you have hardly dared to hope about him.

In the political arena we had stopped expecting anything

302. As I have interpreted this difficult passage, Curio was given credit for checkmating the plans of his pro-Caesarian opponents by standing at a by-election instead of waiting till the following year. Lollius was a former satellite of Clodius. The manuscript reading *laelios* would presumably refer to D. Laelius, Tribune in 54, who is inappropriate.

303. As Tribune in 53 Hirrus had called for Pompey to be made Dictator. From this passage it is inferred that Coelius did likewise, and that his rout in the elections to the Plebeian Aedileship was now taken as a bad sign for Hirrus. How something that happened two years previously could 'suddenly' bring Coelius down is anybody's guess.

fresh. But when the Senate met in the Temple of Apollo[304] on 22 July, and was asked to consider the matter of pay for Pompey's troops, a question was raised about the legion which Pompey lent to C. Caesar[305] – whose was it, and how long would Pompey let it remain in Gaul. Pompey was forced to say that he *would* withdraw the legion, but not immediately under prompting and clamour from his critics. Then he was interrogated about the replacement of C. Caesar, as to which (i.e. on the provinces generally) it was determined that as soon as Pompey returned to Rome a debate should be held on the replacement of provincial governors in his presence (Pompey was about to go to Ariminum to visit his army and went immediately). I think the debate will be on the Ides of August. Presumably something will be decided, or there will be a scandalous veto. For in the course of the discussion Pompey threw out the remark that everyone ought to obey the Senate. For my own part though, I am looking forward to nothing in the world so much as to Consul-Elect Paulus making the first speech.[306]

I am reminding you about Sittius' bond, not for the first time, because I am anxious to make you realize my strong personal concern in that matter. Likewise about panthers – please send for some from Cibyra and have them shipped to me. Another thing, we have had word of the death of the king of Egypt,[307] and it is now taken as certain. Please write to me at length,

304. In the Campus Martius, outside the ancient city boundary, which Pompey, as holding *imperium*, could not enter except by special dispensation.

305. At the beginning of 53 (cf. Caesar, *Bell. Gall.* VI.I).

306. Consuls-Elect spoke first. Paulus (the contemporary spelling was 'Paullus'), a friend of Cicero, had previously been regarded as a firm 'optimate'. In office he took a passive line, allegedly bribed by Caesar. Caelius seems to have had some inkling of his change of front.

307. Ptolemy the Piper. His successors, Ptolemy XIII and Cleopatra, being too young to rule, a regency was established. Caelius was presumably one of the late king's creditors.

advising me how to act and telling me of the state of the kingdom and who is in charge of it.
Kalends of August.

82 (VIII. 9)

CAELIUS RUFUS TO CICERO

Rome, 2 September 51

From Caelius to Cicero greetings.

'So that's how you handled Hirrus, is it?' I hear you saying My dear sir, if you only knew how easy it was, how completely effortless, you would be ashamed to remember that he ever dared to parade as your competitor. After the defeat he's making us all laugh, playing the good citizen and delivering anti-Caesarian speeches in the Senate, denouncing the waiting game, and taking the Consuls to task in no uncertain terms.[308] This defeat has made a completely different man of him. On top of this, he that never showed his face in the Forum and has little experience of law-courts has taken to appearing in freedom suits[309] – but not often after midday.

I told you earlier that there would be a debate on the provinces on the Ides of August, but Consul-Elect Marcellus' trial[310] has upset this timetable. The matter was put off to the Kalends. They had not even been able to get a quorum. I am dispatching this letter on 2 September, and up to that date nothing has been even in main part accomplished. It looks to me

308. For their dilatory handling of the question of Caesar's command.

309. Cases to determine whether a person was free or slave. A man of Hirrus' rank might gain popularity by appearing on behalf of such humble folk.

310. C. Marcellus, Consul in 50, was prosecuted by his unsuccessful competitor M. Calidius for electoral malpractice after the elections, but was acquitted.

as though the entire question will be relegated to next year, and, as far as I can prophesy, you will have to leave a deputy-governor behind you. There is no way clear to the appointment of a successor, because the Gauls, for which a veto is in readiness, are being linked with the other provinces. I am sure of this. That is another reason why I am writing to you, so that you prepare yourself for this outcome.

In almost every letter I have written to you I have mentioned the subject of panthers. It will be little to your credit that Patiscus has sent ten panthers for Curio and you not many times as many.[311] Curio has given me those same animals and another ten from Africa – in case you imagine that country estates[312] are the only form of present he knows! If you will but keep it in mind and send for beasts from Cibyra and write to Pamphylia likewise (they say the hunting is better there), the trick will be done. I am all the more exercised about this now because I think I shall have to make all my arrangements apart from my colleague.[313] Do be a good fellow and give yourself an order about it. You generally like to be conscientious, as I for the most part like to be careless. Conscientiousness in this business is only a matter of saying a word so far as you are concerned, that is of giving an order and commission. As soon as the creatures are caught, you have the men I sent in connection with Sittius' bond to look after their feeding and transport to Rome. Indeed, if you hold out any hope when you write, I think I shall send some more men over.

M. Feridius, a Roman Knight, is going to Cilicia on personal business. He is the son of a friend of mine, and is a worthy and energetic young man. May I recommend him to you and re-

311. i.e. 'for me'.

312. Apparently with reference to some incident otherwise unrecorded. Curio's plan for a redistribution of land in Campania (cf. p. 172), even if already formed and known to Caelius, would hardly have been known to Cicero.

313. M. Octavius.

quest you to admit him to your circle? He hopes that by a kindness which you can render with ease and propriety[314] some lands held in tenancy by communes will receive exemption from tax. You will be obliging worthy people, who do not forget a service.

I wouldn't have you think that Favonius[315] was passed over by the groundlings. All the best people didn't vote for him. Your friend Pompey is openly against Caesar being elected Consul while he retains his province and army. But speaking in the Senate he himself said that no decree should be passed at present, while Scipio proposed that the question of the Gallic provinces should be brought before the House on the Kalends of March, with no other item attached. His speech cast a gloom over Cornelius Balbus, and I know he has remonstrated with Scipio. Calidius gave an excellent performance in his own defence; as prosecutor he was pretty unimpressive.

83 (VIII. 5)

CAELIUS RUFUS TO CICERO

Rome, mid September 51

From Caelius to Cicero greetings.

How worried *you* may be about the prospects of peace in your province and the adjacent areas I don't know, but for my part I am on tenterhooks. If we could so manage that the size of the war should be proportionate to the strength of your forces and could achieve as much as requisite for glory and a Triumph while avoiding the really dangerous and serious clash,

314. The lands may have been owned by Feridius senior and let to local civic corporations.

315. This satellite of Cato had been defeated in the elections to the Praetorship.

it would be the most desirable thing in the world. But I know that as matters stand any move by the Parthians will mean a major conflict; and your army is hardly capable of defending a single pass. Unfortunately nobody allows for this; a man charged with public responsibility is expected to cope with any emergency, as though every item in complete preparedness had been put at his disposal. Furthermore, I do not see any prospect of your being relieved because of the controversy about the Gallic provinces. Although I expect you have settled in your own mind what you are going to do in this contingency, I thought that, since I see it coming, I ought to inform you, so that you take your decision the further ahead. You know the routine. There will be a decision about Gaul. Somebody will come along with a veto. Then somebody else will stand up and stop any move about the other provinces, unless the Senate has free licence to pass decrees on all of them. So we shall have a long, elaborate charade – so long that a couple of years or more may drag by in these manoeuvres.

If I had anything fresh to tell you about the political situation, I should follow my usual practice and describe in detail both what had happened and what consequences I expected to follow. The fact is that everything has stuck in a kind of trough. Marcellus still goes on pressing his point about the provinces, but so far he has not succeeded in getting a muster of the Senate. This year thus passed, Curio will be Tribune, and the same performance about the provinces will come on the boards. You don't need me to tell you how easy it will be then to hold everything up, and how well this will suit Caesar and those who think of themselves and care nothing about the country.[316]

316. Neither the text nor the general sense is certain. Caelius can hardly mean that Curio in office would play Caesar's game (as in fact he did), for at this time he expected quite otherwise. But Curio was unpredictable and might fish in troubled waters. Perhaps *he* might be the one to 'stand up and stop any move about the other provinces'.

84 (VIII. 8)

CAELIUS RUFUS TO CICERO

Rome, early October 51

From Caelius to Cicero greetings.

Although I have some matters of public import to tell you, I have nothing that I think you will be so pleased to read as the following. Learn that your heart's darling, C. Sempronius Rufus,[317] has been nailed for malicious prosecution to loud applause. The case? He charged his own prosecutor, M. Tuccius, with assault under the lex Plotia after the Roman Games, his idea being that, if no priority prosecution came up,[318] he himself would have to stand trial this year – and what would happen then he knew all too well.[319] He thought he might as well make this little present to his accuser as to anybody. So down he went, with no assistant-prosecutor, and charged Tuccius. As soon as I hear of it I hurry unsummoned up to the defence benches. I get on my hind legs and without a syllable on the matter in hand, I make a thorough job of Sempronius, even including Vestorius and the story of how he claimed to have done you a favour in letting Vestorius keep ***.[320]

317. This man was in Cicero's bad books; cf. *Letters to Atticus* 95 (v.2).2.

318. Why Rufus' prosecution of Tuccius should have had priority is controversial. The Roman Games ended on 19 September.

319. Nothing more is known of Tuccius or his charge, but Caelius' forecast that Rufus would be convicted was probably correct, since he was in exile in 44 (*Letters to Atticus* 368 (XIV.14).2).

320. The nature of Cicero's involvement in this affair being obscure (cf. *Letters to Atticus* 95 (v.2).2), the corrupt text seems incurable.

Now the Forum is full of another great tussle.[321] M. Servilius, having completed a career of general derangement and left nobody anything to sell, was handed over to me – a most unpopular client. Pausanias prosecuting, me defending, on a charge of receiving, Praetor Laterensis dismissed the case *prima facie*. Then Q. Pilius, our friend Atticus' connection, charged him with extortion. It became at once a *cause célèbre* and a verdict of guilty was eagerly canvassed. Tossed up on the crest of this wave, Appius minor lays information concerning money received by Servilius out of his father's property, alleging that HS3,000,000 had been deposited to rig the prosecution.[322] The folly of it surprises you? It would surprise you more if you had heard him speak, the admissions he made about himself and his father – the former idiotic, the latter shocking.

He sends the jury to consider their verdict, the same jury that had assessed the damages. The votes were equally divided. Laterensis, not knowing his law, announced the verdict of each category and, to finish up, 'I shall not call in' – the usual form.[323] He then left the courtroom, and everyone began to look on

321. The facts up to this point may be made out as follows: C. Claudius Pulcher, governor of Asia in 55–53, had been charged with extortion after his return (the case seems to have been slow in getting to court). He had paid over a sum to M. Servilius (probably a former member of his staff) to obtain an acquittal by collusion with the prosecution. He was, however, found guilty and went into exile without leaving enough assets to pay the damages assessed by the court. Pausanias, representing the provincials, then tried to prosecute Servilius on a charge of 'receiving' (i.e. receiving money extorted from the province), but the Praetor, M. Juventius Laterensis, refused leave to proceed, presumably on the ground of insufficient evidence.

322. Appius minor seems to have been allowed to revive Pausanias' charge under particular provisions of the lex Julia, with priority over Pilius' general charge under the same law, since the former stemmed from a previous trial.

323. Of acquittal. An even vote was normally considered as a verdict of acquittal, but the lex Julia, whether by accident or design, seems to have required a majority; an even vote meant that the trial was void.

Servilius as acquitted. Laterensis, having read the hundred-and-first section of the law, which states 'the verdict of the majority of such members of the jury shall be lawful and binding', made his entry in the record – not 'acquitted', but the verdicts of the several categories. Appius again laid his charge; on which Laterensis said that he had arranged matters with L. Lollius and would ***.[324] So now Servilius is neither acquitted nor convicted, and will be handed over to Pilius the worse for wear, to be tried for extortion. Appius, having sworn good faith,[325] none the less did not have the courage to contest the right to prosecute and gave way to Pilius. He himself has been prosecuted for extortion[326] by the Servilii, and on top of this has been charged with assault by a satellite of his own, *.[327] A well-matched pair!

As regards public affairs, for a long while nothing was done pending a decision on the Gallic provinces. But eventually, after many postponements and much grave debate, during which it became quite clear that Cn. Pompeius was in favour of his[328] leaving his command after the Kalends of March, the Senate passed a decree, of which I send you a copy, and recorded resolutions.

Decree of the Senate: Resolutions

On this 29th day of September in the Temple of Apollo. Present at drafting the following: L. Domitius Ahenobarbus, son of Gnaeus, of

324. Laterensis' reaction to Appius' demand for a fresh trial is concealed under a corrupt text, but whatever it was it resulted in the lapse of Appius' charge.

325. As a preliminary to claiming the right to prosecute the extortion case in preference to Pilius. Such contests were settled by vote of the jury.

326. Presumably for misconduct in Asia during his father's governorship.

327. The name, possibly Statius or Suettius, is doubtful.

328. Meaning Caesar.

the tribe Fabia; Q. Caecilius Metellus Pius Scipio, son of Quintus, of the tribe Fabia; L. Villius Annalis, son of Lucius, of the tribe Pomptina; C. Septimius, son of Titus, of the tribe Quirina; C. Lucilius Hirrus, son of Gaius, of the tribe Pupinia; C. Scribonius Curio, son of Gaius, of the tribe Pomptina; L. Ateius Capito, son of Lucius, of the tribe Aniensis; M. Eppius, son of Marcus, of the tribe Teretina.

Forasmuch as M. Marcellus, Consul, did address this House touching the consular provinces, it was thus resolved: that L. Paulus and C. Marcellus, Consuls, having entered upon their office, should on or after the Kalends of March falling in their year of office bring the matter of the consular provinces before the Senate, and that from the Kalends of March onwards they bring no other business before the Senate either previously or in conjunction therewith; further that for the said purpose they may hold a meeting of the Senate upon any comitial day and pass a Decree, and that in bringing the said matter before the Senate they may without forfeit incurred bring persons belonging to the panel of 300 jurors from their several juries to this House being members thereof; further, if there be need that proposals touching this matter be brought before People or Plebs, that Ser. Sulpicius and M. Marcellus, Consuls, the Praetors, and Tribunes of the Plebs, whosoever of them see fit, bring such proposals before People or Plebs; and that if they do not so do, then their successors bring such proposals before People or Plebs. Resolved.

On this 29th day of September in the Temple of Apollo. Present at drafting the following: L. Domitius Ahenobarbus, son of Gnaeus, of the tribe Fabia; Q. Caecilius Metellus Pius Scipio, son of Quintus, of the tribe Fabia; L. Villius Annalis, son of Lucius, of the tribe Pomptina; C. Septimius, son of Titus, of the tribe Quirina; C. Lucilius Hirrus, son of Gaius, of the tribe Pupinia; C. Scribonius Curio, son of Gaius, of the tribe Pomptina; L. Ateius Capito, son of Lucius, of the tribe Aniensis; M. Eppius, son of Marcus, of the tribe Teretina.

Forasmuc has M. Marcellus, Consul, did address the senate touching the provinces, it was thus resolved: that in the judgement of the Senate no person having power of veto or impediment should let or hinder that matters touching the commonwealth be brought before the Senate on the first possible occasion and that a Decree of the

Senate be passed; and that whosoever offers such bar or impediment shall in the judgement of the Senate have acted against the commonwealth. If any person shall cast his veto against this Decree of the Senate, it is the Senate's pleasure that a Resolution be recorded and that the matter be brought before the Senate on the first possible occasion.

The above Decree of the Senate was vetoed by the following Tribunes of the Plebs: C. Coelius; L. Vinicius; P. Cornelius; C. Vibius Pansa.

It is likewise the Senate's pleasure as touching soldiers serving in the army of C. Caesar that the cases of any such who have completed their terms of service or who can show cause wherefore they be discharged be brought before this House to the end that their cases be taken under consideration and cognizance. If any person shall cast his veto against this Decree of the Senate, it is the Senate's pleasure that a Resolution be recorded and that the matter be brought before this House on the first possible occasion.

The above Decree of the Senate was vetoed by the following Tribunes of the Plebs: C. Coelius; C. Vibius Pansa.

It is likewise the Senate's pleasure as touching the province of Cilicia and the eight remaining provinces now governed by former Praetors with propraetorian rank that such persons as have held the office of Praetor but have not previously held command in any province, being eligible under the Senate's Decree[329] for dispatch to provinces with propraetorian rank, shall be dispatched to the aforesaid provinces as by lot determined. If the number of persons qualified under the Senate's Decree for such appointment be less than the number required to proceed to the aforesaid provinces, then persons having been members of the Board of Praetors standing next in order of seniority, such persons having previously held provincial office, shall proceed to provinces as by lot determined. If their number be in-

329. Voted in 53 to impose a five-year interval between the holding of a Consulship or Praetorship and the assumption of a province. The rule did not become effective until the following year when it was enacted by law (see n. 238).

sufficient, then members of each Board of Praetors in succession, not having previously held provincial office, shall be admitted to the lot, until the requisite number be completed. If any person cast his veto against this Decree of the Senate, let a Resolution be recorded.

The above Decree of the Senate was vetoed by the following Tribunes of the Plebs: C. Coelius; C. Pansa.

Moreover, certain remarks of Cn. Pompeius have been noted, and have greatly raised public confidence. He said that before the Kalends of March he could not in fairness take a decision about Caesar's provinces, but that after this date he would have no hesitation. Asked what would be the position if vetoes were cast at that point, he replied that it made no difference whether C. Caesar was going to disobey the Senate or was putting up someone to prevent the Senate from passing a decree. 'And supposing,' said another questioner, 'he chooses to be Consul[330] *and* keep his army?' To which Pompey, as gently as you please: 'And supposing my son chooses to take his stick to me?' These utterances of his have produced an impression that Pompey is having trouble with Caesar. So it looks to me as though Caesar is now ready to settle for one of two propositions – either to stay where he is and forgo his candidature this year,[331] or, if he can secure election, to retire from his command. Curio is making ready for all-out opposition to him. What he may be able to accomplish I don't know, but it is clear to me that he cannot come to grief even if he achieves nothing, his sentiments being sound.

Curio is behaving handsomely to me, and has made me a somewhat onerous present in the shape of the African panthers which were imported for his show. Had he not done that, one might have let the thing go. As it is, I have to give it. So, as I have asked you all along, please see that I have a few beasts from your part of the world. And I commend Sittius' bond to

330. i.e. to get himself elected.

331. This can only mean 'the current electoral year', i.e. 50.

your kind attention. I have sent out my freedman Philo and a Greek, Diogenes, and given them a message and a letter for you. Please look after them and the object of their errand. How important that is to me I have explained in the letter which they will deliver to you.

85 (II. 9)

CICERO TO CAELIUS RUFUS

Camp near Mopsuhestia (?), about 8 October 51

From M. Cicero, Proconsul, to M. Caelius, Curule Aedile-Elect greetings.

First my due and joyful congratulations on your present dignity and also on what may be expected to follow.[332] That they are rather late in coming is not the result of any negligence on my part but of my ignorance of all that goes on. I am in a region where news comes in very slowly, because of its remoteness and the banditry in the country. And not only do I congratulate you, I cannot find words to express my gratitude for the manner of your election, which has given us, as you wrote to me,[333] something to laugh at for the rest of our lives. When I first heard the news, I was transformed into the man himself[334] (you know whom I mean), and found myself playing all those *jeune premier* roles which he is so fond of performing.[335] It's

332. After election to the Curule Aedileship Caelius could look forward to higher things in due course – the Praetorship, even the Consulship. Or perhaps Cicero is simply referring to his entry into office.

333. See p. 152.

334. Hirrus.

335. The point of this passage is not entirely clear. It has been supposed that Hirrus was fond of quoting or reciting from Latin comedies;

hard to put into words, but I saw you in imagination and it was as though I was talking to you: 'Well done, egad! A famous piece of work!' The thing came to me so unexpectedly that I went on to that bit that goes 'A quite amazing thing today...' Then, all of a sudden, 'I walked on air. Glee! Glee!' And when I was taken to task for almost losing my wits with excess of jubilation, I defended myself: 'Joy overmuch, I judge...' In short, in laughing at him I almost came to *be* the man.

But more of this and much else, to you and concerning you, as soon as I get a minute to spare. My dear Rufus, you are fortune's gift to me. You raise me in men's eyes, you punish not only my enemies but my enviers, making some of them sorry for their villainies and others for their ineptitudes.

86 (II. 10)

CICERO TO CAELIUS RUFUS

In camp near Pindenissum, 14 November 51

From M. Cicero, Imperator, to M. Caelius, Curule Aedile-Elect greetings.

Just see how letters fail to reach me! For I cannot believe that you have sent none since you were elected Aedile, after so important and felicitous an event – expected as regards yourself, but as regards Hillus (I can't pronounce my 'r's[336]) by me quite unforeseen. And yet it is a fact that no letter of yours has come to my hand since those magnificent elections, which sent me into transports of delight. It makes me afraid that the

but why from these particular roles? Had he a propensity to pose as a dashing young gallant (he must have been in his thirties)? The authorship of the first two quotations is unknown. The third comes from Caecilius, the fourth from Trabea.

336. Neither, we gather, could Hirrus.

same may be happening to *my* letters – I have never sent a letter home without another for you, than whose friendship nothing in life is dearer to me or more agreeable.

But back to business (I *can* pronounce my 'b's!).[337] Your prayer is answered. You say you would have liked me to have just enough trouble to provide a sprig of laurel,[338] but you are afraid of the Parthians, because you have little confidence in the forces at my disposal. Well, so it has turned out. On the news of war with Parthia I marched to the Amanus, relying on certain narrow passes and the mountainous character of the country, at the head of an army tolerably well provided with auxiliary forces and fortified by a certain prestige attaching to my name among those who knew me not. There is a good deal of talk in this part of the world – 'Is that the man to whom Rome . . .?', 'whom the Senate . . .?' (you can fill in the gaps). By the time I reached the Amanus, the range of mountains which Bibulus and I share between us, divided at the watershed, our friend Cassius had driven the enemy back from Antioch in a successful action (a very pleasing piece of news to me) and Bibulus had taken over the province.

Meanwhile I harried the people of the Amanus, who are perpetually at war with us, with my entire force. Many were killed or taken prisoner, the rest scattered. Their strongholds were taken by surprise assaults and burned. So in due recognition of a victorious campaign I was saluted 'Imperator' at Issus, where, as I have often heard you say, Clitarchus told you that Darius was defeated by Alexander. I then led my army into the most hostile part of Cilicia, where I am laying siege to the town of Pindenissum, a very strong place indeed, with ramps, casemates, and towers. The siege is now in its twenty-fifth day; judged by scale and difficulty it is a major operation,

337. Literally 'there is nothing wrong with my speech'; i.e. the topic of Hirrus dismissed (*ad rem redeamus*), Cicero has no more trouble with his 'r's.

338. i.e. a Triumph; cf. p. 159.

one to bring me great glory in everything but the name of the town. If I take it, as I hope to do, *then* I shall send an official report. I am telling you all this now, so that you may be hopeful that you are getting what you prayed for.

However, to return to the Parthians, we can feel tolerably pleased with the final result of this summer's operations. Next summer is an alarming prospect. So keep alert, my good Rufus. First try to get my successor appointed. But if, as you write and I suppose, that is going to be rather sticky, see that my tenure is not extended, which is easy. On politics, as I wrote to you earlier, I expect from your letters the present and still more the future. So *please* write everything to me in full detail.

87 (VIII. 10)

CAELIUS RUFUS TO CICERO

Rome, 17 November 51

From Caelius to Cicero greetings.

We have been uncommonly alarmed by dispatches from C. Cassius and Deiotarus. Cassius has written announcing that Parthian forces are this side of the Euphrates, Deiotarus that they are advancing through Commagene into our province. For my part, the principal fear I had as regards yourself (knowing the extent of your military resources) was that this flare-up might endanger your reputation. If your military resources had been greater, I should have felt anxious about your personal safety, but, being as meagre as they are, I thought they augured retreat, not battle. I was nervous about the way such news would be received and how far the necessity would be appreciated. Nervous I still am, and I shall not stop worrying until I hear you are on Italian soil.

However, the news about the Parthian crossing has given rise to a variety of talk. One man is for sending Pompey out, another says Pompey ought not to be moved away from Rome. Another school of thought would like to send Caesar with his army, another the Consuls. But nobody wants to see persons not holding office appointed by senatorial decree. Moreover, the Consuls are afraid that the decree for their military appointment may not be carried, and that they will be insultingly passed over and the business handed to somebody else. For that reason they don't want the Senate to meet at all, carrying this attitude so far as to suggest a lack of conscientiousness in the public service. However, whatever their motive – whether negligence or inertia or the fear I have suggested – it is respectably cloaked under the current opinion that they are uncovetous men who don't want a province.

No dispatch has come in from you, and but for the subsequent arrival of Deiotarus' letter people were beginning to believe that Cassius had invented the war so that his own plunderings would be attributed to hostile devastations – he was supposed to have let Arabs into the province and reported them to the Senate as Parthian invaders. So let me advise you to let us have a full and carefully worded account of the state of affairs out there, whatever it is, so that there is no talk of your having played into somebody's hands or kept silent about what we ought to know.

Now we are at the end of the year – I am writing this letter on 17 December. It's quite plain to me that nothing can be done before the Kalends of January. You know Marcellus, how slow and ineffective he is, and Servius too – a born procrastinator. How do you imagine they are behaving, how do you rate their capacity to put through something they don't care about,[339] when they are handling what *does* interest them[340] so slackly as to give an impression of disinclination? When the

339. Superseding Caesar.
340. The eastern command.

new men come into office, if the Parthian war is on, that question will monopolize the first months. On the other hand, if there is no war out there, or if it is on a scale which you two[341] or your successors can handle with small reinforcements, I envisage that Curio will make his weight felt in two directions: first he'll try to take something away from Caesar, then to give something to Pompey, any little *douceur*, however trifling. Paulus, moreover, talks unconscionably about a province.[342] Our friend Furnius[343] means to oppose his appetite. More I cannot conjecture.

So much I know. Other possibilities I do not see. That time brings many novelties and changes plans I am well aware, but whatever happens, it will take place within this framework. One addition to C. Curio's programme: the Campanian land.[344] They say that Caesar is not worried, but that Pompey is strongly opposed, not wishing to have the land lying unoccupied for Caesar to play with when he gets back.

As regards your departure from Cilicia, I cannot promise to procure the appointment of a successor, but at least I will guarantee that there will be no prorogation. It will be for you to judge whether you want to maintain your attitude, if circumstances and the Senate bring pressure to bear and we cannot decently refuse. *My* obligation is to remember your parting adjuration not to let it happen.

341. Cicero and Bibulus.

342. He wanted a province after his Consulship despite the law requiring a five-year interval (how he justified this is unknown). Cicero thought he might get Cilicia (*Letters to Atticus* 115 (VI.1).7).

343. Now Tribune-Elect.

344. Curio, still at any rate ostensibly playing an 'optimate' game, was now proposing to interfere with Caesar's agrarian legislation, as Cicero had thought to do in 56.

88 (VIII. 6)

CAELIUS RUFUS TO CICERO

Rome, February 50

From Caelius to Cicero greetings.

Doubtless the news will have reached you that Appius has been charged by Dolabella. I must say that the feeling against him is not what I anticipated. Appius has behaved rather sensibly. The moment Dolabella approached the bench,[345] he crossed the city boundary and gave up his claim to a Triumph, thereby blunting sharp tongues and looking readier for the fray than his prosecutor had expected. His hopes are now mainly pinned on you. I know you don't dislike him. How far you want to put him under obligation rests with you. If you had not had a quarrel with him in the past, you would have a freer hand altogether. As it is, if you demand the letter of the law, the standard of abstract justice without compromise, you will have to be careful not to let it look as though the reconciliation on your side was less than suitably candid and sincere. Moreover, you can safely go the other way, if you want to do him any favours, for nobody is going to say that connection and friendship deterred you from your duty. It comes to my mind that between the preliminary application and the laying of the charge[346] Dolabella's wife left him. I remember the commission you gave me as you were leaving,[347] and I don't suppose you

345. i.e., the Praetor's tribunal, for permission to proceed – the first step in a prosecution.

346. The second step, perhaps involving a detailed specification of the charge; but the procedure is not exactly known.

347. Cicero's parting commission may have been general – to keep an eye open for an eligible match for Tullia.

have forgotten what I wrote to you.[348] Now is not the time to enter into further details. The only advice I can give you is this: even if you are not against the idea in principle, don't show your hand in any way just now. Wait and see how he comes out of this case finally. It would not be good for your reputation if the thing leaks out; and if any hint is forthcoming, it would get more publicity than would be decent or expedient.[349] And *he* won't be able to keep quiet about a development which will chime so conveniently with his own hopes and will be all the more in the public eye as he carries his business through – particularly as he's a fellow who would hardly hold his tongue about such a matter even if he knew that talking would be the ruin of him.

Pompey is said to be greatly exercised on Appius' behalf. They even think he will send one of his sons over to you. Here we are acquitting everybody. To be sure there are screens to protect every dirty scandal. Our Consuls are paragons of conscientiousness – up to date they had not succeeded in getting a single decree through the Senate except about the Latin Festival![350] Our friend Curio's Tribunate is an utter frost. But the stagnation of everything here is indescribable. If I didn't have a battle on with the shopkeepers and inspectors of conduits, a coma would have seized the whole community. Unless the Parthians liven you up a bit over there, we are as dead as dormice – though even without the Parthians Bibulus has somehow or other contrived to lose the odd cohort in the Amanus, so it is here reported.[351]

A propos of what I wrote above about Curio being frozen

348. Caelius' letter, referred to here and in Letter 73 (III.10; see p. 137), may have raised Dolabella's name for the first time.

349. As Appius' prosecutor, Dolabella would be 'in the news', and his engagement to Tullia would attract the more attention on that account.

350. Fixing its date, a matter of no political consequence.

351. Cf. *Letters to Atticus* 113 (V.20).5.

up, he's warm enough now – being pulled to pieces most ardently. Quite irresponsibly, because he hadn't got his way about intercalation, he has gone over to the democrats and started talking in favour of Caesar. He has brandished a Road Bill (not unlike Rullus' Agrarian Bill)[352] and a Food Bill, which tells the Aediles to distribute.[353] He had not done this when I wrote the earlier part of this letter.

If you do take any steps to help Appius, be a good fellow and put in a word with him for me. I recommend you to keep your hands free about Dolabella. That is the right line both from the standpoint of the matter I am talking about and from that of your dignity and reputation for fair dealing.

It will be little to your credit if I don't have any Greek[354] panthers.

89 (II. 14)

CICERO TO CAELIUS RUFUS

Laodicea, mid March (?) 50

From M. Cicero, Imperator, to M. Caelius, Curule Aedile, greetings.

M. Fabius is a man of fine character and culture, and on very close terms with me. I have a quite exceptional regard for him, for his brilliant intellect and scholarly attainments go along with unusual modesty. I want you to take up his case[355] as

352. Successfully opposed by Cicero in 63. The resemblance probably lay in the wide powers proposed for the commissioners who were to execute the bill.

353. i.e. making the Aediles responsible for the regular distributions of free or subsidized grain.

354. i.e. Asiatic as opposed to African.

355. Cf. Letter 114 (IX.25).

though it was an affair of my own. I know you great advocates – a man must commit murder if he wants your services. But in the present instance I take no excuse. If you care for me, you will put everything aside when Fabius wants your services.

I am eagerly and longingly awaiting news of Rome, and especially want to know how you are. Because of the severity of the winter it is a long time since any news reached us.

90 (II. 11)

CICERO TO CAELIUS RUFUS

Laodicea, 4 April 50

M. Cicero, Imperator, to M. Caelius, Curule Aedile, greetings.

Would you ever have thought that I could find myself short of words – and not only the kind of words you orators use, but even this vernacular small change? The reason is that I am on tenterhooks to hear what is decreed about the provinces. I have a marvellous longing for Rome, and miss my family and friends, you especially, more than you would believe. I am sick and tired of the province. I think I have gained a reputation here such that rather than seek to add to it I should beware of fortune's turns. Besides the whole thing is unworthy of my powers. I am able to bear, am used to bearing, greater loads in the service of the state. Then again, the threat of a great war hangs over us; this I believe I escape if I leave by the appointed day.

About the panthers, the usual hunters are doing their best on my instructions. But the creatures are in remarkably short supply, and those we have are said to be complaining bitterly because they are the only beings in my province who have to fear designs against their safety. Accordingly they are reported to have decided to leave this province and go to Caria. But the matter is receiving close attention, especially from Patiscus. Whatever comes to hand will be yours, but what that amounts to I simply do not know. I do assure you that your career as Aedile is of great concern to me. The date is itself a reminder – I am writing on Great Mother's Day.[356] On your side, please send me an account of the whole political situation as full as you can make it. I shall consider what I hear from you as my most reliable information.

91 (VIII. 1)

CAELIUS RUFUS TO CICERO

Rome, mid April 50

From Caelius to Cicero greetings.

Your Supplications[357] have given us a nasty headache – short, but sharp. We found ourselves in a very knotty situation. Curio was most anxious to oblige you, but, finding his comitial days taken away from him on all sorts of pretexts, he said he could not possibly allow Supplications to be decreed.[358] If he did, he would appear as losing by his own fault the advantage offered him by Paulus' lunacy,[359] and would be thought to be betraying the public interest. So we got down to a compromise. The Consuls gave an assurance that they would not

356. 4 April, the first day of the festival of Cybele. Her games, as well as the Roman ones, seem to have been the responsibility of the Curule Aediles.

357. Caelius, like Vatinius, prefers the plural.

358. Because the celebrating of a Supplication would take up 'comitial days' on which he could pursue his legislative programme.

359. Probably with reference to further deferment of the question of Caesar's command for which Paulus, now in Caesar's interest, had been in some degree responsible.

make use of these Supplications for the present year. You really have cause to thank both the Consuls, Paulus to be sure more than his colleague. Marcellus merely replied to Curio that he was not building any hope on these Supplications, whereas Paulus said definitely that he would not announce them for this year.

It was reported to us that Hirrus proposed to speak at some length. We got hold of him. Not only did he not do so, but when the question of sacrificial victims[360] was under discussion and he could have held up the business by demanding a count, he kept quiet. He merely assented to Cato, who after speaking of you in flattering terms declared himself against the Supplications. Favonius joined them to make a third. So you must thank them all according to their various characters and habits of conduct: Cato and his associates, because they merely signified their sentiments but did not put up a fight for their opinion, though it was in their power to obstruct; Curio, because he turned aside from his programme for your sake. Furnius and Lentulus[361] canvassed and worked shoulder to shoulder with me as though it was their own affair, which was right and proper. I can also say a good word for Cornelius Balbus, who worked assiduously. He spoke strongly to Curio, telling him that if he acted in any other way he would be doing Caesar an ill turn; moreover, he called his good faith[362] in question. Domitius, Scipio, and co. had indeed voted in favour, without wanting the business to go through. So they kept interrupting in order to provoke a veto. Curio riposted very neatly that he had all the greater pleasure in *not* casting a veto because he could see that some of the supporters of the motion did not want it to take effect.

As for the political situation, all conflict is directed to a single

360. In decreeing the Supplication the Senate would also specify the number and quality of the animals to be sacrificed as thank-offerings.

361. Spinther.

362. Towards Caesar, whom Curio was now supporting.

question, that of the provinces. As things stand so far, Pompey seems to be putting his weight along with the Senate in demanding that Caesar leave his province on the Ides of November. Curio is resolved to let that happen only over his dead body, and has given up the rest of his programme. Our friends (well you know them) do not dare to push the matter to extremities. This is the tableau, the *tout ensemble*: Pompey pretends that he is not attacking Caesar, but making a settlement which he thinks fair to him; he says that Curio is out to make strife. At the same time he regards the idea of Caesar being elected Consul before he hands over his province and army with strong disfavour and positive apprehension. He gets a pretty rough reception from Curio, and his whole third Consulate is being hauled over the coals. Mark my words, if they use all means to suppress Curio, Caesar will come to his Tribune's[363] rescue. If, as seems probable, they are afraid to do that, Caesar will stay as long as he pleases.

The various speeches made in the Senate are in the abstract of city news. Pick out the worthwhile items for yourself. You can pass over a lot, such as who was hissed at the games and the quantity of funerals and other nonsenses. Most things in it are of use. Anyway, I prefer to err on the generous side – better you should hear what doesn't interest you than that some matter of consequence be left out.

I am glad you are attending to the Sittius business. But since you suspect that the persons I sent are not altogether trustworthy, please act as though you were my agent.

363. Literally 'veto-caster'.

92 (VIII. 7)

CAELIUS RUFUS TO CICERO

Rome, the day after the preceding

From Caelius to Cicero greetings.

How soon you want to leave your present whereabouts I don't know, but for my part, the more successful you have been so far the more I want it. As long as you remain out there, I shall be on thorns about the risk of a Parthian war, for fear some alarm may wipe the grin off my face. This letter will be rather brief – I am giving it without notice to one of the tax-farmers' couriers, who is in a hurry. I gave a longer one to your freedman yesterday.

Nothing new has happened really, unless you want to be told such items as the following – which, of course, you do. Young Cornificius has got himself engaged to Orestilla's daughter. Paula Valeria, Triarius' sister, has divorced her husband for no reason the day he was due to get back from his province. She is to marry D. Brutus. There have been a good many extraordinary incidents of this sort during your absence which I have not yet reported. Servius Ocella would never have got anyone to believe he went in for adultery, if he had not been caught twice in three days. Where? Why, just the last place I should have wished – I leave something for you to find out from other informants! Indeed I rather fancy the idea of a Commander-in-Chief enquiring of this person and that the name of the lady with whom such-and-such a gentleman has been caught napping.

93 (II. 13)

CICERO TO CAELIUS RUFUS

Laodicea, early May 50

From M. Cicero, Imperator, to M. Caelius, Curule Aedile, greetings.

Your letters, as they reach me, are few and far between – perhaps they are not getting through – but delightful. The last one[364] for instance, how wise, how full of friendship and counsel! I had in point of fact determined to act in every way on the lines you recommend, but my resolutions are strengthened when I find that wise and loyal advisers are of the same opinion.

I have a real regard for Appius, as I have often told you, and as soon as we buried our hatchet I perceived the beginning of a corresponding feeling on his side. As Consul he showed me consideration and became a pleasant friend, not without an interest in my literary pursuits. That friendliness on my side was not wanting *you* can testify. And now, I suppose, Phanias corroborates, like a witness in a comedy.[365] And I do assure you that I valued him the more because I saw he had an affection for you. Further, that I am devoted to Pompey you know, and you are aware of my affection for Brutus.[366] Why on earth should I *not* be gratified to welcome the friendship of such a man – in the prime of life, wealthy, successful, able, surrounded by children, by connections of blood and marriage, and by

364. Letter 88 (VIII.6).

365. The Witness (e.g. to the long-lost heroine's identity) was a stock role in Attic New Comedy and 'Phanias' a common dramatic name.

366. One of Appius' daughters was married to Pompey's elder son, another to M. Brutus.

friends – a colleague too, who has put his learned work to the glory of our College in the form of a compliment to me? I have written at some length on this topic because your letter suggested the shadow of a doubt in your mind about my feelings towards him. I suppose you have heard some story. If so, believe me, it is untrue. There is some dissimilarity, generally speaking, between his administration of the province and my own ordinances and principles. Hence perhaps some have suspected that I differ from him out of personal animus, not from theoretical disagreement. But I have never said or done anything with a wish to injure his reputation, and after this recent trouble and our friend Dolabella's precipitate behaviour, I am ready with my intercession in his hour of danger.

In the same letter you speak of a 'community coma'. Well, I was glad of it. It was good news that inactivity had cooled our friend to freezing point. The last little page in your own hand gave me quite a jolt. You don't say so! Curio now standing up for Caesar? Who would have thought it? – except me! For upon my soul, I *did* think it. Powers above, how I should enjoy a laugh with you!

I have completed the assizes, put money into the communal treasuries, assured the tax-farmers of their arrears even for the previous quinquennium without a word of complaint from the provincials, and made myself pleasant to private individuals from the highest to the lowest. So I propose to set out for Cilicia on the Nones of May. Then, as soon as I have touched the fringe of a summer campaign and settled the troops in their stations, I shall vacate the province in conformity with the Senate's decree. I am anxious to see you in office and feel a marvellous longing for Rome and for all my folk, you especially.

94 (VIII. 13)

CAELIUS RUFUS TO CICERO

Rome, early June 50

From Caelius to Cicero greetings.

I congratulate you on the connection you are forming with a very fine fellow,[367] for that, upon my word, is what I think him. In some respects he has done himself poor service in the past, but he has already shaken off these failings with the years and, if any traces remain, I feel sure that your association and influence and Tullia's modest ways will soon remove them. He is not recalcitrant in bad courses or lacking in the intelligence to perceive a better way. And the capital point is that I am very fond of him.

You will like to know that our friend Curio has done very nicely with his veto on the provinces. When the question about the veto was put (this was done in accordance with the Senate's decree) and M. Marcellus' proposal to the effect that representations should be made[368] to the Tribunes was the first pronounced, the House voted it down in large numbers. Pompey the Great's digestion is now in such a poor way that he has trouble finding anything to suit him![369] They have come round to accept that a person should be allowed to stand for office without handing over his army and provinces. How Pompey is going to take this I'll tell you when I know. As for what is to happen if he either resists in arms or just lets it go, you rich

367. Dolabella.

368. The stock phrase for putting pressure upon a Tribune to withdraw his veto, backed by the threat of suspension from office or other coercive action by the Senate.

369. Pompey was actually in poor health and soon afterwards fell seriously ill.

old gentlemen can worry! As I write, Q. Hortensius is at death's door.

95 (II. 12)

CICERO TO CAELIUS RUFUS

Camp on the River Pyramus, 20 (?) June 50

From M. Cicero, Imperator, to M. Caelius, Curule Aedile, greetings.

I am worried about affairs in Rome, with reports of rowdy meetings and a very disagreeable Feast of Minerva[370] – I have no more recent news. But the most worrying thing of all is that, whatever there may be to laugh at in all this unpleasantness, I cannot laugh at it with you – there is in fact a good deal, but I dare not put such things on paper. I do take it hard that I have not yet had a line from you about these matters. When you read this, I shall already have completed my year's assignment, but I hope that a letter from you will meet me on the road to tell me about the whole political situation, so that I don't come to Rome as a complete foreigner. Nobody can do this better than yourself.

Your Diogenes, whose manners I can commend, left me along with Philo for Pessinus. They were going to Adiatorix, despite reports which held out no hope of a kind or affluent reception there.

Rome! Stick to Rome, my dear fellow, and live in the limelight! Sojourn abroad of any kind, as I have thought from my youth upwards, is squalid obscurity for those whose efforts can win lustre in the capital. I knew this well enough, and I only wish I had stayed true to my conviction. I do assure you that

370. 19–23 March. The disturbances were probably due to Curio's activities as Tribune.

in my eyes all I get from the province is not worth a single stroll, a single talk with you. I hope I have won some credit for integrity, but I should have gained as much of that by despising the province as I have by saving it from ruin. You suggest the hope of a Triumph. My Triumph would have been glorious enough; at any rate I should not have been so long cut off from all that is dearest to me. However, I hope to see you soon. Send me letters worthy of yourself to meet me on my way.

96 (II. 15)

CICERO TO CAELIUS RUFUS

Side, 3 or 4 August 50

From M. Cicero, Imperator, to M. Caelius, Curule Aedile, greetings.

Your negotiation with Curio on the matter of the Supplication was a model of thoughtfulness and discretion. The result is indeed to my satisfaction. I am pleased that the thing has been settled so quickly, and also that your and my angry rival[371] gave his assent to the fervid encomiast of my official record.[372] You may take it therefore that I am hoping for the sequel.[373] Be ready to play your part.

I am glad you speak so well of Dolabella, glad too that you are fond of him. As for the features which you hope may be toned down by my dear Tullia's good sense, I know which of your letters[374] to turn up. For that matter you ought to read the letter *I* sent to Appius at the time on receipt of yours! But

371. Hirrus.

372. Cato.

373. A Triumph, which would no doubt have been forthcoming but for the Civil War.

374. It has not survived.

what is one to do? Such is life. The Gods bless what is done! I hope to find him an agreeable son-in-law, and there your kindly tact will help us much.

The political situation is very much on my mind. I wish Curio well, I want to see Caesar respected, I can lay down my life for Pompey; but nothing is closer to my heart than the commonwealth itself. You do not make very much of your own political role. I fancy you find yourself torn between loyalties, as a good citizen and as a good friend.

On vacating the province I left my Quaestor Coelius in charge. A boy,[375] you may say! Well, but he is Quaestor, he is a young man of noble family, and I am following an almost universal precedent. Nor had I anyone available for the appointment who had held a higher office. Pomptinus had left long before. My brother Quintus could not be prevailed upon – but even if I *had* left him, unfriendly tongues would be saying that I had not really vacated my province after a year, as the Senate had determined, since I had left an *alter ego* behind me. They might perhaps have added that the Senate had designated as provincial governors persons who had not previously held such office, whereas my brother had been governor of Asia for three years. And then, as things are, I have no need to worry; if I had left my brother in charge, I should have had all manner of apprehensions.[376] Lastly, I did not so much act of my own volition as follow the example of the two most powerful men of our day, who have made friends of every Cassius and Antonius[377] who comes their way. I did not so much want to attract the friendship of a young man as not to alienate him. You have no choice but to approve my decision, because it cannot be changed.

375. In fact, Coelius must have been about thirty.

376. Cf. *Letters to Atticus* 121 (VI.6).4.

377. Q. Cassius Longinus and M. Antonius (Mark Antony) had been chosen as their Quaestors by Pompey and Caesar respectively. Normally Quaestors were assigned by lot.

What you wrote to me about Ocella was none too clear, and there was nothing in the Gazette![378] Your official actions are so well known that Matrinius is news even this side of Mt Taurus.[379] As for me, unless the Etesians hold me back, I hope I shall see you all in the near future.

97 (VIII. 14)

CAELIUS RUFUS TO CICERO

Rome, c. 8 August 50

From Caelius to Cicero greetings.

What a spectacle you have missed here! If you've made Arsaces[380] prisoner and stormed Seleucia, it wasn't worth the sacrifice. Your eyes would never have been sore again if you'd seen Domitius' face when he heard of his defeat.[381] The polling was heavy, and support for the candidates quite on party lines. Only a tiny minority gave their backing in conformity with personal loyalties. Accordingly Domitius is my bitter enemy. He has not a friend in the world whom he hates more than me![382] – all the more so because he regards himself as having been robbed of the Pontificate[383] and me as the author of the outrage. Now he is furious at the general rejoicing over his

378. This seems to be a joke; cf. p. 180.

379. Nothing is known of this incident.

380. i.e. the King of Parthia. The Parthian kings bore the name of the founder of their line in addition to their individual names, like the Ptolemies of Egypt.

381. As a candidate for the vacancy in the Augural College created by the death of Hortensius. He was beaten by Mark Antony.

382. Cf. Letter 20 (I.9).2.

383. The reading is conjectural. If right, it refers to a previous failure of Domitius to gain a place in the College of Pontiffs, of which he later became a member.

discomfiture and at the fact that Antony had only one more ardent supporter (Curio) than myself. As for young Cn. Saturninus, he has been charged by none other than Cn. Domitius.[384] To be sure his past makes him far from popular. We are now waiting for the trial. Actually there is good hope for him after Sex. Peducaeus'[385] acquittal.

On high politics, I have often told you that I do not see peace lasting another year; and the nearer the inevitable struggle approaches, the plainer the danger appears. The question on which the dynasts will join issue is this: Cn. Pompeius is determined not to allow C. Caesar to be elected Consul unless he surrenders his army and provinces; whereas Caesar is persuaded that he cannot survive if he leaves his army. He makes the proposition, however, that both surrender their military forces. So this is what their love-affair, their scandalous union, has come to – not covert backbiting, but outright war! As for my own position, I don't know what course to take; and I don't doubt that the same question is going to trouble you. I have ties of obligation and friendship with these people. On the other side, I love the cause but hate the men.

I expect you are alive to the point that, when parties clash in a community, it behoves a man to take the more respectable side so long as the struggle is political and not by force of arms; but when it comes to actual fighting he should choose the stronger, and reckon the safer course the better. In the present quarrel Cn. Pompeius will evidently have with him the Senate and the people who sit on juries,[386] whereas all who live in present fear and small hope for the future will rally to Caesar. His army is incomparably superior. To be sure there is time

384. L. Domitius' son. Cn. (Sentius) Saturninus had no doubt supported Antony.

385. Not Cicero's former Praetor or his son (see Glossary of Persons), but perhaps a supporter of Caesar who became governor of Sardinia in 48. The circumstances of his trial are unknown.

386. i.e. the rich and respectable.

enough to consider their respective resources and choose one's side.

I almost forgot the most interesting item of all. Did you know that Appius is performing prodigies of censorial vigour – works of art, size of estates, debt are all grist to his mill. He is convinced that the Censorship is face cream or washing soda, but I fancy he is making a mistake; in trying to scrub out the stains he is laying open all his veins and vitals.[387] Make haste in God's name and man's and get here as soon as you can to laugh at our frolics – at Drusus trying offences under the lex Scantinia,[388] at Appius taking official action about works of art.[389] Believe me, you must hurry. Our friend Curio is considered to have shown good sense in not pressing his point about pay for Pompey's troops.

Well, to sum up: what do I think will happen? If neither of the two goes off to the Parthian war, I see great quarrels ahead in which strength and steel will be the arbiters. Both are well prepared, morally and materially. If it were not for the personal risk involved, Fate is preparing a mighty and fascinating show for your benefit.

98 (VIII. 12)

CAELIUS RUFUS TO CICERO

Rome, c. 20 November 50

From Caelius to Cicero greetings.

I am mortified to have to admit and complain to you about

387. Or 'flesh'.

388. See Glossary of Terms. Drusus was apparently a notorious offender.

389. Appius had allegedly plundered Greece to assemble his own art-collection.

the scurvy treatment I have received from Appius. The man is a monster of ingratitude. Just because he is indebted to me for important favours,[390] he turned against me; and being too much of a skinflint to bring himself to repay them, he declared covert war on me – not so covert though but that I heard tell of it from many quarters and saw his malevolence plainly enough for myself. But when I found that he had been sounding his colleague[391] and that he had talked openly to certain persons and was colloguing with L. Domitius (a bitter enemy of mine these days) with the idea of presenting this little *douceur* to Cn. Pompeius – well, I could not bring myself to tax him personally and ask a man who I thought owed me his life not to do me harm. So what did I do? Notwithstanding my reluctance, I spoke to a number of Appius' friends who had personal knowledge of what I had done for him, as though enquiring as to the true facts. Finding that he did not even consider me worth the trouble of an explanation, I chose to put myself under an obligation to his colleague (an almost total stranger to me and none too well disposed, because I am a friend of yours) rather than subject myself to the sight of that supercilious monkey. When he heard of that, he flew into a rage and went on bawling that I was trying to pick a quarrel so as to use a show of enmity as a pretext for victimizing him if he failed to meet my wishes in a matter of money. Since then he has been continually sending for Servius Pola, the professional prosecutor, and talking with Domitius. They were looking for a charge on which they could put him up to prosecute me, but were puzzled to find one. So they thought they would have me put in court on a charge which they could not decently name (?).[392] They are having the effrontery to get me summoned under the lex

390. Probably with reference to efforts on Appius' behalf when he was under prosecution; see p. 175.

391. L. Calpurnius Piso Caesoninus, Consul in 58, elected Censor along with Appius in 51.

392. Text and sense doubtful.

Scantinia at the end of my Circus Games.[393] The words were hardly out of Pola's mouth when I charged Censor Appius under the same statute! It's the greatest success I ever saw. All Rome (and not just the lower orders) approves; so that Appius is more upset by the scandal than by the prosecution. Furthermore, I have instituted a claim against him for a chapel[394] that is in his house.

I[395] am much put out by the delay of this slave who is bringing you my letter. After receiving my earlier letter,[396] he took more than forty days before setting out. I don't know what else I can write to you. You know that they are marking time at home (?). You are holding things up (?).[397] I am much looking forward to your return, and am eager to see you, as soon as possible. I ask you to take my injuries to heart, as you judge that I am in the habit of taking yours and of avenging them.

99 (XV. 7)

CICERO TO C. MARCELLUS

Between Iconium and Cybistra, early September 51

From M. Cicero, Proconsul, to C. Marcellus, Consul-Elect, greetings.

The news of your election as Consul gave me great happiness. I wish the Gods may prosper you in that high office, and that you may discharge it in a manner worthy of yourself and your father. You have always had my affection and regard, and in all

393. i.e. the Roman Games, which ended on 19 September.

394. Claimed as public property.

395. This postscript seems to have been added a day or two later.

396. Letter 97 (VIII.14).

397. Apparently a reference to Tullia's wedding. But the text is very doubtful.

the vicissitudes of my career I have had evidence of your warm affection for me. From your father also I have received a great many kindnesses – defence in bad times, furtherance in good. So I am, and ought to be, devoted to your family – the more so as that venerable and excellent lady, your mother, has shown an active concern for my welfare and standing beyond what could be expected from her sex. Accordingly I would earnestly solicit your regard and protection during my absence.

100 (XV. 8)

CICERO TO C. MARCELLUS (SENIOR)

Between Iconium and Cybistra, early September 51

From M. Cicero, Proconsul, to his Colleague C. Marcellus, greetings.

I am marvellously pleased to hear that your son Marcellus has been elected Consul and that the joy you most longed for is indeed yours. My happiness is both for his own sake and because I consider you deserving of every possible good fortune. In my trials as in my successes you have always shown me conspicuous good-will; indeed I have found your whole family most active and ardent for my welfare and my standing. I shall accordingly be grateful if you will convey my congratulations to that highly respected and excellent lady, your wife Junia. As for yourself, let me request you to continue to favour me in my absence with your regard and protection.

101 (XV. 9)

CICERO TO M. MARCELLUS

Between Iconium and Cybistra, September (early or middle) 51

From M. Cicero, Proconsul, to M. Marcellus, Consul, greetings.

I am thoroughly delighted that with C. Marcellus' election to the Consulship you have reaped the reward of your family affection, patriotism, and your own most distinguished and meritorious record in that office. Of sentiment in Rome I have no doubt; as for me, far away as I am, dispatched by none other than yourself to the ends of the earth, I assure you I exalt it to the skies in praises most sincere and well grounded. I have had a very particular regard for you from your childhood. On your side, you have ever desired and believed me to stand high in all respects. And what has now happened, whether we call it your achievement or an expression of the sentiments of the Roman people concerning you, very sensibly augments and enhances my affection for you, and it gives me the keenest pleasure when I hear from persons of the highest perspicacity and probity that in all our words, acts, pursuits, and habits I resemble you – or you resemble me. If only you add one more thing to the splendid achievements of your Consulship, I shall feel that you have left me nothing further to wish for – I mean the early appointment of a successor to my post, or at any rate no extension of the term which you fixed for me by decree of the Senate and by law.

Take care of your health and favour me in my absence with your regard and protection.

I still do not think I should write officially on the reports reaching me about the Parthians, and for that reason I prefer not to write to you on the subject either, even as a close personal friend, for fear that a letter to the Consul might be interpreted as an official communication.

102 (XV. 12)

CICERO TO L. PAULUS

Between Iconium and Cybistra, September (early or middle) 51

From M. Cicero, Proconsul, to L. Paulus, Consul-Elect, greetings.

I never had a doubt but that the Roman People would enthusiastically and unanimously elect you Consul in recognition of your great services to the state and the exalted position of your family. All the same, my happiness when I heard the news was more than you can well conceive. I wish the Gods may prosper you in your high office and that you may discharge it in a manner worthy of yourself and your forbears. I only wish I could have been on the spot to see the day for which I have always longed, and to do you yeoman service in return for your signal acts of good-will and kindness towards me. That opportunity was snatched away from me by the sudden, unforeseen chance which sent me on service abroad; but I trust I may still see you as Consul administering the commonwealth in a manner worthy of your standing. To that end I earnestly beg of you to use your best efforts and prevent any unfairness to me or any extension of my year's term. If you do that, you will generously crown your past tokens of good-will.

103 (XV. 3)

CICERO TO CATO

Camp near Iconium, 3 September (or shortly after) 51

From M. Cicero to M. Cato greetings.

In view of the close relations between us I feel I should write to inform you that a mission from Antiochus of Commagene has arrived in my camp near Iconium on 3 September with the news that the Crown-Prince of Parthia, who is married to a sister of the King of Armenia, has arrived on the banks of the Euphrates with a massive Parthian army and a large force in addition, drawn from many different nationalities; that he has already begun the passage of the river; and that there is talk of the King of Armenia invading Cappadocia.

I have not written an official dispatch for two reasons. The envoys says that the King of Commagene himself sent messengers and a letter to the Senate immediately; and I expect that Proconsul M. Bibulus, who left by sea from Ephesus for Syria about the Ides of August, has already arrived in his province, since he had favourable winds. I presume that everything will be more reliably reported to the Senate in a dispatch from him. In such a situation, with a war on so large a scale, my own principal preoccupation is to hold by gentleness and moderation, through the loyalty of our subjects, what I can hardly hold by the troops and resources at my disposal. I hope that, as in the past, I shall have your regard and protection in my absence.

104 (XV. 1)

CICERO TO THE MAGISTRATES AND SENATE

Near Cybistra, 18 September 51

From M. Tullius Cicero, son of Marcus, Proconsul, to the Consuls, Praetors, Tribunes of the Plebs, and Senate, greetings.

I trust you are well. I and the army are well.

Although receiving clear reports that the Parthians had crossed the Euphrates with virtually their entire force, I supposed that M. Bibulus, Proconsul, would be able to give you more reliable information on these matters, and therefore decided that it was unnecessary for me to send an official account of reports which concerned a province other than my own. Subsequently, however, the information reached me on unimpeachable authority, by emissaries, verbal reports, and letters. Bearing in mind the importance of the matter, as also that I have no news as yet of Bibulus' arrival in Syria and that I may almost be said to carry joint responsibility with him in the conduct of this war, I thought it my duty to write apprising you of my intelligence.

Envoys from King Antiochus of Commagene were the first to announce to me that large forces of Parthians had begun to cross the Euphrates. On receiving this report, I decided that it would be best to wait for something more reliable, since there were those who thought the king was not entirely to be trusted. On 18 September, as I was leading my army into Cilicia, I received a letter on the borders of Lycaonia and Cappadocia from Tarcondimotus, who is considered to be our most faithful ally beyond Taurus and a true friend to Rome. This told me that Pacorus, son of King Orodes of Parthia, had crossed the Euphrates with a very large force of Parthian cavalry and pitched camp at Tyba, creating great turmoil in the province of Syria. On the same day I had a letter on these same matters from Iamblichus, Phylarch of the Arabs, who is generally thought to be loyal and friendly to our country.

After receiving this intelligence, I determined to march to the Taurus, for several reasons. I realized that our subjects were in a wavering mood, poised in expectation of change; but I trusted that those with whom I had already been in contact and who had perceived the gentleness and integrity of my government had become more friendly to Rome, and that the loyalty of Cilicia would be strengthened if that area shared in the benefits of my equitable administration. I also wanted to crush the rebellious elements in the Cilician nation and to let the enemy in Syria know that on receipt of the aforesaid intelligence a Roman army was not merely not retreating but actually approaching closer.

If, however, my advice carries any weight with you, especially in circumstances which you have heard by report but which I have almost before my eyes, I would emphatically urge and warn you to take thought for these provinces even at this all too late hour. You are not ignorant of the resources and defensive forces with which you sent me out to face the prospect of a major war. It was not blind folly but a sense of shame that prevented me from declining the task; for I have never thought any danger grave enough to care to evade it by failing in obedience to your authority.

The present situation is this: Unless you send to these provinces without loss of time an army as large as you usually send to cope with war on a grand scale, there is the gravest risk that all the provinces on which the revenues of Rome depend may have to be given up. You should rest no hopes whatever on the local levies. Their numbers are small, and those there are scatter at sight of danger. My gallant colleague, M. Bibulus, gave his verdict on this description of troops in Asia, when he declined to hold a levy, although you had given him permission. As for the auxiliaries supplied by our allies, the harshness and injustices of our rule have rendered them either so weak as to be of little use or so disaffected that it would appear imprudent to expect anything from them or entrust anything to them. I think we can fully depend on the loyalty of King Deiotarus and such forces as he commands. Cappadocia is a vacuum; the remaining kings and rulers are undependable in point both of resources and of loyalty. Few as our numbers are, I shall assuredly not be found wanting in courage, nor yet, I trust, in judgement. What will happen no man can tell. I pray that I may be able to provide for our safety, as I certainly shall for our honour.

105 (XV. 2)

CICERO TO THE MAGISTRATES AND SENATE

Camp near Cybistra, 21 or 22 September 51

From M. Tullius Cicero, son of Marcus, Proconsul, to the Consuls, Praetors, Tribunes of the Plebs, and Senate, greetings.

I trust that you are well. I and the army are well.

On arriving in my province on 31 July, no earlier date being practicable by reason of the difficulties of travel both by land and sea, I considered that I should best conform to my duty and the public interest by making appropriate provisions for the army and for military security. Having made my dispositions with care and diligence rather than plenitude of means, I received reports and letters almost daily concerning a Parthian invasion of the province of Syria. I therefore thought it proper to march through Lycaonia, Isauria, and Cappadocia, since it was strongly suspected that, if the Parthians attempted to leave Syria and break into my province, they would come by way of Cappadocia, where there was least to stop them.

Accordingly I and my army marched through that part of

Cappadocia which adjoins Cilicia and pitched camp near Cybistra, a town lying close to the Taurus mountains, in order that Artavasdes, King of Armenia, whatever his disposition might be, should know that a Roman army was not far from his frontiers, and that I should have King Deiotarus close at hand, a most faithful and friendly ally to our country, whose advice and material support might be of service to the commonwealth.

While stationed in that spot, having previously sent a force of cavalry on to Cilicia so that the news of my arrival might strengthen morale generally in the communes situated in that region and at the same time I might get early intelligence of events in Syria, I thought it proper to devote the three days of my halt in this camp to an important and necessary duty. I had your resolution charging me to take good care of King Ariobarzanes Eusebes and Philorhomaeus, to defend his welfare, security, and throne, and to protect king and kingdom; to which you added that the welfare of this monarch was a matter of great concern to the People and Senate – something that had never before been decreed by our House with respect to any monarch. I therefore considered it incumbent upon me to convey your mandate to the king, and to promise him my faithful protection and care, adding that, since his personal welfare and the security of his realm had been commended to me by yourselves, I should be glad to learn his wishes, if any.

When I had addressed the king to this effect in the presence of my Council, he began his reply with a proper expression of profound gratitude to yourselves, and then proceeded to thank me also. He felt it as a most important favour and a very high compliment that his welfare should be of so much concern to the Senate and People of Rome, and that I should be at such pains to demonstrate my sense of obligation and the weight attaching to your recommendation. At first he gave me to understand, to my great satisfaction, that he had no knowledge or even suspicion of any plots against his life or throne. I congratulated him, and said I was delighted to hear it, at the same time urging the young man to remember the sad end that had overtaken his father;[398] he should guard himself vigilantly and take good heed for his safety, conformably to the Senate's admonition. He then took his leave, and returned to the town of Cybistra.

On the day following, however, he arrived in my camp along with his brother Ariarathes and some older persons, friends of his father's. In a state of tearful agitation, as were also his brother and their friends, he appealed to me in the name of my pledged word and your commendation. When I asked in some surprise what had happened, he said that he had received information of a manifest conspiracy, which had been kept secret prior to my arrival because those who might have revealed it were afraid to speak. But now, in the hope of my protection, a number had plucked up courage to come to him with what they knew. Among them was his brother, who loved him dearly and who had a strong sense of family loyalty. He was alleging (and Ariarathes confirmed the king's words in my presence) that he had been invited to aspire to the throne. This could not have come to anything while his brother was alive; but until now he had been too much afraid to bring the facts into the open. Having heard this speech, I admonished the king to take every precaution for his own safety and exhorted the tried friends of his father and grandfather to take warning by the tragic fate of the former and defend the life of their sovereign with every care and safeguard.

The king then asked me for some cavalry and cohorts from my army. I was aware that under your decree I had not only a right but a duty to agree. But in view of the reports coming in daily from Syria, the public interest demanded that I should conduct the army to the borders of Cilicia as soon as possible. Moreover, now that the plot had been exposed, the king did not appear to me to need a Roman army; his own resources seemed adequate for his protection. I therefore urged him to

398. Ariobarzanes II, murdered by conspirators.

make the preservation of his own life his first lesson in the art of ruling. He should exercise his royal prerogative against the persons whom he had found organizing the conspiracy against him, punishing where punishment was necessary and relieving the rest of apprehension. He should use the sanction of my army to intimidate the guilty rather than for actual combat. But all would understand, knowing the terms of the Senate's decree, that if need arose, I should come to the king's defence on your authority.

So I leave him in good heart. I am breaking camp and setting out on my way to Cilicia, leaving Cappadocia amid a general persuasion that by your policy and an amazing, if not providential, accident my advent has rescued the king from the immediate danger of a conspiracy – one upon whom unsolicited you conferred the royal title in the most honourable terms, whom you recommended to my protection, and whose welfare you decreed to be of great concern to you. I have deemed it appropriate to send you an account of the incident to enable you to appreciate from what nearly happened your own foresight in providing long in advance against that very contingency. And I have been all the more studious to inform you because I believe I have seen in King Ariabarzanes such evidences of character, intelligence, loyalty, and good-will towards your House as appear to justify the care and concern you have lavished upon his welfare.

106 (XV. 14)

CICERO TO CASSIUS

Cilicia, late October (?) 51

From M. Cicero, Imperator, to C. Cassius, Proquaestor,[399] greetings.

399. In Syria.

Your recommendation gives me a friend in the person of M. Fabius; but I am none the richer on his account. These many years past he has been mine absolutely, highly regarded by me for his good nature and attentive courtesy. However, I have become much the more his friend for having perceived what an exceptional regard he has for you. So his own disposition towards you, now that I am thoroughly aware of it, has been in some degree a better passport to my favour than your letter, though that too has had its effect. Anyhow, as to Fabius I shall spare no effort to comply with your request.

For many reasons I am sorry you were unable to meet me. Fond of you as I have long been, I should have liked to see you after so considerable an interval; I should have liked to congratulate[400] you in person as I did by letter; I should have liked to exchange views on such of our several concerns as either of us cared to raise; lastly, I should have liked to see a further strengthening of our friendship, which has been fostered on both sides by substantial services but interrupted, as to daily contact, by lengthy periods of separation.

Since that was not to be, we shall make the best of correspondence and get pretty well the same results apart as if we were together. Of course the satisfaction of seeing you cannot be enjoyed by letter; and the satisfaction of congratulating you would be more full-bodied if I were looking you in the eye as I did it. However, I have done so once, and I do so again. Yes, I congratulate you upon the magnitude of your success, and no less upon its timeliness, for you are leaving for Rome with the thanks and plaudits of your province ringing in your ears.

Then there is the third point – the exchange of views about our concerns which would have taken place had we met must be managed by correspondence. On all grounds but one I am strongly of the opinion that you should make haste back to Rome. When I left, all was quiet so far as you were concerned, and your recent brilliant victory will clearly shed lustre on your

400. On his successful action against the Parthian invaders.

advent. But if those near to you[401] are under fire, we must pause. Should it be such as you can cope with, then make haste – it will be the brightest feather in your cap. But if it's too powerful for that, you must consider. It would be a pity to arrive just at the least favourable moment. The matter is entirely for you to judge. You know your own strength. If you *can*, there is credit and popular approval to be had. But if you really cannot, you will find the talk less annoying elsewhere.

As for me, my plea in this letter is the same as in my last. Strain every nerve to prevent any prolongation of my present office, which both Senate and People fixed for one year. I press you on this point feeling that my worldly welfare depends on it. You can look to our friend Paulus, a thorough well-wisher of mine. There is Curio, there is Furnius. Do try your hardest, in the persuasion that it means everything to me.

The last of the points I mentioned was the strengthening of our friendship. On that little need be said. As a boy you drew towards me, and on my side I always believed that I should be proud of you. You also defended me in my darkest days. After you went abroad, I formed a very close friendship with your connection[402] Brutus. In your joint talents and energy I think I have a rich prospect of pleasure and prestige; and I earnestly ask you to confirm that opinion by your zeal. Send me a letter at once, and when you are back in Rome write as often as you can.

401. As often the plural probably refers to an individual, Cassius' cousin Q. Cassius Longinus. He seems to have been threatened with prosecution in respect of his ill-treatment of provincials in Spain, where he had served as Pompey's Quaestor.

402. Cassius had married Brutus' half-sister Junia, sometimes called Tertulla.

107 (II. 7)

CICERO TO CURIO

In camp at Pindenissum, soon after 17 December 51

From M. Cicero, Imperator, to C. Curio, Tribune of the Plebs, greetings.

Belated congratulations usually pass unrebuked, especially if the omission is not due to negligence – I am far away and news reaches me late. At all events I do congratulate you, and pray that your Tribunate will earn you everlasting credit. And I urge you to guide and govern all your actions by your own good sense, not to be carried away by the counsels of others. No one can advise you more wisely than yourself; if you listen to yourself, you will never go wrong. I do not write this inadvisedly. I am aware whom I am addressing, I know your spirit and intelligence. I have no fear of your acting timidly or foolishly, if you defend what you yourself feel to be right.

You see, I am sure, the political situation which you have chosen (not happened) to enter – for by your own decision, not by chance, you have brought your term of office to coincide with the very crisis-point.[403] I do not doubt that you are bearing in mind the power of circumstances in politics, the shifting nature of affairs, the uncertainty of events, the instability of men's sentiments, the snares and falsehoods of which life is full. But do, I beg you, give care and consideration to – nothing new, only what I wrote to start with: be your own confidant and counsellor. Listen to yourself, defer to yourself. It would not be easy to find one better able to advise others than you, and assuredly no one will better advise yourself. Ah, why am I not there as a spectator of your laurels, as sharer, partner, agent in your plans? Not that you stand in any need of such; but the

403. See p. 154.

measure and strength of my affection would lend me power to help you with advice.

I shall be writing more later on. In a few days' time I shall be sending couriers of my own household, since I wish to present in a single letter a full report to the Senate of the entire summer's operations, which I have conducted with considerable success and to my own satisfaction. As for your Priesthood,[404] you will learn from the letter I have given to your freedman Thraso how much attention I have given to this delicate and difficult matter.

My dear Curio, I have a solemn plea to make to you in the name of the unbounded kindness you bear me and I no less bear you, not to allow my tenure of this tiresome provincial post to be extended for any additional period. I took this up with you in person when I had no idea that you would be Tribune of the Plebs for the year in question, and have often mentioned it in my letters. But at that time I asked you as a member of the Senate, though to be sure a young man of the highest birth and personal influence; now I ask you as Tribune, and what is more as Tribune Curio. I do not want anything new decreed, which is apt to be difficult, but just the opposite. I want you to defend the Senate's decree and the laws of the land, and I want the terms on which I came here to stand intact. Allow me once more to make this pressing request of you.

108 (XV. 10)

CICERO TO C. MARCELLUS

Tarsus, 51 (end) or 50 (beginning)

From M. Cicero, Imperator, to C. Marcellus, son of Gaius, Consul, greetings.

404. This must refer to Curio's election to the College of Pontiffs, of which his father had been a member.

Since my dearest wish has come to pass, namely that the good-will of all the Marcelli, and the Marcellini[405] too – for the friendly disposition of your house and name towards me has always been extraordinary – since, I repeat, it has come to pass that the good-will of your entire family can find its fulfilment through your consular office, with which my own military achievements and the credit and honour thereto appertaining have so opportunely coincided, allow me to request you to ensure that, when my dispatch has been read to the Senate, a decree[406] follows in terms as handsome as possible. That will be very easily done, for the House, as I confidently anticipate, will receive such a proposal without disfavour.

If my relations with yourself were any less close than with the rest of your family, I should make the latter my advocates with you – you know that they have a special regard for me. From your father I have received the most signal favours; no better friend either to my survival or to my advancement can be named. As for your cousin,[407] I suppose nobody is ignorant of his attachment to me, now and always. In fact your whole family circle has always showered favours of the greatest consequence upon me. And yet *you* have yielded to none of your relatives in your regard for me. May I therefore specially request you to desire me to gain all possible distinction through your agency, and both in the matter of a decree of Supplication and in all others to consider my reputation as sufficiently commended to your care?

405. A branch of the Marcellus family which had passed by adoption into the Cornelii Lentuli. The best known of its members is Cn. Cornelius Lentulus Marcellinus, Consul in 56.

406. For a Supplication.

407. M. Marcellus, Consul in 51.

109 (XV. 13)

CICERO TO L. PAULUS

Tarsus, 51 (end) or 50 (beginning)

From M. Cicero, Imperator, to L. Paulus, Consul, greetings.

I should have wished above all things to be with you in Rome for many reasons, but especially to give you clear token of the good-will I owe you both in your candidature for the Consulship and in your conduct of the office. Of your prospects of election I was always well assured, but still I wished to put my shoulder to the wheel. In office I certainly hope that you are having a comparatively easy time; but it irks me that when I was Consul and you were a young man I saw proof of your good-will, while at my present time of life I am unable to show you corresponding proof of mine.

However, I think it must be fated somehow that you are always given opportunity to do me honour, whereas I find nothing but the will with which to requite you. You added lustre to my Consulship and to my return from exile; my time for military achievement has just coincided with *your* Consulship. So it is that, although your exalted position and dignity on the one hand and on the other the great honour I have in view, in which my public reputation is so largely involved, seem alike to require me to press a request upon you in as many words as I can muster – a request, namely, that you ensure the passage of a decree concerning my successes in the most complimentary terms – yet in fact I dare not press you strongly for fear of seeming either to forget your consistent behaviour towards me through the years or to suppose that *you* have forgotten it.

Accordingly, I shall do as I imagine you would have me do, and be brief in addressing a request to one whose past kindnesses towards me are known to all mankind. If the Consuls in office were not who they actually are, you, my dear Paulus, would be the man to whom I should be sending to secure their most friendly dispositions towards me. As it is, the highest power and the highest influence are yours, and the relations between us are universal knowledge. Therefore I earnestly beg you to ensure that a decree in the most complimentary terms goes through concerning my successes, and as rapidly as possible. That they are worthy of recognition and congratulation you will find from the dispatch which I have addressed officially to you and your Colleague and the Senate. And I hope you will regard yourself as having undertaken to look after all other concerns of mine, my reputation above all. In particular I trust you will take care that my tenure is not extended, as I requested in my previous letter. I want to *see* you Consul, and while you are in that capacity to attain all my hopes, not only in my absence, but also on the spot.

110 (XV. 4)

CICERO TO CATO

Tarsus (?), late December 51

From M. Cicero, Imperator, to M. Cato, greetings.

Your exalted prestige and the respect which I have always held for your outstanding personal qualities make me feel it to be highly important to me that you should know of my achievements and not be unaware of the equity and moderation which has characterized my care for our subjects and my administration of my province. For I believe that when you are acquainted with those things I shall find it easier to win your approval for what I have at heart.

Arriving in my province on 31 July, I saw that in view of the advanced season I ought to join my army with all speed. I spent two days at Laodicea, then four at Apamea, three at Synnada, and as many at Philomelium.[408] There were large gatherings in these towns, and I relieved many communes of oppressive imposts, harsh interest dues, and wrongful debt. Before my arrival the army had been scattered by a mutiny or something of the kind. Five cohorts had taken up a position near Philomelium without a Legate or Military Tribune, without even a Centurion, in command. The remainder of the army was in Lycaonia. I ordered my Legate, M. Anneius, to take these five cohorts to join the main body, and having concentrated the entire force to encamp near Iconium in Lycaonia.

Anneius faithfully carried out his orders, and on 24 August I reached the camp, having in the interval (in accordance with the Senate's decree) raised a strong force of reservists and a quite serviceable body of cavalry along with auxiliaries voluntarily supplied by free peoples and allied kings. Meanwhile, after I had reviewed the army and begun the march to Cilicia on the Kalends of September, a mission sent to me by the King of Commagene announced in a great state of excitement (but correctly enough) that the Parthians had crossed over into Syria. I was much alarmed by the news both for Syria and for my own province, and indeed for the rest of Asia. I therefore thought it best to take my army through that district of Cappadocia which adjoins Cilicia. Had I descended into Cilicia, I should have had no difficulty in holding Cilicia itself because of the natural features of Mt Amanus (there are two entries into Cilicia from Syria, both so narrow as to need only small forces to block them – there is no more defensible a position than Cilicia against an attack from Syria); but I was concerned about Cappadocia, which lies open from the Syrian side and is bordered by kings who, even if they are friendly to us, dare not be openly

408. The dates ran: Laodicea 31 July – 3 August; Apamea 5–9 August; Synnada 10–14 August; Philomelium 16–20 August. Cicero seems here to give one day too many to Apamea.

hostile to the Parthians. Accordingly I pitched camp in a corner of Cappadocia not far from the Taurus near the town of Cybistra, where I could at once protect Cilicia and hold Cappadocia, thus applying a brake to any changes of policy on the part of the neighbouring potentates.

In the midst of this agitation, with war on a grand scale in imminent prospect, King Deiotarus sent a mission to tell me that he proposed to march to my camp with his entire forces. It is not without good warrant that you and I and the Senate have always held him in the highest esteem, for he is both notably well-disposed and loyal to Rome and remarkable for his lofty spirit and sound judgement. Impressed by this gesture of friendly zeal, I wrote to thank him and to urge him to make haste.

Having made a stay of five days at Cybistra for military reasons, I unexpectedly came to the rescue of King Ariobarzanes, whose welfare had been commended to me by the Senate at your instance, from the immediate threat of a conspiracy, not only saving his life, but consolidating his authority as ruler. Metras and Athenaeus (the latter the subject of your special recommendation to me), both sentenced to exile by the cruelty of Athenais,[409] were established by me in high favour and influence at court. There was the prospect of a major war flaring up in Cappadocia, should the High Priest[410] defend himself by force of arms, as was generally thought likely; for the young man had horse, foot, and money in readiness, and was supported by those who wanted a change of régime. I so managed that he withdrew from the kingdom. The full authority of the Palace was safeguarded without turmoil or violence, and the king settled in his royal estate and dignity.

409. The Queen-Mother.

410. Of Ma-Bellona at Comana, whose power in Cappadocia was second only to the king's. We do not know his name. Archelaus, with whom he is commonly confused, was High Priest of a similar establishment at Comana in Pontus.

Meanwhile, I learned from many letters and reports that a large Parthian and Arab force had approached the town of Antioch, and that a large body of their cavalry, which had penetrated Cilicia, had been cut to pieces by squadrons of my horse and the Praetorian Cohort, which had been left in garrison at Epiphanea. Seeing that the Parthians had turned away from Cappadocia and were not far from the borders of Cilicia, I led my army to the Amanus by the longest marches I could achieve. On arrival there I learned that the enemy had withdrawn from Antioch, and that Bibulus was in the town. I informed Deiotarus, who was already hastening to join me with a large and reliable body of horse and foot along with his entire forces, that there appeared to be no reason for him to absent himself from his kingdom; if there was any new development I should send him a letter and messengers immediately.

I had come with the intention of lending aid to either province, if occasion arose. Moreover, I had already decided that the pacification of the Amanus and the removal of the traditional enemy from those mountains was of great importance to both. I therefore proceeded with this objective. Pretending to withdraw from the mountains and make for other parts of Cilicia, I pitched camp near Epiphanea, one day's march from the Amanus. On 12 October, as evening drew on, I marched the army in light equipment so rapidly during the night that by daybreak on 13 October I was moving up the mountain. The cohorts and auxiliary formations were divided into three forces, one commanded by my brother Quintus (Legate) along with myself, another by Legate C. Pomptinus, the third by Legates M. Anneius and L. Tullius. We took many of the enemy by surprise, cutting off their escape and killing or taking them prisoner. Erana, the capital of the Amanus region, which was more like a city than a village, together with Sepyra and Commoris, fell to us after a strenuous and lengthy resistance (Pomptinus was in that part of the mountains) lasting from early twilight till four in the afternoon; a large number of the enemy were slaughtered. We also took a number of strongholds by storm, and burned them. After these operations we pitched camp for four days near Alexander's Altars[411] in the foothills of the Amanus, employing the whole period in destroying whatever was left in the mountains and devastating the countryside – that part of the mountains which falls within my province.

These operations concluded, I led the army against Pindenissum, a town of the Free Cilicians. It was in a situation of great strength, perched high up, and inhabited by a race who have never yielded obedience even to the native kings. They were harbouring deserters and eagerly looking forward to the arrival of the Parthians, so that I considered it a matter of imperial prestige to curb their presumption, whereby others not well affected to the rule of Rome would be more easily discouraged. I surrounded the place with a rampart and moat, protecting these with six blockhouses and a very large camp, then pressed the assault with an earthwork, penthouses, and towers, using artillery and archers in large numbers. By dint of much personal effort and without putting our subjects to any trouble or expense, I finished the operation in fifty-seven days. Every part of the city was demolished or burned and the population driven to surrender to me. They had neighbours no less guilty and presumptuous than themselves, the inhabitants of Tebara, from whom I received hostages after the capture of Pindenissum. I then dismissed the army to winter quarters, putting my brother Quintus in charge of stationing the troops in villages which had either been captured or were still in a state of unrest.

Now I should like you to realize that, if a motion concerning these performances is put to the Senate, I shall take it as a signal compliment if, when your turn comes, you will support the honour proposed for me. And although I am aware that personages of the highest dignity often address and receive requests in

411. Set up by Alexander the Great on the bank of the river Pyramus to commemorate his victory over the Persians at Issus.

such cases, I conceive that from me to you a hint is more appropriate than a request. After all, I am writing to one whose motions in the House have again and again done me honour, and who both there and at public meetings has praised me to the skies in language of unstinted panegyric. I have always attached so much weight to your words that a single one of them tinctured with eulogy of myself has represented to my mind the summit of attainment. Finally, I recall that in opposing the grant of a Supplication to a most worthy and illustrious gentleman[412] you said you would have supported it had the motion been based on his achievements as Consul in Rome; and you likewise voted a Supplication[413] to me as a civilian in unprecedented terms – not as having served the commonwealth well (that has been said of many others), but as having saved it. I pass over the fact that you took upon yourself my unpopularity and danger and all the various turns of fortune that have befallen me, and that you were very ready to go a long way further in that direction had I permitted it; that finally, you looked upon my enemy[414] as yours, and gave your approval to his destruction (yes, I fully appreciated how much you were doing for my sake), when you defended Milo's action in the Senate. On my side there has been forthcoming this much (and I do not regard it as a favour but as testimony of a sincerely held opinion), that I have not confined myself to tacit admiration of your extraordinary qualities (that, after all, is universal), but have publicly exalted you beyond any man we have seen or of whom history tells us. This I have done in all my speeches, whether addressing the Senate or pleading in court, in all my writings, Greek or Latin, in fact throughout the entire range of my literary output.

Perhaps you will wonder why it is that I should set so much store by this bauble of congratulation and honour from the

412. Probably Lentulus Spinther.
413. In 63.
414. P. Clodius.

Senate. I will be candid with you – our philosophical pursuits, our mutual good offices, our close friendship, the ties too between our parents, make that only fitting. If there was ever a man indifferent by nature, and still more (so at least *I* fancy) by understanding and instruction, to empty plaudits and the talk of the crowd, I may surely claim to be such a man. My Consulship stands witness. In that office, as in the rest of my career, I confess that I sought eagerly after the sources from which true glory might arise; but glory in and for itself never seemed to me worth the pursuing. I waived a well-appointed province and the clear prospect of a Triumph. Finally, I did not reach out my hand for a priestly dignity when in your opinion, I believe, it could have been mine without any great difficulty.[415] But after the wrong I suffered (*you* always call it a calamity for the state, but for myself no calamity, even an honour) it has been otherwise. I have been ambitious to receive tokens of esteem, the more flattering the better, from the Senate and People of Rome. Accordingly in this later period I was desirous of becoming Augur, something I had formerly disregarded; and I now think the honour customarily conferred by the Senate for military successes worth my seeking, although I waived it aside in days gone by.

I wrote just now that I would not make a request. For all that, I *do* request you earnestly for your benevolent assistance in this wish of mine, which is not without an element of an injured man's craving for balm to heal his wound. I do so, however, always supposing that you find my modest exploits not altogether paltry and contemptible – of such a kind and measure, on the contrary, that many have won the highest distinctions from the Senate for achievements by no means comparable. Furthermore, I think I have observed (you know how attentively I listen to you) that in conceding or withholding such distinctions it is your practice to pay greater regard to a commander's conduct, his principles and way of life, than to

415. Cf. *Letters to Atticus* 25 (11.5).2.

his operations in the field. If you apply such considerations in my case, you will find that with a weak army I made fair and clean administration my strongest bulwark against the threat of a major war. Thus aided, I obtained results which no legions could have secured. I found our subjects thoroughly alienated and disloyal; I have made them thoroughly well-affected and reliable, winning over their minds, poised as they were in expectation of change, to a sentiment of good-will towards the old régime.

But I have written too much about myself, especially to you, the one man to whose ears all our subjects bring their grievances. You will learn of it all from those who feel that my system of government has brought them back to life. All, virtually with one accord, will describe my administration to you in such terms as I should most like to hear. In particular, two communities who call you their patron, the island of Cyprus and the kingdom of Cappadocia, will tell you about me. So, I believe, will King Deiotarus, with whom you have the most intimate of connections. Are not these things of greater moment? Is it not true that in all ages fewer have been found capable of conquering their own passions than of defeating hostile armies? If so, when you have added to military achievements these rarer and more difficult kinds of merit, it will surely be in your character to rate those very achievements of higher account and desert than they would otherwise have appeared.

In conclusion, as though lacking confidence in the efficacy of my plea, let me make Philosophy my advocate with you – than which nothing in my life has been more precious to me, nor have the Gods bestowed any greater gift upon mankind. Think then of the pursuits and acquirements we have in common and to which we have been devoted heart and soul since we were boys. We two almost alone have brought the old authentic philosophy, which some regard as an amusement of leisure and idleness, down into the market-place, into public life, one might almost say into the battlefield. This companionship of ours pleads with you on behalf of my renown. I do not think Cato can in conscience say no.

Take it then, if you please, that, should the honour for which I ask in my dispatch be accorded to me by your voice in the House, I shall regard myself as having attained my dearest wish through the weight of your prestige and through your good-will towards me.

III (XV. 5)

CATO TO CICERO

Rome, latter April 50

From M. Cato to M. Cicero, Imperator, greetings.

Patriotism and friendship alike urge me to rejoice, as I heartily do, that your ability, integrity, and conscientiousness, already proved in great events at home when you wore the gown of peace, are no less actively at work in arms abroad. Accordingly, I did what my judgement allowed me to do: that is to say, I paid you tribute with my voice and vote for defending your province by your integrity and wisdom, for saving Ariobarzanes' throne and person, and for winning back the hearts of our subjects to a loyal support of Roman rule.

As for the decree of a Supplication, if *you* prefer us to render thanks to the Immortal Gods in respect of provision taken for the public good by your own admirable policy and administrative rectitude, not at all the result of chance, rather than to put it down to your own credit – why, I am very glad of it. If, however, you regard a Supplication as an earnest of a Triumph, and on that account prefer the praise to go to accident[416] rather than to yourself, the fact is that a Triumph does not always follow a Supplication. On the other hand, the Senate's judgement that a province has been held and preserved by its governor's mild and upright administration rather than by the swords of an army or the favour of the Gods is a far greater distinction than a Triumph; and that is what I proposed in the House.

I have written to you at some length on this subject (contrary to my normal habit) so that you may realize, as I most earnestly hope you will, my anxiety to convince you of two things: firstly, as touching your prestige, I desired what I conceived to be most complimentary to yourself; secondly, I am very glad that what you preferred has come to pass.

Goodbye, remember me kindly, and follow your chosen course, rendering to our subjects and to the state their due of a strict and conscientious administration.

112 (XV. 6)

CICERO TO CATO

Tarsus, late July 50

From M. Cicero to M. Cato greetings.

I think it is Hector in Naevius who says 'Glad thy praise doth make me, father, praise from one that praisèd is.'[417] Praise is pleasant, you will agree, when it comes from those who have themselves led honoured lives. Yes, I assure you that the congratulatory terms of your letter and the testimonial you gave

416. Cato as a Stoic believed in a Providence, but in ordinary language and thought the ideas of fate, providence, gods, and fortune were much confused at this period.

417. See p. 62.

me in the House represent to my mind the sum of attainment. I am particularly flattered and gratified to feel that you were glad to accord to friendship what you would have had no hesitation in according to truth. And if many (not to say all) members of our society were Catos (the marvel being that it has produced *one*), how could I think of comparing the triumphal car and crown with an encomium from you? To my way of thinking, and by the unbiased and delicate standards of a philosopher, nothing can be more complimentary than that speech of yours of which my friends have sent me a copy.

But I have explained the reason for my inclination (I will not say 'desire') in my previous letter. Perhaps you did not find it altogether convincing; at any rate it means that I do not regard the honour[418] as something to be unduly coveted, but at the same time that, if proffered by the Senate, I feel I ought by no means to spurn it. I trust, furthermore, that in view of the labours I have undertaken for the public good the House will deem me not unworthy of an honour, especially one so commonly bestowed. If it so turns out, all I ask of you is that (to use your own very kind expressions), having accorded to me what in your judgement is most complimentary to myself, you should be glad if what I prefer comes about. Your actions, your views as expressed in the Senate, your letter, and the very fact that you were present at the drafting of the decree are clear evidence to me that the grant of the Supplication in my honour was agreeable to you. For I am well aware that such decrees are usually drafted by the closest friends of the persons honoured.

I shall see you soon, as I hope, and only pray we meet in a better political atmosphere than I fear we shall.

418. A Triumph.

113 (VII. 32)

CICERO TO VOLUMNIUS EUTRAPELUS

Laodicea (?), February or March 50 (?)

M. Cicero to Volumnius greetings.

As you headed your letter in familiar style (and quite right) without first name, I was at first inclined to wonder whether it might not be from Senator Volumnius, with whom I have much acquaintance. But its *eutrapelous* quality[419] gave me to understand that it was yours. The contents all made most agreeable reading, with one exception: as my agent-in-charge you are not careful enough in protecting my property – my *salt mines*![420] You say that since my departure every witticism, whosever it be, not excluding even Sestius' efforts,[421] is fathered upon me. Well, do you allow this? No opposition, no resistance?

I *had* hoped to have left my various categories of *bons mots* so clearly branded as to be recognizable at sight. But since Rome is so full of scum that the most banausic[422] of jests will find someone to relish its elegance, in friendship's name bestir yourself! If there be no pungent *double entendre*, no tasteful hyperbole, no pretty pun,[423] no comical surprise; if the other

419. 'Eutrapelia', defined by Aristotle as 'cultured insolence'. The *cognomen* 'Eutrapelus' was personal and descriptive, Volumnius being a well-known wit.

420. 'Salt' (*sal*) = 'wit'.

421. P. Sestius notoriously lacked *sal* (cf. *Letters to Atticus* 141 (VII. 17).2).

422. The Greek word used means 'charmless'.

423. Strictly, a joke depending on letter-substitution, as in Manutius' example from Terence *inceptio est amentium, haud amantium.*

varieties which I discussed through Antonius'[424] mouth in the second volume of my treatise *On the Orator* shall not appear neatly pointed and *secundum artem*: why you may go bail that the thing is not mine.

As to your grumbles about the trials, I am much less concerned. Every defendant may go to the devil for aught I care. Selius[425] may wax eloquent enough to prove himself freeborn – it doesn't worry me. But my property in wit is another matter. Let us protect that for pity's sake! Get any court order you like. The only rival I fear in this field is yourself, the rest I despise. You think I'm poking fun at you? Very good, I perceive *now* that you are a man of sense.

But really, joking apart, your letter struck me as most entertaining and elegant reading. One part though, however amusing (and it was certainly that), did not make me smile. I am anxious for that friend of ours[426] to carry all possible weight in his career as Tribune, both for his own sake (as you know, I am very fond of him) and also, I may add, for the sake of the commonwealth, which, however poor my return, I shall never cease to love.

Well, my dear Volumnius, now that you have made a start and see that I appreciate it, write to me as often as you can about affairs in Rome and the political situation. I enjoy the way your letters talk. Furthermore, do encourage and confirm Dolabella in his sentiments towards me, which I perceive and judge to be those of sincerely affectionate good-will. Make him mine entirely – not, to be sure, that anything is lacking. But keenly desirous as I am, I don't think I am labouring the point unduly.

424. Apparently a slip on Cicero's part. The section on jokes in the *de Oratore* is in fact given to C. Julius Caesar Strabo.

425. Unknown.

426. Curio.

114 (IX. 25)

CICERO TO PAPIRIUS PAETUS

Laodicea, mid March (?) 50

From Cicero, Imperator, to Paetus.

Your letter has made a first-rate general out of me. I had no idea you were such a military expert – evidently you have thumbed the treatises of Pyrrhus and Cineas.[427] So I intend to follow your precepts, with one addition – I mean to keep a few boats handy on the coast. They say there's no better weapon against Parthian cavalry! But why this frivolity? You don't know what sort of Commander-in-Chief you have to deal with. In my command here I have put into practice the whole *Education of Cyrus*,[428] a work which I read so often that I wore out the book. But we'll joke another time when we meet, as soon I hope we shall.

Now stand by for orders (or rather to obey them), to use the ancient expression.

I have a great deal to do with M. Fabius, as I think you know, and a great regard for him as a man of the highest integrity and unusual modesty, also because he helps me very effectively in my controversies[429] with your Epicurean boozing-partners. After he joined me at Laodicea and I asked him to stay with me, he received a quite appalling letter, a bolt from the blue, informing him that a farm near Herculaneum, which he owns jointly with his brother, Q. Fabius, had been put up for sale by

427. King Pyrrhus of Epirus wrote a treatise on tactics, and his minister Cineas epitomized a work on strategy by one Aelian.

428. Xenophon's work on the Ideal Ruler (cf. *Letters to Atticus* 23 (II.3).2), much of which is concerned with the Ruler as General.

429. Perhaps with reference to the *de Republica*. M. Fabius Gallus was an Epicurean and a *littérateur*.

the latter. M. Fabius has taken this very much to heart. He believed that his brother, who is not remarkable for good sense, had been instigated by his (Marcus') enemies to take this extraordinary step.

Now, my dear Paetus, be a friend and take the whole affair upon yourself, and relieve Fabius of the worry. We need your name and sound judgement, and your personal influence too. Don't let the brothers get into litigation and become embroiled in discreditable lawsuits. Mato and Pollio[430] are Fabius' enemies. Briefly, I assure you that I cannot write down in full how much you will oblige me if you put Fabius' mind at ease. He thinks, and persuades me, that it all depends on you.

115 (II. 18)

CICERO TO Q. THERMUS

Laodicea, early May 50

From M. Cicero, Imperator, to Q. Thermus, Propraetor, greetings.

I am very happy to find you appreciative of the service I rendered Rhodo and of my other acts of good-will towards you and yours – gratitude is a great point with you. Please rest assured that my solicitude for your credit increases every day, though your own integrity and clemency have so enhanced it that any addition seems impossible. But constantly thinking of your interests as I do, I grow more and more convinced of the soundness of the view I originally intimated to our friend Aristo when he came to see me, that you would make formidable enemies if you put a slight upon a powerful young nobleman.[431] And it *will* be a slight, make no mistake. You have

430. Unknowns, unless Pollio is the famous Asinius Pollio.

431. L. Antonius, Thermus' Quaestor. Cicero advises that he be left in charge of the province of Asia after Thermus' departure.

nobody of superior official rank available, and the young man in question has a better claim than your excellent and irreproachable Legates from the very fact (to say nothing of family) that he is Quaestor and *your* Quaestor. I am well aware that nobody's grudge can hurt you, but I should none the less be sorry to see you an object of resentment to three brothers of the highest birth and no mean qualities of enterprise and eloquence, especially if their resentment was justified. It is apparent that they will become Tribunes of the Plebs in three successive years.[432] Who can tell what sort of political conditions lie ahead? To me they seem likely to be disturbed. So why should I want you to fall in the way of tribunician menaces, especially when you can give a Quaestor preference to quaestorian Legates without a word of criticism from anybody? If he proves himself worthy of his forbears, as I expect and hope he will, some part of the credit will go to you. If he stumbles, the damage will be entirely his, not yours at all.

I feel it right to let you know such thoughts as cross my mind and seem to concern you, because I am leaving for Cilicia. Whatever you do, the Gods be with it! But if you listen to me, you will keep clear of feuds and take thought for a quiet future.

116 (II. 19)

CICERO TO COELIUS CALDUS

Camp on the Pyramus, c. 22 June 50

From M. Tullius, son of Marcus, grandson of Marcus, Imperator, to C. Coelius Caldus, son of Lucius, grandson of Gaius, Quaestor, greetings.

432. Apparently an inference from the fact (not otherwise established) that L. Antonius' two elder brothers, Marcus (Mark Antony) and Gaius, had been Quaestors in 52 and 51 (or, more probably, both in 51). Marcus stood successfully for the Tribunate in 50.

After I received the most welcome news of your appointment by lot as my Quaestor, it was my expectation that the more time you spent with me in the province the more pleasure I should derive from that event. I felt it very important that the close tie which chance had established between us should be supplemented by personal intercourse. But time passed, and no word of your arrival reached me either from yourself or any other person; so I began to fear, as I still do, lest it might turn out that I left the province before you entered it. I have received a letter from you while in camp in Cilicia on 21 June. It is most kindly expressed, clear evidence of a conscientious and talented writer; but it contains no indication of the place and date of dispatch or of when I may expect you; neither could the bearer, who did not receive it from your own hand, enlighten me as to where and when you sent it.

Despite my uncertainty on these points, I judge it proper to send you orderlies and lictors of mine with a letter. If you receive it in good enough time, you will greatly oblige me by joining me in Cilicia as soon as possible. Your cousin Curius,[433] who, as you know, is a close friend of mine, and your relative C. Vergilius, also one of my nearest intimates, have written to me at length about you. Their words carry great weight with me, as a particular recommendation from such friends ought to do; but most of all I am impressed by your letter, especially by what you say of your own standing and our association. No Quaestor more welcome could have fallen to me. Therefore whatever I can do by way of compliment to you shall be done, and my sense of your personal and family status[434] shall be made plain to all. But this will be easier for me if you join me in Cilicia, which I believe will be in my and the public interest and most of all in your own.

433. Usually but not very plausibly identified with M'. Curius of Patrae.

434. In fact Coelius' nobility was of recent vintage, starting with his grandfather, Consul in 94.

117 (II. 17)

CICERO TO CN. (?) SALLUSTIUS[435]

Tarsus, c. 18 July 50

From M. Cicero, Imperator, to Cn. (?) Sallustius, Proquaestor,[436] greetings.

Your orderly delivered your letter to me at Tarsus on 17 July. I shall reply point by point, as that seems to be what you wish.

I have heard nothing about my successor, and I am not expecting any appointment. There is no reason why I should not leave on the day fixed, especially now the Parthian danger is out of the way. I hardly expect to make any considerable halts. I think I shall touch at Rhodes for the sake of our two boys, but that is not certain. I want to get back to Rome as soon as possible. However, the ordering of my journey will depend upon the political situation and the state of affairs in the capital. Your successor cannot possibly make such good time as to enable you to meet me in Asia.

As regards the rendering of accounts, there would have been some convenience in making no return, for which you say you have Bibulus' licence. But I hardly think you can take that course in view of the lex Julia. Bibulus has his own reasons for not observing that law,[437] but I think you should be very careful to observe it.

You say that the garrison ought not to have been withdrawn

435. Almost certainly not Cicero's friend of that name nor yet the historian C. Sallustius Crispus. The manuscripts have 'CANINI SALUSTIO'.

436. In Syria.

437. Bibulus denied the validity of Caesar's legislation as Consul, since it had been passed in defiance of his own religious veto.

from Apamea.[438] I find that your opinion is generally shared, and I am sorry that this step has caused some untoward talk among the ill-disposed. But nobody except yourself seems to be in any doubt as to whether or not the Parthians have crossed the river. Accordingly, under the impression of the general, unambiguous report, I have dismissed all the defensive forces which I had prepared in great strength.

It would not have been correct for me to send you my Quaestor's accounts, and in any case they are not ready. I intend to deposit them at Apamea. Not a penny of my booty has been or will be touched by any person except the City Quaestors, which is to say the Roman People. I propose to take sureties at Laodicea for all public moneys, so that both the state and I myself may be insured against transport risks. As for the 100,000 drachmae you mention, I am unable to oblige anyone in such a matter. All moneys are handled by the Prefects or the Quaestor; booty by the former, funds assigned to me by the latter.

You ask my opinion about the legions which have been decreed for Syria. I was previously doubtful whether they would be coming. Now I have no doubt that they will *not* be coming, if the news that all is quiet in Syria arrives beforehand. I suppose your successor Marius will be delayed because the Senate instructed him to accompany the legions.

Having replied to one letter, I come to the other. You request me to recommend you to Bibulus as warmly as possible. The will on my side is not lacking, but I think I have a bone to pick with you in this connection. Of all Bibulus' entourage you are the only one who had never told me how causelessly unfriendly his disposition towards me is. Any number of people have let me know that, when Antioch was in great danger and great hope rested on me and my army, he used to say that he would

438. Not the Phrygian city mentioned in the next paragraph, nor, as usually supposed, Apamea on the Orontes, but another place of the same name on the east side of the Euphrates.

sooner anything than appear to have stood in need of help from me. I was not annoyed with you for keeping silent from a sense of your duty as Quaestor towards your official superior, although I heard of the treatment to which you were subjected. As for Bibulus, although he wrote to Thermus about the Parthian war, he never sent a line to me, whom he knew to be directly involved in the danger of that war. He only wrote to *me* about an Augurate for his son. Out of pity,[439] and because I was always very friendly to him, I was at pains to write to him in the kindest possible way. If he has a spite against the whole world, which I never supposed to be the case, I do not so much resent his behaviour to me. But if he is unfriendly to me in particular, a letter of mine will not do you any good: I may add that in the dispatch which Bibulus sent to the Senate (a) he took sole credit for a thing we did jointly – he says that *he* took steps to see that moneys were exchanged at a profit to the state; (b) with reference to an action entirely mine, my declining to make use of Transpadane auxiliaries, he writes that *he* has relieved the state of that obligation also; (c) on the other hand he makes me share in something for which he was solely responsible: 'When we asked for an additional issue of grain for the auxiliary cavalry,' says he. His pettiness of spirit, the paltry, piddling character of his very malice, comes out when he calls Ariobarzanes in his dispatch not 'King' but 'son of King Ariobarzanes', because the Senate had granted him the royal title through me and had recommended him to my care. Persons of this mentality are not improved by being asked favours. However, I have complied with your wish and written a letter addressed to him. When you get it, you will do what you please.

439. Bibulus had just lost two sons, murdered in Egypt.

118 (XV. 11)

CICERO TO C. MARCELLUS

Tarsus, late July 50

From M. Cicero, Imperator, to C. Marcellus, Consul, greetings.

All my friends have told me in their letters (though the facts speak loudly enough for themselves) of the interest you have taken in the honour[440] conferred upon me. As Consul you have shown the same concern for my distinction and advancement in dignity as you always showed in the past, together with your parents and your whole family circle. Accordingly no service on my part can exceed your deserts, and there is none which I shall not zealously and gladly render. When one owes a favour, personalities make a great difference, and there is no man in respect to whom I have been more content to be in that position. Our common pursuits and the kindness I have received from your father and yourself had already attached me to you, but to this has now to be added what is in my eyes the greatest bond of all – your past and present administration of the commonwealth, which is as precious to me as anything in the world. I have no reluctance to owe you in my single person just as much as the whole body of honest citizens. Accordingly let me wish you such results as you deserve and as I believe will be yours.

As for me, I look forward to seeing you shortly, if I am not delayed on the voyage, which is just coinciding with the Etesians.

440. The Supplication.

119 (XIV. 5)

CICERO TO TERENTIA

Athens, 16 October 50

From Tullius to his dear Terentia greetings.

If you and our beloved Tullia are well, darling Marcus and I are well too.

We arrived in Athens on 14 October, having experienced pretty unfavourable weather at sea – it has been a slow, disagreeable voyage. Acastus met us with letters as we came ashore. He had been three weeks on the way, which is pretty good going. I got your letter, in which you appear to be afraid that your earlier letters have not been delivered All of them were in fact delivered. You covered all items most carefully, and I was most grateful. Nor was I surprised at the shortness of the letter which Acastus brought. After all, you are now expecting me in person, or rather *us* in person, and very impatient we are to see you both – though I well see what sort of situation we are coming home to. Letters brought by Acastus from many friends tell me that war is on the horizon, so that, once I arrive, I shall not be able to disguise my sentiments. But we must take what fortune sends, and I shall try to come all the faster so that we can consult together about the whole position. I shall be glad if you will come to meet us as far as you can without detriment to your health.

About the Precius[441] bequest (I am really sorry to get it – I was very fond of him), would you please see that, if the auction takes place before my arrival, Pomponius or, if he can't manage it, Camillus looks after my interest? When I am safely back I shall see to the rest myself. If you have already left Rome, please arrange this all the same. If the Gods are

441. Cf. *Letters to Atticus* 123 (VI.9).2.

kind, we hope to be in Italy about the Ides of November.

Now my darling and most longed-for Terentia, if you both love us, take care of yourselves. Goodbye.

Athens, 16 October.

120 (XVI. 1)

CICERO TO TIRO

Between Patrae and Alyzia, 3 November 50

From Tullius to his dear Tiro best greetings, also from my son Marcus, and my brother and nephew.

I thought I could bear the want of you not too hardly,[442] but frankly I find it unendurable; and though in view of the honour I have in prospect it is important for me to get back to Rome as soon as possible, I feel I did wrong to leave you. However, since it seemed to be your definite inclination not to sail until your health was recovered, I approved your plan; nor am I changing now, if you are still of the same mind. But if, after you are able to take nourishment, you think you can overtake me, the decision is in your hands. I am sending Mario to you with the intention that he should either join me in your company as soon as possible or return to me at once, if you stay on.

Now do understand that, provided it can be managed without detriment to your health, there is nothing I want more than to have you with me; but that if you find you need to stay a little longer at Patrae to convalesce, there is nothing I want more than for you to be well again. If you take ship straight away, you will catch us up at Leucas. If you want to get back your strength, however, you must take good care

442. Tiro had been left behind sick at Patrae.

that you have suitable companions, good weather, and the right sort of boat. Only, if you love me, my dear Tiro, do be sure not to let Mario's arrival and this letter affect your judgement. If you do what is best for your health, you will best comply with my wishes. So think it over in that clever head of yours. I miss you, but I love you. Loving you, I want to see you fit and well; missing you, I want to see you as soon as possible. The former, therefore, must come first. So make it your chief concern to get well. Of your countless services to me this will be the one I shall most appreciate.

3 November.

121 (XVI. 2)

CICERO TO TIRO

Alyzia, 5 November 50

From Tullius to his dear Tiro greetings.

I can't and don't want to write to you how I feel. I will only say that it will be to our very great pleasure, both yours and mine, if I see you in good health as soon as possible. Two days after leaving you we put in at Alyzia, within 120 stades[443] distance of Leucas. At Leucas I expect I shall see you in person or get a letter from you by Mario. As you care for me, so be sure to look after your health – or as you know I care for you.

Nones of November, from Alyzia.

443. About fourteen English miles.

122 (XVI. 3)

CICERO TO TIRO

Alyzia, 6 November 50

From Tullius and Marcus to their dear Tiro greetings, also from Quintus senior and junior.

We stayed at Alyzia (from where I sent you a letter yesterday) for one day, because Quintus had not come up with us. That was the Nones of November. From there I am dispatching this letter as we leave before daybreak on the 6th.

If you love us all, and especially me, your schoolmaster, get back your strength. I am looking forward in great suspense, first of course to seeing you, but, if not that, to seeing Mario with a letter from you. We all, and I especially, are anxious to see you as soon as possible, but fit and well, my dear Tiro. So no hurry. I shall see you soon enough if you are in good health. I can do without your manifold usefulness, but I want you to be well again, first for your sake and then for my own.

My dear Tiro, goodbye.

123 (XVI. 4)

CICERO TO TIRO

Leucas, 7 November 50

From Tullius to his dear Tiro best greetings, also from Marcus and my brother Quintus and Quintus junior.

I read your letter with varying feelings. The first page upset me badly, the second brought me round a little. So now, if not before, I am clear that until your health is quite restored you should not venture upon travel either by land or water. I shall see you soon enough if I see you thoroughly strong again.

You say the doctor has a good reputation, and so I hear myself; but frankly, I don't think much of his treatments. You ought not to have been given soup[444] with a weak stomach. However, I have written to him at some length, and also to Lyso.[445] To Curius, who is a most agreeable fellow, very obliging and good-natured, I have written a great deal, including the suggestion that, if you agree, he should move you over to his house. I am afraid our friend Lyso is a little casual. All Greeks are; also, he has not replied to a letter he received from me. However, you commend him; so you must judge for yourself what is best. One thing, my dear Tiro, I do beg of you: don't consider money at all where the needs of your health are concerned. I have told Curius to advance whatever you say. I imagine the doctor ought to be given something to make him more interested in your case.[446]

Your services to me are beyond count – in my home and out of it, in Rome and abroad, in private affairs and public, in my studies and literary work. You will cap them all if I see you your own man again, as I hope I shall. I think it would be very nice, if all goes well, for you to sail home with Quaestor Mescinius. He is not uncultivated, and he seemed to me to have a regard for you. But when you have given every possible attention to your health, *then* my dear Tiro, attend to sailing arrangements. I don't now want you to hurry in any way. My only concern is for you to get well.

Take my word for it, dear Tiro, that nobody cares for me who does not care for you. Your recovery is most important

444. Or 'gravy' or 'sauce'.

445. Cicero's host at Patrae in whose house Tiro was staying.

446. Apparently the doctor (whose name was Asclapo; cf. Letter 286 (XIII.20)) was not charging a special fee. He may have looked after Lyso's household for a regular payment.

to you and me, but many others are concerned about it. In the past you have never been able to recruit yourself properly, because you wanted to give me of your best at every turn. Now there is nothing to stand in your way. Put everything else aside, think only of your bodily well-being. I shall believe you care for me in proportion to the care you devote to your health.

Goodbye, my dear Tiro, goodbye and fondest good wishes. Lepta sends you his, so do we all. Goodbye.

7 November, from Leucas.

124 (XVI. 5)

CICERO TO TIRO

Leucas, 7 November 50

From Tullius and Marcus and the Quinti to their nicest and best of Tiros best greetings.

Look what a charmer you are! We spent two hours at Thyrreum,[447] and our host Xenomenes is as fond of you as though he had been your bosom companion. He has promised you everything you need, and I believe he will be as good as his word. I think it would be a good plan for him to take you to Leucas when you are stronger, to finish your convalescence there. You must see what Curius and Lyso and the doctor think. I wanted to send Mario back to you for you to send him to me with a letter when you were a little better, but I reflected that Mario could bring me only one letter, and I expect them one after another.

So do what you can, and, if you care for me, see that Acastus goes down to the harbour every day. There will be plenty of folk to whom you can safely give a letter and who will be glad

447. On the outward journey in 51.

to carry it to me. For my part I shall take advantage of every traveller to Patrae.

I pin all my hope of your getting proper treatment and attention on Curius. He has the kindest of hearts and the truest affection for me. Put yourself entirely in his hands. I had rather see you fit and well a little later on than weak straight away. So attend to nothing except getting well – I shall attend to the rest.

Goodbye once again.

Leaving Leucas, 7 November.

125 (XVI. 6)

CICERO TO TIRO

Actium, 7 November 50

From Tullius and Marcus and the Quinti to Tiro best greetings.

This is my third letter to you in one day. I am writing it more to keep up my established practice, having happened on a bearer, than because I have anything to say. Well then, yet again: as you care for me, so take care of yourself. Add this to your countless services to me; it will be the most agreeable to me of them all. When you have done (I hope) thinking about your health, think about arrangements for sailing too. Please give all travellers to Italy letters to me, just as I never fail to take advantage of anyone going to Patrae. Look after yourself, my dear Tiro, do. Seeing that bad luck has prevented you sailing with me, you have no reason to hurry or to bother about anything except getting well.

Goodbye once more.

7 November, from Actium, in the evening.

126 (XVI. 7)

CICERO AND HIS SON TO TIRO

Corcyra, 16 November 50

From Tullius and Marcus to their dear Tiro greetings.

We have been held up at Corcyra for a week. Quintus senior and junior are at Buthrotum. We are dreadfully anxious about your health, but not surprised that there has been no letter from you; for the sailing winds from your present whereabouts are the same winds but for the want of which *we* should not be stuck at Corcyra. So look after yourself and get strong, and when your health and the time of year enable you to make the voyage conveniently, rejoin us who love you dearly. Nobody loves us who is not fond of you. Everybody will be glad to see you and looking forward to your return. Take care of your health.

Goodbye again, dear Tiro.

16 November, from Corcyra.

127 (XVI. 9)

CICERO TO TIRO

Brundisium, 26 November 50

From Tullius and Marcus to their dear Tiro best greetings.

As you know, we left you on 2 November. We reached Leucas on 6 November and Actium on the 7th, where we stayed over the 8th on account of the weather. Thence on the 9th we had a beautiful voyage to Corcyra. At Corcyra we stayed until the 15th, held up by weather. On the 16th we moved on 120 stades to Corcyra Harbour near Cassiope. Contrary winds held us there until the 22nd. Meanwhile many travellers who were too impatient to wait were shipwrecked. That day we weighed anchor after dinner. A gentle southerly breeze was blowing, the skies were clear. Sailing at our ease through the night and the next day, we reached Italy at Hydrus, and on the day following (24 November) under the same wind arrived at Brundisium at 10 a.m. Terentia, who thinks a great deal of you, entered the town at the same time as ourselves.

At Brundisium on 26 November a slave of Cn. Plancius gave me at long last the letter from you that I had been waiting for so impatiently, dispatched on the Ides of November. It greatly relieved my anxiety – if only the relief had been total! However, Doctor Asclapo definitely assures us that you will soon be well.

Now I do not think I need urge you to apply all possible care to the business of convalescing. I know your good sense, your temperate habits, and your affection for me. I know you will do everything in your power to be with us at the earliest possible moment. But at the same time I should not want you to be in any sort of hurry. I wish you had stayed away from Lyso's concert – you might have had a fourth weekly crisis.[448] However, since you chose to put good manners before your health, be careful in future. I am sending word to Curius to do something for the doctor and advance you what you need, with a promise that I shall repay to anyone he designates. I am leaving a horse and mule for you at Brundisium. I am afraid there will be great alarms and excursions in Rome after the Kalends of January. I shall take a moderate line in all things.

The only other thing is to ask and beg you not to take ship without proper care. Sailors with their money to make are apt to be in a hurry. Take no chances, my dear Tiro. You have a long, difficult voyage ahead. If possible, go with Mescinius –

448. Illnesses were supposed to reach a crisis every seventh day.

he is not one to take chances with the sea. If not, then with some man of position whom the skipper will respect. If you take every care about this and render yourself up to me safe and sound, I shall have all I ever want of you.

Again, dear Tiro, goodbye. I have written to the doctor, to Curius, and to Lyso most particularly about you. Goodbye and good wishes.

128 (v. 20)

CICERO TO MESCINIUS RUFUS

Outside Rome, c. 5 January 49

From Cicero to Rufus.

One way or another I should have met you if you had chosen to go to the place arranged. Regardful of my convenience, you did not want to put me about; but I should like you to believe that, if you had sent me word, I should have set your wish above my convenience.

It would be easier for me to reply to your letter in detail if my Secretary,[449] M. Tullius, were here. As to him, I am fully assured that so far as the rendering of accounts goes (on other matters I cannot speak for certain) he has not intentionally done anything contrary to your financial interest or reputation. Further, I can assure you that, if the old law and ancient custom were still in force, I should not have rendered my accounts without previously comparing and making them up with you, suitably to the intimate connection between us. Now that the lex Julia makes it necessary to leave accounts in the province and present an identical copy to the Treasury, I did in the province what I should have done at Rome if the previous practice had still held good. Nor did I do it in such a way as to oblige you to

449. See Glossary of Terms.

conform to my pattern, but on the contrary gave you a latitude which I shall never regret having given. I put my Secretary, of whom I see you now entertain suspicions, entirely in your hands. You associated with him your brother,[450] M. Mindius. The accounts were made up in my absence with your co-operation. All I did was to read them, and I regarded the book I received from my Secretary as coming from your brother also. If this was a compliment, I could not have made you a greater; if an act of trust, I placed almost more trust in you than in myself; if the object was to ensure that nothing should be presented other than to your credit and advantage, I had nobody more proper to the business than the person to whom I gave it. At any rate what the law required was done; I deposited accounts, made up and compared, with the two communes which appeared to me most suitable since it had to be done in this way, namely Laodicea and Apamea. So on this point my first answer is that, although for good reasons I was in a hurry to present my accounts, I should have waited for you, if I had not looked upon the accounts left behind in the province as already rendered. Therefore ★★★.

As for what you write about Volusius, this does not concern the accounts. I was advised by experts, including the greatest expert of them all and my very good friend, C. Camillus,[451] that the debt could not be transferred from Valerius[452] to

450. i.e. brother (or cousin) by adoption, or brother (or cousin) adopted into another family, or half-brother.

451. He seems to have acted as Cicero's agent-in-charge (*procurator*) in Rome during the Proconsulate.

452. Probably the P. Valerius mentioned in *Letters to Atticus* 114 (V.21).13 as a penniless dependent of King Deiotarus. He seems to have acted as an agent of Q. Volusius, one of Cicero's following (cf. ibid. 6), in a speculation on a public (revenue?) contract and to have given as sureties certain of the principal members of Cicero's staff. When Valerius failed to pay the Treasury, the sureties became liable. The manoeuvre by which Cicero extricated them is not clearly stated. According to an interpretation first advanced in 1961 he reckoned money paid by Valerius in respect of an earlier contract as discharging the debt.

Volusius, and that Valerius' sureties were liable (the amount was not HS3,000,000, as stated in your letter, but HS2,000,000). For the money was paid to me in the name of Valerius as purchaser. That part of it which was arrears I entered in the accounts. But writing as you do, you rob me of the satisfaction of liberality, conscientiousness, and a measure of business sense (though I set little enough store by *that*). (a) Liberality: you prefer to suppose that it was thanks to my Secretary, and not to me, that my Legate, M. Anneius, and my Prefect, Q. Lepta, were relieved of a very heavy liability, which moreover they should not in fairness have incurred. (b) Conscientiousness: you suppose that I neither knew nor thought about a matter so gravely involving my duty, and with such dangerous potentialities, but presented whatever my Secretary thought fit without even having him read it over to me. (c) Business sense: you imagine that the procedure which I rather intelligently thought out was not so much as thought about. Actually the plan of freeing Volusius was mine, and it was I who devised the expedient whereby Valerius' sureties and T. Marius[453] himself escaped so severe a penalty. That expedient has been universally approved, applauded in fact; and, if you want the truth, my Secretary was the only one who, as I could see, was not too happy about it. But I took the view that an honourable man should have regard to the financial welfare of so many friends or fellow-countrymen, seeing that the public kept its due.

As regards Lucceius (?), what happened was that the money was deposited in a temple at the instance of Cn. Pompeius. I acknowledged that this was done on my instructions. Pompey has used the money, just as Sestius[454] has used the sum you

453. Unknown.

454. We know no details about these two deposits. P. Sestius was appointed governor of Cilicia in the second week of January, but was still in Italy.

deposited. But so far as I can see, all this has nothing to do with you. I should be very sorry, however, that I inadvertently omitted to add that you deposited the money in the temple on my instructions, were it not that there is the most weighty and unimpeachable documentary evidence showing to whom that money was given as well as the senatorial decrees and the written authorities, yours and mine, on which it was handed over to P. Sestius. Seeing that all this was unmistakably attested in a number of places, I did not put in a supplement which would have been of no advantage to you. But I wish I had, since you evidently regard it as an omission. You say that *you* had better enter it so, and I quite agree; there will not be the least discrepancy on this point between your accounts and mine. You will add that it was on my instructions; and I, though I did not so add, have no reason to deny it; nor, if I *had* such a reason, should I deny it against your wish.

The entry concerning the HS900,000 was certainly made in the form in which you, or your cousin, wanted it made. However, if there is any point which even at this stage I might be able to correct in presenting the accounts, since you thought the entry about the contribution rather maladroit(?), I shall have to consider what is legally permissible, as I have not taken advantage of the senatorial decree. At all events I don't think you should have entered these items from my rendered accounts under the heading of 'money levied', unless I am in error – I am not the world's greatest expert. One thing you must never doubt, that I will do anything I think your interests or even your wishes require, if I possibly can.

With reference to what you say about bounties,[455] I must tell you that I have given in the names of the Military Tribunes, Prefects, and my personal staff only. Here I was under a mis-

455. Gratuities or other benefits given or promised to military and other personnel by a governor during his term of office. A list had to be presented to the Treasury. Apparently this could be done either by the Governor himself or by his Quaestor.

apprehension. I thought I had time at my disposal in which to present the list. But I was later informed that it had to be sent in within thirty days after I rendered the accounts. I was extremely sorry that those bounties should not have stood to your credit rather than mine, having myself no axe to grind. However, on the Centurions and the staffs of the Military Tribunes we are still uncommitted, bounties in this category not being specified in the statute.

That leaves the matter of the HS100,000.[456] I remember getting a letter from you on this point written from Myrina, and the mistake was not mine but yours. The persons to blame, if blame there was, appeared to be your brother and Tullius. Correction being impossible, because I deposited my accounts before leaving the province, I believe I did reply in as accommodating a fashion as I could, in accordance with my personal feelings and my financial expectations at that time. But I do not consider myself as bound by the accommodating terms of my letter then, nor today, having received your letter about the HS100,000, do I feel myself in the position of persons to whom letters these days spell trouble![457] You should also bear in mind that I deposited the whole of the sum which had legally accrued to me with the tax-farmers at Ephesus, that it amounted to HS2,200,000, and that Pompey has taken the lot.[458] Whether I like that or whether I lump it, you ought to take a matter of HS100,000 coolly enough. You should set it off against your allowances or my liberality. Suppose you had made me a loan of that HS100,000, you have too amiable a disposition and

456. This sum would seem to have been entered in the accounts by error as due from Mescinius to the Treasury.

457. Debtors. With war about to break out creditors were trying to call in their loans.

458. This was not so. A year later the money was still in Ephesus (*Letters to Atticus* 211 (XI.1).2); shortly afterwards Cicero withdrew half of it and lent it to Pompey. But he may have told Pompey that it was at his disposal.

too much affection for me to wish to take my property at valuation at this time – as for cash, I couldn't raise it if I wanted. But don't think I mean all this seriously; no more do I suppose you were serious either. All the same, if you think it would be of any use, I'll send Tullius over to you, when he gets back from the country.

There is no reason why I should want this letter torn up.

129 (XIII. 55)

CICERO TO MINUCIUS THERMUS

Tarsus (?), 51 (end) or 50 (early)

From Cicero to Thermus, Propraetor, greetings.

When I spoke to you in Ephesus about the affair of my Legate, M. Anneius, I formed the impression that you were very anxious to oblige him for his own sake. But I think so much of him that I feel I must leave nothing undone which might be to his benefit, and I have sufficient confidence in your regard for me to feel sure that my recommendation will serve to enhance your friendly sentiments towards him in no small measure. I have long had a regard for M. Anneius. My opinion of him is evident from the fact that I offered him his present post of my own accord after refusing many applications for it. And now that he has been with me on active service in the recent operations, I have so highly approved his courage, skill, loyalty, and personal good-will towards me that nobody stands higher in my esteem.

You know that he has a dispute with the people of Sardis. I explained the case to you in Ephesus, but you will acquaint yourself more easily and accurately face to face. For the rest, I give you my word that for some time I could not make up my mind just what to write to you. Your manner of administering justice is well-known, and redounds to your great credit; and in this case all we need is for you to follow your usual judicial practice. However, I am not unaware of the weight of a governor's influence, especially of one so upright, responsible, and merciful as you are universally acknowledged to be. May I therefore request you in virtue of the very close connection between us and our many equal and mutual good offices to exert your benevolent influence on M. Anneius' behalf, so as to make it clear to him that you are his friend (which he does not doubt – he has often talked to me) and have become much more so as a result of this letter of mine. In the whole sphere of your authority you could do nothing to oblige me more. As for Anneius himself, he is an excellent fellow and does not forget a kindness. I imagine you make no doubt that your friendly efforts will be well placed.

130 (XIII. 53)

CICERO TO MINUCIUS THERMUS

Province of Cilicia, 51 or 50

From Cicero to Thermus, Propraetor, greetings.

I have long been on very familiar terms with L. Genucilius Curvus, a very worthy gentleman who never forgets a service. I thoroughly recommend him to you, and put him in your hands. In the first place, I hope you will accommodate him in all respects so far as your conscience and dignity will allow – and allow they always will, for he will never ask you for anything unbecoming to your character, or for that matter his own. In particular, however, I would recommend to your notice his affairs in the area of the Hellespont with the request that he enjoy rights over certain lands as decreed and granted him by the township of Parium, rights which in the past have always been undisputedly his; further, that if he has any dispute with a native of the Hellespont, you remit it for settlement to that district. But since I am most warmly recommending to you all that he is and has, I do not think I need write in detail of his various concerns. Let this be the long and the short of it: whatever service, kindness, or compliment Genucilius receives at your hands, I shall regard it as rendered to myself and my personal interests.

131 (XIII. 56)

CICERO TO MINUCIUS THERMUS

Province of Cilicia, 51 or 50

From Cicero to Thermus, Propraetor, greetings.

Cluvius of Puteoli pays me much attention, and we are on a very familiar footing. He is convinced that unless he settles some business which he has in your province during your period of office through my recommendations, he may as well give it up for lost. Now since a friend of mine, one who never grudges a service, places such a burden on my shoulders, I for my part shall place it on yours in consideration of the very good turns you have done me in the past – but with the proviso that I don't want to put you to any serious trouble.

The towns of Mylasa and Alabanda owe Cluvius money. Euthydemus told me when I was in Ephesus that he would see that Mylasian counsel were sent to Rome. This has not been done. I hear that *envoys* have been dispatched, but prefer counsel so that something can be settled. Accordingly, may I request you to direct both Mylasa and Alabanda to send counsel to Rome? Furthermore, Philocles of Alabanda has given Cluvius a mortgage, which has now expired. I should be grateful if you would see that he either gives up the property and hands it over to Cluvius' agents or else pays the money; also that the towns of Heraclea and Bargylia, which likewise owe money, either pay up or secure the debts on their revenues. The town of Caunus also owes money, but they say they have been keeping it on deposit. Would you please make enquiries, and if you find that they have not been authorized to keep it on deposit by edict or decree, please see that Cluvius does not lose the interest, according to your rule?

I am all the more concerned about these matters because our friend Pompey's interests are also involved and because he seems to me to be even more exercised than Cluvius himself.[459] I very much want him to feel content with us. Let me again earnestly beg your assistance in these matters.

132 (XIII. 54)

CICERO TO MINUCIUS THERMUS

Laodicea, February–April 50

From Cicero to Thermus, Propraetor, greetings.

Among the many things you have done as a result of my recommendations I am particularly obliged for your most handsome treatment of M. Marcilius, son of my friend and interpreter. He has come to Laodicea and told me how very grateful he is to you, and to me because of you. For the future, let me request you, since your kindness is not falling on stony ground, to be all the readier to accommodate its recipients, and, so far as your conscience will allow, to see that the young man's mother-in-law is not prosecuted. My recommendation of Marcilius is now much more enthusiastic even than before, because I have found Marcilius senior in the course of a long

459. It has been plausibly supposed that Cluvius was merely Pompey's agent.

term of service quite remarkably (I might almost say unbelievably) loyal, honest, and well-conducted.

133 (XIII. 57)

CICERO TO MINUCIUS THERMUS

Laodicea, early April (?) 50

From Cicero to Thermus, Propraetor, greetings.

Every day I learn from letters and reports that a major war is in progress in Syria. That makes me all the more insistent in asking you as a friend to send me back my Legate, M. Anneius, as soon as possible. His services, advice, and military experience may clearly be invaluable to me and to the state. If he had not had so much at stake, nothing would have induced him to leave me or me to let him go. I propose to set out for Cilicia about the Kalends of May. M. Anneius should return to me before that date.

I have already both spoken and written to you very particularly about his business with the people of Sardis, and I would again beg you to see that he settles it in a manner befitting the justice of his case and his personal dignity. From what you said when I talked to you in Ephesus I understood that you were very anxious to oblige M. Anneius for his own sake. But please take it that you can do nothing more agreeable to me than if I understand that thanks to you he has personally settled the business to his satisfaction, and I beg you once again to bring that about as soon as possible.

134 (XIII. 65)

CICERO TO P. SILIUS

Province of Cilicia, 51 or 50

From M. Cicero to P. Silius, Propraetor, greetings.

With P. Terentius Hispo, who works for the Grazing Rents Company[460] as their local manager, I have a great deal of familiar contact, and each of us is indebted to the other for important services, equal and mutual. His reputation very largely depends on his concluding tax agreements with the communes still outstanding. I do not forget that I tried my own hand at the business in Ephesus and was quite unable to get the Ephesians to oblige. However, according to the universal persuasion and my own observation, your complete integrity combined with your remarkable civility and gentleness have earned you the heartiest compliance of the natives with your every nod. I would therefore particularly request you as a compliment to me to make it your wish that Hispo should get this credit.

Furthermore I am closely connected with the members of the Company, not only because it is under my patronage as a whole but because I am on very close terms with many of them individually. So you will both do my friend Hispo a good turn at my instance and strengthen my relations with the Company. You yourself will reap a rich reward from Hispo's attentiveness (he is very appreciative of a service) and from the influence of the Company members, persons of the highest consequence. You will also do me a great kindness. For you may take it that within the whole sphere of your provincial authority you could do nothing that would oblige me more.

460. i.e. a Roman company which bought the right to collect these rents from the provincials.

135 (XIII. 61)

CICERO TO P. SILIUS

Province of Cilicia, 51 or 50

From M. Cicero to P. Silius, Propraetor, greetings.

I think you know that I was on very familiar terms with T. Pinnius, as he himself has testified in his will, under which I am appointed both guardian and second heir. His son, a remarkably studious, erudite, and modest young man, is owed a large sum by the people of Nicaea, about eight million sesterces, and, so I hear, they are particularly desirous to pay him. Not only the other guardians, who know how much you care for me, but the boy himself is convinced that you will do anything for my sake. You will therefore deeply oblige me if you see to it (so far as your conscience and dignity will allow) that as much of the amount as possible is paid to Pinnius as soon as possible on behalf of the people of Nicaea.

136 (XIII. 62)

CICERO TO P. SILIUS

Province of Cilicia, 51 or 50

M. Cicero to P. Silius, Propraetor, greetings.

I was truly beholden to you in the matter of Atilius[461] – thanks to you I saved a respectable Roman Knight from ruin, though I came late upon the scene. And, to be frank, I have

461. Possibly this had to do with the business mentioned in *Letters to Atticus* 94 (V.1).2.

always considered you as quite at my command because of your exceptionally close and friendly relations with our good Lamia. So you see that, having thanked you for relieving me of all anxiety, I go on to offer a piece of impertinence! But I shall make amends by ever cultivating your friendship and protecting your interests with all the devotion in the world.

If you care for me, be sure to think of my brother Quintus as you do of myself. In that way you will pile one great favour on top of another.

137 (XIII. 63)

CICERO TO P. SILIUS

Laodicea, 4 April (?) 50

From M. Cicero to P. Silius, Propraetor, greetings.

I never thought to find words failing me, but in recommending M. Laenius[462] fail me they do. So I shall explain the case to you briefly, but in terms which will make my sentiments quite clear. You would hardly believe how much I and my dearest brother think of M. Laenius. That arises from his many services, but also from his sterling character and exceptional modesty. I was most reluctant to let him go, both because of the charm of his familiar companionship and because I was glad to avail myself of his sound and loyal advice.

But I am afraid you may be thinking that the words I said would fail me are now all too abundant! I recommend him as you will understand that I am bound to recommend a person of whom I have written the foregoing. And I most earnestly request you to expedite the business he has in your province, and to tell him in person what you consider to be proper. You will find him the soul of good nature and generosity. So I beg

462. A friend of Atticus, in Cilicia on business.

you to send him back to me as soon as you can, free and unencumbered, with his affairs settled thanks to you. My brother and I will be very much beholden.

138 (XIII. 64)

CICERO TO P. SILIUS[463]

Laodicea, April (?) 50

From M. Cicero to P. Silius, Propraetor, greetings.

My friend Nero has told me of his gratitude to you in quite extraordinarily glowing terms. No compliment, he says, which you could possibly have offered him was overlooked. Nero himself will richly repay you, for nobody has a better memory for a service than this young man. But I do assure you that you have greatly obliged me as well. In the whole range of our aristocracy there is no man I value more. And so you will oblige me greatly if you will do certain things which he has asked me to raise with you.

First, will you please hold over the matter of Pausanias of Alabanda until Nero arrives – I know he is very anxious to help him and so I beg this favour of you earnestly. Next, will you kindly regard the people of Nysa as specially recommended to your favour? Nero has the closest ties with them and is most active in championing their interests. So please let the commune understand that in Nero's patronage they have a most powerful protection. I have often recommended Servilius Strabo to you, and do so now the more emphatically because Nero has taken up his case. All we ask is that you handle the matter, lest otherwise you leave an innocent man to the rapacity

463. For several reasons I have suggested that this letter is mistakenly addressed, and that it was really written to the governor of Asia, Minucius Thermus.

of a successor who may not be like yourself. That will oblige me, and I shall feel that your good nature has had its way.

The sum and substance of this letter is to ask you to continue to confer all possible favours upon Nero, as you have made it your practice to do already. Your province, unlike mine, offers a wide scope to a talented and disinterested young nobleman to recommend himself and advance his reputation. With your backing, which I am sure will be and has already been forthcoming, he will be able to confirm the loyalty of the distinguished body of clients inherited from his ancestors and attach them by favours personal to himself. If you help him in this respect as actively as you have promised, your kindness will be excellently placed with Nero; but I too shall be very greatly beholden.

139 (XIII. 9)

CICERO TO CRASSIPES

Rome (?), 54 (?)[464]

From Cicero to Crassipes greetings.

I have already recommended the Company of Bithynia[465] to you in person as strongly as I could, and it was evident to me that of your own volition as well as in consequence of my recommendation you were anxious to accommodate the Company in any way in your power. However, since those concerned consider it very much to their advantage that I

464. The letter is usually assigned to the end of 51 or the beginning of 50. Although I believe this to be erroneous, I have kept it among the correspondence of the Proconsulate because its date is most conveniently considered (in my commentary) in that context.

465. Apparently a consortium of companies operating in Bithynia, where Crassipes was serving as Quaestor.

should also declare to you by letter my friendly disposition in their regard, I have not hesitated to write these lines.

I have always been very ready to study the interests of the tax-farmers as a class, which is only right in view of the important services they have rendered me. But I should like it to be clear to you that I have a special regard for this Company of Bithynia. The quality of the membership in itself makes the Company an important section of the community (it is a consortium of all the other companies) and, as it happens, it contains a great many very good friends of mine. I would mention one of them in particular who has a special responsibility at the present time, namely the Chairman, P. Rupilius, son of Publius, of the Tribe Menenia.

In view of the above, let me particularly request you to give your most generous support to the Company's agent, Cn. Pupius, assisting him in every way you can. I hope you will ensure, as you easily can, that his employers are thoroughly satisfied with his services, and will be good enough to protect and further their business interests as far as possible – and I am not unaware how much a Quaestor can do in that direction. I shall be greatly beholden. I can also promise and guarantee from experience that if you oblige the Company of Bithynia you will find that its members have good and grateful memories.

140 (XIII. 58)

CICERO TO C. TITIUS RUFUS

Laodicea, February 50

From M. Cicero to C. Titius Rufus, son of Lucius, Praetor Urbanus, greetings.

L. Custidius is a member of my Tribe, a native of my town, and my good friend. He has a case, which he will be submitting to your judgement. Allow me to recommend him to you within the limits imposed by conscience on your side and propriety on mine, merely asking that he find access to you easy and obtain his fair demands with your good-will; and that he have reason to feel that my friendship, even at so great a distance, is advantageous to him, especially where you are concerned.

141 (XIII. 59)

CICERO TO CURTIUS PEDUCAEANUS

Laodicea, February 50

M. Cicero to M. Curtius Peducaeanus, Praetor, greetings.

I have a unique regard for M. Fabius.[466] My personal intercourse with him is of the closest, and our friendship goes back a very long way. I do not make any request as to your verdict on the matters he has at issue (you will follow your edict and rule, as your conscience and dignity require), but only ask that he find access to you as easy as possible and obtain such points as shall appear just with your good-will, so that he may feel that my friendship, even at a long distance, is of advantage to him, particularly where you are concerned. This I beg of you as a special favour.

142 (XIII. 48)

CICERO TO C. SEXTILIUS RUFUS

Italy, beginning of 49

From Cicero to C. Sextilius Rufus, Quaestor, greetings.

466. Gallus; cf. p. 221.

I recommend all the inhabitants of Cyprus to your favour, but more especially those of Paphos. Anything you do for them I shall greatly appreciate. I am all the more ready to recommend them to you because I think it is to the advantage of your own reputation (which I have much at heart) that on your first arrival in the island as Quaestor you should set a pattern for others to follow. This I think you will the more easily achieve if you see fit to follow the enactment of your friend P. Lentulus and my own ordinances. I am confident that this will tend much to your credit.

143 (XVI. 11)

CICERO TO TIRO

Outside Rome, 12 January 49

From Tullius and Marcus, Terentia, Tullia, and the Quinti to Tiro best greetings.

Although I miss your timely service at every turn, your continued ill-health distresses me for your sake more than for my own. But seeing that the violence of the disease has turned into a quartan[467] fever (so Curius writes), I trust that with care you will soon be stronger. Only be considerate of others as you always are, and think of nothing at the present time except how best to get well. I know well enough how painfully you are missing us. But all will be easy if you regain your health. I don't want you to hurry for fear of your exposing yourself to the miseries of sea-sickness while you are still an invalid, and of your having a dangerous winter voyage.

I arrived outside Rome on 4 January. They streamed out to meet me on the road – a most flattering welcome. But I have fallen right into the flames of civil conflict, or rather war. I

467. It had previously been a tertian.

should dearly have liked to heal the mischief, and I believe I could, had not the personal desires of certain people (there are warmongers on both sides) stood in my way. To be sure, our friend Caesar has sent a threatening, harsh letter to the Senate, and persists in his shameless determination to hold his army and province in defiance of the Senate, and my friend Curio is egging him on. Our friend Antony and Q. Cassius[468] have gone to join Caesar along with Curio. They were not expelled by violence of any kind but left after the Senate had charged the Consuls, Praetors, Tribunes, and us Proconsuls to see that the state took no harm.[469] Never was the community in greater peril, never did bad citizens have a leader more ready to strike. Not but what preparations are going forward actively on our side too. This is taking place by the authority and zeal of our friend Pompey, who late in the day has begun to be afraid of Caesar.

Despite these commotions the Senate in large numbers has demanded a Triumph for me. But Consul Lentulus, to make it a bigger favour on *his* part, said he would put the matter before the House as soon as he had cleared up necessary state business. I am showing no undue eagerness, which makes my public influence the greater. Italy has been divided into districts, each under an appointed supervisor. I am taking Capua.[470]

I wanted you to know these facts. On your side, once again, see that you get well, and send me a letter as often as you have anybody to bring one. Again, goodbye.

Dispatched 12 January.

468. Both Tribunes.

469. The so-called 'Ultimate Decree of the Senate', amounting to a declaration of martial law.

470. The controversial matter of Cicero's command in Campania is discussed in my C.U.P. edition of the *Letters to Atticus*, Vol. IV, Appendix II.

144 (XIV. 18)

CICERO TO TERENTIA AND TULLIA

Formiae, 22 January 49

From Tullius to his dear Terentia, and her father to his darling daughter, and Marcus to his mother and sister best greetings.

My dear hearts, I think you should yet again carefully consider what you are to do – whether you should stay in Rome or with me or in some place of safety. The decision is yours as well as mine.

The points that occur to me are these: Thanks to Dolabella[471] you can stay in Rome safely, and your doing so might help us if there is any outbreak of violence or looting. But on the other hand I am concerned when I observe that all honest men have left Rome and have their womenfolk with them. Moreover, this district where I am is full of towns friendly to me and also of properties of mine, so that you could be with me a good deal, and when we are separated could live comfortably in places of our own. Frankly I have not yet made up my mind which is the better course. You must observe what other ladies of your rank are doing, and take care that when and if you do want to leave you don't find the way barred. Do please consider the matter again together and with our friends. Tell Philotimus to see that the house is barricaded and guarded and please arrange reliable couriers, so that I get some sort of a letter from you every day. But your chief care must be for your health, if you want us[472] to keep ours.

22nd, from Formiae.

471. Now one of Caesar's supporters.
472. Cicero and his son.

145 (XIV. 14)

CICERO TO TERENTIA AND TULLIA

Minturnae, 23 January 49

From Tullius to Terentia, and from her father to Tullia, his two dear hearts, and from Marcus to his best of mothers and darling sister best greetings.

If you are well, we are well.

The decision as to what you should do is now yours, not mine only. If Caesar is going to come back to Rome in civilized fashion, you can safely stay at home for the present. But if in his madness he is going to give the city over to plunder, I am afraid that even Dolabella's protection may not be enough for us. I also have the fear that we may soon be cut off, so that when and if you want to leave you may not be able. There remains the question, on which you yourselves will be the best judges, whether other ladies in your position are staying in Rome. If they are not, you should consider whether *you* can do so without discredit. As things now stand, provided that we can hold this area, you can stay very nicely with me or at my properties in the country. There is also the danger of a food shortage in Rome in the near future. I should like you to discuss these points with Pomponius and Camillus and any others you think proper, and, in fine, to keep stout hearts. Labienus[473] has improved the situation, and Piso[474] too helps by leaving Rome and branding his son-in-law as a criminal.

My dearest hearts, write to me as often as you can to tell me

473. Caesar's principal lieutenant, who went over to Pompey on the outbreak of war.

474. L. Piso Caesoninus, Consul in 58, whose daughter Calpurnia was married to Caesar.

how you are and what is going on in Rome. Quintus senior and junior and Rufus send you their greetings.

Goodbye.

23 January, from Minturnae.

146 (XVI. 12)

CICERO TO TIRO

Capua, 27 January 49

From Tullius to his dear Tiro greetings.

My existence and that of all honest men and the entire commonwealth hangs in the balance, as you may tell from the fact that we have left our homes and the mother-city herself to plunder or burning. We have reached the point when we cannot survive unless some God or accident comes to our rescue.

From the day I arrived outside Rome all my views, words, and actions were unceasingly directed towards peace. But a strange madness was abroad. Not only the rascals but even those who pass for honest men were possessed with the lust of battle, while I cried aloud that civil war is the worst of calamities. Swept along by some spirit of folly, forgetting the name he bears and the honours he has won, Caesar seized Ariminum, Pisaurum, Ancona, and Arretium. So we abandoned Rome – whether wisely or courageously it is idle to argue.

You see our predicament. To be sure, he is offering terms: that Pompey go to Spain, that the levies already raised and the forces at our disposal be dismissed. On his side he will hand over Further Gaul to Domitius and Hither Gaul to Considius Nonianus, their appointed governors; he will come to Rome to stand for the Consulship, and no longer desires his candidature to be accepted *in absentia*; he will canvass for the period of three market days in person. We have accepted the terms, on condition that he withdraws his forces from the places he has occupied so that a meeting of the Senate may be called in Rome, free of duress, to discuss these same terms. If he complies, there is hope of peace, though not peace with honour, since the conditions are dictated; but anything is better than to be as we are. On the other hand, if he refuses to abide by his own terms, war is ready to hand. Caesar, however, will not be able to bear the brunt of it, especially having run away from his own terms. Only we must cut him off so that he cannot get to Rome, which we trust can be done. For we are raising levies on a large scale, and think he is afraid that if he advances on the capital he will lose the Gallic provinces. Both,[475] except for the Transpadanes, are thoroughly disaffected towards him, and he has six legions and large auxiliary forces to his rear in Spain, commanded by Afranius and Petreius.[476] If he does not come to his senses, it looks as though he can be crushed – let us only hope without harm to the capital. He has had a body-blow in the defection of T. Labienus, the most distinguished of his officers, who has refused to be party to his criminal enterprise and joined us. Many are said to be about to follow Labienus' example.

I am still in command of the coast, which I exercise from Formiae. I did not wish to take a more important charge, in order that my letters and exhortations to peace may carry the greater weight with Caesar. But if war is to be, I envisage myself as commanding an army and specified legions. To add to my vexations, my son-in-law Dolabella is with Caesar.

I wanted you to be aware of these facts. Mind you don't let them upset you and hinder your recovery. I have very

475. i.e. Cisalpine and Transalpine Gaul.
476. Pompey's Legates.

particularly recommended you to A. Varro, whom I know to be very fond of me and anxious to assist you, asking him to interest himself in your health and sailing arrangements and in general to take you under his wing. I am sure he will do everything. He gave his word, and spoke to me very nicely.

Since you could not be with me when I most needed your services and loyalty, mind you do not hurry or be so foolish as make the voyage either as an invalid or in winter. I shall never think you have been too long in coming if you come safe and sound. I have not yet met anyone who had seen you later than M. Volusius, from whom I received your letter. That does not surprise me. I don't suppose that my letters either are getting through to you in the depth of winter. But do your best to get well, and once you *are* well and the voyage can be made safely, make it then. My son Marcus is at Formiae, Terentia and Tullia are in Rome. Take care of your health.

27 January, from Capua.

147 (XVI. 8)

Q. CICERO TO TIRO

Rome or Campania, January 49

From Q. Cicero to Tiro greetings.

Your health makes us terribly anxious. Travellers report 'no danger, but it will take time', which is a great consolation. Still it's a huge anxiety, if you are going to be away from us for long. Missing you brings home to us how useful and pleasant it is to have you. But though I long to see you with my every thought, I do ask you in all sincerity not to venture upon so long a journey by water and land in winter unless you are thoroughly strong, and not to take ship without careful preliminary enquiries. Cold is hard enough for an invalid to avoid in town houses; how much more difficult to escape the inclemency of the weather at sea or on the road! As Euripides says, 'Cold is a tender skin's worst enemy.'[477] How much trust you put in him I don't know, but *I* look upon every verse he wrote as an affidavit. Mind you get well, if you love me, and come back to us as soon as possible hale and hearty.

Love us and goodbye. Young Quintus sends you his love.

148 (VII. 27)

CICERO TO T. FADIUS

Early 49

From M. Cicero to T. Fadius greetings.

I am surprised that you should reproach me, when you have no right to do so; but even, if you *had* the right, it would ill become you. You say you paid me many attentions when I was Consul, and that Caesar will restore you.[478] You say a great deal, but nobody gives you credit.[479] You say you stood for the Tribunate on my account. A pity you are not Tribune all the time, then you would not be looking for an intercessor![480] You say I don't dare to speak my mind – as though my answer to your impudent request smacked of timidity!

The above is just to let you see that even in the style in which

477. From one of the lost plays.

478. From exile; cf. Letter 51 (v.18).

479. Latin *credit* = (a) 'believes', and (b) 'lends money to'. Fadius had apparently asked Cicero to stand surety and, on receiving a negative answer, written again in terms which put Cicero in a rage. The harsh, offensive tone of this letter is unique in his correspondence.

480. *intercessor* = (a) 'one who (as Tribune) casts a veto', and (b) 'surety'.

you aspire to shine you are a total failure. If you had expostulated with me in civil fashion, I should willingly and easily have cleared myself. I am not ungrateful for what you did, but I *am* vexed at what you wrote. And I am much surprised that you take me, to whom my fellows owe their freedom, for no better than a slave. If the information[481] you say you gave me was false, what do I owe you? If it was true, you are in an excellent position to testify what the Roman People owes *me*.

149 (VIII. 15)

CAELIUS RUFUS TO CICERO

Central or north Italy, c. 9 March 49

From Caelius to Cicero greetings.

Have you ever seen a more egregious ass than your Cn. Pompeius? What a commotion he has created, and he such a fraud! And have you ever read or heard tell of a leader more energetic in action or more moderate in victory than our Caesar? And what about these troops of ours who have finished a war by the use of their legs, in the roughest and coldest country and the filthiest winter weather – do you think they feed on sugar-plums?[482] 'What's all this brag?' you may say. If you only knew how I am beset with anxieties, you would find this bragging of mine, which has nothing to do with *me*, quite funny. I cannot explain to you what I mean otherwise than in person, and I hope this will shortly be possible – he has decided to recall me to Rome when he has driven Pompey out of Italy.

481. Evidently in connection with Catiline's conspiracy.

482. Literally 'rounded apples', a variety mentioned by Varro, Columella, and others. Such things were served at dessert, not the kind of fare to interest tough soldiers (like Agesilaus of Sparta; see Plutarch's Life of him, 36).

That business, I imagine, is already done, unless Pompey has preferred to stand siege in Brundisium. Hang me if my mortal impatience to see you and exchange all our most intimate thoughts is the least important reason for my hurry to be back! I have a great many such thoughts, but I'm terribly afraid that when I see you the usual thing will happen – I'll forget the lot!

Be that as it may, what have I ever done to deserve the bad luck of this compulsory journey back to the Alps? The Intimilii[483] are up in arms, for no very momentous reason: Demetrius, Bellienus' slave-boy,[484] being stationed there with a detachment of troops, was bribed by the opposite party to seize and strangle one Domitius, a notable of the district and a host of Caesar's. The people rushed to arms. Now I have to trudge there through the snow with *[485] cohorts. You'll remark that the Domitii[486] are coming to grief all along the line. Well, I could wish our scion of Venus had shown as much spirit in dealing with *your* Domitius as Psecas'[487] offspring showed with this one!

Please give my regards to your son.

150 (IV. I)

CICERO TO SERVIUS SULPICIUS RUFUS

Cumae, c. 21 April 49

M. Cicero to Ser. Sulpicius greetings.

My friend C. Trebatius has written informing me that you

483. A people in Liguria.

484. The man was no doubt a freedman.

485. A number is missing.

486. An allusion to the capture of L. Domitius Ahenobarbus and his army at Corfinium. Caesar ('our scion of Venus', the supposed ancestress of the Julian clan) let him go free.

487. Typical name for a woman slave (cf. Juvenal, VI.491).

enquired of him as to my present whereabouts. He says you are sorry your health did not permit you to see me when I came to the neighbourhood of Rome,[488] and that you would like to take counsel with me at the present time, if I come nearer, on what both of us ought to do.

My dear Servius, if only we could have conferred together before the disaster (one has to use such words)! Surely we should have lent some succour to the foundering commonwealth. Even before my return I knew you to be a champion of peace both during and after your Consulship, foreseeing these calamities, as you did, long in advance. As for me, though I approved your policy and shared your views, it was no use. I arrived on the scene too late and stood alone, regarded as a newcomer to the situation, finding myself surrounded by an atmosphere of insensate bellicosity. Now that it no longer seems in our power to be of any assistance to the commonwealth, if there is any step we can take for our personal benefit (not with the object of retaining any part of our former status, but so as to mourn with what dignity we may), there is no man in the world with whom I should think it more appropriate to take counsel than yourself. You do not need to be reminded of the examples of famous men, whom we should resemble, or of the precepts of learned men, to whom you have always been devoted. Indeed I should myself have written to you earlier expressing the opinion that your attendance in the Senate, or rather the meeting of Senators,[489] would serve no useful purpose, but that I was afraid of offending one who desired me to follow your example. When the person to whom

488. Cicero had stayed outside the old city boundary so as not to lose his *imperium* and so forfeit the hoped-for Triumph.

489. Convened at the beginning of April 49, when Caesar returned to Rome. The Consuls and many other magistrates having left Italy with Pompey, Cicero considered the meetings to be irregular, even though the Senate could constitutionally be summoned by a Praetor in default of Consuls.

I refer asked me to come to the Senate, I made it plain that I should say exactly what you have said on the subject of peace and the Spanish Provinces.[490]

You see the situation. The whole world is ablaze with war, distributed into military commands. Rome lies abandoned to fire and plunder; statutes, courts, law, credit have ceased to exist. I cannot imagine anything to hope for, I can scarcely any longer imagine anything I dare to pray for. But if you in the fullness of your wisdom think it useful for us to confer, I will come nearer Rome, though I have it in mind to go still further away and hate to hear the very name of the city. I have asked Trebatius to be good enough to forward any communication you may wish to send me, and would request you to do this, or else, if you prefer, to send me some trustworthy person from your entourage. That way it may not be necessary for you to leave Rome or for me to go there. I feel well assured (in saying which I allow you no less than, perhaps presumptuously, I claim for myself) that whatever we decide by mutual consent will be universally approved.

Goodbye.

151 (IV. 2)

CICERO TO SERVIUS SULPICIUS RUFUS

Cumae, 28 or 29 April 49

M. Cicero to Ser. Sulpicius greetings.

On 28 April I received your letter at my house near Cumae. Having read it, I apprehend that Philotimus has not acted very sensibly in forwarding the letter to me instead of coming in

490. Cicero's interview with Caesar on 28 March is described in *Letters to Atticus* 187 (IX.18).

person, when he had, as you say, a message from you covering all points. I realize that your letter would have been longer if you had not expected him to carry it to its destination. However, after I read it, your lady wife Postumia and our dear Servius[491] met me. They thought you should come to Cumae, and urged me to write to you to that effect.

You ask my advice. It is such as I can more easily take myself than offer to another. What course could I venture to recommend to one so respected and wise as yourself? If we ask which is the most clearly right, the answer is obvious. If we ask which is the most expedient, it is doubtful. But if we are the men we surely should be and judge nothing to be expedient except what is right and honourable, there can be no question how we ought to act.

You judge that your situation and mine are allied, and it is assuredly true that with the best intentions we both went astray in much the same way. Both of us made concord the sole object of our policy; and as nothing could have been more to Caesar's own advantage, we expected actually to earn his gratitude by defending peace. You see the extent of our miscalculation, and the point to which the situation has deteriorated. And you perceive not only the steps which are being, and have already been, taken but the future course and issue of affairs. So one must either approve current proceedings or live amongst them, even though one disapproves. The first plan seems to me dishonourable, the second dangerous as well. I am left to conclude that the right course is to go abroad. That would seem to leave two questions, what plan of departure to adopt and what part of the world to head for. To be sure there was never a sadder business, or a more difficult problem either. Every possible decision runs into some major difficulty.

As for yourself, the advice which I venture to offer is this: if you have already settled what you think you ought to do and your plan is not of a nature to fit in with mine, you should

491. Sulpicius' son.

spare yourself this troublesome journey. If, on the other hand, you have something on which you wish to confer with me, I shall wait for you. I beg you will come as soon as you conveniently can; I gathered that both Servius and Postumia would like you to do so.[492]

Goodbye.

152 (V. 19)

CICERO TO MESCINIUS RUFUS

Cumae, c. 28 April 49

Cicero to Rufus.

Although I never doubted your warm regard for me, I see it every day more plainly. This is the fulfilment of the promise you made in one of your letters, that you would be more zealous in your attentions to me than you had been in Cilicia (not that in my judgement the solicitude you showed out there admits of any addition) in proportion as your choice in friendship could be more freely exercised. Your earlier letter gave me great pleasure. I found that you had waited for my coming, which was friendly of you, and that, when the matter turned out otherwise than you had expected, you were heartily glad of my advice. And from this last letter of yours I appreciate with satisfaction your sound principles and your sense of friendly obligation. As for the first, I perceive that you hold, as all brave and good men ought to hold, nothing expedient but what is right and honourable. As for the second, you promise that you will be my companion in whatever I decide to do; nothing can be more agreeable to me, nor, I fancy, more creditable to you.

492. The interview took place, but led to nothing; cf. *Letters to Atticus* 206 (x.14) and 207 (x.15).2.

My resolution[493] was taken long ago. If I did not write to you about it earlier, it was not that it seemed best to keep you in the dark, but because its communication at such a time has somewhat the air of a reminder of obligation, or rather of an urgent demand of the recipient to take a share in hazard and toil. But since your friendly disposition, kindness, and good-will towards me are what they are, I gladly welcome such a spirit – but with one qualification (for I am not going to put aside my feeling of delicacy in making a request): if you carry out your promise, I shall be deeply grateful, and if you do not, I shall understand. I shall take it that you could not bring yourself to deny me (hence the promise), nor yet to deny your fears (hence the withdrawal). To be sure the matter is of great moment. The right course is plain, the expedient doubtful; and yet, if we are the men we ought to be, worthy of our studies and our books, we cannot doubt that whatever is most right is also most advantageous.

So, if it is to be you and I together, you will join me immediately. If, however, you concur in my plan and destination, but cannot manage it straight away, I shall keep you fully informed. I shall count you as my friend, whatever you decide; but if you decide the way I would fain hope, as a friend indeed.

153 (VIII. 16)[494]

CAELIUS RUFUS TO CICERO

Liguria (?), c. 16 April 49

From Caelius to Cicero greetings.

Much agitated as I am by your letter,[495] in which you make it

493. To join the republicans overseas.

494. This letter is also included in the correspondence with Atticus (200 A (X.9 A)), to whom Cicero sent a copy.

495. Not extant.

plain that you have none but gloomy ideas in mind but do not say in detail what they are, and yet do not conceal the general nature of your intentions, I am writing this letter to you straight away.

I beg and implore you, Cicero, in the name of your fortunes and your children, to take no step which will jeopardize your well-being and safety. I call Gods and men and our friendship to witness that I have told you how it will be, and that it is no casual warning I give; having met Caesar and found what his disposition is likely to be once victory is won, I am telling you what I know. If you suppose that Caesar will continue his policy of letting opponents go free and offering terms, you are making a mistake. He thinks and even talks of nothing but ruthless severity. He left Rome angry with the Senate, he is thoroughly incensed by these vetoes.[496] Believe me, the time for intercession will be past.

Accordingly, if you care for yourself, for your only son, for your household, for your remaining hopes, if I and your excellent son-in-law have any influence with you, whose careers you surely do not wish to ruin by forcing us to hate or abandon the cause with which our welfare is bound up or else to harbour an undutiful wish contrary to *your* welfare ★★★. Finally, consider that any odium which may attach to your hesitancy has already been incurred. When Caesar's prospects were doubtful, you were unwilling to harm him; to go against him now, in his hour of victory, and to join a routed party which you did not choose to follow when they were fighting back, is the acme of folly. Don't be so much afraid of failing the 'right' side as to think too little about making the right choice. But if I cannot persuade you altogether, do at least wait until it is known how things go with us in Spain. You may take my word for it that these provinces will be ours as soon as Caesar arrives. What hope your friends will have with Spain lost I do not know,

496. The Tribune L. Metellus had been obstructing Caesar in the Senate.

and what sense it makes for you to join a hopeless party on my honour I cannot imagine.

What you conveyed to me without putting it into words Caesar had heard already. He scarcely said good day to me before he told me what he had heard about you. I professed ignorance, but asked him all the same to write to you in terms best adapted to induce you not to leave. He is taking me with him to Spain. Otherwise, before returning to Rome, I should have hurried to you wherever you were, and urged my plea in person, and held you back with all my might.

Think, Cicero, again and yet again before you bring utter ruin on yourself and your family, before you plunge with your eyes wide open into a situation from which you see there is no escape. If, however, you are worried by what the optimates may be saying, or if you find the arrogance and bounce of certain people too much for you, my advice is to choose some town well away from the war while these issues are deciding. It will not be long before they are settled. If you do that, I shall judge you to have acted wisely and you will not offend Caesar.

154 (II. 16)

CICERO TO CAELIUS RUFUS

Cumae, 2 or 3 May 49

From M. Cicero, Imperator, to M. Caelius, greetings.

Your letter would have given me great distress, were it not that by now the power of reason has dispelled all vexations and inveterate despair of the world has hardened my mind against new sorrows. All the same, I do not know how you came to form the suspicion of which you write from my last letter. What did that contain apart from complaint against the times we live in? And that surely weighed no less upon your mind than upon mine. I have not formed so poor an opinion of your intellectual acumen as to suppose you blind to what I see myself. But I *am* surprised that you, who ought to know me thoroughly, could have been led to believe me so improvident as to desert the rising sun for the setting and almost set, or so unstable as to throw away the hard-won favour of an eminently successful personage, to turn false to myself, and to take part in civil war, a course which I have always shunned from the very first.

Well then, what is this 'melancholy' project of mine? To withdraw, it may be, to some place of solitude. You must know how the unseemly behaviour of insolent upstarts irritates my spleen (you used to have a similar organ), even my eyes. Then there is this tiresome parade of lictors and the military title[497] by which I am addressed. If I could shed this load, I should be content with a hiding-place in Italy, however exiguous. But these laurels[498] of mine obtrude themselves upon the eyes of my ill-wishers, even on their petty little tongues. And yet I never entertained a thought of leaving without your and your associates' approval. But you know my little properties. I must stay on them, so as not to be a nuisance to my friends. The fact that I find it most convenient to stay on those which are near the coast makes some people suspect that I want to take ship. After all, perhaps I should not mind doing that if I could sail to peace. As for war, the idea is incongruous – especially to fight against one who I trust is satisfied with my conduct, on the side of one who cannot now be satisfied whatever I do.

Furthermore, you have been in a particularly good position to see into my mind ever since you visited me at Cumae. I did not conceal from you what T. Ampius had said. You saw how much I disliked the idea of abandoning the capital after I heard of it. Did I not assure you that I would put up with anything rather than leave Italy to join in civil war? Well then, what has

497. Imperator.

498. On the lictors' *fasces*, in token of victory.

occurred to change my decision? Has not everything rather tended to confirm me in my views? I hope you will believe my assurance, which I think conforms to your own opinion, that I seek nothing from this unhappy situation except to convince the world at last that peace was my chief desire and that, since all hope of peace disappeared, civil war has been my chief aversion. I do not think I shall ever wish to change this resolution. I remember how our old friend Q. Hortensius used to plume himself in this connection, because he had never taken part in a civil war. Mine will be the brighter glory in that *his* conduct was put down to lack of spirit, whereas I do not think the same can be thought of me.

Nor am I alarmed by the bogies which you, in all loyalty and affection, bring out to frighten me. In this world-wide commotion every sort of distress can be seen hanging over every head. For my part, I should have been only too glad to have saved the country from this fate at the cost of private and domestic misfortunes of my own, even those of which you warn me to beware. I am glad you care for my son. If a free constitution survives in any form, I shall leave him a sufficient inheritance in the memory of my name. If there is to be none, nothing will happen to him outside the general lot of his countrymen. You also ask me to think of my son-in-law. He is a fine young man and very dear to me. Knowing as you do my affection for him, and still more for my Tullia, can you doubt that I am most keenly concerned on his behalf? – all the more so because I was flattering myself with one ray of hope amidst the general misery, that my dear Dolabella (*our* dear Dolabella, I should say) would free himself from the difficulties in which his openhanded ways had involved him. You should inform yourself what sort of days he went through while he was in Rome, how painful to himself and how embarrassing even for me as his father-in-law.

Accordingly, I am not waiting for the outcome of this Spanish affair, which I am sure is going exactly as you say, and

I am making no shrewd calculations. If there is to be a civic community one day, there will presumably be a place in it for me. If not, I expect you yourself will come and join me in the lonely retreat in which you will hear that I have settled down. But perhaps I am just a prophet of woe and all this will have a happier ending. I remember how despairingly old men talked when I was young. Perhaps I am doing as they did and indulging the weakness of my age. I wish it may be so; but I doubt it.

I expect you have heard that Oppius' purple-bordered gown is a-weaving. Our friend Curtius has a double-dyed one in mind, but the dyer is keeping him waiting.[499] There's a pinch of seasoning, just to show that I like to laugh even when I am exasperated. I recommend you to pay attention to what I have written about Dolabella as though it were your own affair.

Now this is my final word: I shall do nothing wildly or hastily. All the same, I beg you to stand by me and my children, in whatever part of the world we may be, as our friendship and your honour shall require.

155 (XIV. 7)

CICERO TO TERENTIA

Aboard ship, Caieta, 7 June 49

From Tullius to his dear Terentia best greetings.

All the miseries and cares with which I plagued you to des-

499. The purple-bordered gown (*toga praetexta*) was worn by, among others, members of the four principal priestly colleges. One of these, the Augurs, also wore a distinctive gown, the *trabea*, of purple and yellow. Oppius and Curtius Postumus were friends of Caesar ('the dyer'), and apparently expecting priestly office as indicated.

peration (and very sorry I am for it) and Tulliola too, who is sweeter to me than my life, are dismissed and ejected. I understood what lay behind them the day after our parting. I threw up pure bile during the night, and felt an instantaneous relief as though a God had cured me. To that God you will make due acknowledgement in piety and purity after your custom.

I trust we have a very good ship – I am writing this directly after coming aboard. I shall next write many letters to our friends, commending you and our Tulliola most earnestly to their care. I should give you words of encouragement to make you both braver if I had not found you braver than any man. And after all, I trust things are now in better train. You, I hope, will be as well off as possible where you are, and I shall at last be fighting for the commonwealth alongside my peers. First and foremost, I want you to take care of your health. Second, if you agree, please use the country houses which will be farthest away from army units. The farm at Arpinum with the servants we have in town will be a good place for you if food prices go up.

Darling Marcus sends you his best love. Once again take care of yourself and goodbye.

Dispatched 7 June.

156 (VIII. 17)

CAELIUS RUFUS TO CICERO

Rome, January (?) 48

From Caelius to Cicero greetings.

To think then that I was in Spain instead of at Formiae when you left to join Pompey! If only Appius Claudius had been on our side or C. Curio on yours! It was my friendship with him that little by little landed me in this god-forsaken camp. I realize now that pique and affection robbed me of my good sense. And then, you, when I visited you that night as I was leaving for Ariminum[500] and you gave me a peace-message for Caesar, and played your fine patriotic role – you neglected the duty of a friend, you did not think of *me*! I don't say all this because I doubt our party's success. But, believe me, death is better than the spectacle of these people.

But for the fear of your party's ferocity we should have been thrown out of here long ago, for apart from a few capitalists there's not a man or a class here that is not for Pompey. Thanks to *me*, the lower classes especially, and the general public, which used to be on our side, are now on yours.[501] You ask why. No, you and your friends must wait and see. I'll make you win in spite of yourselves. Cato and company will be smiling on me yet! You folk are fast asleep. You don't seem to me to understand conditions over here as yet – where we are vulnerable, how weak we are. And I shall not be doing this in the hope of any reward, but from what is apt to be the most powerful motive with me – indignation and outrage.

What are you and your friends doing over there? Waiting for a battle? There lies Caesar's *forte*. I don't know about your army, but our fellows are desperate fighters and accustomed to take cold and hunger in their day's work.

500. On 7 January, along with Curio and the Tribunes Mark Antony and Q. Cassius. This is the only record of Caelius' interview with Cicero.

501. As Praetor Caelius had started an agitation for the relief of debtors.

157 (IX. 9)

DOLABELLA TO CICERO

Caesar's camp near Dyrrachium, May 48

From Dolabella to Cicero greetings.

If you are well I am glad. I myself am well and so is our Tullia. Terentia has been rather out of sorts, but I know for certain that she has now recovered. Otherwise all your domestic affairs are in excellent shape.

You did me an injustice if at any time you suspected that in advising you to throw in your lot with Caesar and with me, or at least to retire into private life, I was thinking of party interests rather than of yours. But now, when the scales are coming down on our side, I imagine that only one thing can possibly be thought of me, namely, that I am proffering advice to you which it would be contrary to my duty as your son-in-law to withhold. On your side, my dear Cicero, you must take what follows, whether it meets with your approval or not, in the persuasion that I have thought and written it out of the most sincere loyalty and devotion to yourself.

You see Cn. Pompeius' situation. Neither the glory of his name and past nor yet the kings and nations of whose dependence he used so often to boast can protect him. Even the door of an honourable retreat, which humble folk find open, is closed to him. Driven out of Italy, Spain lost, his veteran army taken prisoner, he is now to crown all blockaded in his camp, a humiliation which I fancy has never previously befallen a Roman general. Do therefore, as a man of sense, consider what he can have to hope or we to fear; so you will find it easiest to take the decision most expedient for you. One thing I beg of you; if he does manage to escape from his present dangerous position and takes refuge with his fleet, consult your own best interests and at long last be your own friend rather than anybody else's. You have done enough for obligation and friendship; you have done enough for your party too and the form of commonwealth of which you approved. It is time now to take our stand where the commonwealth is actually in being rather than, in following after its old image, to find ourselves in a political vacuum.

Therefore, dearest Cicero, if it turns out that Pompey is driven from this area too and forced to seek yet other regions of the earth, I hope you will retire to Athens or to any peaceful community you please. If you decide to do that, please write and tell me, so that if I possibly can I may hasten to your side. Any concessions that you need from the Commander-in-Chief to safeguard your dignity you will yourself obtain with the greatest ease from so kindly a man as Caesar; but I believe that *my* petitions will carry more than negligible weight with him.

I trust to *your* honour and kindness to see that the courier I am sending you is able to return to me and brings a letter from you.

158 (XIV. 6)

CICERO TO TERENTIA

Pompey's camp, 15 July 48

To my family, greetings.

It is not often that I have anyone to take a letter, nor have I anything I want to write about. From the last letter I received from you I learned that it was impossible to sell any property. So I shall be grateful if you and the others will consider how to meet the claims of the person[502] whose claims you know I

502. Dolabella, to whom money was due in respect of Tullia's dowry; cf. *Letters to Atticus* 212 (XI.2).2.

want met. As to what you say about our girl thanking you, I am not surprised that you should give her good reason to do that. If Pollex has not yet left, please pack him off as soon as possible. Take care of your health.

Ides of July.

159 (XIV. 12)

CICERO TO TERENTIA

Brundisium, 4 November 48

From Tullius to his dear Terentia greetings.

I hope your joy at our safe arrival in Italy may be a lasting one. But distracted as I was by my unhappiness and the cruel ill-treatment of my family, I am afraid I may have taken a road with no easy outcome. So help me as far as you can – though what you can do I cannot imagine. There is no reason for you to leave home at present. It is a long, unsafe journey, and I do not see what good you can do if you come.

Goodbye.

Dispatched 4 November from Brundisium.

160 (XIV. 19)

CICERO TO TERENTIA

Brundisium, 27 November 48

From Tullius to his dear Terentia greetings.

In my own deep distresses Tullia's illness is an agony to me. There is no need for me to write any more to you on the subject, for I am sure that you are no less gravely concerned. As for your joint wish that I should come nearer Rome, I see that I ought to do so; and I should have done so already, but have been held up by various obstacles which even now have not been cleared. However, I am expecting a letter from Pomponius, and shall be grateful if you will see that it is forwarded as quickly as possible.

Take care of your health.

161 (XIV. 9)

CICERO TO TERENTIA

Brundisium, 17 (?) December 48

Tullius to his dear Terentia best greetings.

In addition to my other distresses I am now worried about Dolabella's and Tullia's illnesses. In general, I just don't know what plans to make or what to do about anything. I hope you will take care of your own health and Tullia's.

Goodbye.

162 (XIV. 17)

CICERO TO TERENTIA

Brundisium, 23 (?) December 48

From Tullius to his dear Terentia greetings.

I hope you are well, as I am.

I should write to you at greater length and more often if I had anything to say. As it is, you see how matters stand. Of my own sorry state Lepta and Trebatius will tell you. Be sure to take care of your health and Tullia's.

Goodbye.

163 (XIV. 16)

CICERO TO TERENTIA

Brundisium (?), 4 January 47 (?)

From Tullius to his dear Terentia greetings.

I hope you are well, as I am.

In my present circumstances I have no reason to expect anything in the way of a letter from you or to write to you myself. And yet somehow I do expect letters from home and write when I have a bearer.

Volumnia[503] ought to have been more ready to oblige you than she was; and what she did do might have been done with more care and circumspection. However, we have more important matters to occupy and vex us. They are overwhelming me, as was the purpose of those who forced me away from my original intention.

Take care of yourself.

4 January.

164 (XIV. 8)

CICERO TO TERENTIA

2 June 47

From Tullius to his dear Terentia greetings.

I hope you are well, as I am.

I want you to take the greatest care of your health, for I have been told both by letter and word of mouth that you had a sudden attack of fever. Thank you for informing me so

503. Probably Volumnia Cytheris (see Glossary of Persons).

promptly about Caesar's letter.[504] In future too, please let me know if there is anything needful or any new development. Take care of yourself.

Goodbye.

Dispatched 2 June.

165 (XIV. 21)

CICERO TO TERENTIA

Brundisium, June (early) 47

From Tullius to his dear Terentia greetings.

I hope you are well, as I am.

Do your best to regain your health. Please make all necessary provisions and arrangements as circumstances require and write to me as often as possible on all points.

Goodbye.

166 (XIV. 11)

CICERO TO TERENTIA

Brundisium, 14 June 47

From Tullius to his dear Terentia greetings.

I hope you are well, as I am.

Tullia joined me on 12 June. She is so wonderfully brave and kind that it gives me even greater pain to think that through my carelessness she is placed far otherwise than befitted a girl of her station and so good a daughter.

504. Cf. *Letters to Atticus* 227 (XI.16).1.

I am thinking of sending Marcus to Caesar, and Cn. Sallustius with him. I shall send you word when he leaves. Take good care of your health.

Goodbye.

14 June.

167 (XIV. 15)

CICERO TO TERENTIA

Brundisium, 19 June 47

Tullius to Terentia greetings.

I hope you are well.

As I wrote to you earlier, I had decided to send Marcus to Caesar, but changed my mind because there are no reports of his coming home. On other matters there is nothing new, but Sicca will tell you what I wish and think expedient at this time. I still have Tullia with me. Take good care of your health.

Goodbye.

19 June.

168 (XIV. 10)

CICERO TO TERENTIA

Brundisium, 9 July 47

From Tullius to his dear Terentia greetings.

I wrote to Pomponius, later than I ought, telling him what I thought should be done.[505] When you have had a talk with

505. Concerning Tullia's divorce from Dolabella.

him, you will understand my wishes. There is no need to write more explicitly, since I have written to him. Please send me a letter as soon as possible on this and other matters. Take good care of your health.

Goodbye.

9 July.

169 (XIV. 13)

CICERO TO TERENTIA

Brundisium, 10 July 47

From Tullius to his dear Terentia greetings.

As regards what I wrote in my last letter about sending notice of divorce, I don't know how powerful he is at the present time[506] nor how excited the state of popular feeling. If he is likely to be a formidable enemy, don't do anything – perhaps he will take the initiative even so. You must judge of the whole position and choose whatever you think the least of evils in this wretched situation.

Goodbye.

10 July.

170 (XIV. 24)

CICERO TO TERENTIA

Brundisium, 11 August 47

From Tullius to his dear Terentia greetings.

I hope you are well, as I am.

506. Dolabella was Tribune in 47.

I have nothing definite yet either about Caesar's arrival or the letter which Philotimus is said to have.[507] If anything definite comes along, I shall let you know at once. Take good care of your health.

Goodbye.

11 August.

171 (XIV. 23)

CICERO TO TERENTIA

Brundisium, 12 August 47

From Tullius to his dear Terentia greetings.

I hope you are well, as I am.

I have at last received a letter from Caesar, quite a handsome one. He is said to be arriving in person sooner than was expected. I shall let you know when I have decided whether to go to meet him or to wait for him here. Please send the couriers back as soon as possible. Take good care of your health.

Goodbye.

Dispatched 12 August.

172 (XIV. 22)

CICERO TO TERENTIA

Brundisium, 1 September 47

From Tullius to his dear Terentia greetings.

I hope you are well, as I am.

507. Cf. *Letters to Atticus* 232 (XI.23).2.

I am expecting our couriers any day. When they arrive, perhaps I shall know better what to do, and I shall at once inform you. Take good care of your health.

Goodbye.

Kalends of September.

173 (XIV. 20)

CICERO TO TERENTIA

Near Venusia, 1 October 47

From Tullius to his dear Terentia greetings.

I think I shall get to Tusculum either on the Nones or on the following day. Kindly see that everything there is ready. I may have a number of people with me, and shall probably make a fairly long stay there. If there is no tub in the bathroom, get one put in; likewise whatever else is necessary for health and subsistence.

Goodbye.

Kalends of October, from the district of Venusia.

174 (XV. 15)

CICERO TO CASSIUS

Brundisium, August 47

M. Cicero to C. Cassius greetings.

Both of us, hoping for peace and hating civil bloodshed, decided to hold aloof from persistence in an unnecessary war.

But as I am regarded as having taken the lead in that course, perhaps my feeling towards you in this context should hold more of responsibility than of expectation. And yet I often recall how in talking familiarly to each other, you to me no less than I to you, we were both led to the persuasion that our verdict, if not the entire issue, might properly be decided by the result of a single battle. Nor has anyone ever fairly blamed us for taking this view, excepting those who think the commonwealth had better be wiped out altogether than survive in an enfeebled and attenuated form. For my part I saw no hope (obviously) from its destruction, but great hope from its remnants.

The sequel, however, was unexpected – the wonder is that such events could happen rather than that we did not see them coming and, being but human, could not divine them. For my part, I confess my forecast was that, once the fated and fatal battle, so to speak, had been fought, the victors would turn their attention to the general survival and the vanquished to their own. At the same time I thought that both the one and the other depended upon swift action by the victorious leader. Had that been forthcoming, Africa would have experienced the clemency which Asia came to know, as did Achaia also, whose ambassador and intercessor was, I believe, none other than yourself. But the crucial moments were lost, the moments which matter most, especially in civil warfare. A year intervened, leading some to hope for victory and others to care nothing even for defeat. The blame for all these calamities lies at fortune's door. Who could have expected that the main hostilities would have been so long held up by the fighting at Alexandria, or that this what's-his-name, Pharnaces, would menace Asia so formidably?

We thought alike, but we fared differently. *You* made for a quarter[508] where you would be present at the making of decisions and able to foresee events to come, the best comfort for

508. Cassius had joined Caesar in the East.

an anxious mind. *I* made haste to meet Caesar in Italy (so we thought), on his way home after sparing many valuable lives, and to urge him to peace – spurring a willing horse, as they say. The consequence was that I have been, and still am, at a vast distance away from him. I am living amidst the groans of Italy and the pitiful plaints of Rome. Perhaps I and you and every man, each according to his powers, might have done something to help, if authoritative backing had been available.

So I would ask you, in virtue of your unfailing kindliness toward me, to write to me and tell me what you see and feel, what you think I have to expect and ought to do. A letter from you will mean a great deal to me. I only wish I had followed the advice in that first letter of yours from Luceria.[509] I should have kept my standing and avoided all unpleasantness.

175 (IX. 1)

CICERO TO VARRO

Rome, 47 (late) or 46 (early)

From Cicero to M. Varro greetings.

The letter which you sent to Atticus and which he read to me informed me of your doings and whereabouts, but as to when we are to see you, I could not so much as make a guess from that letter. However, I am coming to hope that your advent is not far away.[510] I wish I may find some comfort in it, though our afflictions are so many and so grievous that nobody but an arrant fool ought to hope for any relief. And yet either you may

509. The letter here referred to must have advised Cicero to stay out of the war. It was probably written in February 49, just before the fall of Corfinium. Pompey set up his headquarters at Luceria about 25 January.

510. Varro may not yet have returned to Italy.

be able to help me or perhaps I may in some way be able to help you. For I should tell you that since my return I have restored my relations with my old friends, that is to say my books. Not that I had renounced their companionship because I was annoyed with them – it was because they gave me a sense of shame. I felt that in casting myself into a turmoil of events with altogether untrustworthy associates I had failed in obedience to their precepts. They forgive me. They call me back to the old intercourse and tell me that you in staying faithful to it were wiser than I. And so I have made my peace with them and we are together again. That is why I think I may properly hope that once I see you I shall find both present and impending troubles easy to bear.

So whatever rendezvous you favour, be it Tusculum or Cumae,[511] or my house or yours, or (what would be my last choice) Rome, you may be sure I shall make it appear the most convenient for both of us, only provided we are together.

176 (IX. 3)

CICERO TO VARRO

Rome, c. 18 April 46

From Cicero to Varro.

Although I have nothing to write about, I could not let Caninius[512] go to you without giving him something. So what *should* I write? What I think you want to read, that I shall be coming to visit you soon. But pray ask yourself whether it is quite proper for us to be down there[513] at such a time of national convulsion. We shall be giving a chance for gossip to those who

511. Both Cicero and Varro had villas in both areas.
512. No doubt L. Caninius Gallus.
513. On the coast of Campania.

don't know that, wherever we are, our style and way of living remain the same. And yet, what does it matter? They will gossip about us anyway. When all mankind is wallowing in every sort of crime and outrage, I hardly suppose we need concern ourselves overmuch about possible aspersions on our idleness, whether by ourselves or in one another's company. Yes, I shall follow you[514] and take no notice of these ignorant barbarians. However melancholy the times, and melancholy indeed they are, our pursuits seem somehow to yield more generous rewards now than they did in days gone by. Perhaps it is because we have no other means of relief; or perhaps the severity of the disease puts us in need of the medicine, and its strength, which we did not perceive when we were well, is now manifest.

But why am I now sending such reflections to *you*, who have them home-grown – an owl to Athens?[515] No reason, to be sure, except for you to write a line in return, and to expect me. So please do.

177 (IX. 2)

CICERO TO VARRO

Rome, c. 22 April 46

From Cicero to Varro.

Your (and our) friend Caninius called upon me late one evening and told me that he would be leaving betimes next day to join you; so I said I would give him something to carry, and asked him if he would kindly call for it in the morning. I wrote a letter[516] that night; but he did not come back after all

514. Down to Cumae.
515. Like 'coals to Newcastle'.
516. Letter 176 (IX.3).

and I assumed he had forgotten. I should have sent you the letter all the same by messengers of my own, had I not heard from Caninius that you would be leaving Tusculum[517] early the following day. Well, a few days later who should arrive at my house early in the morning out of the blue, when I was least expecting him, but Caninius? He said he was just off to join you. My letter was by now *passée*, particularly as such important news had come in since I wrote it; but still I did not want my midnight oil to be wasted, and so I gave it to Caninius as it stood. But I also said certain things to him, knowing him to be a man of culture and a very warm friend of yours, which I expect he has passed on to you.

To you I have the same advice to offer as to myself. Let us avoid men's eyes, even if we cannot easily escape their tongues. The jubilant victors[518] regard us as among the defeated, whereas those who are sorry for the defeat of our friends feel aggrieved that we are still among the living. Perhaps you will wonder why, with this going on in Rome, I am not elsewhere like you. Well, and have you yourself, a shrewder man than I or any other, foreseen everything, has *nothing* turned out contrary to your expectations? I can hardly believe that. Whose eyes are so preternaturally sharp[519] as to avoid every obstacle, every pitfall, in darkness such as this? In point of fact it did cross my mind long ago that it would be nice to get away somewhere, so as not to see or hear what was being done and said in Rome. But I made difficulties for myself. I thought that whoever came my way would suspect or, even if he did not suspect, would say, as might suit his individual purpose, 'Aha! He took fright, that's why he ran away; or else he's up to something, has a boat all ready.' Even the most charitable (and per-

517. For Cumae. In fact, Varro's departure was postponed.

518. The news of Caesar's victory over the republicans at Thapsus reached Rome about 20 April.

519. Literally 'who is such a Lynceus?' The Argonaut Lynceus could see in the dark.

haps best acquainted with the kind of man I am) would have thought that I was leaving because I could not stand the sight of certain persons. With all this in mind I stay on in Rome. And after all, long custom has imperceptibly anaesthetized my spleen.

So my conduct is explained. Now my counsel to *you* is to lie low for the present where you are,[520] while these rejoicings are at boiling-point and also until we hear just how the affair has been settled – for settled I believe it is. A great deal will depend on the victor's disposition and the way things turned out. I have my own guess to be sure, but am waiting for news.

No, I don't think you ought to go to Baiae,[521] unless rumour itself grows hoarse. Even when we go away from here, it will be more seemly to appear to have chosen that part of the world for weeping rather than for bathing. But you will judge better than I. Only let us be firm on one point – to live together in our literary studies. We used to go to them only for pleasure, now we go for salvation. If anybody cares to call us in as architects or even as workmen to help build a commonwealth, we shall not say no, rather we shall hasten cheerfully to the task. If our services are not required, we must still read and write 'Republics'. Like the learned men of old, we must serve the state in our libraries, if we cannot in Senate-House and Forum, and pursue our researches into custom and law.[522]

Such are my sentiments. You will oblige me greatly if you will write and tell me what *you* are going to do and what you think best.

520. At Tusculum.

521. The fashionable resort (as distinct from Varro's own villa at Cumae).

522. Cicero may have resumed work on his unfinished treatise *On Laws*.

178 (IX. 7)

CICERO TO VARRO

Rome, May (late) 46

Cicero to Varro.

I was at dinner with Seius when a letter from you was delivered to each of us. Yes, I think it's seasonable now.[523] As for the difficulties I put up previously, I'll confess my craftiness. I wanted to have you near by in case some chance of good turned up. 'Two heads',[524] you know. Now, since all is settled, we must hesitate no longer – full speed ahead.[525] When I heard about L. Caesar junior,[526] I said to myself 'What can I, his father, look for?'[527] So I go dining every night with our present rulers. What am I to do? One must go with the times.

But joking aside (especially as we have nothing to laugh about), 'Africa, grim land's a-tremble in terrific tumult tossed.'[528] There is nothing 'negative'[529] that I don't apprehend.

523. To go to Campania.

524. *Iliad* x.224: 'When two go together, one notices before the other.'

525. Literally 'with horse and foot', i.e. without any holding back. 'We must make friends with the winning party' is implied.

526. i.e. about his death in Africa. Cicero, perhaps mistakenly, implies that this took place by Caesar's orders.

527. i.e. 'what have *I* got to expect?' Cicero recalls this scrap of Terence's *Girl from Andros* (112) (probably without remembering its dramatic context, which is foreign to his point) because 'father' suggests an old man as compared to a young one.

528. From Ennius' *Annals*.

529. A Greek term from Stoic philosophy, which recognized virtue as the only good but allowed that other things (e.g. health, wealth, and their opposites) were on one side or other of complete indifference. Varro was an expert on Greek philosophy.

In answer to your questions as to date, route, and destination, we know nothing yet. Even as to Baiae,[530] some think he may come by way of Sardinia. That is one of his properties that he has not yet inspected. It's the worst he owns, but he doesn't despise it. I myself, to be sure, think he's more likely to travel by way of Sicily. But we shall soon know. Dolabella is coming, and I expect he will be our schoolmaster. 'The teacher's oft inferior to the taught.'[531] However, if I know what you have decided, I shall try to accommodate my plans to yours. So I expect to hear from you.

179 (IX. 5)

CICERO TO VARRO

Rome, May (late) 46

From Cicero to Varro.

The Nones? Yes, that will be very seasonable, I think, literally as well as politically speaking.[532] So I approve your date and shall keep it in view myself. As for our line of conduct,[533] we ought not in my opinion to regret it, even if those who took a different line were not regretting *that*. It was not

530. There seems to have been a rumour that Caesar would land at Baiae. He did in fact come by way of Sardinia and landed at Ostia.

531. A Greek line from an unknown dramatic source. Cicero had given Dolabella lessons in rhetoric (cf. Letter 192 (VII.33)).

532. Literally 'not only because of the circumstances (*tempus*) of the commonwealth but because of the time (*tempus*) of year'. 5 June by the calendar in 46 represented 7 April, a pleasant time for a visit to the Bay of Naples. The reference to politics means, I think, that it would be wise to take the proposed holiday before Caesar's return.

533. In supporting Pompey in the first place and in withdrawing from the war after Pharsalia.

hope, but duty, whose call we followed; and it was not duty, but despair, that we abandoned. We had a tenderer conscience than those who never stirred from home and a sounder sense of reality than those who, after the loss of our resources, did not return there. But what I find hardest to stomach is the censure of do-nothings. However things stand, I have more respect for the men who perished in the war than time for persons who cannot forgive us for being alive.

If I have leisure for a visit to Tusculum before the Nones, I shall see you there. If not, I shall follow you to Cumae, and let you know in advance, so that the bath be ready.

180 (IX. 4)

CICERO TO VARRO

Tusculum, end of May or beginning of June 46

From Cicero to Varro.

'Concerning things possible', let me tell you that I pronounce with Diodorus.[534] So if you are coming, you may be sure that it is necessary for you to come; if you are not coming, it is impossible for you to come. Now ask yourself which pronouncement you prefer, Chrysippus' or this – which our friend Diodotus used to be unable to stomach. But we will talk of these matters as well as others when we have time to spare. This too is possible according to Chrysippus.

Thank you for what you have done about *[535] – I had asked

534. Fourth-century philosopher. His so-called 'Master Argument' sought to prove that what is or will be actual is possible, and that what is not going to be actual is not possible. It was contraverted by the great third-century Stoic Chrysippus, who defined the possible as that which was capable of being actual (if circumstances did not prevent it).

535. 'Coctius' in the manuscripts is not attested as a Roman name. Perhaps it should be 'Cottius'.

Atticus too to attend to that matter. If you don't come to me I shall run over to you. If you have a kitchen garden in your library we shall lack for nothing.[536]

181 (IX. 6)

CICERO TO VARRO

Rome, June (latter half) 46

From Cicero to Varro.

Our friend Caninius told me from you to write if there should be anything which I thought you ought to know. Well, the arrival is awaited – that is no news to you. But when he wrote, as I suppose, that he would be coming to his place at Alsium,[537] his friends wrote to dissuade him, telling him that there were many people thereabouts whose presence would be annoying to him, and many whom *his* presence would annoy; Ostia, in their opinion, would make a more convenient landing-place. I do not myself see what odds it makes, but Hirtius told me that both he and Balbus and Oppius wrote advising him in this sense – persons whom I know to be fond of you.

I wanted you to hear of this so you should know where to arrange to stay, or rather so you should make arrangements in both localities, since what *he* will do is uncertain. At the same time I have shown off to you the familiar footing on which I stand with these gentry, and how I am taken into their counsels. I see no reason why I should object to that. It is one thing to put up with what has to be put up with, another to approve what ought to be disapproved – though for my part I don't any

536. Having food for both mind and body. Even so a rather obscure remark.

537. Or 'the district of Alsium'.

longer know what to disapprove of, except the beginnings of it all, which were a matter of volition. I saw (you were away) that our friends were desirous of war, whereas the person we are expecting was not so much desirous as unafraid of it. That then came within the scope of design, all else followed inevitably. And victory had to fall to one side or the other.

I know that your heart was always as heavy as mine. Not only did we foresee the destruction of one of the two armies and its leader, a vast disaster, but we realized that victory in civil war is the worst of all calamities. I dreaded the prospect, even if victory should fall to those we had joined. They were making savage threats against the do-nothings, and your sentiments and my words were alike abhorrent to them. As for the present time, if our friends had gained the mastery, they would have used it very immoderately. They were infuriated with us. One might have supposed that we had taken some resolution for our own safety which we had not advised them to take for theirs, or that it was to the advantage of the state that they should go to brute beasts[538] for help rather than die outright or live in hope – admittedly no very bright hope, but still hope.

We live, it may be said, in a state that has been turned upside down. Undeniably true. But that bears hard on persons who have not prepared resources for themselves against all life's contingencies. Here is the point to which the flow of these remarks, more prolix than I wished, has been tending. I have always thought you a great man and I think you so now, because in this stormy weather you almost alone are safe in harbour. You reap the most precious fruits of learning, devoting your thoughts and energies to pursuits which yield a profit and a delight far transcending the exploits and pleasures of these worldlings. These days you are now spending down at Tusculum are worth a lifetime by my reckoning. Gladly would I leave all earthly wealth and power to others, and take in

538. The elephants of King Juba of Numidia, an ally of the republicans.

exchange a licence to live thus, free from interruption by any outside force. I am following your example as best I can, and most gladly find repose in literary studies. Surely nobody would begrudge us this. Our country will not or cannot use our services, so we return to a mode of life which many philosophers (mistakenly perhaps, but many) have considered actually to be preferred to the political. The state now grants its permission. Are we not then at liberty to give full rein to pursuits which in the judgement of great thinkers carry a sort of exemption from public employment?

However, I am going beyond Caninius' commission. *He* asked me to write if anything came to my knowledge of which you were unaware; and here am I telling you what you know better than I, your informant. So I shall do what I was asked, and see that you are not left in ignorance of any items relevant to the present situation that may come my way.

182 (V. 21)

CICERO TO MESCINIUS RUFUS

Rome, mid April 46

From M. Cicero to L. Mescinius greetings.

Many thanks for your letter. It told me what I thought even before I read it, that you have a great desire to see me. That I welcome, but at the same time I don't allow you any priority in such a feeling. To be with you is my ardent wish, by all my hopes I swear it. Even when there was a greater plenty of good men and good citizens and of pleasant and friendly company, I liked nobody's society better than yours and few people's so well. But now, when some are dead, others away, others changed towards me, upon my soul I would rather spend a day with you than this whole period with most of those whose company I keep perforce. Don't imagine that solitude is not more agreeable to me (though I am not allowed it) than the talk of my usual visitors, one or two at most excepted.

And so I take refuge, as I would advise you to do, in my literary dabbling, and also in my political conscience. I am one, as you are in an excellent position to judge, that never put his own interest before his countrymen's. Had a personage[539] for whom you never much cared (you cared for *me*) not been jealous of me, it would be well with him and with all honest men today. I am one that wished no man's violence to prevail over public tranquillity and honour; but when I found the armed might which I had always dreaded more potent than the union of honest men of which I had myself been the architect, I was for peace, however unfair the terms, rather than a trial of force against a stronger adversary. But of this and much besides we shall soon be able to talk together.

The only thing that keeps me in Rome, however, is the expectation of events in Africa, where a crisis seems to be imminent. I feel it is of some moment to me (though what actual difference it makes I hardly see, but even so) not to be far away from my friends' advice, whatever news comes in from that quarter. The situation is now such that, although there may be a good deal to choose between the causes of the combatants, I think the victory of either will amount to pretty much the same.

But the fact is that my spirit, which was perhaps inclined to frailty when the issue was in doubt, has been much stronger in despair. Your earlier letter strengthened it still further, for it showed how bravely you bore your ill-usage;[540] and it did me good to see how your fine culture, and especially your literary work, stood you in good stead. For, to tell the truth, I thought you a trifle too easily hurt, like nearly all of us who have lived

539. Pompey.

540. Though back in Italy, Mescinius had been in some way penalized by Caesar, perhaps forbidden to return to Rome.

an independent life in a happy community under a free constitution. But as we observed moderation in the good days gone by, so we ought to take our present adversity, or rather utter ruin, with fortitude. In the midst of disaster we gain one advantage at least: death, which even in the days of our happiness it was incumbent on us to despise on the ground that it would be devoid of consciousness, we ought in our present plight not merely to despise but positively to pray for.

If you care for me, enjoy your present leisure, and persuade yourself that no matter for fear or trembling can befall a man apart from fault and wrongdoing; and of this you are free, and always will be. If I feel I can safely do so, I shall join you shortly, and if anything occurs to alter my intention, I shall let you know immediately. Eager to see me as I should like you to be, in your poor state of health you must not stir from where you are without first writing to me and asking what I wish you to do. I hope you will continue to care for me, and pay proper regard to your health and peace of mind.

183 (VII. 3)

CICERO TO M. MARIUS

Rome, mid April 46

From M. Cicero to M. Marius greetings.

Considering, as I very often do, the general miseries in which we have been living for so many years and, as I see it, shall continue to live, I am apt to call to mind the last time we were together. I remember the very day – 12 May in the Consulship of Lentulus and Marcellus.[541] I had come down to my place near Pompeii that evening, and found you there to meet me in

541. i.e. 49; see *Letters to Atticus* 208 (x.16).4.

a troubled state of mind – troubled by the thought of my duty, and my danger too. You were afraid that if I stayed in Italy I should be failing in my duty, whereas if I set off for the war you were disturbed by the risk I should run. No doubt you saw on that occasion that I too was in such a state of mental turmoil that I could not work out what was best to do. However, I preferred to yield to the claims of honour and reputation than to calculate for my own safety.

I came to regret my action, not so much on account of my personal hazard as of the many deplorable aspects of the situation which confronted me on arrival. To begin with, the forces fell short both in numbers and in fighting spirit. Secondly, apart from the Commander-in-Chief and a few besides, all (I am referring to the principal figures) showed their greed for plunder in the war itself, and talked in so bloodthirsty a style that I shuddered at the prospect of *victory*. Moreover, those of the highest rank were up to their ears in debt. In a phrase, nothing good except the cause. With these things before my eyes, I started by recommending peace, of which I had always been an advocate. When Pompey showed himself strongly averse to that policy, I set myself to recommend delaying tactics. At times he tended to favour this course and seemed likely to make it his policy. Perhaps he would have done so, had not the result of a particular engagement[542] given him confidence in his troops. From then on that great man ceased to be a general. With his raw medley of an army he fought a pitched battle against the hardiest soldiers in the world, and was defeated. Even his camp was lost. He fled shamefully, alone.

For me that was the end of the war. Our full strength had proved no match for the enemy. I saw no prospect of getting the upper hand after a shattering reverse. I withdrew from the conflict. What were the choices? To die on the battlefield, or to fall into some trap, or to come into the hands of the victor, or

542. At Dyrrachium in July 48.

to take refuge with Juba, or to select a place of virtual exile, or suicide. Nothing else surely, if one would not, or dared not, trust oneself to the victor. Of all the aforesaid evils exile is as tolerable as any – especially an innocent exile, with no stain of discredit, and (let me add) exile from a country that holds nothing one can look upon without distress.

For my part, I preferred to be with my own people, and my own belongings too – if anything belongs to anybody nowadays. All that has happened I foretold. I came home, not that the life there offered was particularly attractive, but still, if there was to be some shape or form of free constitution, I wanted to feel as though I was living in my country; and if not, it would serve as a place of exile. I saw no reason to take my life, though many reasons to pray for its ending. It's an old saying that when a man is no longer what he was he has nothing to live for. However, there's a great comfort in having nothing with which to reproach oneself; and I have two further supports, conversance with noble arts and the glory of great achievements. Of the first I shall never be deprived in life, of the second not even in death.

In writing all this I have not spared words. I have thus imposed upon you because I know how deeply you care for me and for the commonwealth. I wanted you to be acquainted with my whole mind and purpose, to know in the first place that I never wished any man to have more power than the state entire; but when by the fault of somebody or other a single person became too strong to resist, I was for peace. With the loss of the army and of the leader upon whom all our hopes were pinned I wanted an end to the war for all concerned; unable to bring that to pass, I made an end for myself individually. At present, if this is a body politic, I am a citizen; if it is not, I am an exile in no worse a place than if I had betaken myself to Rhodes or Mytilene.

I would rather have discussed all this with you in person; but since time was dragging on, I thought it desirable to do so by letter, in order to give you something to say if you should happen to fall in with people who speak ill of me. There are those who hold it an offence in me to be alive, even though my destruction would have brought no advantage to the commonwealth. I am well aware that they think the death-roll not long enough. Had those upon it listened to me, they would at least be living honourably, however harsh the terms of peace, proved weaker in military strength but not in the justice of their cause.

So here you have a wordier letter, it may be, than you would have wished. I shall believe you think so, unless you send me a longer one in return. I have certain matters I want to clear up; that done, I hope I shall see you shortly.

184 (XVI. 19)

CICERO TO TIRO

Tusculum, July (?) 46

From Tullius to his dear Tiro greetings.

I am looking forward to a letter from you on many topics, but to you in person even more. Make Demetrius my friend, and do any other good work you can. I won't urge you about Aufidius' debt, for I know you have it in mind. But get a settlement. If you are taking time on that account, I accept your excuse; but if that is not detaining you, hurry. I am impatiently looking forward to a letter.

Goodbye.

185 (XVI. 22)

CICERO TO TIRO

Tusculum, July (?) 46

From Tullius to his dear Tiro greetings.

From your letter I trust that you are better, certainly I very much hope so. Mind you consider that in every way, and don't take it into your head that you are acting against my wishes in not being with me. You *are* with me if you are looking after yourself. So I want you to care for your health rather than for my eyes and ears. Of course I enjoy hearing and seeing you, but that will be a much greater pleasure if you are fit and well.

I am idling here because I don't write anything myself, though I am reading with great gusto. If the copyists up there can't make out my handwriting, you will put them right. There *is* a rather difficult inset which I don't find easy to read myself, the story about Cato as a four-year-old.[543] See about the dining-room, as you are doing. Tertia will be there, provided that Publilius[544] is not invited.

That fellow Demetrius was never a Phalereus[545] but now he is an absolute Bellienus![546] So I appoint you my deputy – you show him the courtesies. 'Though to be sure . . .,' 'All the same

543. Cicero had recently written a 'Eulogy of Cato' (now lost). The story of the four-year-old Cato's defiance of Poppaedius the Marsian is told by Valerius Maximus (III.I.2) and Plutarch in his Life (2).

544. The manuscripts have 'Publius' (a common mistake). Why (Junia) Tertia objected to Publilius is unknown.

545. i.e. a man of polish and wit, qualities for which Demetrius of Phalerum was celebrated.

546. i.e. an assassin; cf. Letter 149 (VIII.15). He could bore his company to death.

. . .,' 'As to that . . .' – you know how it goes on. Still, if you have any talk with him, please write and tell me, so that I get a theme for a letter and as long as possible a letter of yours to read.

Look after your health, my dear Tiro. You can do nothing to please me more.

Goodbye.

186 (XVI. 17)

CICERO TO TIRO

Tusculum, July (?) 46

From Tullius to Tiro greetings.

I see your game! You want your letters too put into rolls. But just a moment, you yardstick of my literary style, where did you come by so bizarre a phrase as 'faithfully[547] studying my health'? What is 'faithfully' doing in such a context? The home territory of the word is the performance of a duty, but it makes many excursions into other fields. For example, it can be applied to acquired knowledge or a house or a vocation or a piece of land within the bounds of decent metaphor as approved by Theophrastus.[548] But of this when we are together.

I have had a visit from Demetrius, from whose company on the road I disengaged myself rather neatly. Of course you could not have seen him. He will be in Rome tomorrow, so see him you will. For my part, I intend leaving here early the day after.

Your health makes me very anxious, but study it and leave

547. *fideliter.* Tiro no doubt meant 'conscientiously'. Cicero seems to have taken him to mean that he was giving his health *its* due.

548. He had discussed metaphor in his treatise *On Speech.*

nothing undone. *Then* you may feel that you are with me and that I am more than satisfied.

Thank you for helping Cuspius, whose hearty well-wisher I am.

Goodbye.

187 (V. 16)

CICERO TO TITIUS[549]

Rome (?), late summer or autumn 46 (?)

From M. Cicero to Titius greetings.

Of all men I am the least suited to console you, since I am so grieved by your distress that I stand in need of consolation myself. But seeing that my grief falls shorter than yours of the ultimate bitterness of sorrow, I have concluded that our friendship and my anxiety for your welfare make it wrong to be silent so long in your heavy affliction, and require me to proffer a measure of comfort, which may alleviate, if it cannot heal, your pain.

There is a very well-worn form of consolation which we should always have on our lips and in our minds. We must remember that we are but men, the law of whose birth requires that our lives be a target for all the darts of fortune. We must not rebel against the condition to which we are born. We must bear less hard those misfortunes which we cannot by any prudence avoid. We must recall the experiences of our fellows, and reflect that nothing new has befallen us. But more efficacious perhaps than these and other forms of consolation em-

549. Not certainly identifiable with any of the other Titii who crop up at this period. He had apparently lost two or more sons in an epidemic; cf. the reference in *Letters to Atticus* 247 (XII.10).

ployed by the wisest of mankind and consigned to memory in their writings should be the actual state of our community in these chaotic and desperate times. In the world of today those who have never raised children are most to be envied, and those who have lost them less to be commiserated than if they had been thus bereaved in a well-ordered commonwealth, or indeed in any commonwealth properly so called.

If it is the sense of your own loss that grieves you, if it is your own fate you lament, then I fear your pain cannot easily exhaust itself altogether. On the other hand, if the sting lies in your grief for the sad lot of the departed, a sentiment more closely in keeping with affection, it is another matter. I will not dwell on the arguments I have often heard and read in books to the effect that there is no evil in death, because if any consciousness remains thereafter, we should not think of it as death but as immortality, whereas if all consciousness disappears, misery unfelt should not be deemed misery at all; but this I can declare without hesitation, that to my mind at any rate whoever has left behind him the present political turmoil, and all that is in preparation, looming ahead of us, has been cheated of *nothing*. There is no place any more for honour, uprightness, manliness, honest pursuits and liberal accomplishments; none even for personal independence and existence as a citizen. I give you my word that whenever in this terrible year of pestilence I have heard of the death of a young man or a boy, I have considered him as snatched by the Immortal Gods from these calamities and from a life of which all the terms were in his disfavour.

If only you can be divested of the idea that some evil has befallen those dear to you, that in itself will very sensibly diminish the sum of your sorrow. There will then remain the simple burden of your own grief, in which *they* will have no part; it will pertain to you individually. Now to bear the troubles chance has brought upon you more hardly than is fitting, when they involve no unhappiness or evil for those you loved, is really unworthy of the responsibility and sound sense which you have shown since your childhood days. The character you have always presented in public and in private requires you to maintain your dignity and faithfully to follow the pattern you have set. For it is our duty by reason and wisdom to anticipate the effects of time, which by its mere efflux cancels our deepest sorrows. After all, there was never a woman bereaved of children so frail of spirit that she did not in the end set a term to her mourning. Surely then *we* should apply in advance by using our reason what the passing of the days will bring; we ought not to wait for time to produce the medicine which our intelligence can supply to hand.

If this letter has done you good, I feel that I have achieved something worth praying for. But perhaps it has had but little effect, in which case I have at least discharged the duty of a sincere friend and well-wisher. That I have ever been such to you I hope you believe, and are confident that I shall so remain.

188 (IX. 21)

CICERO TO PAPIRIUS PAETUS

Date uncertain

From Cicero to Paetus greetings.

Really? You think you are out of your mind to be imitating my 'verbal thunderbolts'?[550] You would be if you could not make a success of it. Since in fact you actually go one better, you should make fun of me rather than yourself. So you don't

550. The context can only be guessed. Perhaps Paetus had been sent a copy of a Ciceronian speech and tried to produce something in the same vein. Cicero writes more than once of Demosthenes' 'thunderbolts' (*fulmina*).

need that quotation from Trabea.[551] The 'miss' was rather mine. But tell me now, how do you find me as a letter-writer? Don't I deal with you in colloquial style? The fact is that one's style has to vary. A letter is one thing, a court of law or a public meeting quite another. Even for the courts we don't have just one style. In pleading civil cases, unimportant ones, we put on no frills, whereas cases involving status or reputation naturally get something more elaborate. As for letters, we weave them out of the language of everyday.

Be that as it may, my dear Paetus, what possessed you to say that all the Papirii without exception were plebeians? They were in fact patricians, one of the Lesser Clans.[552] The roll begins with L. Papirius Mugillanus, who was Censor along with L. Sempronius Atratinus, having previously been his colleague in the Consulship in the year 312 after the foundation of Rome.[553] But in those days you used to be called Papisii. Thirteen held curule office between him and L. Papirius Crassus, the first of the race not to be called Papisius. He was appointed Dictator with L. Papirius Cursor as his Master of the Horse in the year 415 after the foundation,[554] and four years later became Consul with Kaeso Duilius. Cursor[555] followed him, a very distinguished official career. Then came L. Masso, of aedilician rank, and many Massos after him. All the foregoing were patricians, and I hope you will have their portraits in your hall.

Then follow the Carbos and the Turdi. These were plebeians, and I advise you to ignore them. For with the exception of the

551. Perhaps the quotation warned against reaching beyond one's grasp.

552. According to tradition King Tarquinius Priscus appointed a number of new Senators whose clans were called *gentes minores*.

553. = B.C. 443, by inclusive reckoning from a foundation date 754.

554. = B.C. 340.

555. Son of the Cursor just mentioned.

C. Carbo[556] who was killed by Damasippus, not one of the Carbos was an asset to his country. We knew Cn. Carbo[557] and his brother the wag – a pair of rascals if ever there was one. Of my friend who is still with us,[558] Rubria's son, I say nothing. There were the three famous brothers, C., Cn., and M. Carbo. Marcus, a great thief, was condemned after his career in Sicily on a charge brought by P. Flaccus. Gaius[559] is said to have swallowed Spanish Fly when prosecuted by Crassus. He was a seditious Tribune of the Plebs and was believed to have murdered P. Africanus. As for the man[560] who was put to death at Lilybaeum by our friend Pompey, he was in my opinion as arrant a rascal as ever breathed. His father before him was prosecuted by M. Antonius and is thought to have been acquitted by shoe-blacking.[561]

So I recommend you to 'revert to the *patres*'.[562] The plebeians were an unconscionable lot, as you see.

556. Surnamed Arvina. He was killed by the Marian leader L. Junius Brutus Damasippus in 82.

557. Probably not the Marian leader mentioned below, but a person otherwise unknown, perhaps son of the 'great thief', Marcus. His brother can be identified with a C. Carbo who seems to have been Tribune in 89 and a supporter of Sulla.

558. Another Gaius, perhaps son of the 'wag', who was condemned (probably in 58) for extortion in his province of Bithynia. Caesar may have brought him back from exile.

559. Father of Arvina.

560. Gnaeus, the Marian leader, son of the second of the three brothers. Pompey executed him in 81.

561. Generally supposed to mean that he poisoned himself like his brother Gaius, but such a coincidence could hardly have failed to attract notice in our sources. Probably the reference is to some sort of tampering with the voting tablets at the trial. The charge probably concerned his defeat by the Cimbri in 113.

562. Probably a facetious echo of a technical phrase. In default of patrician magistrates the auspices were said to 'revert to the Fathers' (i.e. the patrician members of the Senate); cf. *Letters to Marcus Brutus* 9 (XIII or I.5).3.

189 (IX. 22)[563]

CICERO TO PAPIRIUS PAETUS

46–44

From Cicero to Paetus.

I like your modesty! – or rather your freedom of language. But after all, this found favour with Zeno, a clever man, no getting away from it, though our Academy is mightily at loggerheads with him – but as I say, the Stoics hold it proper to call everything by its name. Their argument runs like this: There is no such thing as obscene or indecent language. For if there is anything shocking in obscenity, it lies either in the matter or in the word; there is no third possibility. Now it does not lie in the matter. Accordingly, there are accounts of the actual process, not only in Comedy (e.g. *The Demiurge*:[564] 'T'other day, as luck would have it...' – you know the solo,[565] you remember Roscius – 'so she left me bare': the whole speech is guarded as to the words, but pretty shameless as to the matter) but in Tragedy too.[566] What else is this bit: 'When one woman' (mark it now) 'sleeps in two beds'? Or

His daughter's (?) bed
This man did enter?

563. This exposition of the Stoic doctrine that 'the wise man will call a spade a spade' was provoked by the word *mentula* (cf. para. 2) in a letter from Paetus. That Cicero controverts or refutes the doctrine is a hallucination of certain annotators, though he does state (not very solemnly) a personal preference for 'Plato's modesty'. The whole thing is a *jeu d'esprit*.

564. By Sex. Turpilius, second-century writer of Latin comedies.

565. *canticum* (lyric monologue).

566. The sources of the following quotations are unknown.

Or 'Me, a virgin all unwilling, Jupiter did rudely force.' 'Force' is very well. And yet it means the same as the other word, which nobody would have tolerated. You see therefore that, although the matter is the same, there is not thought to be any indecency because the words are different. Therefore it does not lie in the matter.

Still less does it lie in the words. For if that which is signified by a word is not indecent, the word which signifies it cannot be indecent either. You say 'seat', using a transferred word: why not use the proper one? If it's indecent, you should not use the first even; if not, you should use the second. The ancients used to call a tail a penis – hence 'penicillus'[567] from the similarity. But nowadays 'penis' is an obscene word. And yet Piso Frugi in his *Annals* complains of young men being 'devoted to the penis'. What you call by its proper name[568] in your letter he more guardedly called 'penis'; but because many others did the same, it became no less obscene a word than the one you have employed. Again, 'When we[569] wanted to meet you' is an ordinary enough phrase. Is it obscene? I remember an eloquent Consular[570] once saying in the Senate 'Shall I call this or that[571] the more reprehensible?' Most obscene, was it not? no, you say, for he didn't intend it so. Very well then, obscenity does not lie in the word; and I have shown that it does not lie in the matter. Therefore it lies nowhere.

'Provide for the continuation of your family.' What a respectable phrase! Fathers even ask their sons to do it. But they dare not utter the word for this 'provision'. Socrates was taught the lute by a very celebrated player whose name was Connus. Do you think that obscene? When we say 'terni'[572]

567. ='paintbrush'.
568. *mentula.*
569. *cum nos* pronounced like *cunnos.*
570. Possibly Cicero himself; cf. *Letters to Atticus* 44 (11.24).3.
571. *(il)lam dicam* pronounced like *landicam.*
572. 'Three each'.

there's nothing to shock; but when we say 'bini'[573] is it obscene? 'Yes,' you say, 'to a Greek.' Then there is nothing in the word, since *I* know Greek, and I still say to you 'bini', and you behave as though I spoke in Greek instead of in Latin. Take 'ruta' and 'menta'; both all right. But if I want a word for 'little mint' corresponding to 'rutula',[574] I can't have it. 'Tectoriola'[575] is a nice enough word. Try to make a diminutive from 'pavimentum' in the same way: you can't. Don't you see that it's all nonsense, that indecency does not exist either in word or matter, and therefore does not exist at all?

So we utter obscenities when we use respectable words. Take 'divisio'. A respectable word, wouldn't you say? But it contains an obscenity, just like 'intercapedo'. Are these words obscene? Our practice is really comical. If we say 'he throttled his father', we don't apologize; but if we say something about Aurelia or Lollia,[576] an apology is due. Indeed even quite innocent words have come to count as obscene. 'Battuit', somebody says; shameless! 'Depsit': much more so! Yet neither word is obscene. The world is full of fools. 'Testes' is a perfectly respectable word in a court of law, elsewhere *not* too respectable. Lanuvian bags are respectable, Cliternian not. Why even an action is sometimes respectable, sometimes indecent, is it not? It's shocking to break wind. Put the culprit naked in the bath, and you won't blame him.

So there you have a Stoic lecture: 'The Sage will call a Spade a Spade.' What a multitude of words out of one of yours, to be sure! I like you to have no inhibitions when you are addressing me. For myself, I adhere (and shall so continue, since it is my habit) to the modesty of Plato. That is why I have written to you in guarded language on a theme which the

573. 'Two each'. *bini* phonetically = Greek *binei*.

574. 'Little rue'. The corresponding diminutive from *menta* would be *mentula*.

575. Diminutive of *tectorium*, 'wall-plaster'.

576. The notorious wives of Catiline and A. Gabinius.

Stoics handle with complete freedom. But they also say that we ought to break wind and belch with equal unconstraint. So let us respect the Kalends of March![577]

Remember me kindly and keep well.

190 (IX. 16)

CICERO TO PAPIRIUS PAETUS

Tusculum (?), mid July 46

Cicero to Paetus greetings.

Your letter gave me great pleasure. In the first place I was touched by the affection which prompted you to write, because you were afraid that Silius'[578] report had caused me some anxiety. You had written to me previously on the subject, sending two copies of your letter separately, so that I could well see how much it disturbed you; and I had replied in detail in such a way as to remove your concern, or at any rate to relieve it, so far as possible in such a case and at such a time.

But since your latest letter also shows how deeply you are taking this matter to heart, let me assure you, my dear Paetus, that whatever art could do (we cannot nowadays rely on the weapon of good judgement, a degree of artifice and ingenuity is called for) – anyhow, all that pains could effect towards gaining and gathering the good-will of these gentry[579] has been achieved by me, no effort spared; and I do not think I

577. The date of the *Matronalia* (festival of married women, on which husbands and lovers gave presents to their ladies).

578. Probably the ex-governor of Bithynia; possibly a former officer of Caesar, T. Sil(l)ius. His report seems to have concerned some sharp saying of Cicero which had been passed on to Caesar. Paetus was afraid it might give offence.

579. The leading Caesarians.

have wasted my endeavours. The courtesies and attentions I receive from all who stand high with Caesar are such that I believe they have an affection for me. Admittedly it is no easy matter to distinguish the genuine article from the sham, unless a situation happens to arise in which the gold of loyal attachment is discerned in the fire of danger – all other signs being common to both. But one circumstance goes far to prove to my own mind that their regard is sincere and genuine: my position and theirs being what they respectively are, these people have no motive to dissemble.

As for the All-Powerful, I see no reason why I should be apprehensive, unless it be that all becomes uncertain when the path of legality has been forsaken, and that there is no guaranteeing the future of what depends on someone else's wishes, not to say whims. However, I have done nothing to offend Caesar's personal sensibilities. In that very particular I have been extremely careful to regulate my conduct. Time was when I thought that free speech became me, for was not the existence of freedom in the community due to my work? Now that freedom is lost, I think it no less becomes me to say nothing offensive to his sentiments or those of the people he likes. But if I were to disclaim the authorship of certain pungent or amusing remarks, I should have to renounce my reputation as a wit. Well, I should not object to the latter, if the former lay within my power. But Caesar himself is a keenly discriminating connoisseur. Your brother[580] Servius, in my judgement a man of outstanding literary culture, could easily pronounce that Plautus did not write one line or did write another, because his taste has been refined by observation of the styles of poets and by constantly reading their work. In the same way I hear that, having in his day compiled volumes of *bons mots*,[581] Caesar will

580. Or 'cousin', Ser. Claudius; cf. *Letters to Atticus* 20 (I.20).7.

581. According to Suetonius' biography (56.7) Caesar made a collection of witticisms as a boy or young man; along with other of his *juvenilia* Augustus forbade it to be published.

reject any specimen offered him as mine which is not authentic. He does this all the more now because his intimates are in my company almost every day. Talk of this and that produces many casual remarks which perhaps strike these people when I say them as not deficient in polish and point. They are conveyed to him with the rest of the day's news, according to his express instructions. Thus it is that if he hears anything about me from some other source he does not think it worth his attention.

So I don't need your Oenomaus;[582] not but what your Accian lines come à propos. But where is the envy? What is there about me nowadays to inspire such a sentiment? However, suppose there were all manner of things: I find that those philosophers who alone to my mind grasp the essence of virtue hold that the wise man is answerable for nothing save guilt. But of that I conceive myself doubly free, both in that my sentiments were thoroughly sound and because, when I saw that the strength to assert them was lacking, I did not think it right to struggle against superior force. Therefore I certainly cannot be said to have failed in the duty of a good citizen. All that remains is not to act or speak foolishly or rashly against the powers that be. That too I reckon part of wisdom. For the rest, what this or that person says I have said, how *he* takes such reports, how trustworthy are these associates of mine who pay me such assiduous attention and courtesy – for all this I cannot answer.

So I comfort myself with the consciousness of my motives in the past and the regulation of my conduct in the present, and I may apply that simile of Accius' to fortune instead of merely

582. Paetus had cited lines from Accius' tragedy *Oenomaus*, to the effect that *invidia* (envy, jealous ill-will) made no more impression on a strong mind than waves upon a rock (see next paragraph). Cicero remarks that he does not in fact have to fear *invidia*, and would rather apply the simile to fortune. The quotation was clearly intended to encourage Cicero, not to warn him. It should not be identified with the only surviving fragment of the play, in which there happens to be mention of a rock.

to envy; fickle and feeble as she is, I hold that she must break against a firm, constant mind like a wave against a rock. The records of Greece are full of instances of how men of the highest wisdom bore despotic régimes, whether at Athens or Syracuse,[583] and managed amidst the servitude of their communities to keep in some sort their personal liberty. Am I to suppose myself incapable of preserving my position while neither offending any man nor impairing my dignity?

Now I come to your jests, seeing that you have followed up Accius' *Oenomaus* with a mime *à la mode* instead of the old-fashioned Atellane farce.[584] What's this about Pompilius[585] and half-a-crown[586] and a plate of salt fish *au gratin*?[587] In days gone by I used to put up with that kind of thing, being an easy-going fellow, but times are changed. Hirtius and Dolabella are my pupils in oratory, but my masters in gastronomy. I expect you have heard, if all news travels to Naples, that they practise declaiming at my house, and I practise dining at theirs. As for making me an affidavit of insolvency, you'd be wasting your time. When you had money, a profitable little deal would make you all the closer. But now, when you are losing your pile so philosophically, why not take the view that when you entertain me you are being served with a valuation?[588] Such a

583. Socrates at Athens under the Thirty, Plato at Syracuse under the two Dionysii.

584. The former were both more witty and more indecent than the latter.

585. M. Demmel's correction *Pompilium* for *popillium* is most attractive. In his work on Grammarians (8) Suetonius tells us that M. Pompilius Andronicus was a devoted Epicurean, that he spent his later life at Cumae, and that he was poor and needy. Each of these three details helps to qualify him as a prospective guest at Paetus' dinner-table.

586. Literally 'a denarius'; Paetus would naturally mention price in telling Cicero what kind of meal he might expect.

587. A poor man's dish of which Paetus was particularly fond; cf. *Letters to Atticus* 370 (XIV.16).1.

588. By Caesar's legislation creditors were obliged to take their debtors' property in settlement at valuations based on pre-war prices.

knock actually hurts less coming from a friend than from a debtor. Not that I am demanding the sort of banquet that produces a great quantity of left-overs; but what there is must be sumptuous and elegant. I remember your reciting Phamea's dinner to me. Yours may start earlier,[589] but the rest should be in the same style. However, if you insist on bringing me back to your friend Matris'[590] bill of fare, all right, I'll put up with that too. I should like to see anybody with the courage to dare to serve me with the things you mention, or even with octopus the colour of vermilioned Jupiter![591] No, no, you'll never dare! The report of my stylish new ways will reach you before I arrive, and make you shake in your shoes. And don't go building hopes on the *hors d'œuvres*. I have done away with that entirely. I used to half-ruin my appetite with your olives and sausages in the old days!

But what am I saying? I only wish I may be able to come down! As for yourself, let me dispel your alarm; go back to your old salt fish *au gratin*. My visit shall put you to no expense except that you will have to heat a bath. All else shall be as usual between you and me. I was only joking.

Thank you for taking so much trouble and writing so amusingly about Selicius' country house. In view of what you say, I think I'll pass it by. I have plenty of salt, but not enough salt-cellars![592]

589. 'The grander the dinner party at Rome the earlier it began' (Tyrrell and Purser).

590. Celebrated Athenian (or Theban) plain-liver of uncertain date, who ate nothing but figs and drank nothing but water.

591. i.e., probably, in a red sauce. In ancient times the clay image of Jupiter was given a new coat of vermilion paint on festal days.

592. i.e., if the conjecture *salinorum* is right, silver ('siller', money), salt-cellars being normally made of that metal. 'Salt' here has a double meaning, 'wit' (of which Paetus provided a sufficiency in his letter) and (of a villa) 'elegance' (Paetus having presumably praised the villa as having 'plenty of salt').

191 (IX. 18)

CICERO TO PAPIRIUS PAETUS

Tusculum, c. 23 July 46

Cicero to Paetus greetings.

While I was at a loose end at Tusculum, having sent my pupils to meet their friend[593] with the idea that they should at the same time put me in the best possible odour with him, I received your most charming letter. It appears then that my plan meets with your approbation: like Dionysius the tyrant,[594] who is said to have opened a school at Corinth after his expulsion from Syracuse, I have set up as a schoolmaster, as it were, now that the courts are abolished and my forensic kingdom lost. Well, I too am pleased with my plan, which brings me many advantages. To begin with, I gain some protection against the hazards of these times, which is what is most needed just now. What that amounts to I don't know; all I can see is that nobody else has yet produced a plan which I consider superior to mine – unless perhaps it would have been better to die. Better to die in one's bed, I admit it; but that did not happen. At the battle I was not present. The others – Pompey, your friend Lentulus,[595] Scipio, Afranius – came to miserable ends. But Cato's, you say, was splendid. Well, that will be open to me any time I choose. I have only to see that it does not become so much a matter of necessity for me as it was for him. I am doing just that. This then to begin with.

593. i.e. Hirtius and Dolabella to meet Caesar on his return from Africa. When he says he sent them Cicero is probably joking – they would naturally go anyway.

594. Dionysius II of Syracuse; cf. *Letters to Atticus* 176 (IX.9).1.

595. L. Lentulus Crus, Consul in 49.

Next, I benefit directly, first in health, which I lost when I gave up my exercises; and then my oratorical faculty, if I had any, would have dried up had I not gone back to these exercises. There is a final point, which *you* might perhaps put first: I have already polished off more peacocks than you young pigeons. While you enjoy Haterius' legal gravity[596] in Naples, I regale myself with Hirtius' gravy here. Be a man then, and come along! Let me teach you the principia you want to learn – though it will be a case of teaching my grandmother.[597] But, as I see the situation, if you can't sell your valuations[598] or fill a pot with sixpences,[599] you have got to move back to Rome. Better die of stomach-ache here than starvation down there. I see you have lost your money, and I expect it is just the same with your friends. So if you don't look ahead, it's all up with you. You can get up on that mule, which you say you still have left after spending your gelding on food, and ride to Rome. There will be a chair for you in school as assistant-master next to mine, and a cushion will follow.

192 (VII. 33)

CICERO TO VOLUMNIUS EUTRAPELUS

Rome, end of July (?) 46

From Cicero to Volumnius greetings.

In missing my declamations you lose nothing at all. As for

596. Literally 'Haterian law', Haterius being presumably a jurist. There is a play on two senses of *ius*, 'law' and 'sauce'.

597. Literally 'of the pig teaching Minerva' – a proverbial saying. The pig was regarded as the most stupid of animals.

598. i.e. properties compulsorily accepted in lieu of debts.

599. i.e. 'if you don't have enough money to fill a pot with silver coins (*denarii*)'.

your envying Hirtius if you were not so fond of him, you had no cause for such a feeling, unless perhaps you envied him his own oratorical gifts rather than the privilege of listening to me. As for myself, my charming friend, I am simply nothing; or if not that, I am disgusted with my own performance, now that I have lost my ol stable-mates who made me show my paces – to your applause. If ever I do strike out anything worthy of my reputation, I groan to think that

> On feathered, not on armoured forms I ply
> These shafts, my glory humbled,

as Philoctetes[600] says in Accius.

None the less, my whole horizon will brighten if you come. But, as you realize yourself, you are coming into a rush of pressing affairs. If I dispose of these satisfactorily, I shall bid a long farewell to Forum and Senate-House, and shall pass much of my time with you and our common admirers. Your friend Cassius and our friend Dolabella (I should rather say 'our' in both cases) are devoted to the same pursuits[601] and find in me a very well-disposed audience. We need your delicately filed and polished critical judgement and that recherché learning before which I often check my own exuberant tongue. For my part I am quite determined, if only Caesar either permits or welcomes my resolution, to lay aside the role in which he himself has often approved me and to bury myself in literary work, enjoying an honourable retirement in your company and that of other devotees of letters.

I wish you had not been afraid that I might read your letters like books,[602] if (as you say) they should happen to be on the lengthy side. In future do please depend upon it that the longer the letters you write the better I shall like them.

600. In a play of that name.

601. Apparently literary and philosophical rather than oratorical.

602. i.e. as too long to be read at one sitting. The reading is conjectural.

193 (IX. 20)

CICERO TO PAPIRIUS PAETUS

Rome, early August 46

From Cicero to Paetus.

I was doubly delighted with your letter – laughed myself, and saw that you are now capable of laughing. As a light-armed buffoon,[603] I did not object to your pelting me with insults.[604] What does vex me is that I have not been able to get down to your part of the world as I had arranged. You would have found me a comrade[605] in arms rather than a guest. And what a warrior! Not the man you used to lay low with your *hors d'œuvres*. I bring an appetite unimpaired to the eggs,[606] and so carrry on the good work down to the roast veal. 'What an accommodating fellow!' you used to say of me. 'What an easy man to entertain!' Not any more! I have dropped all my concern for public affairs, all preoccupation with what to say in the Senate, all study of briefs, and flung myself into the camp of my old enemy Epicurus. I don't aim at the excesses of Rome, however, but at *your* elegance – your former elegance, I mean, when you had money to spend (though, to be sure, you never owned more real estate[607] in your life).

603. Paetus had apparently called Cicero *scurra veles* ('skirmisher jester'), perhaps because he had begun the fight. The verb *velitari* is used elsewhere of verbal skirmishing.

604. Untranslatable pun on *malis* (with a short 'a') = 'abuse' and *malis* (with a long 'a') = 'apples' (which might be thrown at a buffoon).

605. Literally 'tent-mate'. The military metaphor continues, but the word may imply a longer stay than would be normal for a guest.

606. Here regarded as beginning the main meal, as opposed to the *hors d'œuvres*. The roast veal would be the last course, followed by dessert (*mensae secundae*).

607. Which Paetus had been forced to take from his debtors.

So be prepared! You are dealing with a hearty eater, no longer wholly ignorant of what's what; and you know how opsimaths assert themselves. You had best forget about your little baskets[608] and your scones. I have acquired enough of the the art by now to dare invite your friend Verrius and Camillus (the very acme of refinement and elegance!) on several occasions. More, I even had the audacity to give a dinner to Hirtius (think of it!) – no peacock, though. At that meal nothing proved beyond my cook's powers of imitation except the hot sauce.

So this is the way I live nowadays. In the morning I receive callers – both honest men (numerous, but depressed) and these jubilant victors, who, I must say, are most obliging and friendly in their attentions to me. When the stream has ceased to flow, I absorb myself in literary work, writing or reading. Some of my visitors listen to me as a man of learning, because I know a little more than themselves. All the rest of the time is given to the claims of the body. As for my country, I have already mourned her longer and more deeply than any mother ever mourned her only son.

But if you are my friend, take care of your health, or I shall be consuming your substance while you lie flat on your back. For I have made up my mind not to spare you, well or sick.

194 (IX. 19)

CICERO TO PAPIRIUS PAETUS

Rome, mid August 46

From Cicero to Paetus.

Still up to your tricks? You intimate that Balbus was satisfied

608. Containing dates, as at Trimalchio's feast (Petronius, 40.3), or something of the kind. The meaning of the word translated 'scones' is doubtful.

with a modest little spread. I suppose you imply that when kings[609] are so temperate, Consulars should be much more so. What you don't know is that I fished the whole story out of him – he came straight from the City gate, let me tell you, to my house (I'm not surprised that he didn't rather go to his own, but I *should* have expected him to go to his sweetheart).[610] My first four words were: 'What of old Paetus?' And *he* said he'd be hanged if he had ever had a better time. If you have achieved this by talk, you will find me no less discriminating a listener. But if the credit goes to your cuisine, I must ask you not to rate balbutients[611] above orators. Every day one thing after another holds me up. But if I get clear and can pay a visit to your part of the world, I shall take very good care not to let you think I have given you insufficient notice.[612]

195 (IX. 17)

CICERO TO PAPIRIUS PAETUS

Rome, late August or early September 46

Cicero to Paetus.

Aren't you a comedian? After a visit from our friend Balbus you ask *me* what I think is going to happen about these towns and lands![613] As though I know anything that he doesn't

609. *rex* is often applied to a rich and powerful personage, but has special reference here to Balbus' relations with the despot Caesar; cf. *Letters to Atticus* 259 (XII.12).1.

610. Play on *suam (domum)*, 'to his house', and *ad suam*, 'to his mistress'.

611. *balbus* = 'stammerer'.

612. And so provide an excuse for meagre entertainment.

613. Paetus was afraid that land belonging to municipalities or private individuals might be confiscated by Caesar for distribution to his veterans.

know! Or as though, if ever I *do* know anything, I don't get my information from him! On the contrary, if you are a friend of mine, you tell me what is going to happen to us! After all, you had him in your power, you could have pumped him, drunk if not sober. But as for me, my dear Paetus, I am not inquisitive about such matters. For almost four years past the fact that we are still alive is a bonus to which we are not entitled – that is, if to survive freedom can be called a bonus or a life. Moreover, I fancy I know the answer too: what will happen will be whatever those who have the power want to happen. And power will always lie with armed force. So we ought to be content with whatever is allowed us. Anybody unable to put up with life on these terms should have taken leave of it.

They *are* surveying land at Veii and Capena. That is not so far from Tusculum. But I have no fears. I enjoy while I am able. I pray I may always be able. But if my prayer is not granted, well, as a man of courage and a philosopher, I thought life a very fine thing. Therefore I cannot but feel beholden to the man to whose favour I owe it. Even if he were to will that the state be such as he perhaps desires and as all of us ought to pray for, there is nothing he can do. He has too many associates to whom he has tied himself.

But I am going further than I meant – after all, I am writing to *you*. However, you may take my word for it that not only I, who am not in his counsels, but the great man himself does not know what will happen. We are his slaves, he is the slave of circumstances. So he cannot know what circumstances will demand, and we cannot know what he has in his mind.

If I have not replied sooner, it is not because I am habitually lazy, particularly where writing is concerned, but, having nothing solid to go on, I was reluctant to cause you anxiety by expressing a doubt or to raise your hopes by a positive statement. I will only add the bare truth, that so far I have heard nothing in recent times about the danger you fear. But you are a man of sense, and as such you should pray for the best, contemplate the worst, and bear whatever betide.

196 (IX. 15)

CICERO TO PAPIRIUS PAETUS

Rome, first (?) intercalary month 46

Cicero to Paetus greetings.

I am replying to two letters of yours. I received one of them four days ago by Zethus, the other was brought by your courier Phileros.

Your earlier letter had made it plain to me that my concern for your health was very welcome to you. I am glad you appreciated it, but, believe me, you could not appreciate it as it really is from a letter. I find myself the object of attention and regard from a fair number of persons (I cannot say otherwise), but none of them all is more agreeable to me than you. That you love me, and have done so steadily and long, is certainly important, perhaps the most important thing of all; but in this you are by no means alone. What is singular to yourself is that *you* are so lovable, such pleasant company, so agreeable in every way. And then there is the salt of your wit – not Attic, but genuine old Roman, saltier than the Athenian variety. For my part, make what you will of it, I am marvellously fond of pleasantries, our native brand most of all, especially in view of its present decline; for adulterated as it had already become after the influx of the foreign element into our city, it is now with the accession of the trousered tribes from over the Alps so overwhelmed (?) that no trace of the old gay charm is any more to be found. So when I see you, I imagine I have the wits of bygone days, Granius,[614] Lucilius, and their like – indeed, to say the truth, Crassus[615] and Laelius and *their* like – all before my eyes. Confound me if I have anyone but you in whom I can recognize the image of the good old home-bred humour! When these charms of wit are combined with so hearty an affection for myself, do you wonder that your serious illness threw me into such a panic?

In your second letter you excuse yourself. You say you were not dissuading me from buying a place in Naples, but encouraging me to spend my time in Rome. That was what I took you to mean; but I also understood (as I understand from this later letter) that you thought I do not have the right to abandon metropolitan life, as I conceive myself entitled to do, not altogether indeed, but to a great extent. You talk to me of Catulus and those days. Where is the resemblance? At that time I myself did not care to be absent too long from watching over the commonwealth. I was sitting in the poop, you see, with the helm in my hands. But now I have scarcely so much as a place in the hold. Do you suppose there will be any the fewer senatorial decrees if I am in Naples? When I am in Rome, up and down the Forum, decrees are drawn up at the residence of your admirer, my very good friend.[616] What is more, when it happens to occur to him, I am put down as present at drafting, and I hear of some decree, allegedly passed on my motion, reaching Armenia and Syria before I know that there has been so much as a mention of the matter concerned. You must not think I am joking. Let me tell you that letters have been brought to me before today from monarchs at the other end of the earth, thanking me for my motion to give them the royal title, when

614. The sharp-tongued auctioneer of Puteoli; cf. *Letters to Atticus* 28 (II.8).2.

615. L. Crassus, the orator. He and Laelius were men of high birth and official rank.

616. Doubtless Cornelius Balbus.

I for my part was unaware of their very existence, let alone of their elevation to royalty.

Very well then. Despite the foregoing, as long as our new Prefect of Morals[617] remains in Rome, I shall defer to your advice. But when he is gone, I'll betake myself to your mushrooms. If I have a house, I shall make the daily maximum under the sumptuary law[618] last ten days. But if I don't find anything to my taste, I've decided to make my home with you – I know I could do nothing that would please you more! I am now giving up hope of Sulla's house, as I said in my last letter, but still I have not quite abandoned it. Would you please inspect the place with the builders, as you say? If there is nothing wrong with the walls or roof, I shall find no fault with the rest.

197 (IX. 26)

CICERO TO PAPIRIUS PAETUS

Rome, shortly before 17 November (true calendar) 46

From Cicero to Paetus greetings.

I am scribbling the lines of which you are reading a copy on my tablets[619] after taking my place at dinner at two-thirty of the afternoon. If you wish to know where, my host is Volumnius Eutrapelus. Your friend Atticus and Verrius are on either side of me. Does it surprise you that we have become such a merry lot of slaves? Well, what am I to do? I ask *you*, since you are going to philosophy lectures. Am I to torture and torment myself? What should I gain? And how long should I keep it

617. Caesar was so appointed for three years by the Senate after his victory in Africa.

618. Caesar's.

619. See Glossary of Terms.

up? You may advise me to spend my life in literary work. Surely you realize that this *is* my only occupation, that if I did not spend my life in that way I could not live at all. But even literary work has, I won't say its saturation-point, but its due limit. When I leave it, little as I care about dinner (the one problem *you* put to philosopher Dio),[620] I really do not see anything better to do with the time before I go to bed.

Well, to the rest of my tale. Cytheris lay down next Eutrapelus. 'So?' I hear you say, '*Cicero* at such a party,

> 'He the admired, upon whose countenance
> The Greeks all turned their eyes?'[621]

I assure you I had no idea *she* would be there. But after all, even Aristippus the Socratic did not blush when someone twitted him with keeping Lais as his mistress. 'Lais is my mistress,' said he, 'but I'm my own master' (it's better in the Greek;[622] make your own rendering, if you care to). As for me, even when I was young I was never attracted by anything of that sort, much less now that I'm old. It's the party I enjoy. I talk about whatever comes uppermost, as they say, and transform sighs into shouts of laughter. Do you manage matters better, actually making mock of a philosopher? When he put his question whether anybody had anything to ask, you called out 'Who's going to ask me to dinner? Been wondering all day.'[623] The poor dunderhead[624] thought you would be enquiring whether there is one sky or an infinite number. What business is that of

620. Otherwise unknown; but see below.

621. Source unknown.

622. The Latin means literally 'I possess Lais but am not possessed by her'. In the Greek *ekhomai* has a double sense, 'I am possessed by' and 'I cling to'.

623. The lecturer asked '*numquid quis quaerit?*' ('any questions?'). Paetus replied '*cenam quaero*', 'I'm looking for a dinner'.

624. Cicero was fond of so referring to Epicurean philosophers because of their professed hostility to culture; cf. n. 230.

yours? But, confound it, is a dinner any business of yours, especially one in *this* house?[625]

Well, so life passes. Every day a bit of reading, or a bit of writing. Then, since something is due to my friends, I dine with them. We don't go beyond the law, if there is such a thing nowadays, we even stop short of it, and that by a considerable margin. So you don't have to dread my arrival. You'll receive a guest with a small appetite for food, but a large one for frolic.

198 (IX. 23)

CICERO TO PAPIRIUS PAETUS

Cumae, 22 November (true calendar) 46

From Cicero to Paetus.

I arrived at Cumae yesterday and shall perhaps be with you tomorrow. But when I know for certain, I shall send you word a little beforehand. To be sure, when M. Caeparius met me in Poultry Wood[626] and I asked after you, he told me you were in bed with the gout in your feet. I was properly sorry of course, but decided to come all the same – to see you, visit you, and even dine, for I don't suppose your cook is a fellow-sufferer. Expect a guest then – a small eater and a foe to sumptuous banquets.

625. The house of such a person as Eutrapelus.
626. Silva Gallinaria, a pine forest on the coast north of Cumae.

199 (VII. 4)

CICERO TO M. MARIUS

Cumae, 21 or 22 November (true calendar) 46

From M. Cicero to M. Marius greetings.

On 21 November I arrived at my place near Cumae with your, or rather our, friend Libo. I mean to go on to Pompeii straight away, but shall send you word in advance. I always wish you to keep well, but particularly during my visit; for you see what a long time it is since we were last in one another's company. So if you have an appointment with the gout, please put it off for another day. Take care of yourself then, and expect me in two or three days' time.

200 (VII. 28)

CICERO TO M. CURIUS

Rome, August (?) 46

From M. Cicero to Curius greetings.

I remember the time when I thought you were out of your mind to prefer life with your friends over there to life with us. When Rome was Rome, it would have been a much more suitable residence for a person of your culture and social gifts than the whole Peloponnesus, let alone Patrae. Today, on the contrary, I applaud your foresight then in betaking yourself to Greece when affairs here were in wellnigh hopeless case; and at the present time I think you not only sensible to be absent but happy too – though I don't know how a man of any sense *can* be happy at the present time.

However, what you have done, and were free to do, by locomotion, i.e. to live 'where nevermore of Pelops' line . . .' (you know how it goes on),[627] I am achieving more or less in a different way. After receiving my friends' morning calls, which are in even greater numbers than of yore because they seem to see a loyal citizen as a bird of good omen,[628] I bury myself in my library. And so I produce books – of their importance you will perhaps judge; for from a conversation you had with me at your house, when you were taking me to task for my gloom and despondency, I understood you to say that you wondered what had become of the spirit you saw in my writings.

But the truth is that I mourned in those days for the commonwealth, which for benefits conferred as well as received was dearer to me than my life, and that now, though solaced not only by reflection, which ought to be man's most efficacious comforter, but by time, which is wont to bring healing even to fools, I still grieve to see our common heritage so fallen to pieces that we are not even left the hope of better things in days to come. Nor does the fault now at any rate lie with our all-powerful governor (unless in the sense that there ought not to be any such person). No, events have so fallen out, part by chance but part also by our own fault, that recrimination is idle. I see no hope remaining. So, to go back to my starting-point, if calculation made you leave Rome, you are a sensible man; if chance, a lucky one.

627. Cf. *Letters to Atticus* 366 (XIV.12).2. The 'sons of Pelops' will represent the people now dominant in Rome.

628. Literally 'a white bird'. A white *crow* stood for something impossible or at any rate extremely rare, but the idea of rarity is not in Cicero's phrase, though implicit in the context.

201 (V. 13)

CICERO TO LUCCEIUS

Summer or autumn 46 (?)

From M. Cicero to L. Lucceius, son of Quintus, greetings.

The consolation you offer in your letter is in itself most welcome, showing, as it does, the most sincere good-will combined in equal measure with good sense. But the feature of your letter from which I have especially derived benefit was its revelation of your splendid disregard for human vicissitudes and your admirable readiness and equipment to meet the blows of fortune. This I hold to be the highest glory of wisdom, to depend upon oneself alone, and not to let externals govern one's ideas of the good life and the bad. This conception had not altogether fallen out of my mind, where indeed it had taken deep root, but the storm of calamities bursting all around had in some degree shaken its hold. I perceive that you aim to lend it support, and in your latest letter I am conscious that you have done so effectively and helped me a great deal. So I feel bound to say again and again, and not merely to intimate but to declare, that nothing could have been more welcome to me than your letter.

The arguments which you have so gracefully and copiously brought to bear have indeed their consolatory effect; but nothing is more effective than my perception of *your* steadfastness and imperturbability of spirit. I should be deeply ashamed if I did not imitate it. And I account myself even braver than you, my instructor in fortitude, in that *you* appear to cherish a hope that things will one day improve; the chances of gladiator fights and your other similitudes and the arguments you assemble in discussing the topic tell me not to despair utterly of the commonwealth. No wonder then that you should be braver than I, since you have some hope; the wonder is that any hope remains to you. Can you say of any part that its decline does not amount to total annihilation? Survey all the members of the body politic with which you are well acquainted: I am sure you will find none that is not shattered or enfeebled. I should pursue the theme, if I saw all this more plainly than you see it, or could recall it without distress – though that is an emotion which according to your counsels and precepts must be utterly cast aside.

Therefore I shall bear domestic troubles[629] as you recommend, and public calamities a little more bravely, it may be, than my mentor himself. For you are comforted, so you say, by a measure of hope; whereas I shall be brave even in total despair, as, notwithstanding your hope, you enjoin and instruct me, offering me the agreeable recollections of a clear conscience and of those achievements which you were foremost to encourage. For I have done some service to my country; certainly no less than I owed her, and more, I suppose, than has ever before been demanded of a man's spirit and brain. You will forgive me for claiming something on my own behalf. You hope that the thought of these things will relieve my sore heart; in the mention of them also there is balm.

Therefore I shall follow your counsel. As far as I can, I shall withdraw myself from all that troubles and torments, transferring my mind to those pursuits by which prosperity is embellished and adversity aided. I shall be with you as much as the age and health of both of us allow. And if we cannot be together as much as we should wish, we shall so enjoy our unity of heart and our common studies that we shall never seem to be apart.

629. Terentia, Quintus, and Tullia (Dolabella) may all be in mind.

202 (IV. 3)

CICERO TO SERVIUS SULPICIUS RUFUS[630]

Rome (?), first half of September (?) 46

From M. Cicero to Ser. Sulpicius greetings.

Every day I hear reports from many informants that you are deeply troubled in mind, suffering a distress somehow over and above the general portion of afflictions. I am not at all surprised, and I might almost say that I recognize my own condition in yours. And yet I am sorry that a man so almost uniquely wise as you should not rather take satisfaction in the good things that are his than grieve over the ills of others. For myself, I will not allow that any man has been harder hit than I by the dire disaster that has overtaken the commonwealth. None the less, I now have much to console me, above all the knowledge of my past policies. Long before the storm broke, I saw it brewing as from a high tower – and that not simply by my own vision but far more by the aid of your admonitions and warnings. I was away, it is true, during a great part of your Consulship, but in my absence I was informed of the line you took, how you tried to guard against this disastrous war and foretold it; and I was myself on the spot in the early months of your term of office, when you gave the Senate the fullest warning. I remember how you rehearsed all the civil wars of former days, and told your audience both to fear the calamities they remembered and to be sure that, as the men of the past, with no such precedents in our history to follow, had perpetrated these atrocities, any subsequent armed oppressor of the commonwealth would be far worse to endure. People think they have a right to do what others have done, but they also

630. Now governor of Achaia by Caesar's appointment.

put in some contribution, say rather a large contribution, of their own.

So you must bear in mind that those who refused to follow your lead and listen to your advice have perished by their own folly when they might have been saved by your wisdom. You will ask what consolation that thought brings you in these dark days, when our country lies in ruins. Indeed it is a sorrow almost beyond comfort – the utter loss of all, and the despair of recovery. Yet in the judgement of Caesar himself and the estimation of all our countrymen your integrity, wisdom, and high standing shine like a lamp when all other lights are extinguished. These things should count much towards alleviating your troubles. As for absence from your family and friends, it should be the easier to bear because you are also away from many severe vexations. I should tell you about them all, if I were not reluctant to have you learn in absence what you do not see, and are on that account happier, I think, than we who do.

I judge my words of consolation well placed in so far as they tell you, from a true friend, of considerations which may serve to lighten your troubles. All other sources of comfort lie in yourself. I know them, and they are not small; or rather to my way of thinking, they are by far the greatest of all. I experience them every day and value them so highly as to see my salvation in them. I well remember how keen a student *you* have been from childhood in every branch of letters, how eagerly and attentively you learned all that the wisest of mankind have handed down to show us how to live. These studies could be useful and delightful in the height of prosperity; but in times like these we have nothing else to ease our hearts. I will not presume. I will not urge a man of your attainments and disposition to have recourse to the pursuits to which you have given your energies from your earliest years. I shall only say something I think you will approve: seeing that there is no further place in Senate-House or Forum for the craft which I have studied, *I* have devoted all my time and attention to philosophy. Little more scope is left for your branch of knowledge,[631] in which you have attained such outstanding distinction, than for mine.[632] So, not to offer you counsel, I feel sure that you are engaged in the same pursuits as myself. Even if they do little good, they distract the mind from its anxiety.

Your son Servius engages and excels in all the pursuits of a gentleman, especially in the one in which I have told you my heart finds ease. In my regard for him I yield to you and to nobody else; and he requites me. He thinks, as is plain to see, that in paying attention and respect to me he is doing what most pleases you.

203 (IV. 4)

CICERO TO SERVIUS SULPICIUS RUFUS

Rome, late September or early October 46

From M. Cicero to Ser. Sulpicius greetings.

I accept the excuse you make for often sending me identical[633] letters, but I accept that part of it only in which you say that letters are not always delivered to me because of the negligence or dishonesty of those who take charge of them. The other part, in which you write that you often send identically phrased letters because of your 'verbal poverty', I neither recognize nor approve. I myself, whom you jestingly (so I suppose) credit with verbal riches, acknowledge that I am not altogether unprovided with words (no need for false modesty!); but also, and with no false modesty, I readily yield the palm to the spareness and elegance of *your* compositions.

631. Jurisprudence.
632. Oratory.
633. i.e. virtually identical. The letters would not be actual duplicates.

I had all along approved the considerations which led you, as you say, not to refuse this job in Achaia, but my approval was notably confirmed after reading your most recent letter. All the reasons which you advance are thoroughly valid, eminently worthy of your reputation and wisdom. I do not at all agree with your judgement that the matter has turned out otherwise than you had supposed. But in the general perturbation and chaos, when all lies overthrown and prostrate in the wake of a hideous war, each man reckons his own whereabouts as the worst of places and himself as the most wretched of beings. That is why you regret your decision and why we at home seem happy to you; whereas to us *you* seem, not indeed trouble-free, but happy by comparison with ourselves. And your state is better than ours in this very respect, that you dare to put your discontents[634] on paper, whereas we cannot even do that without risk. It is the fault, not of the victor, who is as moderate as could be, but of the victory itself. In civil war victory is always insolent.

On one point we have had the advantage of you. We learned of your colleague Marcellus' restitution a little sooner than you, and I will add furthermore that we saw *how* the matter was handled. For I do assure you that since the start of these calamities, that is, since force of arms first came to be arbiter of constitutional right, no other piece of public business has been transacted with dignity. Caesar himself, after complaining of Marcellus' acerbity (that was the word he used) and lauding your fair-mindedness and wisdom in the most complimentary terms, suddenly and unexpectedly declared that, if only for the omen's sake, he would not say no to the Senate's petition on Marcellus' behalf. This was after the House had risen in a body and approached Caesar in supplication, which they did when L. Piso had made mention of Marcellus in his speech and C. Marcellus had fallen at Caesar's feet. All in all, it seemed to me a

634. These would concern private or provincial matters which might safely be put on paper.

fine day's work; I thought I saw some semblance of reviving constitutional freedom.

Accordingly, after all those called upon to speak ahead of me had expressed thanks to Caesar except Vulcatius (*he* said he would not have done it in Caesar's place), my name was called; and I changed my resolution. I had determined to hold my peace for ever, not, let me say, from sluggishness, but because I remembered the station that used to be mine and is mine no longer. This resolution of mine was overborne by Caesar's magnanimity and the Senate's solicitude. So I expressed gratitude to Caesar at considerable length,[635] and I am afraid I may have thus forfeited in other contexts the decent retirement which was my only consolation in adversity. However, now that I have escaped his displeasure (he might have thought I did not regard the present régime as constitutional if I never broke silence), I shall do this in moderation, or rather on the near side of moderation, so as to meet his wishes on the one hand and the claims of my literary pursuits on the other. From my childhood I have taken pleasure in every liberal art and branch of knowledge, most of all in philosophy; but my devotion to this study grows upon me every day. I suppose I have reached an age ripe for wisdom; and the evils of the times are such that nothing else can relieve one's mind of its burdens. I see from your letter that business is distracting you from this pursuit, but the lengthening nights will soon be some help.

Your boy, Servius, our boy rather, is most attentive to me. His sterling worth and high character, and more particularly his devotion to literary studies, are my delight. He often confers with me about the question of your staying on or coming home. So far I take the view that we should do nothing but what appears most in accord with Caesar's wishes. The state of affairs is such that, if you were in Rome, nothing could give you pleasure except your family and friends. That aside, the best feature in the scene is himself. Other persons and things are

635. The speech is extant (*pro Marcello*).

such as one would prefer to learn of by report than see, if it were necessary to do one or the other. This advice of mine is by no means agreeable to *me* – I am anxious to see you, but counsel for your good.

Goodbye.

204 (XII. 17)

CICERO TO CORNIFICIUS[636]

Rome, September (middle) 46

From Cicero to his Colleague Cornificius greetings.

I am truly gratified by your remembrance of me, which you signify in your letter. Let me ask you to keep it in being. I do so, not as doubting your constancy, but as a common form.

Reports of disturbances have reached us from Syria.[637] As you are nearer their source than we, I am more concerned on your account than on my own. Rome is profoundly quiet. One would prefer some action, of a wholesome and honourable sort. I hope there will be such – Caesar evidently has it in mind.

You may be interested to learn that, profiting by your absence, I have taken the opportunity and licence, so to speak, to write more adventurously. Most of the results, it is true, might pass muster even with you. But my latest work is a treatise 'On the Best Style of Oratory',[638] a subject on which I have often suspected that you are not altogether at one with my judgement – a case, naturally, of an expert differing from one not wholly without claim to that description. I hope you will befriend the book because you really like it; but if not that,

636. Now governing Cilicia.

637. First news of the soldiers' mutiny headed by Caecilius Bassus seems to have reached Rome shortly before Cicero wrote.

638. Known as *The Orator*; the title was decided later.

then for my sake. I shall ask your people to copy it if they please, and send it to you. For I fancy that, even if the contents do not quite meet with your approval, any product of my pen will be agreeable to you in your present isolation.

In commending your reputation and consequence to my care you follow the general form of courtesy; but I hope you will believe not only that I set great store by the mutual affection which I am conscious exists between us but also that in the brilliance of your talents, your devotion to culture, and the prospect of a splendid political future you stand second to none in my estimation and comparable to few.

205 (XII. 18)

CICERO TO CORNIFICIUS

Rome, September (end) or October (beginning) 46

From Cicero to his Colleague Cornificius greetings.

The latest point in the letter I most recently received from you is the one which I shall answer first (I have observed that you great orators do this now and then). You complain that you don't hear from me. The fact is that I have never failed to send a letter when notified by your people that someone was going.

I think I may gather from your letter that you will take no hasty step and make no definite decision until you know the upshot of this Caecilius Bassus fellow. That is what I had expected, counting upon your good sense, and your most welcome letter has confirmed it. I would particularly ask you to write as often as you can, so that I know what you are doing and what is going on, also your further intentions.

Although I was sorry indeed to say goodbye to you, I consoled myself at the time with the belief that all was completely quiet where you were going, and that on the other hand you were leaving the threat of serious trouble behind you. In both respects the opposite has happened. War has broken out there, peace has ensued here. But it is a peace in which many things would displease you if you were on the spot – things, however, which do not please Caesar either. This is what always happens at the end of a civil war. It is not just a matter of the victor's wishes coming into effect; he also has to humour the people with whose assistance the victory has been gained. For my part, I have grown so thick a skin that at our friend Caesar's show[639] I saw T. Plancus[640] and heard Laberius' and Publilius' verses with perfect composure.[641] Let me tell you that what I lack most is someone with whom to laugh at all this in an intimate, sophisticated way. You will fill the gap, if you come back as soon as possible. I think it is to your own interest that you should do so as well as to mine.

206 (XII. 19)

CICERO TO CORNIFICIUS

Rome, December 46

From Cicero to Cornificius greetings.

I was delighted to read your letter. What pleased me most was to know that mine had been delivered. I did not doubt that you would be glad to read it, but I was uneasy about its safe delivery.

Your letter tells me that the present war in Syria and the province itself have been entrusted to you by Caesar. I wish you good luck and success in that responsibility; and I feel

639. The *ludi Victoriae Caesaris,* instituted in honour of Caesar's victory at Thapsus.

640. Bursa, restored by Caesar from exile.

641. Cicero had to sit through the mimes lest his absence should offend the Dictator.

sure you will have it, counting as I do on your diligence and good sense. But what you say about the possibility of a war with Parthia has alarmed me not a little, for I could guess for myself the size of your forces, and now learn it from your letter. So I pray that nation makes no move for the time being, before the legions which I hear are being brought to your support actually reach you. If you do not have troops enough to engage on equal terms, I trust you won't fail to follow M. Bibulus' tactics, who shut himself inside an extremely well-fortified and well-provisioned town[642] so long as the Parthians remained in the province.

But you will be better able to decide this in the light of the situation at the time. I shall be wondering anxiously what you are doing, until I know what you have done. I have taken every opportunity of sending you a letter and request you to do the same. Above all please write to your people in such a way as to let them know that I am one of their number.

207 (XV. 21)

CICERO TO TREBONIUS[643]

Rome, beginning of December 46 (?)

From M. Cicero to C. Trebonius greetings.

It was a pleasure to read your letter, and a great pleasure to read your book. But there was a touch of pain too, for, having inflamed my eagerness to increase our intercourse (our *affection* admitted of no addition), you then go away. Missing you as sorely as I do, you leave me only one consolation – that long, frequent letters will mitigate the sense of loss we both feel in

642. Antioch.

643. On his way to Spain, where Caesar's last campaign against the resurgent republicans was about to begin.

each other's absence. I can vouch to you for my part, and to myself for yours too; for you have left me in no doubt how much you care for me. Suppose I put out of account what you did in full public view, when you made my enemy[644] yours, defended me in your speeches, as Quaestor took upon yourself the duty of the Consuls on my behalf and the public's, and as Quaestor refused to obey the orders of a Tribune, even though your colleague obeyed them. Suppose I forgot matters of recent date, which I shall always remember – your concern for me at the war, your gladness at my return, your anxiety and distress when you were told of *my* anxieties and distress, your intention to visit me at Brundisium had you not suddenly been ordered to Spain. Leaving all this aside (and I must needs value it as highly as I value my existence as a man and a citizen), this book[645] you have sent me, what a declaration of your affection! To begin with, you find wit in every saying of mine – another perhaps would not; and then, these things, whether witty or only so-so, become irresistible when you are their *raconteur*. In fact the laugh is nearly all over before *I* come on the scene. I should have a heart of stone not to love you simply for thinking so long about me and me only, as in writing these pieces you necessarily did. But you could not have thought what you have put down on paper without the most sincere affection. So I cannot suppose that anybody loves himself more than you love me. I wish I could repay your affection in all other ways, but at least I shall repay it with my own; and, after all, I feel sure that this by itself will be all the return you desire.

I come now to your charming and communicative letter, to which there is no necessity for me to reply at great length. I sent that letter to Calvus[646] with no more idea that it would get

644. Clodius. We are not otherwise informed of Trebonius' activities as City Quaestor (apparently in 60, or perhaps 58).

645. A collection, as appears, of Ciceronian witticisms, each in its anecdotal setting.

646. The poet and orator, C. Licinius Macer Calvus, now dead.

into circulation than the one you are reading at this moment. Now our way of writing when we think we shall be read only by our addressee is not the same as when we write for a multitude of eyes. If I praised his talent more generously than in your opinion the truth could warrant, it was first and foremost because such was really my opinion. Calvus' intellect was keen and quick; he followed a style in which, though he failed in judgement (a strong point with him), he none the less succeeded in the manner of his choice; his reading was wide and recondite. But he lacked force, and I was urging him to make good the deficiency. Now in trying to rouse a man and spur him on, it works wonders if you mingle some praise with your admonitions. So that's what I think of Calvus, and why I wrote as I did. I praised in order to exhort; and I did think very highly of his talent.

It remains for me to let my affection follow you on your way, to look forward hopefully to your return, to remember you faithfully in your absence, and to mitigate all sense of loss by sending and receiving letters. I hope you will often think of all you have done for me and tried to do. *You* are at liberty to forget it, but for me to forget would be a sin. So you will not only rate me an honourable man but conclude that I have a deep affection for you.

Goodbye.

208 (XV. 20)

CICERO TO TREBONIUS

Rome, shortly after the foregoing

From M. Cicero to C. Trebonius greetings.

I have entrusted my *Orator*, as I have entitled it, to your friend Sabinus. His race gave me the notion that he would make a trustworthy messenger – unless he has taken a leaf out of the candidates' book, and laid hold of the name incontinent![647] But his modest face and his firm, even way of talking seemed to have something of Cures.[648] But that's enough of Sabinus.

My dear Trebonius, when you left Rome you poured some oil on the flame of my affection; and so, to make it easier for me to bear the smart of missing you, salute me with letters in plenty, on the understanding that the same shall be forthcoming on my side. To be sure, you ought to be more assiduous in this office than I for two reasons: firstly, because, whereas in the old days people in Rome used to write to their friends in the provinces about politics, it is now for you to write to me, for the body politic is over there with you; secondly, because I can give you your due by other services while you are away, but I do not see how you can give me mine except by writing letters.

You will be writing me the rest of your news later on, but now I want first of all to know what sort of a journey you are having, where you saw Brutus,[649] and how long you spent with him. Then, when you are further on your way, tell me about military matters and the whole situation, so that I can make an estimate of how we stand. I shall consider I know just as much as I learn from your letters.

Take care of your health and the affection which you so generously bestow on me.

647. The *cognomen* 'Sabinus' suggested Sabine origin, and Sabinum was traditionally the home of the old-time virtues. Or had Sabinus merely assumed his *cognomen*, like certain candidates for office (possibly an allusion to C. Calvisius Sabinus)? Perhaps, however, he was a slave.

648. Ancient chief town of the Sabines.

649. Now governing Cisalpine Gaul.

209 (VII. 23)

CICERO TO M. FABIUS GALLUS

Rome, December 46

From Cicero to M. Fabius Gallus greetings.

I had just got in from Arpinum when I was handed a letter from you. By the same bearer I received a letter from Avianius,[650] containing a very handsome offer to debit me after he arrives from any date I please. Now pray put yourself in my shoes. Can you reconcile it with your sense of decency or with mine to ask for credit in the first place, and in the second for more than a year's credit? But everything would be straightforward, my dear Gallus, if you had bought what I needed and within the price I had wished to pay. Not but what I stand by these purchases you say you have made, indeed I am grateful. I fully understand that you acted out of good-will, affection indeed, in buying the pieces which pleased you (I have always regarded you as a very fine judge in any matter of taste), and which you considered worthy of me. But I hope Damasippus doesn't change his mind, for, frankly, I don't need any of these purchases of yours. Not being acquainted with my regular practice you have taken these four or five pieces at a price I should consider excessive for all the statuary in creation. You compare these Bacchantes with Metellus'[651] Muses. Where's the likeness? To begin with, I should never have reckoned the Muses themselves worth such a sum – and all Nine would have approved my judgement! Still, that would have made a suitable acquisition for a library, and one appropriate to my interests. But where am I going to put Bacchantes? Pretty

650. Doubtless the sculptor, C. Avianius Evander; cf. Letter 314 (XIII.2). Gallus had bought some statues from him on Cicero's behalf.

651. Probably Metellus Scipio.

little things, you may say. I know them well, I've seen them often. I should have given you a specific commission about statues which I know, if I had cared for them. My habit is to buy pieces which I can use to decorate a place in my palaestra,[652] in imitation of lecture-halls. But a statue of Mars! What can I, as an advocate of peace, do with that? I'm glad there was none of Saturn – I should have thought those two between them had brought me debt! I had sooner have had one of Mercury[653] – we might fare better in our transactions with Avianius!

As for that table-rest which you had earmarked for yourself, if you like it, you shall have it; but if you have altered your mind, I'll keep it of course. For the sum you have spent I should really have much preferred to buy a lodge at Tarracina,[654] so as not to be continually imposing on hospitality. To be sure, I realize that my freedman is to blame (I had given him quite definite commissions), and Junius too – I think you know him, Avianius' friend. I am making some new alcoves in the little gallery of my house at Tusculum, and I wanted some pictures for their decoration – indeed, if anything in this way appeals to me, it is painting. However, if I have to keep these things of yours, please let me know where they are, and when they are sent for, and by what mode of transport. If Damasippus changes his mind, I shall find some Damasippus *manqué*, even if it means taking a loss.

You write again about the house. I had already given directions on this head to my girl Tullia as I was leaving – I got your letter that same hour. I had also taken it up with your friend

652. Probably in his house on the Palatine; cf. *Letters to Atticus* 24 (II.4).5.

653. The god of gain. In astrology Saturn and Mars generally bring the opposite.

654. Cicero had recently visited his Campanian villas and will have stayed at Tarracina *en route*; perhaps Gallus was his host.

Nicias, since he is on familiar terms with Cassius,[655] as you know. On my return, before I read this last letter of yours, I asked Tullia how she had got on. She said she had gone to work through Licinia (I have an impression, though, that Cassius does not have a great deal to do with his sister), and that Licinia in her turn said that while her husband was away (Dexius has left for Spain) she did not venture to move house in his absence and without his knowledge. I take it very kindly that you set so much store on our friendly day-to-day intercourse that you took a house so as to live not only in my neighbourhood but in my actual company, and that you are in such a hurry to move. But on my life I won't admit that you are any more eager for that arrangement than myself. So I shall try every way, conscious as I am of what it means to me and to both of us. If I have any success, I'll let you know. Write back on all points and inform me, if you will, when I am to expect you.

210 (VII. 26)

CICERO TO M. FABIUS GALLUS

Tusculum, late 46 or early 45

From Cicero to Gallus greetings.

For ten days my stomach had been seriously out of order, but as I did not have a fever I could not convince the folk who wanted my services that I was really sick. So I took refuge here at Tusculum, after two days of strict fasting – not so much as a drop of water! Famished and exhausted, I was craving your good offices rather than expecting you to demand mine. I

655. Probably not C. Cassius, but perhaps his younger brother Lucius.

am terrified of all forms of illness, but especially of dysentery – your master Epicurus gets a rough handling from the Stoics for complaining of trouble with his bladder and his bowels, the latter being according to them a consequence of over-eating and the former of an even more discreditable indulgence! Well, I was really afraid of dysentery. However, I think I am better for the change, or maybe the mental relaxation; or perhaps the malady is simply wearing itself into abatement.

But in case you wonder how this happened or what I did to deserve it, the Sumptuary Law, supposed to have brought plain living, has been my downfall. Our *bons vivants*, in their efforts to bring into fashion products of the soil exempted under the statute, make the most appetizing dishes out of fungi, potherbs, and grasses of all sorts. Happening on some of these at an augural dinner at Lentulus' house, I was seized with a violent diarrhoea, which has only today begun (I think) to check its flow. So: oysters and eels I used to resist well enough, but here I lie, caught in the toils of Mesdames Beet and Mallow! Well, I shall be more careful in future. As for you, you heard of it from Anicius (he saw me in the qualms), and that should have been reason enough for a visit, let alone a letter.

I intend to stay here until I have convalesced, having lost strength and weight. But I expect I shall recover both easily enough, once I have thrown off the attack.

211 (XIII. 68)

CICERO TO SERVILIUS ISAURICUS

Rome, October (?) 46

M. Tullius Cicero to P. Servilius Isauricus, Proconsul and Colleague, best greetings.

I am extremely grateful for your letter giving the stages of your voyaging;[656] it showed that you have not forgotten our friendly relations, and nothing could be more agreeable to me than that. For the future, I shall be even more grateful if you will write to me as friend to friend on public matters, that is to say the state of the province and the rules you institute. I shall hear all this from many informants (your light does not shine under a bushel), but I should like most of all to learn about it from your letters.

On my side, I shall not often be giving you my views on high politics because of the risk attached to such letters, but I shall write fairly often about what is going on. In spite of all, I think I see a hope that our colleague[657] Caesar will try, and is already trying, to get us some sort of a constitutional system. It would have been very desirable that you should have been present and party to his plans. But if it is more to your advantage, to your honour that is to say, to govern Asia and care for a part of our state interests that has suffered so severely, I too am bound to prefer what will benefit you and your reputation.

Whatever may seem to me to concern your public standing shall receive my most active care. In particular, I shall pay every respect and attention to your illustrious father, as is my duty in view of our old friendship, the kindness I have received from you both, and his own eminence.

212 (XIII. 77)

CICERO TO P. SULPICIUS RUFUS[658]

Rome, autumn 46

From M. Cicero to P. Sulpicius, Imperator, greetings.

Though I do not go to the Senate very often nowadays, I felt

656. To his province of Asia.

657. As Augur.

658. Now governor of Illyricum. His relationship to the jurist, Ser. Sulpicius Rufus, is uncertain.

after reading your letter that I should be failing in my obligations to our old friendship and the many good offices we have rendered one another if I was not present when the honour was conferred upon you. So present I was, and happy to vote for your Supplication. Nor shall a time ever come when I shall not play my part in furthering your interest or your reputation or your dignity. I should be glad if you would so inform your friends, so that they know of my disposition towards you and feel entitled to call upon me without hesitation if you should stand in need of any service.

M. Bolanus is an honourable, gallant, in every way respectable gentleman, and an old friend of mine. I recommend him to you warmly. You will oblige me very much if you let him realize that this recommendation has been of great assistance to him, and you will find himself an excellent, most appreciative person. I can promise you that his friendship will bring you no small gratification.

There is another matter in which I would earnestly request you to put yourself to some trouble, in virtue of our friendship and your unfailing readiness to serve me. My library, worth a considerable sum, was in the charge of a slave of mine called Dionysius.[659] Having pilfered a large number of books and anticipating a day of reckoning, he ran away. He's now in your province. Many people, including my friend M. Bolanus, saw him at Narona, but believed his story that I had given him his freedom. If you see to it that he is returned to me, I cannot tell you how much it will oblige me. In itself it is no great matter, but I am intensely vexed. Bolanus will tell you where he is and what can be done. If I recover the fellow thanks to you, I shall regard you as having done me a very great favour.

659. Cf. Letter 255 (v.9).

213 (XV. 18)

CICERO TO CASSIUS[660]

Rome, December 46

From M. Cicero to C. Cassius greetings.

This letter would have been longer, if I had not been asked for it just as your post was leaving – longer, anyhow, if I had had any bavardage to hand, since writing *au sérieux* is hardly possible without risk. Is joking possible then, you will ask. Well, it certainly isn't very easy, but we have no other means of diversion from our troubles. Where then is philosophy? Yours[661] is in the kitchen, mine is a scold – to be a slave makes me ashamed of myself. So I make believe to be otherwise occupied, so as not to have Plato's[662] reproaches in my ears.

Of Spain nothing certain yet, no news at all in fact. I am sorry for my own sake that you are away but glad for yours. But the courier is getting impatient. So keep well and fond of me, as you have been from a boy.

214 (XV. 17)

CICERO TO CASSIUS

Rome, January (beginning) 45

M. Cicero to C. Cassius greetings.

Your couriers are a queer set – not that *I* mind; but when they

660. Now in Brundisium.

661. Cassius had joined the Epicureans, whose master had written 'the beginning and root of all good is the pleasure of the belly'.

662. The founder of the Academic school to which Cicero belonged.

go away they demand a letter, while when they arrive they bring none. Even so, it would be more convenient if they gave me a little time to write, but they arrive with their travelling caps on and say their party is waiting for them at the city gate. So you must forgive me. You are going to get a second short letter. But you may look forward to full amends. Though I can't think why *I* am apologizing to *you*, when your people come to my house empty-handed and go back with letters.

Here in Rome (just to write you something after all) we have a death to talk about – P. Sulla senior. Some say it was bandits, others overeating. The public doesn't care which, as there's no doubt that he's ashes. You will bear the news like the philosopher you are. Still, the town has lost a *personnage*. They think Caesar will take it hard – he'll be afraid the public auctions[663] may go with less of a swing. Mindius Marcellus[664] and Attius the perfumer are delighted to have shed a competitor.

From Spain nothing new, but keen expectancy of news. Rumours tending to gloom, but nobody to vouch for them. Our friend Pansa left Rome[665] in uniform on 30 December, an unmistakable illustration of what you have latterly begun to question – that Right is to be chosen *per se*. He has given a helping hand to many persons in distress and behaved like a human being in these bad times; accordingly he went off in astonishingly good odour with honest men.

So you are still at Brundisium. I heartily approve and rejoice. Upon my word, I think you will do wisely to avoid worry to no purpose. We who care for you will be glad if you do. And in future, when you send a line home, be a good fellow and remember me. I shall never knowingly let anybody go to you without a letter from me.

Goodbye.

663. Sales of confiscated property.

664. Later a naval commander in the service of his friend and fellow-townsman, Octavian. Nothing is known of Attius.

665. We do not know where he was going.

215 (XV. 16)

CICERO TO CASSIUS

Rome, January (middle) 45

From M. Cicero to C. Cassius greetings.

I think you must be a trifle ashamed of yourself now. Here comes a third letter down upon you before you have produced so much as a sheet or a line! However, I am not pressing you. I shall expect a longer letter, or rather I shall require one. As for me, if I always had a bearer, I should dispatch them three an hour. I don't know how it is, but when I write something to you, I seem to see you here in front of me. I am not speaking according to the doctrine of appearances of images, to use the terminology of your new friends, who think that even mental appearances are aroused by Catius' *spectres*. For, in case you have not noticed it, what the Sage of Gargettus,[666] and Democritus before him, called 'images'[667] are termed 'spectres' by the late lamented Catius, Insubrian and Epicurean. Now even granting that those 'spectres' could strike the eyes, because they run upon the pupils of their own accord, I for one don't see how they can strike the mind – you will have to teach me when you are safely home again. Are we really to suppose that your 'spectre' is in my control, so that as soon as I take a fancy to think about you, up it comes? And not only you, who are in my heart all the time, but if I start thinking about the island of Britain, will its image fly into my brain?

But of all this later on. I am just testing your reactions. If

666. Epicurus belonged to the Attic district ('deme') of Gargettus.

667. Greek *eidôla. spectrum* in classical Latin occurs only in this letter and Cassius' reply. Perhaps Catius coined it (from *specio*, 'look at'). On the theory of visual perception through images see *Letters to Atticus* 23 (II.3).2.

you are nettled and upset, I shall continue and file a claim for your restitution to the philosophical persuasion[668] from which you have been ousted 'by violence, by force of arms'.[669] In this formula they don't usually add 'during the current year', so that if it is now two or three years since you were seduced by the wiles of Miss Pleasure into serving notice of divorce on Lady Virtue,[670] my action will still lie.

But to whom am I talking? Why, to the most gallant gentleman alive, whose every action since entering public life has been in the fullest accord with his splendid reputation. I am afraid that even this system of yours must have more spunk in it than I had supposed, that is if you are really an adherent.

'How on earth did he come to think of that?' you will be wondering. Why, because I have nothing else to write about. Of politics I can write nothing, for I do not care to write what I feel.

216 (XV. 19)

CASSIUS TO CICERO

Brundisium, January (last half) 45

From C. Cassius to M. Cicero greetings.

I trust you are well.

You may be sure that nothing I do in this sojourn of mine abroad is done more willingly than writing to you. It is as though I was chatting and joking with you in the flesh. That

668. What this was is uncertain. Perhaps, like Brutus, Cassius had been an adherent of Antiochus of Ascalon's 'Old Academy', which was close to Stoicism.

669. Cf. Letter 36 (VII.13). It seems to be implied that Cassius' conversion was in some way due to the Civil War.

670. See p. 59

does not, however, come about because of Catius' 'spectres' – in return for him I'll throw so many clodhopping Stoics back at you in my next letter that you'll declare Catius Athenian born!

I am glad that our friend Pansa left Rome in uniform amid general good-will, both for his own sake and, let me add, for all our sakes. For I trust people will realize how intense and universal is hatred for cruelty and love for worth and clemency, so that they will see how the prizes most sought and coveted by the wicked come to the good. It is hard to persuade men that Right[671] is to be chosen *per se*; but that Pleasure and Peace of Mind are won by virtue, justice, and Right is both true and easily argued. Epicurus himself, from whom all these sorry translators of terms, Catius, Amafinius, etc., derive, says: 'To live pleasurably is not possible without living rightly and justly.' Thus it is that Pansa, whose goal is Pleasure, retains Virtue; and those whom you and your friends call Pleasure-lovers are Right-lovers and Justice-lovers, practising and retaining all the virtues. And so Sulla[672] (whose judgement[673] we must respect) saw that the philosophers were at loggerheads: instead of trying to discover *what* was good, he went and bought up all the goods he could find! Indeed I have borne his death with fortitude. However, Caesar will not let us miss him long – he has other victims of justice to offer us in his place. Nor will *he* miss Sulla's activity in the auction rooms – he will only have to look at Sulla junior.

Now to get back to public affairs, let me know in your reply how things are going in Spain. I'm devilish worried, and I'd rather have the old easy-going master than try a cruel new one. You know what a fool Gnaeus[674] is, how he takes cruelty

671. *to kalon*; cf. *Letters to Atticus* 134 (VII.11).1. – Capitals indicate Greek terms.

672. Cf. Letter 214 (XV.17).

673. Perhaps in allusion to Sulla's conviction on charges of electoral malpractice in 66.

674. Pompey's elder son.

for courage, how he thinks we always made fun of him. I'm afraid he may answer our persiflage with his sword, hobbledehoy-fashion. If you love me, tell me what is going on. Ah, how I should like to know your frame of mind as you read this! Anxious or easy? I should know by the same token what I ought to do.

Not to be too prolix, goodbye. Go on caring for me. If Casear has won, expect me quickly back.

217 (IX. 10)

CICERO TO DOLABELLA[675]

Rome, beginning of 45

From M. Cicero to P. Dolabella greetings.

I dare not let our friend Salvius[676] leave without giving him something in the way of a letter to you, though upon my word I have nothing to write except that I am marvellously fond of you; and of that I am sure you are convinced without my writing a word. In point of fact I have better cause to expect to hear from you than you from me. Nothing is afoot in Rome which I judge you would care to know, unless perhaps you wish to known that I am appointed arbiter between our friend Nicias and Vidius. The latter, I believe, is producing a couple of lines registering a payment to Nicias, who on his side Aristarchus-like obelizes these same. My job is to decide like a critic of old whether they are the poet's own or interpolated.

I expect you may ask now whether I have forgotten those mushrooms at Nicias' and the giant snails with * * *.[677] Come now, do you suppose that my old austerity has been so

675. Now with Caesar in Spain.
676. Probably Caesar's freedman, not Atticus' slave.
677. Several words are corrupt in the manuscripts.

thoroughly shaken off that even in a court of law there isn't a remnant to be seen of my former grave demeanour? Never mind, I shall give our charming little *copain* back as good as new. I shan't be so foolish as to find against him only for you to rehabilitate him for fear Plancus Bursa be left without a school-master.[678]

But here I go rambling on and on, when I don't know whether your mind is at ease or whether you are anxiously employed on some substantial bit of military business. So when I am assured of finding you in a mood to laugh, I shall write more at length. However, I want you to know that there was much public concern about P. Sulla's death before it was known for certain. Now they have stopped wondering *how* he met his end. What they know is all they want to know. I bear the event philosophically, apart from one misgiving – I'm afraid Caesar's auctions may go with less of a swing.

218 (VI. 18)

CICERO TO Q. LEPTA

Rome, January 45

From Cicero to Lepta.

As soon as your letter came to hand by your man Seleucus, I at once sent a note to Balbus enquiring what the law[679] had to say. He replied that practising auctioneers[680] are debarred

678. Cicero playfully writes as though Nicias was facing a criminal charge and would go into exile if he lost the case. Nicias was a scholar, the obnoxious Bursa an ignoramus.

679. Evidently a new law of Caesar, drafted (presumably by Balbus) but not yet promulgated. The provision respecting auctioneers may have been taken over from earlier legislation.

680. Their trade was not highly regarded, perhaps because they made money out of the distress of others – debtors forced to sell their property.

from membership of a town council, but that the bar does not apply to persons who have practised in the past. So your friends and mine can set their minds at rest. It would have been intolerable, after all, if persons who had once practised as auctioneers were not allowed to sit on their town councils, while currently practising inspectors of entrails[681] were appointed members of the Roman Senate.

No news of Spain. But it is generally accepted that Pompey has a large army, as Caesar himself sent his people a copy of a letter of Paciaecus' stating the number of legions as eleven. Messalla[682] too has written to Q. Salassus[683] that his brother, P. Curtius, has been executed in front of the army by Pompey's orders on a charge of conspiring with certain Spaniards to seize Pompey, when he entered some town or other to obtain supplies, and hand him over to Caesar.

As regards your own affair (your standing surety for Pompey), when your co-surety Galba (a gentleman who cannot be accused of carelessness where his finances are concerned) gets back, I shall be in constant touch with him to see if a solution can be found. He seemed confident that it could.

I am greatly pleased that you think so well of my *Orator*. I do flatter myself that I have put into that book whatever judgement I may possess on the subject of public speaking. If it is as you say you find it, then I too amount to something. If not, I am content that my reputation for sound judgement and the book shall suffer in exactly the same proportion. I hope our little boy[684] has already developed a taste for such compositions. Though he has still to grow up, there is something to be said for letting his ears buzz with utterances of this kind.

My Tullia's confinement has kept me in Rome. But even now

681. *haruspices* practised the Etruscan system of divination from the entrails of sacrificial animals.

682. M. Valerius Messalla Rufus, Consul in 53.

683. Q. Curtius Salassus was a Prefect under Antony in 41.

684. Lepta's son.

that she has, as I hope, fairly well regained her strength, I am still kept here waiting to extract the first instalment[685] out of Dolabella's agents. And in point of fact I am not the gadabout I used to be. My buildings and the freedom from distraction were what I used to enjoy. Well, I have a town house as pleasant as any of my country places, and greater freedom from distraction than anywhere in the wilds. So even my literary work is not hampered, and I employ myself in it without any interruptions. I fancy therefore that I shall see you here before you see me there.

Your charming boy should learn Hesiod by heart and never forget 'Sweat before virtue', etc.[686]

219 (XVI. 18)

CICERO TO TIRO

Rome (?), 46 or 45 (?)

From Tullius to Tiro greetings.

Well then! Isn't that as it should be? *I* think so, and should like to make it 'to his dear Tiro'.[687] However, let us beware of jealous malice, if you wish – the malice I have often despised.

I am glad your perspiration has done you good. If my place at Tusculum has done you good too, heavens, how much

685. Of Tullia's dowry. She and Dolabella were now divorced.

686. 'The Gods set sweat in front of excellence', from Hesiod's *Works and Days* (289).

687. Tiro seems to have suggested that the heading of Cicero's previous letter, 'Tullius to Tiro greetings', was too familiar. To all other correspondents except his wife and brother Cicero uses his *cognomen*. Yet earlier letters to Tiro were similarly headed, and most of those after his manumission add *suo* ('his dear'). Perhaps the letter to which Tiro referred had to be shown to a third party.

better I shall love it! But if you love me, and if you don't you make a very pretty pretence of it, which after all answers nicely – well, however that stands, humour your health. In your devotion to me you have not hitherto devoted yourself enough to that. You know what it requires – digestion, no fatigue, a short walk, massage, proper evacuation. Mind you come back in good shape. I should love not only you but my house at Tusculum the more.

Prod Parhedrus to hire the garden himself. That will give the gardener a jolt. That rascal Helico used to pay HS1,000 when there was no sun-trap, no drain, no wall, no shed. After all my expense is this fellow going to make fools of us? Give him a hot time, as I did Motho[688] and in consequence have more flowers than I can well use.

I should like to know what is happening about Crabra,[689] even though nowadays water is really too plentiful. I shall send the sundial and the books when the weather is clear. But have you no books with you? Or are you composing something Sophoclean? Mind you have results to show.

Caesar's familiar A. Ligurius is dead, a good fellow and a friend of mine. Let me know when we are to expect you. Look after yourself carefully.

Goodbye.

220 (XVI. 20)

CICERO TO TIRO

Rome (?), shortly after the foregoing

From Tullius to Tiro greetings.

On my life, my dear Tiro, I am anxious about your health.

688. Perhaps gardener at the house on the Palatine.

689. The Aqua Crabra, an aqueduct running into Rome, supplied water to the villa, for which Cicero paid.

But I am sure that, if you continue to exercise the same care, you will soon be strong again. Put the books[690] away. Do the catalogue when Metrodorus[691] likes, since you have to live under his ordinance. Deal with the gardener as you think best. You can see the gladiators on the Kalends and return the following day. That is my advice – but as you please. Look after yourself carefully if you care for me.

Goodbye.

221 (VI. 22)

CICERO TO CN. DOMITIUS AHENOBARBUS

Rome (?), May (?) 46

From Cicero to Domitius.

I was not deterred from sending you a letter after your return to Italy by the fact that you had sent none to me. But I knew neither how to make you any promise, being myself in need of everything, nor how to advise you, when I was short of advice myself, nor how to comfort you in the midst of such afflictions. The present situation in these respects is no better, it is far more hopeless even. However, I prefer to write an empty letter than not to write at all.

Even if I saw that you had tried to take upon yourself for the sake of the commonwealth a greater burden of duty than you would have been able to sustain,[692] I should still urge you in every way I could to accept life as it is on the conditions on

690. Not Cicero's library at Tusculum but those mentioned in the previous letter.

691. Tiro's doctor.

692. i.e. 'had gone to Africa in 48 to carry on the fight against Caesar'. Cicero's convoluted way of putting this shows that he felt himself on dangerous ground.

which it is offered you. But you set a term to the course you so well and gallantly undertook, the same that Fortune herself decreed as the final limit to our struggles.[693] Therefore I implore and conjure you in the name of our old association and friendship, and of the abundant good-will I bear you and you equally bear me; preserve yourself for me, for your mother,[694] your wife, and all your family, to whom you are and have ever been most dear. Think of your own safety and that of those near to you, who depend on you. Make use now of what you have learned, those admirable teachings handed down by the wisest of mankind which from youth up you have absorbed into your memory and knowledge. Bear the loss of persons bound to you by good-will and good offices, signal in measure and number, if not with equanimity, then at any rate with fortitude.

What *I* can do I do not know, or rather I am conscious that it is all too little. But I promise you to do whatever in my judgement conduces to your safety and dignity with the same devotion that *you* have always shown to practical effect in *my* affairs. This disposition of mine I have freely conveyed to that excellent lady your mother, who bears you so deep an affection. If you write to me, I shall execute your wishes as I understand them. But if you do not write, I shall none the less pay most zealous and particular heed to everything that seems to me for your advantage.

Goodbye.

693. The defeat at Pharsalia.
694. Cato's sister Porcia.

222 (VI. 10. 4–6)

CICERO TO TREBIANUS[695]

Rome, August (?) 46

From M. Cicero to Trebianus greetings.

I should have written sooner, if I had seen what type of letter to write. In circumstances like these the part of friends is either to offer comfort or to make promises. I have not been doing the former, because I heard from many quarters of the courage and good sense with which you bear the times' ill-usage, and how efficacious a consolation you find in the consciousness of your past actions and motives. If you do this, you reap the reward of the noble studies in which I know you have always been engaged, and I earnestly urge you so to do.

Moreover you are very well versed in affairs and in all the lessons that history teaches, nor am I myself a novice in these matters, having engaged both in study, though less perhaps than I could wish, and in practical experience of affairs even more than I could wish. And I give you this pledge: the harsh ill-usage you now suffer will not long continue. The personage whose power is greatest seems to me to be inclining ever more and more towards justice and his own natural disposition; and the cause itself is such that it must soon revive and be constituted once more, along with freedom, which cannot lie for ever in the dust. Each day brings some act of unexpected lenity or liberality. All this depends on shifts of circumstances which are often slight, and so I shall keep my eyes open for every movement and let no opportunity slip of helping and alleviating your condition.

So I hope the other type of letter which I mentioned will

695. This Pompeian exile is otherwise unknown.

become easier for me every day, and that I shall also be in a position to make promises. That I shall do more gladly in deeds than in words. I would ask you to believe that (at least so far as I have been able to judge) you have more friends than most people who are, and have formerly been, in the same case as yourself; and that I yield to none of them. Keep a brave and lofty spirit – that depends on you alone. What depends on fortune will be governed by circumstances, and our calculations will provide for it.

223 (VI. 10. 1–3)

CICERO TO TREBIANUS

Rome, September (?) 46

From M. Cicero to Trebianus greetings.

How highly I regard you and always have, and how highly I have come to realize you regard me, I am my own witness. Your decision to continue fighting in the civil war, or rather the chance which led you to do so, was always a great distress to me; and the result, that the recovery of your position and status is taking longer than is right and than I should have wished, is a matter of no less concern to me than my misfortunes always were to you. Therefore I have freely opened my mind to Postumulenus, to Sestius, very often to our friend Atticus, and most recently to your freedman Theudas. I have told each one of them more than once that I am anxious to do my duty by you and your children in every way I can. I should like you to write to your people and tell them to regard my time, advice, money, and loyalty (these at least are under my own control) as at their disposal for all purposes. If my public and private influence counted for what it should in a commonwealth to which I have done such service, you too would be what you were – most worthy of any rank, however exalted, and assuredly by far the most distinguished member of your own order. But both of us have come down in the world at the same time and for the same reason. So I promise you the commodities I have just mentioned, which still belong to me, as well as those others which I fancy I retain in some degree as relics of my former status. Caesar himself, as I have had numerous opportunities to recognize, is not unfriendly to me; and almost all his most intimate associates happen to be bound to me by considerable services rendered in the past, and pay me assiduous attention and regard. If an opening occurs for me to make representations concerning your circumstances, I mean your status as a citizen, in which all else is included (and the way they talk makes me every day more hopeful of this), I shall make them personally and work hard.

There is no need to enter into details. My zeal and good-will are yours in entirety. But it is very important that all your people should know (your letters can make it clear to them) that everything that is Cicero's is at Trebianus' disposal. The point is that they must think nothing too difficult for me to undertake with pleasure on your behalf.

224 (VI. 11)

CICERO TO TREBIANUS

Tusculum (?), June (first half) 45 (?)

From M. Cicero to Trebianus greetings.

My feelings towards Dolabella used to be merely of regard. I *owed* him nothing, for it had never so happened that I had need of his services, and he was indebted to me for standing by him in his ordeals.[696] But now, by his superlative response

696. Cf. p. 137.

both previously in the matter of your estate and at the present time in that of your restoration, his kindness has placed me under so powerful an obligation that there is no man to whom I am more beholden. On this my hearty congratulations – and I would rather *you* congratulated me than thanked me. Thanks I do not at all crave, and congratulations you can offer in all sincerity.

For the rest, now that your high character and standing have cleared the way for your return to your family and friends, as a wise and high-minded man you must forget what you have lost and think of what you have recovered. You will live with your people and with me. You have gained more in respect than you have lost in possessions. And possessions themselves would be more enjoyable if there were a commonwealth.

Our friend Vestorius has written to me that you express the utmost gratitude to myself. Such acknowledgement on your part is very agreeable to me, and I am particularly willing that you make it among others to our friend Siro. One likes what one does to win approbation, and the approbation of a very wise man is especially welcome.

I am looking forward to seeing you as soon as possible.

225 (IV. 13)

CICERO TO NIGIDIUS FIGULUS

Rome, August (?) 46

From M. Cicero to P. Figulus greetings.

I have been asking myself this long while past just what to write to you, but nothing comes to mind – not any particular thing to say, not even a *manner* of writing normally used in correspondence. Circumstances have taken away one element[697] customary in the letters we used to write in happier

697. Jokes.

days. Fortune has made it impossible for me to write or even think in that vein. There remains a gloomy, doleful sort of letter-writing, suited to the times we live in. That too fails me. It should include either the pledge of some assistance or comfort for your distress. Now as for promises, I can make none, for I myself am in like case and support my misfortunes by others' means. I am more often inclined to complain of the life I lead than to be thankful for living at all.

True, I personally have suffered no conspicuous private injury, and I can think of nothing to wish for at such a time which Caesar has not spontaneously granted me. But my troubles are such that I feel guilty in continuing to live. I lack not only many personal intimates, snatched from me by death or scattered in exile, but all the friends whose good-will I won when I defended the state with you at my side. I live among the wreckage of their fortunes,the plundering of their possessions. To hear of it would be sad enough, but I have actually before my eyes the heartrending spectacle of the dissipation of their estates – the men who were my helpers when I put out that fire[698] in days gone by. In the city where not long ago I stood high in influence, respect, and fame, I now have none of these things. I do indeed enjoy the greatest consideration from Caesar himself, but that cannot counterbalance the violence, the total revolution of environment. Deprived, therefore, as I am of everything to which I had been accustomed by nature, inclination, and habit, I cut a sorry figure in other men's eyes, so at least I fancy, and in my own. Born as I was for action, incessant action worthy of a man, I now have no way to employ my energies or even my thoughts. I, who once had it in my power to help the obscure and even the guilty, now find myself unable even to make a kindly promise to P. Nigidius, the most accomplished and the most stainless man of our time, once so influential and assuredly so good a friend of mine.

698. Catiline's conspiracy. Cicero is said to have relied much on Nigidius' advice at that time.

This sort of letter-writing, therefore, is ruled out. It remains for me to offer you comfort and to try by reasoned argument to divert you from your troubles. But you have in the highest degree, if ever any man had, the faculty of consoling yourself or another. Therefore I shall not touch that side of the subject which starts from recondite philosophical theory. That I shall leave entirely to you. *You* will see what is worthy of a man of sense and courage, what is demanded of you by dignity, elevation of mind, your past, your studies, the pursuits in which you have distinguished yourself from childhood upwards. I merely assure you of what my understanding and intuition tell me, being in Rome and keeping a close eye on the course of events: that you will not have to bear your present troubles much longer, but that those that you share with us may be with you always.

To begin with the personage whose word is law, I think I see his mind and that it is favourable to your cause. These are not idle words. The less I have of his intimacy, the more curious I am to probe. It is only because he wants to make it easier for himself to give discouraging answers to people with whom he is more seriously annoyed that he has so far been slow to release you from your unpleasant predicament. But his friends, especially those he likes best, speak and feel about you with remarkable warmth. To that we can add the popular sentiment, or rather the universal consensus. Even the Republic, which counts for little enough at the moment but must count for something some day, will exert whatever power she may have to win your pardon from these very people in whose hands she lies, and, believe me, it will not be long.

So I will now go back on my tracks and make you a promise, which earlier in this letter I refrained from doing. I shall both cultivate his intimates, who have no small regard for me and are much in my company, and find a way into familiar intercourse with himself, from which a sense of shame on my part has deterred me hitherto. Assuredly I shall follow any path which I think likely to lead to our goal. In this whole sphere I shall do more than I venture to put on paper. Other kinds of service, I am sure, are at your disposal in many quarters; but from me they are most heartily at your command. Of my possessions there is none that I would not as soon were yours as mine. On this and all related points I say little only because I would rather have you expect to enjoy your own, as I am confident you will.

It only remains for me to beg and implore you to be of excellent courage and to remember not only the lessons you have learned from other great men but those of which you are yourself the author, the products of your intellect and study. If you put them all together, you will be in the best of hope; and, come what may, good or bad, you will bear it with philosophy. But all this you know better than I, or rather better than any man. For my part I shall attend with all zeal and diligence to whatever I find to concern you, and shall treasure the memory of your kindness to me in the darkest days of my life.

226 (VI. 12)

CICERO TO AMPIUS BALBUS

Rome, August or September (?) 46

From Cicero to Ampius best greetings.

I congratulate you, my dear Balbus, and in all sincerity. For I am not so foolish as to wish you temporary enjoyment of an illusory happiness, only to be dashed of a sudden and to fall so low that nothing later on could lift you into equanimity. I have pleaded your cause more openly than my present circumstances warranted, for I thought more of my fondness for you and the uninterrupted affection which you have been so sedulous to foster than of the debility which has overtaken my personal influence. All that concerns your return and restoration has been promised and confirmed, positively and definitely. I was present, observing and taking note.

The fact is, opportunely enough, that I have Caesar's intimates all linked to me in familiar intercourse and friendship, and stand with them second only to Caesar himself. Pansa, Hirtius, Balbus, Oppius, Matius, and Postumus carry their regard for me to really extraordinary lengths. If I had had to bring this about by my own exertions, I should not regret my trouble, considering the times we live in. But I have done nothing in the way of time-serving. With all of them I have friendships of long standing; and I have pleaded with them incessantly on your behalf. But my principal reliance has been on Pansa, who is most zealous for your welfare and anxious to please myself; for he has influence with Caesar founded on respect no less than personal liking. And I am very pleased with Tillius Cimber. When all is said, petitions founded on obligation carry more weight with Caesar than those of self-interest; and because Cimber had such an obligation, he carried more weight than he would have carried on behalf of any other person.

A passport was not granted straight away because of the unconscionable rascality of certain people, who would have resented the granting of a pardon to 'the Trumpet of the Civil War', as they call you, and who talk at large as though they were not glad enough that the war took place. It therefore seemed best to proceed discreetly and on no account to let it be generally known that your case had already been settled. But it will go through very soon; indeed I have no doubt that by the time you read these lines the thing will have been done. Pansa, a responsible and reliable person, assured me, in fact guaranteed, that he would procure the passport in no time. Nevertheless I thought I should tell you all this, for the way your dear Eppuleia spoke and Ampia's[699] tears make it evident that you are not in such stout heart as your letters suggest. Moreover, they think your trouble of mind will grow much worse now that they are no longer with you. So I considered it highly desirable to relieve your anxiety and distress by giving you the facts fully and definitely, since definite they are.

You know that in my earlier letters I have sought to console you as a brave, sensible man rather than hold out any assurance of restoration, apart from what I thought should be hoped for from the commonwealth itself, once this conflagration has been extinguished. Remember your own letters, in which you have always shown me a lofty spirit, steadfast and ready for whatever might betide. That gave me no surprise, recalling as I did that you have been engaged in public affairs from your youth upwards, that your periods of office have coincided with the very crises of our national fortunes and existence,[700] and that you embarked on this very war prepared for the role not only of happy winner but, should it so fall out, of philosophic loser. Since, furthermore, you devote your literary activity to recording the deeds of brave men for posterity, it behoves you to consider it your duty not to present yourself as in any way dissimilar to the objects of your eulogies.

Such words, however, would be more appropriate to a state of things which you have already left behind you. As matters now stand, you have only to prepare yourself to bear conditions here along with us. If I knew any remedy for them, I should pass it on to you. But the one refuge is learning and literary work, which we have always pursued. Merely a source of pleasure in good times, it now appears as our life-line.

But to return to my starting-point: have no doubt that all is settled for your restoration and return.

699. Ampius' wife and (probably) daughter. Apparently they had been with him but had recently returned to Italy.

700. Ampius was Tribune in Cicero's Consulship (63) and Praetor in Caesar's (59).

227 (VI. 13)

CICERO TO Q. LIGARIUS

Rome, August or September (?) 46

From Cicero to Ligarius.

In your present circumstances I owed it to our friendship to write to you something that might bring comfort or help, but hitherto I have not done so, because I did not see how my words could assuage or alleviate your distress. But now that I have begun to entertain high hopes that we shall soon have you back in your rightful place, I feel I must make clear to you both my opinion and my disposition.

First then, let me say that, as my understanding and perception tell me, Caesar will not be over-hard on you. Circumstances, time, public opinion, and, I think, his own nature make him more lenient every day. This I feel where others are concerned, and as regards yourself I also hear it from his most intimate friends. Ever since the news[701] arrived from Africa, I have never stopped pleading with them in conjunction with your brothers. *Their* high character, family feeling, conspicuous affection for you, and assiduous, unflagging concern for your rehabilitation are producing an effect; so much so that I believe there is nothing which Caesar himself will not concede. But if it goes more slowly than we wish, the heavy pressure of business upon him as the recipient of all petitions has made access to him more difficult, and at the same time he was especially irritated by the resistance in Africa, and seems inclined to prolong the anxieties of those who he feels caused himself protracted difficulty and annoyance. But in this too I understand that every day makes him more tolerant and forgiving. So

701. Of the battle of Thapsus (6 April); or possibly of Ligarius' subsequent capture at Hadrumetum.

trust me, and make a mental note of my assurance that you will not long remain in your present disagreeable position.

Having told you what I think, I shall make plain my friendly disposition towards you by deed rather than word, though if I had as much say as I ought to have in a state which I have served as you rate my services, you too would not be in this unpleasant situation. The same cause that has brought your civic existence into peril has dissolved the power I used to have. Nevertheless, whatever the shadow of my old prestige and the residue of my influence may count for, my zeal, advice, time, influence, money, and loyalty shall be at the disposal of your excellent brothers in all things.

You have always had a stout heart. Keep it now, partly for the reasons I have given and partly because of the political aims and sentiments you have always held. In view of these, not only ought you to hope for a favourable outcome now but, even if everything were against you, the consciousness of your past acts and motives should strengthen you to bear whatever may betide with fortitude and magnanimity.

228 (VI. 14)

CICERO TO Q. LIGARIUS

Rome, end of November 46

From Cicero to Ligarius.

Be assured that I am devoting all my effort, all my time, attention, and energy to your restitution. I have always had the greatest regard for you, and the conspicuous family loyalty and fraternal affection shown by your brothers, whose friendship I have embraced no less warmly than your own, do not permit me to omit any act or occasion of service and good-will towards you. But what I am doing, and have done, on your behalf I prefer you to learn from their letters rather than from mine. My hope, or rather, my confident assurance, of your restoration is what I want personally to make clear to you.

If any man tends to be apprehensive in affairs of moment and danger, always fearing the worst rather than hoping for the best, I am that man. If this is a failing, I confess that I am not immune from it. But I tell you this: on 26 November, at your brothers' request, I paid Caesar a morning visit. I had to put up with all the humiliating and wearisome preliminaries of obtaining admission and interview. Your brothers and relations knelt at his feet, while I spoke in terms appropriate to your case and circumstances. When I took my leave, it was with the persuasion, not only from Caesar's words, gentle and gracious as these were, but from the look in his eyes and many other indications more easily perceived than described, that there was no doubt about your reinstatement.

So keep a brave and lofty spirit. If you have been taking the foulest weather with philosophy, take the fairer with good cheer. Despite what I have told you, I shall lend my support to your cause as though it was one of the utmost difficulty, and shall continue to plead for you most gladly, not only with Caesar himself but with all his friends, whom I have found very friendly to me.

Goodbye.

229 (IV. 8)

CICERO TO M. MARCELLUS

Rome, August 46

From M. Cicero to M. Marcellus greetings.

I do not venture to offer advice to a man of your exemplary sagacity, or encouragement to the noblest and bravest of souls; and certainly I must not attempt consolation. If you are bearing all that has befallen as I am told you are, I ought rather to congratulate you on your manly spirit than to comfort your distress. If, on the other hand, you are bowed by the weight of the public calamities, I cannot boast such ingenuity as to find comfort for you when I can find none for myself. All that remains then is for me to proffer and render my services to you in all things and to be at the disposal of your family in any way they may desire, holding myself bound to do on your behalf not only whatever I can but what I cannot as well.

One thing though I will say, and you may take it as a piece of advice or as an expression of opinion, or you may suppose that the good-will I have for you made it impossible for me to keep silence: I hope you will come round to the view I take in my own case, that if there is to be some form of commonwealth, you ought to be in it, as one of its leaders in virtue of public opinion and reality, but of necessity yielding to the conditions of the time; whereas if there is no commonwealth, Rome is still a better place than any other, even for passing one's exile. After all, if liberty is our object, where does this ruler's writ not run? But if we are merely looking for a place to live, what is more pleasant than hearth and home? But believe me, even he in whom all power resides is well disposed towards talent; and as for birth and rank, he cherishes them so far as circumstances and his own political position allow.

But I am saying more than I had intended. Let me return then to the single point, that I am at your service. I shall stand with those near to you, if near they really are. Otherwise, I shall at any rate do no less in all things than is due to our friendship and mutual affection.

Goodbye.

230 (IV. 7)

CICERO TO M. MARCELLUS

Rome, September (?) 46

From M. Cicero to M. Marcellus greetings.

Your policy hitherto, as I understand it, is one with which I do not venture to find fault – not that I do not disagree with it, but because I think too highly of your wisdom to prefer my opinion to yours. However, the length of our friendship and your notable kindness towards me, of which I have had evidence ever since you were a boy, urge me to write to you in terms which I believe to be conducive to your welfare and judge not incompatible with your honour.

I very well remember that I am addressing a man who saw the seeds of these calamities long before they ripened; nor do I forget your fine and splendid record as Consul. But this is not all. I also saw your dissatisfaction, the utter lack of confidence you always felt in the way the civil war was conducted, in Cn. Pompeius' forces, in the type of army he led. I think you remember that I held the same views. Accordingly, you took little part in the conduct of operations, and I was always careful to take none. We were not fighting with the weapons with which we might have prevailed – policy, prestige, cause. In these lay our superiority, but we fought with brute force, in which we were outmatched. So we were vanquished, or, if moral standing cannot be vanquished, at any rate broken and cast down. Your reaction to that outcome cannot fail of high and universal acclaim. With the hope of victory you discarded the desire of combat, and showed that a wise man and a patriot will join with reluctance in the opening stages of a civil war, but willingly decline to pursue it to the end. Those who followed a different plan from yours manifestly split into two categories. Some, those who betook themselves to Africa, tried to resuscitate the war; others, like myself, committed themselves to the victor. You chose a middle way; you thought the former course savoured of obstinacy, the latter perhaps of pusillanimity.

I allow that your plan is generally, or shall I say universally, judged wise, and that many think it high-minded and courageous as well. But there is a limit, so at least it seems to me, to your present line of conduct; especially as I believe there is nothing except lack of will to hinder you from the enjoyment of all that is yours. For it is my understanding that the personage in whose hands power lies would not be hesitating but for one reason, a fear that you might not regard it as a favour at all.

My own opinion on this subject it is needless to state, since my action is manifest. None the less, even suppose you had determined to prefer perpetual absence to the sight of what you did not wish to see, you ought still to have reflected that, wherever you were, you would be in the power of the very man whose presence you avoided. Assume it were the case that he would be content to let you live a quiet, independent life far from your country and all that is yours, you would still have to ask yourself whether you would rather live in Rome, in your own house, under whatever conditions, than in Mytilene or Rhodes. But the power of him we fear is world-wide. Do you not prefer safety at your own hearth to danger at a stranger's? For my part, I would rather face death, if need were, at home in my country than as a stranger in a foreign land.

This view is shared by all who care for you – a mighty throng, to match your great and splendid qualities. We are also thinking of your private fortune, which we do not want to see dissipated. True, you can suffer no damage of a permanent sort, because neither the ruler of the commonwealth nor the commonwealth itself will tolerate that. All the same, I do not wish to see the pirates make an onslaught on your estate. I should not baulk at naming them if I were not confident that you know whom I mean.[702]

Here your best of cousins, C. Marcellus, intercedes for you as none other, with anxious thought, yes, and constant flow of tears. I stand next in solicitude and distress, but in supplication I am less forward because, having needed intercession myself, I do not have the right of approach, and my influence is that of a member of a vanquished party. But my counsel and zeal are at Marcellus' disposal. Your other relatives do not call me in. I am ready to do anything.

231 (IV. 9)

CICERO TO M. MARCELLUS

Rome, shortly after the foregoing

From M. Cicero to M. Marcellus greetings.

It is only a very few days since I gave Q. Mucius a letter for you of considerable length in which I made clear how I thought you ought to feel and what I thought you ought to do. But since your freedman Theophilus is setting out, whose loyalty and good-will towards you I have plainly seen, I did not wish him to go to you without a letter from me.

So once again, I urge you on the same points as in my previous letter, to choose without delay to live in whatever commonwealth we have. You will perhaps see much that you do not like, but no more than you *hear* every day. And it is not worthy of you to be affected by one sense only, that of sight, and to be less troubled when you perceive the very same thing

702. We do not know. M. Marcellus himself complains of the disloyalty of his family and friends, apart from his cousin (Letter 232 (IV.11)).

with your ears, although what is so perceived is apt to seem even bigger than it really is.

Perhaps you are afraid of having yourself to say things you do not mean, or do things you disapprove. Well, in the first place, to yield to the pressures of the time, that is, to obey necessity, has always been considered a wise man's part. In the second, this particular evil, at present anyway, is not in the case. One is not free, it may be, to say what one thinks, but one is quite free to keep silence. All power has been handed over to one man; and he follows no counsel, not even that of his friends, except his own. It would not have been very different if *our* leader[703] ruled the commonwealth. In the war, when all of us were united in danger, he followed his own judgement and that of certain persons by no means conspicuous for their good sense. Are we to suppose that he would have been more democratically minded in victory than he was when the issue hung in the balance? When you were Consul he did not follow your admirable advice; and when your cousin administered the office under your guidance, he would not make you his counsellors. If he were now supreme, do you suppose he would feel any need of our opinions?

In civil war, never once experienced by our forbears but often by our own generation, all things are sad, but none sadder than victory. Even if it goes to the better party, it makes them more fierce and violent; though they may not be so by nature, they are forced to it willy-nilly. For the victor has often to act even against his inclination at the behest of those to whom he owes his victory. Did you not see as I did how cruel that other victory would have proved? Would you *then* have kept away from your country for fear of seeing what you would not have liked? 'No,' you will say, 'for I myself should have retained my wealth and status.' Surely to a man of your moral stature his own affairs count as trifles, his deeper concern is for the commonwealth.

703. Pompey.

And then, where does this policy of yours end? So far your conduct is approved, and even your fortune is held to be good in the circumstances: the first, because you joined in the opening of the civil war of necessity and wisely declined to persevere to the end; the second, because you have retained your high standing and reputation in honourable retirement. But now no place should have more charms for you than your country, and you must not love her the less because her beauty is marred. You ought rather to pity her, and not deprive her of the sight of you also, bereft as she is of so many illustrious children.

Furthermore, if refusal to supplicate the victor was nobility of spirit, are you sure it is not pride to spurn his generosity? If it is wisdom to keep away from your country, is it not insensibility not to miss her? If you may not be able to enjoy public life, is it not foolish to refuse to enjoy your private fortune?

The capital point is this: if you feel the life you are leading suits you better, you must still consider whether it is equally secure. Swords are loose in their scabbards nowadays; but abroad there are fewer scruples to check a deed of violence.

In my concern for your safety I can claim to rival, or at any rate to approach, your cousin Marcellus. It is for you to take thought for your present circumstances, your status as a citizen, your life, and your estate.

232 (IV. 11)

M. MARCELLUS TO CICERO

Mytilene, October 46

From Marcellus to Cicero greetings.

That your advice has always weighed heavily with me you can judge from all previous experience, but the matter in hand is a notable example. My cousin C. Marcellus, who is dearly fond of me, not only advised, but begged and implored me; yet he could not persuade me until your letter determined me to follow your joint judgement rather than any other.

The letters I have had from you both tell me how the affair went through. I cordially accept your congratulations because of the friendly spirit in which they are offered; but I am far more pleased and grateful to find that, when so very few of my friends and relatives and connections sincerely wished for my restoration, you have shown such conspicuous affection and good-will towards me. As for the rest, it is such that, given the times, I was quite well content to do without it. But *this* is another matter; without the good-will of such men and such friends as you, nobody, in my judgement, can truly live, whether in good fortune or bad. So herein I do congratulate myself; and I shall not fail to give you substantial proof that the man to whom you have rendered your service is your very sincere friend.

Goodbye.

233 (IV. 10)

CICERO TO M. MARCELLUS

Rome, December 46 (?)

From Cicero to Marcellus greetings.

I have no news to give you, and was in fact beginning to expect a letter from you, or rather you yourself in person; but since Theophilus is leaving, I could not let him go without something in the way of a letter. Be sure then to come as soon as you can. Your coming, believe me, is eagerly awaited, not only by us your friends but by every man in Rome. I am sometimes visited by a sneaking apprehension that you are disposed to take your time about your homecoming. If your eyes were your only organ of perception, I should quite forgive you for preferring to avoid the sight of certain individuals. But things heard are not much less vexatious than things seen, and I suspect that your early arrival will be much to the advantage of your private estate; and the same applies from all other points of view. So I have thought it right to say a word in season. But having made my opinion plain, I leave the rest to your wise consideration. I should, however, be grateful if you would let me know when we may expect you.

234 (VI. 6)

CICERO TO A. CAECINA[704]

Rome, October (?) 46

From M. Cicero to A. Caecina greetings.

I fear you may think me negligent, which I have no business to be towards a friend to whom I am bound by many obligations and by pursuits in common; still, I fear you find me a neglectful correspondent. I should have written long ago and often but that, as my hopes rose higher day by day, I wanted to send you a letter of congratulation rather than one of moral encouragement. As matters stand, I hope to congratulate you soon, and so I defer that theme to another occasion.

In *this* letter I think I should use yet again the influence I command with you, not indeed as one much wiser than the ordinary but as a most sincere friend, to fortify your spirit; though, from what I hear and hope, it is very far from feeble. I shall not console you as a man undone beyond all hope of recovery, but as one of whose rehabilitation I feel no more doubt than I remember you used to feel of mine. For I recall

704. Now in Sicily, awaiting Caesar's permission to return to Italy.

that, after my expulsion from the commonwealth by those who believed it could not fall so long as I stood upright, many travellers coming to me from Asia, where you were at the time, told me how confidently you predicted my speedy and glorious return. Now if *you* had a system which did not mislead you, based on the marvellous lore of Etruria as imparted to you by your noble and excellent father, no more shall I be led astray by my prophetic skill. I gained it not only from the admonitions and precepts of sages and by assiduous theoretical study, as you know, but also by my long experience as a statesman and the remarkable vicissitudes of my career. My reliance upon it is the more secure because in all these dark and perplexed transactions it has never once deceived me. I would give you examples of my predictions, were I not afraid of being thought to have manufactured them *ex post facto*. However, there are witnesses in abundance to attest that I originally advised Pompey against allying himself with Caesar, and later against dissolving the alliance. I saw that the alliance broke the power of the Senate, whereas its dissolution spelt civil war. I was on the closest terms with Caesar, and held Pompey in the greatest regard; but my advice was loyal to Pompey and salutary to both.

Of my other previsions I say nothing, because I would not have our present ruler, who has been very good to me, think that I gave counsels to Pompey which, had Pompey heeded them, would have meant that he himself would indeed be enjoying a position of distinction and leadership in civil life, but would not be holding so much power as is now his. I recommended that Pompey should go to Spain.[705] Had he done so, there would have been no civil war. I did not so much contend that Caesar should be granted permission to stand for office in his absence as that his candidature should in fact be admitted, seeing that at Pompey's own urging during his Consulship the

705. Perhaps in January 49, immediately before war broke out. Earlier Cicero had been against Pompey going to Spain (cf. *Letters to Atticus* 104 (v.11).4).

People had so ordered.[706] A pretext[707] for war arose. Did I leave anything undone in the way of warning or protest in advocating the most inequitable peace as preferable to the most righteous of wars? My advice was overborne, not so much by Pompey, on whom it made an impression, as by persons who in reliance on Pompey's generalship conceived that victory in such a war would be highly opportune for their personal affairs and ambitions. When hostilities were joined I remained passive, and I stayed in Italy as long as I was able after they had been shifted elsewhere. But sensibility prevailed with me over fear. I was ashamed to fail Pompey in his hour of need, when he in time gone by had not failed me. Duty then, or my reputation with the honest men, or sensibility carried the day. Like Amphiaraus[708] in the plays I set out

witting full well,
To bane right plain to see.

And no reverse befell us in that war which I did not predict.

Well then, since after the manner of augurs and astrologers I have established with you, as a public Augur, the credit of my augural and divinatory claims on the basis of my past predictions, my prophecy will be entitled to respect. I do not make it from the flight of one kind of ominous bird or the left-hand cry of another, as our system prescribes, nor yet from *tripudia solistima* or *sonivia*;[709] I have other signs to watch – no

706. In 52 the ten Tribunes had carried a law allowing Caesar to stand for the Consulship *in absentia*. Pompey backed it and Cicero assisted (*Letters to Atticus* 124 (VII.I).3).

707. The flight of the two Tribunes, Antony and Q. Cassius, to Caesar's camp on 7 January 49.

708. In the legend of the Seven against Thebes the seer Amphiaraus was persuaded by his wife Eriphyle to join the Argive expedition though he knew it would end in disaster. The quotation that follows may be from Accius' tragedy *Eriphyle*.

709. Omens taken from food dropping from the mouths of the sacred chickens.

surer, perhaps, but less difficult to perceive and less readily mistaken. For the purpose of my divining the signs are observed in two categories, one deriving from Caesar's personality, the other from the general nature of political conditions. In Caesar we find a mild and merciful disposition, as portrayed in your excellent volume of *Remonstrances*.[710] Moreover, he is remarkably partial to outstanding talents like your own. He also defers to a widespread sentiment, when it is just and inspired by principle, not frivolous or self-interested; and in that connection he will be powerfully impressed by the united voice of Etruria. Why then have these factors hitherto failed of their due effect? Because he reckons he will be unable to resist a multitude of claims if once he gives way to you, with whom he is supposed to have more right to be angry. You will ask what in that case we have to hope for from an angry arbiter. This: he will realize that he is going to draw his praises from the fountain that sprinkled him with cold water. Finally, he is a very clever, far-sighted man. He realizes that a man like you, of birth easily the highest in your part of Italy, which is a very far from contemptible part, and in our common body politic equal to any of the best of your generation in talent, influence, and public reputation, cannot be barred from the commonwealth in the long run. He will not wish you to owe your eventual restoration to time rather than to himself straight away.

Having spoken of Caesar, I pass to the nature of things and circumstances. Nobody is so unfriendly to the cause which Pompey espoused with more spirit than forethought as to dare to call us bad citizens or scoundrels. In this connection I often admire Caesar's responsibility, fairness, and good sense. He never mentions Pompey's name except in the most respectful

710. Caecina had written a 'very libellous' (so Suetonius, *Iul.* 75) book against Caesar during the war. Later he tried to make amends by a book of 'Remonstrances' (*querelarum*), extolling Caesar's merciful disposition.

terms. It may be said that he has committed many acts of harshness towards Pompey, but these were the work of war and victory, not of Caesar personally. And think how he has taken us into his favour: Cassius made his Legate, Brutus appointed to Cisalpine Gaul, Sulpicius to Greece, Marcellus, against whom he was especially incensed, restored in a fashion most honourable to Marcellus himself. All this I mention to show that it would be intolerable to the nature of things and political circumstances and incompatible with existing policy or any change of policy (a) that all men engaged in the same cause should not receive the same treatment and lot, and (b) that honest men and good citizens, to whom no stigma of disgrace has been attached, should not return to a community which has readmitted so many found guilty of heinous crimes.

There then is my augury. If I felt any uncertainty about it, I should not employ it in preference to a different consolation, which I might easily offer a brave man to sustain his spirits. If you took up arms for the state (as you then thought) in a full assurance of victory, your conduct would not be particularly praiseworthy; but if you recognized the possibility of defeat, the issues and events of warfare being uncertain, you ought not to have been fully prepared for good fortune but quite unable to bear bad. I should also speak of the comfort you should find in your conscience, and the pleasure in adversity which literary work should provide. I should recall the melancholy fates not only of men long dead but of your own late leaders and comrades. I should cite many celebrated names from the history of foreign peoples; for a reminder of the common law, so to speak, and the condition of humanity makes sorrow weigh less heavily. I should also set forth our mode of life here, where all is turmoil and confusion. After all, one cannot but miss a ruined commonwealth less keenly than a sound one. But nothing in this style is called for. As I hope, or rather as I perceive, we shall shortly see you restored to your rights.

Meanwhile, I long ago promised you in your absence and

that present mental and physical image of you, your steadfast and excellent son, my support and friendly offices, my time and trouble; and they have been at your disposal. I do so now in larger measure, because Caesar's attitude towards me is every day more expressive of the warmest friendship, while his intimates pay me a quite unparalleled regard. Whatever influence I come to have with him, whether public or private, it shall be for your behoof. Do you keep up your spirits, not only in fortitude of mind but in the brightest of hope.

235 (VI. 8)

CICERO TO A. CAECINA

Rome, December 46

From Cicero to Caecina.

Largus, who is much concerned for your welfare, told me when we met that the Kalends of January had been fixed as the limit of your stay. Having observed in all sorts of contexts that Caesar is in the habit of confirming arrangements made by Balbus and Oppius in his absence, I made strong representations to them that as a favour to myself you should be allowed to stay in Sicily as long as we wished. Usually I find they readily agree to anything that does not fall foul of their own ideas, or else they say no and give their reason. But to this request of mine, or rather urgent demand, they made no immediate reply. However, later the same day they came back, and gave me their assurance that you shall stay in Sicily as long as you like, personally guaranteeing that you will incur no disfavour thereby.

Now that you know what you *may* do, I think I ought to tell you what in my view you ought to do. After the aforesaid transactions I received a letter from you in which you ask my advice; do I think you should stay where you are in Sicily or set off to see to what remains of your business in Asia? This deliberation on your part did not seem to me consistent with what Largus had said. He had spoken to me as though it was not open to you to stay in Sicily indefinitely, whereas you pose your question as though you had permission. But whichever is right, for my part I think you should remain in Sicily. Its proximity allows frequent interchange of letters and messengers, and is thus an advantage in the process of gaining your pardon. It will also enable you to come back quickly when that goes through, as I hope it will, or the business is settled in some other way. Therefore I strongly advise you to remain.

I shall particularly recommend you to my friend T. Furfanus Postumus and to his Legates, who are also friends of mine, when they return – they are all at Mutina. They are excellent people, with a regard for men like yourself and closely attached to me. Anything that occurs to me in furtherance of your interests I shall do without prompting. Certain points may lie outside my knowledge; once my attention is drawn to such, I shall press harder than anybody. I shall speak of you personally to Furfanus in a way which will make it needless for you to have a letter addressed to him from myself; but since your people thought it desirable that you should have a letter of mine to present to him, I have complied with their wish. I append a copy of the letter.

236 (VI. 9)

CICERO TO FURFANUS POSTUMUS

Rome, December 46

From M. Cicero to Furfanus, Proconsul, greetings.

My familiar friendship with A. Caecina has always been of

the most intimate. I had a great deal to do with his father, a gallant and distinguished gentleman, and have entertained a warm regard for Caecina himself ever since he was a boy, both for the high promise I saw in him of exceptional character and oratorical ability and from the closest association in common pursuits as well as the usual offices of friendship. There is no man with whom I have lived on closer terms.

There can be no need for me to write at greater length. You see how compelling an obligation I have to make every effort on behalf of his welfare in person and estate. It remains to say that, aware as I am from many indications of your sentiments concerning the plight of honest men and the misfortunes of the commonwealth, I shall only ask you to let my recommendation go to increase in a measure proportionate to the regard I know you have for me the good-will which you will bear Caecina spontaneously. You can render me no greater service.

Goodbye.

237 (VI. 7)

A. CAECINA TO CICERO

Sicily, December or early January 46

From Caecina to Cicero greetings.

As regards the delay in forwarding the book[711] to you, do please forgive our nervousness and sympathize with our situation. I hear that my son was afraid, and not unreasonably so,

711. Not the book of 'Remonstrances', which Cicero had already seen and praised, but a new production. From what follows it appears to have contained praise of Cicero, though less lavish than its author would have wished, and criticism of others. Since Caecina was a noted orator, it may have been on the subject of eloquence.

that if the book got out, this might do me a stupid damage, seeing that it is the reader's attitude rather than the writer's that counts. And after all, I am still suffering for my pen.[712] Mine is a strange fate. A *lapsus calami* is removed by an erasure, folly is punished by talk; whereas my mistake is corrected by exile! And the sum total of my offence is that as a fighting soldier I said nasty things about the enemy! None of us, I dare say, but made his vows to Victory – *his* victory – and, even when offering a sacrifice to the Gods in some other connection, used at the same time to pray for Caesar's speedy defeat. If he does not think of this, he's a happy man all round! If he knows and is persuaded of it, why is he angry with somebody for writing something to his displeasure, when he has pardoned all the folk who often prayed heaven for his destruction?

But to resume, the reason for our nervousness was this: I have written about yourself, sparingly and gingerly enough upon my word,[713] not only keeping myself in check but almost running the other way. Now we all know that this type of composition[714] calls for freedom, indeed for excitement and enthusiasm. Restraint is thought out of place in an *attack* upon another person; all the same one has to be on one's guard against degenerating into bullying. Praise of *self* is held to be fraught with embarrassment – the vice of arrogance is at its heels. Only praise of others is regarded as completely uninhibited, for any stinting is ascribed to fickleness or jealousy. But perhaps it was more agreeable and convenient to you so. What I could not do supremely well it would have been best to leave alone, but the second-best kindness was to do it very sparingly. Anyhow, restrain myself I did. Much I toned down, deleted much else, and there was a good deal that never got on paper. Think of a ladder. If you take away some of the rungs, and hack into others, and leave others loose, you will be setting a booby-

712. i.e. the attack on Caesar written during the war.
713. Inhibited presumably by fear of offending Caesar.
714. Eulogy of another person.

trap, not constructing a means of ascent. So with my literary endeavour. Clogged and fractured by so many adversities, how can it produce anything fit to hear or worthy of approval?

Coming to the name of Caesar himself, I tremble from head to foot for fear, not of punishment, but of his critical opinion. Of Caesar I know personally nothing at all. Imagine my feelings when I take counsel with myself: 'He'll like *that*. But *this* word might be misconstrued. Well then, suppose I change it – but I'm afraid I may make matters worse.' Now then, I praise so-and-so: am I giving offence? Again, when I criticize, suppose he doesn't like it. He persecutes a fighting man for his pen; what will he do to a beaten enemy, still under sentence of banishment? You yourself add to my apprehension, when I see you in your *Orator* making Brutus your shield and casting about apologetically for a partner.[715] When every man's advocate behaves so, what am *I* to feel, your old client[716] and now every man's? Armed against all contingencies by superlative genius, you may not know by experience how difficult it is to make a tolerable showing in such a torment of self-induced anxiety and groping surmise, writing for most of the time not as one's judgement directs but with a view to the probable effect on another person's mind. I *feel* it. However, I did tell my son to read the volume to you and then take it away, or else to give it to you on condition that you undertook to correct it, that is, to make a totally different book of it.

Concerning the trip to Asia, despite the urgent and compelling character of my business, I have done as you commanded.

I do not need to urge you on my own behalf. You see that the time has arrived when a decision on my case must be made. There is no call, my dear Cicero, for you to wait for my son. He is a young man. Eagerness, youth, and anxiety make it

715. In allusion to Cicero's statement in the *Orator* (35) that his eulogy of Cato was written at Brutus' instigation.

716. Probably a reference to Cicero's (extant) speech on behalf of the writer's father.

impossible for him to think everything out. *You* must carry the whole affair. My entire hope lies in you. In your sagacity you know the kind of thing that gives Caesar pleasure and wins him over. The whole campaign must start with you and be conducted by you to the finish. You have much influence with himself, and more with his whole circle. If only you make up your mind that it is not only your business to do what is asked of you (though that is a great deal in all conscience), but that the whole load is yours to bear, you will succeed. Or do I act like a fool in my present sorry state, or presume too far upon friendship, when I saddle you so? But your habit of conduct offers an excuse for both. You are so indefatigable on your friends' behalf that they have come not merely to hope for your help as I do, but to demand it as I am doing.

As for the book which my son will give you, let me beg of you not to let it get into circulation, or else to revise it in such a way that it can do me no damage.

238 (XIII. 66)

CICERO TO SERVILIUS ISAURICUS

Rome, December 46 (?)

From M. Cicero to P. Servilius greetings.

Since A. Caecina is a particularly attached client of your family, and since I know how loyal you are to those connected with you and how merciful to the unfortunate, I should not be recommending him to you, were it not that the memory of his father, who was on very close terms with me, and his own adversity affects me as it ought in the case of a person with whom I have the most intimate and comprehensive ties of common pursuits and good offices. May I request you with all urgency – I could ask nothing with more earnestness and concern of mind – to let my letter add a little extra to what you would have done of your own accord, without anybody's recommendation, for so eminent and worthy a person in distress, hoping that on this account you will assist him all the more actively in any way you can?

If you had been in Rome, my opinion is that we should actually have obtained A. Caecina's pardon through your intercession. However, I have high hopes of this, founded on the merciful disposition of your colleague.[717] As matters stand, since in his reliance on your sense of justice he has chosen your province as his securest haven, I would entreat you once again to assist him in gathering together the remnants of his old business, and to give him in other ways the benefit of your shield and support. You can do nothing to oblige me more.

239 (VI. 5)

CICERO TO A. CAECINA

Rome, January 45 (?)

From M. Cicero to A. Caecina greetings.

Whenever I see your son, and I see him practically every day, I promise him my zeal and service, without reservation as to work or pressure of business or time; my personal and public influence I promise with the reservation 'so far as it extends, so far as I can'.

I have read, and am reading, your book carefully, and am keeping it most carefully in custody. Your affairs and fortunes are the object of my closest solicitude. They look to me to be in daily process of easement and amelioration; and I notice that many people have them much at heart. I am sure your son has

717. Caesar, as Consul in 48.

written to you in detail of the support given by these persons and of his own hopes.

As for what lies in the sphere of conjecture, I do not pretend myself to see more ahead than I take to be apparent to your vision and understanding. But since it may be that you consider the prospects under a greater mental stress, I think I ought to set out my impressions. The nature of things and the trend of events make it impossible that this plight in which you and others find yourselves should be of long duration. So cruel an injustice to good citizens in a good cause cannot last. The hope we entertain in all such cases is reinforced by that which applies peculiarly to yourself: not only on account of your standing and wealth, distinctions you possess in common with others, but what is additional and special to yourself, your outstanding talents and qualities, attributes of much importance, I do assure you, in the eyes of the personage in whose power we lie. You would not have been a moment in your present predicament if he had not thought himself injured by the very gift[718] of yours that pleases him. But his resentment grows milder every day, and his associates intimate to me that your literary reputation will in fact count with him heavily in your favour.

First, then, you must keep a stout heart and a lofty spirit. One born, educated, taught, and I may add, proved, as you have been can do no less. Second, you must be confidently hopeful, for the reasons I have given. Please rest assured that I am most ready to assist you and your children in every way. I owe it to our long-standing affection, and my habits of behaviour to my friends, and your many services to me.

718. Skill as a writer.

240 (IV. 14)

CICERO TO CN. PLANCIUS

Rome, winter of 46–45 (?)

From M. Cicero to Cn. Plancius greetings.

I have received two letters from you, dispatched at Corcyra. In one you felicitate me on hearing that I maintain my former standing. In the other you wish me good fortune and prosperity in the step I have taken.[719]

Well, if 'standing' means to feel as a loyal citizen and to have one's sentiments approved by honest men, then I do maintain my standing. But if it consists in the power to implement one's feelings, or even to speak freely in their defence, not a vestige of standing is left us. We have good cause for satisfaction if we can discipline our own selves to bear calmly evils both present and imminent. That is no easy matter in a war which threatens to end in massacre from one side or in slavery from the other.[720] In this peril I take some comfort in recollecting that I foresaw these consequences in the days when I feared our party's success as well as its disaster, and perceived the deadly danger involved in settling a constitutional issue by force of arms. If such force brought victory to those with whom I had associated myself, not desiring war but hoping for peace, I saw none the less the cruelty with which angry, greedy, and unbridled men would exploit it. On the other hand, I realized what their defeat would cost in the lives of our countrymen, some of the highest and some of the best too, men who, when I declared these views and advised in their own best interests, preferred

719. Cicero had divorced Terentia and married his young ward Publilia, only to divorce her a few months later.

720. Caesar was now fighting his last campaign against the republicans in Spain. Their victory would mean massacre, Caesar's slavery.

to have me considered unduly timid than reasonably far-sighted.

As for your felicitations on the step I have taken, I am sure your good wishes are sincere. But I should not have taken any new decision at so sad a time, if on my return I had not found my household affairs in as sorry a state as the country's. In my own house I knew no security, had no refuge from intrigue, because of the villainy of those to whom my welfare and estate should have been most precious in view of the signal kindnesses I had showered upon them. Therefore I thought it advisable to fortify myself by the loyalty of new connections against the treachery of old ones.

But there's enough or perhaps too much about *my* affairs. As for yours, I would have you think as you should, that is, you must not suppose that you have anything specially to fear. If there is to be a settlement of the community, of whatever nature, you will clearly be free of all hazards. One party is now appeased, as I gather, and the other you have never offended. As for my own disposition towards you, I should like you to feel assured of my support for your estate, reputation, and civil rights in all matters where it seems required. I am well aware of my present position and capabilities, but I can promise my service and advice, and certainly my zeal. I hope you will keep me informed as fully as possible of your activities and plans.

Goodbye.

241 (IV. 15)

CICERO TO CN. PLANCIUS

Rome, winter of 46–45

From M. Cicero to Cn. Plancius greetings.

A very brief letter from you has come to hand. I was unable to learn from it what I wanted to know; I did learn what I have never doubted. That is to say, it does not tell me with what courage you are facing the common lot of affliction, but your affection for me is plain to see. The latter, however, I knew. If I knew the former, I should frame my letter accordingly.

Nevertheless, although I have previously written what I thought proper to write, I feel I should now briefly advise you that you ought not to regard yourself as in any peculiar danger. All of us are in great danger, but we share it in common. So you must not demand a special, privileged lot, or reject the common one. Therefore let us feel towards one another as we have always felt. I hope you do, and can answer for myself.

242 (VI. 1)

CICERO TO TORQUATUS[721]

Rome, early January 45

From M. Cicero to A. Torquatus greetings.

In the present state of universal upheaval each one of us thinks his own lot the hardest and would rather be anywhere but where he is. Even so, I have no doubt that residence in Rome is

721. In Athens.

the worst of all for an honest man at the present time. True, wherever a man may be, his feelings are the same; public and private ruin fills him with the same bitterness. But the eyes add to the pain, forcing us to look at what others only hear and forbidding us to turn our thoughts away from our sorrows. So although you must be suffering from the absence of much that you miss, do free your spirit from the distress which I hear weighs upon you most heavily – that you are not in Rome. Painfully as you miss your people and possessions, the objects of your regret continue in their usual state, and would be in no better if you were here. They are in no special danger, and in thinking of what is yours you ought not to claim a privileged lot or reject the common one.

As for yourself, dear sir, when you revolve the situation, it would ill become you to take despair or fear into your mental council-chamber. The individual[722] who has been less fair to you hitherto than your personal eminence made incumbent has given no small indications of a softening in his attitude towards you. Yet he himself, from whom men beg their lives, has no plain assurance for his own. Bearing in mind that no war has a certain issue, I perceive that you have nothing to fear from the victory of the one side, apart that is from involvement in a universal destruction; from that of the other[723] I am sure that you yourself have never apprehended any danger.

There remains the possibility that what I am placing almost in the light of a consolation may constitute your chief torment – the general danger to the commonwealth. For so vast an evil I fear that, much as philosophers have to say on the subject, no true consolation is to be discovered, excepting one; and the efficacy of that one is in proportion to each individual's spiritual strength and energy. If an honest heart and rectitude of conduct suffice for the good and happy life, I ask myself whether it be not blasphemy to speak of a man who can rest upon an ex-

722. Caesar.

723. The republicans, whose cause had revived in Spain.

cellent political conscience as unfortunate. After all, I do not suppose it was for the prizes of victory that we left country, children, and estate years ago. We thought we were fulfilling a valid and sacred duty to the commonwealth and to our own public characters, and in thus acting we were not so deluded as to take victory for granted. So if what we knew *might* happen when we first embarked upon the struggle has come to pass, we ought not to let it deject us, as though a thing had come about which we never reckoned within the bounds of possibility. Let us then follow the dictates of truth and reason, not holding ourselves answerable for anything for which we are not to blame, and, so long as we are blameless, bearing all the chances of mortality with sober composure. The purport of what I am saying is that, when all is lost, virtue must still be thought capable of resting upon its own support. But if there is some hope for our communal affairs, you must have your share in it, whatever the nature of the settlement is to be.

As I write, it crosses my mind that it was you who used to challenge *my* despair, and whose bracing words raised me from hesitation and despondency. It was not our cause with which I found fault in those days, but the conduct of it. I saw that it was too late for us to oppose the military power which we ourselves had long ago made strong, and I was sorry that constitutional questions should be decided by spears and swords rather than by our counsels and characters. When I foretold what has come about, I had no prophetic vision; perceiving what *could* happen, and would be disastrous if it did, I feared it, especially since, if I had been obliged to predict the final outcome one way or the other, I could have predicted that which actually occurred with greater confidence. For while we were superior in matters extraneous to the battlefield, we were weaker in military experience and in the calibre of our troops. Well, pray now yourself take the courage which you used then to think I ought to display.

I write in this strain because your man Philargyrus told me

(in reply to my searching enquiries about you and, as it seemed to me, in a spirit of thorough loyalty) that you were subject to fits of rather severe depression. This ought not to happen. You ought not to doubt that either you will take your proper place in the commonwealth, if there is one, or, if that is lost, your state will be no more unhappy than anyone else's. You have two special reasons for self-control just now, when all of us are holding our breath in suspense: the city where you are residing is the mother and nurse of reason and restraint applied to the conduct of life; and you have Ser. Sulpicius, for whom you have always had a unique regard, at your side. I am sure his good-will and wisdom are a comfort to you. If we had followed his weighty advice, we should have succumbed to the power of a citizen[724] rather than to the sword of a conqueror.

But perhaps all this has been more prolix than was necessary. Let me put what is of greater moment more succinctly. I have nobody to whom I owe more than to yourself. There were others [725] to whom I owed much, you know how much; but the chances of this war have swept them away. Of my position at this time I am well aware. But nobody is in so sorry a case but that he can do yeoman service, if he applies himself wholeheartedly to the matter in hand. I hope you will believe that anything I can give in advice, time, and devotion at least is yours and your children's by right.

724. More strictly, 'a civilian'.
725. Pompey, Lentulus Spinther, Milo.

243 (VI. 3)

CICERO TO A. TORQUATUS

Rome, January 45

From M. Cicero to A. Torquatus greetings.

In my earlier letter I wrote at considerable length, more out of friendly feeling than because the case required it. Your manly spirit needed no fortifying by me; and in my present forlorn and unhappy predicament I am poorly qualified to fortify another. Now too I should be brief. If many words were unnecessary then, they are no more necessary today; if they were needed then, what I wrote is sufficient, particularly as no new development has supervened. Every day, to be sure, we hear some part of the events which I imagine are reaching your ears, but the sum total remains the same, as does the final outcome. I see it in my mind as plain as what we see with our eyes, but I am sure I see nothing which is not equally visible to you. The outcome of the battle nobody can divine, but I see the outcome of the war; or if not that, at any rate I see what the victory of either side will mean – and, after all, one or the other must win. Perceiving this very plainly, I find the picture such that, if what is presented as the ultimate terror[726] comes to pass even sooner, it will be no misfortune. For to live what would then be life is misery indeed; whereas no wise man ever counted it misery to die, even for the happy. But you are in a city where one fancies the very walls can say these things, only more, and more eloquently.

One thing I can tell you confidently, though it is a poor comfort that is founded on the miseries of others: you are in no greater danger now than any one of those who fought on or of those who gave up. The former are fighting, the latter fear

726. Death.

the victor. But that is a poor comfort. There is a better, of which I hope you avail yourself, as I certainly do. While I exist, nothing will give me pain, since I have nothing with which to reproach myself; and if I cease to exist, I shall feel nothing at all. But here I go again, sending an owl to Athens![727]

You and your family and your possessions are all the objects of my closest care, and shall be while I live.

Goodbye.

244 (VI. 4)

CICERO TO A. TORQUATUS

Rome, January 45

From M. Cicero to A. Torquatus greetings.

I have no news to tell you and anyhow, if there were any, I know your own people keep you informed. Of things to come it is always difficult to speak, but sometimes a guess can land near the mark, when the nature of the matter makes it possible to foresee the outcome. Now so much only seems clear, that the war will not last long – though even that is not everybody's opinion. At the time of writing I think something decisive has already taken place, but *what* – that is hard to guess. In every war the God of Battles fights in both ranks, and the outcome of a battle is always in doubt. But at the present time the forces on both sides are said to be so large and so ready to fight to the death that whichever of the two wins it will be no matter for surprise. One general conviction gains ground with every passing day: that even though there may be a certain amount to choose between the causes for which they are in arms, the victory of either side will amount to much about the same. One

727. See n. 515. Here the saying has additional point, in that Torquatus *was* in Athens.

set[728] we have by now pretty well experienced. As for the rival leader,[729] the formidable figure of an angry conqueror sword in hand is in everybody's mind.

Here I may seem to be adding to your distress, which I ought to console and alleviate. I must admit that I find no consolation for our common calamities, save one; but that one, if we can make it ours, is sovereign, and I myself have recourse to it more and more every day. I mean that the consciousness of honest intentions is a sovereign consolation in adversity, and that there is no great calamity apart from guilt. We are free of that. On the contrary our hearts have always been in the right place, and the issue of our course of action is deplored rather than the course itself. Having done our duty, let us bear the event without too much repining. However, I do not take it upon myself to console you for the common afflictions. They are such that consolation demands a greater intellect than mine, endurance an exceptional courage. But anyone may easily show why you ought not specially to distress yourself. A certain personage[730] has been slower to come to your relief than we might have expected, but I have no doubts about his purpose concerning your rehabilitation. As for the others,[731] I do not suppose you are waiting for me to express my opinon.

There remains the pain you feel at so long an absence from your friends and family – a loss indeed, especially those quite delightful boys. But as I wrote to you earlier, the times are such that every man thinks his own lot the hardest and would least wish to be where he actually is. For my part I rate us who are in Rome as most to be pitied, not merely because in all calamities it is more bitter to see than to hear but also because we are more exposed to every sudden, dangerous accident than if we were elsewhere.

728. The Caesarians.
729. Cn. Pompeius the younger.
730. Caesar.
731. The republicans.

Yet I, your comforter, have felt my grief assuaged not so much by the books to which I have always been devoted as by the passing of time. You remember how sorely distressed I was. My first consolation is that I saw further than others in desiring peace, on terms however unfavourable. That was chance, not any prophetic gift of mine; and yet the credit I get for foresight gratifies my vanity. And then, a comforting reflection which you and I have in common, if I were to be called upon to meet life's end, I should not be torn away from a commonwealth which I should grieve to lose, especially as the condition will be entirely unconscious. My age helps too, and all the years behind me. There is satisfaction in the thought of a race well run; I must not be afraid of violence at a juncture which I have now almost reached in the course of nature. Finally, when I think of the great man,[732] I might even say men, who perished in this war, I should feel shameless if I rebelled against a like fate, should it be forced upon me. To be sure I set all manner of contingencies before my mind; no catastrophe so terrible that I do not envisage it as imminent. But since fearing hurts us more than the actuality of what we fear, I desist. Besides, the impending doom will be painless, indeed it will be the end of pain.

However, I have written enough in this strain, or rather more than was necessary. But it is my friendly concern, not loquacity, that make my letters long.

I was sorry to hear of Servius' departure from Athens, for I don't doubt that you found daily meetings and talks with so close a friend and so excellent and wise a man a great solace. Let me hope that you fall back upon your own strength of mind, as is your duty and your wont. I shall give zealous and sedulous attention to anything I think to be your wish, or of concern to you and yours. In so doing I shall emulate your good-will towards me, but shall not equal your deserts.

Goodbye.

732. Pompey.

245 (VI. 2)

CICERO TO A. TORQUATUS

Atticus' villa near Nomentum, April 45

From M. Cicero to A. Torquatus greetings.

I beg you not to suppose that, if my letters come less frequently than of yore, it is because I have forgotten you. The cause lies in my poor health, though now I think it has a little improved, and my absence from Rome, which prevents me hearing of travellers to your whereabouts. So I want you to be sure once for all that I keep you in mind with the most friendly feelings and pay as much attention to all your affairs as to my own.

Considering the bad times we live in, you ought not, believe me, to take it hard that your case has hitherto gone through more ups and downs than was generally hoped or expected. There are three possible futures for the commonwealth: oppression in endless armed conflict, eventual revival when arms are laid aside, and complete annihilation. If arms are to prevail, you should not fear the side which is pardoning you, nor yet that which you assisted. If arms are laid aside on terms, and the state breathes once more, you will be free to enjoy your rank and fortune. If, however, the sum of things goes down to destruction, the end feared long ago by a very wise man, M. Antonius,[733] when he surmised the vast calamities to come, well then, you have the consolation (a sad one indeed, especially for a man and a Roman like yourself, but necessary) that in what happens to all the individual has no special reason for distress.

If you will carefully consider the significance implicit in

733. The orator (see Glossary of Persons).

these few words (more it would not have been wise to commit to a letter), you will realize, as I am sure you do without any letter of mine, that you have something to hope and nothing, in this or any other state of the commonwealth, to be afraid of; and that if all goes to ruin, you must bear what fortune sends, especially as your conscience is clear. For you would not wish to survive the commonwealth, even if that were possible. But I have written enough on this topic.

Please write and tell me of your doings and your future whereabouts, so that I may know where to write to or where to go.

246 (VI. 21)

CICERO TO TORANIUS[734]

Rome, January 45

From Cicero to Toranius.

As I write these lines to you, it looks as though the final issue of this most disastrous of wars is approaching; or it may be that a decisive action has already taken place. But every day I recall how you and I alone in that great army shared each other's views, and saw, as no one else did, with what an infinity of evil that war was charged. All hope of peace being excluded, even victory was bound to prove a most bitter experience, fraught with destruction to the vanquished and slavery to the victors. In those days such paragons of courage and wisdom as Domitius and Lentulus[735] used to call me timid – and so indeed I was; I was afraid that what has happened

734. C. Toranius had probably been Quaestor in 73 and Plebeian Aedile in 64, the latter as colleague of C. Octavius, who left him guardian to his son, the future Augustus. He was now in Corcyra.

735. Lentulus Crus, Consul in 49.

would come to pass. But today I have no fears, and am ready for any outcome. When it still seemed possible to make some provisions against the future, I was sorry to see the chance neglected. But now that all is topsyturvy and nothing can be achieved by policy, resignation to whatever may betide appears the only rational course; especially as death is the end of all, and my conscience tells me that I took thought for the dignity of the commonwealth so long as I could and, when that was lost, was fain to save its existence.

I have written thus, not in order to talk about myself, but to put the same thoughts into your mind, since your view and aims were very close to mine. It is a great consolation to remember that one has meant well and honestly, even though things have fallen out awry. I only hope we may one day enjoy some form of settled constitution and talk over our anxieties, as we did in the days when we were thought timid because we said that what has come would come.

As for your affairs, I assure you that you have nothing to fear apart from the destruction of the whole commonwealth. As for me, I hope you will determine that, so far as I can, I shall ever stand by you, and by the cause of your restoration, and by your children.

Goodbye.

247 (VI. 20)

CICERO TO TORANIUS

Summer of 45

From Cicero to Toranius.

Three days ago I gave a letter for you to Cn. Plancius' boys so I shall now write more briefly; and whereas in my earlier letter I offered you comfort, I am now going to offer advice.

I think you have no better course than to wait where you are until you can decide what to do. Besides the risk in a long, stormy voyage along a coast very poorly provided with harbours, which you will thus avoid, there is the infinitely important consideration that, when you do hear something definite, you can set out straight away from your present place of residence. Also there is no reason why you should be all agog to put yourself in their way as they[736] approach. And I have many other apprehensions, of which I have told our friend Cilo. In short, you could have found no more convenient place to stay in these distressing circumstances; for it is one you can leave and go wherever may be advisable with the maximum of ease and expedition. If *he* returns on time, you will be close at hand; whereas if something hampers or delays him (many things can happen), you will be where you can get all the news. This really does seem to me best.

For the rest, as I have often borne in upon you in my letters, I hope you will make up your mind that you have nothing to fear in your present situation over and above the general fate of the community. That, no doubt, is a very hard one, but considering the character of our lives and the age we have now reached, we ought to bear with fortitude anything that happens to us for which we are not responsible. All your family here are well. They miss you and love you and cherish you with the fondest affection. See you keep fit and do not move from where you are without good reason.

736. Caesar and his party returning from Spain.

248 (IV. 5)

SERVIUS SULPICIUS RUFUS TO CICERO

Athens, mid March 45

From Servius to Cicero greetings.

When the report reached me of the death of your daughter Tullia, I was indeed duly and deeply and grievously sorry, and I felt that the blow had struck us both. Had I been in Rome, I should have been with you and shown you my grief in person. And yet that is a melancholy and bitter sort of comfort. Those who should offer it, relations and friends, are themselves no less afflicted. They cannot make the attempt without many tears, and rather seem themselves to stand in need of comfort *from* others than to be capable of doing their friendly office *for* others. None the less, I have resolved to set briefly before you the reflections that come to my mind in this hour, not that I suppose you are unaware of them, but perhaps your grief makes them harder for you to perceive.

What reason is there why your domestic sorrow should affect you so sorely? Think how fortune has dealt with us up to now. All that man should hold no less dear than children – country, dignity, standing, distinctions – has been snatched away from us. Could this one further mishap add appreciably to your grief? How should not any heart practised in such experience have grown less sensitive and count all else as of relatively little consequence?

But I suppose you grieve for *her*. How often must you have thought, and how often has it occurred to me, that in this day and age they are not most to be pitied who have been granted a painless exchange of life for death! What was there after all to make life so sweet a prospect for her at this time? What did she have or hope? What comfort for her spirit? The thought perhaps of spending her life wedded to some young man of distinction? Do you suppose it was possible for you to choose from this modern generation a son-in-law suitable to your standing, to whose protection you could feel safe in confiding your child? Or the thought of bearing children herself, whose bloom would cheer her eyes, sons who could maintain their patrimony, would seek public office in due course, and act in public affairs and in their friends' concerns like free men? Was not all this taken away before it was granted? The loss of children is a calamity, sure enough – except that it is a worse calamity to bear our present lot and endure.

I want to tell you of something which has brought *me* no slight comfort,[737] in the hope that perhaps it may have some power to lighten your sorrow too. As I was on my way back from Asia,[738] sailing from Aegina towards Megara, I began to gaze at the landscape around me. There behind me was Aegina, in front of me Megara, to the right Piraeus, to the left Corinth; once flourishing towns, now lying low in ruins before one's eyes. I began to think to myself: 'Ah! How can we manikins wax indignant if one of us dies or is killed, ephemeral creatures as we are, when the corpses of so many towns lie abandoned in a single spot? Check yourself, Servius, and remember that you were born a mortal man.' That thought, I do assure you, strengthened me not a little.[739] If I may suggest it, picture the same spectacle to yourself. Not long ago so many great men died at one time, the Roman Empire was so gravely impaired, all its provinces shaken to pieces; can you be so greatly moved by the loss of one poor little woman's frail spirit? If her end had not come now, she must none the less have died in a few years' time,

737. If Sulpicius had suffered a bereavement we do not know what it was.

738. i.e. from Samos. Sulpicius will have been returning to Rome in the autumn of 47.

739. Byron refers to this passage in *Childe Harold* (Canto V, stanza 4), as does Sterne, *Tristram Shandy*, V, 3, who probably got it from Burton.

for she was mortal. You too must take your mind and thoughts away from such things, and dwell instead on recollections worthy of the character you hold. Tell yourself that she lived as long as it was well for her to live, and that she and freedom existed together. She saw you, her father, Praetor, Consul, and Augur. She was married to young men of distinction. Almost all that life can give, she enjoyed; and she left life when freedom died. How can you or she quarrel with fortune on that account?

And then, do not forget that you are Cicero, a man accustomed to give rules and advice to others. Do not be like a bad physician, who professes medical knowledge to his patients but does not know how to treat himself. Rather lay to your heart and place before your mind the precepts you are wont to offer others. There is no grief that is not lessened or softened by the passage of time. For *you* to wait for this time to pass, instead of anticipating the result by your own good sense, does you discredit. And if consciousness remains to those below, loving you as she did, dutifully fond as she was of all her family, *she* assuredly does not wish you to act so. Listen then for her dead sake, for the sake of others, your well-wishers and friends who are sad for your grief, and for your country's sake, so that if need arise she may have the benefit of your service and counsel. And then, since in the pass to which we have come we must not disregard even *this* aspect, do not let anyone suppose that it is not so much a daughter you are mourning as the public predicament and the victory of others.

I am ashamed to write at greater length to you on this matter, lest I seem to doubt your good sense, and so I shall end my letter with one final observation. We have seen more than once how nobly you sustain prosperity, and how great the glory you gain thereby. Let us recognize at last that you are no less able to bear adversity, and that you count it no heavier load than you should, lest of all fine qualities you may seem to lack this only.[740]

740. Livy wrote of Cicero that he bore none of his misfortunes like a man except death.

As for me, I shall inform you of what is going on here and of the state of the province when I hear that your mood is calmer.

Goodbye.

249 (IV. 6)

CICERO TO SERVIUS SULPICIUS RUFUS

Atticus' villa near Nomentum, mid April 45

From M. Cicero to Ser. Sulpicius greetings.

Yes, my friend, I wish you had been with me, as you say, in my most grievous affliction. How much your presence would have helped me by consolation and by sorrow well-nigh equal to my own I readily recognize from the measure of easement I felt when I read your letter. You have written the words that could alleviate mourning and your own no small distress has given you the means of comforting mine. But your son Servius has shown by every friendly attention that could be rendered at such a time how much he thinks of me and how welcome he believes such a disposition on his part will be to you. I have often felt more pleasure in his attentions than I feel now (as you may imagine), but never more grateful.

Not only am I comforted by your words and (I might almost say) your fellowship in sorrow, but by your counsel as well. I feel it discreditable in me not to bear my bereavement as so wise a man as you considers it should be borne. But sometimes I am overwhelmed, and scarcely offer any resistance to grief, because I have no such solaces as others in similar plight, whose examples I set before my mind, did not lack. Q. Maximus[741] lost a son of consular rank, high reputation, and splendid record.

741. Q. Fabius Maximus 'Cunctator'.

L. Paulus[742] lost two in a single week. Then there was Galus in your own family[743] and M. Cato,[744] who lost a son of the highest intellectual and moral qualities. But they lived in periods when the honourable standing they enjoyed in public life assuaged their mourning. *I* had already lost those distinctions which you yourself mention and which I had gained by dint of great exertions. The one comfort still left to me was that which has now been snatched away. Neither my friends' concerns nor the administration of the state detained my thoughts. I had no wish to appear in the courts, I could not endure the sight of the Senate-House. I considered, as was the fact, that I had lost all the fruits of my work and success. However, I reflected that I shared this situation with yourself and certain others; I conquered my feelings and forced myself to bear it all patiently. But while I did so, I had a haven of refuge and repose, one in whose conversation and sweet ways I put aside all cares and sorrows.

Now this grievous blow has again inflamed the wounds I thought healed. When in the past I withdrew in sadness from public affairs, my home received and soothed me; but I cannot now take refuge from domestic grief in public life, to find relief in what it offers. And so I stay away from home and Forum alike, for neither public nor private life can any longer comfort the distress which each occasions me.

All the more then do I look forward to your return and desire to see you as soon as possible. No abstract reflection can bring me greater comfort than our fellowship in daily life and talk. However, from what I hear, I hope your arrival is imminent. One reason among many why I am anxious to see you as soon as may be is that I should like us to ponder together how we

742. L. Aemilius Paulus, victor of Pydna.

743. i.e. *gens*. C. Sulpicius Galus was Consul in 166.

744. The Censor. Cicero had collected many such examples in his lost 'Consolation', addressed to himself.

should best pass through this present time, all of which must be accommodated to the wishes of a single individual. He is a man of sense and generosity, and I think I have cause to believe him no enemy of mine and a very good friend of yours. Even so, what line we are to take needs careful consideration. I am not thinking of any positive action, but of retirement by his leave and favour.

Goodbye.

250 (IX. 11)

CICERO TO DOLABELLA

Atticus' villa near Nomentum, April (late) 45

From Cicero to Dolabella greetings.

I would rather my failure to write had been due to my own death than to the grievous calamity which has come upon me. I should surely bear it less hard if I had you beside me. Your wise words and signal affection for me would be a great solace. However, I shall soon be seeing you, so we think here. You will find me in a state which offers plenty of scope for your assistance. Not that I am so far broken down as to forget my human lot or to think it right to sink under fortune's blows. But the gaiety and charm which people saw in me, and you in particular used to find agreeable, is all swept away. My fortitude and resolution, however, if I ever possessed those qualities, you will recognize as no whit diminished.

You tell me that you have to fight my battles.[745] I am less concerned that you should rebut my detractors than anxious that your affection for me should be recognized, as it surely is.

745. Against his nephew, the younger Q. Cicero, now also with Caesar's forces in Spain. Reports of his evil tongue had arrived from other quarters (cf. *Letters to Atticus* 346 (XIII.37).2).

Let me earnestly request you to act accordingly, and to forgive the brevity of this letter. I expect we shall shortly be together, and I have not yet sufficiently regained my strength for writing.

251 (V. 14)

LUCCEIUS TO CICERO

Rome, 9 May 45

From L. Lucceius, son of Quintus, to M. Tullius, son of Marcus, greetings.

I hope you are well, as I am – that is, I am in my usual state of health, but just a little worse even than usual.

I have often asked after your whereabouts in the hope of seeing you. I was surprised that you have not been in Rome[746] since you left, and it still surprises me. What chiefly draws you away I am not sure. If you enjoy solitude while writing or engaged in one of your usual occupations, I am glad and make no criticism of your plan. Nothing can be more agreeable even in calm, prosperous times, let alone in these dark days of mourning, especially as yours is a weary mind, needing rest now from the heavy pressure of affairs, and a well-instructed one, ever creating something to delight others and shed lustre on yourself.

If, on the other hand, as before you left, you have abandoned yourself to tears and sorrow, I grieve in your grievous pain; but, if you allow me to speak my mind plainly, I cannot help taking you to task. For consider: Will you, whose intelligence pierces the darkest abstrusities, alone be blind to the obvious? Will you not understand that you gain nothing by constant complaining, that you double the cares which your good sense enjoins you to make lighter?

746. i.e. even for a short visit.

If advice can be of no avail, then I ask as a personal favour and beg of you, if you have any regard for me, to loose yourself from the bonds of your distresses and come back to live with us and to your normal way of life, both that which you share with the rest of us and that which is personal and peculiar to yourself. I am anxious not to importune you, if you find my concern irksome; and I am anxious to turn you from perseverance in this course. These two conflicting desires confuse me. As to the latter, I hope you will comply with my request, if you can; or else, as to the former, I hope you will take no offence.

Goodbye.

252 (V. 15)

CICERO TO LUCCEIUS

Astura, mid May 45

From M. Cicero to L. Lucceius, son of Quintus, greetings.

All your affection stands revealed from every angle in the letter I have lately received from you, an affection not unknown to me indeed, but none the less welcome and wished for; I should say 'pleasant', had I not lost that word forever. The reason is not only the one which you suspect, and for which, in terms of the most loving gentleness, you take me in effect severely to task; it is also that the remedies appropriate to my grievous wound no longer exist. For consider: Am I to have recourse to my friends? How many do I have? You know, for most of them were yours too. Some have perished, others have somehow grown less feeling. With you, it is true, I could live, and should greatly so desire. Old acquaintance, affection, habit, community of pursuits – what tie, pray, is wanting to our attachment? Can we then be together? Upon my word, I do not know what hinders us. Yet the fact is that hitherto we have not been so, neighbours though we were at Tusculum and Puteoli – of Rome I say nothing, for where the Forum is common ground there is no need to live next door.

But by some malign chance our lot has fallen in times when, at what should be the crown of our careers, life itself seems a dishonour. Bereft of embellishment and solace indoors and out, what refuge could I find? Books, to be sure. I go to them constantly; what else am I to do? And yet they too seem somehow to bar my way to haven and refuge, and almost to reproach me for lingering in a life that has nothing to offer save the protraction of sad days.

In these circumstances are you surprised that I stay away from Rome, where my home can afford me no pleasure, while I am mortally weary of times and men, of Forum and Senate-House? So I go to my books, on which I spend all my time, not looking for a lasting cure but only for brief forgetfulness of pain. But if you and I had done what continual alarms prevented us even thinking of, and had been always together, your health would be no burden to me nor my mourning to you. Let us, as far as may be, bring that to pass. Both of us will surely find our account in it. I shall see you soon then.

253 (IV. 12)

SERVIUS SULPICIUS RUFUS TO CICERO

Athens, 31 May 45

From Servius to Cicero cordial greetings.

I know that my news will not be of the most agreeable[747] to

747. An odd meiosis; but Sulpicius' writing is not of the most sensitive.

you and other friends. But chance and nature are our masters. Stand the matter how it may, I feel it my duty to inform you.

On 23 May I took ship from Epidaurus to Piraeus, where I met my colleague M. Marcellus, and spent the day there to be with him. I took leave of him the following day, intending to travel from Athens to Boeotia and conclude what remained of my assizes. He proposed, as he told me, to sail round Cape Malea towards Italy. Two days later I was about to set out from Athens, when about three o'clock in the morning a friend of his, P. Postumius, arrived to tell me that my colleague[748] M. Marcellus had been attacked with a dagger by P. Magius Cilo, a friend of his, after dinner, and had received two wounds, one in the stomach and one in the head behind the ear. He hoped, however, that there was a chance for his life. Magius had later committed suicide, and he himself had been sent to me by Marcellus to tell me what had occurred and ask me to send him doctors. Accordingly, I collected some doctors and set out straight away for Piraeus as day broke. I was not far away, when a boy of Acidinus' met me on the road with a note which stated that Marcellus had breathed his last shortly before dawn. So a very eminent man has been tragically murdered by a villain. He was spared by the respect of his enemies only to meet his death at the hand of a friend.

None the less I proceeded to his tent. I found two freedmen and a handful of slaves. They said the rest had fled in a panic, because their master had been killed in front of his tent. I had to bring him back to the city in the litter in which I myself had travelled, using my own bearers; and there I saw to his funeral, on as handsome a scale as the resources of Athens could provide. I could not induce the townspeople to grant him burial within the city precincts; they pleaded a religious bar, and it is a fact that they had never given such permission in the past. The next best thing they did allow, to bury him in a public hall, whichever I wished. So I chose a spot in the most celebrated hall in the

748. As Consul in 51.

world, the Academy. There we cremated him, and I later saw to it that the people of Athens should arrange for the erection of a monument to him in marble on the spot. So I have done all that in me lay for my colleague and kinsman, in life and in death.

Goodbye.

Dispatched 31 May, Athens.

254 (IX. 8)[749]

CICERO TO VARRO

Tusculum, 11 or 12 July 45

From Cicero to Varro.

To dun a man for a present, though promised, is in poor taste – even the crowd does not demand a show[750] unless stirred up to it. None the less my impatience for the fulfilment of your promise[751] impels me – not to dun, but to remind you. And I am sending you four monitors[752] not of the most bashful. I am sure you know how assertive this younger Academy[753] can be; well, the quartet I am sending you has been summoned from its

749. This letter, of which Cicero wrote to Atticus (333 (XIII.25).2) that he would never take so much trouble over anything again, accompanied the presentation of the four Books of his dialogue *Academic Questions*. Varro had a major role in the final version.

750. *munus* has the double meaning of 'present' and 'show'; cf. Letter 47 (II.3).

751. Several years previously Varro had promised to dedicate his work *On the Latin Language* to Cicero; cf. *Letters to Atticus* 320 (XIII.12). 2.

752. The four Books of the *Academic Questions*.

753. The sceptical school of Arcesilas and Carneades. Elsewhere Cicero calls it the 'New Academy'.

headquarters. I am afraid they *may* dun you, but I have charged them to *request*. To be sure, I have been waiting quite a while and holding back, so as not to address a piece to you before I received one and thus repay you as nearly as possible in your own coin. But since you are proceeding rather slowly (and that is to say, as I interpret, carefully), I could not refrain from advertising the bond of common pursuits and affection between us by such a form of composition as lay within my powers. Accordingly, I have staged a conversation between us at Cumae, Pomponius also being present. I have assigned the exposition of Antiochus' tenets (being under the impression that you approve of them) to your role, that of Philo's to my own. I dare say you will be surprised when you read to find that you and I have discussed a subject which in fact we never *have* discussed; but you know the conventions of Dialogue. In future, my dear Varro, we shall have talks in plenty, if so minded, between ourselves and to please ourselves. Late in the day perhaps. But let the public destiny answer for what is past; the present is our own responsibility. If only we could pursue these studies together in peaceful times and a settled, if not satisfactory, state of the community! And yet, if that were so, there would be other claims upon us, calling us to honourable responsibilities and tasks. As matters stand, why should we desire life without our studies? For my part, I have little enough desire for it even with them; take them away, and I should lack even that little. But all this we will talk over together and often.

All good luck to your change of residence and your new purchase. I think you are doing wisely. Take care of your health.

255 (V. 9)

VATINIUS TO CICERO

Narona, 11 July 45

From Vatinius, Imperator, to his friend Cicero greetings.

I trust you are well, as I am and my army.

Do you keep up your practice of standing by old clients? If so, here comes one of them by the name of P. Vatinius, who wants an advocate to take his case! Surely you won't turn your back now I stand well in the world after taking me on when it was touch and go. As for me, whom should I choose and turn to but my old defender, who taught me how to win? When I think what a combination of powerful persons you disregarded to save my life, I can hardly doubt your readiness to smash and squash a set of petty backbiters with their spiteful tittle-tattle, when it's a question of an honour.[754]

Well then, if you love me as you usually do, let me put myself wholly in your hands. Look upon this load, such as it is, as yours to shoulder, a task you ought to perform for the sake of my standing. You know that somehow or other my career is apt to find tongues to carp at it – truly no fault of mine, but what difference does that make if the thing happens just the same, fated as it were? If anyone *does* show a disposition to stand in my light, may I ask you to defend me in my absence with no less than your usual generosity? I am appending the text of my dispatch to the Senate on my military operations for your perusal.

They tell me that a runaway slave[755] of yours, a reader, is with the Vardaei. You gave me no commission about him, but I have

754. A Supplication for Vatinius' military successes in Illyricum.
755. Cf. Letter 212 (XIII.77).

none the less issued instructions in advance that he be searched for by land and sea, and no doubt I shall find him for you, unless he has made off into Dalmatia – though even there I shall winkle him out sooner or later. Don't forget me.

Goodbye.

11 July, from camp at Narona.

256 (V. 10a. 3)

VATINIUS TO CICERO

Narona, early November 45

Caesar is treating me badly so far. He is still not putting the motion about my Supplications and my Dalmatian successes. One might think I had not done fully enough in Dalmatia to entitle me to a Triumph![756] Or am I supposed to wait until I have finished the whole war? Dalmatia has twenty towns of ancient foundation, more than sixty adopted later into the confederacy. If no Supplications are decreed me until I take them all, then I am on a very different footing from other generals.

257 (V. 11)

CICERO TO VATINIUS

Rome, early December (?) 45

From M. Cicero to Vatinius, Imperator, greetings.

It is no surprise to me to find you appreciative of my good offices, for I know you of old as the most grateful of mankind,

756. Vatinius was finally granted a Triumph by the Triumvirs in 42.

and I have never been behindhand in proclaiming it. You not only felt but *showed* your gratitude to me in deed, and in more than ample measure. Accordingly, in all your future concerns you shall find my devotion no less and my sentiments towards you unchanged.

As soon as I had read your letter, in which you commend to me your excellent lady Pompeia, I had a word with our friend Sura and asked him to tell her from me to let me know of any service she might require, and to promise that I should give my most sedulous endeavours to perform her wishes. And so I shall, and, if need appears, I shall see her in person. But will you please write and tell her that she must not consider anything too big or too small? I shall find nothing too difficult and nothing beneath my attention. No part I take in your affairs will appear to me either troublesome or unbecoming.

Do please settle this affair of Dionysius. I shall honour any undertaking you make him. If he behaves like the scoundrel he is, you shall lead him captive at your Triumph. Deuce take these Dalmatians, who are giving you so much trouble! But, as you say, they will soon be in the bag and will shed lustre on your successes, for they have always been accounted a warrior race.

258 (v. 10b)

VATINIUS TO CICERO

Narona, 5 December 45

After the Supplications in my honour were decreed, I set out for Dalmatia. I took six towns by storm. The single town of *, the biggest of the lot, was captured by me four times over, for I took four towers and four walls and their whole citadel, from which snow, frost, and rain dislodged me. Thus, my dear Cicero, I had to leave the town I had taken and the war I had won; it was too bad. Please plead my cause with Caesar, if need arises, and regard me as yours to defend on all fronts, believing that you have no more devoted friend than me.

Goodbye.

Dispatched Nones of December, from Narona.

259 (V. 10a. 1–2)

VATINIUS TO CICERO

Narona, late December 45 or January 44

From Vatinius to his friend Cicero greetings.

I trust you are well, as I am and my army.

So far I cannot fish anything out about your man Dionysius, especially as the Dalmatian cold, which drove me out from there, has frozen me up here too. But I shall not give up till sooner or later I winkle him out. But you are a hard taskmaster! You write me what reads like a very earnest intercession on behalf of Catilius. Get along with you, and our friend Sex. Servilius too! Upon my word, I think a lot of him, as you do. But is this the kind of client and case you people take on – a monster of savagery, who has murdered and kidnapped and ruined all those freeborn men and matrons and Roman citizens, and laid whole districts waste? This ape, this worthless ruffian, bore arms against me, and I took him prisoner of war. But really, my dear Cicero, what can I do? Upon my word, I am anxious to obey your every command. My own right to inflict condign punishment upon him as my captive, which I was going to exercise, I forgo in deference to your request. But what am I to say to those who demand redress by process of law for the plunder of their property, the seizure of their ships, the slaughter of brothers, children, and parents? Upon my word, I could not face it out, not if I had the impudence of Appius, whose shoes I wear.[757] Well then, I shall spare no pains to meet your wishes, as I know them. He is defended by Q. Volusius, a pupil of yours[758] – perhaps that circumstance may rout the other side. There lies the best hope. You will defend me in Rome, if need arises.

260 (VII. 24)

CICERO TO M. FABIUS GALLUS

Tusculum, 22 August 45

From M. Cicero to M. Fabius Gallus greetings.

Everywhere I turn I come across traces of your affection, as most recently in the affair of Tigellius.[759] I could see from your letter that you have been very much concerned. So I thank you for the kind intention. But on the matter itself, one or two observations. Cipius I think it was who said on a certain occasion 'I am not asleep to everybody.'[760] Just so, my dear Gallus, *I* am not a slave to everybody. Though I don't know why I talk of slavery. In the old days, when I was supposed to be an autocrat, I was never so courted as I now am by Caesar's closest intimates, all except your friend. I consider myself so much the

757. Literally 'into whose place I was elected'. Vatinius had succeeded to the vacancy in the College of Augurs left by Ap. Pulcher's death in 48.

758. He may have taken lessons in declamation from Cicero, like Hirtius and Dolabella.

759. On this see *Letters to Atticus* 347 (XIII.49).

760. The story (or an allusion to it) could be found in Lucilius. Cipius pretended to be asleep at dinner so that he could ignore his wife's misbehaviour. But when a slave tried to make off with some wine, he started up with the words quoted.

luckier, not to have to put up with the fellow – more pestilential than his native climate![761] I regard him as knocked down to the highest bidder all those years ago in Licinius Calvus' Hipponactean advertisement![762]

However, let me tell you about his grievance. I had taken on Phamea's case, for his own sake – he was quite a friend of mine. He came and told me that the judge had fixed a day for the hearing, being the very day that the jury had to consider their verdict in P. Sestius' case.[763] I replied that I could not possibly manage it; if he picked any other day he liked, I should not fail him. However, conscious of having a nephew, a pretty performer on the flute and a tolerable hand with the oil-can,[764] he took his leave, in something of a huff, I thought. So there you are: 'Sardinians for sale, each worse than t'other.'[765] You now know my side, and can see how unreasonable this beggar on horseback is being.

Send me your 'Cato'[766] – I am anxious to read it. It's a disgrace to us both that I have not read it already.

761. Sardinia was notoriously unhealthy.

762. Calvus had composed a lampoon upon Tigellius after the manner and in the metre of the sixth-century Hipponax of Ephesus. The first line is preserved: 'Sardinian Tigellius for sale – stinking goods!'

763. Sestius was accused of electoral corruption in 52.

764. Presumably in training athletes. But Manutius' conjecture *cantorem* ('singer') for *unctorem* ('anointer') is attractive.

765. A proverb quoted elsewhere and variously interpreted.

766. After Cato's death in April 46 there was a brisk output of pamphlets for and against his character and record. Cicero's had appeared about a year previously.

261 (VII. 25)

CICERO TO M. FABIUS GALLUS

Tusculum, 23 or 24 August 45

From Cicero to M. Fabius Gallus greetings.

Don't distress yourself about the letter which you are so sorry you tore up. I have it safe at home.[767] You can ask for it any time you like. As for your word of warning, I'm very grateful, and hope you will always so favour me. Apparently you are afraid that, if we make mock of your friend, we may come to laugh – *sard*onically![768]

Attention now! No more writing![769] Here comes the beak, sooner than expected! It's the cat for Catonians, I fear.

My dear Gallus, that part of your letter from 'all goes downhill' onwards – depend upon it, it's the best thing ever. This for your private ear, keep it to yourself – not a word to your freedman Apella even. Nobody but us two talks in this style – good or bad, that's another question; but whatever it is, it's *ours*. So press on and don't budge a nail's breadth, as they say, from your pen. The pen makes the author! For my own part, I work o'nights nowadays as well as in the day-time.

767. i.e. a copy. The letter was probably Letter 260 (VII.24).

768. The Greek phrase *sardonion gelan*='to laugh scornfully' or 'bitterly' ('the wrong side of one's mouth') was variously explained in antiquity. Cicero of course alludes to the Sardinian origin of Tigellius.

769. Literally 'hands off the tablet'. When the schoolmaster comes in the boys must stop writing their exercise. The schoolmaster here is Caesar.

262 (VI. 19)

CICERO TO LEPTA

Astura, August (end) 45

From Cicero to Lepta.

Glad to hear that Macula has behaved as he should.[770] I always thought his Falernian place suitable for a lodge, provided there is enough shelter for my entourage. In other respects I don't dislike the place. But I shall not on that account give up your Petrine establishment – the house and amenities generally are for residence, not just a lodge.

I have spoken to Oppius about a Curatorship of the royal shows[771] (Balbus I have not seen since you left; the gout in his feet is so bad that he doesn't want visitors). To be sure, I think you would be wiser to forget the whole thing. You will stand no chance of gaining the object for which you put yourself to such drudgery. He[772] has so many intimates that there is more likelihood of one dropping out than of any opening for a newcomer, especially one who has nothing to contribute except his services; and as for them, he will think he has conferred a favour (if he so much as knows of it) rather than received one. However, we'll try to find something that looks well; otherwise I think that, far from seeking such employment, you should steer clear of it.

770. Probably a relative of Lepta who had died leaving him money; cf. the beginning of *Letters to Atticus* 65 (III.20). Lepta seems to have suggested that Cicero might like to acquire part of the estate, a small property in the Falernian district eastward of Sinuessa, as a lodge for use on his journeys up and down the Appian Way; cf. Letter 339 (XII.20).

771. Cf. *Letters to Atticus* 338 (XIII.46).1. 'Royal', of course, is a hostile reference to Caesar, called *rex* in *Letters to Atticus* 346 (XIII.37)2.

772. Caesar.

I think I shall stay at Astura until I learn his route and time of arrival.

Goodbye.

263 (IX. 12)

CICERO TO DOLABELLA

A villa, December 45 (?)

From Cicero to Dolabella.

I congratulate our Baiae if, as you say, it has suddenly become a healthy spot.[773] But perhaps it is out of fondness and flattery towards yourself; perhaps the place has forgotten its nature so long as you are there. If that is the explanation, I am not in the least surprised that even air and soil put aside their natural properties for your benefit.

Contrary to what I thought, I find I have with me the little speech in defence of Deiotarus[774] which you were asking for, and so I am sending it to you. Please bear in mind, when you read it, that the case was a meagre, paltry affair, hardly worth writing up. But I wanted to send my old friend and host a little present – on the light, coarse-spun side, as his own presents are apt to be.

I wish you good sense and courage, so that your moderation and steadiness will bring shame on the misconduct of others.

773. The apparent implication that this most famous of Roman pleasure-resorts was unhealthy is surprising.

774. Accused of an attempt on Caesar's life. Cicero's defence survives.

264 (VII. 29)

MANIUS CURIUS TO CICERO

Patrae, 29 October 45

From his friend Curius to M. Cicero greetings.

I trust you are well.

I say '*his* friend', for I am yours in usufruct, though I belong to our good Atticus by right of ownership. You have the enjoyment, and he the title. If he puts the goods up for sale as a job lot, he won't get much by it. But *I* advertise that everything I am and have, my entire place in society, comes from you. That's worth something! So, Cicero mine, carry on your good work. Keep me in good shape, and give me a first-class recommendation to Sulpicius' successor,[775] thus making it easier for me to obey your precepts, and see you gladly come spring, and pull up stakes here, and take my all safely home.

Only, exalted friend, please don't show Atticus this letter. Leave him in his delusion. Let him go on thinking me a man of honour, not one to cover two walls from the same pot of whitewash.

And so, patron mine, a very good day to you. Give my regards to my good friend Tiro.

Dispatched 29 October.

775. As governor of Achaia. His name was Acilius.

265 (VII. 30)

CICERO TO MANIUS CURIUS

Rome, January 44

From Cicero to Curius greetings.

Not so. I no longer urge you or ask you to come home. On the contrary, I am anxious to take wing myself and go to some place 'where nevermore of Pelops' line I'll hear the name or deeds'.[776] You cannot imagine the sense of personal dishonour I feel at living in the Rome of today. Farsighted indeed you turn out to have been when you fled this country. Although the happenings here are painful enough in the report, yet it is more tolerable to hear of them than to see them. At least you were not in the Campus when the elections to the Quaestorship began at nine o'clock in the morning. A chair of state had been placed for Q. Maximus, whom these people used to call Consul. His death was announced, and the chair removed. Whereupon *he*,[777] having taken auspices for an assembly of the Tribes, held an assembly of the Centuries,[778] and at one o' clock of the afternoon declared a Consul elected, to remain in office until the Kalends of January, the next morning that was to be. So in the Consulship of Caninius[779] you may take it that nobody had breakfast! However, at any rate no crime was committed during the same period – the Consul's vigilance was extraordinary. Throughout his entire term of office he never closed an eye! You find such things laughable, for you are not on the

776. See n. 627.

777. Caesar.

778. For the election of a Consul. Quaestors were elected by the Assembly of Tribes.

779. C. Caninius Rebilus.

spot; if you were here to witness, you would have to weep. What if I were to tell you the rest? Incidents of the same character are innumerable. I could not bear them, if I had not brought my boat into the harbour of philosophy, and if I did not have our dear Atticus to share my pursuits. You say you belong to him by legal ownership, but to me by use and enjoyment. I am quite satisfied with that position. What a man uses and enjoys *is* what belongs to him. But of this more anon.

Acilius, who has been sent to Greece with an army, is under a great obligation to me, having been twice defended by me in better days on a capital charge. He is not without a sense of gratitude, and pays me many attentions. I have written to him on your behalf with all care and am enclosing my letter herewith. I should be glad if you would write and tell me how he receives it, and what promises he makes you.

266 (XIII. 50)

CICERO TO ACILIUS

Rome, January (beginning) 44

From Cicero to Acilius greetings.

In view of your habitual courtesy towards me, of which I had full experience throughout the time of my residence in Brundisium, I have made bold to write to you without ceremony and almost as of right on any matter which deeply concerns me.

Manius Curius, who is in business at Patrae, is on the closest and most familiar terms with me. I am indebted to him for many services, as he is to me. And, what is most important, there is a cordial and reciprocal affection between us. That being so, if you pin any hopes upon my friendship, if you wish to make me even more grateful for the services you so readily rendered me in Brundisium (though most grateful I am), and if you see that all those near to you hold me in affection, then of your favour grant me this request: Keep Manius Curius in good fettle, as the phrase goes, safe and sound and free of all embarrassment, loss, and trouble. I give you my personal guarantee (and all your people will undertake as much on my behalf) that my friendship and your good offices to me will yield you no small returns and no slight pleasure.

Goodbye.

267 (VII. 31)

CICERO TO MANIUS CURIUS

Rome, February 44

From Cicero to Curius greetings.

I readily perceive from your letter that you have a great regard for me, and that you are aware of my affection for yourself. It has always been my endeavour that this should be so. Having both achieved this result, we now have only to vie with one another in acts of friendship, a contest in which the victory of either will leave me equally content.

Just as well that you had no need to give my letter to Acilius. I understand from yours that you did not much require Sulpicius' help,[780] because your affairs have contracted to a point at which, as you say, 'there is neither head nor foot to them'[781] – for my part I wish they had *feet*, to bring you home at long last. You see how the sources of ancient wit have dried up. Our friend Pomponius can truly say 'Save that we few keep the

780. Cf. Letter 283 (XIII.17).

781. i.e. 'they are worth nothing'.

ancient Attic glory living still.'[782] He is your successor, and I am his. Pray then come back, so that the seed of wit at least does not perish along with the commonwealth.

268 (XIII. 43)

CICERO TO Q. GALLIUS[783]

Rome, winter of 47–46

From M. Cicero to Q. Gallius.

I hope your affection for me, which to be sure has long been apparent, will be shown in many contexts, but here you have a matter in which you can easily demonstrate your good-will towards me. A friend of mine, L. Oppius, son of Marcus, is in business at Philomelium. I recommend him to you very specially, all the more so because, besides the regard I have for himself, he is managing the affairs of L. Egnatius Rufus. Now Egnatius is of all Roman Knights on the most familiar terms with me; daily intercourse and many important services rendered have created a close attachment.

So I am asking you to look kindly on Oppius, who is on the spot, and to protect Egnatius' interests in his absence just as though his affairs were mine. I should be grateful if, to aid your memory, you would write a few lines to be delivered to you in the province – but write in such terms that, when you read them, you can readily recall the urgency of this recommendation of mine. This I beg of you as a special favour.

782. Source unknown.

783. The manuscripts vary and the name of the addressee (also in Letter 270 (XIII.44)) may have been Q. (?) Quintius Gallus – an unknown. In any case he was about to join Q. Marcius Philippus, governor of Cilicia, as Quaestor or Legate.

269 (XIII. 74)

CICERO TO Q. PHILIPPUS

Rome, early 46

From M. Cicero to Q. Philippus, Proconsul, greetings.

Although, in view of your attentiveness to me and the friendship between us, I do not doubt that you are bearing my recommendation in mind, I would none the less recommend to you yet again my friend L. Oppius, who is on the spot, and the affairs of my very good friend L. Egnatius, who is not. My connection with the latter is so close and familiar that I should not be more concerned if my own money were at stake. So you will greatly oblige me if you make clear to him that your affection for me is as great as I myself believe it to be. You can do nothing to oblige me more, and I beg it of you earnestly.

270 (XIII. 44)

CICERO TO Q. GALLIUS

Rome, early 46

From Cicero to Gallius greetings.

Letters from yourself and from my good friend L. Oppius have informed me that you have been mindful of my recommendation, which in view of your notable good-will towards me and the attachment between us did not at all surprise me. However, I should like once again to recommend L. Oppius, who is on the spot, and the affairs of my very close friend L. Egnatius, who is not. My connection with the latter is so close and intimate that I should not be more concerned if my own money were at stake. So you will very much oblige me if you make it clear to him that your affection for me is as great as I myself believe it to be. You can do nothing to oblige me more, and I beg it of you earnestly.

271 (XIII. 45)

CICERO TO APPULEIUS

Rome, 46

From Cicero to Appuleius, Proquaestor.[784]

Of all Roman Knights L. Egnatius stands on the most familiar footing with me, and I recommend to you his slave Anchialus and his business affairs in Asia as warmly as if I were writing of my personal interests. I should like you to be aware that apart from a great deal of day-to-day contact we are indebted to one another for important services mutually rendered. So let me earnestly request you to let him understand that I have written to you in appropriately pressing terms – for as to your friendly disposition towards me he is in no doubt. May I particularly beg this favour of you?

Goodbye.

784. Evidently in the province of Asia. He cannot be securely identified with any of the contemporary Ap(p)uleii.

272 (XIII. 46)

CICERO TO APPULEIUS

Rome, 47–46

From Cicero to Appuleius greetings.

L. Nostius Zoilus is my co-heir and the estate is that of his former master. I mention these two particulars so you may know that I have cause to be his friend and may judge him a man of good character to be favoured by his ex-master with such a mark of esteem. So I recommend him to you as though he were one of my own domestic circle. It will be very agreeable to me if you will let him understand that this recommendation has done him great service with you.

273 (XIII. 73)

CICERO TO Q. PHILIPPUS

Tusculum (?), summer of 46

From M. Cicero to Q. Philippus, Proconsul, greetings.

I congratulate you on your safe return from your province to the bosom of your family with your reputation and the public interest unimpaired. If I had been in Rome, I should have seen you, and thanked you in person for taking care of my very good friend L. Egnatius in his absence and of L. Oppius on the spot.

My relations with Antipater of Derbe[785] are not only of hospitality, but of the most familiar acquaintance. I heard that

785. 'A local dynast in south Lycaonia, holding Derbe and Laranda, both places of some consequence' (R. Syme).

you have been very angry with him and was sorry for it. On the merits of the case I can make no judgement, apart from my persuasion that, being the man you are, you have done nothing without due consideration. But in virtue of our old friendship, I would urgently request you to spare his sons, who are in your hands, if only as a favour to me, unless you think your reputation would thereby be in any way compromised. If *I* thought that, I should not dream of asking you – your credit would be of much more consequence in my eyes than the connection I have mentioned. But I am persuaded (I may be wrong) that such action will bring you commendation rather than criticism. If it is not troubling you too much, I should be glad to learn from you what can be done, and what you can do for my sake – of your will I have no doubt.

274 (XIII. 47)

CICERO TO P. SILIUS

Date uncertain

From Cicero to Silius greetings.

Why should I recommend to you a person for whom you yourself have a regard? However, to let you know that I have not only a regard but an affection for him, I am writing you these lines. Of all your good offices, which are many and great, it will be to me the most agreeable if you will deal with Egnatius so as to make him feel that I am fond of him and that you are fond of me. I beg this of you as a special favour.

You may take it that those plans[786] of mine have fallen through. Well, let me apply the proverbial comfort – it may all be for the best. But of this when we meet. Be sure to keep your affection for me, and be satisfied of mine for you.

786. Reference uncertain.

275 (XIII. 78)

CICERO TO A. ALLIENUS

47–46? (perhaps c. 62)

From M. Cicero to Allienus[787] greetings.

Demetrius of Sicyon is not only a former host of mine, but a familiar friend, which not many (especially Greeks) can say. He is a most honest, worthy, and sedulously hospitable person, and pays me particular respect and attention and regard. You will find that he is the leading man, not only in his own town, but almost in Achaia as a whole. I would only open the door and pave his way into your acquaintance. Once you get to know him, your own disposition will do the rest: you will judge him worthy of your friendship and hospitality. So may I request you after reading this letter to take him under your wing, and promise to do all you can for him for my sake? As for what may follow, if, as I am confident will be the case, you find him deserving of your friendship and hospitality, I would ask you to make much of him and include him in your circle. I shall be greatly obliged.

Goodbye.

787. The following letter (276 (XII.79)) is addressed to Allienus as Proconsul, which he was, in Sicily, in 48–46. But the recommendation of a citizen of Sicyon suggests that this letter belongs to an earlier period in his career when he may have been serving in Greece. He was probably Quaestor *c.* 62.

276 (XIII. 79)

CICERO TO A. ALLIENUS

Rome, 47–46

From M. Cicero to Allienus, Proconsul, greetings.

I think you know how high a regard I had for C. Avianius Flaccus, and I heard from his own lips (he was an excellent man, most appreciative of a kindness) how handsomely you treated him. His sons are thoroughly worthy of their father, and very dear friends of mine. May I recommend them to you as warmly as I possibly can? C. Avianius is in Sicily, Marcus is here with us. I beg you to enhance the standing of the former, who is on the spot, and to protect the interests of both. You can do nothing in your present province to oblige me more, and I do most particularly request it of you.

277 (XIII. 10)

CICERO TO M. BRUTUS

Rome, early (?) 46

From Cicero to Brutus greetings.

When your Quaestor, M. Varro,[788] was setting off to join you I did not think he needed any recommendation. Traditional usage, I thought, was in itself sufficient to recommend him to you – which, as you are aware, has decreed that the relationship of Quaestor to superior should stand next to that of children to

788. M. Terentius Varro Gibba. Brutus was governor of Cisalpine Gaul.

parents. But Varro himself is persuaded that a carefully drafted letter of mine concerning him will carry great weight with you, and urges me to write as fully as possible. So I have thought it better to comply with my friend's wish, since he attaches so much importance to it.

To show you then that in so doing I am fulfilling an obligation, let me mention that when M. Terentius first entered public life he sought my friendship. Then, when he had established himself in the world, two additional circumstances served to increase my good-will towards him. One was that he was engaged in my own chosen avocation,[789] in which even today I take most pleasure, showing natural ability, as you know, and considerable application; the other, that at an early age he involved himself in the companies managing public contracts – to my regret, for he lost a great deal of money. However, the common interest of a class which stands very high in my regard made our friendship the firmer. Then, after a record of highly conscientious and creditable activity on both benches,[790] he applied himself to a political career (that was before this recent constitutional upheaval), and regarded the office as the most honourable reward of his hard work. I may add that latterly he travelled from Brundisium with a letter and oral message from myself to Caesar. I was impressed by his friendly spirit in undertaking this mission and the conscientiousness with which he discharged and reported it.

I had intended to deal specifically with his good character and personality after explaining the reason why I have so high a regard for him, but it seems to me that in doing the latter I have sufficiently covered the former. However, I do specifically promise and personally guarantee that he will make you a pleasant and useful associate. You will find him a man of modesty and good sense, a stranger to any form of self-seeking, active and painstaking furthermore in the highest degree.

789. Forensic oratory.

790. As prosecutor and defender.

I ought not to promise what you will have to judge for yourself when you come to know him well. Still, in all new associations something depends on the nature of the first approach, the sort of recommendation which opens as it were the door of friendship. That was my purpose in this letter. It should have been achieved, to be sure, by the official bond automatically; all the same, that bond will be none the frailer for this extra link. So if you think as much of me as Varro believes and I myself am conscious that you do, I trust you will make it your business to show me as soon as possible that this recommendation of mine has proved as advantageous to him as he expects (and I do not doubt) it will.

278 (XIII. 11)

CICERO TO M. BRUTUS

Rome, 46

From Cicero to Brutus greetings.

I have always noticed the particular care you take to inform yourself of all that concerns me, so I do not doubt that you not only know which township I hail from but also know how attentively I look after the interests of my fellow-townsmen of Arpinum. All their corporate income, including the means out of which they keep up religious worship and maintain their temples and public places in repair, consists in rents from property in Gaul.[791] We have dispatched the following gentlemen, Roman Knights, as our representatives to inspect the properties, collect sums due from the tenants, and take general cognizance and charge: Q. Fufidius, son of Quintus; M. Faucius, son of Marcus; Q. Mamercius, son of Quintus.

791. Cisalpine.

May I particularly request of you in virtue of our friendship to give your attention to the matter, and to do your best to see that the business of the municipality goes through as smoothly and rapidly as possible with your assistance. As for the persons named, let me ask you to extend them, as you naturally would, all possible courtesy and consideration. You will attach some worthy gentlemen to your connection and your favour will bind a township which never forgets an obligation. As for myself, I shall be even more beholden than I should otherwise have been, because, while it is my habit to look after my fellow-townsmen, I have a particular concern and responsibility towards them this year. It was my wish that my son, my nephew, and a very close friend of mine, M. Caesius, should be appointed Aediles this year to set the affairs of the municipality in order – in our town it is the custom to elect magistrates with that title and no other. You will have done honour to them, and above all to me, if the corporate property of the municipality is well managed thanks to your good-will and attention. May I again ask you this favour most earnestly?

279 (XIII. 12)

CICERO TO BRUTUS

Rome, same date as preceding

From Cicero to Brutus greetings.

In a separate letter I have recommended the representatives of the people of Arpinum jointly to your favour as warmly as I was able. In this letter I am recommending Q. Fufidius, with whom I have all manner of friendly ties, individually and with special warmth; not in any way to detract from the force of my other recommendation, but to add this one. He is the stepson of my particular friend and connection M. Caesius, and served with me as Military Tribune in Cilicia. His conduct in that capacity was such as to make me feel that I had not conferred a favour but received one. Furthermore, a point to which you attach special importance, he is not without a leaning towards our favourite pursuits. So I hope you will give him the most generous of welcomes, and do your best to ensure that his activity in a mission which he undertook contrary to his own convenience in deference to my wishes may shine as conspicuously as possible. He is desirous (the natural instinct of a man of mould) to gain all the commendation he can from me, his instigator, and from the municipality. In that he will succeed, if through this recommendation of mine he enlists your goodwill.

280 (XIII. 13)

CICERO TO M. BRUTUS

Rome, 46

From Cicero to Brutus greetings.

L. Castronius Paetus is without question the leading man in Luca, a gentleman of distinction and consequence, always ready to serve a friend – a thoroughly honourable man, whose virtues (if it be anything to the purpose) are set off by worldly fortune. He is also an intimate of mine; in fact there is no member of our order[792] whom he cultivates more assiduously. So I recommend him as my friend and worthy to be yours. Any service you render him will, I feel sure, tend to your own gratification, as it will certainly oblige me.

Goodbye.

792. The senatorial.

281 (XIII. 14)

CICERO TO M. BRUTUS

Rome, 46

From Cicero to Brutus greetings.

L. Titius[793] Strabo, one of our most respected and distinguished Roman Knights, is on intimate terms with me, and we can claim from one another all that belongs to the closest of connections. He is owed money in your province by P. Cornelius. Vulcatius, as City Praetor, has remitted the matter for adjudication in Gaul.

May I request you particularly (more so than if the case were mine, in so far as one is more respectably concerned about a friend's money than about one's own) to see that the affair is settled? Take it up personally and put it through. Try to arrange, so far as seems to you right and fair, that Strabo's freedman, who has been dispatched for the purpose, settles the business on the most favourable terms and collects the cash. I shall be deeply beholden, and you yourself will find L. Titius well worthy of your friendship. Let me once more earnestly beg of you to attend to this, as you habitually do to any wish of mine within your knowledge.

793. Perhaps 'Tidius'; he may have been the father of the person mentioned in Letter 376 (XII.6).

282 (XIII. 29)

CICERO TO L. PLANCUS

Rome, 46 (early)

From M. Cicero to L. Plancus greetings.

I am sure you know that among the connections you inherited from your father I stand pre-eminently close to you, not only on such grounds as present the façade of an intimate association, but on those of familiar intercourse – for, as you are aware, I had such a relationship, most valid and most delightful, with your father. Such were the origins of my affection for yourself. It strengthened my association with your father, the more so because I observed that, from the time when you were old enough to discriminate in your regard for this person or that, I was the object of your special notice and fond attention. Add to this the strong attachment of common pursuits, important in itself, and of such pursuits and accomplishments as automatically link those who share the love of them in the bonds of familiar friendship.

I expect you are wondering where this long-drawn exordium may be tending. Well, let me begin by assuring you that I have not mentioned these points without good and ample reason.

I am on the closest terms with C. Ateius Capito. You know the vicissitudes of my career. In all the various advancements and tribulations which have come my way C. Capito has been mine to command. His spirit and his time, his public and personal influence, even his private fortune, have been at my service in good times and bad.

Capito had a relative, T. Antistius. As Quaestor he was appointed by lot to Macedonia, and was in charge of that province, no one having come to replace him, when Pompey and his army arrived. There was nothing Antistius could do. Given the opportunity, he would have preferred above all things to rejoin Capito, whom he loved as a father, especially as he knew how deeply attached Capito was and has always been to Caesar. But taken as he was by surprise, he touched only such employment as he could not refuse. When money was minted at Apollonia, I cannot assert that he was not in charge, and I cannot deny that he was present, though for no more than two or perhaps three months. After that he kept away from the army and shunned all activity. I hope you will take my word for this as an eye-witness. He saw my despondency in that war, and shared all his thoughts with me. So he hid himself in a corner of Macedonia as far away as possible from the army, so as not to be present at any activity, let alone in command. After the battle he went to Bithynia, to a person with whom he had connections, A. Plautius. There Caesar saw him, and without a word of harshness or reproof told him to return to Rome. Directly afterwards he fell ill, and never recovered. He arrived in Corcyra a sick man, and there died. Under his will, made in Rome in the Consulship of Paulus and Marcellus, he left Capito five-sixths of his estate. The remaining sixth is left to persons whose portion may be confiscated to the state without exciting any complaint. It amounts to HS3,000,000. But this is Caesar's business.

Now, my dear Plancus, I appeal to you in the name of my friendship with your father and our mutual affection, of our studies and the whole tenor of our lives in which we are so much alike: I beg you with all possible earnestness and urgency to take this matter up and regard it as mine. Press with all your strength. Bring it about that by dint of my recommendation, your active support, and Caesar's good favour C. Capito enjoys his relative's estate. If you grant me this, I shall feel that you have spontaneously laid in my lap all the advantages which, in your present plenitude of influence and power, I could have had of you for the asking.

There is a point which I hope will help you, one of which Caesar himself is in the best possible position to judge. Capito has always cultivated and regarded Caesar. But Caesar himself is witness to that. I know what an excellent memory he has, so I do not attempt to brief you. When you speak to Caesar, assume on Capito's behalf just so much as you find *his* recollection acknowledges. For my part, let me put before you what I have been able to test in personal experience – how much weight it should carry you must judge. You are not unaware what party and cause I championed in public life, and on what persons and classes I relied for support and protection. Please believe me when I say that in this very war any action of mine not in accordance with Caesar's wishes (and I know Caesar realizes that such action was very much contrary to my own inclination) was taken by the advice, instigation, and influence of others; whereas the fact that I was the most moderate and temperate member of that party was due above all to the influence of Capito. Had my other friends been similarly minded, I might have done something for the state and should certainly have greatly benefited myself.

If you put this matter through, my dear Plancus, you will confirm my hopes of your kindly disposition towards me, and in Capito himself you will add to your connection a most appreciative, serviceable, and excellent person by conferring upon him so eminent a favour.

283 (XIII. 17)

CICERO TO SERVIUS SULPICIUS RUFUS

Rome, 46

From Cicero to Servius Sulpicius greetings.

There are many good reasons for the regard I have for Manius Curius, who is in business in Patrae. My friendship with him is of very long standing, begun when he first entered public life; and at Patrae his whole house was open to me in this recent terrible war, as well as on several earlier occasions. Had I needed, I should have used it like my own. But my principal link with Curius has, if I may so put it, a more sacred character; for he is a great intimate of our friend Atticus, whom he cultivates and regards more than anybody in the world.

If you happen to have made Curius' acquaintance already, I imagine that this letter comes too late; for he is so agreeable and attentive that I expect he will have recommended himself to you by now. If that is so, I would none the less earnestly request of you that any measure of good-will you have bestowed upon him prior to this letter of mine may be supplemented as largely as possible by my recommendation. If, on the other hand, his modesty has deterred him from putting himself in your way, or if you do not yet know him sufficiently, or if for some particular reason he requires a recommendation out of the common, then there is no man whom I could recommend to you more cordially or on better grounds. I will do what those who recommend a friend in conscience and simplicity ought to do – I will give you, or rather I do give you, my pledge and personal guarantee that Manius Curius' personality, character, and manners are such as will make you deem him, once you get to know him, worthy both of your friendship and of so studied a recommendation. Certainly I shall be deeply grateful if I find that my letter has carried as much weight with you as at the moment of writing I am confident it will.

284 (XIII. 18)

CICERO TO SERVIUS SULPICIUS RUFUS

Rome, 46

From Cicero to Servius greetings.

I won't acknowledge that your kind and charming letter gave more pleasure to our friend Atticus, whose delight I witnessed, than to myself. Our gratification was about equal, but I was the more amazed. Had you *answered* Atticus handsomely, after a request or at any rate a hint (not that we had any doubt but that you would), I should have been beholden; but you have actually written to him of your own accord, and shown him by letter such a wealth of good-will when he was not expecting it! I ought not to make a request of you in order to make you the more zealous on *my* account, for your promises go to the limit of liberality. I ought not even to thank you for what you have done for Atticus' sake and of your own volition. But this I will say, that I am deeply grateful for it. Such an expression of your esteem for my dearest friend cannot but give me the liveliest satisfaction; and, that being so, I must needs be grateful.

And yet we are so close that I may allow myself a slip when I am writing to you. So I shall proceed to do both the things I have said I must not do. I hope you *will* enhance what you have told Atticus you are ready to do for his sake by any additional favours your affection for me can prompt. And whereas I did not venture a moment ago to thank you, thank you now I do. I want you to feel that when you oblige Atticus by your good offices in connection with his affairs in Epirus or elsewhere you will by the same token be obliging me.

285 (XIII. 19)

CICERO TO SERVIUS SULPICIUS RUFUS

Rome, 46

From Cicero to Servius greetings.

With Lyso of Patrae I have an old tie of hospitality, a connection which I believe should be religiously observed. But that applies to a good many individuals, whereas the intimacy existing between myself and Lyso has no parallel among my other relationships of this sort. It has been so greatly furthered by his many services and by daily intercourse that our familiarity could not be closer. He has been in Rome for almost a year, constantly in my company. We were very hopeful that as a result of my letter of recommendation you would use your best endeavours to protect his interests while he is away; and so you have. All the same, remembering that all power resides in a single pair of hands and that Lyso had been on our side, serving in our ranks, we dreaded what each day might bring. However, his own distinction and the efforts of myself and his other erstwhile guests have carried the day. Caesar has acceded to our petitions in full, as you will gather from the letter which he has dispatched to you.

And now, far from at all abating my previous recommendation as though all our objectives were already achieved, I want to urge you all the more pressingly to take Lyso into your patronage and connection. When his fortunes hung in the balance, I was chary of saying too much to you in case of some mischance which even you would be powerless to remedy. But now that his status is secure, I most earnestly and particularly ask you for all possible assistance. Not to make a catalogue, I commend his whole household to your favour, including his young son, whom my client C. Maenius Gemellus adopted under the laws of Patrae, when he himself had become a citizen of that place during his unhappy exile. I trust that in this same matter of Maenius' inheritance you will defend his cause and rights.

The capital point is that you should admit Lyso, whom I know to be an excellent and appreciative fellow, into your connection. If you do, I have no doubt that you will form a regard for him, and in due course recommend him to others with sentiments and judgement corresponding to my own. This I ardently desire. And I also have some apprehension that, if in any particular you appear to have done less for him than you conceivably might, he will suspect that the perfunctory style of my letters has been to blame rather than your unmindfulness of myself. For how much you think of me he has been able to perceive from your own letters as well as my day-to-day conversation.

286 (XIII. 20)

CICERO TO SERVIUS SULPICIUS RUFUS

Rome, 46

From Cicero to Servius greetings.

Asclapo, a physician of Patrae, is on familiar terms with me. I liked his company, and had favourable experience of his professional skill when members of my household[794] were taken sick. He gave me satisfaction in this connection as a knowledgeable doctor, and also a conscientious and kindly one. Accordingly I am recommending him to you, and would request you

794. Tiro in 50–49, possibly others.

to let him understand that I have written about him with some particularity, and that my recommendation has been to his no small advantage. I shall be truly obliged.

287 (XIII. 21)

CICERO TO SERVIUS SULPICIUS RUFUS

Rome, 46

From Cicero to Servius greetings.

M. Aemilius Avianianus has cultivated my acquaintance from his early youth and always held me in regard. He is an honourable man and a very amiable one, most conscientious in serving his friends by every means in his power. If I thought he was now in Sicyon and had not heard that he is still staying where I left him, at Cibyra, there would be no need for me to write to you about him at any length. For I am sure that his own personality and manners without anybody's recommendation would have made you as fond of him as I and his other friends. But as I believe him to be away, let me warmly recommend to you his household in Sicyon and his interests – more especially his freedman C. Avianius Hammonius, whom I also recommend to you in his own right. I like him for his exceptional conscientiousness and fidelity towards his former master; moreover, he has rendered me personally important services, making himself available to me in the most difficult period of my life with as much loyalty and good-will as if I had given him his freedom. So let me ask you to support the said Hammonius in his former master's affairs, as the agent of the person whom I am recommending to you, and also to hold him in regard for his own sake and admit him to your circle. You will find him a modest, serviceable person, worthy of your regard.

Goodbye.

288 (XIII. 22)

CICERO TO SERVIUS SULPICIUS RUFUS

Rome, 46

From Cicero to Servius greetings.

I have a warm regard for T. Manlius, who carries on business at Thespiae. He has always made a point of cultivating my acquaintance and showing me courtesy, nor is he a stranger to our studies. Furthermore, Varro Murena takes the liveliest interest in his welfare. Although fully confident in the effect of his own letter of recommendation to you on Manlius' behalf, Varro was of the opinion that a letter of mine would contribute something additional. As for me, my friendship with Manlius and Varro's urgency have induced me to write to you as pressingly as I can.

So then, I shall be deeply obliged if you will give as much attention to this recommendation of mine as you have ever given to such a document; that is to say, if you will assist and further T. Manlius as much as possible in any way consistent with your honour and dignity. And I assure you that you will reap from his own most appreciative and amiable character the reward you are accustomed to expect from the services of honourable men.

289 (XIII. 23)

CICERO TO SERVIUS SULPICIUS RUFUS

Rome, 46

From Cicero to Servius greetings.

L. Cossinius, a friend of mine and a member of my Tribe, is

on very friendly terms with me. We have an old-established acquaintance, and our friend Atticus has made me see even more of Cossinius than I otherwise should. His whole family circle has a regard for me, in particular his freedman L. Cossinius Anchialus, a person very highly thought of by his master and his former master's connections, of whom I am one. I recommend him to you as warmly as I could if he was my own freedman and he stood in the same relation to me as to his former master. You will very much oblige me if you will admit him to your friendship and give him your assistance in any matter wherein he may require it, so far as you can do so without inconveniencing yourself. I shall be greatly obliged, and you will be glad of it later on, for you will find him a very worthy, amiable, and attentive person.

290 (XIII. 24)

CICERO TO SERVIUS SULPICIUS RUFUS

Rome, 46

From Cicero to Servius greetings.

In the consciousness of duty performed, I was already happy to remember the pains with which I had recommended to you my host and friend Lyso; but after learning in a letter from him that he had fallen under some unmerited suspicion on your part, I was glad indeed to have taken such trouble in recommending him. He tells me that my recommendation has been of the greatest help to him, because you had been informed that he was in the habit of speaking disrespectfully about you in Rome. To be sure, he writes that with your usual kindness and good nature you accepted his exculpation. None the less I should, and do, thank you most warmly for paying so much attention to my letter as to put aside after reading it all offence arising from the suspicion of Lyso which you had previously entertained. I also hope that you will believe me when I assure you that *nobody* (and in writing this I am not defending Lyso any more than the community at large) has ever spoken of you in other than the most complimentary terms. As for Lyso, who has been with me almost daily, my constant companion, he used to belaud your every act and word, not only because he thought I enjoyed listening to such talk but because he enjoyed the talking even more.

Your treatment of him is such that he no longer requires any recommendation from me and thinks that *one* letter of mine has accomplished all he needed. None the less I would particularly ask you to continue to favour him with your good offices and liberality. I should tell you what kind of a man he is, as I did in my previous letter, if I did not suppose that you know him well enough by now from personal acquaintance.

291 (XIII. 25)

CICERO TO SERVIUS SULPICIUS RUFUS

Rome, 46

Cicero to Servius greetings.

Hagesaretus of Larissa received substantial favours at my hands when I was Consul and held them in grateful memory, paying me the most sedulous attention thereafter. I recommend him to you warmly as my host and friend, an honourable man who knows the meaning of gratitude, a leading member of his community, thoroughly worthy of your friendship. You will deeply oblige me if you make him sensible that my present recommendation has carried great weight with you.

292 (XIII. 26)

CICERO TO SERVIUS SULPICIUS RUFUS

Rome, 46

From Cicero to Servius greetings.

I am bound to L. Mescinius by the fact that he was my Quaestor; but he has made that claim, to which I have always attached the importance prescribed by our traditions, all the more valid by his own merits of character and manners. I have no more familiar or pleasant companion.

I think he is confident that you will be glad to do for his own sake all you properly can, but he hoped that a letter from me would carry much additional weight with you. That was his own impression, and in his familiar intercourse with me he had often heard me refer to the close and delightful connection between us.

Accordingly let me request you, with all the warmth which you will naturally understand to be appropriate in the case of so strong and familiar a connection, to smooth and straighten his affairs in Achaia, which arise from the fact that he is heir to the estate of his brother M. Mindius,[795] who was in business at Elis. This you can do by your influence and advice as well as by your official power and prerogative. We have instructed all our agents in these affairs to submit any disputed points to you as umpire and (so far as may be consistent with your convenience) as final arbiter. May I beg you most earnestly to take this responsibility upon yourself as a compliment to me?

One further point: should any parties show an unaccommodating disposition and prove unwilling to reach a settlement out of court, you will oblige us very greatly (provided you see nothing inconsistent therein with your own high standing) by

795. See n. 450.

referring them to Rome in view of the fact that a Senator is involved. In order that you may take this course with the less hesitation, we have obtained a letter from Consul M'. Lepidus addressed to yourself – not directing you on any point (that we should consider less than respectful towards you), but a sort of letter of recommendation as it were.

I could say how wisely you will be placing such a favour with Mescinius. But I am sure you know that, and besides it is for myself that I am asking. For I hope you will take it that I am as much concerned for his interest as he is himself. But while I am anxious for him to come into his own with as little trouble as possible, I am also concerned to have him think that he owes this in no trifling degree to my present recommendation.

293 (XIII. 27)

CICERO TO SERVIUS SULPICIUS RUFUS

Rome, 46

From Cicero to Servius greetings.

I might legitimately send you many letters of this kind in identical terms, thanking you for paying such careful attention to my recommendations, as I have done in other cases and shall clearly often be doing. None the less I shall not spare my pains. Like you jurists in your formulae I shall treat in my letters 'of the same matter in another way'.

C. Avianius Hammonius has written to me in transports of gratitude on his own behalf and that of his former master, Aemilius Avianianus. He writes that he himself on the spot and the interests of his absent ex-master could not have been dealt with more handsomely or with more flattering consideration. That makes me happy for their sakes. Close friendship and connection led me to recommend them to you, for of all my most intimate and familiar friends M. Aemilius is the nearest,[796] bound to me by substantial favours on my part, and the most grateful, I might almost say, of all those who may be thought to owe me anything. But it makes me far happier to find you so cordially disposed towards me that you do more for my friends than perhaps I should do myself, if I were on the spot. For I imagine that in serving them I should feel more hesitation as to how far I should go than you feel in serving me.

But of course you realize that I am grateful. What I ask you to believe is that they too are men of gratitude, which I hereby solemnly assure you is so. I hope you will try as far as you conveniently can to see that they settle whatever business they have on hand while you are governor of Achaia.

I have the closest and most agreeable association with your son Servius, and take great pleasure in observing his fine and upright character as well as his abilities and exceptional appetite for learning.

294 (XIII. 28)

CICERO TO SERVIUS SULPICIUS RUFUS

Rome, 46

From Cicero to Servius greetings.

I am generally ready enough to ask your assistance when any of my friends stands in need, but it is with far greater readiness that I write to thank you when you have acted on my recommendation, as you always do. The gratitude expressed to me by everyone I recommend to you, even without special emphasis, passes belief. All this makes me beholden, but most of all in the case of Mescinius. He tells me that as soon as you read my letter

796. Nothing is heard of this Aemilius except in letters of recommendation.

you immediately promised his agents all they asked, and that you actually did far more and better than your word. I hope you realize (I feel I cannot say it too often) that I am most deeply beholden on this score.

It makes me all the happier because I am clear that Mescinius himself will prove a source of great satisfaction to you. He is a man of fine, upright character, in the highest degree obliging and attentive, and he shares those literary interests which used to be our diversion and are now our very life. As for the future, I hope you will increase your benefactions to him by all means befitting yourself. But I have two specific requests. Firstly, if security has to be given in respect of final settlement of any claim, please see that security is given on my guarantee. Secondly, the estate consists, as near as makes no matter, of those items which Mindius' widow, Oppia, has made away with; please assist and find some means whereby the woman may be brought to Rome. It is our opinion that, if she thinks this is going to happen, we shall settle the business. Let me beg you most particularly to gain us this point.

In confirmation of what I have written above, let me personally guarantee that your past and future good offices to Mescinius will be well placed, and that you will find for yourself that you have obliged a most grateful and agreeable individual. I want this to add something to what you have done on *my* account.

295 (XIII. 28a)

CICERO TO SERVIUS SULPICIUS RUFUS

Rome, 46

From Cicero to Servius greetings.

The Lacedaemonians are confident, I imagine, that their own

prestige and that of their forefathers is all the recommendation they need to your sense of duty and justice, nor was I in any doubt, knowing you so well, that you are fully conversant with the rights and deserts of peoples. Accordingly, when Philippus of Lacedaemon asked me to recommend his community to you, I replied, though conscious of my great obligations to them, that the Lacedaemonians require no recommendation where you are concerned.

So please take it that I regard all the communities of Achaia as fortunate, considering the disorders of the present time, in having you as their governor; and, further, that I judge you to be of your own accord a good friend, now and in the future, to the people of Lacedaemon, better versed as you are in the whole history of Greece as well as Rome than any man alive. Let me then request only this: when you do for the Lacedaemonians what your conscience, your dignity, and your sense of justice will demand, indicate to them, if you please, that you are not sorry to understand that I too shall take it kindly. I have an obligation to let them feel that their interests concern me. Allow me to ask this as a particular favour.

296 (XIII. 67)

CICERO TO SERVILIUS ISAURICUS

Rome, 46–44

From M. Cicero to P. Servilius, Proconsul, greetings.

In all my province of Cilicia (to which, as you know, three districts of Asia were assigned) there was nobody with whom I was on a more friendly footing than with Andro, son of Artemo, of Laodicea. He was my host in that town and one that eminently suited my way of life and daily habit. Since leaving the province, I have come to value him far more even than at the time, having experienced in many contexts his grateful disposition and mindfulness of me. I was therefore very glad to see him in Rome. You, who have done good turns to so many people in your province, are well aware that the proportion of the grateful is less than overwhelming.

I have written the above to let you realize that my concern is not idle, and so that you yourself may account him worthy of your hospitality. You will oblige me very much indeed if you make it plain to him how much you think of me; that is to say, if you take him under your wing, and help him in every way you can with propriety and without inconvenience to yourself. That will oblige me indeed, and I would earnestly beg you so to do.

297 (XIII. 69)

CICERO TO SERVILIUS ISAURICUS

Rome, 46–44

From Cicero to his Colleague P. Servilius best greetings.

C. Curtius Mithres is, as you know, the freedman of my very good friend Postumus, but he pays as much respect and attention to me as to his own ex-master. At Ephesus, whenever I was there, I stayed in his house as though it was my home, and many incidents arose to give me proof of his good-will and loyalty to me. If I or someone close to me want anything done in Asia I am in the habit of writing to Mithres and of using his faithful service, and even his house and purse, as though they were my own.

I have told you this at some length to let you understand that I am not writing conventionally or from a self-regarding motive, but on behalf of a really intimate personal connection.

Accordingly may I request you, as a compliment to me, to accommodate Mithres in the dispute he has on hand with a certain citizen of Colophon concerning a country property, and in all other matters, so far as your conscience will permit and so far as you conveniently can – though from my knowledge of him he has too much sense of propriety to be burdensome to you in any respect. If my recommendation and his own worth win him your good opinion, he will feel that he has gained every purpose. So I do particularly ask you to take him under your wing and include him in your circle.

I shall give my most careful and devoted attention to anything that I think you would like or that appears to concern you.

298 (XIII. 70)

CICERO TO SERVILIUS ISAURICUS

Rome, 46–44

From M. Cicero to his Colleague P. Servilius best greetings.

Your good-will towards me is no secret, and so it happens that many persons want to be recommended to you by me. Sometimes I comply without much discrimination, but mostly for my friends, as in the present instance; for with T. Ampius Balbus I have the closest friendship and connection. His freedman, T. Ampius Menander, is a worthy, modest person, of whom both his ex-master and I have an excellent opinion. I specially recommend him to you. You will particularly oblige me if you will accommodate him as and when you can without trouble to yourself; and I beg you so to do as a special favour.

299 (XIII. 71)

CICERO TO SERVILIUS ISAURICUS

Rome, 46–44

From M. Cicero to his Colleague P. Servilius best greetings.

I cannot help recommending a good many people to you, since our friendship and the good-will you have for me is common knowledge. Still, though I am bound to wish well to all those I recommend, they do not all have the same claim on me.

T. Agusius was my companion in my time of tribulation. He shared all my journeys by land and water, all my fatigues and dangers. He would not have left my side now, if I had not given him leave. Accordingly I recommend him to you as a member of my domestic circle with whom I have the most intimate connection. You will oblige me very much indeed if you treat him so as to let him understand that this recommendation has been to his no small help and advantage.

300 (XIII. 72)

CICERO TO SERVILIUS ISAURICUS

Rome, 46–44

From M. Cicero to his Colleague P. Servilius greetings.

I recommended the financial interests of my friend Caerellia – her investments and property in Asia – to you, when we were together at your place in the suburbs, as warmly as I was able; and you, conformably to your habit and the constant flow of your signal services to me, undertook most handsomely to do all I asked. I expect you remember – I know you rarely forget. However, Caerellia's agents write that, because of the size of your province and the quantity of business, you should be frequently reminded.

May I request you therefore to bear in mind the ample undertaking you gave me to do all that your conscience would permit? I believe (but it is for you to consider and judge) that you have a great opportunity to accommodate Caerellia, arising out of the Senate's decree in respect of C. Vennonius' heirs. You will interpret that decree in the light of your own wisdom – I know you have always held the authority of the House in high regard. For the rest, please take it that any kindness you may do Caerellia will greatly oblige me.

301 (XIII. 30)

CICERO TO ACILIUS

Rome, 46–45

From Cicero to Acilius, Proconsul,[797] greetings.

L. Manlius Sosis was formerly a citizen of Catina, but became a Roman citizen along with the rest of the Neapolitan community and a town-councillor at Naples, having been enrolled as a citizen of that municipality before the franchise was granted to the allies and the Latins. His brother recently died at Catina. We do not expect any dispute to arise as to his title to the estate, and he is in possession of it at the present time. However, since he also has some old affairs of business in his part of Sicily, I beg to recommend to your notice this matter of his brother's estate and all other concerns of his, above all the man himself. He is

797. In Sicily.

an excellent person, a familiar friend of mine, conversant with the literary and scholarly pursuits in which I chiefly delight.

Let me then ask you (whether or not he goes to Sicily) to be aware that he is one of my closest and most intimate friends, and to let him understand by the way you treat him that my recommendation has been of substantial assistance to him.

302 (XIII. 31)

CICERO TO ACILIUS

Rome, 46–45

From Cicero to Acilius, Proconsul, greetings.

I am on very familiar terms with C. Flavius, a respected and distinguished Roman Knight. He was a great friend of my son-in-law, C. Piso, and both he and his brother L. Flavius are sedulous in their attentions to me. I hope therefore that as a compliment to me you will treat C. Flavius in the most handsome and flattering fashion in all respects consistent with your honour and dignity. Nothing could oblige me more. But furthermore I assure you (and I do so, not from any interested motive, but out of friendship and attachment, also because it is the truth) that C. Flavius' sense of obligation and attentive courtesy, together with the eminence and influence he enjoys among men of his own rank, will be a source of much gratification to yourself.

Goodbye.

303 (XIII. 32)

CICERO TO ACILIUS

Rome, 46–45

From Cicero to Acilius, Proconsul, greetings.

In the rich and famous community of Halaesa I have the closest ties of hospitality and friendship with two persons, M. Clodius Archagathus and C. Clodius Philo. But I feel some uneasiness in recommending so many people to you in special terms in case I may appear to be placing all my recommendations on a level from a self-regarding motive – not but that your response is more than gratifying both to myself and to all connected with me.

Anyhow, please take it that the family to which I refer, and these members of it especially, are bound to me by length of acquaintance, good offices, and good-will. Therefore I particularly ask you to accommodate them in all respects, so far as your conscience and dignity will allow. I shall be very sincerely beholden if you do.

304 (XIII. 33)

CICERO TO ACILIUS

Rome, 46

From Cicero to Acilius, Proconsul, greetings.

I am on a very familiar footing with Cn. Otacilius Naso, as familiar in fact as with any gentleman of his rank. His attractive manners and worth of character make my daily contacts with him very agreeable. You will not need to wait and see what words I use to recommend one with whom I am on such terms. He has affairs of business in your province, to which his freedmen Hilarus, Antigonus, and Demostratus are attending. I recommend to you these persons and all Naso's affairs exactly as though they were my own. You will oblige me deeply if I find that this recommendation has carried much weight with you.

Goodbye.

305 (XIII. 34)

CICERO TO ACILIUS

Rome, 46–45

From Cicero to Acilius, Proconsul, greetings.

My relations of hospitality with Lyso,[798] son of Lyso, of Lilybaeum, go back to his grandfather. He is most attentive to me, and I find him worthy of his grandfather and father – it is a very distinguished family. Therefore I particularly recommend his property and domestic circle to your notice, and earnestly request you to make him realize that my recommendation has tended to his great honour and advantage in your eyes.

306 (XIII. 35)

CICERO TO ACILIUS

Rome, 46–45

From Cicero to Acilius, Proconsul, greetings.

C. Avianius Philoxenus is an old host of mine and, apart

798. Nothing to do with Lyso of Patrae.

from relations of hospitality, my very good friend. Caesar through my good offices entered him as a citizen of Novum Comum.[799] He took the name of Avianius because of his especially close relations with Avianius Flaccus, a very good friend of mine, as I think you know. I have put all these facts together to let you understand that this recommendation of mine is outside the ordinary.

May I therefore request you to accommodate him in all respects, so far as you can do so without trouble to yourself, and to admit him to your circle? Let him understand that this letter of mine has been very useful to him. I shall be greatly beholden.

307 (XIII. 36)

CICERO TO ACILIUS

Rome, 46–45

From Cicero to Acilius, Proconsul, greetings.

I have old ties of hospitality with Demetrius Megas, and no native of Sicily is on such familiar terms with me. At my request Dolabella obtained the franchise for him from Caesar – I was party to the matter. So now his name is P. Cornelius. And when Caesar, on account of certain mercenary fellows who were selling his favours, gave orders for the removal of the plaque on which the names of grantees of citizenship had been engraved, he told the same Dolabella in my presence that he need not worry about Megas. In his case the favour held good.

I wanted you to know this, so that you should regard him as a Roman citizen, and in all other respects I recommend him as

799. Caesar had enrolled five hundred distinguished Greeks in his colony of Novum Comum under a law passed during his Consulship, though they did not settle there. Their Roman citizenship was now, of course, established.

warmly as I have ever recommended anyone. I shall be very much beholden to you if you deal with him so as to let him understand that my recommendation has been a great asset to him.

308 (XIII. 37)

CICERO TO ACILIUS

Rome, 46–45

From Cicero to Acilius, Proconsul, greetings.

Let me particularly recommend to you my host and friend Hippias, son of Philoxenus, of Calacte. As the matter has been represented to me, his property is being held by the state under a different name in violation of the laws of Calacte. If that is true, the nature of the case entitles him to your assistance as a just magistrate even without any recommendation of mine. But whatever the position, allow me to request you, as a compliment to me, to extricate him from his difficulty, and to accommodate him in this and other matters as far as your conscience and dignity will allow. I shall be truly beholden.

309 (XIII. 38)

CICERO TO ACILIUS

Rome, 46–45

From Cicero to Acilius, Proconsul, greetings.

L. Bruttius, a young Roman Knight of quality in every sense of the word, is one of my most familiar friends and most sedulous in his attentions to me. I was a great friend of his father's from the time when I was Quaestor in Sicily. Bruttius himself is now with me in Rome, but I beg to recommend to you his domestic circle, property, and agents with all possible warmth. I shall be very much beholden if you will let Bruttius understand that my recommendation has been of great assistance to him, as I undertook that it would be.

310 (XIII. 39)

CICERO TO ACILIUS

Rome, 46–45

From Cicero to Acilius, Proconsul, greetings.

There is an old connection between myself and the Titurnius family. Its only surviving representative is M. Titurnius Rufus, whom I am in duty bound to protect and assist to the best of my ability. It rests with you therefore to let him feel that he has in me a sufficiently powerful patron. Accordingly I recommend him to you warmly and request you to let him understand that this recommendation has been greatly to his advantage. I shall be truly beholden.

311 (IX. 13)

CICERO TO DOLABELLA

Rome, 46 (end) or 45 (beginning)

From Cicero to Dolabella greetings.

C. Subernius of Cales is a friend of mine and very closely attached to my intimate friend Lepta. In order to escape the war he went to Spain with M. Varro before its outbreak, and was living in a province where, after Afranius' defeat, none of us supposed there would be any fighting; but, as luck would have it, he found himself in the very trouble which he had tried so hard to avoid. The war which suddenly flared up caught him unawares; started by Scapula, it later gained such momentum under Pompey[800] that he could not possibly extricate himself from this wretched environment. The case of M. Planius Heres, also of Cales and a close friend of Lepta's, is almost identical.

I recommend both these persons to you, and I could not do so with a greater measure of sincere concern and anxiety. I am interested for their own sake; friendship and humanity alike move me strongly on their behalf. But when Lepta is so profoundly concerned (his whole fortune seems to be at stake), my concern must approach, or even equal, his. Therefore I should like you to persuade yourself that, often as I have experienced the warmth of your affection for me, I shall judge of it particularly in this affair. Accordingly I request you, or beg you if you will allow me, to save these unhappy persons, whose calamities are due to fortune, which there is no avoiding, rather than to any fault of their own, and to make it your wish that through you, I may confer this favour not only upon the principals, friends of mine as they are, but upon the town of Cales, with which I have a close connection, and upon Lepta, who matters to me most of all.

What I am about to say is probably not very relevant to the matter at issue, but still it can do no harm to mention it. One of the two has very little money, the other hardly up to Knight's qualification. Since, then, Caesar has generously granted them their lives and there is nothing much else which can be taken from them, get them permission (if you love me as much as I am sure you do) to return to Italy. There is nothing in that which need take up much time, except the journey; and this they are ready to undertake in order to live with their families

800. Cn. Pompeius the Younger.

and die at home. Once again I earnestly ask you to try your utmost, or rather to *do* it, for I am satisfied that you have the power.

312 (XIII. 52)

CICERO TO REX[801]

46–45(?)

From Cicero to Rex greetings.

A. Licinius Aristoteles of Malta has a very old-established tie of hospitality with me, and is furthermore attached to me by much familiar personal contact. That being so, I don't doubt that he is sufficiently recommended to your favour. Indeed I am told on all hands that a recommendation from me counts for a great deal with you. I obtained his pardon from Caesar – he had been much with me, and actually stayed in the cause longer than I did, which I imagine will make you think all the better of him. So make him understand, my dear Rex, that this letter has tended greatly to his advantage.

313 (XIII. 49)

CICERO TO CURIUS[802]

Date uncertain

From Cicero to Curius, Proconsul.

Many ties of long standing go to form my connection with Q. Pompeius, son of Sextus. He has been in the habit of protect-

801. Presumably in an official position in Sicily.

802. Nothing is known of Curius or his province or the person recommended.

ing his financial interests, personal influence, and prestige by means of my recommendations; and now that you are in charge of the province, a letter from me should surely gain him enough to let him feel that he has never been better recommended to any governor. Therefore I particularly request you, bound as you are in virtue of our connection to pay as much regard to my friends as to your own, to take Pompeius under your especial patronage, so that he himself realizes that nothing could have been more to his advantage and distinction than my recommendation.

Goodbye.

314 (XIII. 2)

CICERO TO MEMMIUS[803]

Date uncertain

From Cicero to Memmius greetings.

C. Avianius Evander, who is residing in your family chapel, is a person with whom I have a good deal to do and I am on very friendly terms with his former master, M. Aemilius. May I therefore particularly request you to accommodate him in the matter of his residence as far as you can without inconveniencing yourself? It is rather sudden for him to move back on the Kalends of July, because he has a number of commissions on hand for various patrons. Modesty forbids me to ask you at much length, but I am sure that if the matter is of no consequence to you, or not much, you will feel as I should feel if you made any request of me. I shall certainly be most grateful.

803. Possibly son of the recipient of Letter 63 (XIII.1).

315 (XIII. 3)

CICERO TO C. MEMMIUS

Date uncertain

From Cicero to Memmius greetings.

A. Fufius is one of my inner circle, most attentive and devoted to me. He is a learned, highly cultivated person, thoroughly worthy to be your friend. I hope you will treat him in accordance with the promise you made me orally. I shall take it *most* kindly. Furthermore you will permanently attach to yourself a very serviceable and punctilious gentleman.

316 (XIII. 16)

CICERO TO CAESAR

Rome(?), winter of 46–45

From Cicero to Caesar greetings.

Young P. Crassus was my favourite among the whole range of our aristocracy. From his earliest youth I had good hopes of him, but he rose really high in my estimation when I saw how well you thought of him. Even during his lifetime I had a great regard and liking for his freedman Apollonius. He was warmly attached to Crassus, and admirably fitted to join him in his liberal interests, so naturally Crassus was very fond of him. After Crassus' death I thought him all the worthier of admission to my patronage and friendship because he felt it proper to pay respect and attention to those whom Crassus had loved and who had loved him in return. Accordingly he joined me in

Cilicia, where his loyalty and good sense proved very useful to me in many connections. And I believe that in the Alexandrian War such service as his zeal and fidelity could render you was not lacking.

Hoping that you are of the same opinion, he is leaving to join you in Spain, mainly on his own initiative, but not without encouragement from me. I did not promise him a recommendation, not that I did not think it would carry weight with you, but because a man who had seen military service at your side and whom Crassus' memory made one of your circle did not seem to me to need one. And if he did wish to make use of recommendations, I knew he could obtain them elsewhere. But I am glad to give him a testimonial of what I think of him, since he makes a point of it and my experience has shown me that you pay attention to such.

I know him to be a scholar, devoted to liberal studies from boyhood. For he was much in my house from an early age with Diodotus the Stoic, a most erudite person in my opinion. Now his imagination has been captured by your career, and he wants to write an account of it in Greek. I think he can do it. He has a strong natural talent cultivated by practice, and has for a long time been engaged in this type of literary work. To do justice to your immortal fame is his passionate ambition.

Well, there you have my considered testimony, but your own keen discernment will provide you with a much easier means of assessing the matter. And after all, I do recommend him to you, having said I should do no such thing. Any kindness you do him will particularly oblige me.

317 (XIII. 15)

CICERO TO CAESAR

c. May(?) 45

From Cicero to Caesar, Imperator, greetings.

Allow me to recommend Precilius to you with peculiar warmth, the son of a very worthy gentleman who is connected with you and intimate with me. I have an extraordinary regard for the young man himself because of his modesty, amiability, and notably affectionate disposition towards me; and experience has taught me to appreciate his father's unfaltering goodwill. For, mark you, he is the one man above all others who used to jeer and gird at me because I would not join you despite your most flattering invitations. But 'the heart within my breast he ne'er did sway'. For I used to hear our men of light and leading clamouring

> 'Be bold, and earn the praise of men unborn.'[804]
> He spake; but grief's dark mist the other cloaked.[805]

But he comforts me too. Burned child as I am, they are still trying to kindle the fire of ambition in my heart:

> No sluggard's fate, ingloriously to die,
> But daring that which men to be shall learn.[806]

That is the way they talk. But, as you see, I am not so responsive nowadays. So I turn from Homer's magniloquence to the sound precepts of Euripides:

> Who for himself's not wise, his wisdom scorn,[807]

804. *Odyssey*, I.302 (Athene to Telemachus).
805. *Odyssey*, XXIV.315 (of Laertes).
806. *Iliad*, XXII.304 f. (Hector is speaking).
807. Cf. Letter 27 (VII.6).

a verse which old Precilius extols in fine style, and says that a man may look 'both to front and rear',[808] and yet at the same time 'e'er be the first, o'ertopping all the rest'.[809]

But to go back to my starting point: I shall be truly grateful if you will take the young fellow under your wing with the kindness which is so conspicuous a trait of yours, and add my recommendation to crown the good-will which I suppose you to bear the Precilii for their own sakes. I have written you an unconventional sort of letter to let you understand that this is no ordinary recommendation.

318 (XIII. 4)

CICERO TO VALERIUS ORCA[810]

Between November 46 and July 45(?)

M. Cicero to Q. Valerius Orca, son of Quintus, Legate *pro praetore*, greetings.

I have a very close connection with the people of Volaterrae. Having received an important favour at my hands, they repaid me most amply, never stinting their support either in my advancements or in my tribulations. But even if there was nothing between me and them, I should advise and urge you out of my warm affection for you and my consciousness of your high regard for me to consider their financial welfare – especially as they have an almost peculiarly strong claim to maintain their rights. By the grace of the Immortal Gods they es-

808. *Iliad*, I.343=*Odyssey*, XXIV.452.

809. *Iliad*, VI.208=XI.784. This had been Cicero's watchword in his early days; cf. *Letters to his Brother Quintus* 25 (III.5)4.

810. Cf. Letter 57 (XIII.6). Orca was now apparently in charge of the assignment of land in Etruria to Caesar's veterans.

caped the harsh measures of the Sullan period;[811] and they were defended by me during my Consulship with the enthusiastic support of the People of Rome.

When the Tribunes of the Plebs brought forward a highly iniquitous bill concerning their lands, I had no difficulty in persuading the Senate and People of Rome to decree the preservation of Roman citizens to whom fortune had been merciful. During his first Consulship C. Caesar approved my action in his agrarian bill, and gave the town and district of Volaterrae permanent security from any such threat. So I cannot doubt, when I see him acquiring new connections, that he wishes his old benefactions to stand. Accordingly your good sense will instruct you either to take your cue from the leader in whose wake and under whose command you have gained such high preferment, or at least to leave the whole case open for him to determine. Moreover, you ought surely to feel no doubt about the desirability of placing so important, well-established, and respectable a community as Volaterrae under a lasting obligation to yourself by conferring a signal favour.

What I have written so far is in the nature of exhortation and counsel. What follows is petitionary. I would not have you think that I am merely advising you in your own interests, and not also asking you for a favour which I personally need. Well then, I shall be greatly beholden if you decide to preserve the people of Volaterrae in complete safety and integrity. To your honour, justice, and benevolence I commend their dwellings, abodes, property, and fortunes, which the Immortal Gods and the leading men in our commonwealth have maintained intact with the wholehearted approbation of the Senate and People of Rome.

If the conditions of today permitted me to defend the people

811. Sulla had passed a law depriving the Volaterrans of Roman citizenship and confiscating their land in punishment for their long resistance to his army. But the law seems to have remained inoperative as to the first and only partially operative as to the second.

of Volaterrae as it has been my habit to support those with whom I have connections, conformably to the resources which used to be at my command, I should not fail to engage in every service, every contest indeed, in which I might possibly be of use to them. But I am confident that with yourself my voice is at the present time no less powerful than it always was with all honest men. Therefore let me request you, in the name of the close connection and reciprocally equal good-will that exists between us, to deserve well of the people of Volaterrae. Let them think that a divine providence has placed this business in charge of the man with whom of all others I, their constant champion, might exercise most influence.

319 (XIII. 5)

CICERO TO VALERIUS ORCA

46–44

From Cicero to Q. Valerius Orca, Legate *pro praetore*, greetings.

That my friendship with you should be as widely known as possible is not disagreeable to me. At the same time I have not on that account (as you are in the best possible position to judge) stood in the way of your carrying out the task you have undertaken loyally and conscientiously in accordance with the will of Caesar, who has entrusted you with so important and difficult a commission. Although I receive many requests from many people in their confidence of your friendly disposition towards me, I take good care not to embarrass you in the execution of your duty by solicitations of mine.

I have been on intimate terms with C. Curtius[812] since early youth. His iniquitous deprivation in Sulla's time was a grief to

812. Known only from this letter.

me; and when it appeared that persons who had suffered a similar injustice were allowed to return to their country, though with the loss of their entire fortunes, a concession which was universally welcomed, I lent my assistance in his rehabilitation. He owns a property in the district of Volaterrae into which he put what remained from the wreck of his estate. Caesar has now appointed him a member of the Senate, a rank which he can scarcely support if he loses this property. It is very hard that, having been raised in station, he should be at a disadvantage in fortune; and it is highly incongruous that a Senator by Caesar's favour should be evicted from land which is under distribution by Caesar's orders. However, I do not care to dwell on the rights of the matter, or I might seem to have prevailed with you in virtue of a strong case rather than by my personal influence. So let me particularly request you to regard C. Curtius' estate as mine, to do for C. Curtius' sake whatever you would do for mine, and, having done it, to consider that whatever comes to him through my intervention is a gift from you to me. This I most earnestly beg of you.

320 (XIII. 7)

CICERO TO C. CLUVIUS[813]

Rome, autumn 45

From Cicero to Cluvius greetings.

When you called upon me at my house just before you left for Gaul (a token of our friendship and an example of your unfailing attentiveness to me), I spoke to you about the leased land in Gaul belonging to the town of Atella, and made my deep concern for the town plain to you. Bearing in mind your

813. Evidently in charge of land assignments in Cisalpine Gaul.

particularly friendly disposition towards myself, I think it incumbent upon me to write to you after your departure in greater detail, since the matter involves both a major financial interest of a highly respected township with which I have close ties, and an imperative obligation on my side – although I am not unaware of the nature of the present situation and the extent of your powers, and perfectly understand that C. Caesar has assigned you a piece of business, not asked you to exercise your discretion. I am therefore requesting of you only so much as I think you can perform, and will gladly perform for my sake.

And first I would ask you to believe, what is the fact, that the finances of the municipality depend entirely on this rent, and that in these days they are labouring under very heavy burdens and are involved in serious difficulties. Many others seem to be in a similar situation, but I do assure you that this particular town has been exceptionally unfortunate. I do not go into details for fear I might seem to be casting aspersions on persons whom I have no wish to offend when I complain of the distresses of those connected with me. If I was not very hopeful that we shall establish the town's case to C. Caesar's satisfaction, there would be no reason for me to trouble you at present. But I am confidently persuaded that he will take into account the high standing of the community, the equity of their cause, and also their disposition towards himself. Therefore I do not hesitate to urge you to leave the case open for him to determine.

I should make this appeal to you even if I had not heard that you had so acted in another case, but I became more hopeful of your granting it after I was told that you had made the same concession to the people of Regium. Even though they have a certain connection with you, your affection for me constrains me to hope that what you do for your own connections you will do for mine – especially as I am asking this only for Atella, though several communities connected with me are in similar trouble. I do not think you will suspect me of so proceeding without good reason, or of soliciting you from a trivial desire to increase my popularity. Still, I hope you will believe me when I give you my word that I am under a great debt to this municipality. In my advancements as in my tribulations their devotion towards me has on every occasion been quite outstanding.

Accordingly, let me beg you most earnestly, in virtue of the intimate bond between us and your signal and unfailing good-will towards me, to grant what I ask, realizing that the finances of a municipality with which I am closely linked by mutual relations, services, and good-will are here at stake. You may take it that, if we get what we hope from Caesar, we shall regard ourselves as owing it to your kindness; and if not, that we shall take the will for the deed, considering that you will have done your best to get it for us. I myself shall be deeply grateful, and an excellent and highly respected body, one too that well knows the meaning of gratitude and is thoroughly worthy to be connected with you, will be bound to you and yours for all time by a signal benefaction.

321 (XIII. 8)

CICERO TO M. RUTILIUS[814]

46–44

From M. Cicero to M. Rutilius greetings.

Conscious of my regard for you and aware by experience of your good-will towards myself, I do not hesitate to lay before you the request I have to make.

How highly I regard P. Sestius is best known to myself; how highly I ought to regard him is known to you and all the world.

814. Evidently another land commissioner. The area in which he operated is unknown.

Learning from other sources of your eagerness to be of service to me, he has requested me to write to you most particularly about a matter concerning Senator C. Albanius, whose daughter was the mother of that excellent young man L. Sestius, P. Sestius' son. I mention this to let you know that, besides my obligation to concern myself on Sestius' behalf, Sestius has a like obligation towards Albanius.

The affair in question is as follows: C. Albanius received certain properties at valuation from M. Laberius, which properties had been purchased by Laberius from Caesar out of Plotius' estate. If I were to say that it is contrary to public interest that those properties should be brought under assignment, it would look as though I were not asking a favour but giving you instruction. All the same, I may point out that Caesar wishes the Sullan sales and assignments to be valid in order that his own may be thought more secure. If properties sold by Caesar himself are to be brought under assignment, what sort of title will his sales carry in future?

But you in your wisdom will consider that aspect of the matter. *I* am simply making a request of you (and I could make none with more earnestness and sincerity, or in a juster cause) to spare Albanius and not to touch the properties formerly belonging to Laberius. You will make me not only very happy but also rather proud to have been the means of enabling P. Sestius to meet the needs of a close connection, owing him as I do more than any other man. Allow me to ask you most pressingly so to do. You can confer upon me no higher favour, and you will find me most grateful.

322 (VI. 15)

CICERO TO MINUCIUS BASILUS

Date uncertain[815]

From Cicero to Basilus greetings.

Congratulations. I am delighted on my own account. Be sure of my affection and active concern for your interests. I hope I have *your* affection, and want to hear what you are doing and what is going on.

323 (VI. 16)

POMPEIUS BITHYNICUS[816] TO CICERO

Sicily, c. end of March(?) 44

From Bithynicus to Cicero greetings.

If my friendship with you did not rest on many good grounds peculiar to ourselves, I should go back to its origins and speak of our parents. But that I take to be appropriate when family friendship has not been followed up by personal good offices. Therefore I shall be content with our personal friendship, and relying thereupon would ask you to defend my interests during my absence, wherever there may be need, in the persuasion, I hope, that no service you render will ever lose its freshness in my memory.

Goodbye.

815. There are serious objections to the common view that this evidently hasty note refers to Caesar's assassination.

816. See Glossary of Persons.

324 (VI. 17)[817]

CICERO TO POMPEIUS BITHYNICUS

c. May(?) 44

From Cicero to Bithynicus greetings.

There are all manner of reasons why I am anxious to see the commonwealth settled at long last, but, believe me, the promise you make in your letter adds one to their number, causing me to long for that event yet the more. For you write that, if it comes about, you will be much in my society. Your wish is most gratifying to me, and you express it in the spirit of our friendship and of the opinion which that fine man, your father, held of me. You may be assured that, although those whom events made, or make, powerful are more closely attached to you than I in respect of the magnitude of what they have conferred upon you, none stands nearer in friendship. I am therefore gratified by your mindfulness of our connection and your wish to strengthen it still further.

325 (XI. 1)

D. BRUTUS TO M. BRUTUS AND CASSIUS

Rome, c. 22(?) March 44[818]

From D. Brutus to his friend Brutus and to Cassius greetings.

Let me tell you how we stand. Yesterday evening Hirtius was at my house. He made Antony's disposition clear – as bad

817. Evidently not a reply to the preceding, though probably belonging to the same period.

818. At least half-a-dozen dates have been assigned to this letter, of

and treacherous as can be. Antony says he is unable to give me my province,[819] and that he thinks none of us is safe in Rome with the soldiers and populace in their present agitated state of mind. I expect you observe the falsehood of both contentions, the truth being, as Hirtius made evident, that he is afraid lest, if our position were enhanced even to a moderate extent, these people would have no further part to play in public affairs.

Finding myself in so difficult a predicament, I thought it best to ask for a Free Commission[820] for myself and the rest of our friends, so as to get a fair excuse for going away. Hirtius promised to get this agreed to, but I have no confidence that he will, in view of the general insolence and vilification of us. And even if they give us what we ask, I think it won't be long before we are branded as public enemies or placed under interdict.

You may ask what I advise. I think we must give way to fortune, leave Italy, go to live in Rhodes or anywhere under the sun. If things go better, we shall return to Rome. If moderately, we shall live in exile. If the worst happens, we shall take any and every means to help ourselves. Perhaps one of you will wonder at this point why we should wait till the last moment instead of setting something on foot now. Because we have nowhere to base ourselves, except for Sex. Pompeius[821] and Caecilius Bassus – I imagine their hands will be strengthened when this news about Caesar gets through. It will be time enough for us to join them when we know what their power amounts to. I shall give any undertaking you and Cassius wish on your behalf. Hirtius demands that I do this.

Please let me have your reply as soon as possible. I don't doubt that Hirtius will inform me on these points before ten

---

which Cicero no doubt received a copy from the recipients. I accept the view that it was written soon after the disturbances which followed Caesar's funeral on 20 March.

819. Cisalpine Gaul according to Caesar's assignment.

820. See Glossary of Terms under 'Legate'.

821. Pompey's younger son, still fighting in Spain.

o'clock. Let me know where we can meet, where you wish me to come.

After Hirtius' latest talk I have thought it right to demand that we be allowed to stay in Rome with a public bodyguard. I don't suppose they will agree – we shall be putting them in a very invidious light. However, I think I ought not to refrain from demanding anything that I consider fair.[822]

326 (IX. 14)[823]

CICERO TO DOLABELLA

Pompeii, 3 May 44

From Cicero to his friend Dolabella, Consul, greetings.

Content as I am, my dear Dolabella, with *your* glory, and finding as I do sufficient cause in that for delight and rejoicing, yet I cannot but confess that my cup of happiness is filled to overflowing by the popular opinion which makes me a sharer in your laurels. Every single person I have met (and I meet a great many every day, for a large number of the best people come hereabouts for their health, and I have many visits in addition from friends in the neighbouring towns) has first praised you sky high in the most glowing terms and then in the same breath expressed deep gratitude to me, not doubting, so they say, that it is in conformity with my precepts and advice that you are showing yourself so admirable a citizen and so outstanding a Consul.

822. This paragraph is probably not, as generally supposed, a postscript added after Hirtius' return, since it does not say what answer Hirtius brought back.

823. This letter is also found in the Atticus series, 371A (XIV.17A). Dolabella, who became Consul after Caesar's death, had drastically repressed some pro-Caesarian demonstrations in Rome.

I can reply with perfect truth that what you do you do by your own judgement and volition, needing nobody's advice. In fact, however, I neither give a direct assent, in case I might detract from your credit by letting it appear to have proceeded entirely from my counsels, nor yet a very vigorous disclaimer, for I am fond, perhaps too fond, of glory. And yet it detracts nothing from your prestige to have a Nestor to consult, as did the King of Kings, Agamemnon himself, without any loss of dignity. As for me, it is a proud thing that a young Consul should win such laurels as, so to speak, a pupil from my school.

I visited L. Caesar on his sick bed at Naples. His whole body racked with pain though it was, he had scarcely greeted me before he exclaimed 'Oh my dear Cicero, congratulations! If I had as much influence with my nephew[824] as you have with Dolabella, we might now be out of our troubles. As for your Dolabella, I congratulate him and thank him. He is the first Consul since yourself who deserves the name.' Then he went on to speak at large of your action and achievement, which he called as magnificent, distinguished, and publicly salutary as any in history. And this is the sentiment expressed by all.

Now please allow me to accept this counterfeit inheritance, so to speak, of an acclaim which does not belong to me, and admit me to some small partnership in your triumph. Not but what, my dear Dolabella – for I have written the above only in jest – I would sooner transfer to you all the credit for my own achievements, if any such there be, than divert any part of yours. You cannot but know how deep my regard for you has always been; but your recent exploits have kindled in me such enthusiasm that no affection was ever more ardent. Nothing, believe me, is more beautiful, fair, and lovable than manly virtue. As you are aware, I have always loved M. Brutus for his fine intellect, the charm of his manners, and his outstanding uprightness and reliability. Yet the Ides of March added so much to my love for him that I was astonished to find room for

824. Mark Antony, the other Consul.

increase where I had long believed all was full to overflowing. Who would have thought that the love I bore you admitted of any accession? Yet the accession is such that it seems to me as though I only now feel love where formerly I felt affectionate regard.

There is no need for me to urge you to cherish the high standing and glory you have won. Why should I, in hortatory fashion, remind you of famous names? I can quote none more famous than your own. You yourself should be your model, it is yourself you have to emulate. After such exploits you no longer have the *right* to fall below your own standard. Exhortation is therefore superfluous, felicitation rather is called for. In your case, and I dare say in yours only, the extreme of penal rigour has brought not merely no odium but actual popularity, delighting the lower orders as well as all honest folk. If this had come to you by a stroke of luck, I should congratulate you on your good fortune; but you owe it to your generous courage and, no less, to your ability and sound judgement. I have read your speech, an excellently conceived performance. How cautiously you felt your way towards the issue, now approaching, now drawing back, so that by common consent the simple facts of the case showed the time to be ripe for your punitive action!

So you have rescued Rome from danger and her inhabitants from fear. You have done a vast deal of good, not only for the present occasion, but as a precedent for the future. Having done that, you should understand that the commonwealth rests upon your shoulders, and that those men from whose initiative freedom has sprung are deserving, not only of your protection, but of your favour. But on these matters more when we meet; soon, I hope. Lastly, my dear Dolabella, as the commonwealth's guardian and mine, see that you take the utmost care for your own safety.

327 (XII. 1)

CICERO TO CASSIUS

Pompeii, 3 May 44

Cicero to Cassius greetings.

Believe me, Cassius, I never stop thinking about you and our friend Brutus, that is to say about the whole country, whose only hope lies in you both and in D. Brutus. I myself now feel more optimistic after the splendid performance of my dear Dolabella. The rot in Rome was spreading and getting more virulent every day, so that I for one was alarmed for the city and for public order inside it. But this has been so effectually suppressed that I think we may now reasonably consider ourselves safe for all time to come from that most squalid of threats at any rate.

The tasks that remain are many and serious, but all depends on you three. However, let me set out the position item by item.[825] As things have gone so far, it appears that we are free of the despot, but not of the despotism. Our king has been killed, but we are upholding the validity of his every regal nod. And not only that, but we sanction measures which he himself would not be taking if he were alive on the pretext that he had them in mind. I see no end to the business. Laws are posted up, exemptions granted, large sums of money assigned, exiles brought home, decrees of the Senate forged – it seems we are merely rid of the disgust we felt for an abominable individual and of the mortification of slavery, while the state still lies in the chaotic condition into which he flung it.

You and your friends must straighten out the whole tangle. You must not think that you have done enough for your

825. With what follows cf. *Letters to Atticus* 368 (XIV.14).2.

country already. She has indeed had more from you than it ever entered my mind to hope, but she is not satisfied; she wants great things from you, proportionate to the greatness of your hearts and service. So far she has avenged her injuries by the death of the tyrant at your hands, nothing more. What of her dignities? Which of them has she recovered? The right to obey a dead man, whom she could not tolerate alive? Are we defending the paper memoranda of one whose laws graven on bronze we ought to annul? Oh yes, we have so decreed.[826] When we did that, we bowed to circumstances, which in politics count for a great deal. But some people are abusing our facility without restraint or gratitude.

But of this and much else when we meet, soon. Meanwhile, please believe that I have your public standing very much at heart, both for the sake of the commonwealth, which has always been dearer to me than anything else in the world, and for that of our mutual affection. Take care of your health.

Goodbye.

328 (XII. 16)

TREBONIUS TO CICERO

Athens, 25 May 44

From Trebonius to Cicero greetings.

I trust you are well.

I arrived in Athens on 22 May,[827] and there saw what I most desired to see, your son devoting himself to liberal studies and bearing an exemplary character. How much pleasure this gave

826. In the temple of Tellus on 17 March, when the Senate confirmed Caesar's 'acts'.

827. Trebonius was on his way to take over the province of Asia.

me you can appreciate even without my telling you. You are not unaware how much I think of you and how warmly I welcome any gratification that comes your way, even the most trifling, let alone such a blessing as this. Such is the long-standing and sincere affection between us. Do not suppose, my dear Cicero, that I tell you this because it is what you want to hear. This young man of yours (or rather ours, for you can have nothing I do not share) could not be more popular with every-body in Athens, nor more enthusiastically attached to the studies for which you care most, that is to say, the highest. And so I am delighted to congratulate you, as I can sincerely do, and myself no less, upon the fact that in him we have a young man for whom it is a delight to care, since care for him we must however he had turned out.

When he let fall in conversation with me that he would like to visit Asia, I not only invited but requested him to do so during my term as governor of the province. You should have no doubt that I shall stand towards him in your stead with a father's care and affection. I shall also see that Cratippus comes with him, so you need not think that in Asia he will be taking a vacation from the studies to which he is spurred by your encouragement. He is evidently a willing student, advancing at the double. I shall be continually encouraging him to further progress through daily study and practice.

As I write this letter, I do not know how you at home are faring politically. I hear some reports of unrest. Naturally I hope they are untrue, and that we can at last enjoy freedom in peace and quiet. Up to date I have been very far from that good fortune. However, I got a modicum of relaxation during the voyage, and have fitted together a little present for you after my fashion – I have cast a *bon mot* of yours, one very complimentary to myself, into verse, and written it down for you below. If you think certain words in this little piece rather *risqués*, the turpitude of the figure[828] I am somewhat freely

828. Probably Antony.

assailing will be my excuse. You will also make allowance for my irascibility, which is justified against persons and citizens of this type. And then, why should I not be allowed as much licence as Lucilius? Even granted that he hated his targets as much as I, it certainly cannot be claimed that the people he attacked with such licence of language deserved it more.

As you have promised me, you will give me a place in your conversation-pieces as soon as possible. I am sure that, if you write anything on Caesar's death, you will not let me take the smallest share of the event, and of your affection.

Goodbye, and consider my mother and family as commended to your care.

Dispatched 25 May, from Athens.

329 (XI. 2)

M. BRUTUS AND CASSIUS TO ANTONY

Lanuvium, May (end) 44

From Brutus and Cassius, Praetors, to M. Antonius, Consul.

Were we not convinced of your good faith and friendly intentions towards us, we should not write you this letter, which, since you are in fact thus disposed, you will doubtless take in the best of part. We are informed by letters that a large number of veterans has already gathered in Rome, and that a much larger number is expected before the Kalends of June. It would be out of character for us to entertain any doubt or apprehension concerning yourself. But having placed ourselves in your hands and dismissed our friends from the municipalities on your advice, having done that moreover not only by edict but in private letters, we surely deserve to share your confidence, particularly in a matter which concerns us.

Therefore we request you to inform us of your disposition towards us, whether you think we shall be safe among such a multitude of veteran soldiers, who are actually thinking, so we hear, of replacing the altar.[829] It is not easy to believe that anyone who desires our security and dignity can desire and approve of that.

The event shows that peace has been our aim from the beginning, and that we have had no object in view but the freedom of the community. Nobody can deceive us except yourself, a thing surely abhorrent to your manly and honourable spirit. Still, no other man has the means to trick us, for we have trusted, and shall continue to trust, only you. Our friends are deeply anxious on our behalf. They have every confidence in your good faith, but it is in their minds that the crowd of veterans can more easily be impelled by others in any direction they please than held in check by you.

We request you to give us your reply on all points. As for the allegation that the veterans were summoned because you intended to bring matters to their advantage before the Senate in June, it is a quite frivolous and nugatory excuse. Who do you suppose is likely to be obstructive, since, as for ourselves, it is certain that we shall hold our peace? None should believe us over-anxious to preserve our lives, for nothing can happen to us without universal ruin and chaos.

829. A funeral monument to Caesar in the Forum which became an object of popular cult until it was demolished by Dolabella.

330 (XVI. 23)

CICERO TO TIRO

Tusculum, May (end) 44

From Cicero to Tiro greetings.

Yes, please get the declaration[830] done if you can, though with a sum of this sort no declaration is necessary – but do it all the same. Balbus writes to me that he has had an attack, so severe that he can't talk. Antony can do as he likes about the law,[831] so long as I am allowed to stay in the country. I have written to Bithynicus.[832]

Servilius I leave to you, since you think old age worth having.[833] To be sure our good Atticus, having found me susceptible to scares in the old days, still thinks it is so and doesn't see my proof-armour of philosophy. And, truth to say, being a nervous fellow himself he plays alarmist. However, I certainly want to keep my old-established friendship with Antony – we have never had a quarrel – and shall write to him, but not till I have seen you. Not that I am taking you away from your bond[834] – charity begins at home.[835] I expect Lepta

830. Perhaps the public registration of a transfer of assets.

831. Perhaps a bill for the distribution of all available public lands among veterans and the poor.

832. Not necessarily Pompeius Bithynicus. The purpose of Cicero's letter is unknown.

833. The elder Servilius Isauricus had recently died at a great age. Tiro seems to have relayed a talk with Atticus, who was afraid that Cicero might take fright at some current 'scare'. Tiro may have added that Cicero ought not to worry and that he would very likely live to a ripe old age, like Servilius.

834. Some private business of Tiro.

835. Cicero quotes a Greek proverb meaning literally 'the knee is nearer than the shin'.

tomorrow and *.[836] I shall need the sweet of your conversation to counteract the bitter of his company.

Goodbye.

331 (VII. 22)

CICERO TO TREBATIUS

Rome, 44(?)

From Cicero to Trebatius greetings.

You made game of me yesterday over our cups for saying that it was a moot point whether an heir can properly take action for theft in respect of a theft previously committed.[837] So when I got home, though late and well in tipple, I noted the relevant section[838] and send you a transcript. You will find that the view which, according to you, has never been held by anybody was in fact held by Sex. Aelius, Manius Manilius, and M. Brutus.[839] However, for my part I agree with Scaevola and Testa.

836. The manuscripts are corrupt at this point, but the person concerned is probably either Q. Cicero senior or his son; cf. *Letters to Atticus* 404 (XV.26).1.

837. i.e. in the interval between the testator's death and the heir's taking possession. A theft committed during the testator's lifetime *was* actionable.

838. No doubt in Scaevola the Pontifex's great treatise on civil law.

839. Three eminent second-century jurists.

332 (VII. 21)

CICERO TO TREBATIUS

Tusculum, June (latter half) 44

From Cicero to Trebatius greetings.

I have given you an account of Silius' case.[840] Since then he has been at my house. When I told him that in your opinion we could safely make the stipulation ('if Q. Caepio,[841] Praetor, under his edict has given me possession of the estate of Turpilia'), he said that Servius does not agree that the will of a person not possessing testamentary capacity has any existence in law, and that Offilius says the same. He told me that he has not spoken to you, and asked me to commend to you himself and his case.

My dear Testa, there is no better man alive than P. Silius and no better friend to me, yourself however excepted. I shall therefore be deeply obliged if you will go to see him and promise your services. But if you love me, no delay! I ask this as a most particular favour.

333 (VII. 20)

CICERO TO TREBATIUS

Velia, 20 July 44

From Cicero to Trebatius greetings.

I have found Velia[842] all the more likeable a place because I

840. The legal details are too complicated to go into here.
841. i.e. M. Brutus, the City Praetor.
842. Cicero was on his way to Athens, though he got no further than Syracuse; cf. *Letters to Atticus* 415 (XVI.7).1. It is not clear that he stayed in Trebatius' house.

saw how much Velia likes you. But I need not talk of you, who are liked by all the world – your man Rufio[843] is as much missed, my word upon it, as if he were one of ourselves. But I don't blame you for taking him along to your building operations. Velia is as respectable a place as the Lupercal,[844] but still I prefer Rome to everything down here. But if you will take my advice, as you generally do, you will hold on to your paternal property (the good folk of Velia are somewhat apprehensive), and not forsake the noble river Hales and the house of the Papirii.[845] To be sure it contains a lotus, a plant which captivates even strangers[846] – though if you cut it down, you will see a long way further than your nose! But there is a great deal to be said, particularly in times like these, for having a refuge – a town full of people who care for you and a house and land of your own, that too in a retired, healthy, and pleasant locality. And I feel that I myself have some stake in the matter, my dear Trebatius. However, you must keep well and look after my affairs and expect me back, Gods willing, before mid-winter.

I have taken away a book, from Nico's[847] pupil, Sex. Fadius – 'Nico on Heavy Eating'. What a charming physician, and how docile a patient he would find me! But our friend Bassus told me nothing about that book – though he seems to have told you![848]

The wind is getting brisker. Take care of yourself.

27 July, Velia

843. A slave or freedman of Trebatius.

844. A grotto at the foot of the Palatine, where the she-wolf was supposed to have suckled Romulus and Remus. Presumably Trebatius was building in its vicinity.

845. Presumably Trebatius' house, called after its previous owners.

846. With allusion to the lotus-eaters in the *Odyssey*.

847. Prescriptions by a physician so called are cited by Celsus. Nothing else is known of Fadius or Bassus.

848. Perhaps with the implication that Trebatius knew all about 'Heavy Eating'.

334 (VII. 19)

CICERO TO TREBATIUS

Regium, 28 July 44

From Cicero to Trebatius greetings.

This will show how highly I regard you – as indeed I ought, for your affection is no less warm than my own; but anyhow, that request of yours to which to your face I said something a little like no, and at any rate did not say yes – in your absence I could not let it go unanswered. As soon as my boat left Velia, I set to work on writing up Aristotle's *Topics*.[849] The town itself, in which you are so well-loved a figure, reminded me of you. I am sending the book to you from Regium, written in as clear a style as the material admits.[850] If you find it in places hard to follow, you must remember that no technical subject can be acquired by reading, without an interpreter and a certain amount of practice. You will not have far to go for an illustration – can your Civil Law be learned from books? There are any number of them, but they need a teacher and experience. However, if you read and re-read carefully, you will understand everything correctly by your own efforts. But only practice will make the 'topics' present themselves to your mind automatically when a question is proposed. I shall keep you hard at it, if I get back safely and find all safe with you.

28 July, Regium

849. In fact Cicero's *Topics* (on the sources of proof, *topoi*) is not based on Aristotle's work of the same name, which he had perhaps never seen. He seems to have used Antiochus of Ascalon, who claimed to be following Aristotle.

850. A somewhat defensive qualification. The *Topics* is the most difficult of Cicero's works, the examples being taken from Roman law in compliment to Trebatius.

335 (XI. 29)

CICERO TO OPPIUS

Anagnia(?), July (beginning) 44

From Cicero to Oppius greetings.

As our friend Atticus knows, I have been hesitating about this whole project of going abroad, because many considerations occurred to me on either side. Your judgement and advice have now come massively into the scales to put an end to my indecision. You have written your opinion in plain terms and Atticus has reported to me what you said to him. I have always had the highest respect for your sagacity in framing advice and your honesty in giving it, which I experienced most notably when I wrote to you at the beginning of the Civil War to ask you what you thought I should do – join Pompey or stay in Italy. You recommended me to think of my reputation; from which I understood your opinion, and admired your scrupulous honesty as an adviser. For although you believed that your greatest friend[851] would have preferred it otherwise, you thought more of my duty than of his wishes.

For my part, I had a regard for you even before that time and have always felt that you had a regard for me. When I was away and in great danger, I remember how you cared for and protected my absent self and my family on the spot. To our familiar association since my return, and to my sentiments and public expressions about yourself, we can call everybody who notices such things to witness. But the weightiest tribute you paid to my good faith and consistency was after Caesar's death, when you gave me your friendship without reserve. If I do not justify your choice by the most hearty good-will towards you

851. Caesar.

and by all friendly offices in my power, I shall consider myself a poor creature indeed.

On your side, my dear Oppius, you will maintain your affection (I say this more as a conventional form than because I suppose you need any reminder), and give me your support in all my concerns. I have asked Atticus to make sure you don't lack information about them. Expect a more substantial letter from me as soon as I get a little time to spare.

Take care of your health – you can do me no greater favour.

336 (XI. 3)

M. BRUTUS AND CASSIUS TO ANTONY

Naples, 4 August 44

From Brutus and Cassius, Praetors, to Antonius, Consul, greetings.

We trust you are well.

We have read your letter. We find it very similar to your edict, offensive and menacing, a letter which ought never to have been sent by you to us. We, sir, have done nothing to provoke or annoy you, nor did we suppose that you would be surprised if, as Praetors and gentlemen of a certain station, we put forward in an edict a request to you as Consul. If you resent our venturing it, permit us to be sorry that you grudge even so small a licence to Brutus and Cassius.

You say that you have made no protest concerning our levies of troops and money, our tampering with the loyalty of the armed forces, and our dispatching of messengers overseas. We believe in the excellence of your motives, but at the same time we do not acknowledge any of these allegations; we also find it surprising that, having held your peace on these matters, you should not have been able to control your spleen so far as to refrain from throwing Caesar's death in our teeth.

One point we must ask you yourself to consider: is it tolerable that Praetors should not be permitted in the interests of concord and freedom to abate the rights of their office by edict[852] without a Consul threatening military violence? You must not count upon such a threat to intimidate us. It would be unworthy and unbecoming in us to be cowed by any personal danger; and you, sir, should not claim authority over those to whom you owe your freedom. Suppose we desired on other grounds to stir up civil war, your letter would have no effect. Free men are not impressed by threats. But you are perfectly well aware that we cannot be driven into any course, and it may be that your present menacing behaviour is designed to make our deliberate choice look like fear.

To summarize our position, we are desirous to see you an important and respected member of a free commonwealth. We are not fastening any quarrel upon you. At the same time, our freedom means more to us than your friendship. On your part, consider what you undertake and what you can sustain. Bear in mind, not only the length of Caesar's life, but the brevity of his reign. We pray heaven that your counsels may be salutary to the commonwealth and to you. If it should be otherwise, then we pray that they may bring you as little hurt as possible without detriment to the public safety and honour.

4 August.

852. Brutus and Cassius had put out an edict to the effect that they were inhibited from carrying out their duties as Praetors and were ready to retire into voluntary exile.

337 (XVI. 21)

M. CICERO JUNIOR TO TIRO

Athens, August(?) 44

From Cicero junior to his beloved Tiro greetings.

I was eagerly expecting couriers every day, and at last they have come, forty-five days after leaving home. I was delighted by their arrival. My kindest and dearest father's letter gave me great pleasure, and then your own most agreeable letter put the finishing touch to my happiness. I am no longer sorry to have made a break in our correspondence, rather the contrary, since as a result of my letters falling silent I am repaid by this example of your good nature. I am truly delighted that you have accepted my excuses without question.

I don't doubt that you are pleased with the reports you are hearing of me, dearest Tiro, and that they are such as you wished to hear. I shall make sure and work hard to see that this tiny new image of mine goes on getting bigger and bigger[853] as the days go by. So you can carry out your promise to be my publicity agent with every confidence. Young men make mistakes, and mine have brought me so much unhappiness and torment that I hate to think of what I did, or even hear it mentioned. Very well do I know that you shared my worry and unhappiness, as well you might, for you wanted all to go right for me not for my sake only but for your own too, because I have always wanted you to have a part in any good things that come my way. Well, since I gave you unhappiness then, I shall make sure to give you twice as much happiness now.

I can tell you that Cratippus and I are very close, more like

853. Literally 'is doubled more and more', a phrase of which Cicero senior would hardly have approved.

father and son than teacher and pupil. I enjoy hearing him lecture, and quite delight in his own pleasant company. I spend all day with him and often part of the night, for I beg him into dining with me as frequently as possible. Now that he has got into the habit, he often drops in on us at dinner unawares, and then he puts off the grave philosopher and jokes with us in the most genial way. So you must try to meet him as soon as possible – he is such a pleasant, excellent man.

As for Bruttius,[854] what can I say? I never let him out of my sight. He lives simply and strictly, and he is the best of company too. Fun goes hand in hand with literary study and daily disputation. I have rented a lodging for him near mine, and as he is a poor man, I help him as best I can out of my own meagre funds. Also I have started regular declamation in Greek with Cassius,[855] and I want to practise in Latin with Bruttius. Some people whom Cratippus brought over from Mytilene, scholars whom he entirely approves of, are my friends and daily associates. I see a lot of Epicrates too (a leading man in Athenian society), and Leonides, and people of that sort. So as to myself – *voilà*!

As for what you say about Gorgias,[856] he *was* useful to me in declamation practice, but I have put obedience to my father's directions above all other considerations. He had written telling me *sans phrase* to get rid of Gorgias at once. I thought I had better not boggle over it – if I made too much fuss, he might think it suspicious. Also it came to my mind that I should be taking a lot upon myself in judging my father's judgement. All the same, I am very grateful for your concern and advice.

I quite accept your excuse about shortage of time. I know how busy you generally are. I'm really delighted to hear that

854. Nothing more known, but no doubt an Italian.

855. Another unknown professor of rhetoric.

856. Later a noted rhetorician in Rome, he is said by Plutarch ('Life of Cicero', 24) to have led M. Cicero junior into bad ways and to have received an angry letter (in Greek) from his father.

you have bought a property, and hope it turns out a successful investment. Don't be surprised at my congratulations coming at this stage in my letter – that was about the point where *you* put the news of your purchase. Well, you are a landed proprietor! You must shed your town-bred ways – you are now a Roman squire! How amusing to picture the delightful sight of you now! I imagine you buying farm tackle, talking to the bailiff, hoarding pips at dessert in your jacket pockets! But seriously, I am as sorry as you that I was not there to lend you a hand. However, dear Tiro, I *shall* help you, provided luck helps me, especially as I know you have bought the place to share with us.

Thank you for attending to my commissions. But do please get a clerk sent out to me, preferably a Greek. I waste a lot of time copying out my notes.

Take care of your health first and foremost, so that we can be students together. I commend Anterus[857] to you.

338 (XVI. 25)

M. CICERO JUNIOR TO TIRO

Athens, autumn(?) 44

From Cicero junior to his dear Tiro greetings.

Your excuse for letting your correspondence with me lapse is fair and sufficient, but I beg of you not to do this often. Even though I am kept informed of political rumours and reports and my father constantly writes to me about his sentiments towards me, a letter from you, no matter what or how trivial the topic,

857. Presumably the slave who carried the letter. The form *Anterum* here seems to come from a hybrid form 'Anterus' (instead of 'Anterōs'), which is also found in inscriptions.

has always been most welcome to me. So since I miss your letters above all things, don't let your obligation to write be fulfilled in the making of excuses, but by a steady stream of letters.

Goodbye.

339 (XII. 20)

CICERO TO CORNIFICIUS

Rome, 2 September 44(?)[858]

From Cicero to Cornificius.

Thank you for your letter – but you should not have been so rude to my little lodge at Sinuessa.[859] The insult will rankle with my poor little house, unless you make an *amende honorable* at Cumae or Pompeii. So that is what you must do; also you must remember me kindly, and prod me with a literary effort. I find it easier to answer a challenge than to issue one. However, if you drag your feet (a tendency of yours), I shall be the one to prod. Your laziness will not make an idler of *me*. More when I have time to spare – I scribbled this in the Senate.

858. Perhaps written at a sitting of the Senate on that day, after Cornificius had set out for his province of Africa.

859. Perhaps acquired from Lepta; cf. Letter 262 (VI.19). Evidently Cornificius had declined an invitation to use it on his way south.

340 (X. 1)

CICERO TO PLANCUS

Rome, September 44

From Cicero to Plancus.

I have been away, *en route* for Greece; and ever since the voice of the commonwealth called me home half way through my journey, Mark Antony has not left me a quiet moment. His insolence – but that is a common fault, say rather his atrocity – has reached such proportions that he cannot bear anybody to look like a free man, let alone speak like one. My greatest concern is not for my own life. As for that, I have run my race, whether in respect of years or achievements or (if that too be relevant) glory. But the thought of my country, and above all the prospect of your Consulship,[860] my dear Plancus, makes me anxious – it is so far away that I must pray rather than hope to be granted breath until that time comes for the commonwealth. For what hope can there be in a commonwealth where all lies crushed by the armed force of a violent, licentious individual, where neither Senate nor People has any power, where neither laws nor law-courts exist, nor any semblance or trace whatsoever of a free community?

Well, I imagine you are sent all the news of the day, so there is no point in my going into details. But the steadfast and indeed increasing affection I have entertained for you ever since you were a boy prompts me to urge and admonish you to consecrate all your thoughts and care to the commonwealth. If it lasts until your time comes, its guidance will be easy; but to make it last great fortune as well as great pains is required.

However, I hope we shall see you back some considerable

860. By Caesar's appointment Plancus and D. Brutus were to hold the Consulship in 42.

time before then. Apart from my obligation to think of the commonwealth I also take a strong and sympathetic interest in your future dignity. My advice and zeal, my time and service, my effort and industry, are entirely devoted to your advancement. Thus I conceive I shall most easily render what is due both to the commonwealth, which is most dear to me, and to our friendship, which I hold us bound religiously to maintain.

I am not surprised, but I am happy, that you value our friend Furnius as highly as his own goodness and high standing deserve. Please believe that any good opinion or good office you bestow upon him is in my estimation bestowed upon myself.

341 (X. 2)

CICERO TO PLANCUS

Rome, c. 19 September 44

From Cicero to Plancus greetings.

As a friend I should not have failed to support the decree in your honour,[861] had I been able to enter the Senate in security and dignity. But it is dangerous for any man of independent political views to move about in public when swords are drawn with complete impunity; and it does not seem to comport with my dignity to make a speech in a House where men-at-arms would hear me better and at shorter distance than members.

In private matters you shall find me always zealous to serve you; and even in matters public, if there be some compelling occasion for me to take part, I shall never fail you in your career, even at risk to myself. But in matters which can just as well be settled in my absence I would ask you to wish me to consider my own safety and dignity.

861. Probably for a Supplication in honour of Plancus' military successes in Rhaetia.

342 (XI. 4)

D. BRUTUS TO CICERO

Cisalpine Gaul, September 44

From D. Brutus, Imperator, Consul-Elect, to Cicero greetings.

If I had any doubt of your sentiments towards me, I should use many words in requesting you to defend my public standing; but the fact surely is as I am convinced, that you have my interests at heart.

I marched against the Alpine tribes, not so much in quest of the title Imperator, as desiring to satisfy my men and make them firm for the defence of our concerns. I think I have succeeded; for they have had practical experience of my liberality and spirit. I have made war on the bravest warriors in the world, taken many strong places, laid many areas waste. My dispatch to the Senate is not unwarranted. Support me with your voice in the House. In so doing you will be serving the common cause in no small measure.

343 (XI. 6)

CICERO TO D. BRUTUS

Rome, September or October (beginning) 44

From M. Cicero to D. Brutus, Imperator, Consul-Elect, greetings.

Arriving in Rome five days after leaving Mutina, our friend Lupus had an interview with me the following morning, at which he set forth your message very carefully and delivered your letter. When you commend your public standing to my care, I feel that you are also commending my own, which is truly no more precious to me than yours. Therefore you will gratify me highly if you will rest assured that my counsel and support shall at no point be lacking to promote your credit.

344 (XII. 2)

CICERO TO CASSIUS

Rome, c. 25 September 44

From Cicero to Cassius greetings.

I am very glad to find that my vote and speech[862] meet with your approval. If I had been able to make such speeches often, the recovery of liberty and constitution would have been no problem. But a crazy desperado, far more wicked even than he whom you called the wickedest man ever killed, is looking for a starting-point for a massacre. In charging me with having instigated Caesar's slaying he has no other object than to incite the veterans against me (a risk which I am not afraid to take so long as he honours me with a share in the glory of your exploit). Accordingly, neither Piso, who was the first to make an (unsupported) attack on him, nor I, who followed Piso's example a month later, nor P. Servilius, who came after me, can enter the Senate in safety. The gladiator is looking for a massacre, and thought to make a start with me on 19 September. He came prepared for the occasion, having spent several days in Metellus' villa[863] getting up a speech. How could that be done in an orgy of drink and debauchery? So, as I wrote to

862. The First Philippic, Cicero's first public challenge to Antony, delivered on 2 September.

863. Metellus Scipio's villa at Tibur, bought by Antony after its confiscation.

you earlier, everyone thought he was not speaking but vomiting – according to habit![864]

You say you are confident that with my prestige and eloquence something can be achieved. Well, something *has* been achieved, if we allow for the deplorable state of affairs. The People of Rome realizes that there are three Consulars who cannot come to the Senate in safety because they felt as loyal citizens and spoke their minds. Beyond that you must expect nothing. Your relative[865] is delighted with his new connection, and so he is no longer interested in the Games, and is ready to burst at the endless applause they give your brother. Your other connection[866] likewise has been cajoled by new memoranda of Caesar's. Such things are tolerable, but it is surely not to be borne that a certain person[867] should expect the Consulship for his son in your and Brutus' year, and give out that he is this brigand's humble servant on that account. As for my good friend L. Cotta, to use his own phrase, he is in a state of fatalistic despair, and rarely comes to the Senate any more. L. Caesar, an excellent citizen and a brave man, is tied by ill health. Ser. Sulpicius has great prestige and loyal sentiments, but he is away. As for the rest,[868] the Designates[869] excepted, you'll forgive me[870] but I

864. Antony's tendency to vomit in public is featured in the Second Philippic and attested in Plutarch's life of him.

865. L. Aemilius Paulus, whose brother Lepidus was married to a sister of Cassius' wife Junia Tertia. Lepidus' son had recently been betrothed to a daughter of Antony. Presumably Paulus was generally fond of shows, but now avoided them for fear of popular demonstrations.

866. C. Marcellus, Consul in 50, whose mother was a Junia, perhaps Junia Tertia's aunt.

867. L. Marcius Philippus, Consul in 56. His son of the same name was Praetor in 44 and so would be eligible for the Consulate in 41, which would be the earliest possible year for M. Brutus and Cassius.

868. Men appointed under Caesar's régime or recalled by him from exile.

869. A. Hirtius and C. Vibius Pansa (for 43); also, but absent from Rome, D. Brutus, Plancus (for 42).

don't reckon them as Consulars. Such are the men to whom the country looks for guidance; even for good times an all too meagre number, but for desperate times – I say no more.

So all our hope lies in yourselves.[871] If you are keeping away for your safety's sake, even that hope fails. On the other hand, should you be planning something worthy of your glory, I hope I may be alive to see it; but if I am not, at any rate the state will soon regain its rights through you.

Your family can count on me now and in the future. Whether they consult me or not, my loyalty and good-will to you shall not be wanting.

Goodbye.

345 (XII. 3)

CICERO TO CASSIUS

Rome, early October 44

From Cicero to Cassius greetings.

Your friend[872] gets crazier every day. To begin with he has inscribed the statue[873] which he set up on the Rostra 'To Father and Benefactor' – so that you are now set down, not only as assassins, but as parricides to boot! I say 'you', but ought rather to say 'we', for the madman declares that I was the promoter of your noble enterprise. If only I had been! He would not be giving us any trouble then. But all that is your responsibility,

870. The judgement logically applied to Cassius' connection by marriage, Lepidus, though he was absent from Rome; as also to P. Servilius, married to another sister of Junia Tertia, though Cicero includes him as a Consular above.

871. M. Brutus and Cassius. Both were leaving, or had already left, Italy for the East.

872. Antony.

873. Of Caesar.

and now that it is past and gone, I only wish I had some advice to offer you. But I cannot even think what to do myself. What can be done against violence except by violence?

Their whole plan is to avenge Caesar's death. On 2 October Antony was brought before a public meeting by Cannutius. He came off ignominiously indeed, but still he spoke of the country's saviours in terms appropriate to her betrayers. Of myself he declared unequivocally that everything you and your friends did and Cannutius is doing was on my advice. As a specimen of their behaviour in general, take the fact that they have deprived your Legate[874] of his travelling allowance. What do you suppose they infer by that? Presumably that the money was being conveyed to a public enemy.

It is a lamentable picture. We could not tolerate a master, so we are in bondage to our fellow-slave. However, hope still remains in your valour (though for me it is a case of wishing rather than of hoping). But where are your forces? For the rest I prefer you to consult your own conscience rather than listen to words of mine.

Goodbye.

346 (XII. 22)

CICERO TO CORNIFICIUS

Rome, not long after 19 September 44

From Cicero to Cornificius greetings.

Here I have a fight on my hands with a most rascally gladiator fellow, our colleague[875] Antony. But it is no fair match – words

874. Cassius had been appointed governor of Cyrene. The names of his Legates are unknown.

875. As Augur.

against weapons. However, he also makes speeches to public meetings, about you! Not with impunity – he shall find to his cost what sort of people he has provoked! However, I suppose you get details of all that *has* happened from other correspondents; it is my business to inform you of what is going to happen, and that is hard to guess at present.

The whole country is under heel. The honest men have no leader, our tyrannicides are at the other end of the earth. Pansa's sentiments are sound, and he talks boldly. Our friend Hirtius is making a slow recovery. What will come of it I simply don't know, but the only hope is that the People of Rome will at last show themselves like their ancestors. I at any rate shall not fail the commonwealth, and shall bear with courage whatever may befall, provided that I am not to blame for it. Of one thing you may be sure – I shall protect your reputation and prestige to the best of my ability.

347 (XII. 23)

CICERO TO CORNIFICIUS

Rome, c. 10 October 44

From Cicero to Cornificius greetings.

Tratorius has given me a comprehensive picture of your situation as governor and the state of your province. Outrages everywhere! But the higher your standing, the less you should acquiesce in what has happened to you. What *your* lofty spirit and intellect bear equably *you* should not on that account let go unpunished, even though it need not cause you pain. But of this later.

I feel sure that the city gazettes are sent to you. If I thought otherwise, I should give you the particulars myself, especially about Caesar Octavian's attempt.[876] The general public thinks Antony has trumped up the charge because he wants to lay hands on the young man's money; but intelligent and honest men both believe in the fact and approve. In a word, high hopes are set on him. He will do anything, it is thought, for honour and glory. As for our friend Antony, he is so conscious of his unpopularity that after catching his would-be murderers in his house he does not dare to make the matter public. So on 9 October he set off for Brundisium to meet the four Macedonian legions.[877] He intends to buy their good-will, and then to march them to Rome and set them on our necks.

Such is the political situation in outline, if a political situation can exist in an armed camp. I often feel sorry for you, because you are too young to have sampled any part of a free state in sound working order. Formerly it was at least possible to hope, but now even that has been torn from us. What hope is left, when Antony dares to say in a public meeting that Cannutius is trying to make a place for himself with people who can have no place in the community so long as he, Antony, remains a member of it?[878]

For my part, I take all this and whatever else can happen to mortal man with profound thankfulness to philosophy, which not only diverts me from anxiety but arms me against all assaults of fortune. I recommend you to do the same, and not to reckon as an evil anything devoid of culpability. But you know all this better than I.

I always thought well of our friend Tratorius, and I have been particularly impressed by his thorough loyalty, conscientiousness, and good sense in your affairs.

Take good care of your health. You can do nothing to please me more.

876. To have Antony assassinated.

877. Legions sent to Macedonia to take part in Caesar's projected war against Parthia and recently brought to Italy by Antony.

878. Caesar's assassins.

348 (XI. 27)

CICERO TO MATIUS

Tusculum, mid October(?) 44

From M. Cicero to Matius greetings.

I have not yet quite made up my mind whether our good Trebatius, a zealous and affectionate friend to both of us, has brought me more vexation or pleasure. He paid me an early morning visit at my house at Tusculum, where I had arrived the previous evening, although his health was still not fully restored. On my scolding him for not taking proper care of himself, he answered that he had never felt more impatience for anything than for an interview with me. 'Why, has something happened?' I asked. And he laid before me your grievance.

Before replying to that, I will make a few observations. As far back into the past as my memory extends, no friend of mine is older than yourself. But length of acquaintance is something which many share in some degree, affection is not. I cared for you from the first day we met and believed that you cared for me. Your subsequent departure for a long period, together with my pursuit of a political career and the difference between our modes of life, debarred us from cementing our friendly feelings by constant intercourse. But I had fresh evidence of your disposition towards me many years before the Civil War, when Caesar was in Gaul. Through your efforts Caesar came to look upon me as one of his circle, the object of his regard and friendly attentions; a result which you considered highly advantageous to me and not disadvantageous to Caesar himself. I pass over our many familiar interchanges in those days by word of mouth and correspondence, for graver matters followed.

At the outset of the Civil War, when you were on your way to join Caesar at Brundisium, you paid me a visit in my house at Formiae.[879] That to begin with meant a good deal, especially at such a time. And then, do you suppose I have forgotten your kindly advice and talk? I remember that Trebatius was present during all this. Nor have I forgotten the letter[880] you sent me after you had met Caesar in the Trebula district, I think it was.

Then followed the time when, whether impelled by my sensitivity to criticism or by obligation or by fortune, I went to join Pompey. Your devoted service was never wanting either to me in my absence or to my family on the spot. In the judgement of them all, neither they nor I had a better friend.

I arrived in Brundisium. Do you think I have forgotten how swiftly, the moment you heard the news, you rushed over to me from Tarentum, how you sat beside me, talking and encouraging me in the dejection to which fear of the common calamities had reduced me?

At long last we took up residence in Rome. Our familiar friendship was now complete. In the most important matters, in determining how to conduct myself towards Caesar, I availed myself of your advice; in others, of your good offices. Was there any man but me, Caesar excepted, whose house you chose to frequent, and often spend many hours in the most delightful conversation? It was at that time, if you recall, that you prompted me to compose these philosophical works of mine. After Caesar's return I doubt if you had any object so much at heart as that I should be on the best possible footing with him. In that you had succeeded.

You may wonder where all this discourse (longer than I had envisaged) is tending. The truth is, I am astonished that you, who ought to know all this, should have believed me guilty of any action against the spirit of our friendship. For besides the well-attested and manifest facts which I have mentioned above,

879. Cf. *Letters to Atticus* 178 (IX.11).2.

880. Presumably *Letters to Atticus* 184 (IX.15 a).

I have many others of a less conspicuous nature in mind, such as I cannot easily express in words. All about you delights me, but your most notable characteristics attract me most: loyalty to friendship, judgement, responsibility, steadfastness on the one hand, charm, humanity, literary culture on the other.

And so, to revert to your grievance, in the first place I did not believe you cast a vote on that law;[881] and in the second, if I had believed it, I should never have supposed you to have acted without some legitimate reason. Your standing brings all you do into notice, and the malice of the world sometimes presents your actions as more uncompromising than they really were. If such things don't come to your hearing, I don't know what to say. For my own part, if ever I hear anything, I defend you as I know you are in the habit of defending me against *my* ill-wishers. This I do in two ways: there are some things I deny outright, as this very matter of the vote, others in which I claim you are acting out of loyalty and good nature, for example your superintendence of the Games.[882]

But a scholar like yourself will not be unaware that if Caesar was a despot, which seems to me to be the case, your ethical position can be argued in two ways. On the one side it can be maintained (and this is the line I take) that in caring for your friend even after he is dead you show commendable loyalty and good feeling. According to the other view, which is adopted in some quarters, the freedom of one's country should come before a friend's life. I only wish that my argumentations arising from such talk had been conveyed to you. At any rate no one recalls more readily and more often than I the two facts which above all others redound to your honour, namely, that yours was the weightiest influence both against embarking on a civil war and in favour of a moderate use of victory.

881. A recent law, possibly one of Antony's redistributing provincial commands (certainly not Caesar's law on debt, as sometimes supposed).

882. Celebrated by Octavian in memory of Caesar and in honour of his victory from 20 to 30 July; cf. *Letters to Atticus* 379 (XV.2).2.

In this I have found nobody who did not agree with me.

So I am grateful to our good friend Trebatius for giving me occasion to write this letter. If you do not believe in its sincerity, you will be setting me down as a stranger to all sense of obligation and good feeling. Nothing can be more grievous to me than such a verdict, or more uncharacteristic of yourself.

349 (XI. 28)

MATIUS TO CICERO

Rome, in reply to the foregoing

Matius to Cicero greetings.

Your letter gave me great pleasure, because it told me that you think of me as I had expected and desired. Although I was not in any doubt on this score, the high importance I attach to your good opinion made me anxious that it should remain unimpaired. My conscience assured me that I had not been guilty of any act which could give offence to any honest man. I was therefore all the less disposed to believe that a man of your great and many-sided attainments would let himself be persuaded of anything hastily, especially in view of my ready and never-failing good-will towards yourself. Now that I know this is as I hoped, I will make some reply to the charges which you, as befitted the singular kindness of your heart and the friendly relations between us, have often rebutted on my behalf.

I am well aware of the criticisms which people have levelled at me since Caesar's death. They make it a point against me that I bear the death of a friend hard and am indignant that the man I loved has been destroyed. They say that country should come before friendship – as though they have already proved that his death was to the public advantage. But I shall not make debating points. I acknowledge that I have not yet arrived at that philosophical level. It was not Caesar I followed in the civil conflict, but a friend whom I did not desert, even though I did not like what he was doing. I never approved of civil war or indeed of the origin of the conflict, which I did my very utmost to get nipped in the bud. And so, when my friend emerged triümphant, I was not caught by the lure of office or money, prizes of which others, whose influence with Caesar was less than my own, took immoderate advantage. My estate was actually reduced by a law of Caesar's,[883] thanks to which many who rejoice at his death are still inside the community. For mercy to our defeated fellow-countrymen I struggled as for my own life.

Well then, can I, who desired every man's preservation, help feeling indignant at the slaughter of the man who granted it – all the more when the very persons[884] who brought him unpopularity were responsible for his destruction? 'Very well,' say they, 'you shall be punished for daring to disapprove of our action.' What unheard-of arrogance! Some may glory in the deed, while others may not even grieve with impunity! Even slaves have always had liberty to feel hope or fear or joy or sorrow of their own impulse, not someone else's. That freedom the 'authors of our liberty', as these persons like to describe themselves, are trying to snatch from us by intimidation. But they are wasting their breath. No threats of danger shall ever make me false to obligation and good feeling. I never thought an honourable death a thing to shun, indeed I should often have welcomed it.

Why are they angry with me for praying that they may be sorry for what they have done? I want every man's heart to be sore for Caesar's death. But I shall be told that as a citizen I ought

883. On debt.

884. Such as D. Brutus, who had 'taken immoderate advantage' of their position as leading Caesarians.

to wish the good of the commonwealth. Unless my past life and hopes for the future prove that I so desire without words of mine, then I do not ask anyone to accept it because I say so. Therefore I earnestly request you to consider facts rather than words, and, if you perceive that it is to my advantage that things go as they should, to believe that I cannot have any part or lot with rascals.[885] Is it likely that in my declining years I should reverse the record of my youth (*then* I might have been pardoned for going astray) and undo the fabric of my life? Nor shall I give any offence, except that I grieve for the tragic fate of a great man to whom I was intimately bound. But if I were differently disposed, I should never deny what I was doing, and risk being thought a rascal for my misconduct and a cowardly hypocrite for trying to conceal it.

Well, but I superintended the Games for Caesar's Victory given by his young heir. That was a matter of private service, which has nothing to do with the state of the commonwealth. It was, however, an office which I owed to the memory and distinction of a dear friend even after his death, and one which I could not deny to the request of a most promising young man, thoroughly worthy of the name he bears. Also I have often called on Consul Antony to pay my respects; and you will find that those who think *me* a poor patriot are continually flocking to his house to make their petitions or carry off his favours. The presumption of it! Caesar never put any obstacle in the way of my associating with whom I pleased, even persons whom he himself did not like. And shall the people who have robbed me of my friend try to stop me with their carping tongues from liking whom I choose?

However, I don't doubt that the moderation of my career will be a strong enough defence against false reports in time to come; and I am equally confident that even those who do not love me because of my loyalty to Caesar would rather have

885. i.e. subversive elements. Matius is here asserting his loyalty to established order.

friends like me than like themselves. If my prayers are granted, I shall spend the remainder of my days quietly in Rhodes; but if some chance interferes with my plan, I shall live in Rome as one whose desire will ever be that things go as they should.

I am most grateful to our friend Trebatius for revealing the straightforward and amicable nature of your sentiments towards me, thus adding to the reasons why I ought to pay respect and attention to one whom I have always been glad to regard as a friend.

I bid you goodbye and hope to have your affection.

350 (XVI. 24)

CICERO TO TIRO

Arpinum, November (middle) 44

From Tullius to Tiro greetings.

I sent Harpalus to you this morning, but having a suitable bearer, though nothing new to say, I thought I would write to you again on the same subjects – not that I doubt your conscientiousness, but the thing is so important. The fore and aft (as the Greek saying has it) of my letting you go away was that you should put my affairs straight. Offilius and Aurelius must be satisfied at all costs. If you cannot extract the full amount from Flamma,[886] I hope you will get some part of it. Above all the payment on the Kalends of January must be cleared. Settle the assignment and use your judgement about the cash payment. So much for domesticities.

As for public affairs send me full, reliable reports – on Octavian, on Antony, on the state of public opinion, on what you think will happen. I can hardly stop myself hurrying up to

886. On these transactions see *Letters to Atticus* 294 (XII.52).1.

town, but I am waiting to hear from you. You may be interested to know that Balbus *was* at Aquinum when you were told so, and Hirtius the next day; both on their way to the waters, I suppose – but let them do what they like. See that Dolabella's agents get a reminder. You will also ask Papias for payment.

Goodbye.

351 (XVI. 26)

Q. CICERO TO TIRO

44(?)[887]

From Quintus to his dear Tiro best greetings.

A second packet has reached me with no letter from you, and my thoughts have drubbed you with reproaches, though I *say* nothing. You cannot hope to escape punishment for this offence if you conduct your own case. You must call Marcus in and see whether he can prove you innocent with a speech long pondered in the watches of many a night. I really do beg of you – I remember how our mother in the old days used to seal up the empty bottles, so that bottles drained on the sly could not be included with the empties – so you likewise write, even though you have nothing to write about, so that you are not suspected of having scraped an excuse to cover your idleness. Your letters always tell me things most true and agreeable.

Love me and goodbye.

887. The letter is usually assigned to 44, but may be much earlier, perhaps written during Quintus' service in Gaul.

352 (XVI. 27)

Q. CICERO TO TIRO

December(?) 44

From Q. Cicero to his dear Tiro best greetings.

By your letter you have given me a fine drubbing for my idleness. My brother wrote more charily, no doubt because he did not like to say too much and was pressed for time. You handle the same material, but give the naked truth without varnish, especially about the Consuls-Elect. I know them through and through. They are riddled with lusts and languor, utter effeminates at heart. Unless they retire from the helm, there is every risk of universal shipwreck. It is incredible the things they did to my knowledge on active service, with the Gauls encamped right opposite. Unless a firm line is taken, that bandit[888] will woo them over by comradeship in vice. The position must be fortified by the Tribunes or by private initiative. As for that precious pair, you would hardly trust one with Caesena or the other with the cellars of Cossutius' taverns.[889]

As I have said, you are the apple of my eye. I shall see you all on the 30th and smother *your* eyes in kisses, even though I first sight you in the middle of the Forum.

Love me. Goodbye.

888. Antony.

889. Caesena was a small town in Cisalpine Gaul south of Ravenna. Cossutius' taverns were probably in the same area, which produced a noted wine. Possibly Quintus was staying there. He seems to mean that Hirtius was feeble and incompetent, Pansa a drunkard; cf. *Letters to Atticus* 409 (XVI.1).4.

353 (XI. 5)

CICERO TO D. BRUTUS

Rome, 9 December (or shortly after) 44

From M. Cicero to D. Brutus, Imperator, Consul-Elect, greetings.

When our friend Lupus arrived from you and spent some days in Rome, I was where I thought I should be safest.[890] That is how it came about that Lupus went back without a letter from me, although he had seen to it that I received yours. I returned to Rome on 9 December and made it my first business to meet Pansa without delay. From him I received news of you such as I was most desirous to hear.

You stand in no need of encouragement, any more than you wanted it in your late exploit, the greatest in history. Yet I think I should briefly intimate that the People of Rome look to you to fulfil all their aspirations, and pin upon you all their hope of eventually recovering their freedom. If you bear in mind day and night, as I am sure you do, how great a thing you have accomplished, you will not be likely to forget how much remains for you still to do. If the personage[891] with whom you have to deal obtains a province (I was always his friend until I saw him waging war upon the state not only without concealment but with relish), I see no further hope of survival.

Therefore I implore you (and I am echoing the entreaty of the Senate and People of Rome) to liberate the state forever from despotic rule. Let the end chime with the beginning. Yours is this task, yours the role. Our community, or rather all nations of the earth, expect this of you, indeed they demand it.

890. In Arpinum.

891. Antony, who had marched north in order to dispossess D. Brutus of Cisalpine Gaul.

But as I have already said, you need no encouragement, so I shall not spend many words in offering it. That which properly concerns me I will do, namely, promise you all my devoted service, all my care and consideration, in all that shall tend to your credit and glory. Therefore I hope you will believe that both for the sake of the commonwealth, which is dearer to me than my life, and also because I wish you well personally and desire your further advancement, I shall not fail at any point to support your patriotic designs, your greatness, and your glory.

354 (XI. 7)

CICERO TO D. BRUTUS

Rome, mid December 44

From M. Cicero to D. Brutus, Imperator, Consul-Elect, greetings.

Lupus asked myself, Libo, and your cousin Servius to meet him at my house. I think you will have heard the view I expressed from M. Seius, who was present at our colloquy. Other matters you will be able to learn from Graeceius, although he left just after Seius.

The main point, which I want you thoroughly to grasp and remember in the future, is that in safeguarding the liberty and welfare of the Roman People you must not wait to be authorized by a Senate which is not yet free. If you did, you would be condemning your own act, for you did not liberate the commonwealth by any public authority – a fact which makes the exploit all the greater and more glorious. You would also be implying that the young man, or rather boy, Caesar had acted inconsiderately in taking upon himself so weighty a public cause at his private initiative. Further, you would be implying that the soldiers, country folk but brave men and loyal citizens, had taken leave of their senses – that is to say firstly, the veterans,[892] your own comrades in arms, and secondly the Martian and Fourth Legions, which branded their Consul as a public enemy and rallied to the defence of the commonwealth. The will of the Senate should be accepted in lieu of authority when its authority is trammelled by fear. Lastly, you are already committed, for you have twice taken the cause upon yourself – first on the Ides of March, and again recently when you raised a new army and forces. Therefore you should be ready for every contingency. Your attitude must be, not that you will do nothing except on orders, but that you will take such action as will earn the highest praise and admiration from us all.

355 (x. 3)

CICERO TO PLANCUS

Rome, shortly after 9 December 44

From Cicero to Plancus greetings.

I was delighted to see Furnius for his own sake, and all the more so because as I listened to him I felt I was seeing *you*. He gave me an account of your military prowess, your rectitude in the administration of your province, and your good sense in all spheres. He spoke further of your agreeable personality in familiar intercourse, which was no news to me, and added that you had treated him most handsomely. All this I heard with pleasure, the last item with gratitude as well.

My friendly connection with your family, my dear Plancus, came into being some time before you were born. My affection towards yourself dates from your early childhood. When you

892. Settled in Caesar's Campanian colonies. They had rallied to Octavian early in November and were later joined by two of the four 'Macedonian' legions, the Martian and Fourth.

became a grown man, my desire and your choice established a familiar friendship. For these reasons I take the most lively interest in your standing in the world, which I hold to be mine also. Guided by ability and accompanied by good fortune you have achieved the highest success in everything you attempted, and you have gained these triumphs as a young man in the face of much jealousy, which you have overcome by capacity and energy. Now, if you will listen to me, your truly affectionate friend, who could allow no man pride of place with you in virtue of old association, you will derive all further advancement to the end of your days from the establishment of the best form of constitution.

You are of course aware, for nothing could escape you, that there was a time when the world thought you too much at the service of the times. I should have held that opinion myself, if I had taken acquiescence on your part for approval. But, perceiving your sentiments as I did, I considered that you took a realistic view of your power to influence events. Now the case is altered. You will form your own judgement on all questions, and it will be unconstrained. You are Consul-Elect, in the prime of life and the flower of oratorical talent, at a time when the commonwealth is so sorely bereft of men of such calibre. In heaven's name, throw your thoughts and solicitude into the channel which will bring you to the highest honour and glory. To glory there is only one path, especially now, when the body politic has so many years been torn asunder: good statesmanship.

Affection, rather than any notion that you were in need of admonition and advice, made me think fit to write to you in this strain. I know you drink in such ideas from the fountains at which I myself imbibed them. Therefore I will go no further. At this time I thought I ought to intimate that much, to advise you of my affection rather than to advertise my wisdom. Meanwhile I shall most zealously and faithfully attend to any matters which I judge to bear upon your personal standing.

356 (XI. 6a)

CICERO TO D. BRUTUS

Rome, 20 December 44

From M. Cicero to D. Brutus, Imperator, Consul-Elect, greetings.

The Tribunes summoned a meeting of the Senate by proclamation for 20 December with the intention of bringing the question of a bodyguard for the Consuls-Elect before the House. I had determined not to come to the Senate before the Kalends of January, but seeing that your proclamation[893] was published on that very day, I felt I should never forgive myself if the meeting passed without any reference to your immortal services to the state (which would have happened if I had not attended), or even if you did come in for honorific mention and I were not there.

Accordingly, I arrived at the House early. When my presence was noticed, members gathered in large numbers. Of my part in the Senate's proceedings concerning you[894] and my subsequent speech[895] before a large public meeting I prefer you to learn from other correspondents. But I hope you will believe that I shall always take up and maintain with the utmost enthusiasm whatever may tend to the advancement of your public standing, which is already of the highest. I know that I shall have many fellow-labourers in this field, but I shall strive for the foremost place among them.

893. In which D. Brutus declared that he would hold Cisalpine Gaul for the Senate and People (cf. *Phil.* III.8).

894. The Third Philippic was delivered at this meeting.

895. The Fourth Philippic.

357 (XII. 22a)

CICERO TO CORNIFICIUS

Rome, c. 21 December 44

From Cicero to Cornificius greetings.

On 20 December a well-attended meeting of the Senate accepted my proposals on certain urgent and important matters, including one to the effect that provincial governors should remain at their posts and hand over authority only to successors appointed by senatorial decree. I made this motion in the public interest, but I assure you that I was also actuated in no small measure by concern for the preservation of your personal consequence. Accordingly, I would ask you for the sake of our affection and exhort you for the sake of the commonwealth to allow no person any jurisdiction in your province and always to make your own public standing your primary consideration – and no man could stand higher. I will be candid, as our friendship requires. In the matter of Sempronius[896] you would have gained a great deal of credit in all quarters if you had paid heed to my letter. But that is a thing of the past and of no great moment, this is really important: be sure to keep your province in the state's control.

I should have written more if your people had not been in a hurry. So please make my excuses to our friend Chaerippus.

896. Perhaps C. Sempronius Rufus. His matter is obscure (cf. Letters 373 (XII.25), 433 (XII.29)).

358 (x. 4)

PLANCUS TO CICERO

Gaul, December (end) 44

From Plancus to Cicero.

Very many thanks for your letter, which I notice you wrote as a result of your talk with Furnius. As for myself, I have an excuse to plead for the time I have allowed to go by – I heard you had set out, but did not know of your return much before I was apprised of it in your letter. I mention this because even the slightest failure in due attention to you could not but make me feel most deeply to blame. I have many reasons to be punctilious – your relations with my father, the respect I have paid you since childhood, your reciprocal affection for me.

Therefore, my dear Cicero, be assured that (as our respective ages allow) in cultivating your friendship I have invested you, and only you, with the sacred character of a father. Your counsels all appear to me full no less of sincerity, which I measure by my own conscience, than of the wisdom for which you are distinguished. If my disposition were otherwise, your admonition would assuredly suffice to check it; and if I were hesitating, your exhortation would be enough to urge me forward in pursuit of what *you* hold to be best. But as it is, what is there to draw me in a different direction? Your affection leads you to estimate such advantages as I possess (whether the gift of kindly fortune or the product of my own effort) beyond their worth; but even my worst enemy would admit that only the world's good opinion seems wanting.

Therefore rest assured of one thing: all that my strength can compass, my prudence foresee, and my counsel suggest, shall ever be at the service of the commonwealth. I am not unaware of your sentiments. If I could have you with me in person, as *I* should so much wish, I should never dissent from your policies; and as it is, I shall take good care not to let any of my actions give you fair ground for censure.

I am waiting for news of all manner of things – what is toward in Cisalpine Gaul, and what in Rome this January. Please send me word, so that I know. Meanwhile I have a heavy and anxious task on my hands here, to guard (while others misbehave themselves) against the danger that the peoples of this country may see their opportunity in our calamities. If I am as successful in this as I deserve, I shall assuredly not disappoint you, whom I am most especially anxious to content, or the whole body of honest men.

Keep well and remember me kindly, as I do you.

359 (x. 5)

CICERO TO PLANCUS

Rome, January (middle) 43

From Cicero to Plancus greetings.

I have received two letters from you, duplicates. That in itself showed me how punctilious you are. I appreciated your anxiety that the letter I so eagerly awaited should duly reach me. The letter itself gave me a two-fold satisfaction; and when I try to make a comparison, I find it hard to decide which I should esteem the more precious, your affection for me or your spirit of patriotism. To be sure (in my judgement at all events) love of country transcends all other sentiments; but affection and friendly attachment undeniably exercise a greater charm. And so your reminder of my relations with your father, of the good-will you have bestowed upon me since your childhood, and of other points relevant to the theme, made me a happier man than you can well believe. But, again, the declaration of your political attitude, now and in time to come, pleased me exceedingly. My happiness was all the greater because this came as an addition to what had gone before.

So I urge you, my dear Plancus, nay more, I *beg* you, as I did in the letter to which you have replied so kindly, to bend all your thoughts and mental energy upon public affairs. There is nothing that can so richly reward you or so redound to your glory; nor in the whole range of human activities is there one more splendid and excellent than service to the state. Hitherto (your admirable good nature and good sense allow me to put my thoughts freely into words) you appear to have won brilliant success with luck on your side. That would not, it is true, have been possible without merit. None the less, the greater part of your achievements is credited to fortune and circumstances. But if you come to the aid of the commonwealth in the very difficult circumstances of today, all you do will be properly your own. The universal hatred of Antony (bandits[897] excepted) is extraordinary. Great is the hope pinned upon you and the army under your command, great the expectancy. Do not, in the name of heaven, lose the opportunity to render yourself popular and renowned. I admonish you as a son, I hope for you as for myself, I urge you as one addressing a very dear friend in his country's cause.

360 (XI. 8)

CICERO TO D. BRUTUS

Rome, late January 43

From M. Cicero to D. Brutus, Imperator, Consul-Elect, greetings.

I have had word from your lady Polla to give the bearer a

897. Antony and his followers are often referred to as *latrones* ('brigands'), as being in arms against the public peace.

letter for you if I wished to send something, but at this particular time I have nothing to write. Everything is in suspense while we wait to hear the result of the embassy,[898] of which nothing is reported as yet. However, I think I should tell you to begin with that the Senate and People of Rome is much concerned about you, not only for their own safety's sake but for that of your prestige. The emotion your name inspires is extraordinary. The whole citizen community feels a peculiar affection towards you, hoping and believing that you will now free our country from tyranny as you have already freed her from a tyrant. The levy is proceeding in Rome and all over Italy, if 'levy' is the right word to use when the whole population is freely volunteering in a flush of enthusiasm inspired by craving for liberty and disgust of their long servitude. On other matters it is time for us to be expecting a letter from you with news of yourself and our friend Hirtius and my young friend Caesar. I trust it will not be long before you and they are united in the bond of a common victory.

I have only to add concerning myself something which I hope and prefer you learn from the letters of those near to you, that my support for your public standing is not and never shall be wanting on any occasion.

361 (XII. 24. 1–2)

CICERO TO CORNIFICIUS

Rome, late January 43

From Cicero to Cornificius greetings.

I do not (and in duty I should not) lose any opportunity of

898. Three Consulars, Ser. Sulpicius Rufus, L. Calpurnius Piso, and L. Marcius Philippus, had been sent by the Senate to convey its behests to Antony, now besieging D. Brutus in Mutina (Modena). They returned about 1 February, Sulpicius having died on the journey.

singing your praises and, what is more, of securing practical recognition for you. But I prefer you to learn of my efforts and good offices from the letters of your domestic correspondents rather than from mine. I would, however, urge you to throw your whole mind into the public service. That is worthy of your spirit and intellect, and of the hope of increased prestige which you ought to entertain.

But of this more at some other time. As I write, everything hangs in suspense. The envoys sent by the Senate (not to beg for peace but to give notice of war if he did not comply with their message) have not yet returned. However, on the first occasion that presented itself to defend the commonwealth in my old style I offered myself to the Senate and People of Rome as their leader,[899] and, since I first took up the cause of freedom, I have not let slip the smallest opportunity to champion our corporate existence and liberties. But of this too I would rather you learned from others.

362 (IX. 24)

CICERO TO PAPIRIUS PAETUS

Rome, January 43

Cicero to Paetus greetings.

I should assist your friend Rufus,[900] about whom you now write to me for the second time, to the best of my ability, even if he had done me an injury, seeing how concerned you are on his behalf. But understanding and concluding as I do both from your letters and from one he has sent me himself that he has been greatly exercised about my safety, I cannot but be his

899. In the Third Philippic, delivered on 20 December 44.
900. Otherwise unknown.

friend, not only because of your recommendation (which carries the greatest weight with me, as is right and proper) but from my personal inclination and judgement. For I want you to know, my dear Paetus, that my suspicions and diligent precautions all started with your letter, which was followed by letters to like effect from many other correspondents. Plots were laid against me both at Aquinum and at Fabrateria of which something evidently came to your ears. They[901] put all their energies into catching me unawares, as though they had a presentiment of what a thorn in their flesh I was to become. Unsuspecting as I was, I might have laid myself open but for your admonition. Therefore this friend of yours needs no recommendation to me. I only hope the Fortune of the commonwealth may be such as to enable him to discover that gratitude is a strong point with me. So much for that.

I am sorry to hear that you have given up dining out. You have deprived yourself of a great deal of amusement and pleasure. Furthermore (you will not mind my being candid), I am afraid you will unlearn what little you used to know, and forget how to give little dinner-parties. For if you made such small progress in the art when you had models to imitate, what am I to expect of you now? When I laid the facts before Spurinna and explained to him your former mode of life, he pronounced a grave danger to the supreme interests of the state unless you resume your old habits when Favonius[902] starts to blow; at the present time of year he said he thought it might be borne, if *you* could not bear the cold.

And really, my dear Paetus, all joking apart I advise you, as something which I regard as relevant to happiness, to spend time in honest, pleasant, and friendly company. Nothing becomes life better, or is more in harmony with its happy

901. Partisans of Mark Antony. We hear something of plots against Cicero's person by L. Antonius in the summer of 44; cf. *Letters to Atticus* 385 (XV.8).2, 390 (XV.12).2, *Phil.* XII.20.

902. The west wind, harbinger of spring.

living. I am not thinking of physical pleasure, but of community of life and habit and of mental recreation, of which familiar conversation is the most effective agent; and conversation is at its most agreeable at dinner-parties. In this respect our countrymen are wiser than the Greeks. They use words meaning literally 'co-drinkings' or 'co-dinings',[903] but we say 'co-livings',[904] because at dinner-parties more than anywhere else life is lived in company. You see how I try to bring you back to dinners by philosophizing!

Take care of your health – which you will most easily compass by constantly dining abroad.

But do not suppose, if you love me, that because I write rather flippantly I have put aside my concern for the commonwealth. You may be sure, my dear Paetus, that my days and nights are passed in one sole care and occupation – the safety and freedom of my countrymen. I lose no opportunity of admonition or action or precaution. Finally it is my feeling that, if I must lay down my life in my present care and direction of public affairs, I shall consider myself very fortunate in my destiny.

Once again, goodbye.

363 (XII. 4)

CICERO TO CASSIUS

Rome, 2 or 3 February 43

From Cicero to Cassius greetings.

A pity you did not invite me to dinner on the Ides of March! Assuredly there would have been no leavings! As it is, *your*

903. 'Symposia', 'syndeipna'.
904. *convivia.*

leavings are giving me plenty of trouble – yes, me in particular. True, we have an excellent pair of Consuls, but the Consulars are a shocking collection. The Senate is firm, but firmest in the lowest rank. As for the people, they are magnificently firm and loyal, so is the whole of Italy. The envoys Philippus and Piso have played a disgusting, scandalous role. They were sent to announce certain specific items to Antony according to the will of the Senate. After he had refused to obey any of these, they took it upon themselves to bring back a set of intolerable demands from him to us. Accordingly there is a rally to me, and I have now become a popular favourite in a good cause.

But what *you* are doing or going to do, or even where you are, I don't know. Rumour reports you in Syria, but nobody vouches for it. Reports of Brutus[905] appear more trustworthy in so far as he is nearer Italy. Dolabella is severely censured by persons with some claim to wit for relieving you in such a hurry, when you had been barely thirty days in Syria![906] It is accordingly agreed that he ought not to be let into the province. You and Brutus are highly commended because you are supposed to have raised an army, which nobody expected. I should write more if I knew the facts of the case. As it is, what I write is based on public opinion and rumour. I am eagerly waiting to hear from you.

Goodbye.

905. M. Brutus was now in Macedonia.

906. Under the lex Cornelia a governor must leave his province within thirty days of the arrival of his successor. Cassius, as it seemed, was not to be allowed thirty days from the *start* of his tenure. But the real point of the joke is not obvious. Cassius had no legal claim to Syria, which had been assigned to Dolabella.

364 (x. 28)

CICERO TO TREBONIUS

Rome, 2 February 43

From Cicero to Trebonius greetings.

How I wish you had invited me to that splendid feast on the Ides of March! We should then have had no left-overs! As it is, we are having so much trouble with these that the immortal service which you and your friends rendered the state leaves room for some criticism. And when I think that it was your excellent self who drew that noxious creature[907] aside and that he has you to thank that he is still alive, I sometimes grow half angry with you, which for me is almost sinful.[908] For you have left *me* with more trouble on my hands than everybody else put together.

As soon as the Senate was able to meet in freedom after Antony's ignominious departure, my old spirit returned to me, the spirit which you and that ardent loyalist, your father, always praised and admired. The Tribunes had summoned a meeting on 20 December and put another matter to the House. I then entered upon a comprehensive survey of the whole political situation. I did not mince my words, and, more by will-power than by oratorical skill, I recalled the weak and weary Senate to its old, traditional vigour. That day, and my energy, and the course I took, brought to the Roman People the first hope of recovering their freedom. And from that time forward I have used every possible moment, not only in thought but in action, on behalf of the commonwealth.

907. Antony, who was kept in conversation by Trebonius while the other plotters were disposing of Caesar.

908. Because of the obligations rehearsed in Letter 207 (xv.21).

If I did not suppose you to be receiving all the city affairs and official proceedings, I should recount them myself, although I am immersed in pressing business. But you will learn all that from others – from me, only a few items, and those in brief. We have a courageous Senate, but of the Consulars some are timid and others disloyal. Servius was a great loss. L. Caesar is thoroughly sound, but as Antony's uncle he does not speak very forcibly in the House. The Consuls are admirable, D. Brutus is splendid, young Caesar admirable – I for one have good hopes of him in the future. This much at any rate you may take as certain; if he had not rapidly enrolled veterans, if two of Antony's legions had not put themselves under his orders,[909] and if Antony had not been confronted with this menace, he would have stopped at no crime or cruelty.

Although I suppose you have heard all this, I wished you to know it better. I shall write further as soon as I have more leisure.

365 (XII. 5)

CICERO TO CASSIUS

Rome, early February 43

From Cicero to Cassius greetings.

I dare say it is the winter weather that has so far prevented us getting any certain news of you – your doings and, above all, your whereabouts. But everybody is saying (I imagine because they would like it to be so) that you are in Syria at the head of a force. This report gains the readier credence because it has a ring of probability. Our friend Brutus has won golden opinions. His achievements have been no less important than unexpected, so

909. Cf. n. 892.

that, welcome as they are intrinsically, they are enhanced by their rapidity. If you hold the areas we think you do, the national cause has massive forces at its back. From the shores of Greece down to Egypt we shall have a rampart of commands and armies in thoroughly patriotic hands.

And yet, if I am not in error, the position is that the decision of the whole war depends entirely on D. Brutus. If, as we hope, he breaks out of Mutina, it seems unlikely that there will be any further fighting. In fact the forces besieging him are now small, because Antony is holding Bononia with a large garrison. Our friend Hirtius is at Claterna, Caesar at Forum Cornelium, both with a strong army; and Pansa has got together a large force in Rome, raised by levy throughout Italy. The winter has so far prevented action. Hirtius seems determined to leave nothing to chance, as he intimates in frequent letters to me. Except for Bononia, Regium Lepidi, and Parma, all Gaul is in our hands, enthusiastically loyal to the state. Even your clients[910] beyond the Po are marvellously attached to the cause. The Senate is thoroughly resolute, except for the Consulars, of whom only L. Caesar is staunch and straight. With Servius Sulpicius' death we have lost a tower of strength. The rest are without energy or without principle. Some are jealous of the credit of those whose statesmanship they see gaining approval. But the unanimity of the People of Rome and of all Italy is quite remarkable.

That is about all I wanted you to know. I pray now that from those lands of the sunrise the light of your valour may shine.

Goodbye.

910. Why the Transpadanes are called clients of Cassius is unknown. They were indebted to Caesar the Dictator for Roman citizenship.

366 (XII. 11)

CASSIUS TO CICERO

Tarichea, 7 March 43

From C. Cassius, Proconsul, to M. Cicero greetings.

I trust you are well, as I am, and my army.

Let me inform you that I am leaving for Syria to join Generals L. Murcus and Q. Crispus. These gallant and loyal gentlemen, having heard of events in Rome, have handed their armies over to me, and are themselves discharging their public duties jointly with me in the most resolute spirit. I beg further to inform you that the legion commanded by Q. Caecilius Bassus has joined me, and likewise that the four legions which A. Allienus[911] led from Egypt have been handed over to me by him.

Affairs thus standing, I do not suppose you need any encouragement to defend us in our absence and the state also, so far as in you lies. I want you to know that you and your friends and the Senate are not without powerful supports, so you can defend the state in the best of hope and courage. On other matters my friend L. Carteius will speak to you.

Goodbye.

Dispatched Nones of March from camp at Tarichea.

911. As Dolabella's Legate he was sent to Egypt to bring four legions stationed there to Syria.

367 (XII. 7)

CICERO TO CASSIUS

Rome, 7 March 43

From Cicero to Cassius greetings.

How zealously I have defended your position both in the Senate and before the People I prefer you to learn from your domestic correspondents than from myself. My motion[912] in the Senate would have gone through with ease but for Pansa's strong opposition. After delivering my speech, I was presented to a public meeting by Tribune M. Servilius. I said what I could about you loudly enough to be heard all over the Forum, amid unanimous shouts of approval from the crowd.[913] I have never seen anything like it. I hope you will forgive me for doing this against your mother-in-law's[914] wishes. She is a nervous lady, and was afraid that Pansa might take umbrage. In fact Pansa told a public meeting that your mother and brother too had been against my making my motion. But all this did not affect me; I had other considerations more at heart. I was for the state, as always, and for your dignity and glory.

I hope you will redeem the pledge I gave in the Senate, at some length of discourse, and at the public meeting. I promised, indeed almost guaranteed, that you had not waited and would not wait for our decrees, but would defend the commonwealth on your own initiative in your wonted fashion. Although no news has yet reached us of your whereabouts and the forces at

912. That Cassius should be put in charge of operations against Dolabella. For the wording see *Phil.* XI.29 f. Pansa put through a decree assigning the war to himself and Hirtius after D. Brutus had been relieved.

913. This speech has not survived.

914. M. Brutus' mother, Servilia.

your disposal, I am resolved that all resources and troops in that part of the world are yours, and am confident that you have already recovered the province of Asia for the commonwealth. You must now surpass yourself in adding to your glory.

Goodbye.

368 (x. 31)

POLLIO TO CICERO

Corduba, 16 March 43

C. Asinius Pollio to Cicero greetings.

You must not think it at all strange that I have written nothing on public affairs since war broke out. The pass of Castulo, which has always held up my couriers, has become more dangerous than ever with increasing banditry. Even so, that does not cause nearly so much delay as the pickets posted everywhere by both sides, which examine couriers and stop them proceeding. Had not letters got through by sea, I should be totally ignorant of affairs in Rome. But now that the opening of navigation gives me the chance, I shall write to you most eagerly and as often as I can.

There is no danger of my being influenced by the talk of an individual[915] whom nobody wants in his sight, but who even so is by no means as unpopular as he deserves to be. My own dislike of him is such that anything in common with him would be disagreeable to me. Furthermore, my nature and pursuits lead me to crave for peace and freedom. The outbreak of the former civil war cost me many a tear. But since I could not remain neutral because I had powerful enemies on both sides,

915. Almost certainly the Quaestor (strictly Proquaestor) L. Cornelius Balbus the Younger; cf. Letter 415 (x.32).

I avoided the camp where I well knew I should not be safe from my enemy's[916] plots. Finding myself forced whither I would not, and having no wish to trail in the rear, I certainly did not hang back from dangerous work. As for Caesar, I loved him in all duty and loyalty, because in his greatness he treated me, a recent acquaintance, as though I had been one of his oldest intimates. Where I was allowed to manage as I thought best, my actions were calculated to win cordial approval in the most respectable quarters. Where I obeyed orders, it was at a time and in a manner which made it clear that I had received them with reluctance. The ill-will thereby incurred, highly unjust as it was, was enough to teach me how pleasant a thing is freedom and how miserable life under despotic rule.

If, therefore, we have an attempt to place supreme power once again in the hands of one man, I profess myself his enemy, whoever he is. There is no danger on behalf of freedom from which I shrink or seek to be excused. But the Consuls had not instructed me how to act, either by senatorial decree or by letter. I have finally received one letter, from Pansa, on the Ides of March, in which he urges me to write to the Senate that I and the army under my command will be at their disposal ★★★.[917] That would have been very unhelpful, since Lepidus was declaring in public speeches and in letters to all and sundry that he saw eye to eye with Antony. Where would I get provisions if I led my legions through his province against his will? Or even if I had passed the earlier stages, could I fly across the Alps, which are held by his troops? Add the fact that it was quite impossible for a letter to get through. Couriers are searched at any number of points, and then are actually detained by Lepidus. One thing nobody will question, that before a public meeting in Corduba I declared that I would hand over my province to none but an emissary of the Senate. There is no

916. He cannot be identified.

917. Something like 'which he intimates I should have done at an earlier stage' seems to have dropped out of the text.

need for me to describe the struggle I have had about handing over the Thirtieth Legion.[918] Had I done so, nobody can be unaware how greatly my power to aid the national cause would have been enfeebled. For I assure you that the keenness and fighting spirit of that legion is quite outstanding. So you must think of me as one who is, first, most eager for peace (I am unashamedly anxious that none of our fellow-countrymen should perish) and, second, ready to defend my country's freedom and my own.

I am more gratified than you imagine by your taking my friend[919] into your circle. But I envy him his walks and jests with you. You will ask how highly I value that privilege: if we are ever allowed to live in peace, you will find out by experience. I shall not stir a yard from your side.

What does very much surprise me is that you have not written to me whether I shall help the commonwealth more by staying in my province or by leading my own army to Italy. As for myself, although it is safer and easier for me to stay here, I perceive that at a time like this legions are needed much more than provinces, especially as the latter can be recovered without trouble. So I have decided, as matters stand, to march.[920]

Further, you will learn everything from the letter I have sent to Pansa – I am sending you a copy.

16 March, from Corduba.

918. To Lepidus.

919. Probably the poet C. Cornelius Gallus; cf. end of Letter 415 (x. 32).

920. Yet earlier in his letter Pollio represented that it was quite impossible for him to get to Italy through Lepidus' province without Lepidus' consent; and there is nothing to suggest that this would now be forthcoming. Perhaps he was thinking of a sea route. The letter to Pansa may have made matters clear.

369 (x. 27)

CICERO TO LEPIDUS

Rome, 20 March 43

From Cicero to Lepidus greetings.

The great good-will I bear you makes me very anxious for you to enjoy the highest measure of public esteem. For that reason I was pained by your omission to thank the Senate after having been signally honoured by that body.[921] I am glad that you are desirous of restoring peace between your fellow-countrymen. If you draw a line between peace and slavery, you will do a service to the state and your own reputation. But if the peace you have in view is one which is going to put unbridled autocratic power back into the hands of a desperado, then you should understand that all sane men are of a mind to prefer death to slavery. You will therefore, in my opinion at least, be wiser not to involve yourself in a kind of peacemaking which is unacceptable to the Senate, the People, and every honest man.

However, you will be hearing all this from others, or will be informed by your correspondents. Your own good sense will tell you what is best to do.

921. On Cicero's motion at the beginning of the year the Senate had passed a vote of thanks to Lepidus for his successful conclusion of negotiations with Sex. Pompeius and decreed the erection of a gilded equestrian statue on the Rostra, an extraordinary distinction. On 20 March the Senate considered letters from Lepidus and Plancus advocating peace. Cicero dealt with the former in his Thirteenth Philippic.

370 (x. 6)

CICERO TO PLANCUS

Rome, 20 March 43

From Cicero to Plancus.

Our friend Furnius' account of your political disposition was most agreeable to the Senate and warmly approved by the Roman People. But your letter,[922] which was read out in the Senate, appeared by no means in accordance with Furnius' statement. You wrote as an advocate of peace, at a time when your distinguished colleague[923] is under siege by a band of the foulest brigands. Either they ought to lay down their arms and sue for peace, or, if they demand it fighting, then peace must be had by victory, not by negotiation. However, you will be able to learn from your excellent brother[924] and from C. Furnius how letters about peace have been received, whether yours or Lepidus'. You are well able to think for yourself; and the good-will and loyal good sense of your brother and Furnius will be at your call. None the less, my affection for you prompts me to wish that a word of advice, to which the many ties between us ought to lend some weight, should also reach you from myself.

So, believe me, Plancus, when I say that all the stages of advancement which you have hitherto attained – and most splendid they are – will count but as so many official titles, not as symbols of public esteem, unless you ally yourself with the freedom of the Roman People and the authority of the Senate. At long last pray dissociate yourself from those to whom no choice of yours but bonds forged by circumstances have attached you. In this period of political turmoil a number of

922. See previous note.
923. D. Brutus.
924. L. Plotius Plancus.

persons have been called Consuls, none of whom has been considered a Consular unless he displayed a patriotism worthy of the office. Such a patriot you should show yourself: firstly, in dissociating yourself from all connection with disloyal citizens, persons utterly unlike you; secondly, in offering yourself to the Senate and all honest men as adviser, principal, leader; lastly, in judging peace to consist, not in the mere laying down of weapons, but in the banishment of the fear of weapons and servitude. If such are your acts and sentiments, you will be not only a Consul and a Consular, but a great Consul and Consular. If otherwise, there will be no honour in these splendid official designations; rather they will carry the direst disgrace.

Prompted by good-will, I have written rather gravely. You will prove the truth of my words by experience, in that path of conduct which is worthy of you.

Dispatched 20 March.

371 (x. 8)

PLANCUS TO THE MAGISTRATES, SENATE, AND PEOPLE

Gaul, March (middle) 43

From Plancus, Imperator, Consul-Elect, to the Consuls, Praetors, Tribunes of the Plebs, Senate, and People and Plebs of Rome.

Before I make any promise to any man as to my duty in time to come, it will, I think, be proper to offer my excuses to those, if any there be, who feel that I have kept public expectancy and the hopes of the commonwealth concerning my political sentiments too long in suspense. For I do not wish to appear to have made amends for past shortcomings, but rather to be enunciating in the fulness of time thoughts long pondered in a loyal heart.

I was not unconscious that at such a time of grave public anxiety and national upheaval the profession of loyal sentiments is highly rewarding, and I saw that a number of persons had gained signal honours by this means. Fortune, however, had placed me in a dilemma. I had to choose whether to make promises without delay and thereby create obstacles to my own possibilities of usefulness, or, if I restrained myself in that particular, to gain larger opportunities for service. I preferred to smooth the path of national deliverance rather than that of my personal glory. A man enjoying a position such as mine, after a life such as I think I am generally known to have led, and with such a prospect as I now see before me, is not likely to submit to anything degrading or entertain a mischievous ambition. But a certain amount of time, a great deal of effort, and substantial expenditure of money were requisite, if I was in the end to make good my promises to the state and to all honest men, and to bring to the national cause, not empty hands and loyal sentiments, but the means to aid. I had to confirm the loyalty of the men under my command, who had been repeatedly tempted by lavish offers, inducing them to look to the state for a moderate recompense rather than to an individual for unlimited bounty. I had to confirm the loyalty of a number of communities which during the previous year had been obligated by means of gifts and grants of privileges, inducing them to regard those concessions as void and to make up their minds to seek the same from those better qualified to bestow them. I had to elicit the sentiments of my fellow-governors and commanders in adjoining provinces; for I wished to join with many partners in a league for the defence of freedom, not to share with a few[925] the fruits of a victory disastrous to the world. I had

925. Not the Antonians. Plancus assumes that the Republic will triumph anyhow, but the more of his fellow-commanders who join its cause the less costly the victory. He is thinking of Lepidus and Pollio.

also to strengthen my own position by increasing the size of my army and the numbers of its auxiliary forces, so that, when I came to make open declaration of my views, there might be no danger in the cause I intended to support becoming common knowledge, even though the announcement might be unwelcome in certain quarters.

So I shall never deny that, in order to bring those plans into effect, I made many reluctant pretences and distressful concealments; for I saw from my colleague's[926] predicament how dangerous it was for a loyal citizen to proclaim himself without preparing the ground. That is why the greater part of the communication which I entrusted to my Legate C. Furnius, a gallant and energetic officer, was by word of mouth rather than in writing, in order that it might reach you with less publicity and that I might run less risk. Therein I gave advice as to the measures requisite for the protection of the common safety and for my own equipment, from which it can be seen that the defence of the supreme interests of the state has for a long time past been my vigilant concern.

Now, by the grace of heaven, I am in every way better prepared; and I wish my countrymen not only to entertain good hope of me, but to make up their minds in full assurance. I have five legions under the standards; their own loyalty and valour closely attach them to the state, and my liberality has secured their obedience to myself. My province is in full readiness; all its constituent communities are of one mind, and there is the keenest rivalry in rendering services. I have cavalry and auxiliary forces in such strength as these peoples can muster for the defence of their lives and liberties. As for my personal resolution, I am prepared to defend my province, or to go wherever the public interest may summon, or to hand over my army, auxiliaries, and province, or to turn the whole brunt of the conflict upon myself, if only by such personal hazard I can assure my country's safety or hold back the danger that threatens her.

926. D. Brutus, under siege in Mutina.

It may be that I make these professions when the clouds have already dispersed and national tranquillity has been restored. In that case my credit will be the less, but I shall rejoice in the public good. If, however, I come to take my share in dire and quite undiminished dangers, I commend the defence of my conduct from the malice of jealous tongues to equitable judges. For myself, I can look forward to the preservation of the state as an ample enough return for my services. But I think I ought to ask you to regard as recommended to your favour those[927] who, in deference to me and (what counts for much more) in reliance upon your good faith, have resisted all blandishments and defied all threats.

372 (X. 7)

PLANCUS TO CICERO

Gaul, March (middle) 43

From Plancus to Cicero.

I should be writing at greater length about my plans and rendering you a more extended account of all particulars, thus enabling you better to judge how faithfully I have rendered to the state all that I took upon myself at your instigation and to which I am pledged by my solemn word to you given – I have always wanted your approval no less than your affection, and if in you I have secured a defender when at fault, I have also wished you to be the herald of my good works: but two things make me comparatively brief; first, I have dealt with everything in an official dispatch; second, I have told M. Varisidius, a Roman Knight and my close friend, to come over to you in person, so that you can learn it all from him.

927. His soldiers.

I have felt no small chagrin, I give you my word, when others appeared to be staking out claims to glory ahead of me. But I made myself wait until I should have brought the situation to the point when I could achieve something worthy of my Consulship and the expectations of my friends in Rome. That aim, if fortune does not disappoint me, I hope to accomplish, so that contemporaries shall recognize and posterity remember me as one who has rendered signal service to the state at need.

Let me ask of you to support my public standing and to render me more ardent in the further pursuit of glory by the enjoyment of those rewards which you set before my eyes when you called me to that endeavour. That your power is no less than your will I am well assured. Take care of your health and remember me as affectionately as I do you.

373 (XII. 25)

CICERO TO CORNIFICIUS

Rome, c. 20 March 43

From Cicero to Cornificius greetings.

I received your letter on Bacchus' Day. Cornificius[928] handed it to me three weeks after dispatch, so he told me. There was no meeting of the Senate that day or the next. On Minerva's Day I pleaded your cause at a well-attended session, not without the Goddess' good-will[929] – my statue of her as Guardian of Rome[930] had been blown down in a gale, and that very day the Senate passed a decree to set it up again. Pansa read your dispatch. The House highly approved of it, to my great delight

928. Perhaps son of Cicero's correspondent.

929. *non invita Minerva*; see Letter 64 (III.1).1.

930. Just before leaving Rome for exile in 58 Cicero dedicated a small statue of Minerva Guardian of the City (=Athene Polias) in the temple of Jupiter Capitolinus.

and the discomfiture of the Minotaur (Calvisius and Taurus).[931] A decree in honorific terms was voted concerning you. There was a demand that *they* should be censured as well, but Pansa took a more lenient view.

For my part, my dear Cornificius, the day I first embarked upon the hope of liberty, that 20th of December on which I laid the foundations of a free state while all the rest hung back, that very day I looked carefully ahead and took account of your personal standing – the Senate acceded to my proposal about the provincial governorships' remaining in their present hands. Ever since then I have delivered blow after blow at the position of the person[932] who is acting as governor *in absentia* – an insult to yourself and a defiance of the state. My frequent, I might say daily, denunciations were too much for him. Unwillingly he returned to Rome, and was evicted not merely from the prospect of the province but from the actuality, the possession, by my most just and proper invective.

I am indeed delighted that you have held your distinguished post so ably and have received the highest honours the province has to offer. As for your apologia about Sempronius,[933] I accept it. In those days of slavery we lived in a land of mist. I myself, the inspiration of your conduct and the well-wisher of your public career, was letting myself be carried off to Greece in a mood of anger against the times and despair of freedom, when the Etesian winds, like loyal citizens, refused to escort a deserter of the commonwealth and a contrary southerly gale brought me back to your fellow-tribesmen of Regium. From there I hastened back to my country as fast as sail and oar could take

931. On 28 November 44 Antony had put through a senatorial decree reassigning provincial commands, under which Africa was given to its former governor C. Calvisius Sabinus, a former officer of Caesar's with a distinguished career ahead of him as a partisan of Octavian. Taurus may be T. Statilius Taurus, later to command Octavian's land forces at Actium. The nature of his association with Calvisius is unknown.

932. Calvisius.

933. Cf. n. 896.

me, and the day after my arrival I was the one free man in an assembly of abject slaves. I delivered an attack[934] upon Antony which was more than he could stand. So he poured out all his drunken fury on my single person, at one time trying to provoke me into giving him a pretext for bloodshed, at another laying traps to catch me. I flung the belching, vomiting brute into Caesar Octavian's toils. This extraordinary youngster has raised a force to defend himself and us in the first place and the supreme interests of the state in the second. But for him Antony's return from Brundisium would have been the downfall of Rome. The sequel I think you know. But to return: I accept your explanation about Sempronius. In such confusion you could not have any definite code.

'Now this day brings new life, demands new modes,' as Terence has it.[935] So, my dear Quintus, come aboard with us and stand at the poop. All honest men are now in the same boat. I am trying to keep her on course, and I pray we have a fair voyage. But whatever winds may blow, my skill shall not be wanting. What more can virtue guarantee? Do you keep a brave spirit and a lofty one. Remember that all your personal consequence should be bound up with the common weal.

374 (XII. 28)

CICERO TO CORNIFICIUS

Rome, March (latter part) 43

From Cicero to Cornificius greetings.

I agree with you that the individuals who you say are threatening Lilybaeum[936] ought to have been brought to book

934. The First Philippic.

935. In *The Girl from Andros* (189).

936. Apparently certain Antonian partisans in Africa had been detected in a plot to descend on Sicily.

in Africa. But you were afraid, so you say, of seeming too little inhibited in punitive proceedings; which means that you were afraid of seeming too responsible a citizen, too brave, too worthy of yourself.

I am glad you are reviving for yourself that partnership with me in the preservation of the commonwealth which you have inherited from your father. It will always remain in being between us, my dear Cornificius. I am also glad you feel that expressions of thanks to me on your part are out of place – you and I do not have to do that between ourselves. The Senate would have been reminded more often of what is due to your position but for the fact that in the absence of the Consuls it is only convoked in emergencies. So nothing can be done through the Senate at present either about the HS2,000,000 or the HS700,000. I advise you to levy a tax on the basis of the Senate's decree, or to raise a loan.

I expect you are kept informed of what is going on politically by your correspondents, who should be sending you details of public proceedings. I am hopeful. I am not behindhand with advice, solicitude, and hard work. I declare myself a deadly foe to all enemies of the state. In my view the situation is not a difficult one as it stands; it would have been a very easy one, if certain parties had not been to blame.[937]

375 (X. 10)

CICERO TO PLANCUS

Rome, 30 March 43

From Cicero to Plancus.

Although sufficiently apprised of your political sentiments

937. Probably a reflection on the Consuls; cf. *Letters to Marcus Brutus* I (I or II.I)I.

and intentions by our friend Furnius, I have reached a clearer assessment of your whole attitude after reading your letter.[938] The Fortune of the commonwealth is deciding all points at issue in a single battle (when you read these lines I expect its outcome will have been determined). None the less the widespread report of your sentiments has in itself redounded greatly to your credit. Had we had a Consul in Rome, the Senate would have declared its appreciation of your efforts and preparations and conferred high honours upon yourself. But the time for that has not gone by; indeed, in my judgement it was not yet ripe. For I always consider an honour to be really and truly such when offered and given, not in the expectation of future benefit, but to persons whose great services have made them illustrious.

And so, provided always that some form of free society exists wherein honours can shine, all the highest, trust me, shall be yours in abundance. But an honour truly so called is not an allurement offered at a crisis, but the reward of constant merit. Therefore, my dear Plancus, strive heart and soul for glory, bring aid to your country, succour to your colleague, support to the marvellous union of all nations banded together in spirit. In me you will find one to help your counsels and further your advancement, an ever loyal and loving friend in all things. For to the bonds of affection, good offices, and old acquaintance which link us to one another the love of country has been added, to make your life more precious to me than my own.

30 March.

376 (XII. 6)

CICERO TO CASSIUS

Rome, March (end) or April (beginning) 43

From Cicero to Cassius greetings.

938. Lost.

You will be able to find out the state of affairs at the time this letter was dispatched from C. Tidius Strabo,[939] a good man and an excellent patriot – that he is most anxious to serve you I need hardly say, seeing that he has left home and career expressly in order to join you. I do not even recommend him to you. His own arrival will be recommendation enough.

Of one thing I hope you are thoroughly convinced, that honest men can look for refuge solely to yourself and Brutus, should any reverse unfortunately take place. As I write, the ultimate crisis is upon us. Brutus[940] is hard put to it to hold out any longer at Mutina. If he is saved, we have won. If not, which heaven forfend, there is only one road for us all – to you. Your courage and preparations must be on the scale needed for the recovery of the whole commonwealth.

Goodbye.

377 (X. 12)

CICERO TO PLANCUS

Rome, 11 April 43

From Cicero to Plancus.

I must heartily rejoice for our country's sake that you have brought such large resources to her defence and aid at an almost desperate hour. And yet, as truly as I hope to embrace you victorious in a restored commonwealth, a great part of my happiness is in your prestige, which I know is already of the highest and will so remain. I assure you that no dispatch ever read in the Senate was more favourably received than yours,[941] an effect due not only to the peculiar importance of your public services

939. Cf. n. 793.
940. D. Brutus, distinguished from M. Brutus (above) by the context.
941. Letter 371 (x.8).

but also to the impressiveness of the words and sentiments. It was all no novelty to me, who knew you and remembered the promises you made in your letters[942] to me and had been thoroughly apprised of your intentions by our friend Furnius; but the Senate felt that their expectations had been surpassed – not that they ever doubted your good-will, but they were not altogether clear as to how much you could do or how far you wished to go.

Accordingly, when M. Varisidius gave me your letter on the morning of 7 April and I read it, I was transported with delight; and as I was escorted from my house by a large throng of loyal patriots, I lost no time in making all of them sharers in my pleasure. Meanwhile our friend Munatius[943] called on me as usual, so I showed him your letter – he knew nothing about it beforehand, because Varisidius had come to me first, on your instructions as he said. A little later the same Munatius gave me the letter you had sent him together with your official dispatch for me to read. We decided to lay the dispatch immediately before Cornutus, the City Praetor, who in the absence of the Consuls is discharging consular functions according to traditional practice. The Senate was convoked at once and met in large numbers, attracted by the report of your dispatch and their eagerness to hear it. After the dispatch had been read out, a religious scruple arose: Cornutus was apprised by the Keepers of the Chickens of an inadvertence in his taking of the auspices, and their representations were confirmed by our College.[944] Business was therefore deferred till the following day, on which I had a great struggle with Servilius so that you should get your due. By personal influence he managed to get his motion taken first, but a large majority of the Senate left him and voted

942. Or 'letter'; perhaps the lost letter referred to in Letter 375 (x.10)1.

943. Who this T. Munatius (cf. end of letter) was and how related to Plancus is unknown.

944. The Augurs.

against it. My motion, which was taken second, was gaining widespread assent, when P. Titius at Servilius' request interposed his veto. The matter was adjourned to the day following. Servilius arrived ready for the fray, 'wrath with Jove himself',[945] in whose temple the meeting was taking place. How I tamed him and how vigorously I put down Titius with his veto I prefer you to learn from other correspondents. One thing, though, you may learn from me: the Senate could not have been more responsible, resolute, and disposed to hear your praises than it was on that occasion; and the community at large is no less well disposed towards you than the Senate. Marvellous indeed is the unanimity with which the entire Roman People, and every type and order therein, has rallied to the cause of freedom.

Continue then in your present course, and hand down your name to eternity. Despise all these prizes that have only the semblance of glory, deriving from meaningless badges of distinction; hold them for brief, unreal, perishable things. True dignity lies in virtue; and virtue is most conspicuously displayed in eminent services to the state. Such you have a splendid opportunity to render. You have grasped it; do not let it slip. Make your country's debt to you no less than yours to her. You shall find me prompt not only to support but to amplify your standing. That I consider I owe both to the commonwealth, which is dearer to me than my life, and to our friendship. Let me add that in my recent endeavours for your credit I have had great pleasure in perceiving more clearly what I already knew well – the sound sense and loyalty of T. Munatius, shown in his truly remarkable good-will and devotion to yourself.

11 April.

945. Proverbial for violent anger or truculence; cf. *Letters to Atticus* 165 (VIII.15)2.

378 (x. 30)[946]

GALBA TO CICERO

Camp at Mutina, 15 April 43

Galba to Cicero greetings.

On 14 April, that being the day Pansa was to have joined Hirtius' camp (I was with him, having gone 100 miles to meet him and expedite his arrival), Antony led out two legions, the Second and Thirty-Fifth, and two praetorian cohorts, one his own and the other Silanus', together with part of his reservists. In this strength he advanced to meet us, thinking that we had only four legions of recruits. But the previous night Hirtius had sent us the Martian Legion, which used to be under my command, and the two praetorian cohorts for our better security on the march to his camp.

When Antony's cavalry came into sight, there was no holding the Martian Legion and the praetorian cohorts. We started to follow them willy-nilly, since we had not been able to hold them back. Antony kept his forces at Forum Gallorum, wanting to conceal the fact that he had the legions; he only showed his cavalry and light-armed. When Pansa saw the legion advancing contrary to his intention, he ordered two legions of recruits to follow him. Having traversed a narrow route through marsh and woodland, we drew up a battle-line of twelve cohorts; the two legions had not yet come up. Suddenly Antony led his forces out of the village, drew them up and immediately engaged. Both sides at first fought as fiercely as men could fight. But the right wing, where I was

946. An account of the battle of Forum Gallorum. On 27 April Antony suffered a second defeat (in which, however, the Consul Hirtius was killed) and was forced to raise the siege of Mutina.

placed with eight cohorts of the Martian Legion, threw back Antony's Thirty-Fifth at the first charge, and advanced more than half a mile from its original position in the line. The cavalry then tried to surround our wing, so I started to retire, setting our light-armed against the Moorish horse to stop them attacking our men in the rear. Meanwhile I found myself in the thick of the Antonians, with Antony some distance behind me. All at once I rode at a gallop towards a legion of recruits which was on its way up from our camp, throwing my shield over my shoulders. The Antonians chased me, while our men were about to hurl their javelins. In this predicament some providence came to my rescue – I was quickly recognized by our men.

On the Aemilian Way itself, where Caesar's praetorian cohort was stationed, there was a long struggle. The left wing, which was weaker, consisting of two cohorts of the Martian Legion and one praetorian cohort, began to give ground, because they were being surrounded by cavalry, which is Antony's strongest arm. When all our ranks had withdrawn, I started to retreat to the camp, the last to do so. Having won the battle, as he considered, Antony thought he could take the camp, but when he arrived he lost a number of men there and achieved nothing.

Having heard what had happened, Hirtius with twenty veteran cohorts met Antony on his way back to his camp and completely destroyed or routed his forces, on the very ground of the previous engagement near Forum Gallorum. Antony withdrew with his horse to his camp at Mutina about 10 o'clock at night. Hirtius then returned to the camp from which Pansa[947] had marched out and where he had left two legions, which had been assaulted by Antony. So Antony has lost the greater part of his veteran troops; but this result was achieved at the cost of some losses in the praetorian cohorts and the Martian Legion.

947. Pansa had been taken to Bononia (Bologna), fatally wounded. Galba had evidently not heard of this.

Two eagles and sixty standards of Antony's have been brought in. It is a victory.

16 April, from camp.

379 (X. 9)

PLANCUS TO CICERO

Near Vienne in Gallia Narbonensis, c. 27 April 43

From Plancus to Cicero greetings.

I am happy to feel that the pledges I made to you were not hasty, and that those you gave to others concerning me have not proved idle. At any rate, the earlier I wished you to know my plans before anyone else the greater evidence you have of my affection.[948] I hope you observe how the tale of my services lengthens every day; that you will learn of them in the future I do not hope so much as guarantee.

As for myself, my dear Cicero (so may the state be relieved with my assistance from impending evils), I prize the honours and rewards which you and those with you have to bestow as gifts surely no less precious than immortality itself; at the same time my zeal and perseverance will be no whit relaxed without them. Only if amid the throng of good patriots *my* enthusiasm and exertions shine conspicuous do I wish my standing to be enhanced by your collective support. For myself I covet nothing – that[949] is exactly what I am fighting against. When and what are questions which I am well content to leave to your discretion. No gift that a man receives from his country can appear tardy or trivial.

948. Or (reading *quod* for *quo*) 'you have so much the greater evidence of my affection in that I wished . . .'

949. i.e. personal ambition like Antony's.

By dint of forced marches I have taken my army across the Rhône this 26th of April, and have sent a thousand horse ahead to Vienne by a shorter route. I myself shall not fail in the matter of speed, if I am not held up by Lepidus; but if he blocks my way, I shall act as circumstances suggest. The forces I am bringing are very strong in numbers, character, and loyalty. I ask you to remember me affectionately, if you know that I shall do the like for you.

Goodbye.

380 (XI. 9)

D. BRUTUS TO CICERO

Regium Lepidum, 29 April 43

From D. Brutus to M. Cicero greetings.

How serious a loss the state has sustained in Pansa you doubtless appreciate. It now behoves you to apply your authority and foresight to ensuring that the removal of the Consuls does not give rise to hopes of possible recovery among our enemies. For my part, I shall try to see that Antony is unable to maintain himself in Italy. I shall be after him immediately. I trust I can stop Ventidius[950] slipping away on the one hand, and Antony remaining in Italy on the other. Let me especially ask you to send word to that arrant weathercock Lepidus, so that he does not let Antony join him and perhaps make us fight the war all over again. As for Asinius Pollio, I expect you see well enough what he is likely to do.[951] The legions under Lepidus and Asinius are good and strong, and there are many of them.

950. He was bringing up three legions from Picenum in support of Antony whom he eventually joined at Vada Sabatia (cf. Letter 385 (XI.10)).

951. i.e. join Antony if he got the chance.

I do not write to you thus because I am not sure that these same points have occurred to yourself, but because I am firmly convinced that Lepidus will never behave well, in case you people in Rome feel any doubt about the matter. I also beg you to stiffen Plancus. After Antony's defeat I trust he will not fail the public cause. If Antony gets over the Alps, I have decided to station a force there and to inform you on all points.

29 April, from camp at Regium.

381 (XI. 13b)

D. BRUTUS TO CICERO

Parma, 30 April 43

From D. Brutus, Consul-Elect, to M. Cicero greetings.

The unfortunate people of Parma ***[952]

382 (X. 11)

PLANCUS TO CICERO

Country of the Allobroges, April (end) or May (beginning) 43

From Plancus to Cicero.

Thank you a thousand, thousand times.[953] As long as I live I shall thank you – as for repaying you, I cannot promise. I feel incapable of matching such services as yours – unless, perchance,

952. The rest is lost. Parma, which must have passed into the hands of the republicans (cf. Letter 365 (XII. 5)), had been captured and sacked by L. Antonius.

953. Plancus is answering Letter 377 (X. 12).

as you have so movingly and eloquently written, you will consider yourself repaid so long as I hold them in remembrance. If your own son's standing had been in question, assuredly you could have shown no warmer affection. Your earlier motions in the Senate heaping all imaginable favours on my head, those more recent adapted to the occasion and the wishes of my friends, your unremitting series of speeches concerning me, your altercations with detractors for my sake – how well I know it all! I must study, no light matter, to show myself a patriot worthy of your eulogies and a friend whose gratitude is undying. For the rest, act in the spirit of your bounty, and if in the actual event you find me the man you wished me to be, take me under your protection and patronage.

After taking my forces across the Rhône, I sent my brother ahead with 3,000 horse and myself advanced along the road to Mutina. While on the march, I heard the news of the battle and of Brutus' and Mutina's liberation from siege. It was apparent to me that Antony and the remnants accompanying him had no refuge except in these areas; also that he had two hopes before him, one in Lepidus himself, the other in Lepidus' army, since part of that army is no less rabid than the men who were with Antony. I recalled the cavalry and have myself halted in the Allobrogian country to be ready for anything as circumstances may suggest. If Antony comes here without a following, I believe I can easily cope with him by myself and handle the situation to your and your friends' satisfaction, even though Lepidus' army takes him in. On the other hand, if he brings some force with him and if the veteran Tenth Legion,[954] which I recalled to its duty along with the others, reverts to its former infatuation, I shall still do my best (and I hope with success) to see that no harm comes until forces are sent over from Italy. United we shall have less difficulty in crushing the desperados.

954. Despite Appian's statement (*Civil Wars*, III.83) that this famous legion was under Lepidus' command it seems to have been under Plancus. How otherwise could he have recalled it to its duty?

This I guarantee you, my dear Cicero, that neither courage nor pains shall be lacking on my part. I most earnestly hope that there is no further reason for anxiety. But if any there should be, my spirit, good-will, and endurance on your collective behalf shall be second to no man's. I am doing my best to urge Lepidus too to come into the fold, and am promising him all manner of compliance, if only he chooses to remember his patriotic duty. As coadjutors and intermediaries in this matter I am employing my brother, Laterensis, and our friend Furnius. No private quarrels shall prevent me from co-operating with my worst enemy for the safety of the commonwealth. If these efforts turn out fruitless, none the less I am in excellent heart and perhaps I shall content you all with greater glory to myself.[955]

Take care of your health and remember me kindly, as I do you.

383 (XII. 25a)

CICERO TO CORNIFICIUS

Rome, May (beginning) 43

From Cicero to Cornificius greetings.

You recommend to me P. Luccius, one of my own circle. I shall spare no pains to help him in any way I can.

We have lost our colleagues Hirtius and Pansa at a very unfortunate moment. In their Consulship they gave good service to the state, which is now rid of Antony's brigandage, but not yet completely out of the wood. If permitted, I shall fight the good fight as ever, though I am now very tired. But no weariness should stand in the way of duty and loyalty. Well, enough

955. If Lepidus took the wrong side after all, Plancus would not have to share the credit of victory.

of that. I would rather you heard about me from others than from myself.

Of you we hear what we should most have wished to hear. There are some sinister rumours abroad about Cn. Minucius, whom you praised to the skies in one of your letters. I should be glad if you would let me know the facts, and how things are going over there in general.

384 (x. 14)

CICERO TO PLANCUS

Rome, 5 May 43

From Cicero to Plancus greetings.

Most welcome the report that arrived two days before the victory about the aid you are bringing – your devotion, your speed, your forces! Even after the rout of the enemy all our hopes are pinned on you. The foremost rebel leaders are said to have escaped from the field of Mutina. Now to wipe out the last remnants of mischief is no less thankworthy an achievement than to drive off its beginnings.

For my part I am already awaiting a dispatch from you, as are many others. I hope that Lepidus too will pay heed to the national emergency and co-operate with you in the national interest. Therefore bend your energies, my dear Plancus, to the end that not a spark of this abominable war is left alive. If that is accomplished you will have conferred a superhuman benefit upon the state and will yourself reap immortal glory.

Dispatched 5 May.

385 (XI. 10)

D. BRUTUS TO CICERO

Dertona, 5 May 43

From D. Brutus to M. Cicero greetings.

I think the country owes me no more than I owe you. Be sure that I can be more grateful to you than those ill-natured folk are to me. But if you should think I am saying this for expediency's sake, then have it that I prefer your good opinion to that of the whole lot of them put together. For your judgement of me starts from a sure and true perception. *They* cannot judge so, because they are handicapped by vicious malice and jealousy. Let them interfere to block the conferment of honours upon me, so long as they do not interfere with my ability to do my job to the advantage of the country. Let me set out as briefly as I can the danger in which she stands.

To begin with, I do not have to tell you of the confusion into which the death of the Consuls has plunged affairs in Rome, or of the greedy spirit aroused by the official vacuum.[956] I think I have written enough – as much as can be committed to a letter. After all, I know to whom I am writing.

Now to come back to Antony. He fled with a petty little band of unarmed foot-soldiers, but by throwing open the slave-barracks and laying hands on every sort of manpower he seems to have made up a pretty sizable body. This has been joined by Ventidius' band, which after a very difficult march across the Apennines reached Vada and linked up with Antony there. There is a pretty considerable number of veterans and armed troops with Ventidius.

956. Octavian may already have given signs of his ambition to take one of the vacant Consulships.

Antony must choose between the following plans: (a) He may go to Lepidus if Lepidus is receiving him. (b) He may keep to the Apennines and Alps and use his cavalry, with which he is well provided, in raids to devastate the areas he invades. (c) He may come back to Etruria, because there is no army in that part of Italy. If Caesar had listened to me and crossed the Apennines, I should have put Antony in so tight a corner that he would have been finished by lack of supplies rather than cold steel. But there is no giving orders to Caesar, nor *by* Caesar to his army – both very bad things.

In this situation, as I have said above, if people want to interfere with what concerns me personally, let them. What alarms me is how this situation can be straightened out, or that, when you are in process of straightening it, others may tangle it up. I cannot any longer feed my men. When I put my hand to the work of liberation, I had a fortune of over HS40,000,000. Now my whole estate is encumbered; not only that, but I have involved all my friends in debt. I am maintaining seven legions, you may imagine with what difficulty. If I had Varro's treasure-vaults,[957] I could not stand against the expense.

As soon as I know for certain about Antony I shall send you word. Let me have your kind regard, provided you find a corresponding sentiment on my side.

5 May, from camp at Dertona.

957. Possibly with reference to a fragment of one of Varro's Menippean Satires (ed. Riese, p. 103): 'not by treasure-vaults (*thesauris*) nor by gold is the heart freed of bondage; not the mountains of Persia nor the halls of wealthy Crassus take care and superstition from men's minds'.

386 (XI. 11)

D. BRUTUS TO CICERO

Borders of the Statiellenses, 6 May 43

From D. Brutus, Imperator, Consul-Elect, to M. Cicero, greetings.

A duplicate of the letter which my boys brought from you has been delivered to me. I consider that I owe you a great debt, which it is difficult to pay in full.

I am writing to tell you what is going on here. Antony is on the march, he is going to Lepidus. He has not yet given up hope even of Plancus, as I have perceived from some papers of his which have come my way, in which he entered the names of his various emissaries to Asinius, Lepidus, and Plancus. However, I entertained no misgivings, and sent word to Plancus straight away. And in a couple of days I expect envoys from the Allobroges and the whole of Gaul. I shall send them back home in good heart.

Please look to future action in Rome, so that any necessary steps may be taken in accordance with your views and the public interest. You will counter the world's malice towards me if you can. If that is beyond your power, you will have the consolation of knowing that they cannot by any indignities turn me away from the position I have taken up.

6 May, from camp on the borders of the Statiellenses.

387 (XII. 12)

CASSIUS TO CICERO

Syria, 7 May 43

From Cassius, Proconsul, to his friend M. Cicero, greetings.

I trust you are well, as I am, and my army.

I have read your letter,[958] in which I find evidence once again of your singular regard for me. You would appear not only to wish me well, as you have always done both for my sake and the country's, but to have taken a grave responsibility upon yourself and to be very anxious on my account. Because I felt you were persuaded that I could not stand idly by while freedom was stifled, and because I felt that, suspecting me to be at work, you were anxious about my safety and the outcome of the enterprise, I wrote to you and sent a number of couriers to Rome as soon as I took over the legions which A. Allienus had led from Egypt. I also wrote a dispatch to the Senate, with orders that it should not be delivered until it had been read to you – if my people have seen fit to comply with my instructions. If the letters have not been delivered, I can only suppose that Dolabella, who has villainously put Trebonius to death and seized Asia, has caught my couriers and intercepted the letters.

All the armies that were in Syria are at my orders. I was held up for a short time pending discharge of promises given to the men. Now my hands are free. May I ask you to regard my public standing as entrusted to your care, if you recognize that I have declined no risk or labour for the country's sake? On your encouragement and advice I have taken up arms against a set of savage brigands, and have not only raised armies for the defence of commonwealth and liberty but wrested them from

958. Doubtless Letter 367 (XII.7).

the grip of cruel tyrants. Had Dolabella seized upon these troops before me, he would have strengthened Antony's hands, not only by the arrival of his army on the scene but by the report and expectation of it.

In view of these facts take the soldiers under your protection, if you perceive that they have deserved wonderfully well of the state, and see to it that no man of them regrets having chosen to follow the national cause rather than the hope of spoil and plunder. Likewise defend the standing of Generals Murcus and Crispus, so far as in you lies. As for Bassus, he was sorely reluctant to hand over his legion to me, and if the troops had not sent me their representatives against his will, he would have shut the gates and held Apamea[959] until it was taken by storm. I make these requests of you not only for the sake of the commonwealth, which has always been most dear to your heart, but also in the name of our friendship, which I am confident counts for a great deal with you. Believe me, this army under my command is devoted to the Senate and the loyalists, and most of all to you. By dint of constantly hearing about your friendly sentiments they have developed an extraordinary regard and affection for you. Once they realize that you have their interests at heart, they will feel unbounded gratitude as well.

P.S. I hear that Dolabella has entered Cilicia with his force. I shall set out for Cilicia. I shall try to let you know quickly how I get on. And I hope that luck will be on my side in so far as I deserve well of the commonwealth. Take care of yourself and your affection for me.

Nones of May, from camp.

959. On the Orontes, south of Antioch.

388 (XI. 13)

D. BRUTUS TO M. CICERO

Pollentia, c. 9 May 43

From D. Brutus, Imperator, Consul-Elect, to M. Cicero, greetings.

I have given up thanking you. There is no making adequate return in words to one whom I can scarcely repay in deeds. I want you to concentrate on the matters in hand – nothing will escape your perspicacity if you read my letter carefully.

The reasons why I was unable to pursue Antony at once, my dear sir, were these: I had no cavalry, no pack-animals; I did not know of Hirtius' death, but I did know of Aquila's; I did not trust Caesar until I had met and talked to him. So the first day passed. Early on the next I had a message from Pansa summoning me to Bononia. As I was on my way I received the report of his death. I hastened back to my own apology for an army, as I can truly call it; it is most sadly reduced, and in very bad shape through lack of all things needful. Antony got two days' start of me and made far longer marches as the pursued than I as the pursuer, for he went helter-skelter, while I moved in regular order. Wherever he went he opened up the slave-barracks and carried off the men, stopping nowhere until he reached Vada. I want you to know this place. It lies between the Apennines and the Alps, and its approach offers the greatest difficulties.

When I was thirty miles away from Antony and Ventidius had already joined up with him, a speech of his was brought to me in which he now asked his troops to follow him across the Alps and told them that he had an understanding with Lepidus. There was a shout (coming in volume from Ventidius' men, for Antony has precious few of his own) of 'death or victory in

Italy', and they started begging him to let them march on Pollentia. Unable to hold out against them, he fixed his march for the following day.

On receiving this report I immediately sent five cohorts in advance to Pollentia, and myself set out for the town. My detachment arrived there an hour ahead of Trebellius and a squadron of horse.[960] I felt no small satisfaction, for I think victory depends upon ***.

389 (X. 13)

CICERO TO PLANCUS

Rome, c. 11 May 43

From Cicero to Plancus.

As soon as the opportunity to enhance your standing came my way, I left nothing undone to your honour – no recompense of merit, no verbal accolade. That you will be able to see from the terms of the Senate's decree. They are exactly those of my motion, which I delivered from a script and which a well-attended House adopted with remarkable enthusiasm and unanimity. It was indeed clear to me from the letter you sent me that you find greater satisfaction in the judgement of honest men than in badges of glory. None the less, I felt it incumbent upon us to consider what was due to you from the state, even though you asked for nothing. It is for you to match the end with the beginning. The man who crushes Mark Antony will have won the war. It was Ulysses whom Homer called 'sacker of cities', not Ajax or Achilles.[961]

960. The evidence does not support the view that D. Brutus was deceived by a feint.

961. The passages in the *Iliad* in which Achilles is so called were held by Aristarchus to be spurious.

390 (X. 15)

PLANCUS TO CICERO

Camp on the Isara, 11(?) May 43

From Plancus to Cicero.

After writing the above,[962] I thought that in the public interest you should know the sequel. My assiduity has, I hope, borne fruit both for the state and for myself. Through intermediaries frequently passing to and fro I urged Lepidus to lay aside all quarrel, be reconciled with me, and collaborate in aiding the commonwealth. I exhorted him to think more of himself, his children, and his country than of one ruined, desperate bandit, and told him that if he did so my compliance in all things was entirely his to command.

My representations took effect. Lepidus gave me his word through Laterensis to make war on Antony, if he was unable to bar him from his province. He requested me to come and join forces, particularly as Antony is said to be strong in cavalry, while Lepidus has not even a second-class cavalry force. Even of the few he had, six hundred – the pick of them – had come over to me not long beforehand.

On receiving this intelligence I lost no time, reckoning that Lepidus should be assisted in the flowing tide of his good intentions. I saw the salutary effects to be expected from my arrival on the scene. I should be able to pursue Antony and crush his cavalry with mine, and at the same time the presence of my troops would serve to reform and coerce that portion of Lepidus' army which is tainted with disaffection. I therefore constructed in one day a bridge across the great river Isara on the border of the Allobrogian territory, and led my army

962. The letter to which this is a postscript seems to have been lost (it can hardly be 382 (x.11), written about thirteen days earlier).

across on 9 May. On 11 May, receiving a report that L. Antonius had been sent ahead with some cavalry and cohorts and had reached Forum Julii, I dispatched my brother with 4,000 horse to block him. I shall follow myself by forced marches with four legions without baggage and my remaining horse. Aided, even to a moderate degree, by the fortune of the commonwealth, we shall here find an end to the audacity of the desperados and our own anxiety. If, however, the bandit hears that I am on my way and beats a retreat back to Italy, it will be Brutus' duty to block him. I am sure that Brutus will lack neither skill nor courage. None the less, I shall in that event send my brother with the cavalry in pursuit and for the defence of Italy from devastation.

Take care of your health and remember me kindly, as I do you.

391 (X. 21)

PLANCUS TO CICERO

Camp on the Isara, 13(?) May 43

From Plancus to Cicero.

I should be ashamed to chop and change in my letters, were it not that these things depend on the fickleness of another person. I did everything in my power to combine with Lepidus for the defence of the commonwealth, so that I could oppose the desperados on terms which would leave you at home less cause for anxiety. I pledged myself to all he asked and made other promises voluntarily. The day before yesterday I wrote to you that I was confident of finding Lepidus amenable and of conducting the war in concert with him. I relied on letters in his handwriting and on the assurance given in person by Laterensis, who was with me at the time, begging me to make up my quarrel with Lepidus and to trust him. It is now no longer possible to augur well of him. But at least I have taken, and shall continue to take, good care that the supreme interests of the state are not betrayed by my credulity.

After constructing in one day a bridge over the river Isara, I led my army across in all haste, as the importance of the emergency demanded, since Lepidus himself had requested me in writing to make all speed to go to him – only to be met by his orderly with a letter enjoining me not to come. He wrote that he could settle the business himself, and asked me in the meanwhile to wait on the Isara. I will tell you the rash plan I formed. I decided to go none the less, supposing that Lepidus did not want to share the glory. I reckoned that without in any way detracting from this paltry personage's credit I could be at hand somewhere in the vicinity, so as to come rapidly to the rescue if anything untoward should occur.

That was how in my innocence I gauged the situation. But Laterensis, who is a man of complete integrity, now sends me a letter in his own hand utterly despairing of himself, the army, and Lepidus' good faith, and complaining that he has been left in the lurch. He warns me in plain terms to beware of treachery, says that he himself has kept faith, and urges me not to fail the commonwealth. I am sending a copy of his letter to Titius.[963] All the autograph originals (both those which I believed and those which I considered untrustworthy) I shall give to Cispius Laevus, who has been privy to all these transactions, for him to take to Rome.

There is a further item. When Lepidus was addressing his soldiers, who are disloyal by inclination and have been further corrupted by their officers such as Canidius, Rufrenus, and others whose names you will know when the time comes, these honest patriots roared out that they wanted peace, that they would fight nobody now that two excellent Consuls had

963. Probably Plancus' brother-in-law L. Titius, not the Tribune mentioned in Letter 377 (x.12).

been killed and so many Romans lost to the fatherland, branded wholesale moreover as public enemies and their goods confiscated. Lepidus neither punished this outburst nor remedied the mischief.

For me to go this way and expose my thoroughly loyal army with its auxiliaries and the Gaulish chiefs and the whole province to two combined armies, would clearly be the height of folly and temerity. If I was overwhelmed and had sacrificed the state along with myself, I could expect no pity, much less honour, for such a death. Therefore I intend to go back, and shall not let these desperate men be presented with the possibility of such advantages.

I shall take care to keep my army in suitable locations, to protect my province even if Lepidus' army defects, and to preserve the whole position uncompromised until you send armies to my support and defend the commonwealth here as successfully as you have done in Italy. On behalf of you all I am ready, no man has ever been more so, either to fight it out if I get a fair opportunity, or to stand a siege if it prove necessary, or to die if chance so fall. Therefore I urge you, my dear Cicero, to do your utmost to get an army across the Alps here as soon as possible, and to make haste before the enemy's strength grows further and our men become unsettled. If speed is used in this operation, the state will remain in possession of its victory and the criminals will be destroyed.

Take care of your health and remember me kindly.

392 (x. 21a)

PLANCUS TO CICERO

Camp on the Isara, c. 15 May 43

Would you have me offer you apologies for my brother in a letter – the most gallant of gentlemen and the most forward in every patriotic endeavour? As a result of his exertions he has contracted a slight fever, continuous and pretty troublesome. As soon as he can manage it he will hasten back to Rome without question, so that the state may not lack his services wherever he may be.

Let me ask you to regard my public standing as entrusted to your care. There is no need for me to be covetous, for in you I have a most affectionate friend and (as I prayed you would be) a most influential one. The magnitude and timing of any benefaction you may wish me to owe you will be yours to determine. All I ask is that you take me as Hirtius' successor both in affection on your side and respect on mine.

393 (x. 19)

CICERO TO PLANCUS

Rome, mid May 43

From Cicero to Plancus.

I felt no need for words of thanks from you, knowing how grateful you are in truth and heart. But I must acknowledge that they gave me deep pleasure. I saw your affection for me plain as I see what is in front of my eyes. 'And before?' you may ask. Yes indeed, always, but never more clearly.

Your dispatch[964] made an extraordinarily favourable impression on the Senate, both from the great and momentous news it contained, magnificent evidence of your courage and judgement, and from the impressive quality of sentiments and style. Forward now, my dear Plancus, to finish the last remnants of the war! That will be a most grateful and glorious achievement. I am heart and soul devoted to the commonwealth; yet, truth to tell, I have grown weary in its preservation

964. Not preserved.

and my zeal for my country is not much greater than that which I feel for your glory. The Immortals have given you, as I trust, a golden opportunity to earn it. Grasp that opportunity, I beg of you. The man who crushes Antony will have finished this ghastly and perilous war.

394 (XI. 12)

CICERO TO D. BRUTUS

Rome, c. 13 May 43

From M. Cicero to D. Brutus, Imperator, Consul-Elect, greetings.

I have received three letters[965] from you on the same day: a short one, which you sent by Volumnius Flaccus, and two of more substance, one brought by T. Vibius' couriers, the other sent to me by Lupus.

From what you write and from what Graeceius says, the flames of war, so far from having been extinguished, seem to be blazing higher. Knowing your exceptional perspicacity, I do not doubt you realize that if Antony acquires a position of any strength all your splendid services to the state will be brought to nothing. According to reports reaching Rome and to the universal persuasion here Antony had fled in despair with a few unarmed and demoralized followers. If in fact his condition is such that, as I hear from Graeceius, a clash with him will be a dangerous matter, I do not regard him as having fled from Mutina but as having shifted the war to another theatre. Accordingly, the public mood has changed. There are even those who criticize you men in the field for having failed to pursue Antony. They think that with prompt action he might

965. Letters 380 (XI.9), 385 (XI.10), and 386 (XI.11).

have been overwhelmed. No doubt it is a characteristic of the masses, those of Rome in particular, to exercise their liberties upon the one person of all others through whose agency they have gained them. Even so, care must be taken not to give just grounds for complaint. The case stands thus: the man who crushes Antony will have finished the war. What this means I would rather leave you to consider than put it in plainer language myself.

395 (x. 18)

PLANCUS TO CICERO

Camp on the Isara, 18 May 43

From Plancus to Cicero.

What I had in mind when Laevus and Nerva took their leave you will have learned from the letter I gave them and from their own report – they have been privy to all my actions and plans. I find myself, as a man of honour anxious to do his duty to the state and all honest citizens is apt to find himself, following a dangerous course in earning approval rather than a safe one which might be censurable.

After the departure of my envoys I received two letters in quick succession, one from Lepidus urging me to go to him, the other in still more pressing terms from Laterensis, almost begging and imploring me. His one fear is exactly my own – the fickle and disloyal disposition of Lepidus' troops. I felt I must not hesitate to go to his assistance and face the common peril. No doubt I should be acting more cautiously if I waited on the Isara till Brutus brought his army across the Alps, and then advanced against the enemy with a like-minded colleague and a united and patriotic army (as my men are). But I can see that if Lepidus came to any harm in the right cause, all would be blamed on my obstinacy in not going to the relief of a friend to the public with whom I had a personal quarrel, or on my pusillanimity in deliberately withdrawing myself from the clash in so necessary a conflict.

Accordingly, I have chosen to take a chance, in the hope that my presence will bolster up Lepidus and improve the morale of his army, rather than to be considered over-cautious. I really believe no man was ever in greater anxiety through no fault of his own. If Lepidus' army were elsewhere, it would be plain sailing; but as matters stand, there is great cause for anxiety and great risk. If I had had the luck to meet Antony first, I give you my word he would not have lasted an hour – I have enough self-confidence and enough contempt for his battered forces and that muleteer[966] Ventidius' army to say so much. But I cannot help trembling at the thought of a wound beneath the skin which may do mischief before it can be diagnosed and treated. But if I stayed where I am, it is certain that Lepidus himself and the loyal section of his troops would be in deadly peril. The enemy ruffians too would have gained much in strength if they had drawn forces over from Lepidus. If my arrival dispels these threats, I shall thank my stars and my own resolution, which has spurred me on to this adventure.

Accordingly, this 18th of May I am striking camp on the Isara. I am, however, leaving the bridge which I constructed over the river and two forts at either bridgehead strongly garrisoned, so that when Brutus and his army arrive they will find free passage. I hope myself to effect a junction with Lepidus' forces within eight days of dispatching this letter.

966. Ventidius had at one time made money by contracting for the supply of mules and carts for provincial governors.

396 (X. 34)

LEPIDUS TO CICERO

Pons Argenteus, c. 19 May 43

Lepidus, twice Imperator, Pontifex Maximus, to M. Tullius Cicero, greetings.

I trust you are well, as I am, and my army.

On hearing that M. Antonius was on his way with his forces into my province and had sent L. Antonius ahead with part of his cavalry, I struck my camp at the confluence of the Rhône and the * and started to advance against them with my army. Marching every day, I reached Forum Voconium and took up a position against the Antonii east of the town on the River Argenteus. P. Ventidius joined him with his three legions, and pitched his camp to the east of me. Previously Antony had the Fifth Legion and a great number of men from his other legions, but these latter are unarmed. His cavalry is very strong; the whole of it withdrew without loss from the battle, amounting to more than 5,000 troopers. Numbers of foot and horse have deserted him to join me, and his forces are dwindling every day. Silanus and Culleo have left him. Although they had committed a grave offence against me in going to Antony against my will, yet for mercy and friendship's sake I have spared their lives; but I do not employ them or have them in camp, nor have I given them any charge.

As for this war, I shall not fail the Senate or the commonwealth. I shall keep you informed of my further activities.

397 (XI. 18)

CICERO TO D. BRUTUS

Rome, 19 May 43

From M. Cicero to D. Brutus, Imperator, Consul-Elect, greetings.

From the messages you sent to the Senate by Galba and Volumnius we suspect the nature of the dangers you envisage; but those messages seem apprehensive to a degree unworthy of your and the Roman People's victory. The Senate, my dear Brutus, is brave and has brave leaders; and so they are vexed to be set down by you, whom they judge the bravest man that ever was, as a body of nervous faint-hearts. And really, considering that when you were shut up in the town everybody placed the highest hopes upon your valour, though Antony was flourishing, who could be afraid of anything after his overthrow and your liberation? Nor are we afraid of Lepidus. After declaring his desire for peace when the war was at its height, could anyone suppose him mad enough to declare war on the state when peace, the peace we prayed for, reigned?

At the same time I don't doubt that you see further than we. All the same, this renewal of alarm, following so swiftly upon the thanksgivings which we offered upon your account at every temple, is causing great vexation. So for my part, my wish and hope is that Antony is really down and out. If, however, he manages to collect some sort of power, he shall find that the Senate does not lack for counsel, nor the People of Rome for valour, nor the commonwealth, while you live, for a general.

19 May.

398 (x. 17)

PLANCUS TO CICERO

En route *to Forum Voconii, c. 21 May 43*

From Plancus to Cicero.

On the Ides of May Antony arrived at Forum Julii with his advance guard. Ventidius is two days' march away from him. Lepidus is encamped at Forum Voconii, twenty-four miles from Forum Julii, and has decided to wait for me there, as he has written to me himself. If he and fortune leave me a clear field, I guarantee that I shall quickly finish the job to your collective satisfaction.

I have already told you that my brother has been seriously ill, worn out by the fatigue of continual hurrying to and fro. None the less, as soon as he was able to walk, he was ready to be foremost in every dangerous work, regarding his recovery as for the state's benefit as much as his own. However, I have urged, in fact compelled, him to leave for Rome, on the ground that in his present state of health he would be more likely to wear himself out than to help me in camp; and I thought that a man of his calibre would be needed as Praetor in city affairs, now that the state has been left denuded by the lamentable loss of the Consuls. If anyone at home disapproves of this, let him know that there has been a failure of judgement on my part, not any lack of patriotic loyalty on my brother's.

To resume, Lepidus has complied with my desire that he should send me Apella[967] as a hostage for his good faith and collaboration in the public service. In this connection, I have found L. Gellius, one of the three brothers from Segovia,[968]

967. Presumably a confidential freedman of Lepidus.

968. The reading is very doubtful. If 'Segovia' is wrong, this Gellius may be a son of Gellius Poplicola (see Glossary of Persons) who later served with Brutus and Cassius in the East.

very ready to help. He has been my latest go-between with Lepidus. I think I can say that he has proved himself a good patriot and I am glad to testify accordingly, as I shall readily do for all who deserve it.

Take care of your health and remember me kindly, as I do you. Stand up for me in public (if I deserve it), as you have done hitherto with such notable good-will.

399 (XI. 19)

D. BRUTUS TO CICERO

Vercellae, 21 May 43

From D. Brutus, Imperator, Consul-Elect, to M. Cicero greetings.

Will you be good enough to read beforehand the dispatch I am sending to the Senate and make any alterations you think proper? You will see for yourself that I had no choice but to write it. When I thought I should have the Fourth and Martian Legions with me, as proposed by Drusus and Paulus with the assent of yourself and the rest, I saw less reason for anxiety as to future operations. But now that I am left with a wretchedly appointed body of recruits, I must needs be gravely apprehensive on my own account and that of you all.

The Vicetini show myself and M. Brutus particular attention. May I beg of you not to let any injury come to them in the Senate for the sake of a pack of slaves?[969] They have an excellent case, and are eminently loyal to the commonwealth; and their opponents are a disorderly, thoroughly untrustworthy set.

21 May, from Vercellae.

969. Perhaps contemptuously for freedmen. But they may have been slaves belonging to the municipality, which denied the validity of their manumission.

400 (x. 34a)

LEPIDUS TO CICERO

Pons Argenteus, 22 May 43

M. Lepidus, twice Imperator, Pontifex Maximus, to M. Tullius Cicero greetings.

You and I have always vied in the eagerness of our mutual zeal to do one another service in virtue of the friendship between us, and both of us have been careful to maintain our practice accordingly. At the same time I have no doubt that in the present violent and unexpected political disturbance my detractors have brought you false and unworthy reports concerning me, calculated to give your patriotic heart no small disquiet. My agents have informed me that you have not allowed these rumours to upset you or thought it right to give them hasty credence. For that I am deeply and duly grateful. I also remember your earlier friendly efforts to promote and enhance my standing; they will ever remain firmly rooted in my mind.

I have one earnest request to make of you, my dear Cicero. If in time past my life and endeavour, my diligence and good faith in the conduct of public affairs, have to your knowledge been worthy of the name I bear, I beg you to expect equal or greater things in time to come, and to regard me as deserving the protection of your public influence in proportion as your kindness places me further and further in your debt.

Goodbye.

Dispatched 22 May from camp, Pons Argenteus.

401 (XI. 20)

D. BRUTUS TO CICERO

Eporedia, 24 May 43

From D. Brutus to M. Cicero greetings.

My affection for you and your services to me make me feel on your account what I do not feel on my own – fear. Here is something I have often been told and have not thought negligible – my latest informant is Segulius Labeo (he never acts out of character), who tells me that he has been with Caesar and that a good deal of talk about you took place. Caesar, he says, made no complaints about you to be sure, except for a remark which he attributed to you: 'the young man must get praises, honours, and – the push.'[970] He added that he had no intention of letting himself get the push. I believe that the remark was repeated to him (or invented) by Labeo, not produced by the young man. As for the veterans, Labeo would have me believe that they are grumbling viciously, and that you are in danger from them. He says they are particularly indignant that neither Caesar nor I have been put on the Commission of Ten,[971] and that everything has been placed in the hands of you gentlemen.

When I heard all this, though I was already on the march, I thought it would be wrong for me to cross the Alps yet, before I knew what was going on in Rome. As for the danger to yourself, believe me, they are hoping to gain larger gratuities by talking at large and threatening trouble – they mean to terrorize you and instigate the young man. This whole rigmarole has one origin – they want to make as much profit for themselves as

970. *laudandum, ornandum, tollendum.* The last verb seems to be used with a double meaning, 'exalt' and 'get rid of'.

971. Appointed by the Senate after the battle of Mutina to review Antony's 'acts' as Consul. Decimus seems to have thought that land and gratuities for the republican army were involved, but cf. Letter 411 (XI.21), last paragraph but one.

possible. At the same time I don't want you to be other than circumspect and wary of plots; I can have no greater source of pleasure, nothing more precious, than your life. Only you must be careful that fearing does not give you further cause for fear; and at the same time you should meet the veterans where you can. First, do what they want about the Commission of Ten. Second, with regard to gratuities, you should propose, if you think fit, that the lands of the veteran soldiers who were with Antony be assigned them by the two of us, and, as regards cash, say that the Senate will take time to decide in the light of the financial situation. It occurs to me that the four legions for whom the Senate has voted grants of land can be provided for out of the ⋆ lands and the Campanian land. I think the lands should be assigned to the legions in equal portions, or by lot.

It is not my perspicacity that impels me to write all this, but my affection for you and my desire for public tranquillity, which cannot subsist without you. Unless it is really necessary, I shall not leave Italy. I am arming and equipping my troops. I hope I shall have a not wholly contemptible army to meet all contingencies and attacks. Caesar is not sending me back the legion from Pansa's army.

Please answer this letter at once, and send one of your own people if there is anything especially confidential which you think I ought to know.

24 May, from Eporedia.

402 (XI. 23)

D. BRUTUS TO CICERO

Eporedia, 25 May 43

From D. Brutus to M. Cicero greetings.

We are in good shape here and shall try to be in better.

Lepidus' sentiments seem to me satisfactory. We must put all fear aside and take measures for the public interest without inhibition. But even if everything were against us, with three such large and powerful armies[972] dedicated to the public service you ought to keep your spirit high – high you have always kept it, and now with fortune's help you can raise it higher. As for what I wrote in my own hand in my earlier letter, people talk like this to scare you. Just take the bit between your teeth, and I'll be hanged if the whole pack of them will be able to stand against you when you open your mouth.[973]

As I wrote to you in my earlier letter, I shall stay in Italy till I hear from you.

25 May, from Eporedia.

403 (X. 25)

CICERO TO FURNIUS

Rome, May 43

From Cicero to Furnius greetings.

If, as is generally supposed, it is in the public interest for you to continue as you have begun, still taking an active part in the vitally important operations directed to stamping out the remnants of the war, I think that no course could be better or redound more to your credit and honour; and I consider that your activity, energy, and patriotic spirit should be of more account than a swift attainment of the Praetorship. For I would not have you unaware how much credit you have already won. Believe me, it is second only to Plancus', and that by Plancus' own testimony as well as by report and universal opinion. So if

972. Those of Decimus himself, Plancus, and Octavian.

973. For the singular infelicity of the metaphor Decimus is responsible.

you have any further work to do, I consider it most important that you should go ahead with it. Surely that is the most honourable course, and surely honour must come first. On the other hand, if you think you have done enough for duty and enough for your country, I advise you to lose no time in returning for the elections, since they will be held early; always provided that such haste in the furtherance of your career does not in any degree detract from the reputation we[974] have won. Many famous men, while engaged on public service, have not stood for office in the normal year.[975] That course is all the easier for us because this is not your appointed year in the way that, had you been Aedile, your time would have come two years later. As things stand, you will be looked upon as not letting slip any of the customary, quasi-legal period of candidacy.[976] It also occurs to me that your candidacy will have more *éclat* when Plancus is Consul (though you would have nothing to worry about even without him), if only matters in Gaul have been brought to a satisfactory conclusion.

To be sure, I do not think there is much need for me to write at length to a man of such sense and judgement as yourself. However, I would not have you ignorant of my opinion, the long and short of which is that I should like you in all things to make prestige rather than ambition for office your criterion, and to look for reward in lasting reputation rather than swift attainment of the Praetorship. I asked your very good friends

974. As often, Cicero politely affects to consider his correspondent's affairs as his own.

975. Literally 'the year of their candidature', i.e. in which they attained the qualifying age for this or that office. Since Furnius had been Tribune in 50 he will already have been past the normal minimum age for praetorian candidacy.

976. In common parlance (though not technically) candidacy began long before the official declaration (*professio*). If Furnius stood in 43 he would be a candidate in this customary sense for a much shorter time than was normal, whereas if he waited till the following year he would be regarded as giving himself the benefit of the full period.

my brother Quintus, Caecina, and Calvisius[977] to my house, and said the same to them in the presence of your freedman Dardanus. My words seemed to find favour with them all. But you will judge best.

404 (x. 16)

CICERO TO PLANCUS

Rome, c. 26 May 43

From Cicero to Plancus.

I know of nothing in history, my dear Plancus, more glorious than your dispatch.[978] No happening in my experience has ever been more welcome, more fortunate too in its moment. It was delivered to Cornutus during a well-attended meeting of the Senate, after he had read out a distinctly cold, shuffling communication from Lepidus. Yours was read immediately after, and to loud cheers. The facts themselves and your patriotic zeal and services gave the most lively satisfaction; and furthermore, words and sentiments alike were deeply impressive. The House began to importune Cornutus for an immediate debate on your dispatch. He said he wanted time to consider. There was a great outcry from the entire House, and finally five Tribunes put the question. Servilius, when called upon, proposed an adjournment. I put forward a motion which received unanimous assent. You will learn its terms from the Senate's decree.

You stand in no need of counsel, or rather you have it in abundance. Still, you should make up your mind not to refer any decision to Rome and not to consider yourself obliged to seek the Senate's advice in a situation so fraught with surprises

977. Surely to be distinguished from the obnoxious C. Calvisius Sabinus; cf. Letter 373 (XII.25).

978. Its contents will have corresponded to Letter 390 (x. 15).

and with so little margin for error. You must be your own Senate, and follow wherever the national interest leads you. Let us hear of some fine achievement on your part before we think that it is coming. One thing I promise you: whatever you do will meet with the Senate's approval as not only loyally, but wisely done.

405 (XII. 14)

LENTULUS SPINTHER THE YOUNGER TO CICERO

Perge, 29 May 43

Lentulus to his friend Cicero cordial greetings.

After meeting our friend Brutus and perceiving that his arrival in Asia was likely to be somewhat delayed, I returned to the province to tie up the loose ends of my work[979] and dispatch the money to Rome at the earliest possible moment. Meanwhile I learned that Dolabella's fleet was in Lycia together with more than a hundred freighters in which his army might be embarked. He was reported to have got them together in case his hopes of Syria were disappointed, with a view to going aboard and making for Italy, there to join forces with the Antonii and the other bandits.

This news alarmed me so much that I dropped all else and set out to meet them with a squadron of vessels inferior in number and size. Had I not been obstructed by the Rhodians, perhaps the whole business would be out of the way. Even as it is, the back of it has been nearly broken. Their fleet scattered in alarm at my coming, commanders and men took to flight, and all the freighters without exception fell into our hands. I think I can at least say that I have prevented Dolabella from getting

979. i.e. tax-collecting.

to Italy and reinforcing his associates, so as to make your task the harder – which was my principal fear.

The contempt which the Rhodians have displayed for me and for the state you will see from my official dispatch. Actually I wrote in terms much less emphatic than their infatuation, as I found it, really warranted. That I *did* write something about them you must not be surprised. Their folly is extraordinary. My private injuries have at no time influenced me, but their hostility to our welfare, their partiality to the other side, their obstinate contempt for our leading men, were more than I could tolerate. Not that I regard the whole community as hopelessly depraved. But by a strange fatality the same individuals who formerly refused to admit my father in his flight, and L. Lentulus, Pompey, and other exalted personages likewise, now again either hold magistracies themselves or have the magistrates under their thumb. Accordingly they are behaving with the same arrogant perversity. It is not only desirable in our national interest, it is necessary that their evil disposition should at last be checked and not allowed to flourish with impunity.

As for my own standing, I hope you will always make it your concern, and lend your support to anything tending to my credit whenever you find occasion, both in the Senate and in other contexts. Since Asia has been assigned by decree to the Consuls with licence to appoint a deputy to govern the province pending their arrival, I would ask you to request them to confer this distinction upon me rather than another, and to appoint me as their deputy to govern Asia until one or other of them arrives. They have no cause to hurry out here during their term of office or to send an army. Dolabella is in Syria, and, as you with your prophetic instinct foresaw and publicly foretold, Cassius will crush him while these gentlemen are still on their way. Antioch shut its gates against him and gave him a rough reception when he tried an assault; so, having no other town he could rely on, he betook himself to Laodicea on the Syrian coast. There I trust he will soon be brought to book. He has nowhere to retreat, and he cannot hold out for long against an army the size of Cassius'. Indeed I trust that Dolabella has already been finally crushed.

Thus I do not expect Pansa and Hirtius to leave Rome and hurry to their provinces during their Consulship, but rather to serve their term of office in Rome. And so, if you ask them to put me in charge of Asia in the meantime, I imagine you can gain your point. Furthermore, Pansa and Hirtius promised me in person and wrote to me after I left, and Pansa confirmed to our friend Verrius that he would see that I was not relieved during their Consulship. As for myself, I do assure you that I don't want my tenure extended because I covet provincial office; it has brought me abundance of work, risk, and financial loss. I *am* much concerned that I shall not have undergone all this for nothing, nor be compelled to leave before I have reaped the remaining harvest of my efforts. Had I been able to send the whole of the money I raised, I should be asking to be relieved. As it is, I want to collect and make good the sums I gave Cassius and lost by Trebonius' death, also by Dolabella's ruthlessness or the bad faith of those who broke their word to me and to the state. This cannot be done unless I have time. I hope you will gain it for me, with your usual solicitude.

I conceive my public deserts to be such that I may legitimately expect not only the favour of this assignment but as much as Cassius and the two Bruti, in virtue both of my association in the great deed and danger[980] and of my current zeal and activity. After all, I was the first to break Antony's enactments, the first to bring Dolabella's cavalry over to the national cause and hand them over to Cassius, the first to levy troops for the defence of the whole community against a criminal conspiracy. I alone brought Syria and the armies there to Cassius' side; for

980. Lentulus was one of several who, though not party to the plot against Caesar, joined the assassins immediately and claimed to have been of their number.

if I had not so promptly furnished Cassius with money and troops on so considerable a scale, he would not even have ventured to go to Syria, and Dolabella would now constitute no less serious a threat to the commonwealth than Antony. And I, who have done all this, was Dolabella's familiar friend and companion, closely related by blood to the Antonii, to whose favour moreover I owed my provincial post. But, 'loving my country more', I took the lead in declaring war on all those near to me. Although I do not observe that my conduct has so far brought me any very notable return, I do not give up hope, nor shall I grow tired of persevering in zeal for liberty and in toil and danger as well. At the same time, if I am challenged to further effort by some just and well-merited distinction through the good offices of the Senate and leading loyalists, I shall carry more weight with others and my power to serve the state will be all the greater.

I was unable to see your son when I visited Brutus, because he had already left for winter quarters with the cavalry. But upon my word I am delighted both for your sake and his, and not least for my own, that he should be so well thought of. As a son of yours, and worthy of you, he is like a brother to me.

Goodbye.

Dispatched 29 May, at Perge.

406 (XII. 15)

LENTULUS SPINTHER THE YOUNGER TO THE MAGISTRATES, SENATE, AND PEOPLE

Perge, 29 May and 2 June 43

From P. Lentulus, son of Publius, Proquaestor *pro praetore*, to the Consuls, Praetors, Tribunes of the Plebs, Senate, and People and Plebs of Rome greetings.

I trust you and your children are well, as I am.

After Dolabella's criminal seizure of Asia I made my way to the adjacent province of Macedonia and the national forces under our illustrious fellow-citizen, M. Brutus. From there I worked for the restoration of your authority over the province of Asia and its revenues through the agency of those best able to achieve the same with speed. Dolabella took alarm at this prospect, and evacuated the province before troops could be brought against him, having laid it waste, seized the revenues, and ruthlessly stripped and sold the goods of all and sundry, especially Roman citizens. It appeared to me unnecessary to delay any longer or to wait for troops; and I considered it my duty to return to my post as soon as possible in order to levy the remaining taxes and collect the money I had deposited, also to discover as soon as possible how much of it had been carried off and by whose fault this had occurred, and to inform you of the whole transaction.

Meanwhile, as I was sailing through the islands to Asia, it was reported to me that Dolabella's fleet was in Lycia and that the Rhodians had a number of ships afloat equipped and ready. With a squadron consisting of the vessels which I had brought with me and those collected by Proquaestor Patiscus (an officer with whom I have close ties of political sentiment as well as of personal friendship) I changed course and made for Rhodes. In so doing I relied upon your authority and the Senate's decree pronouncing Dolabella a public enemy, as well as the treaty with Rhodes renewed in the Consulship of M. Marcellus and Servius Sulpicius, under which the people of that island bound themselves to regard as enemies the enemies of the Senate and People of Rome.

I was much deceived in my expectation. So far from our reinforcing our fleet with a Rhodian contingent, our troops were actually refused access to the town, the harbour, and the roadstead outside the town, as also supplies and even water. I myself gained admittance with difficulty, in one little boat on each occasion. I put up with this unseemly treatment and the derogation to the majesty, not merely of my official prerogative, but of the Empire and People of Rome, because an intercepted letter had apprised me that, if Dolabella gave up hope of Syria and Egypt (as he must), he was ready to embark with his entire band of ruffians and all his money, and make for Italy; for which purpose he had requisitioned freighters, none of less than 2,000 amphorae,[981] and kept them in Lycia under guard with his fleet.

Alarmed at such a prospect, Fathers Conscript, I preferred to swallow insults and try every means of prevention, even at the cost of my dignity. I was accordingly admitted into their town and Senate in the manner of their choice, and there I pleaded the national cause to the best of my ability, and gave a full exposition of the impending danger, should that bandit embark with all his following. But I found the Rhodians utterly wrong-headed, convinced that preponderance of force lay anywhere but with the honest men, refusing to believe that the present union and concert of all classes for the defence of freedom had come about spontaneously, confident that the apathy of the Senate and its supporters still continued and that nobody could have dared to pronounce Dolabella a public enemy. In short, they gave more credence to every rascally fabrication than to the true facts as presented by myself.

This attitude had been in evidence even before my arrival. After the shocking murder of Trebonius and all his other heinous crimes a couple of Rhodian delegations set out to meet Dolabella – contrary to precedent, moreover, and their own laws, and against the orders of the magistrates then in office. Whether their conduct is due to apprehensions for their possessions on the mainland, as they like to allege, or to mental aberration, or to the domination of a clique who similarly insulted exalted personages on a former occasion and hold the principal offices just at this time, the fact is that, without

981. About 52.4 tons.

precedent and with no provocation on my part, they have refused the assistance they might easily have rendered in my own immediate danger and in that which hung over Italy and Rome, should the traitor and his rebel following have sailed for Italy after his expulsion from Asia and Syria.

In some quarters the magistrates themselves were suspected of having deliberately detained us so as to give time for news of our approach to reach Dolabella's fleet. Some subsequent events lent colour to this suspicion, especially the fact that Dolabella's Legates, Sex. Marius and C. Titius, suddenly left the fleet and took flight from Lycia in a warship, abandoning the freighters which they had collected at no small expense of time and trouble. Accordingly, when I arrived in Lycia from Rhodes with the squadron I already had, I took over the freighters and returned them to their owners. My principal fear, that Dolabella and his ruffians might get to Italy, was thus at an end. I pursued the fleet in its flight as far as Side, which district forms the border of my province.

There I learned that part of Dolabella's ships had fled in various directions and the remainder made for Syria and Cyprus. After their dispersal, knowing that a very large naval force under the orders of our distinguished fellow-citizen and general, C. Cassius, would be to hand in Syria, I returned to my post. I shall take good care that my zeal and diligence shall be forthcoming in your service, Fathers Conscript, and the state's, and shall collect as large a sum as I can with all possible speed, and forward it to you with complete accounts. As soon as I have made a rapid tour of the province and found out who has kept faith with me and the state in preserving intact the funds I deposited, as well as the villains who went to Dolabella with the public money in their hands as an offering with which to buy their way into a partnership of crime, I shall apprise you accordingly. If of your good pleasure you take drastic measures with the latter as they have deserved and strengthen my position by your authority, it will be easier for me to levy the taxes still due and to keep safe those levied already. In the meanwhile, I have raised a necessary guard on a voluntary basis, thus enabling myself to look after the revenues with less trouble and to defend the province from any harm.

After this dispatch was written, about thirty soldiers recruited by Dolabella in Asia arrived in Pamphylia in flight from Syria. They reported as follows: Dolabella went to Antioch in Syria. Refused admittance, he made several attempts to enter by force, but was repulsed every time with heavy casualties. After losing about 600 men and abandoning his disabled, he fled from Antioch at night in the direction of Laodicea. Almost all his Asiatic troops deserted that night. About 800 of them returned to Antioch and surrendered to the officers left by Cassius in charge of the city, while the rest crossed the Amanus into Cilicia (they themselves claimed to be part of this body). Cassius and his entire force were reported to be four days' march from Laodicea when Dolabella was moving towards the place.

In the light of this news I am confident that the nefarious bandit will be brought to book sooner than was anticipated.

2 June, at Perge.

407 (x. 20)

CICERO TO PLANCUS

Rome, 29 May 43

From Cicero to Plancus.

Reports coming in from Gaul are so uncertain that what to write to you I cannot tell. Sometimes we get satisfactory accounts of Lepidus, sometimes the reverse. As for yourself, rumour speaks with one tongue to the effect that you can be neither tricked nor overcome. Fortune has some part in the latter; for the former your own prudence is alone responsible.

However, I have received a letter from your colleague dispatched on the Ides of May in which he says you have written to him that Lepidus is not letting Antony in. I shall be better assured of that if you write the same to me. Perhaps you do not much care to do so because the optimism of your earlier letter[982] turned out to be unfounded. My dear Plancus, you could make a mistake like everybody else; but anyone can see that you are not to be tricked. But *now* there can be no excuse even for a mistake. There's a common proverb scolding people who trip twice over the same stone. If, however, the fact is as you have written to your colleague, then all our worries are over; but they will not be until you have told us that it is so.

My view is, as I have often told you, that the man who crushes its remnants will be the winner of the entire war. I pray you are that man, and believe you will be. That you appreciate my efforts on your behalf (which certainly could not have been greater) as highly as I expected you would does not in the least surprise me, but makes me very happy. If all goes well in your quarter, you will find them greater and more effective.

29 May.

408 (x. 35)

LEPIDUS TO THE MAGISTRATES, SENATE, AND PEOPLE

Pons Argenteus, 30 May 43

M. Lepidus, twice Imperator, Pontifex Maximus, to the Praetors, Tribunes of the Plebs, Senate, and People and Plebs of Rome greetings.

982. Letter 390 (x.15).

I trust you and your children are well, as I am and my army.

I call Gods and men to witness, Fathers Conscript, how my heart and mind have ever been disposed towards the commonwealth, how in my eyes nothing has taken precedence of the general welfare and freedom. Of this I should shortly have given you proof, had not fortune wrested my decision out of my hands. My entire army, faithful to its inveterate tendency to conserve Roman lives and the general peace, has mutinied; and, truth to tell, has compelled me to champion the preservation in life and estate of so vast a number of Roman citizens.

Herein, Fathers Conscript, I beg and implore you to put private quarrels aside and to consult the supreme interests of the state. Do not treat the compassion shown by myself and my army in a conflict between fellow-countrymen as a crime. If you take account of the welfare and dignity of all, you will better consult your own interests and those of the state.

Dispatched 30 May from Pons Argenteus.

409 (x. 33)

POLLIO TO CICERO

Corduba, early June 43

From Pollio to Cicero best greetings.

I trust you are well, as I am and my army.

News of the battles at Mutina reached me later than it should thanks to Lepidus, who held up my couriers for nine days. To be sure, it is desirable to hear of so grievous a public calamity as late as may be; that is to say, for those who can do nothing to help or remedy. I only wish you and your colleagues had ordered me back to Italy in the same decree in which you summoned Plancus and Lepidus. Surely the state would not then have suffered this blow. Some may be rejoicing at the moment, because the leaders and veterans of Caesar's party appear to have perished, but they must needs be sorry ere long, when they contemplate the desolation of Italy. For the flower of our soldiers, present and to come, has perished, if there is any truth in the reports.

I did not fail to realize how useful I could have been to the state if I had joined Lepidus. I should have dispelled all his hesitation, especially with Plancus to help me. But when he wrote me letters of the kind you will read, similar no doubt to the speeches which he is said to have delivered at Narbo, I had to stroke him the right way if I wanted to get provisions on my way through his province. I was also afraid that if the decisive battle took place before I had completed my intention, detractors of mine might put the opposite construction on my patriotic purpose, because of my former friendship with Antony – though no closer than Plancus had with him.

Accordingly, in April I dispatched two couriers in two ships from Gades with letters to yourself, to the Consuls, and to Octavian, asking to be informed how I could best help the commonwealth. But according to my reckoning the ship left Gades on the same day that Pansa joined battle; for before that day there had been no navigation since last winter. Far removed as I certainly was from any suspicion of a coming civil upheaval, I had stationed my legions in winter quarters in the interior of Lusitania. And both sides were in such a hurry to come to grips, one might think their worst fear was of a settlement to the war without maximum loss to the commonwealth. However, if haste was called for, Hirtius evidently showed the highest qualities of generalship throughout.

According to letters and reports coming in to me from Lepidus' part of Gaul, Pansa's army has been cut to pieces, Pansa is dead of his wounds, the Martian Legion has been destroyed in the same battle together with L. Fabatus, C. Peducaeus, and D. Carfulenus. In Hirtius' battle I hear that the Fourth Legion and all Antony's legions alike have suffered severely, as also Hirtius', and that the Fourth was cut to pieces by the Fifth after capturing Antony's camp; that Hirtius too lost his life there, and Pontius Aquila; and that Octavian also is said to have fallen. If these reports are true, which heaven forfend, I am sorry indeed. I further hear that Antony has ignominiously abandoned the siege of Mutina, but that he has 5,000 horse and three well-armed legions under the standards and one under P. Bagiennus, along with a considerable number of unarmed men; that Ventidius too has joined him with the Seventh, Eighth, and Ninth Legions; that, if he has nothing to hope for from Lepidus, he will go to all lengths and stir up the native tribes, even the slaves; that Parma has been sacked; and that L. Antonius has occupied the Alps.

If these reports are true, then none of us must lose time or wait for what the Senate decrees. The nature of the case compels all who wish the survival of the empire, or even the very name, of the Roman People to rush to quench the devouring flames. I hear that Brutus[983] has seventeen cohorts and two legions of recruits, not up to strength, which Antony had raised; though I make no doubt that all the survivors of Hirtius' army will flock to join him. I see little hope in a levy, especially as the most dangerous thing of all would be to give Antony time to recover. The season of the year, moreover, gives me greater freedom of action because the grain is now in the fields or on the farms. So I shall explain my plans in my next letter. I do not wish to fail the commonwealth, nor to survive it. But what irks me most is that the distance to my whereabouts is so long and the route so unsafe that all news reaches me forty days, if not more, after it has happened.

983. i.e. D. Brutus.

410 (XI. 26)

D. BRUTUS TO CICERO

Camp in the Alps, 3 June 43

From D. Brutus to M. Cicero greetings.

Greatly as I am distressed by what has happened, I take some comfort in the general realization that my fears of it were not idle. Let them deliberate whether to bring over the legions from Africa and Sardinia or not, whether to summon Brutus or not, whether to give me pay for my troops or decree it! I am sending a dispatch to the Senate. Believe me unless all these steps are taken as I say, we shall all find ourselves in great danger. I beg of you, let the Senate be careful in choosing the men for the job of conducting the legions to me. Both loyalty and speed are needful.

3 June, from camp.

411 (XI. 21)

CICERO TO D. BRUTUS

Rome, 4 June 43

From M. Cicero to D. Brutus, Imperator, Consul-Elect, greetings.

Confound that Segulius,[984] the most arrant scoundrel alive or dead or yet to be! Do you really suppose that he talks only to you or to Caesar? He has told the same tale to every person he could find to listen to him. But I am properly grateful to you,

984. Cf. Letter 401 (XI.20).

my dear Brutus, for wanting me to know of this piece of tittle-tattle, such as it is – a notable mark of your affection.

As for this same Segulius' story that the veterans are grumbling because you and Caesar are not on the Commission of Ten, I only wish *I* was not on it! A most tiresome business! However, I did move that a vote should be taken on generals in command of armies, but was met by an outcry from the usual quarters. So you two were actually excluded specifically, against my strong opposition. Let us then pay no attention to Segulius. He's out for news and a new deal – not that he squandered his share (which was nil) in the old deal, but he *has* wolfed down what he got out of this latest new one![985]

You say that you have some fears on my account, feeling for me what you do not feel for yourself. Excellent and dearest Brutus, I hereby absolve you of all fear concerning me. As regards foreseeable dangers, I shall not be caught napping; and as for those which will not admit of precaution, I am not worrying so very much about them. After all, I should be presumptuous if I claimed more than can be granted to humanity by the nature of things.

You advise me to have a care lest fearing give me further cause for fear, a wise and friendly precept. But as you are generally admitted to be an outstanding example of the courage that is never frightened or discomposed, I should like you to believe that I am not far your inferior in this quality. Therefore I fear nothing and shall beware of everything. But you must take care, my dear Brutus, that the fault be not yours in future, if I should have any fears. Even if I were a timid man, I should cast all fear aside when I thought of your resources and your Consulship, especially as everyone (and I myself above all) is persuaded that you have a singular regard for me.

I emphatically agree with your advice in what you write about the four legions and the assignment of lands by the two

985. i.e. Segulius, a poor man before the Civil War, had profited from the Caesarian victory, but squandered his gains.

of you. For that reason, when certain of my colleagues were nibbling at the agrarian business, I thwarted it and reserved the whole matter for your two selves.

If anything of a secret and, as you say, 'recondite' nature arises, I shall send you a letter by one of my own people for more trustworthy delivery.

4 June.

412 (XI. 24)

CICERO TO D. BRUTUS

Rome, 6 June 43

From M. Cicero to D. Brutus, Imperator, Consul-Elect, greetings.

Take note: I used to be a trifle irritated by the brevity of your letters. Now I look upon myself as a chatterbox, so I shall follow your example. How much you have said in a few words![986] – that you are in good shape and trying to be in better every day, that Lepidus' sentiments are satisfactory, that we ought to place unlimited confidence in the three armies. Even if I were a timid man, this epistle of yours would have swept all apprehensions out of my mind; but, as you advise, I have taken the bit between my teeth. After all, I placed my entire hopes in you when you were a prisoner, so you can imagine my feelings now. I long to hand over my patrol to you, dear sir, but only if I can do so while remaining true to my own resolution.

You say you will stay in Italy until you hear from me, if the enemy allows. You will not be doing wrong, for there is much afoot in Rome. But if the war can be finished by your advent, let nothing come before that. You have been decreed the funds

986. In Letter 402 (XI.23).

most immediately available. Servius[987] is devoted to you. I am not behindhand.

6 June.

413 (XI. 14)

CICERO TO D. BRUTUS

Rome, 7 June 43

From M. Cicero to D. Brutus, Consul-Elect, greetings.

I am wholeheartedly delighted, my dear Brutus, that you approve of my views and proposals on the Commission of Ten and the honours for the young man.[988] And yet, what is the use? Believe me, Brutus, as one not given to self-depreciation, I am a spent force. The Senate was my right arm, and it has lost its cunning. Your splendid break-out from Mutina and Antony's flight with his army cut to pieces had brought such high hopes of assured victory that there was a universal slackening of energy, and those vehement harangues of mine look like so much shadow-boxing.

However, to come back to the business in hand, those who know the Martian and Fourth Legions say that they cannot be brought to join you on any terms.[989] The money you require *can* be looked to, and will be. As regards sending for Brutus and keeping Caesar to protect Italy, I entirely agree with you. But, as you say, you have your detractors – I withstand them very easily, but still they hold things up. The legions from Africa are expected.

987. Ser. Sulpicius Rufus, son of the Consul of 51. He was D. Brutus' cousin.

988. Octavian. D. Brutus' letter to which Cicero refers is lost.

989. They put themselves under Octavian.

But there is general amazement at the revival of the war in the north. Nothing was ever so unexpected. When the victory was announced on your birthday,[990] we looked to the re-establishment of freedom for centuries to come. Now these new alarms undo all that was done. You wrote to me in the letter you dispatched on the Ides of May that you had recently heard from Plancus that Lepidus is not harbouring Antony.[991] If that is so, all will be easier; if otherwise, we have a big job on our hands, but I am not afraid of the outcome. That is your part. I can do no more than I have done. But I am anxious to see you the greatest and most famous of us all, as I expect I shall.

414 (x. 23)

PLANCUS TO CICERO

Cularo, 6 June 43

From Plancus to Cicero.

Never, my dear Cicero, shall I regret the grave risks I am taking for my country's sake, provided that I am free of the reproach of rashness if anything happens to me. I should confess to a mistake due to imprudence if I had ever in my heart trusted Lepidus. After all, credulity is an error rather than a sin, and one which slides into an honourable mind with peculiar ease. But it was not through any such tendency that I was almost hoodwinked, for I knew Lepidus only too well. The truth is that sensitivity to criticism, a most dangerous proclivity in military operations, impelled me to take this chance. I was afraid that, if I stayed where I was, some detractor might think I was too obstinately holding a grudge against Lepidus, and

990. The date is uncertain, perhaps 26 April.
991. Cf. Letter 407 (x.20).

even that my inertia was responsible for the enlargement of the conflict.

Accordingly, I led my forces almost within sight of Lepidus and Antony, and took up a position at a distance of forty miles from which I could either make a rapid approach or a successful retreat. Further, I chose a position with a river to my front which would take time to cross, hard by the Vocontii, through whose territory I could count on a free and trustworthy passage. Lepidus made strenuous efforts to lure me on, but finally giving up hope of success he joined forces with Antony on 29 May, and they advanced against me on the same day. This intelligence reached me when they were twenty miles away. I took good care, under providence, to retreat rapidly, but without letting my departure look in any way like a flight, so that not a soldier nor a trooper nor an item of baggage was lost or intercepted by those red-hot rebels. So on 4 June I recrossed the Isara with my entire force and broke the bridge which I had constructed, so as to give people time to readjust while I myself effect a junction with my colleague. I am expecting him three days after the dispatch of this letter.

I shall always acknowledge the good faith and conspicuously patriotic spirit of our friend Laterensis. But his over-tenderness towards Lepidus undeniably made him less alert to perceive the dangers in which we stood. When he saw that he had been the victim of a deception, he tried to turn against himself the weapon which he might with greater justice have used to destroy Lepidus, but he was interrupted in the act. He is still alive, and is said to be likely to live.[992] However, I have no certain information on the latter score.

The traitors are deeply chagrined at my escape from their clutches. They came at me with the same fury that stirred them against their country, angry besides on several recent counts arising from these transactions: namely, that I had continually taken Lepidus to task and urged him to stamp out the war, that

992. He died.

I censured the talks that were going on, that I refused to allow envoys sent to me under safe conduct from Lepidus into my sight, that I arrested C. Catius Vestinus, Military Tribune, carrying a letter to me from Antony, and treated him as an enemy. It gives me some satisfaction to think that at any rate their disappointment will annoy them in proportion to the viciousness with which they attacked me.

For your part, my dear Cicero, continue as hitherto to furnish us here in the front line with vigilant and energetic support. Let Caesar come with the very dependable force under his command, or, if he is personally prevented for some reason, let his army be sent. He is himself perilously[993] involved. All the elements that were ever likely to appear in the camp of the desperados to fight against their country have now joined forces. Why should we not use every means we possess to save Rome? As for me, if you at home do not fail me, I need hardly say that I shall do my patriotic duty to the very uttermost.

Of yourself, my dear Cicero, I do assure you I grow fonder daily; and every day your good offices sharpen my anxiety not to forfeit one jot of your affection or esteem. I pray that I may be able in person to add by my devoted services to the pleasure you take in your benefactions.

6 June, from Cularo, on the border of the Allobrogian territory.

415 (X. 32)

POLLIO TO CICERO

Corduba, 8 June 43

From C. Asinius Pollio to Cicero.

My Quaestor Balbus has taken himself off from Gades, and

993. This can hardly refer to plots by Antony against Octavian's life. Plancus is merely pointing out incidentally that Octavian had a personal interest in doing everything possible to achieve victory.

after three days' hold-up off Calpe due to weather has crossed over into King Bogud's territory[994] with his pockets very nicely lined – a large sum in cash, a mass of gold, and a bigger mass of silver, all collected from the public revenues – without even giving the troops their pay. With the rumours that are coming in, I don't yet know whether he will be returning to Gades or going to Rome – he changes his plans on every new report in the most contemptible fashion.

The following exploits, on the model of C. Caesar as he himself boasts, are in addition to his pilferings and robberies and floggings of provincials: At the games which he gave at Gades he presented a gold ring[995] to an actor, one Herennius Gallus, on the last day of the show, and led him to a seat in the fourteen rows (that being the number he had assigned to the Knights). He extended his own term of office on the Board of Four.[996] He held elections, that is to say he returned his own nominees, for two years in two days. He brought back exiles, not those of recent years but agitators responsible for the massacre or expulsion of the Senate during Sex. Varus' Proconsulate.[997]

For other proceedings he could not even quote Caesar's precedent. He put on a play at the show about the journey he made to persuade Proconsul L. Lentulus to change sides,[998] and what is more, burst into tears during the performance at the poignant memory of his adventures. At the gladiators a Pompeian soldier called Fadius, who had been forced to join the troop, twice fought to a finish without pay. Being unwilling to bind himself over as a gladiator, he besought the people to protect him. Balbus had his Gaulish horse charge the crowd (some stones had been flung at him when Fadius was

994. Mauretania.

995. The badge of a Knight.

996. The governing magistrates of the town.

997. In 56 or 55. Nothing is known of this incident.

998. Shortly before the battle of Pharsalia the younger Balbus secretly entered Pompey's camp and talked to Lentulus Crus.

being hauled off), and then carried the man off to the Gladiator School, where he had him buried in the ground and burned alive. While this was going on, Balbus walked up and down after lunch barefoot, his tunic loose and his hands behind his back. The poor fellow kept crying out pitifully that he was a Roman citizen born. 'Off you go then!' said Balbus. 'Appeal to the People!'[999] He even threw Roman citizens to the wild beasts, among them a certain pedlar who went round auction-sales, a very well-known character in Hispalis – because he had a deformity! Such is the monster I have had to deal with!

More of him, however, when we meet. What is of greater importance at the moment, you gentlemen must decide what you want me to do. I have three reliable legions. One of them, the Twenty-Eighth, was summoned by Antony at the start of the war with a promise that the day they arrived in his camp he would give them 500 denarii per man; further, that when he had won, they should have the same bounties as his own legions – and these, as anyone may guess, would be absolutely unbounded. The men were much excited, and I give you my word I had a hard job of it to hold them in check. I should not have succeeded, if I had kept them together – certain cohorts mutinied individually. He has been continually inciting the other legions too with letters and unlimited promises. Lepidus has been no less insistent, urging me by letters (his own and Antony's) to send him the Thirtieth.

You must then consider this army, which I have refused to sell for any rewards or to reduce out of fear of the dangers held over my head in the event of these people winning the war, as kept and preserved for the commonwealth. On the evidence of my obedience to the orders you have actually given you must believe that I should have obeyed any I had received. I have kept this province free of disturbance and the army under my control, I have not stirred outside my province borders,

999. A Roman citizen had the right of appeal to the People against a sentence of death or flogging.

have dispatched not a single legionary or even auxiliary to any destination, and have punished any troopers I found leaving. For all of which I shall feel sufficiently recompensed if the commonwealth is saved. But had the commonwealth and the majority of the Senate known me better, they would have gained more from me.

I am sending you for your perusal a letter I wrote to Balbus when he was still in the province. If you want to read the play too, ask my friend Cornelius Gallus for it.

8 June, from Corduba.

416 (XII. 8)

CICERO TO CASSIUS

Rome, c. 9 June 43

From Cicero to Cassius greetings.

I expect you have learned from the gazette, which I am sure is sent to you regularly, of the criminal behaviour of your relative Lepidus, his egregious faithlessness and fickleness. After the war had been finished, as we thought, we find ourselves waging it afresh, and pin all our hopes on D. Brutus and Plancus, or, if you will have the truth, on you and M. Brutus – not only for immediate refuge, should some reverse unfortunately occur, but for the assurance of freedom in perpetuity.

Satisfactory reports concerning Dolabella are reaching us here, but without reliable authority. You are in grand repute, let me tell you, both on present estimate and in expectation of things to come. Set that thought before you, and strive on to the heights! There is nothing that the People of Rome does not judge you capable of achieving and maintaining.

Goodbye.

417 (XII. 30)

CICERO TO CORNIFICIUS

Rome, c. 9 June 43

From Cicero to Cornificius greetings.

So! Nobody brings you a letter of mine except people with lawsuits! Such letters, to be sure, you get in plenty - it is your own doing that nobody thinks himself recommended to you without a letter from me. But has there been a single occasion when one of your people told me of a bearer and I did not write? Now that I cannot talk to you face to face, what could I like better than writing to you or reading your letters? My trouble is rather that I have such a press of matters to keep me occupied that I am given no chance of writing to you at will, or I should be bombarding you with letters, or rather with pamphlets. *You* should be the challenger, for, busy as you are, you have more time to call your own than I - or if you too have none, don't have the effrontery to nag me and dun me for letters when you write so few yourself. Even earlier on I was under very heavy pressure of work, because I felt it my duty to give my whole mind to the national struggle, but at the present time the pressure is far greater. We are like relapsed invalids, who get much worse after an apparent recovery. Our troubles weigh heavier now that we have to set about fighting a resurrected war after the old one had been all but finished and done with.

Well, so much for that. Now please assure yourself, my dear Cornificius, that I am not so poor-spirited, not to say unfeeling, as to be capable of letting you outmatch me either in friendly services or in affection. Of your affection I had no doubts before, but thanks to Chaerippus I know it far better than I did. What a good fellow he is! I always liked him, but now I find him absolutely charming. Upon my word, he made me see your every look to the life, let alone conveying your mind and words. So don't be in any apprehension as to my feeling irritated at your sending me the same letter you sent to others. True, I should have liked a special letter to myself individually, but it was not a very strong reaction and it was an affectionate one.

As regards the expenses to which you say you are being put, and have already been put, for military purposes, I am afraid I cannot help you. The Senate is bereaved, both Consuls lost; and the Treasury is in terribly low water. Efforts are being made to raise money from all sources in order to discharge promises given to the soldiers who have deserved so well. I don't think it can be done without a special levy.

With regard to Attius Dionysius, I imagine there is nothing in it since Tratorius said nothing to me about it. As for P. Luccius, I won't allow that you are any more anxious to help him than I am – he is a friend of mine. But when I pressed the receivers for a postponement, they explained to my satisfaction that the arbitration agreement and their oath would not allow them to do it. So I think Luccius had better come over. To be sure, if he has paid attention to my letter, he should be in Rome by the time you read this.

You write on other points, especially money, which you thought you might be able to obtain from Pansa (not knowing of his death) through my mediation. Had he lived, you would not have been disappointed, for he had a high regard for you. But now that he is dead, I do not see what can be done.

As regards Venuleius, Latinus, and Horatius,[1000] I emphatically approve of your decision. On one point I am not too happy – you say that to spare these people's feelings you have also withdrawn lictors from your own Legates. Persons deserving respect ought not to have been put on a par with

1000. Apparently three Legates left in the province by the previous governor Calvisius Sabinus.

those deserving the opposite. And I think that if the latter do not leave the province in accordance with the Senate's decree, they should be compelled to do so.

The above more or less answers the letter which I have received in two copies. As for all else, please rest assured that my own public standing is not more precious to me than yours.

418 (XI. 13a)

D. BRUTUS AND PLANCUS TO THE MAGISTRATES, SENATE, AND PEOPLE

Cularo, c. 10 June 43

*** had come to hope, thinking Plancus' four legions no match for their total force and not believing that an army could be brought over from Italy at such speed. But so far the Allobroges and our entire cavalry, which had been sent there in advance, are holding them presumptiously enough, and we are confident that they can be held more easily when we arrive. All the same, even if by some chance they cross the Isara, we shall take very good care that they do the state no damage.

We would have you be of good courage and in the highest hopes for the national cause, seeing as you do that we and our armies stand shoulder to shoulder, notably united and ready for any sacrifice on your behalf. Even so, you should by no means relax your efforts, and should take care that in military force and all other respects we are as well equipped as possible to join battle in your defence against a criminal combination of enemies, who have suddenly turned to threaten their country with the forces which they have for long been assembling under cover of the public interest.

419 (XII. 13)

CASSIUS PARMENSIS TO CICERO

Crommyacris, 13 June 43

C. Cassius, Quaestor, to M. Cicero greetings.

I trust you are well, as I am.

I am rejoicing not only at the national salvation and victory, but at the renewal of your glory. You have excelled yourself; Rome's greatest Consular has surpassed her greatest Consul. My joy and admiration know no bounds. Surely a mysterious blessing of providence rests upon your valour, as we have often found; your gown is more fortunate than the arms of any other man – in which garb you have once again snatched our almost vanquished country from the hands of her enemies and restored her to us. So now we shall live as free men. I shall now have your testimony – the word of the greatest of Romans and to me (as you came to know in our country's darkest hours) the dearest – your testimony to my affection for yourself and for the commonwealth, with which you are identified. There are words concerning me which you often promised not to say while our bondage continued, but to pronounce when they should be to my benefit. For my part, I do not so much desire to have them now spoken aloud as to know that you feel them in your heart. I would rather myself be recommended to your good opinion according to my just deserts than be recommended by you to the good opinion of the world. I want you to set down my latest actions as no sudden or incongruous departure, but as conformable to the ideas which you are witness that I entertained; and to think me deserving of advancement to a fine prospect of service to my country and a prospect not negligible of service to you.

You have children,[1001] dear sir, and blood-relations who do you credit and of whom you are deservedly very fond. Next to them in your affections should stand those who emulate your patriotic ideals. I wish you to have many such, and yet I do not think I am shut out by a vast crowd. You will, I trust, find time to take my outstretched hand and advance me to such stations as you may wish and think proper. My spirit you have perhaps seen reason to approve. As for my talents, however humble, it can at least be claimed that the long years of servitude let them seem less than they really were.

Having launched all available ships from the coast of the province of Asia and the islands, and held a levy of rowers fairly quickly despite the stubbornly uncooperative attitude of the communes, I went in pursuit of Dolabella's fleet, which was under the command of L. Figulus. While often holding out hopes that he might change sides, he kept drawing away all the time until he finally betook himself to Corycus, where he blocked the harbour and shut himself inside. I left them there, because I thought it better to join the land army, and because another fleet, raised in Bithynia last year by Tillius Cimber, was sailing up behind me under the command of Quaestor Turullius. I therefore made for Cyprus, and have thought proper to write to Rome as soon as possible with information of what I learned there.

Like our treacherous allies the people of Tarsus, the Laodiceans, who are far more wrongheaded than they, have called in Dolabella of their own motion. From these two communes he has raised the semblance of an army with a quantity of native troops. He is encamped in front of the city of Laodicea, and has demolished part of the wall, thus joining camp and town. Our friend Cassius has pitched camp with ten legions, twenty auxiliary cohorts, and 4,000 horse about twenty miles away at Paltus. He reckons to win a bloodless victory, for the price of grain with Dolabella has gone up to twelve drachmae. Unless

1001. In fact only one, but the plural is often so used.

he brings in a supply in Laodicean ships, he must starve to death before long; and Cassius' very sizable fleet, commanded by Sextilius Rufus, and the three others which I myself, Turullius, and Patiscus have brought to join him, will have no trouble in preventing Dolabella from importing. So you may be of good cheer, confident that, following your example in Italy, we for our part shall soon succeed in solving the commonwealth's problems.

Goodbye.

Dispatched Ides of June, from Crommyacris, Cyprus.

420 (XI. 25)

CICERO TO D. BRUTUS

Rome, 18 June 43

From M. Cicero to D. Brutus greetings.

I have been waiting to hear from you every day. All of a sudden our friend Lupus has given me notice to write to you if I have anything I want to say. In point of fact I haven't – I know that the news of the day is sent to you, and perceive that empty chat in correspondence is not to your liking – but I did not want to write nothing at all. But I study to be brief, as your pupil.

Let me tell you then that all hopes rest on you and your colleague. Of Brutus there is no certain news as yet. As you recommend, I am continually urging him in private letters to join the common fight. I only wish he were here now. I should then be less apprehensive about the internal mischief in Rome, which is no light matter. But what am I doing? I am not copying your laconism – here is the second little page on its way! Victory and goodbye!

18 June.

421 (XII. 9)

CICERO TO CASSIUS

Rome, June (middle or end) 43

From Cicero to Cassius greetings.

The brevity of your letters makes me too write more briefly; and, to tell the truth, nothing very much occurs to me to write about. I am sure our news reaches you in the gazette, and of yours I know nothing. It is as though Asia were sealed off. Nothing gets through to us except rumours that Dolabella has been crushed – consistent enough, but so far unvouched for.

As for us, just when we thought the war was finished, we have suddenly been plunged into grave anxiety by your connection Lepidus. You must therefore realize that the state's best hope lies in you and your men. True, we have strong armies, but though all goes well, as I trust it may, it is highly important that you should come. The hope for a free constitution is meagre (I do not like to say non-existent), but, such as it is, it is bound up with the year of your Consulship.

Goodbye.

422 (XI. 15)

CICERO TO D. BRUTUS

Rome, late June 43

From M. Cicero to D. Brutus, Consul-Elect, greetings.

Although your letters give me great pleasure, your asking your colleague Plancus to write to me and make your excuses in the midst of your heavy preoccupations gave me more. He did so faithfully. I am deeply touched by your attention and thoughtfulness. The full and friendly co-operation between you and your colleague, as declared in your joint dispatch, has been warmly welcomed by the Senate and People of Rome.

As for the future – carry on, my dear Brutus, and try now to excel, not others, but yourself. I ought not to write any more, especially to you from whom I plan to take lessons in brevity. I eagerly await a letter from you – one such as I most pray for.

Goodbye.

423 (X. 22)

CICERO TO PLANCUS

Rome, late June 43

From Cicero to Plancus.

In you and your colleague lie all our hopes, with the favour of heaven. Your concert, declared to the Senate in your joint letters, has given the liveliest pleasure both to the Senate and the community at large.

As for what you wrote to me with reference to the agrarian matter,[1002] if the Senate had been consulted, it would have followed the proposer of the motion most complimentary to you – and no doubt he would have been none other than I myself. But the speeches dragged on and business was held up, so that the matters submitted to the House never came to an issue. Therefore your brother Plancus and I think it best to make do with the Senate's decree as it stands – who[1003] pre-

1002. The distribution of land to Plancus' troops. His letter on the subject has not survived.

1003. Perhaps Servilius Isauricus; cf. Letter 377 (X.12).

vented its being drafted as we desired, you will, I suppose, have learned from your brother's letter.

However, if you have any further desires in respect to the Senate's decree or any other matter, the attachment which all honest men feel for you is such (rest assured of it) that every conceivable distinction, of whatever type or eminence, is yours for the asking.

I eagerly await a letter from you – one such as I most pray for. Goodbye.

424 (X. 26)

CICERO TO FURNIUS

Rome, June (end) 43

M. Cicero to C. Furnius greetings.

When I read your letter in which you declared that the choice lay between giving up Narbonese Gaul and fighting a risky battle, I found the former alternative the more alarming. I am not sorry it has been avoided. You write of the good understanding between Plancus and Brutus; therein lies my greatest hope of victory. As for the loyal spirit of the Gauls, we shall know one day, as you say, who has done most to evoke it – but, take my word for it, we know already. And so the final passage in your most agreeable letter put me out of humour. You write that if the elections are put off till August, you will soon be here, and if they have already taken place, sooner still, since you have been a fool at the risk of your neck long enough.

Oh my dear Furnius, for one so adept in getting up other people's cases, how little you know of your own! Do you at this moment regard yourself as a candidate? Are you thinking of hurrying back for the elections, or staying in your own house if they have taken place already – so as not to be an idiot and risk your life into the bargain, as you put it? I do not believe that these are your true sentiments. I know all your impulses to glory. But if you really feel as you write, then I do not blame *you* so much as the opinion I formed of you. Will you allow precipitate impatience to gain an insignificant office (if you were to come by it in the ordinary way), vulgarized as it is,[1004] to draw you away from the shining honour with which all men are rightly and properly gilding your name? As though what signifies is whether you become Praetor this year or next, not that you should deserve so well of the state as to be judged most worthy of every distinction! Don't you know how high you have climbed or don't you think it of any consequence? If you don't know, I forgive you, the fault is ours. But if you do realize it, is any Praetorship sweeter to you than duty, the goal of the few, or glory, the goal of all mankind? I and Calvisius,[1005] a man of the soundest judgement with a great affection for you, scold you every day over this. However, since the elections are keeping you on tenterhooks, we are doing our utmost to stave them off till January, which we consider would be in the public interest for many reasons.

I wish you victory then, and goodbye.

425 (XII. 10)

CICERO TO CASSIUS

Rome, c. 1 July 43

From Cicero to Cassius greetings.

Lepidus, your relation[1006] and my friend, was declared a

1004. Caesar had increased the number of Praetors from eight to sixteen. The competition in 43 was keen, however (cf. Letter 435 (XI. 17)).

1005. Cf. n. 977.

1006. The wives of Lepidus and Cassius were sisters, half-sisters to M. Brutus.

public enemy by unanimous vote of the Senate on 30 June, as also those who defected from the commonwealth along with him. They have, however, been given until the Kalends of September to come to their senses. The Senate is in stout heart to be sure, but principally because they expect succour from you. At the time of writing we have a major war on our hands through Lepidus' criminality and fickleness.

Satisfactory reports come in every day about Dolabella, but still without known source or authority – just hearsay. Even so, your letter[1007] dispatched from camp on the Nones of May has produced a universal conviction in the community that he has already been crushed, and that you are on your way to Italy with your army, so that we shall rely upon your advice and prestige, if operations here have by then been satisfactorily concluded, or upon your army, if anything goes awry, as is apt to happen in war. As for that army, I shall give it every subvention I can. The time for that will arrive when it becomes clear to what extent this army will assist the national cause, or has already done so. Hitherto we hear only of enterprises – fine and splendid to be sure, but we are waiting for results; some I am confident have already materialized or soon will. Your vigour and generous courage are indeed admirable. We pray therefore to see you in Italy as soon as possible. We shall think we have a free constitution, if we have you two.

We had won a splendid victory, if Lepidus had not harboured Antony as he fled, stripped of his power and unarmed. Hence Lepidus is more hated in the community than ever Antony was; for whereas Antony stirred up war in a country that was already in turmoil, Lepidus has done so in time of peace and victory. Our Consuls-Elect stand against him, and we have great hopes of them, but suspense and anxiety too, since the results of a battle are never certain beforehand.

Believe then that all depends on you and your brother-in-law, that you are expected – Brutus indeed from day to day.

1007. Letter 387 (XII.12).

Even if, as I hope, you arrive after our enemies have been defeated, the commonwealth will rise again and settle down in some tolerable shape under your leadership. There are a great many evils that will call for remedy, even if the commonwealth shall come to seem pretty well emancipated from the villainies of its enemies.

Goodbye.

426 (x. 29)

CICERO TO APPIUS PULCHER MAJOR

Rome, 6 July 43

Cicero to Appius greetings.

Of my zeal for your welfare and restitution I believe your relatives' letters will have told you. I am sure that I have more than contented them; and signal as is their good-will towards you, I cannot admit that any one of them is more anxious for your welfare than I. *They* must grant that at the present time I have more power than themselves to serve you, as I have never ceased and shall continue to do, and have already done in a matter of the greatest consequence,[1008] thereby laying the foundations of your welfare. On your side, be of good cheer and courage, and be confident that you may count on me in all matters.

6 July.

1008. Just what this was cannot be determined.

427 (XI. 22)

CICERO TO D. BRUTUS

Rome, June or July 43

From M. Cicero to D. Brutus greetings.

I have the closest relations with Appius Claudius, son of Gaius, established by our many services to one another, rendered and received. May I particularly request you, whether for the sake of your own kindly nature or for my sake, to use your weighty public influence for his preservation? You are well known as a very brave man, and I want you to be considered a very merciful one. It will be a fine feather in your cap that a young man of the highest family should owe his civic existence to your kindness. His case ought to be improved by the fact that he joined Antony from a motive of filial affection on account of his father's restoration. So you will be able to put forward *some* excuse, even if you do not think it entirely convincing.

A nod from you can retain in the community a man of the highest birth, abilities, and character, one moreover with a strong sense of obligation and gratitude. Let me request you to do so in all possible earnestness and sincerity.

428 (X. 24)

PLANCUS TO CICERO

Camp in Gaul, 28 July 43

Plancus, Imperator, Consul-Elect, to Cicero greetings.

I cannot refrain from thanking you with respect to your

services in this matter or that, but I assure you I do so with a sense of shame. The intimate friendship which by your choice binds you and me does not seem to require expressions of gratitude. And it goes against the grain to acquit myself of your splendid benefactions with so cheap a commodity as words. I prefer to prove myself grateful in person by diligent and assiduous observance. If life is granted me, my devotion to you will transcend all gratitude of friends, all duteous observance of kin. For I should be hard put to it to say whether your affection and esteem will tend more to my lasting honour or to my pleasure from day to day.

You have been attending to my soldiers' interests. It was not for the sake of personal power (for I know that none but patriotic thoughts are in my mind) that I wished them to be provided for by the Senate, but, firstly, because I considered they deserved it; secondly, because I wished to strengthen their attachment to the commonwealth against all contingencies; and lastly, to enable me to guarantee you that their future behaviour will correspond to their past, proof against all solicitations from any quarter.

So far we have maintained the situation here entirely uncompromised. I trust that this course meets with approval from you and your fellows, although I know the general and understandable impatience for a victory so much to be prayed for. If these armies meet with a reverse, the state has no large reserves in readiness to withstand a sudden onslaught by those rebels and traitors. I think you know our forces. There are three veteran legions in my camp and one of recruits – a very fine one, the best of the lot.[1009] In Brutus' camp there is one veteran legion, one of two years' service, and eight of recruits. The combined army is therefore very strong numerically, but meagre from the standpoint of reliability. We have seen only too often how much reliance can be placed on raw troops in battle.

If the power of our armies were augmented by the veteran

1009. i.e. of the recently recruited legions.

African army or by Caesar's army, we should have no misgivings in staking the fate of the commonwealth on a decision. And we observe that in Caesar's case the distance is considerably less. I have continually urged him by letter, and he has never stopped affirming that he is coming without delay; but in the meanwhile I perceive that his mind has been diverted from that intention and shifted to other projects. However, I have sent our friend Furnius to him with a letter and an oral message in the hope that he may possibly be able to achieve something.

You are well aware, my dear Cicero, that so far as affection for Caesar is concerned you and I are partners. Even during the late Caesar's lifetime, as an intimate of his, I was bound to have a care and regard for the young man. So far as I could tell, his disposition was eminently moderate and gentle. By Caesar's decision and that of you all he has been given the place of Caesar's son, and I think it would be to my discredit, considering the conspicuously friendly relations between Caesar and myself, if I did not look upon him as such. At the same time (and whatever I write to you, believe me, is written more in sorrow than in any spirit of ill-will), the fact that Antony is alive today, that Lepidus is with him, that they have armies by no means contemptible, that their hopes and audacity run high – for all this they can thank Caesar. I will go no further back than the time when he himself professed to me to be coming: if he *had* chosen to come, the war would by now have been either quashed altogether or thrust back into Spain (a province thoroughly unfriendly to them) with heavy loss on their side. What he can be thinking of or whose advice has turned him away from so glorious a course, so necessary moreover and salutary to himself, and diverted him to this notion of a six-months' Consulship, which to the general consternation he is pushing with such tasteless persistence, is more than I can fathom. I imagine his connections can do a good deal in this matter, for the commonwealth's sake and his own; but you too, I think, can do most of all, since you have done more for him than for anyone in the world except myself – for I shall never forget the magnitude and number of my obligations to you. I have charged Furnius to go into these matters with him. If he pays as much attention to me as he ought, I shall have done *him* a great service.

Meanwhile we are bearing the brunt of the war in a situation of considerable difficulty. We do not see our way quite clear to a decisive engagement, and on the other hand we have no intention of risking further damage to the national cause by taking to our heels. If Caesar considers his own best interests, or if the African legions come up quickly, we shall free you from anxiety on this side.

Please maintain your regard for me, and be sure that I am thoroughly yours.

28 July, from camp.

429 (XII. 21)

CICERO TO CORNIFICIUS

Rome(?), 44–43

From Cicero to Cornificius.

My friend C. Anicius, a man of quality in every sense of the word, has been appointed to a Free Commissionership to Africa for purposes of private business. I shall be grateful if you will give him every assistance, and do all you can to facilitate the smooth transaction of his affairs. In particular (something he has very much at heart) I would ask you to look after his personal dignity, and to do for him what I myself used to do for all Senators in my province without being asked – I granted them lictors, having received the same privilege myself and knowing it had been commonly done by persons of the highest eminence. So please do this as a friend, my dear Cornificius, and have regard for his prestige and material interests in all other respects. I shall take it very kindly.

Take care of your health.

430 (XII. 24.3)

CICERO TO CORNIFICIUS

44 or 43

I should like to recommend to you in the strongest possible way a very good friend of mine, T. Pinarius. I have a very warm regard for him, both for his generally admirable character and because of the pursuits we have in common. He is acting as accountant and general agent for our friend Dionysius,[1010] for whom you have a considerable, and I a very special, affection. I ought not to recommend his affairs to *you*, but I do. So please see that Pinarius' letters (he is a very grateful sort of person) give me evidence of your interest both in him and in Dionysius.

431 (XII. 26)

CICERO TO CORNIFICIUS

Rome, spring of 43

From Cicero to Cornificius greetings.

Q. Turius, an honest and respectable gentleman who had business affairs in Africa, left as his heirs Cn. Saturninus, Sex. Aufidius, C. Anneus, Q. Considius Gallus, L. Servilius Pos-

1010. Cf. Letter 417 (XII.30).

tumus, and C. Rubellinus – men of his own stamp. From what they tell me I gather that an expression of thanks would be more to their purpose than a recommendation. They are so loud in praise of the handsome way you have treated them as to make it evident to me that you have done more for them than I should dare to ask. Dare, however, I shall, knowing how much weight my recommendation will carry. Let me therefore request of you that your generosity, shown in ample measure without any letter of mine, may be increased as substantially as possible by what I now write. The main point of my recommendation is that you should not allow Q. Turius' freedman, Turius Eros, to appropriate the estate, as he has done hitherto, and that in all other respects you regard the heirs as specially recommended by me. You may expect much gratification from the attentions of such distinguished persons. Let me again ask you very particularly to be good enough to act accordingly.

432 (XII. 27)

CICERO TO CORNIFICIUS

Rome, spring of 43

From Cicero to Cornificius greetings.

Sex. Aufidius is most attentive to me – my nearest intimates hardly more so – and there is no more distinguished member of the equestrian order. His personality is a singularly judicious blend of moral strictness and unselfish courtesy. Let me recommend to you his affairs in Africa in all earnestness and sincerity. I shall be deeply obliged if you make it apparent to him that my letter has carried great weight with you. My dear Cornificius, I ask this as a particular favour.

433 (XII. 29)

CICERO TO CORNIFICIUS

Rome, spring(?) of 43

From Cicero to Cornificius greetings.

To say nothing of yourself, who are thoroughly familiar with all that concerns me, I suppose there is no man in all Rome who is ignorant of my friendship with L. Lamia. It came before the public eye on a grand stage when he was banished from Rome by Consul A. Gabinius for his free and intrepid defence of my status as a citizen. That was not the origin of our affection; on the contrary, he was ready to face any risk on my behalf just because of its strength and long standing. Besides these acts of friendship, or rather these benefactions, a most agreeable intimacy exists between us, and Lamia's society really gives me as much pleasure as that of anyone in the world.

After all this you will not be waiting to see what terms I use in recommending him. Where such affection exists, you know what terms are appropriate, and you are to suppose that I have used them all. I would only ask you to believe that if you protect Lamia's interests and assist his agents, freedmen, and household as occasion may require, I shall be more beholden to you than if your generosity had to do with my own finances. Knowing what a good judge of men you are, I do not doubt that you would do your utmost for Lamia's own sake without any recommendation from me. To be sure, I have been told that you are under the impression that Lamia witnessed the drafting of a certain decree derogatory to yourself. In fact, he never on any occasion witnessed a drafting that year;[1011] further-

1011. Literally 'when they (i.e. Antony and Dolabella) were Consuls', i.e. from 15 March 44 to the end of the year.

more, all manner of forged decrees were registered at that time. You might as well suppose that I was present at the drafting of that decree about Sempronius,[1012] whereas in fact I was not even in Rome, as I wrote to you at the time just after the event.

But enough of that. Let me ask you again, my dear Cornificius, to look upon all Lamia's affairs as though they were mine, and to make sure that he realizes that this recommendation has been of the greatest service to him. You can do nothing to oblige me more.

Take care of your health.

434 (XI. 16)

CICERO TO D. BRUTUS

Rome, May or June 43

From M. Cicero to D. Brutus, Consul-Elect, greetings.

A great deal depends on *when* this letter is delivered to you – whether at a time when you have something on your mind or when you are quite free from anxiety. I have accordingly instructed the bearer to watch for the right moment to hand you his charge, for a letter delivered unseasonably often annoys us like an inopportune visitor. But if, as I hope, you have nothing to worry and distract you and my messenger chooses a sufficiently tactful and convenient time to make his approach, I am confident that the request I have to put to you will be readily granted.

L. Lamia is standing for the Praetorship. He is the most familiar friend I have. Our intimacy goes back a long way, and we have had a great deal to do with one another; but what counts most is that his friendship gives me as much pleasure as

1012. Cf. n. 896.

anything in life. Furthermore, I am indebted to him for a great kindness and service. In Clodius' time, when he was a leading member of the Order of Knights and took a most active part in the campaign for my restoration, he was banished from town by Consul Gabinius, something that had never previously happened to a Roman citizen in Rome. The people of Rome remembers this; for *me* not to remember it would be shameful indeed.

Therefore, my dear Brutus, I want you to believe that *I* am standing for the Praetorship. To be sure, Lamia is a most distinguished and influential figure, with a splendid aedilician show to his credit. But I have taken the whole business upon myself, as though none of that were in the case. Now you control the Centuries of Knights[1013] and reign supreme in them. If you think as much of me as I know you do, send to our friend Lupus and tell him to make certain of these Centuries for us. I shall not keep you with further words. Let me just put down in conclusion what I feel. Though I expect of you any and every service, there is nothing, dear sir, that you could do to please me more.

435 (XI. 17)

CICERO TO M. BRUTUS

Rome, May or June 43

From M. Cicero to M. Brutus[1014] greetings.

L. Lamia is my most intimate friend. He has rendered me

1013. i.e. 'Knights with public horse', consisting of young aristocrats and distinguished members of the *ordo equester*.

1014. The manuscripts say 'Decimus Brutus'; but this and the preceding letter could not have been written to the same person.

great services, I will not say as a friend but as a benefactor, and they are very well known to the People of Rome. Having fulfilled his duty as Aedile with a splendid show, he is standing for the Praetorship, and everyone is aware that he lacks neither public respect nor popularity. But the competition for the office seems to be becoming so unbridled that I fear anything may happen and feel I must take the whole business of Lamia's candidature upon myself.

How substantially you can help me in this matter I can easily perceive, nor do I doubt your good-will towards me. Please believe then, my dear Brutus, that I have nothing to ask of you with greater urgency, and that you can do nothing to please me more than if you assist Lamia in his candidature with all your power and zeal. And I earnestly request you so to do.

INTRODUCTION TO CICERO'S LETTERS TO HIS BROTHER QUINTUS

Marcus Cicero's only brother, Quintus, was about two years his junior. They grew up together, and when Marcus went on his eastern travels in 79 Quintus accompanied him. Some ten years later he married the sister of Marcus' closest friend, T. Pomponius Atticus. The marriage, which M. Cicero is said on good authority to have engineered, was a failure, although it lasted nearly a quarter of a century and produced a son. Pomponia was somewhat older than her husband and they made a cantankerous pair from the first.

Following in his elder brother's wake, Quintus embarked on a political career, although he had no taste for public speaking, and stood successfully for Quaestor, Aedile, and Praetor (the last during Marcus' Consulship in 63). In 61 he went out to the province of Asia as Proconsul, a post which he held for the exceptional period of three years. It says much for his integrity as a governor that he was genuinely annoyed when the Senate extended his term a second time. His return from Asia in 58 coincided with his brother's journey into exile. Back in Rome, Quintus was for some time anxious about a threatened prosecution for maladministration in his province, perhaps to be conducted by a nephew of P. Clodius. When nothing came of it, he was able to devote himself wholeheartedly to the campaign for Marcus' restoration. On one occasion his efforts nearly cost him his life, when he was left for dead on the scene of a riot.

After Marcus' return in 57, Quintus remained for nearly two more years in Italy, with a brief interval of overseas employment in 56, when Pompey stationed him in Sardinia to supervise grain supplies. In the spring of 54 he joined Caesar's staff in Gaul as Legate, where he distinguished himself by a heroic defence of his camp against a rebel tribe. Caesar congratulated him publicly and gives the episode handsome recognition in his *Commentaries*, qualified however by criticism of a subsequent piece of negligence on Quintus' part, which nearly led to a disaster. With his later career down to his death in the Proscriptions of 43 we are not here concerned.

Quintus shared his brother's and brother-in-law's interest in Hellenic culture and was himself a prolific versifier, whiling away inactive spells in Gaul by translating Sophocles' plays into Latin. Twenty uninspired hexameters about the signs of the zodiac, taken from an unknown poem, are attributed to him. We also have four short letters from him in the collection *ad Familiares* (44, 147, 351, 352) and a tract on electioneering couched in the form of a letter of advice to his brother on his consular candidature in 64, generally known as *Commentariolum Petitionis* ('A Short Memorandum on Standing for Office'). But the authenticity of this last is in serious doubt.

Down to the closing years of their lives the relationship between the brothers remained on the whole close and affectionate, though indications of friction and latent resentments on Quintus' part are not lacking. For details I must refer to my biography, from which I quote the following summary: 'The deplorable marriage, which Marcus Cicero had made and striven to keep in being for his own reasons, friction over Statius, disappointments in Gaul, untoward incidents in Cilicia, Quintus' strange passivity in the early months of the Civil War – all this and much more of which we are not informed may have gone to nourish an ulcer in Quintus' mind: the mind of a small man, irritable, querulous, and weak; a severe magistrate, who spoiled his son and let himself be run by a slave; a good man in a battle or a riot, but a rabbit in front of his wife; ambitious, but inhibited by a distrust of his talents, which were not of the first order, and handicapped by the unlucky accident of birth, which had made him a bigger man's younger brother.' The outcome was a prolonged and bitter quarrel during the

Civil War, which was never more than superficially patched up.[1]

The three 'Books' of Cicero's letters to Quintus may well have been published by Tiro, like the *Letters to Friends*. The first in the series is no ordinary letter but a tract, presumably meant for at least private circulation, which might have been entitled 'Advice to a Governor' and could be regarded as a *quid pro quo* for the *Commentariolum*, if the latter were certainly authentic. A second, genuinely private letter belongs to this period. Then come two letters from exile, followed by the remaining nineteen, which date from the end of 57 to the end of 54.

The text on which my translation is based that is of W. S. Watt (Oxford Classical Text series, 1958).[2] A few significant departures are mentioned in footnotes.

1. The orthodox view, at least until 1971, that the reconciliation between the brothers was genuine and complete cannot be entertained by anyone who has read the contemporary letters to Atticus with attention and without sentimental prejudice.

2. The occasional discrepancies that will be noted between this translation and my edition of the Latin text of these letters with commentary (Cambridge, 1980) are mostly due to second thoughts.

CICERO'S LETTERS TO HIS BROTHER QUINTUS

1 (I. 1)

CICERO TO HIS BROTHER

End of 60 or beginning of 59

From Marcus to his brother Quintus greetings.

I don't doubt that this letter will be outpaced by many messengers, indeed by Rumour herself with her well-known speed, and that you will hear from others beforehand that our loss and your labour[1] have been extended for a third year. Still, I thought it proper that this tiresome news should reach you from me as well as others. After all, in writing to you previously, not once but a number of times, I have held out to you the hope of an early homecoming after others had already despaired of it. That was not just to amuse you as long as possible with a pleasant notion but because the Praetors and I were both working so hard for it that I felt sure the thing could be done.

Well, unfortunately, neither the Praetors' influence nor my own zeal has had any success. It is hard not to feel irked. However, we have had too long a training in the conduct of great affairs and the bearing of great responsibilities to lose heart and strength in our vexation. And in one respect I should be taking it harder than you, since it is the misfortunes for which they are ourselves to blame that ought to distress people the most. It *was* my fault that, against your urgings before you set out and later by letter, you were not relieved the previous year. Thinking of the welfare of the provincials, opposing the effrontery of certain businessmen, and seeking to add to our prestige by your abilities, I acted unwisely, all the more so as I ran the risk of that second year entailing a third.

1. As Proconsul in Asia.

I acknowledge my error. Now it is for you, with your great good sense and your kind heart, to take good care to correct my lack of foresight by your pains. If you gird up your loins to the business of gaining approval all round and try to excel, not others, but yourself; if you urge your whole mind and concern and thought into one ambition – to do yourself the utmost credit in all things: then take my word for it, a single added year of work will bring us happiness for many years ahead and glory to those who come after us as well.

Well then, this is the first thing I ask of you: let there be no inner withdrawal or discouragement. Don't allow yourself to be submerged beneath the flood of a great responsibility. Stand up and face it, contend with business as it comes or even go out to meet it. Success in your sphere of public service is not in the hands of chance, it mainly depends on thought and application. If you were conducting some big, dangerous war and I saw your command extended, I should be alarmed, because I should realize that it also meant an extension of fortune's power over ourselves. But as matters stand, fortune has no part, or only a very small part, in the public responsibility which has been entrusted to you. It seems to me to lie wholly in your own ability and discretion. We do not, I think, have to fear a hostile ambuscade or a pitched battle or the desertion of allies or want of means to pay and feed our troops or a mutiny. Such things have happened time and time again to very wise men; they could not overcome fortune's onset any more than the best of seamen can master a violent storm. *Your* portion is perfect peace and calm; and yet if the helmsman falls asleep he could go to the bottom in such weather, while if he keeps wide awake he may actually enjoy it.

Your province consists of a native population the most highly civilized in the world and of Romans who are either tax-farmers, and thus very closely connected with us, or wealthy businessmen who think they owe the safety of their money to my Consulship. Ah, but they get into disputes among themselves, often do each other harm leading to mighty contentions. Well, I am not under the impression that you have no responsibilities at all! I do realize that you have a very great responsibility, calling for the highest qualities of judgement. But remember that in my opinion it is a good deal more a matter of judgement than of luck. After all, it is not too difficult to control the people under you if you control yourself. Self-control may be a great and difficult achievement for others, is so indeed, most difficult; but for you it has always been quite easy, and why not? You have a nature which would surely have tended to gentleness even without instruction; and instruction such as yours might lend some grace even to the most faulty of natures. In the future, as now, you will resist the temptations of money, pleasure, and every sort of appetite. Small fear then of your finding yourself unable to restrain a crooked businessman or an over-acquisitive tax-farmer! As for the Greeks, when they look at you leading the life you do, they will think you are a character from an ancient story or a divine being come down from heaven into the province.

I do not write all this to tell you how to behave, but to make you glad of your behaviour, past and present. It is a fine thing to have spent two[2] years in Asia in supreme authority without letting any of the commodities in which your province abounds draw you away from the strictest uprightness and integrity – neither statue nor painting nor cup nor fabric nor slave, neither beauty of person nor financial arrangement. And it is a rare and enviable piece of good fortune that your ability, discretion, and self-restraint are not hidden away in some dark corner but placed in the full light of Asia, for the most brilliant of provinces to see and for all peoples and nations to hear tell of: how no man is afraid of your progresses or put to crushing expense or disturbed by your arrival; how there is hearty rejoicing in public and private wherever you go, for you enter

2. 'Three' according to the manuscripts.

a city as a protector, not a tyrant, and a house as a guest, not a looter.

However, experience has doubtless taught you that in these matters it is not enough for you to have such virtues yourself; you must look carefully around you, so that as guardian of your province you are seen to take responsibility to the provincials, the Romans, and the commonwealth not only for your individual self but for all your subordinate officials. To be sure you have Legates who of their own volition will pay regard to your good name. Tubero is first among them in official rank, personal consequence, and age. I imagine that as a historian he can choose many a figure from his own chronicles whom he is wishful and able to imitate. Allienus is ours in spirit and good-will, and in the way he takes our lives as models for his own. As for Gratidius[3] what shall I say? I am sure that his brotherly affection for us will prompt concern for our reputation along with the concern he feels for his own. You have a Quaestor[4] whom you did not choose of your own judgement but acquired by the luck of the draw. It behoves him to exercise discretion of his own accord and to defer to your rules and advice. If it were by any chance the case that the moral standards of one or other of these gentlemen left something to be desired, you would put up with his disregard of regulations which apply to him as an individual, but not allow him to use for profit the authority which you confer upon him as appropriate to his rank. Now that our modern ways have leaned so far in the direction of excessive lenity and popularity-mongering, I would not really have you examine every dark patch and search their pockets man by man; better to assign to each one an amount of responsibility commensurate with the trust he inspires.

Very well, you will answer for the officers whom the state itself gives you as your companions and assistants within the

3. M. Gratidius, a relative of the Ciceros.

4. His name is unknown.

limits I have just laid down, and no further. What of those whom you have chosen to be with you as part of your household entourage or to do necessary jobs – members of the Governor's Staff, as they are usually called? In their case we have to answer not only for everything they do but for everything they say. However, the people with you are people of whom you can easily be fond if they behave well and whom you can even more easily check if they don't pay enough regard to your reputation. When you were new to the job, they could perhaps have taken advantage of your generous instincts – the better a man is, the harder he finds it to suspect rascality in others. Now a third year is opening; let it show the same integrity as the two that preceded it with an even greater measure of watchfulness and care. Let men think of your ears as hearing what they hear, not as receptacles for false, deceitful, profit-seeking whispers. Let your seal-ring be no mere instrument but like your own person, not the tool of other men's wills but the witness of your own. Let your orderly be what our forbears meant him to be. Except for some good reason they gave this function to none but their own freedmen, and that not as a favour but as a task and duty; and their authority over their freedmen differed little from their authority over their slaves. Let your lictor be the servant of *your* clemency, not of his own; let the rods and fasces bear before you insignia of rank rather than power. In a word let the whole province know that the lives, children, reputations, and property of all over whom you rule are most precious to you. Finally let it be believed that, if you get to know of a bribe, you will be the enemy of the giver as well as of the taker. Nor will anybody give a bribe once it becomes clear that as a rule nothing is obtained from you through the agency of people who pretend to have much influence with you. Mind you, what I have been saying does not mean that I want you to be over-austere or suspicious towards your entourage. If any of them in the course of two years has never given you cause to suspect him of money-grubbing, as I hear to be true of Caesius and Chaerippus and Labeo and so judge from my own knowledge of them, I should think it entirely proper to place unlimited trust and confidence in them and in anyone else of the same stamp. But if you find something wrong with a man or scent corruption, don't trust him an inch or put any part of your good name in his keeping.

If, however, you have met someone in the province itself, not previously acquainted with us, who has found his way into your closer intimacy, take care how far you trust him. I don't say that many residents in the provinces are not honest men; but this is something which it is allowable to hope but dangerous to decide. Each man's nature lies hidden under a mass of enveloping pretence, like veils stretched to cover it from sight. Countenance, eyes, expression very often lie, speech yet oftener. These people out of desire for money go without all those amenities from which we cannot bear to be parted.[5] Are you likely to find any man among them to love you, a stranger, sincerely, not just pretending it for his own advantage? That would be most extraordinary in my opinion, especially if these same persons love hardly anybody in a private station but are always fond of every governor. If you have come to know someone in this category as caring more for you than for your temporary position (it is not impossible), by all means write him down as your friend. But unless you see this clearly, there is no class of men with whom as intimates you should be more on your guard. They know all the paths that lead to money, everything they do is for money's sake, and they are not concerned to guard the reputation of someone who will not be with them indefinitely.

Furthermore, much caution is called for with respect to friendships which may arise with certain among the Greeks themselves, apart from the very few who may be worthy of the Greece of old. A great many of these people are false, unreliable,

5. The amenities of life in Italy.

and schooled in over-complaisance by long servitude. My advice is to admit them freely to your company in general and to form ties of friendship and hospitality with the most distinguished; but too close intimacies with them are neither respectable nor trustworthy. They do not dare to oppose our wishes and they are jealous not only of Romans but of their fellow-countrymen.

If I am for watchfulness and care in relationships as to which I fear I may actually be taking too austere a view, how do you think I feel about slaves? We ought to keep them firmly in hand wherever we are, but most especially in the provinces. A great deal can be said by way of advice upon this subject, but the shortest rule and the easiest to follow is this: let them conduct themselves on your journeyings in Asia as though you were travelling down the Appian Way, let them not suppose it makes any difference whether they have arrived in Tralles or in Formiae. If you have an outstandingly faithful slave, employ him in household and private concerns, but don't let him touch any that have to do with the duties of your office or with state business in any shape or form. For much that can safely be entrusted to faithful slaves ought not to be entrusted to them even so, in order to avoid talk and criticism.

Somehow or other as I write I have slipped into the role of mentor, which was not my original intention. Why should I give advice to someone whom I recognize as not inferior to myself in worldly wisdom, especially in this area, and my superior in experience? And yet I had the feeling that you yourself would find more pleasure in doing what you did if it were done on my authority. Well then, here are the foundations of your prestige: first, your own integrity and self-restraint, next a sense of propriety in all your companions, a very cautious and careful selectivity as regards close friendships with Roman residents and with Greeks, and the maintenance of strict household discipline. Such conduct would be creditable enough in our private, everyday lives, but with so wide an authority, amid such a falling-off in moral standards and in a province so rich in temptations, it must surely appear superhuman.

With these principles and this discipline you can safely practise in your decisions and judgements the severity which you have shown in certain matters, by which we have made ourselves some enemies – and very glad I am of it. For you are not to suppose that I pay attention to the grumblings of a fellow called Paconius (not a Greek even, but a Mysian, or rather Phrygian) or the talk of a crazy money-grubber like Tuscenius, whose unsavoury plums you most justly plucked from his disgusting jaws. These and other markedly strict decisions in your province could not easily be sustained against criticism without the highest integrity. So let your judicial rulings be of the strictest, provided that strictness be consistently maintained and never modified by partiality. And yet it is of no great importance that you yourself dispense justice consistently and conscientiously if those to whom you grant some share in this function do not do the like. As it seems to me, the administration of Asia presents no great variety of business; it all depends in the main on the dispensation of justice. The actual knowledge involved, especially in a province, is no problem, but there is need of consistency and firmness to resist even the suspicion of partiality.

Other requisites are readiness to listen, mildness of manner in delivering judgement, conscientiousness in arguing with suitors and answering their complaints. C. Octavius recently gained much public regard by these means.[6] The lictor in his court had nothing to do, the orderly held his tongue, every man spoke as often as he pleased and as long. Perhaps he might have seemed too indulgent, were it not that his indulgence supported his rigour. Sulla's men were obliged to restore what they had stolen by violence and terror. Magistrates who had given wrongful rulings were obliged as private persons to yield obedience conformably to the rules they had made themselves. His rigour

6. As Praetor in 61.

would have seemed harsh, had it not been qualified by a generous seasoning of kindliness.

If such mildness is appreciated in Rome, where people have so much arrogance, such unlimited freedom, such unbridled licence, where moreover there are so many magistrates, so many courts of appeal, where the plebs has so much power and the Senate so much authority, how popular cannot a governor's courtesy be in Asia, with all that multitude of Roman citizens, all those cities and communes, watching the nod of one man – no appeal, no protest, no popular assembly? Only a really great man, gentle by nature and cultivated by instruction and devotion to the highest pursuits, can so behave himself in a position of such power that those under his rule desire no other power than his. Such a one[7] was Cyrus as described by Xenophon,[8] not according to historical truth but as the pattern of a just ruler; in him the philosopher created a matchless blend of firmness and courtesy. With good reason our Roman Africanus[9] used to keep that book always in his hands. It overlooks no aspect of a conscientious and gentle ruler's duty. And if a monarch, who would never be in a private station, so practised these principles, how sedulously ought they to be observed by those to whom official power is granted only for a period, and granted by the laws to which they must eventually return!

I conceive that those who rule over others are bound to take the happiness of their subjects as their universal standard. That this *is* your leading consideration, and has been from the first moment you set foot in Asia, is notorious from consistent report and the talk of all and sundry. Attentiveness to the welfare and needs of those under him is the duty of any ruler, not only over provincials and Roman citizens but even over slaves and dumb animals. I find a universal consensus that you take

7. Supply *ut est* before *Cyrus* in the text.
8. In his *Education of Cyrus*.
9. The younger Scipio Africanus.

all possible pains in that regard. The communes, we are told, are contracting no new debts, and many have been relieved by you of a massive load of old obligations; you have restored a number of ruined and almost deserted cities, including Samos and Halicarnassus, one the most famous city of Ionia, the other of Caria; the towns are free of rioting and faction; you take good care that the government of the communes is in the hands of their leading citizens. Brigandage has been abolished in Mysia, homicides reduced in many areas, peace established throughout the province, banditry quelled not only on the highways and in the countryside but in greater quantity and on a larger scale in the towns and temples; calumny, that cruellest instrument of governors' greed, has been banished, no longer to threaten the reputations, property, and tranquillity of the rich; communal expenses and taxes are equitably borne by all who live within the communal boundaries. You yourself are very easy of access, ready to lend an ear to every grievance, and no man is so poor and forlorn but he is admitted to your house and bedchamber, to say nothing of the tribunal where you receive the public; your entire conduct as governor is free of all trace of harshness and cruelty, entirely pervaded by mercy, gentleness, and humanity.

And then what a boon you conferred on Asia in relieving her from the iniquitous, oppressive Aediles' Tax, thereby making us some powerful enemies. One noble personage is openly complaining that your edict forbidding the voting of public money for shows has picked his pocket of HS200,000. That gives an idea of the sum that would be involved if money were paid out for the benefit of everybody who gave shows in Rome, as had become the practice. However, I found a means of stifling our fellow-countrymen's grumblings on this point – I don't know about Asia, but in Rome my action has been greeted with no little surprise and commendation. I have declined money voted by the communes for a temple and memorial to myself. They had voted it enthusiastically in recognition of their great indebtedness to me and the signal benefits of your government; and the taking of money for a temple and memorial is specifically permitted by law. Moreover, the sum contributed would not have vanished into thin air, but would have remained in the form of temple ornaments, presented, as might well be thought, to the Roman People and the Immortal Gods quite as much as to me. This gift – honourable to myself, legally sanctioned, and made with the good-will of the givers – I thought proper to decline, in order, among other reasons, to mitigate the annoyance of those who had lost what nobody owed them and what they had no right to take.

Accordingly, let me urge you to put your whole mind and heart into continuing upon the lines you have followed hitherto; love those whom the Senate and People of Rome have committed to your charge and authority, protect them in every way, desire their fullest happiness. If the luck of the draw had sent you to govern savage, barbarous tribes in Africa or Spain or Gaul, you would still as a civilized man be bound to think of their interests and devote yourself to their needs and welfare. But we are governing a civilized race, in fact the race from which civilization is believed to have passed to others, and assuredly we ought to give its benefits above all to those from whom we have received it. Yes, I say it without shame, especially as my life and record leaves no opening for any suspicion of indolence or frivolity: everything that I have attained I owe to those pursuits and disciplines which have been handed down to us in the literature and teachings of Greece. Therefore, we may well be thought to owe a special duty to this people, over and above our common obligation to mankind; schooled by their precepts, we must wish to exhibit what we have learned before the eyes of our instructors.

The great Plato, a prince among thinkers and scholars, believed that polities would only be happy either when wise and learned men came to rule them or when rulers devoted all their energies to acquiring virtue and wisdom.[10] That is to say, he laid down that this combination of wisdom and power can bring welfare to communities. Perhaps there was a point in time when our state as a whole had such good fortune;[11] at any rate your province surely has it today, with supreme power vested in one who from boyhood has given the greater part of his time and energy to the acquisition of virtue and culture. So see that this year added to your toil may appear in the light of an extension granted for the salvation of Asia. She has been more fortunate in keeping you than we in bringing you home; then make the happiness of the province console our heartache. Nobody could have taken greater pains to deserve the distinctions which have been conferred upon you[12] in perhaps unprecedented measure, and you should take far greater pains to live up to them. I have already written to you what I feel about honours of this kind. I have always considered them worthless if showered indiscriminately, and trivial if conferred from interested motives. But if they were offered as a tribute to your deserts, as is indeed the case, I thought you should make a point of acting up to them. Since you are living with supreme authority and power in cities where you see your virtues consecrated and deified, you will remember in your every decision, ruling, and act what you owe to such honourable tokens of popular sentiment and esteem. That means you will take thought for all, find remedies for men's misfortunes, make provision for their welfare, aiming to be spoken of and thought of as the father of Asia.

Now there is one great obstacle to this your will and endeavour: the tax-farmers. If we oppose them, we shall alienate from ourselves and from the state a class to which we owe a great deal and which we have brought into alliance with the

10. This famous thought comes from Plato's *Republic* (345 D).

11. When Cicero was Consul!

12. By the provincials.

public interest. On the other hand, if we defer to them all along the line, we shall have to close our eyes to the utter undoing of the people for whose interests, as well as survival, it is our duty to care. If we look facts in the face, this is your only really difficult administrative problem. To have clean hands, to restrain all appetites, to keep your subordinates in order, to maintain an even dispensation of justice, to be willing to look into people's problems and listen to them and see them – all that is admirable rather than difficult. It is not a matter of work but of a certain disposition of mind and purpose. How much bitterness the tax-farmer question creates in the provinces has been illustrated for us by the attitude of some of our countrymen over the abolition of Italian customs. It was not the duty they complained of so much as certain maltreatments at the hands of customs officers. Having heard the complaints of Roman citizens in Italy I do not need to be told what happens to provincials at the ends of the earth. So to manage that you satisfy the tax-farmers, especially when they have made a poor bargain with the Treasury,[13] without letting the provincials go to ruin seems to call for judgement more than human – which is to say, it calls for yours.

Now to begin with, the most painful point to the Greeks is that they have to pay taxes at all. And yet they ought not to feel it so very painfully, since without any Roman Empire they were in just the same case under their own institutions, making their own arrangements. They ought not to turn away in disgust at the word 'tax-farmer', seeing that they proved unable to pay their taxes, as fairly allocated by Sulla, on their own without the tax-farmer's intervention. That Greeks in this capacity make no more easy-going collectors than Romans is well seen from the recent appeal to the Senate by the Caunians and all the islands assigned to Rhodes by Sulla, that they should in future pay their taxes to Rome instead of to Rhodes. And so I say that people who have always had to pay taxes ought not

13. As had actually happened; cf. *Letters to Atticus* 17 (I.17).5.

to shudder at the word 'tax-farmer', that such disgust comes ill from people who were unable to pay their tax by themselves, and that those who have what they asked for should not raise objections. Asia must also remember that if she were not in our empire she would have suffered every calamity that foreign war and strife at home can inflict. Since the empire cannot possibly be maintained without taxation, let her not grudge a part of her revenues in exchange for permanent peace and quiet. Now if they will only tolerate the actual existence and name of the tax-farmer with some degree of equanimity, your policy and wisdom will make all else seem easier to bear. In making their compacts they need not worry about the censorial contract, but rather look to the convenience of settling the business and freeing themselves of its annoyance. You yourself can help, as you have admirably done and are doing, by dwelling on the high status of the tax-farmers as a class and how much we[14] owe them, using your influence and moral authority to bring the two sides together without any show of magisterial power and constraint. You may ask it as a favour from people for whom you have done so much and who ought to refuse you nothing, that they be willing to stretch a point or two in order to let us preserve our friendly relations with the tax-farmers unimpaired.

No doubt these exhortations are superfluous. You can do all this yourself without advice from anybody, in fact to a great extent you have done it already. The most important and respectable companies are constantly expressing their gratitude to me, which I find the more agreeable because the Greeks do the same. It is no easy matter to create harmony where there is an opposition of interest and almost of nature.[15] However, I have not written the foregoing to instruct you (you know the world too well to require anyone's advice), but the writing gave me pleasure, the pleasure of dwelling upon your fine

14. Cicero and his brother.
15. I leave out the word *commodis*.

qualities. Though I must admit that this letter has turned out more lengthy than I expected or should have wished.

There is one point on which I shall continue to offer you advice. I shall never, so far as in me lies, let you be praised with a qualification. All who come from out there are loud in praise of your ability, integrity, and courtesy, but they make one reservation – your tendency to lose your temper. In everyday private life this is regarded as the fault of a weak, unstable mind; but nothing looks so ill as the combination of natural acerbity and supreme power. I won't take it upon myself here to expound to you what philosophers are apt to say on the subject of irascibility, for I don't want to take too long, and you can easily find it in many books. It is the proper function of a letter to inform one's correspondent of what he does not know, and that I think I ought not to leave undone.

Pretty well everyone tells us the same tale. They say that no man could be more agreeable than you when you are not out of temper, but that once irritated by some piece of rascality or perverseness you become so worked up that everybody wonders what has become of your gentlemanly self. Not so much by any appetite for glory as by accident of circumstance we have been led into a way of life which will make us a theme of talk for all time to come. So let us take care that, if we can possibly help it, they don't say 'He had one glaring fault.' I am not urging you to change your disposition and eradicate at one pull a deep-rooted habit. That is perhaps difficult to achieve in every nature and particularly at our time of life. I would only suggest, if you cannot avoid the failing altogether because anger seizes your mind before reason can look ahead to prevent it, that you prepare yourself in advance and make a daily resolve not to lose your temper and in moments of extreme exasperation to be particularly careful to restrain your tongue. To do this, I sometimes think, is as great a moral accomplishment as not to be angry at all. The latter is not exclusively a product of moral strength, it sometimes comes of a phlegmatic humour;

whereas to govern one's spirit and speech in anger, or even to hold one's tongue and keep the spiritual disturbance and passion under one's own control, though not the part of the perfect sage, does imply a mind beyond the ordinary.

However, reports are that you have become much milder and more amenable in this respect. We hear of no violent excitement on your part, no abuse or insults – behaviour far removed from literary culture and civilized manners and no less at odds with official authority and dignity. For implacable anger is the extreme of harshness, while appeasable anger is the extreme of levity; which, however, given the choice of evils, is to be preferred to harshness. Well, your first year produced a great deal of criticism in this regard, I imagine because you had not expected to meet with so much injustice, greed, and insolence and found it more than you could tolerate. The second year was a great improvement; habit, reason, and (as I suppose) my letters having made you more patient and gentle. The third year ought to be so impeccable that nobody will be able to find fault with the smallest detail.

And now I no longer exhort and advise, I beg you as a brother to set your whole mind, your entire thought and concern, on gathering universal praise from every quarter. If the talk and public blazoning of our achievements had not been exceptional, nothing extraordinary, nothing beyond the practice of other governors, would be demanded of you. As it is, the lustre and magnitude of the affairs which have engaged us are such that unless we gain the highest credit from your administration it looks as though we shall hardly be able to avoid bitter censure. Consider our situation: all the honest men wish us well, but also demand and expect of us the utmost in conscientiousness and ability; all the rascals, since we have declared unending war on them, will evidently want only the slightest excuse to censure us. Therefore, since so great a theatre has been given for your virtues to display themselves, the whole of Asia[16] no less, a theatre so crowded, so vast, so expertly critical, and with acoustic properties so powerful that cries and demonstrations echo as far as Rome, pray strive with all your might not only that you may appear worthy of what was achieved here[17] but that men may rate your performance above anything that has been seen out there. As chance has decreed, my public work in office has been done in Rome, yours in a province. If my part stands second to none, make yours surpass the rest. Also reflect that we are no longer working for glory hoped for in the future but fighting for what we have gained, and we are more bound to maintain this than we were to seek it.

If I had anything apart from you, I should want no more than this standing which I have already won. But the case is such that, unless all your acts and words out there match my record, I shall feel I have achieved nothing by those toils and hazards of mine, in all of which you took your part. More than any other you have helped me to gain so great a name; assuredly you will work harder than any other to let me keep it. You should not think only of the esteem and judgement of contemporaries but of posterity too; its judgement, to be sure, will be fairer, freed of detraction and malice. Finally, you ought to reflect that you are not seeking glory only for yourself, though even if you were you would not think lightly of it, especially as you have desired to immortalize your name by your splendid works.[18] But you must share that glory with me and hand it on to our children. If you make too light of it, you will run the risk of seeming to begrudge it to your family as well as of caring too little for yourself.

Now I do not wish it to appear as though my words were meant to wake a sleeper; rather, to spur a runner. As in the past,

16. Of course this refers, as elsewhere, to the Roman province so called.

17. By Cicero as Consul.

18. A compliment to Quintus' literary productions.

so to the end you will make all men praise your justice, temperance, strictness, and integrity. But my deep affection inspires me with an almost infinite appetite for your glory. However, after all, you should now know Asia as well as a man knows his own house; you now have a mass of experience to back your excellent judgement. I suppose then that there is nothing tending to credit which you do not best perceive and which does not enter your mind every day without anybody's prompting. But when I read your letters I seem to hear you talk, and when I write to you it is as though I were talking to you. That is why the longer your letters the better I like them, and why I myself often write rather lengthily.

This lastly I beg and urge of you: like good playwrights and hard-working actors, take your greatest pains in the final phase, the rounding off, of your appointed task. Let this third year of your term as governor be like the third act of a play – the most highly finished, best fitted-out of the three. This you will most easily accomplish if you imagine that I, whose single approval has always meant more to you than that of mankind at large, am ever with you, at your side in anything you say or do.

It only remains for me to beg you to pay particular attention to your health, if you value mine and that of all your folk.

2 (I. 2)

CICERO TO HIS BROTHER

Rome, between 25 October and 10 December 59

From Marcus to his brother Quintus greetings.

Statius arrived at my house on 25 October. I was sorry to see him come because you wrote that you would be plucked to pieces by your entourage while he was gone. On the other hand, I felt it just as well to have avoided the curiosity and crowding around there would have been if he came back with you without having made a previous appearance. The talk has exhausted itself. 'Methought to see a mighty man'[19] – such things have now been said a good many times. And I am glad to have got all that over in your absence.

It was not in the least necessary, however, for you to send him to clear himself to me. To begin with, I never suspected him. What I wrote to you about him did not represent my own opinion. But the success and security of all of us in public life rests not only on the truth but on common report, and that is why I have all along kept you informed of what others were saying, not what I myself was thinking. How much talk there was, and how strongly critical, Statius himself found out on his arrival here. He came along just when certain parties were complaining about him to me, and could see how unfriendly talk made his name its principal target.

What used to disturb me most when I heard that he had more to say with you than befitted the weight of your age, official authority, and worldly wisdom – how many people, do you suppose, have asked me to recommend them to Statius? How often do you suppose he himself in talking to me has innocently used phrases like 'I didn't approve of that,' 'I suggested . . . ,' 'I advised . . .,' 'I warned . . .'? Even if his loyalty in these matters is implicit (which of course I believe, since you are persuaded it is so), the look of the thing, a freedman or slave with so much influence, could not but be highly undignified. I should be wrong if I spoke without good grounds, and wrong if I kept diplomatically silent: please realize that all the grist to the mills of your would-be detractors has been furnished by Statius. Previously I only understood that some people might have been annoyed by your strictness, but after his manumission I saw that those who were had got something to talk about.

19. *Odyssey*, IX.513.

Let me now reply to the letters delivered to me by L. Caesius (I shall do all I can for him since I understand that you so wish). One of them concerns Zeuxis of Blaundus. You say that I have warmly recommended to you an individual who beyond a shadow of doubt murdered his mother. As to that, and to the whole topic, let me tell you one or two things, in case you are surprised that I have become so anxious to curry favour with Greeks. I found that the complaints of these people carried more weight than I liked because of their natural talent for deception; and so I tried in whatever way I could to appease whichever of them I heard complaining about you. First I smoothed down the group from Dionysopolis, who were extremely hostile, and made a friend of their leader, Hermippus, by talking to him and even associating with him on familiar terms. I have showered courtesies on Hephaestius of Apamea, on that little rogue Megaristus of Antandros, on Nicias of Smyrna, on the most arrant good-for-nothings, including Nympho of Colophon. All this I did not do because I have any taste for these specimens or for their whole tribe. On the contrary I am sick and tired of their fribbling, fawning ways and their minds always fixed on present advantage, never on the right thing to do.

But to return to Zeuxis: He was talking about his conversation with M. Cascellius, just the same points as in your letter. So I set myself to stop his gossip and took him into my familiar circle. I don't quite understand this ambition of yours – you write that having sewn up two Mysians in a sack[20] at Smyrna you wanted to show a similar example of your severity in the interior of the province, and for that reason to entice Zeuxis by any means available. Once brought to trial it would not perhaps have been right to let him go, but it was hardly necessary to have him searched for and wheedled into court with soft words, as you put it; particularly as his fellow-Blaundians and

20. The traditional punishment of parricides and matricides.

others give me to understand more and more every day that he is almost more distinguished than his town![21]

It is not as though I am nice only to Greeks. Didn't I try all I knew to propitiate L. Caecilius? What a fellow he is! What fire and fury! Is there anyone except Tuscenius, a hopeless case, whom I haven't mollified? And now down comes Catienus, a mercenary rogue to be sure, but with a Knight's qualification. He too shall be appeased. You bore pretty hard on his father, which I do not criticize – I am sure you had your reasons. But where was the need to write a letter such as you sent Catienus himself: 'that he was building his own gallows, from which you had once before taken him down; you would see to it that he is burned alive to the applause of the whole province'? Why did you have to write to C. Fabius, whoever he may be (that's another letter which T. Catienus is toting around), that 'it was reported to you that taxes were being collected by yon kidnapping villain Licinius and his young sparrowhawk of a son'? You proceed to ask Fabius to burn both father and son alive if he can; if not, he is to send them to you so that they can be burnt up in court. You sent the letter to Fabius as a joke (if you really wrote it), but when folk read it the ferocity of the wording raises a prejudice against you.

If you will recall the advice I have given you in all my letters, you will see that my only criticism has been on the score of harsh language, irritability, and perhaps now and then a lack of care in your official letters. If my counsel had counted more with you in these respects than – shall we say your somewhat hasty temper, or a certain pleasure you take in letting fly, or your gift for pungent and witty expression, we should really have had nothing to regret. You must appreciate the pain I feel when I am told how highly people think of Vergilius and of your neighbour C. Octavius[22] (as for your neighbours on the

21. I understand this to mean that Zeuxis was too insignificant to be worth so much trouble.

22. Governors of Sicily and Macedonia respectively.

other side in Cilicia and Syria,[23] you are not claiming much if you compare yourself favourably with them!). And the distressing thing is that your hands are just as clean as theirs. They put you into the shade by their technique of gaining good-will. And yet they know nothing of Xenophon's Cyrus nor yet his Agesilaus. Nobody ever heard a harsh word from either monarch, autocrats though they were.

Well, I have been telling you all this from the beginning and I am well aware how much good it has done. All the same, in quitting the province, as I understand you are now in process of doing, do leave behind you as pleasant a memory as possible. Your successor[24] is a man of very agreeable manners. Other qualities which you possess will be very much to seek when he arrives. In sending out official letters (I have often written to you about this) you have been too ready to accommodate. Destroy, if you can, any that are inequitable or contrary to usage or contradictory. Statius has told me that they used to be brought to you already drafted, and that he would read them and inform you if they were inequitable, but that before he joined you letters were dispatched indiscriminately. And so, he said, there are collections of selected letters and these are adversely criticized. I am not going to warn you about this now. It is too late for that, and you are in a position to know how many warnings I have given on various occasions and with no lack of particularity. But as I asked Theopompus to tell you at his own suggestion, do see to it through friendly agents (it is easy enough) that the following categories are destroyed: first, inequitable letters; second, contradictory letters; third, letters drafted inappropriately or contrary to accepted usage; and finally, letters insulting to any person. I don't believe all I am told; and if there has been some negligence due to pressure of business, look into it now and set it right. I have read an im-

23. The governor of Syria was Cn. Cornelius Lentulus Marcellinus, Consul in 56. The governor of Cilicia is unknown.

24. T. Ampius Balbus.

proper letter which your nomenclator Sulla is said to have written himself and I have read some angry ones.

The subject of letters is à propos. As I was on this page, Praetor-Elect L. Flavius, a close friend of mine, came to see me. He told me that you had written a letter to his agents which appeared to me quite inequitable, directing them not to touch the estate of L. Octavius Naso, who left Flavius as his heir, until they had paid a sum of money to C. Fundanius; also that you had written directions to the town of Apollonis not to allow Octavius' estate to be touched until Fundanius' debt was paid. This all sounds improbable to me; it is so completely foreign to your usual good judgement. Must the heir not touch the estate? Suppose he denies the debt? Suppose there *is* no debt? Is it usual for a governor to rule that a debt exists? And am *I* not Fundanius' friend and well-wisher, am I not sorry for him? Nobody more. But in some matters the path of justice is not wide enough for favour. Flavius further told me that the letter which he alleged came from you contained a promise 'either to thank them as friends or to make things uncomfortable for them as enemies'. In short, he was much put out and expostulated with me strongly, asking me to write to you most particularly. That I am doing, and I ask you again most earnestly to countermand your order to Flavius' agents about touching the estate, and not to give any further directions to Apollonis against Flavius' interests. I am sure you will do all you can both for Flavius' sake and, no doubt, for Pompey's. Upon my word, I don't wish to appear as obliging Flavius in consequence of your unfairness. On the contrary, I beg you yourself to leave behind you an official declaration in writing in the form of a ruling or a letter which will help Flavius' interests and case. Being most attentive to me and careful of his own rights and dignity, he is greatly put out to find that neither friendship nor justice have counted with you in his favour. I believe that both Pompey and Caesar at some time or other recommended Flavius' interests to you; Flavius himself had written to you, and certainly I did so. So if there is anything you would think proper to do at my request, let this be it. If you love me, spare no pains to ensure that Flavius thanks both you and me as heartily as may be. I could not ask anything of you more urgently.

What you write about Hermia has really vexed me a lot. I had written you a not very brotherly letter – I was annoyed by what Lucullus' freedman Diodotus said, and wrote in some irritation immediately after hearing about the agreement.[25] I wanted to recall it. This unbrotherly letter you must like a good brother forgive.

As for Censorinus, Antonius, the Cassii, and Scaevola, I am very pleased to hear that they are so friendly to you.[26] The remainder of your letter took a graver tone than I could have wished: 'I'll go down with my flag flying',[27] and 'better die once'![28] That is surely overdoing it. My scoldings were full of affection. There *are* some things that I complained of,[29] but of no vast consequence, quite small in fact. Behaving as uprightly as you do, I should never have thought you deserving of the slightest criticism if we did not have many enemies. What I wrote to you in a somewhat warning or reproving strain was written out of the care I take to be always on guard. That I maintain and shall, and I shall continue to ask you to do the same.

Attalus of Hypaepa has been talking to me. He wants you not to stand in the way of his arranging payment of the money decreed for a statue of Q. Publicius. I request accordingly, and

25. The circumstances are unknown.

26. How these young noblemen had shown their friendly feelings is uncertain.

27. Partial quotation of a Greek proverb which means literally: 'Know ye, Poseidon, that the ship when I sink her shall be on an even keel.'

28. From Aeschylus, *Prometheus Bound* (750): 'Better die once for all than be miserable all one's days.'

29. Reading *erant* for *erunt* and *quae ⟨questus sum⟩ sunt nonnulla.*

would advise you not to wish to be responsible for whittling down or obstructing an honour to so worthy a man and so good a friend of ours. Furthermore, a slave called Licinus (you know him) belonging to our friend Aesopus has run away. He was in Athens with Patro the Epicurean posing as a free man, and passed from there to Asia. Later, one Plato of Sardis, an Epicurean, who is a good deal in Athens and was there when Licinus arrived, having later learned that he is a runaway, arrested him and gave him into custody in Ephesus; but from his letter we are not sure whether the fellow was put into gaol or into the mill. However that may be, he is in Ephesus, so will you please search for him and take good care either to send him to Rome or to bring him with you? Don't consider what he's worth – such a good-for-nothing can't be worth much. But Aesopus is so distressed by the slave's criminal audacity that you can do him no greater favour than by getting him back his property.

Now let me tell you what you are most eager to know. Our free constitution is a total loss, so much so that C. Cato, a young harum-scarum but a Roman citizen and a Cato, had a narrow escape with his life when he addressed a public meeting and called Pompey 'our unofficial Dictator' – he wanted to charge Gabinius with bribery and for several days the Praetors would not let themselves be approached or give him a hearing. It was really touch and go with him. You can see from this what the state of the whole commonwealth is like.

As for my own prospects, however, I do not think I shall lack general support. It is amazing how people are coming forward with declarations and offers and promises. For my own part, I am in good hope and even better courage – hope, because I am confident I shall win; courage, because in the present state of the commonwealth I am not afraid of anything, even an accident. Anyway, this is how things stand: If Clodius takes me to court, all Italy will rally and I shall come out of it with much additional *kudos*; if he tries force, I trust to oppose him with force, supported not only by my friends but by outsiders as well. Everyone is pledging himself and his friends, dependants, freedmen, slaves, even money. My old band of honest men is passionately enthusiastic and loyal. Those who were formerly not so well disposed or not so energetic are now joining the honest men out of disgust with our present tyrants. Pompey is lavish with promises, and so is Caesar. If I take their word, I do not on that account relax my preparations in the slightest. The Tribunes-Elect are my good friends. The Consuls[30] show every sign of good-will. Among the Praetors I can count on Domitius, Nigidius, Memmius, and Lentulus[31] as warm friends and vigorous patriots – others too are well enough, but these are outstanding. Courage then and good cheer! On particulars, I shall send you frequent news of what goes on from day to day.

3 (I. 3)

CICERO TO HIS BROTHER

Thessalonica, 13 June 58

From Marcus to his brother Quintus greetings.

My brother, my brother, my brother! Were you really afraid that I was angry with you for some reason and on that account sent boys to you without a letter, or even did not want to see you?[32] *I* angry with *you?* How *could* I be? As though it was *you* who struck me down, *your* enemies, *your* unpopularity, and not *I* who have lamentably caused *your* downfall! That much-lauded Consulship of mine has robbed me of you, and my children, and my country, and my possessions; I only hope it has robbed you of nothing but myself. Sure it is that you have

30. i.e. Consuls-Elect, L. Calpurnius Piso and A. Gabinius.
31. L. Cornelius Lentulus Crus. Praetors=Praetors-Elect.
32. Cf. *Letters to Atticus* 54 (III.9).1.

never given me cause for anything but pride and pleasure, whereas I have brought you sorrow for my calamity, fear of your own, loss, grief, loneliness. *I* not want to see *you?* No, it was rather that I did not want to be seen by you! You would not have seen your brother, the man you left in Rome, the man you knew, the man who saw you off and said goodbye with mutual tears – you would not have seen any trace or shadow of *him*; only a likeness of a breathing corpse.

Would that you had seen me or heard of me dead before this happened! Would that I had left you as the survivor not of my life only but of my standing! But I call all the Gods to witness that one saying called me back from death – everyone told me that some part of your life was bound up in mine. I was wrong, criminally wrong. If I had died, the fact itself would stand as ample proof of my brotherly love for you. Instead, through my fault you have to do without me and stand in need of others while I am alive, and my voice, which has often defended strangers, is silent when my own flesh and blood is in danger.[33]

As for the fact that my boys came to you without a letter, since you see that anger was not the reason, the reason was surely inertia and an endless stream of tears and grieving. You can imagine how I weep as I write these lines, as I am sure you do as you read them. Can I help thinking of you sometimes, or ever think of you without tears? When I miss you, I do not miss you as a brother only, but as a delightful brother almost of my own age,[34] a son in obedience, a father in wisdom. What pleasure did I ever take apart from you or you apart from me? And then at the same time I miss my daughter, the most loving, modest, and clever daughter a man ever had, the image of my face and speech and mind. Likewise my charming, darling little boy, whom I, cruel brute that I am, put away from my arms. Too wise for his years, the poor child already understood what was going on.

33. Quintus had reason to fear that a charge might be brought against him in connection with his record as governor of Asia.

34. Text doubtful.

Likewise your son, your[35] image, whom my boy loved like a brother and had begun to respect like an elder brother. As for my loyalest of wives, poor, unhappy soul, I did not let her come with me so that there should be someone to protect the remnants of our common disaster, our children.

However, I did write to you as best I could and gave the letter to your freedman Philogonus. I expect it was delivered to you later. In it I urge and ask of you, as in the verbal message brought you by my boys, to go straight on to Rome and make haste. To begin with, I wanted you to stand guard in case there may be enemies whose cruelty is not yet satisfied by our downfall. Secondly, I was afraid of the outburst of grief which our meeting would have brought on. As for parting, I could not have borne it, and I feared the very thing you say in your letter, that you might not endure to be separated from me. For these reasons the heavy affliction of not seeing you, which seems the bitterest, saddest thing that could happen to brothers so affectionate and close as we are, was less bitter and sad than our meeting would have been, and still more our parting.

Now if you can do what I, whom you always thought a strong man, am unable to do, then stand up and brace yourself for the struggle you may have to sustain. I should hope (if any hope of mine counts for anything) that your integrity, the affection in which you are held in the community, and in some degree also the pity felt for myself will bring you protection. If, however, it turns out that your hands are free of that danger, you will doubtless do what you think can be done, if anything, about me. I get many letters from many people on the subject and they make themselves out to be hopeful. But for my own part I can't see any grounds for hope, when my enemies are in power and my friends have either deserted or actually betrayed me. Perhaps the idea of my coming home frightens them as involving blame for their own villainy. But please see how things

35. Reading *tuam* ('your') for *meam* ('my') of the manuscripts.

stand in Rome and make them clear to me. In spite of all, I shall go on living as long as you need me, if you have to go through an ordeal. Live any longer in this kind of life I cannot. No worldly wisdom or philosophic instruction is strong enough to endure such anguish. I know I had the opportunity to die a more honourable and useful death, but that is only one of many chances I let slip. If I were to bewail past mistakes, I should only be adding to your sorrow and exposing my own folly. One thing I ought not and cannot do, and that is to linger on in so miserable and dishonourable an existence any longer than your predicament or a well-grounded hope shall demand. Once I was happy indeed, in my brother, children, wife, means, even in the very nature of my wealth,[36] the equal of any man that ever lived in prestige, moral standing, reputation, influence. Now in my abject ruin I cannot bear to mourn myself and mine much longer.

Why then did you write to me about a bill of exchange?[37] As though your resources were not supporting me at present. Ah, how well I see and feel what a wicked thing I did! You are about to pay your creditors with your heart's blood and your son's, while I squandered to no purpose the money which I received from the Treasury on your behalf.[38] However, both M. Antonius and Caepio[39] were paid the sums you had mentioned. As for me, what I have is enough for my present purposes. Whether I am restored or given up for lost, no more is needed.

If you have any trouble, I advise you to go to Crassus and Calidius. How much faith you should put in Hortensius I don't know. He behaved to *me* most villainously and treacherously, while pretending the warmest affection and sedulously keeping

36. Apart from his inherited fortune this was mainly derived from legacies left by grateful clients.

37. Quintus will have offered to negotiate a bill in Rome, the money to be paid to his brother in Thessalonica.

38. Cf. *Letters to Atticus* 26 (II.6).2.

39. Better known as M. Brutus.

up our daily intercourse. Q. Arrius joined him in this. Through their policies and promises and advice I was left in the lurch and fell into my present plight. But you will keep all this under cover, lest it tell against you. Be careful of one thing (and for that reason I think you should conciliate Hortensius himself through Pomponius): that epigram about the lex Aurelia which was attributed to you when you were standing for the Aedileship,[40] mind it doesn't get established by false evidence.[41] My principal fear is that when people realize how much pity your entreaties and your escape from a prosecution is going to arouse for us, they will attack you the more vigorously. I think Messalla[42] is on your side. Pompey, I think, is still pretending. If only you don't have to put all this to the test! I should pray to the Gods for that if they had not given up listening to my prayers. None the less, I do pray that they may be content with these boundless afflictions of ours, which, however, are free from any stigma of wrong-doing. The whole tragedy is that fine actions have been cruelly penalized.

My brother, I need not commend my daughter (and yours) and our Marcus to your care. On the contrary, I grieve to think that their orphaned state will bring you no less sorrow than me. But while you are safe, they will not be orphans. I swear that tears forbid me to write of other things – so may I be granted some salvation and the power to die in my country! Please look after Terentia too, and write back to me on all matters. Be as brave as the nature of the case permits.

Ides of June, Thessalonica.

40. In 66.

41. It can be supposed that the epigram was offensive to Pompey and Crassus, since the lex Aurelia of 70, revising the Roman jury system, was passed in their Consulship with their support. Cicero seems to have feared that Hortensius might confirm its attribution to Quintus out of spite. As an opponent of the law he would be a credible witness.

42. The Consul of 61, as generally supposed. Perhaps more probably Hortensius' nephew Messalla Rufus, Consul in 53.

4 (I. 4)

CICERO TO HIS BROTHER

Thessalonica, c. 5 August 58

From Marcus to his brother Quintus greetings.

Dear brother, if a single act of mine has brought you and all my family low, I beg you not to attribute this to wickedness and evil-doing on my part but rather to imprudence and ill-fortune. My only fault lay in trusting men in whom I thought it would be an abomination to deceive me or even imagined that it was not in their interest to do so. My closest, most intimate, most familiar friends were either afraid for themselves or jealous of me. So I lacked nothing, unfortunate that I was, except good faith on my friends' part and good judgement on my own.

If your own innocence and public compassion prove sufficient to protect you from annoyance at this time, you doubtless perceive whether any hope of deliverance is left for me. Pomponius, Sestius, and our Piso have kept me in Thessalonica so far, telling me not to move further away on account of certain developments. But it is because of their letters rather than from any definite hope that I am waiting for the outcome. What am I to hope for, with my enemy[43] wielding great power, my detractors ruling the state, my friends unfaithful, so many jealous of me? As for the new Tribunes, certainly Sestius is most anxious to help me and so, I hope, are Curtius, Milo, Fadius, and Atilius.[44] But Clodius is in strong opposition, and even after he goes out of office he will be able to stir up public meet-

43. Clodius.

44. i.e. Sex. Atilius Serranus Gavianus, originally friendly to Cicero, though in office he joined Clodius. I read *Atilius* for *Gratidius* (there was no Tribune of that name in 57). Editors read *Fabricius*.

ings with the same gang. And someone will be found to cast a veto.

That is not the prospect that was painted to me when I left Rome. I was often told that I could expect a glorious return within three days. You will ask what I thought myself. Well, a combination of factors upset the balance of my mind: Pompey's sudden desertion, the unfriendly attitude of the Consuls, and even the Praetors, the timidity of the tax-farmers, the sight of weapons. The tears of my family and friends forbade me to go to my death, which would certainly have been the most honourable course and the best way of escaping intolerable distresses. But I wrote to you on the subject in the letter I gave to Phaetho.

As matters stand, if public compassion can alleviate[45] our common plight, yours will doubtless be an incredible achievement, thrust down as you are into an abyss of mourning and trouble the like of which no man has ever known. But if we are really lost, oh, the misery of it! I shall have been the ruin of all my family, to whom in time gone by I was no discredit.

But, as I wrote to you earlier, view the situation thoroughly, take your soundings, and write me the truth; that is what our situation, though not your affection, requires. I shall hold on to life as long as I think that it is in your interest for me to do so or that it should be preserved in hope[46] of better things. You will find Sestius very friendly to us. I think Lentulus, who will be Consul, wishes you well. But actions are not so easy as words. You will see what is needed and how things are.

If nobody scorns your loneliness and our common calamity, something will be achievable through you or not at all. But if our enemies start persecuting you too, don't take it lying down. In your case the weapons will be lawsuits, not swords. But I hope there will be none of that. I beg you to write back to me

45. Perhaps read *potes* for *potest*: 'if through public compassion you can alleviate . . .'

46. I retain the manuscript reading *ad spem*.

on all matters and to believe that, however much I may have lost in spirit, or rather in judgement, my affection and family feeling remain the same.

5 (II. 1)

CICERO TO HIS BROTHER

Rome, shortly before 15 December 57

From Marcus to his brother Quintus greetings.

I dispatched a letter this morning which you will have already read. But Licinius was kind enough to call on me this evening after the Senate had risen to give me the opportunity of writing to you an account of the day's proceedings.

The House met in larger numbers than I thought possible in December just before the holiday. Of the Consulars, there were, besides myself and the two Consuls-Elect, P. Servilius, M. Lucullus, Lepidus, Vulcatius, Glabrio. The ex-Praetors were in good force. In all we were about 200. Lupus'[47] speech was awaited with interest. He dealt with the Campanian Land very fully, to an extremely attentive House. You know the material. He covered all my own contributions. There were some barbs to Caesar's address, some insults to Gellius', some complaints to Pompey's – who was not present. It was getting late when he wound up, and he said he would not ask for a debate since he did not wish to put any pressure on members to make themselves enemies. The high words of days gone by and the present silence told him the feeling of the House. He began to dismiss the meeting. Marcellinus observed: 'I must ask you, sir, not to draw any conclusions as to what we now approve or disapprove of from

47. Lupus, who had just come into office as Tribune, later figures as an adherent of Pompey. Hence probably the interest in his speech.

the fact that we have nothing to say. So far as I myself am concerned, and I imagine the same applies to the rest of the House, I am holding my peace because I do not think the question of the Campanian Land can properly be handled in Pompey's absence.' Lupus then said that he would not detain the House.

Racilius then rose and laid the question of the trials before the House, calling on Marcellinus to open the debate. After a powerful indictment of Clodius' arsons, killings, and stonings he proposed that the City Praetor should personally appoint a jury by lot, and that when this process was complete elections should be held; any person obstructing the trials to be regarded as acting contrary to public order. This proposal was warmly approved. C. Cato spoke against it, as did Cassius,[48] amid loud cries of protest when they put the elections before the trials. Philippus concurred with Lentulus. Then Racilius called upon me first of the private members. I spoke at length on the whole issue of P. Clodius' sedition and banditry, arraigning him like a man in the dock with frequent murmurs of approval from the whole House. Antistius Vetus[49] praised my speech at some length – his was not at all a bad performance. He also took up the question of the trials and said that he would regard it as of primary importance. A vote to that effect was about to take place, when Clodius was called and proceeded to talk out the motion. Racilius' insulting and witty attack had infuriated him. Then his roughs suddenly set up quite a formidable shouting from Ambassadors' Lodge[50] and the steps. I believe they had been stirred up against Q. Sextilius and Milo's friends. On that alarm we broke up in haste, amid loud and general protest.

There you have one day's proceedings. The sequel, I suppose,

48. Unknown. Possibly read *Caninius*.

49. Another Tribune, L. Antistius Vetus, to be distinguished from C. Antistius Vetus of *Letters to Atticus* 363 (XIV.9).3 (this has now been established by E. Badian).

50. 'Graecostasis', a platform from which envoys listened to senatorial debates.

will be deferred till January. Racilius is much the best of the Tribunes, but I think Antistius too will be friendly to us. Plancius, of course, is completely devoted.

If you love me, be sure to be cautious and careful about putting to sea in December.[51]

6 (II. 2)

CICERO TO HIS BROTHER

Rome, 17 January 56

From Marcus to his brother Quintus greetings.

Contrary to my habit when writing to you I am dictating this letter instead of writing it myself, not because of pressure of business (though busy I certainly am) but because I have a touch of ophthalmia.

And first I want to excuse myself and accuse you on one and the same count. Nobody has so far asked me whether I have a message for Sardinia, while I think you often have people who ask you whether you have a message for Rome.

As regards what you write to me on behalf of Lentulus[52] and Sestius, I have talked with Cincius. As the matter stands, it's not any too easy. There must be something about Sardinia which arouses dormant memories. Just as Gracchus the Augur[53] after arriving in that province remembered what had happened to him when he held the consular elections in the Campus Martius contrary to the auspices, so you in your Sardinian leisure seem

51. Quintus was going to Sardinia as Legate to Pompey, now in supreme charge of grain supplies.

52. Which Lentulus is uncertain, and we have no further information about the matter under reference.

53. Father of the Gracchi; Cicero tells the story in his treatise *On the Nature of the Gods* (II.10 f.).

to have brought Numisius'[54] ground-plan and the transactions with Pomponius back to your recollection. But so far I have bought nothing. Culleo's auction has taken place, and the property at Tusculum[55] did not find a buyer. If I can get really good terms, perhaps I shall not let it slip. I keep on urging Cyrus about your building[56] and hope he will do a good job. But everything goes slowly because of the prospect of a madman[57] as Aedile. For it looks as though elections will be held without delay – they have been announced for 20 January. However, I don't want you to be anxious. I shall take all manner of precautions.

As for his Alexandrian majesty, the Senate has passed a decree pronouncing it dangerous for him to be restored 'with a host'.[58] For the rest, there has been a tussle in the Senate as to whether Lentulus or Pompey should restore him, and Lentulus looked like winning his point. In that affair I performed my duty to Lentulus to a marvel, at the same time meeting Pompey's wishes in fine style, but the matter was dragged out by the manoeuvring of Lentulus' ill-wishers. Then followed the comitial days during which the House could not meet. What will come of the Tribunes' freebooting I can't prophesy, but I suspect that Caninius will carry his bill by violence. I can't fathom Pompey's wishes in the matter; but everyone sees what his friends want, and the king's creditors are openly putting up money against Lentulus. He certainly seems to have lost the assignment, which I am very sorry for, though he has given me many good reasons to feel annoyed with him[59] if that were not against my conscience.

54. Presumably an architect.
55. Culleo's, not Cicero's.
56. Cf. Letter 8 (II.4).
57. Clodius.
58. Cf. *Letters to his Friends* 12 (I.1).2.
59. Cicero was dissatisfied with Lentulus Spinther's attitude in respect of his indemnities; cf. *Letters to Atticus* 74 (IV.2).4.

If you have sorted matters out over there, I hope you will board ship at the first spell of fair, settled weather and join me. There are numberless things in which I miss you, every day and in every way. Your folk and mine are well.

17 January.

7 (II. 3)

CICERO TO HIS BROTHER

Rome, 12–15 February 56

From Marcus to his brother Quintus greetings.

I gave you the earlier news in my last. Now for the sequel: On the Kalends of February there was a move to postpone the embassies to the Ides. No conclusion reached that day. On 2 February Milo appeared to stand trial with Pompey as supporting counsellor. M. Marcellus spoke (I had asked him) and we came off creditably. Case adjourned to 7 February. Meanwhile the embassies were postponed to the Ides and the House was asked to consider the Quaestors' provinces and the Praetors' establishments. But business was interrupted by numerous complaints about the state of the commonwealth and nothing done. C. Cato gave notice of a bill to relieve Lentulus of his command, and his son put on mourning.

Milo appeared on 7 February. Pompey spoke – or rather tried to speak, for no sooner was he on his feet than Clodius' gang raised a clamour, and all through the speech he was interrupted not merely by shouting but by insults and abuse. When he wound up (and I will say he showed courage; he was not put off, delivered all he had to say, sometimes even managing to get silence by his personal authority) – well, when he wound up, Clodius rose. Wishing to repay the compliment, our side gave him such an uproarious reception that he lost command of thoughts, tongue, and countenance. That lasted till half past one, Pompey having finished just after midday – all manner of insults, ending up with some highly scabrous verse to the address of Clodius and Clodia. Pale with fury, he started a game of question and answer in the middle of the shouting: 'Who's starving the people to death?' 'Pompey,' answered the gang. 'Who wants to go to Alexandria?' Answer: 'Pompey.' 'Whom do you want to go?' Answer: 'Crassus' (who was present as a supporter of Milo, wishing him no good). About 2.15 the Clodians started spitting at us, as though on a signal. Sharp rise in temperature! They made a push to dislodge us, our side counter-charged. Flight of gang. Clodius was hurled from the rostra, at which point I too made off for fear of what might happen in the free-for-all. The Senate was convened in its House, and Pompey went home. I did not attend, however, not wishing to keep mum about so remarkable an incident nor yet to offend the honest men by standing up for Pompey, who was under fire from Bibulus, Curio, Favonius, and Servilius junior. The debate was adjourned to the following day. Clodius had the trial postponed to Quirinus' Day.

On 8 February the Senate met in the temple of Apollo[60] in order that Pompey could be present. Pompey spoke strongly – nothing concluded that day. 9 February, Senate in temple of Apollo. A decree was passed pronouncing the doings of 7 February contrary to public interest. That day C. Cato delivered a broadside against Pompey – a set speech like a prosecuting counsel's with Pompey in the dock. He said many highly laudatory things about me, which I could have done without, denouncing Pompey's treachery towards me. The ill-wishers listened in rapt silence. Pompey replied warmly, making oblique allusion to Crassus and saying plainly that he intended to

60. Outside the ancient city boundary. As holding *imperium* Pompey could come inside only by special dispensation.

take better care of his life than Africanus had done, whom C. Carbo murdered.[61]

So I think big things are on the way. Pompey has information (and talks about it to me) that a plot against his life is on foot, that Crassus is backing C. Cato and supplying Clodius with funds, and that both are getting support both from Crassus and from Curio, Bibulus, and his other enemies. He says he must take very good care not to be caught napping, with the meeting-going public pretty well alienated, the nobility hostile, the Senate ill-disposed, and the younger generation ill-conditioned. So he is getting ready and bringing up men from the country. Clodius on his side is reinforcing his gang in readiness for Quirinus' Day. With the same date in view we have much the advantage even with Milo's own forces, but a large contingent is expected from Picenum and Gaul, which should further enable us to make a stand against Cato's bills concerning Milo and Lentulus.

On 10 February Sestius was charged with bribery by an informer, Cn. Nerius of the tribe Pupinia, and on the same day with breach of the peace by a certain M. Tullius. He was unwell, so, as was only proper, I called on him immediately and promised him my services without reservation. And I have acted accordingly, contrary to what people were expecting in the belief that I was justifiably annoyed with him.[62] So I figure in his eyes and everyone else's as an eminently forgiving and grateful character. And I shall so continue. The same informer Nerius has produced as deputies Cn. Lentulus Vatia and C. Cornelius of the tribe Stellatina. The same day the Senate passed a decree to the effect that the political clubs and caucuses should be dissolved and a bill put through providing that persons not complying with this ordinance be liable to the same penalty as those guilty of breach of peace.

61. In 129. But murder was never proved.

62. The reason is unknown; cf. the first paragraph of the next letter.

On 11 February I defended Bestia on a bribery charge before Praetor Cn. Domitius in mid Forum. There was a large crowd in court. In the course of my speech I came to the occasion on which Bestia saved Sestius' life when he was lying covered with wounds in the temple of Castor. I took the favourable opportunity to lay down a foundation for my defence of Sestius against the charges which are being got up against him and pronounced a well-deserved eulogy, which was received with great approval by all. Sestius was highly pleased. I tell you all this because you have often referred in your letters to the desirability of preserving good relations with him.

I am writing this before dawn on 12 February. This evening I shall be dining with Pomponius at his wedding.[63]

In the rest of my affairs it is as you foretold when I was far from hopeful – my prestige and influence flourishes. This restitution, in which we both share, is due, my dear brother, to your patience, courage, devotion, and, let me add, your personal charm.

Piso's house (the Liciniana) near the wood[64] has been rented for you, but I hope you will be moving into your own in a few months' time, after the Kalends of July. The Lamiae have taken your house in Carinae – nice, clean tenants. Since your letter from Olbia I have heard nothing from you. I am anxious to know how you are and how you amuse yourself, and above all to see you as soon as possible.

Take care of your health, my dear brother, and don't forget that it's Sardinia where you are, winter time though it be.[65]

15 February

63. To Pilia.

64. Reading uncertain.

65. The climate of Sardinia was notoriously unhealthy, more so, naturally, in summer than in winter.

8 (II. 4)

CICERO TO HIS BROTHER

Rome, mid March 56

From Marcus to his brother Quintus greetings.

Our friend Sestius was acquitted on 14 March, and by a unanimous vote, which was politically of great importance as showing that no difference of opinion exists in a case like this. I have often noticed your anxiety lest I gave a handle to a hostile critic who might accuse me of ingratitude if I did not put up with his unreasonableness in certain respects with the best of grace. Well, you may rest assured that my conduct in that trial has made me pass for a model of gratitude. By my defence I have more than discharged what was due to this peevish personage, and I cut up his overt adversary Vatinius just as I pleased to the applause of Gods and men,[66] which was what he wanted more than anything. What is more, our friend Paulus, who appeared as a witness against Sestius, undertook to prosecute Vatinius if Licinius Macer[67] did not get on with the job; on which Macer rose from Sestius' benches and promised not to fail him. In short, that bullying ruffian left the court much disconcerted and unnerved.

Your son Quintus, who is a fine boy, is getting on famously with his lessons. I notice this more now because Tyrannio is teaching at my house. Building of both our houses goes briskly forward. I have paid your contractor half his money. I hope we shall be under the same roof before winter. I hope we have settled matters with Crassipes about our Tullia, who loves you very much indeed. But it is the two days after the Latin Festival (now ended), which are holy days, and he is just leaving town.

66. In the speech *In Vatinium*.

67. i.e. the poet and orator C. Licinius Macer Calvus.

9 (II. 5)

CICERO TO HIS BROTHER

Rome, March 56

★★★ As for the *abondance* you often talk about, I want it moderately; that is to say, if the animal comes my way I shall be glad to snap it up, but if it stays in hiding I don't intend to flush it out. I am building in three places and refurbishing the rest. I live on a rather more handsome scale nowadays than I used – it was called for. If I had you with me, you[68] would take second place to the builders for a spell! But all this too I hope we shall soon be talking over between us.

The situation in Rome is as follows: Lentulus makes an excellent Consul, and his colleague does not stand in his way – yes, really good, I have never seen a better. He has blocked all the comitial days – even the Latin Festival is being repeated, and no lack of Supplications either. So pernicious bills are blocked, especially Cato's.[69] Our friend Milo has played that patron of gladiators and beast-fighters a fine trick. Cato had bought some beast-fighters from Cosconius and Pomponius and never appeared in public without their armed escort. He could not feed them and was having difficulty in keeping them. Milo got to know, and employed an agent to buy the troupe from Cato, a man who was not a crony of his own and so could do it without arousing suspicion. No sooner had they been led off than Racilius (the only Tribune worth the name at present) gave the show away, announcing by prearrangement with Milo that these men had been bought for himself and putting out an advertisement that he was going to sell 'Cato's troupe' by auction. There was great amusement over that advertisement.

68. I read *dares* for *darem*.

69. Cf. *Letters to his Friends* 15 (I.5a). The references are throughout to the Tribune, C. Cato.

Well, Lentulus has kept this fellow Cato away from legislation, as also some others who have given notice of bills about Caesar – monstrous things, and nobody to veto them. As for Caninius' campaign regarding Pompey, it has fallen quite flat. The proposal finds little favour in itself, Pompey is criticized because of his friendship with P. Lentulus,[70] and frankly his position is not what it was. He has incurred some unpopularity with the vicious elements, the dregs of the mob, because of Milo, while the honest men find him lacking in many respects and blameworthy in many others. The only fault *I* have to find with Marcellinus is his excessive asperity towards Pompey. But the Senate does not disapprove, which makes me all the more glad to withdraw from the Senate-House and public affairs altogether.

In the courts I stand where I stood. My house is as full of callers as in my heyday. One unfortunate incident happened through Milo's imprudence, about Sex. Cloelius[71] – I was against a prosecution at the present time and with weak prosecutors. It only needed three more votes in a deplorable jury. The people are demanding another trial and he will have to be brought back – they won't tolerate it, and look upon him as already convicted since he was almost found guilty by a jury of his own men. In this affair too Pompey's unpopularity stood in our way. The Senators acquitted him by a large margin, the Knights were tied, the Paymaster Tribunes voted guilty. But to make up for this misadventure, my enemies are being convicted every day. Sevius ran on the rocks to my great satisfaction, and the rest are being broken up.[72] C. Cato has told

70. i.e. for acting disloyally by intriguing to get the Egyptian assignment transferred to himself.

71. Read *Cloelio* for *Caelio* etc. in the manuscripts (*Clodio* edd.).

72. The distinction is not wholly clear, but it may be that Sevius (an unknown; most editors read *Servius*, mistakenly identifying with Servius Pola) had been condemned for some non-political offence. His fate, then, was a kind of accident, whereas the other Clodians had been prosecuted by their political enemies on public grounds.

a public meeting that he won't allow elections to be held if his days for moving legislation in the Assembly are blocked. Appius has not yet got back from Caesar.

I am waiting for a letter from you with the greatest impatience. I know that the sea has been closed to shipping up till now, but they say that certain persons arrived in Ostia bringing glowing accounts of you and your great reputation in the province. They also say you are giving out that you will cross at the first sailing. I hope so, and although naturally it is yourself I most want, I am none the less expecting a letter in advance.

Goodbye, dear brother.

10 (II. 6)

CICERO TO HIS BROTHER

En route *to Anagnia, 9 April 56*

From Marcus to his brother Quintus greetings.

I sent you a letter[73] the other day telling you that our Tullia was betrothed to Crassipes on 4 April, along with the rest of the news, public and private. Subsequent items are as follows: On the Nones of April the Senate decreed HS40,000,000 to Pompey as Grain Commissioner. The same day there was a warm debate on the Campanian Land – the shouting in the House was like at a public meeting. The shortage of funds and the high price of grain made the question more acute. I must not fail to mention that M. Furius Flaccus, a Roman Knight and a scoundrel, was expelled from the Capitoline College and the Guild of Mercury,[74] he being present and throwing himself at the feet of every member in turn.

73. Not extant.

74. The *Capitolini* were in charge of the Capitoline Games held every Ides of October. The *Mercuriales* were a corporation of merchants.

On 6 April I gave a dinner for Crassipes to celebrate the engagement. Your and my boy Quintus (a very good boy) could not come because of a very slight indisposition. On the 8th I went to see him and found him quite recovered. He talked to me at length and in the nicest way about the disagreements between our ladies. It was really most entertaining. Pomponia has been grumbling about you too, but we will talk of this when we meet.

On leaving the boy I went over to your site. Work was going ahead with a crowd of builders. I said a few animating words to Longilius the contractor, and he convinced me that he wants to give us satisfaction. Your house will be splendid. One can see more now than we could judge from the plan. Mine too will be built rapidly.

I dined that evening at Crassipes' and after dinner had myself carried to Pompey's, not having been able to meet him during the day because he had been away – I wanted to see him because I was leaving Rome next day and he had a trip to Sardinia in view. So I met him and asked him to send you back to us as soon as possible. 'Straight away,' said he. He would be leaving, he said, on 11 April and taking ship from Labro[75] or Pisae. Now as soon as he arrives, my dear fellow, be sure to take the next boat, provided the weather is suitable.

On 9 April I dictated this letter before daylight and am writing the rest on the road, expecting to stay the night with T. Titius near Anagnia. Tomorrow I intend to stay at Laterium, and then, after five days in the Arpinum area, go on to Pompeii. I shall have a look at my Cumae place on the way back, and so to Rome (since Milo's trial has been scheduled for the Nones of May) on the 6th, then, as I hope, to see you, my dearest and sweetest of brothers. I thought it best to hold up the building at Arcanum pending your arrival.

Be sure to keep well, my dear fellow, and come as soon as you can.

75. No place of this name is otherwise recorded.

11 (II. 7)

CICERO TO HIS BROTHER

Rome, shortly after 15 May 56

From Marcus to his brother Quintus greetings.

At last, your delightful letter! I have been waiting for it so impatiently, and of late apprehensively too. I must tell you that this is the only letter I have had from you since the one dispatched from Olbia which your sailor brought.

Let all else be kept for talk in person, as you say, but one thing I cannot let wait: on the Ides of May the Senate refused Gabinius a Supplication – a magnificent performance! Procilius takes his oath that this has never happened to anyone before.[76] Outside the House it is heartily applauded. To me it is agreeable in itself, and the more so because it was done in my absence – an unbiased judgement, without any aggressive action or influence on my part. I did not attend because it had been reported that the Campanian Land would be debated on the Ides and the day following, as indeed it was. On this question I am muzzled.[77] But I am writing more than I intended – we shall talk.

Goodbye, my best and most longed-for of brothers, and hurry you home. Our boys make the same plea of you. Oh, and of course you will come to dinner when you arrive.

76. In fact there seems to have been only one precedent, that of T. Albucius, Governor of Sardinia *c.* 104.

77. Cf. *Letters to his Friends*, 20 (I.9)5 ff.

12 (II. 8)

CICERO TO HIS BROTHER

Rome, shortly after 11 February 55

From Marcus to his brother Quintus greetings.

I thought you would like Canto II,[78] but I'm very glad you liked it so very much as you say in your letter. You remind me of Indifference[79] and advise me to remember Jupiter's speech at the end of the Canto.[80] Yes, I remember. I wrote it all for myself more than for the rest of the world.

However, the day after you left I paid Pompey a late-night visit in company with Vibullius and spoke to him about those buildings and inscriptions.[81] He answered very kindly and held out great hopes, saying that he would like to discuss it with Crassus and advising me to do the same. I accompanied Consul Crassus from the Senate to his house. He undertook to do his best and said there was something Clodius wanted to get just now through Pompey and himself; if I did not put a spoke in his wheel, he thought I could gain my point without a fight. I put the whole business in his hands and said I would do just as he thought fit. Young P. Crassus, who is devoted to me as you know, was present during our talk. As for what Clodius wants, it's a Free Commissionership (if not through the Senate, then through the Assembly) either to Byzantium or to Brogitarus or

78. Of the poem *On my Vicissitudes*. Cf. *Letters to his Friends* p. 54.

79. I translate a Greek word taken from Stoic terminology and conjectured here by W. Sternkopf in place of *non curantia* in the manuscripts, which seems to be an attempt to render it in Latin. Cicero also uses the word in *Letters to Atticus* 37 (II.17) and in his *Academica* (II.130).

80. Jupiter will have advised the poet to leave politics and devote himself to letters; see end of next paragraph.

81. The reference is obscure, but cf. n. 141.

both.[82] There's plenty of money in it, but that doesn't trouble me too much – even if I don't get what I'm after. However, Pompey has talked to Crassus, and they seem to have taken the thing on. If they do it, fine! If not, let us return to our Jupiter.

On 11 February the Senate passed a decree about bribery on Afranius' motion, which was the one I proposed myself when you were here. But to the loudly voiced disappointment of the House the Consuls did not pursue the proposal of certain members who, after concurring with Afranius, added that the Praetors should remain private citizens for two months after election. There was a flat repudiation of Cato.[83] The fact is, they are all-powerful and want everybody to know it.

13 (II. 9)

CICERO TO HIS BROTHER

Cumae(?), 55(?)

From Marcus to his brother Quintus greetings.

What, *you* afraid of interrupting me? To start with, even if I were occupied in the way you think, you know what 'interrupting an idler' is![84] But upon my word it looks as though you

82. As Tribune Clodius had brought about the recall of some Byzantine exiles and had got Brogitarus appointed High Priest of Cybele at Pessinus. He now proposed to go and 'collect'. Though his business was private, the 'Free Commissionership' would give him official status.

83. Since the Praetors for 55 had not been elected in the previous year they would, failing special provision, take office immediately after election and so become immune from prosecution for electoral malpractice. M. Cato was a candidate, in opposition to the Consuls, Pompey and Crassus, who secured his defeat. He was, however, later elected for the following year.

84. I translate my conjecture *tu scis quid sit interpellare otiantem*, by which Cicero may be supposed to allude to a saying that to interrupt an

are giving me a lesson in this kind of thoughtfulness, for which I have no use when it comes from you. No, no, I hope you will interpose and interrupt and talk me down and talk me out! Nothing would please me better. No moonstruck poet is so willing to recite his latest effusions as I to listen to you talking on any topic, public or private, country or town. It was my stupid diffidence that stopped me from taking you along when I left Rome. You put up an unanswerable excuse the first time, the ill health of our little boy; so I held my tongue. Then again it was the boys, and I said nothing. And now your most agreeable letter bothers me a little, because it looks as though you were afraid, and still are, of being a bother! I should quarrel with you if brotherly love permitted. But mark my words; if ever I suspect anything of the kind again – well, I'll say only this: I shall be afraid when we are together of bothering *you*. That touches you on the raw, doesn't it? Well, that's the way it goes: 'whoso evil speaketh . . .'[85] (I'll never say 'evil doth').

As for our friend Marius, I assure you I should have thrown him into the litter – not the one Asicius[86] had from King Ptolemy (I remember that occasion when I was transporting him from Naples to Baiae in Asicius' eight-bearer palanquin with a hundred swordsmen following; Marius knew nothing about this escort and I laughed till I cried when he suddenly opened the curtains and we both almost collapsed – he with fright and I with laughter). Well, as I say, I should certainly have taken him along to sample the subtlety of his old-time wit and civilized conversation, but I did not like to invite an invalid

idle man was to do him a service. Private study or literary work came under the heading of *otium* ('leisure, idleness').

85. The Greek verse part of which Cicero quotes is from a lost work of Sophocles: 'If what you did was terrible, so must what you suffer be terrible also.'

86. Charged with the murder of the chief of a delegation from Ptolemy the Piper's revolted subjects, he was successfully defended by Cicero.

to a draughty house, still not even roughly finished. It would be a special treat for me to enjoy his company here too – I can tell you that Marius as my neighbour is the pride and glory of my property at Pompeii. I shall take care that Anicius' place is ready for him. As for me, bookworm though I be, I can live with the carpenters, a philosophy which I get, not from Mt Hymettus, but from our native Peak.[87] Marius is not so tough, either in health or nature. As for interruptions, I shall borrow from you people just so much time for writing as you allow, and I hope you don't allow any; that way, if I do nothing, you will be to blame instead of my own laziness.

I am sorry you take the political situation overmuch to heart and that you are a better citizen than Philoctetes, who being wronged wanted to see such sights as are evidently painful to you.[88] Be a good fellow, and hurry over. I shall comfort you and wipe away all sorrows. And bring Marius, if you love me. But make haste, both of you.

The kitchen garden is in good shape.[89]

14 (II. 10)

CICERO TO HIS BROTHER

Rome, early February 54

From Marcus to his brother Quintus greetings.

Your tablets[90] clamorously demanded this letter. Otherwise,

87. Literally 'from our Arx', reading *arce nostra* (written *arcenra*) for the meaningless *araxira* in the manuscripts. There was a place called Arx ('citadel') in the neighbourhood of Arpinum. Cicero means that he did not need Greek philosophy to teach him to put up with inconvenience; early training in his native hill country had done that.

88. Evidently an allusion to a lost play. Sophocles' *Philoctetes* contains nothing relevant.

89. The meaning of the Latin (*hortus domi est*) is uncertain.

90. See Glossary of Terms.

in actual material the day of your departure offers virtually no subject for my pen. But when we are together we are seldom at a loss for talk, and in the same way our letters must sometimes just ramble on.

Well then, the liberties of the good folk of Tenedos have been chopped by their own axe;[91] nobody came to their defence except myself, Bibulus, Calidius, and Favonius. You got an honourable mention from the men of Magnesia by Mt Sipylus; they said you were the only one to stand up to L. Sestius Pansa's demand.[92] If there is anything you ought to know on the remaining days, or for that matter if there is nothing, I shall still write you a daily line. On the 12th I shall not fail you, nor Pomponius either.

Lucretius' poetry is as you say – sparkling with natural genius, but plenty of technical skill.[93] If you read Sallust's *From Empedocles*,[94] I'll rate you both more and less than ordinary humanity.[95]

91. The people of Tenedos seem to have petitioned the Senate for the status of a 'free' community, and to have been summarily refused. The exact origin of the proverbial expression 'axe of Tenedos' is variously explained, but has to do with the eponymous hero of the island, Tenes, who was supposed to have introduced a peculiarly drastic legal code.

92. Nothing is known of Pansa or his demand. He may have been a tax-farmer.

93. According to St Jerome Cicero edited Lucretius' poem *On the Nature of the Universe* after the poet's death.

94. Presumably a Latin translation of the fifth-century philosopher-poet Empedocles. The identity of the translator is unknown.

95. Literally: 'I shall think you a *man* (*virum*), but not a human being.'

15 (II. 11)

CICERO TO HIS BROTHER

Rome, c. 13 February 54

From Marcus to his brother Quintus greetings.

I am glad my letters give you pleasure, though just now I should not have had any subject to write about if I had not had a letter from you.

Appius called a thinly attended meeting of the Senate on the 12th, but it was so chilly that the outcry forced him to dismiss us. As for His Majesty of Commagene,[96] I quite settled his hash and so Appius is paying me extravagant court both in person and through Pomponius. He sees that if I take the same tone in other matters he will have a lean February.[97] I poked fun at the king comically enough, not merely twisting that little town on the Bridge of Euphrates out of his grip but raising a storm of laughter by my jibes at the purple-bordered gown he got during Caesar's Consulship: 'Now as for his request for the renewal of the honours accorded to him, far be it from me to suggest that this House should gainsay his right to give the purple-bordered gown an annual redyeing. But I appeal to members of the nobility here present: you gentlemen drew the line at Oxnose; are you going to accept Commagene ointment?'[98] You perceive the genre and the theme. I cut so many jokes at this

96. Antiochus. He had received the kingdom, formerly part of Syria, when Pompey set up the Roman province at the end of the war against Mithridates.

97. The Senate dealt with foreign delegations in February. As Consul Ap. Claudius Pulcher was in a position to help them gain their petitions, for which, as Cicero implies, he would expect to be paid.

98. It seems that in 59 the king had been accorded the right to wear the purple-bordered gown (*toga praetexta*) worn by Roman curule

inglorious monarch's expense that he was totally exploded. Appius, as I say, was alarmed by this procedure and is smothering me in courtesies. It would be the easiest thing in the world to spoke the other wheels. But no, I shall not offend him,

> lest upon Jove he cry,
> Guardian of Troth, and all the Greeks convoke[99]

– that is, the intermediaries in our reconciliation.

I shall do my best for Theopompus. As for Caesar, I forgot to tell you – yes, I understand what kind of a letter you have been waiting for. But he wrote to Balbus that the parcel containing Balbus' letter and mine was delivered to him completely waterlogged so that he doesn't even know that a letter from me was inside. But he had made out a few words in Balbus' letter, to which he replies as follows: 'I see you have written something about Cicero which I cannot make out. But so far as I could follow it by guesswork, it looked like something I should have wished rather than hoped for.'[100] So I proceeded to send Caesar

---

magistrates, perhaps on a particular annual occasion; and that the Senate had been asked to renew or confirm it. The conjecture *qui Burrhinum* for *quibus r(h)enum* assumes a double pun in Cicero's usual manner. There was a medicament *commagenum*, made from a herb *commagene*; and there was a herb *burrhinon* (*burrhinum*, 'oxnose'; it was otherwise called *bucranion*, 'oxskull'). The missing link will be a low-born person named or nicknamed *Burrhinus*, whose election to a magistracy was resented or ridiculed by the nobility – unless, as suggested by T. P. Wiseman, one Burrienus (or, more likely, Burrenus), City Praetor in 83, is relevant.

99. A quotation from an unknown Latin play. 'Jove, Guardian of Truth' (Jupiter Hospitalis) = Zeus Xenios, defender of the laws of hospitality. The 'Greeks' do not, as commentators naïvely suppose, represent actual Greeks, but, as Cicero expressly says, the intermediaries who had recently reconciled him with Appius, principally Pompey; cf. *Letters to Atticus* 124 (VII.1)3, where, likewise in quotations, the 'Trojan men and dames' stand for public opinion and 'Polydamas' for Atticus.

100. This no doubt referred to Q. Cicero's desire for a command in Caesar's army.

a copy of my letter. And don't be put off by his joke about being hard up. I replied that he had better not spend his last penny depending on *my* strong-box, and some more banter on the same lines – familiar but not undignified. All reports speak of his special regard for me. The letter replying to the point you have in mind should just about coincide with your return to Rome.

I shall write you day-by-day news-letters always provided you supply the couriers. But there's a hard frost ahead. In fact Appius stands in grave danger of seeing his house become a bonfire.[101]

16 (II. 12)

CICERO TO HIS BROTHER

Rome, 14 February 54.

From Marcus to his brother Quintus greetings.

Your 'black snow' made me laugh,[102] and I am very glad to find you so cheerful and ready for a joke. I agree with you about Pompey, or rather you agree with me, for, as you know, I have been chanting your Caesar's praises this long while past. Believe me, he is grappled to my heart and *I* have no intention of disengaging.

Well, now for the Ides. It was the tenth day for Caelius.[103]

101. There is an untranslatable joke here, in the word *urerentur*, which can mean 'may be burned' or 'may be frostbitten'. The meaning is, of course, that Appius' unpopularity was such that a mob might set his house on fire.

102. The point of Quintus' joke is uncertain.

103. An interval of at least ten days was required between arraignment and trial. Nothing is known of the trial here in question.

Domitius[104] didn't have a complement of jurors. I'm afraid that horrible savage Servius Pola may join the prosecution, for our friend Caelius is vigorously assailed by the Clodian clan.[105] There's nothing for certain so far, but we are apprehensive.

That same day a well-attended Senate gave audience to the delegation from Tyre. Numerous Syrian tax-farmers appeared in opposition. Gabinius was hauled over the coals in lively style, but the tax-farmers were harried by Domitius for having escorted him on horseback.[106] Our friend Lamia went a little far. When Domitius said: 'All this is the fault of you Roman Knights. You give lax verdicts,' Lamia retorted: 'We give verdicts, and you give testimonials!'[107] Nothing was concluded that day before nightfall ended the session.

According to Appius' interpretation, he is not debarred by the lex Pupia from holding meetings of the Senate on the comitial days following the Feast of Quirinus, and is actually obliged, as laid down in the lex Gabinia, to hold a meeting every day from the Kalends of February to the Kalends of March for the hearing of embassies.[108] So it's thought that the elections[109] are pushed away into March. All the same, the Tribunes say they intend to bring Gabinius' action before the Assembly on these coming comitial days.

I rake together all I can find to put some news in my letter, but, as you see, I am simply out of matter. So I come back to Callisthenes and Philistus – I can see you have been wallowing

104. A Praetor; or possibly the Consul, L. Domitius Ahenobarbus, mentioned below.

105. Already in 56 Caelius Rufus had been defended by Cicero on a charge instigated by his former mistress Clodia, sister to P. Clodius.

106. Ptolemy the Piper had finally been restored to his throne by Gabinius, now governor of Syria.

107. Cf. *Letters to his Friends*, p. 51.

108. Cf. n. 97.

109. Of magistrates for the current year, whether Praetors or Aediles is uncertain.

in them. Callisthenes is a vulgarian, a 'bastard'[110] author, as certain of his fellow-countrymen have put it. But the Sicilian is capital – full of matter, penetrating, concise, almost a miniature Thucydides. But which of his books you have had (there are two works), or whether you have had them both, I don't know. I prefer his *Dionysius*. Dionysius is a grand old fox and on very familiar terms with Philistus. You add a question – shall you embark on history? You have my full encouragement. And since you are furnishing couriers, you shall have today's chronicle on the Lupercalia.

Have a perfectly delightful time with our young man.

17 (II. 13)

CICERO TO HIS BROTHER

Cumae or Pompeii, May 54

From Marcus to his brother Quintus greetings.

Up to date I have received two letters from you, one dispatched just as we said goodbye,[111] the other from Ariminum; the further letters which you say you sent I have not received.

Except that I lack your company I am in other respects having quite a pleasant time at Cumae and Pompeii and shall be staying in those places till the Kalends of June. I am writing the political book[112] I mentioned earlier, and a pretty sticky, laborious job it is. However, if it turns out satisfactory, the time will have been well spent. If not, I'll toss it into the sea, which is before my eyes as I write, and attack something else, since I can't do nothing.

110. Reading *nothum* for *notum* ('familiar'). In his treatise *On the Orator* (II.58) Cicero says that Callisthenes wrote history 'almost in the fashion of a rhetorician'.

111. Quintus had left to join Caesar for service in Gaul.

112. *On the Republic.*

I shall carefully attend to your charges, both in conciliating people and in not estranging certain persons. But my greatest concern will be to see your boy (*our* boy) every day, which goes without saying, and to look into what he is learning as often as possible. If he is willing to accept it, I shall even offer my services as his teacher, having gained some practice in this employment in bringing our younger boy[113] forward during this holiday season.

On your side, as you say in your letter (though even if you did not say so I know you are doing it most conscientiously), you will of course take care to sort out my commissions and follow them up and do them. When I get back to Rome I shall not let a single courier of Caesar's leave without a letter for you. At present (you will forgive me) there was nobody to take a letter until this M. Orfius, a Roman Knight who is connected with me both on personal grounds and because he comes from the town of Atella, which you know to be under my patronage. So I recommend him to you warmly. He is a man of distinction in his own community and of influence even outside it. Be sure to treat him handsomely and so attach him to yourself. He is a Military Tribune in your army. You will find him grateful and attentive.

Let me earnestly beg you to be very kind to Trebatius.

18 (II. 14)

CICERO TO HIS BROTHER

Rome, beginning of June 54

From Marcus to his brother Quintus greetings.

On 2 June, the day I got back to Rome, I received your letter dispatched from Placentia, and then another dispatched the

113. Young Marcus.

following day from *,[114] together with a letter of Caesar's full of all manner of friendly attention, thoughtfulness, and charm. The things you speak of are indeed important, or rather *most* important, tending powerfully, as they do, to great *kudos* and the highest prestige. But take the word of one you know: what I value most in these matters I already have, and that is, first, yourself so dedicated to the support of our common standing, and second, such affection for me on Caesar's part. That means more to me than all the distinctions he wants me to expect at his hands. The letter he sent along with yours pleased me beyond words. He begins by saying how delighted he was at your arrival and the memory of old affection, then goes on to promise that, knowing how sorely I shall miss you, he will make me glad that in your absence from me you are with him rather than anywhere else.

It is good brotherly advice you give me to make Caesar the one man I exert myself to please, but *now* upon my word the horse is willing. Yes, that I shall do enthusiastically. It often happens to travellers in a hurry that after getting up rather later than they intended they put on speed and thus arrive at their destinations faster even than if they had been astir in the middle of the night. So perhaps with me. In cultivating this man's friendship I have been asleep a long while, though I must admit that you often tried to wake me up. Now I shall compensate my slowness by putting my horse to a gallop – and not just my horse but my poetic chariot, since you say my poem[115] meets with his approval. All you have to do is to give me Britain to paint. I'll use your colours with my brush. And yet . . . Where can I spy the spare time, especially if I stay in Rome, as he asks me to do? Well, I'll see. Perhaps love alone will conquer all obstacles. It often does.

114. 'Blanden(n)o' in the manuscripts; but no place of that name is known.

115. An epic poem addressed to Caesar which Cicero had begun, and eventually finished; cf. Letter 27 (III.7)6.

He actually thanks me for sending him Trebatius, very wittily and kindly, saying that in all his multitudinous entourage there wasn't a man who could draw up a bail-bond. I asked him for a Tribunate for M. Curtius – if I had asked Domitius he would have thought I was making game of him, it's his daily grumble that he can't even appoint a Military Tribune; he even made a joke in the Senate to the effect that his colleague Appius had gone to Caesar for the gift of a Tribune's commission – but for next year. That is how Curtius himself wanted it.[116]

Rest assured that in public life and in my personal feuds I am and shall be just what you recommend, softer than the lobe of your ear. Public affairs stand as follows: there is some hope of elections, but doubtful; some suspicion of a Dictatorship, but that too not definite; peace reigns in the Forum, but it's the peace of a senile community rather than a contented one. In the Senate my speeches are of a nature to win agreement from others rather than from myself.

Such are the sorry works of woeful war.[117]

19 (II. 15)

CICERO TO HIS BROTHER

Rome, end of July 54

From Marcus to his brother Quintus greetings.

This time it will be best-quality pen and ink and ivory-finished paper, since you say you could hardly read my last letter. No, my dear fellow, it was for none of the reasons you

116. Cf. p. 713 and *Letters to his Friends* 26 (VII.5)2.

117. From Euripides' *Suppliant Women* (119).

suppose. I was neither busy nor upset nor annoyed with anybody. It's just that I always take the first pen that comes to hand as though it was a good one.

But now, my best and sweetest of brothers, pay careful attention while I answer that very down-to-earth passage in this same short letter. You ask me to reply in brotherly candour, without concealment or dissimulation or attempt to spare your feelings, to tell you, that is, whether you should hurry back as we had agreed or stay on (given sufficient reason) with a view to disembarrassing yourself. My dear Quintus, if you were enquiring about my wishes on some small matter, I should leave it to you to do as you chose, but at the same time make my own wishes clear. In this matter, however, I take it that you are really asking how I expect next year to turn out: well, definitely a peaceful year for me, or at any rate a very well-protected one. My house, the Forum, the demonstrations in the theatre declare as much every day. And I am not making the mistake I made once before in my consciousness of the forces behind me.[118] What gives me confidence is that I am in Pompey's and Caesar's good graces. But if the madman[119] breaks out in some wild attempt, everything is ready to crush him.

This is my true feeling and judgement, written after a careful survey. You must have no misgivings; I forbid it as a brother, not because that is what you want to be told. To enjoy the pleasure we take in each other's society I should wish you to come home at the time you stated originally, but above that I put what you think to be in your own interest. I also attach great importance to your *abondance* and the liquidation of your debts. Be sure of one thing: once free of embarrassments, we shall be the most fortunate folk in the world, given health. Our habits being what they are, the gaps are small, and if health holds, to fill them is no problem.

118. Reading *nec labor, ut quondam, conscientia* (or *confidentia*?) *copiarum nostrarum*.

119. Clodius.

Bribery is rampant again, dreadful, worse than ever before. On the Ides the rate of interest rose from 4 to 8%[120] because of a coalition between Memmius and the Consuls with Domitius.[121] Scaurus on his own can hardly defeat this. Messalla is a tired horse. I do not speak in hyperbole: they are settling to distribute ten million sesterces among the first Century. It is a flaming scandal. The candidates for the Tribunate have agreed among themselves to deposit HS500,000 each with M. Cato and make him referee of the elections, anyone contravening his rulings to be condemned by him. If these elections go through without corruption, Cato will have achieved more on his own than all the laws and all the juries.

20 (II. 16)

CICERO TO HIS BROTHER

Rome, late August 54

From Marcus to his brother Quintus greetings.

When you get a letter from me in the hand of one of my secretaries you are to infer that I did not have a minute to spare; when in my own, that I had – a minute! For let me tell you that I have never in my life been more inundated with briefs and trials, and in a heat-wave at that, in the most oppressive time of the year. But I must put up with it, since you so advise. I shall not let it appear that *I* have disappointed your[122] joint hopes and plans; and if that prove difficult, at any rate I shall reap a

120. Literally 'from 1/3 to 2/3%' (monthly).

121. There were four candidates for the Consulship of 53: M. Aemilius Scaurus, Cn. Domitius Calvinus, C. Memmius, and M. Valerius Messalla Rufus. On the coalition cf. *Letters to Atticus* 91 (IV.17)2.

122. Quintus' and Caesar's.

rich harvest of influence and prestige from my labour. So I follow your wishes. I take care to offend nobody, to be highly regarded even by those who deplore our having become so closely involved with Caesar, and an object of much attention and friendly feeling from non-partisans or from those whose sympathies actually lie this way. There has been a debate in the Senate lasting a number of days on the bribery question. The most drastic action was called for, the candidates for the Consulship having gone to intolerable lengths. I did not attend. I have decided not to come forward to cure the ills of the body politic without powerful backing.

The day I write this letter Drusus has been acquitted of collusive prosecution by the Paymaster-Tribunes. The overall majority was four, the Senators and Knights having found him guilty. This afternoon I shall be defending Vatinius – an easy matter. The elections have been put off to September. Scaurus' trial[123] will proceed straight away, and I shall not let him down.

I don't at all approve of Sophocles' *Banqueters*,[124] though you evidently gave an entertaining performance.

Now I come to what ought perhaps to have been put first. How pleased I was to get your letter from Britain! I dreaded the Ocean and the island coast. Not that I make light of what is to come, but there is more to hope than to fear, and my suspense is more a matter of anticipation than of anxiety. You evidently have some splendid literary material – the places, the natural phenomena and scenes, the customs, the peoples you fight, and, last but not least, the Commander-in-Chief! I shall be glad to help you, as you ask, in any way you wish, and I shall send you the verses you ask for (an owl to Athens!).[125]

But see here, you seem to be keeping me in the dark. Tell me,

123. For extortion in Sardinia; cf. *Letters to Atticus* 89 (IV.16)6, 90 (IV.15)9, 91 (IV.17)3.

124. Sophocles wrote a satyric play so entitled, but Cicero's meaning is obscure.

125. Cf. *Letters to his Friends*, n. 515.

my dear fellow, how does Caesar react to my verses?[126] He wrote to me that he read the first Canto and has never read anything better than the earlier part, even in Greek, but finds the rest, down to a certain point a trifle 'languid'. The truth, please! Is it the material or the style he doesn't like? No need for you to be nervous – my self-esteem won't drop a hair's-breadth. Just write to me *en ami de la vérité* and in your usual fraternal way.

21 (III. 1)

CICERO TO HIS BROTHER

Arpinum and Rome, September 54

From Marcus to his brother Quintus greetings.

Escaped from the great heat-wave (I don't remember a greater), I have refreshed myself on the banks of our delightful river at Arpinum during the Games period, after putting our fellow-tribesmen in the hands of Philotimus.

I was at Arcanum on 10 September. There I saw Mescidius and Philoxenus and the stream which they are bringing over not far from the house. It was flowing merrily enough, particularly in view of the severe drought, and they said they would be collecting a considerably larger volume of water. All was well at Herus'.[127]

On the Manilius property[128] I found Diphilus, slower than – Diphilus. However, he had nothing left to do except for the baths, promenade, and aviary. I was very pleased with the house, because the paved colonnade is a most imposing feature;

126. The poem *On my Vicissitudes*.

127. 'Herus' was probably the bailiff (therefore a slave). But the name is unexampled. Perhaps it should be 'Herius'.

128. Seemingly near Arcanum and recently acquired by Quintus.

it struck me only this visit, now that its whole range is open to view and the columns have been cleared. All depends on the elegance of the stucco, and that I shall attend to. The paving seemed to be going nicely. I did not care for some of the ceilings and gave orders to alter them.

They say you have written instructions for a small court in a certain area of the colonnade. I like that area better as it is. I don't think there is enough space for a small court, and it is not very usual to have one except in buildings which contain a larger court. Nor could it have adjoining bedrooms and suchlike appurtenances. As it is, it will make a handsome vault or a very good summer-room. But if you feel otherwise, please write back as soon as possible.

In the baths I moved the sweat-bath into the other corner of the dressing-room because in the original position its steam-pipe lay immediately underneath the bedrooms. I was very pleased with a largish bedroom and another bedroom for winter; they are a good size and well situated on the side of the promenade next the baths. The columns placed by Diphilus are neither straight nor properly aligned. He will pull them down, of course. One day he may learn how to use a rule and plumb-line. To be sure, I hope Diphilus' job will be finished in a few months. Caesius, who was with me at the time, is keeping a very watchful eye on it.

From there I set off straight down Steer Street to the Fufidius farm which I bought for you from Fufidius in Arpinum last market day for HS101,000. I never saw a shadier place in summer. There is running water all over and plenty of it. In fact Caesius thinks you will irrigate thirty-five acres of meadow with ease. For my part I'll promise what I better understand, that you will have an exceptionally charming country house when certain extras have been put in – a fish-pond, fountains, a palaestra, a * wood. I hear you want to keep this Bobilius[129] place. You

129. Another property, called after its previous owner. But the name may be corrupt – perhaps 'Babullius'.

will decide for yourself what you think best about that. *[130] says that with the water taken off, and the right to the water legally certified, and a servitude placed on the property, we can still keep our price if we wanted to sell. I had Mescidius with me. He says he agreed with you on three sesterces per foot,[131] and that he has measured the distance by walking as 3,000 paces. It looked more to me, but I will guarantee that the money could not be better invested. I had sent for Cillo from Venafrum, but that very day at Venafrum a tunnel had fallen in, crushing four of his fellow-slaves and pupils.

On the Ides of September I was at Laterium. I examined the road, which I thought good enough to be a public highway, except for 150 paces (I measured it myself) from the little bridge at Furina's[132] temple leading to Satricum. In that stretch powdered earth has been used instead of gravel (that will be altered) and that part of the road has a steep uphill gradient. But I saw that no other direction was possible, especially as you did not want to take it through either Locusta's land or Varro's. Varro had made the road in front of his property in good style, whereas Locusta has not touched his section. I shall tackle him in Rome and think I shall get him moving. At the same time I shall ask M. Taurus, who is now in Rome, about taking a conduit through his farm – I hear he has made you a promise.

Your bailiff Nicephorus impressed me very favourably. I asked him whether you had given him any instructions about that little bit of building at Laterium of which you had spoken to me. He answered that he had contracted to do the job himself for HS10,000, but that you had later made considerable additions to the work and none to the price, so he had done nothing about it. For my part, I am really strongly in favour of making the additions you proposed. True, the house at present

130. The name in the manuscripts appears as 'Calibus'. Purser's correction *Camillus* is the most plausible.

131. For the construction of an aqueduct.

132. Or Furrina, an ancient Roman goddess of whom little is known.

has an air of high thinking which rebukes the wild extravagance of other country houses; but still that addition will be pleasant. I commended the gardener. He has covered everything with ivy, the foundation-wall of the house and the intervals between the columns in the promenade, so that the Greek statues look as though they were doing ornamental gardening and advertising their ivy. Then there is the little dining-room which is cool and mossy to a degree.

That's about all from the country. Philotimus and Cincius are pushing on with the finishing touches to your house, but I often put in an appearance myself, which is easy to do. So please set your mind at rest on that score.

I pardon your continual enquiries about young Quintus, but I hope you on your side will pardon me if I refuse to admit that you love him any more than I do myself. I only wish he could have been with me these days at Arpinum, which he wanted and I no less. So I'd like you to write to Pomponia, if you see fit, and ask her to come with me when I make an excursion and bring the boy. I shall do wonders if I have him by me on vacation – in Rome there isn't a moment to breathe. You know I gave you my word earlier gratis, so you can imagine what will happen now that you have offered me such a splendid fee.

I come now to the letter which I received at Arpinum in several instalments – three letters were delivered to me in one day, apparently dispatched by you simultaneously. One, which was rather long, began by noting that my letter to you bore an earlier date than the one to Caesar. It sometimes happens unavoidably that when Oppius has arranged to send couriers and been given a letter from me, he is held up by something unexpected and dispatches it unavoidably later than he had arranged; and once the letters are handed in, I don't trouble about getting the date changed.

You write about Caesar's warm affection for us. You will cherish that, and I shall do everything in my power to increase it. As regards Pompey, I am and shall be careful to do what you advise. You say you are grateful for my licence to stay on; I miss you very sorely indeed, but still I am partially glad of it. I don't understand your purpose in sending for Hippodamus and certain others. Every one of these gentry expects a present from you to the value of a property in the suburbs. But you don't have to mix up Trebatius in that category. *I* sent him to Caesar, who has already done all I expected of him. If he has not done all that Trebatius expected, I am not obliged to answer for anything and I likewise absolve and acquit you of all responsibility for him. I am tremendously pleased that you say you are rising in Caesar's good graces every day. Balbus, who you say is your helper in this, is the apple of my eye. I am glad that you and my friend Trebonius are such good friends.

As for what you write about the Tribunate, I did request one for Curtius[133] and Caesar wrote to me personally in so many words that one was waiting for Curtius, mentioning his name; and he took me to task for my backwardness in making such requests. If I make one for anybody else (and I have told Oppius to write to Caesar accordingly), I shall not mind a refusal, seeing that the people who pester me *do* mind *my* refusing them. I have a regard for Curtius, as I told himself, not only because you ask me but because of your testimonial, for your letter made it clear to me how zealous he was for my restoration.

As to British matters, I see from your letter that we have no cause for alarm nor for rejoicing either. On public affairs, which you want Tiro to write up for you, I have hitherto written rather perfunctorily because I know that everything, from greatest to least, is reported to Caesar.

I have answered the big letter, now for the little one: First you tell me about Clodius' letter to Caesar. I think Caesar was right to say no to the request you so affectionately made of him and not to write a single word to that embodiment of mis-

133. Cf. Letter 18 (II.14)3.

chief.[134] Next, as to Calventius Marius' speech,[135] I am surprised that you think I should write a rejoinder to that, especially as nobody will read it if I don't reply, whereas all the school-children learn mine against him by heart as though it was part of their lessons. I have begun the work which you are waiting for,[136] but I can't finish it this trip. I have completed the speeches for Scaurus and for Plancius[137] according to demand. I have broken off the poem addressed to Caesar which I had begun, but for you I shall write what you ask[138] (since the very springs are now athirst),[139] if I get any time.

Now I come to the third letter. You say that Balbus will be coming to Rome in good time with a goodly company and that he will be with me constantly until the Ides of May; much obliged, and much pleased to hear it. And then on the same letter, as often in the past, you urge me to go on winning friends and working. I shall. But when are we going to start living?

A fourth letter was delivered to me on the Ides of September, which you dispatched from Britain on 10 August. There was really nothing new in it except about *Erigona*[140] (and when I get her from Oppius I shall send you my opinion, though I don't doubt I shall like her) and (this I almost forgot) about the person who you say wrote to Caesar about the applause for Milo.

134. Quintus in brotherly solicitude had urged Caesar to rebuke or restrain Clodius; but Caesar had thought it best not to reply at all, a decision which M. Cicero approves.

135. L. Calpurnius Piso, Consul in 57, whose maternal grandfather was an Insubrian Gaul named Calventius. Cicero's speech against him, delivered in 55, compares him (naturally to his disadvantage) with Marius, who was responsible for Metellus Numidicus' exile in 100; cf. *in Pisonem*, 20. Piso had evidently published a speech in reply to Cicero's.

136. The treatise *On the Republic*.

137. Part of the former and the whole of the latter are extant.

138. Cf. Letter 24 (III.4)3.

139. Cicero affects to consider Quintus a better poet than himself; cf. ibid.

140. A tragedy composed by Quintus.

Well, I am quite happy that Caesar should think the applause was tremendous. In point of fact, it was; though applause for him seems in a way like applause for me.

Also, a very old letter was delivered to me, a late arrival, in which you remind me about the temple of Tellus and Catulus' portico.[141] Work is going diligently forward on both. I have even put up your statue in the former. You also remind me about a place in the suburbs, but I was never very eager for one and my house now affords me that amenity.

When I returned to Rome on 18 September I found the roof on your house finished. You had not wished it to have any gables above the living-rooms. It now slopes handsomely down to the roof of the lower portico.

Our boy has not been idle with his tutor in rhetoric during my absence. You need have no anxiety about his progress, for you know his abilities and I see his keenness. All else that concerns him I take upon myself and regard as my responsibility.

So far there are three groups out to prosecute Gabinius: L. Lentulus, the Flamen's son, who has already brought a charge of lèse-majesté; Ti. Nero, with some good assistant-prosecutors; and Tribune C. Memmius,[142] with L. Capito. Gabinius arrived in the neighbourhood of Rome on 19 September. It was an ignominious homecoming with hardly a soul to welcome him. But the courts being what they are nowadays I dare not feel confident about anything. He has not yet been charged with extortion because Cato is ill. Pompey is putting a lot of pressure on me for a reconciliation, but so far he has got nowhere, nor ever will if I keep a scrap of personal independence. I am waiting impatiently for a letter from you. It is untrue that I had anything to do with the coalition between the

141. The latter, adjoining Cicero's house on the Palatine, had been destroyed by Clodius. Cicero seems to have been in charge of restoring both.

142. To be distinguished from his relative and namesake, the consular candidate.

consular candidates, as you say you have heard. In view of the nature of the bargains struck in that coalition, which were subsequently made public by Memmius, no honest man could decently have had a hand in it. Besides, it would not have been right for me to take part in coalitions from which Messalla was excluded. He is very pleased with the support I am giving him in all ways. I think Memmius is pleased too. Even Domitius has had many favours from me, things he wanted or asked of me. Scaurus is under a great obligation to me for defending him. So far both the date of the elections and the result are highly uncertain.

Just as I was folding up this letter, couriers arrived from you – on the 20th, twenty-seven days' journey. How anxious I was! And how distressed to read Caesar's charming letter – the more charming the letter, the more distress I feel at the blow which has befallen him. But to come to your letter: First, once again I approve of your staying on, especially as you have discussed it, as you say, with Caesar. I am surprised that Oppius has had any dealings with Publius[143] – I did not want it. Further on in your letter you say that I am to be appointed Pompey's Legate on the Ides of September.[144] That is news to me. I have written to Caesar to say that neither Vibullius nor Oppius has brought any message from Caesar to Pompey about my staying in Rome. What was the reason? Well, it's true that I held Oppius back, because the leading role belonged to Vibullius; Caesar had talked to him in person on the subject, only written to Oppius. No, I cannot have any second thoughts where Caesar is concerned. He comes next with me after you and our children, and only just after. I think I am wise in this (after all, it is time for some wisdom), but my affection is truly kindled.

After I had written these last lines which are in my own hand, your son came over to us for dinner, as Pomponia was dining out. He gave me your letter to read, which he had received

143. Clodius.

144. Cf. *Letters to his Friends*, n. 142.

shortly before – a charming, serious letter upon my word, in the manner of Aristophanes.[145] I was quite delighted with it. He also gave me the other letter, in which you tell him to stick close to me and regard me as his teacher. How pleased they made him these letters, and me likewise! He is the most charming boy, and no one could be fonder of me. I dictated the above to Tiro at dinner, in case the different handwriting may surprise you.

Annalis was very grateful for your letter, grateful to you for taking trouble on his behalf and at the same time for honestly advising him for his own good. P. Servilius senior, speaking of a letter which he says he has had from Caesar, intimates that he is very much obliged to you for having spoken so kindly and with such particularity about his friendly feelings towards Caesar.

When I got back to Rome from Arpinum I was told that Hippodamus had set out to join you. I cannot say that I was surprised by his lack of consideration in leaving to join you without a letter from me. I say only that it vexed me. You see, it had been in my mind for a long time, from what you had written to me, that if there was anything which I wanted conveyed to you with extra care I should give it to him; for in those letters which I send you in the ordinary way the fact is that I write practically nothing which would be awkward if it fell into the wrong hands. Now[146] I am reserving myself for Minucius and Salvius and Labeo. Labeo will either leave late or stay here. Hippodamus did not even bid me goodbye.

T. Pinarius sends me an amiable letter about you, saying that he takes great pleasure in your letters, your conversation, and, not least, your dinners. I always liked him, and his brother is much in my company. So go on being nice to the young man.

I have had this letter in my hands for many days past, and so collected many items at different times. For instance: T. Anicius

145. Probably the comic poet rather than the grammarian.
146. *nunc* seems to have fallen out of the text before *Minucio*.

has often told me that he would not hesitate to buy a suburban property for you if he found one. This talk of his surprises me in two ways. I think it strange that you should write to him about buying a suburban property, whereas not only do you not write about it to *me* but you write in a different sense. I also think it odd that when you write to him you don't remember anything about those letters of his which you showed me at Tusculum or the precept of Epicharmus ('Find how he behaves to others'), that in fact you have as it were obliterated (?), so I suppose, his whole face and talk and mind. But it's your affair. As to suburban property, make sure that I know your wishes, and mind he doesn't do something idiotic.

What else? Oh yes, Gabinius entered Rome after dark on 27 September and today at two o'clock, when he had to appear to answer a charge of lèse-majesté on C. Alfius' order, he was almost crushed by a huge, hostile assembly of the whole people. He cuts the sorriest of figures, but Piso runs him close. I am thinking of putting a marvellous episode into Canto II of my 'Vicissitudes' – Apollo in the assembly of the Gods foretelling the return of the two generals, one of them after losing his army, the other after selling it.

Caesar dispatched a letter to me from Britain on the Kalends of September which I received on 27 September, giving a good enough account of the British campaign. He says that, in case I might wonder why I got no letter from you, you were not with him when he got to the coast. I have not replied, not even to congratulate him, because of his bereavement.[147]

Once again, my dear fellow, I beg you take care of your health.

147. Caesar's daughter and Pompey's wife Julia had recently died.

22 (III. 2)

CICERO TO HIS BROTHER

Rome, 11 October 54

From Marcus to his brother Quintus greetings.

On the evening of 10 October Salvius left for Ostia by boat with the articles you wanted sent to you from Rome. That same day Memmius[148] gave Gabinius a rare pasting at a public meeting; Calidius was not allowed to say a word in his defence. The day following the day that is about to break as I write Memmius, Ti. Nero, and the Antonius brothers (Gaius and Lucius, sons of Marcus) will plead before Cato for the right to prosecute Gabinius. We think it will go to Memmius, though Nero is remarkably keen. In a word, he is properly under pressure – unless our friend Pompey spoils the sport to the disgust of God and man.

Now let me tell you about the fellow's insolence – something to give you a little pleasure in this twilight of the commonwealth. After giving out wherever he went that he was claiming a Triumph and then (good general that he is) suddenly bursting into the enemy capital[149] at night, he didn't trust himself inside the Senate. Not until[150] the statutory tenth day, on which he was required to report the number of sacrificial victims and soldiers, did he creep into a very thin House.[151] As he was about

148. The Tribune.

149. Literally 'into a city' (or 'into Rome'; *in urbem* can mean either) 'full of enemies'.

150. *interim* ('meanwhile') in the manuscripts seems to be wrong. I have conjectured *inde primo*.

151. By entering Rome Gabinius had forfeited his claim to a Triumph, which, in any case, could hardly be taken seriously after the Senate's refusal of his Supplication. Cicero's remarks are therefore ironical. It

to leave he was detained by the Consuls and the tax-farmers brought in. Attacked from all sides as he was, I hit him hardest. Unable to stand it, he called out 'exile' in a quavering voice. Thereupon (Gods above, it was the most flattering thing that ever happened to me) the Senate rose like one man, shouting and physically bearing down on him. The tax-farmers shouted as loud and moved as smartly. To put it in a nutshell, every man of them behaved as though he was you. Outside the House nothing has ever been more talked of. However, I refrain from prosecuting him myself – with difficulty I can assure you, but I refrain. I don't want a fight with Pompey (what's coming over Milo is enough) and there are no juries any more. I'm afraid of a fiasco. And then people are so malicious – I'm nervous that he might gain some advantage with myself as prosecutor. And I don't despair of seeing the thing go through without me, and in some degree with my assistance.

All the candidates for the Consulship have been charged with bribery: Domitius by Memmius,[152] Memmius by Q. Acutius (a good, well-instructed young man), Messalla by Q. Pompeius, Scaurus by Triarius. Something big is on the way, for it looks like the end of either the men or the laws. Efforts are being made to prevent the trials, and there's the prospect of an Interregnum. The Consuls are eager to hold elections, but the defendants don't want them, especially Memmius, because he hopes that when Caesar arrives he will be elected. But he is in remarkably low water. It seems a certainty for Domitius and Messalla. Scaurus has gone flat. Appius says definitely that he will take over from our friend Lentulus[153] without a *lex*

would seem that a general claiming a Triumph was required to give notice within ten days of arrival in the area of Rome how many sacrificial victims he proposed to immolate and how many soldiers would be taking part. The reading *hostium* ('enemies') in Watt's text, instead of *hostiarum* ('victims'), has practically no manuscript authority and is otherwise unsatisfactory.

152. Probably the candidate rather than the Tribune.

153. As governor of Cilicia.

curiata. I almost forgot to say that he was magnificent that day against Gabinius – charged him with lèse-majesté. Members volunteered (?),[154] while Gabinius never said a word.

So much for public affairs. At home all is well. As to the home itself, the contractors are making reasonably good progress.

23 (III. 3)

CICERO TO HIS BROTHER

Rome, 21 October 54

From Marcus to his brother Quintus greetings.

You may take my secretary's handwriting as a sign of how busy I am. I tell you, there is not a day on which I don't make a speech for the defence. So practically everything I do or think about I put into my walking-time.

Our affairs stand as follows: Domestically they are as we wish them. The boys are well, keen at their lessons and conscientiously taught. They love us and each other. The finishing touches to both our houses are in train, but your country residences at Arcanum and Laterium are already all but complete. Furthermore, I wrote to you in full detail about the water and the road in one of my letters,[155] omitting nothing. But I am very anxious and worried by the fact that for more than seven weeks now I have heard nothing either from you or from Caesar. Not a letter, not even a rumour has trickled in from that part of the world. Sea and land out there both make me anxious now, and, as usual when people one is fond of are concerned, I am continually imagining the worst. I won't ask you

154. Literally 'names were given'; but the meaning is uncertain.
155. Letter 21 (III.1).

to write to me about yourself and about what is going on, for you never lose an opportunity; but I do want you to know that I have never been so impatient for anything in my life as I am for a letter from you as I write these lines.

Now let me tell you about politics. Day by day election-days are cancelled by declarations of contrary omens, to the great satisfaction of all honest men. That is because the Consuls are in very bad odour owing to the suspicion that they have sold themselves to the candidates. All four consular candidates have been charged. The cases are difficult to defend, but I am working hard to save Messalla, and that involves the survival of the others. P. Sulla has charged Gabinius with bribery, with his stepson Memmius, his brother Caecilius,[156] and his son Sulla as assistant-prosecutors. L. Torquatus put in a rival claim to prosecute and everyone was glad it failed. You will want to know what is happening about Gabinius. We shall know about the lèse-majesté in three days' time. In that trial he is weighed down by his unpopularity with all classes, and the witnesses are most damaging; the prosecutors are extremely ineffective, the jury is a mixed bag, the President, Alfius, is responsible and firm, Pompey is urgently trying to influence the jurors. I don't know what will happen, but I don't see any place for him in the community. I take a moderate attitude as to his ruin, and a very easy one as to the outcome of events.

That is about all my news. I will add one thing: your (our) boy Quintus is greatly devoted to his tutor in rhetoric, Paeonius, a very good experienced man, I think; but, as you are aware, my method of instruction is a little more scholarly and abstract. Accordingly, I don't want Quintus' progress and the teaching he is getting held up; and the boy himself seems to find the declamatory mode more attractive and agreeable. We have been through it ourselves, so let us allow him to follow in our footsteps. I am confident he will reach the same goal. All the same, when I take him away with me somewhere in the

156. L. Caecilius Rufus, Praetor in 57.

country, I shall introduce him to my method and practice. You have offered me a big fee, and it won't be my fault if I don't earn it.

Do write to me in full detail where you will be spending the winter and with what prospects.

24 (III. 4)

CICERO TO HIS BROTHER

Rome, 24 October 54

From Marcus to his brother Quintus greetings.

Gabinius has been acquitted. To be sure, the prosecutor Lentulus and his assistants were stutterers and the jury was a disgrace. None the less, but for Pompey's incredible lobbying and importunity, also the formidable rumour of a Dictatorship, he would not have answered, not even to Lentulus. Even with such a prosecutor and such a jury he was found guilty by 32 votes out of 70 cast. To be sure, this trial has caused so much scandal that he looks likely to go under in the forthcoming trials, especially for extortion. But you see that we have neither commonwealth nor Senate nor courts of justice, and that none of us has any standing. Further as to the jury, two ex-Praetors sat on it, Domitius Calvinus (who openly voted for acquittal for all to see) and *[157] (when the votes had been counted he slipped off and was the first to bring the good news to Pompey).

Some, like Sallustius, say I ought to have prosecuted. Was I to trust myself with such a jury as this? How should I have looked if he had got away with me conducting the business? But I had

157. The manuscripts have 'Cato'; but M. Cato, who was Praetor in 54, is impossible, C. Cato, Tribune in 56, equally so. Gutta, who appears to have been a candidate for the Consulship of 52 favoured by Pompey (cf. p. 732), is a possibility.

other reasons. Pompey would have felt that it was a fight between him and me, and that the stake was, not Gabinius' survival, but his own prestige. He would have entered Rome, it would have come to a feud. I should have looked like Pacideianus matched against Aeserninus the Samnite.[158] He might have bitten off my ear, and he would certainly have made it up with Clodius. No, I strongly approve of my decision, especially if you don't disapprove of it. Think of what Pompey did. I had shown extraordinary zeal for his advancement, I was under no obligation to him, whereas his to me were unlimited; and yet he couldn't tolerate (I will use no harsher phrase) my political disagreement with himself, and though less powerful then than now he showed what he could do to me at the height of my career. *Now*, when I don't even trouble about having power and the state certainly has none and Pompey alone is all-powerful, was I to lock horns with Pompey himself? For that is what I should have had to do. I don't believe you would have had me take that upon myself. 'One thing or the other,' says that same Sallustius. 'You ought to have defended him and yielded to Pompey's insistence' (he certainly begged me earnestly to do that). What a charming friend Sallustius is! He thinks I ought to have chosen between a dangerous feud and eternal disgrace. For my part, I like this middle way. And I am glad to remember that after I had given my evidence very gravely in accordance with my honour and conscience the defendant said that if he was allowed to remain in the community he would make me amends. Nor did he ask me a single question.

As for the verses you want me to write for you, I lack the leisure, but I also lack divine *afflatus*, which[159] calls not only for time but for a mind free of all anxiety. For I am not altogether

158. Two gladiators in the time of Lucilius. Pacideianus was the more skilful, Aeserninus the more powerful.

159. I translate a reading proposed in *Proceedings of the Cambridge Philological Society*, 7 (1961), p. 4.

without anxiety about next year, though I have no fear. And furthermore, truly without false modesty, I recognize you as my superior in that line of authorship.

As regards filling the gaps in your Greek library and exchanging books and acquiring Latin ones, I should very much like all this done, especially as I too stand to benefit. But I have nobody I can employ on such business, not even for myself. Books, at least such as one would like to have, are not on the market and they can't be obtained except through an expert who is willing to take trouble. However, I'll give an order to Chrysippus and talk to Tyrannio. I shall enquire what Scipio has done about the Treasury,[160] and shall pay what appears proper. As to Ascanio, you will do what you wish – I don't interfere. You are wise to be in no hurry about a suburban property, though I do encourage you to get one.

I am writing this on 24 October, the opening day of the Games, as I leave for Tusculum. I am taking my son with me, to work, not to play. The reason I go no further away, as[161] I should have liked to do, is that I want to put in an appearance for Pomptinus, whose Triumph is on 2 November. And there will be some little trouble, for Praetors Cato and Servilius are threatening to forbid it. I don't know what they can do (he will have Consul Appius with him and most of the Praetors and Tribunes), but threaten they do, especially Q. Scaevola, 'breathing war'.[162]

Take care of your health, my sweetest and dearest of brothers.

160. Nothing is known about this business, but cf. p. 728.
161. Read *quod vellem* for *quam vellem*.
162. Greek. (The Latin equivalent is in *Letters to Atticus* 389 (XV.11).1); cf. Aeschylus, *Agamemnon*, 375, Quintus of Smyrna, I. 343.

25 (III. 5)

CICERO TO HIS BROTHER

Tusculum, end of October or beginning of November 54

From Marcus to his brother Quintus greetings.

You ask what has become of the work[163] which I started to write when I was at Cumae. Well, I have not been and am not idle, but several times already I have changed the whole plan and framework. I had two Books in which I presented a conversation held during the nine-day holiday in the Consulship of Tuditanus and Aquilius,[164] the speakers being Africanus (shortly before his death), Laelius, Philus, Manilius, P. Rutilius, Q. Tubero, and Laelius' sons-in-law, Fannius and Scaevola. The conversation, distributed over nine days and nine Books, concerned the ideal constitution and the ideal citizen. The composition of the work was going forward very nicely and the high rank of the participants lent weight to their words. But when these two Books were read to me at Tusculum in Sallustius' hearing, he pointed out that these matters could be treated with much more authority if I spoke of the state in my own person. After all, he said, I was no Heraclides of Pontus but a Consular, one who had been involved in most important state affairs. Speeches attributed to persons so remote in time would appear fictitious. In my earlier work on the theory of oratory, he said, I had tactfully separated the conversation of the orators from myself, but I had put it into the mouths of men whom I had personally seen. Finally, Aristotle's writings on the state and the pre-eminent individual are in his own person.

This shook me, all the more so as I was debarred from touching upon the greatest upheavals in our community because they

163. *On the Republic.*
164. 129 B.C.

took place after the lifetimes of the interlocutors. In point of fact that was my object at the time, to avoid giving offence in any quarter if I came into contact with our own period. Now, while avoiding this, I shall speak myself in conversation with you; none the less I shall send you what I had begun when I return to Rome. I think you will appreciate that it cost me some heartburning to give up those two Books.

Caesar's affection as expressed in his letter pleases me beyond anything, but I set no great store by the promises he holds out. I am not thirsty for honours nor do I hanker after glory. I look forward to his lasting good-will more than to the outcome of his promises. And yet I live constantly toiling to win friends as though I *were* looking forward to what I do not ask.

As for your request about writing verses, my dear fellow, you cannot believe how short I am of time; and frankly I am not sufficiently stimulated by the theme on which you want me to poetize. Do you ask me for tides[165] and things which I myself cannot even imagine – you, who have excelled everyone in this kind of descriptive eloquence? Even so I should do it as best I could, but, as you are very well aware, poetry calls for a certain *élan* of which the times we live in quite deprive me. To be sure, I am withdrawing from all political concerns and giving myself up to literary work; all the same, I will tell you something which I assure you I used to want to hide from you of all people. My sweetest brother, it wrings my heart to think that we have no commonwealth, no courts of justice, and that these years of my life which ought to be passing in the plenitude of senatorial dignity are spent in the hurly-burly of forensic practice or rendered tolerable by my studies at home. As for my childhood dream, 'Far to excel, out-topping all the rest,'[166] it has perished

165. Reading *ampoteis* (Greek) *et ea quae*. Quintus had invited Cicero to describe British natural phenomena in verse (cf. p. 708), including the ocean tides.

166. Cf. *Letters to his Friends*, n. 809. *pollon* ('far') is here substituted for *aien* ('always').

utterly. Some of my enemies I have refrained from attacking, others I have actually defended. My mind, even my animosities, are in chains. And in all the world Caesar is the only man who cares for me as much as I could wish, or (as others would have it) who wants *me* to care for *him*.[167] And yet nothing of all this is so painful but that I find many consolations to make life easier day by day. But the greatest consolation will be for us to be together. As it is, I have to bear the heavy burden of your absence on top of the rest.

If I had defended Gabinius, as Pansa thought I ought to have done, it would have been my undoing. Those who hate him (and this includes all categories of society) would have begun to hate me – the very person on whose account they hate *him*.[168] I held my horses to admiration, I think, doing just so much as everyone saw I had to do. And in the final sum I am resolutely facing in the direction of tranquillity and peace, as you advise.

As for the books, Tyrannio is a dawdler. I shall speak to Chrysippus. But it is a laborious business and needs somebody who will take a lot of trouble. I know that from my own experience of trying very hard and making no headway. As for the Latin ones, I don't know where to turn, the copies are made and sold so full of errors. None the less, I shall not neglect to do what can be done.

*,[169] as I wrote to you earlier, is in Rome and reports himself as infinitely obliged to you, which is very gratifying.[170] I think our business has been settled by the Treasury during my absence.

You write that you have finished off four tragedies in sixteen days; and are *you* trying to borrow anything from someone else? And are you asking for *Sailors* when you have written an

167. Reading *qui a me amari vellet.*

168. As largely to blame for Cicero's exile.

169. 'Crebrius', according to the manuscripts, which are probably corrupt.

170. Reading *et, quod valde iuvat, omnia debere tibi renuntiat.*

Electra and a ★?[171] Don't be so lazy. And don't suppose that the old maxim 'know thyself' was made only to reduce conceit; it also tells us to know our strong points. But please send me these new ones and *Erigona*. There are your two last letters answered.

In Rome and especially on the Appian Way near the temple of Mars we are having extraordinarily heavy floods. Crassipes' promenade has been swept away along with a great number of residences and shops. The vast expanse of water stretches as far as the public fish-pond. Homer's lines are much quoted:

> An autumn day, when Zeus most mightily
> Doth rain, in ire against unrighteous men,

pat as they are to Gabinius' acquittal:

> Who, rendering crooked judgements openly,
> Drive justice out nor reck of wrath divine.[172]

But I am resolved not to trouble myself about such matters. When I get back to Rome I shall write to you what I observe, especially about the Dictatorship, and shall send letters to Labienus and Ligurius.

I am writing this before dawn by the light of a little lamp with a wooden stand, which delights me because they say you had it made when you were in Samos.

Goodbye, my sweetest and best of brothers.

171. On this passage see *Proceedings of the Cambridge Philological Society*, 7 (1961), p. 5.
172. *Iliad*, XVI.385–8.

26 (III. 6)

CICERO TO HIS BROTHER

Rome, end of November 54

From Marcus to his brother Quintus greetings.

I have no answer to make to your earlier letter, which is full of spleen and grumblings (you say you gave another in similar vein to Labienus the previous day, but that has not yet arrived); for the letter which followed it obliterated all my vexation. I only warn and beg you amid these annoyances and labours and privations to be mindful of our purpose when you went to Gaul. They were no trifling or ordinary advantages that we had in view. What would have seemed worth the price of our separation? Our object was to gain reliable, comprehensive support for our public position and status from the good-will of a very fine and very powerful person. Our capital is invested in hope rather than in money; if that hope were to be abandoned,[173] all else would be saved only to be lost later on. Accordingly, if you will frequently carry your mind back to our old reasoned purpose and hope, you will find it easier to put up with your military labours and the other irritants – which, however, you will lay aside when you so desire; but the time is not yet ripe for that, though it is already drawing near.

I would also advise you not to trust anything to a letter which might embarrass us if it became public property. There are many things of which I had sooner be ignorant than informed, if the information carries risk. I shall write to you at greater length when, as I hope, my boy is himself again and my mind is easy. On your part please see to it that I know to whom I ought

173. Reading *qua relicta reliqua.*

to give the letter which I shall then be sending – should it be Caesar's couriers, so that he forwards it to you straight away, or Labienus'? For where those Nervii of yours live and how far they are away from us I don't know.

It gave me much pleasure to learn from your letter of the courage and dignity of Caesar's bearing in his great sorrow.[174] As for your command that I finish that poem addressed to him which I had begun, my time is much distracted and my mind far more so, but since Caesar knows from my letter to you that I have started on something, I shall go back to what I began and finish it during these leisure days of Supplications. I am very glad that thanks to them our friend Messalla and the others have been relieved of annoyance, and when you folk reckon him as certain of election along with Domitius you don't at all run counter to our opinion. I make myself responsible to Caesar for Messalla's behaviour. But Memmius pins hopes on Caesar's return to Italy, wherein I fancy he is making a mistake. Here at any rate he is in the cold. Scaurus was thrown over by Pompey some time ago.

Business has been adjourned and the elections brought to an Interregnum. There is talk of a Dictator, disagreeable to the honest men; what they are saying is to me still less agreeable. But the whole idea is viewed with alarm, and at the same time it's falling flat. Pompey categorically denies any desire for it. Talking to me himself earlier on he did not use to deny it. It looks as though Hirrus will make the proposal (Gods, what an ass he is! How he loves himself – in which regard he has no competitor!). He got me to frighten off Crassus Junianus,[175] who is at my service. Does he want it or doesn't he? Hard to tell, but if Hirrus is the mover, he will never persuade the world that

174. Julia's death.

175. A Tribune in 53. His full name seems to have been P. Licinius Crassus Junianus (Brutus) Damasippus.

he doesn't. At present they are talking of nothing else in the way of politics; certainly nothing is a-doing.

The funeral of Serranus, Domitius' son,[176] took place on 23 November, a very sad occasion. His father spoke a eulogy of my composition.

Now about Milo: Pompey does nothing to help him and everything to help Gutta.[177] He says that he will see to it that Caesar throws his weight that way. This appalls Milo, as well it may, and he is almost in despair should Pompey become Dictator. If he assists anyone vetoing the Dictatorship with his organized band he fears Pompey's hostility, whereas if he doesn't give such assistance he's afraid it will be carried through by force. He is preparing some most magnificent Games, in fact they will cost as much as any that ever were – which is double and triple folly, for (a) nobody asked him, (b) he had previously given a splendid show, (c) he can't afford it; or rather more than triple because (d) he could have seen himself as an executor, not an Aedile.[178]

That's about all. Take care of your health, my dearest brother.

27 (III. 7)

CICERO TO HIS BROTHER

Rome, December 54

From Marcus to his brother Quintus greetings.

It would not have been right for me to take any of the courses

176. Reading with Münzer *Domiti* for *domestici*. The deceased will have been a son of L. Domitius Ahenobarbus adopted by an Atilius Serranus.

177. Otherwise unknown, unless he is the ex-Praetor mentioned in Letter 24; see n. 157. Milo was standing for the Consulship of 52.

178. Reading *vel quia non postulatos* and *vel magis quam ter, quia potuerat*. But the meaning of *magistrum*, translated 'executor', is uncertain.

with regard to Gabinius which you, in the warmth of your affection, have been considering. 'Then let the earth yawn wide for me.'[179] What I did I did, as everybody feels, with the utmost responsibility and moderation. I have neither borne hard on him nor lent a helping hand. I spoke forcibly on the witness-stand but otherwise held my peace. As for the outcome of the trial, shocking and detrimental as it was, I took it with complete composure. Now at long last I have gained this much: the evils in our public life and the licence of bold, bad men, which used to make me boil with rage, now leave me quite unmoved. For the men and the times could not be worse than they are; so, since public affairs can no longer yield any pleasure, I don't know why I should get my temper up. I have sources of joy in my writings and studies, the leisure of my country houses, and above all else in our children. Milo is my only worry, but I hope his Consulship will put an end to that. I shall make as big an effort in that as I made for my own, and you will help from over there, as you are doing. In this matter, unless sheer violence breaks loose, everything is in good shape with one exception – his pocket. That alarms me. 'Mad he is, past all bearing'[180] – planning a show to cost HS ⋆. His unwisdom in this one particular I shall restrain as best I can, and your force of character[181] should enable you to do the like with effect.

As for the changes in the coming year, I did not mean you to understand anything in the nature of private alarm, I was referring to the general state of the commonwealth. Even though I have no responsibility, I cannot be indifferent. How cautious I want you to be in what you write you may infer from the fact

179. *Iliad*, IV.182=VIII.150.

180. *Iliad*, VIII.355.

181. The conjecture *Nerviorum*, adopted in Watt's text for *nervorum*, would mean that Quintus, whose winter headquarters were among the Nervii, could get rich at their expense and so come to Milo's assistance. *sustinebo*, translated 'I shall restrain', will then have to mean 'I shall support'.

that in writing to you I don't mention even overt political disorders, for fear of the letters getting intercepted and giving offence in any quarter. So I want you to ease your mind of private concern. I know how anxious you are apt to be about public affairs.

I expect to see our friend Messalla made Consul; if by an Interrex he will not be on trial, if by a Dictator he will still be in no danger.[182] Nobody hates him, Hortensius' ardour[183] will have a powerful effect, and Gabinius' acquittal is regarded as a statute of impunity. *En passant*, nothing has so far been done about a Dictator after all. Pompey is away, Appius is stirring the pot, Hirrus making ready, many vetoes are being counted, the public is indifferent, the leaders are opposed, I lie low.

Thank you very much for your promise of slaves.[184] As you say, I am indeed short-handed, both in Rome and on my estates. But, my dear fellow, please don't consider anything to do with my convenience unless it is absolutely convenient and easy for *you*.

I was amused to hear about Vatinius' letter,[185] but I may tell you that he is so attentive to me that I not only swallow those insolences of his but digest them too.

The epic to Caesar which you urge me to finish, finished it I have, a delectable piece, so it seems to *me*. But I am looking for a trustworthy courier for fear it share the fate of your *Erigona*, the only traveller from Gaul under Caesar's government who found the road unsafe. And she at least had an excellent dog to protect her![186]

182. If the elections were held by an Interrex in 53 (as ultimately happened) Messalla would take office immediately the result was declared and would be immune from prosecution at least until the end of his term. But even if they were held before the end of the year Messalla was not likely to be convicted.

183. Hortensius was Messalla's uncle.

184. From Gaul or Britain.

185. Probably a letter to Caesar which had been shown to Quintus.

186. Reading *quid si canem tam bonum non haberet?*, literally 'What

What, demolish the building?[187] I like it better every day. The lower portico and its rooms are coming on particularly well. As for Arcanum, we need Caesar's good taste, or even better taste than his upon my word! Those busts of yours, the palaestra, the fishpool, the canal, call for a multitude of Philotimi – not Diphili![188] However, I shall visit them myself, and send people over, and give instructions.

You would be more indignant about Felix's will than you are if you knew. The document which he thought he signed, in which you were firmly down for a twelfth share, he did not in fact sign, being misled by an error of his own and of his slave Sicura's;[189] the one he signed was contrary to his wishes. But to the devil with him! So long as we stay healthy!

I love your son as you ask and as he deserves and as I ought, but I am letting him go because I don't want to take him away from his teachers and because his mother ⋆ is leaving. Without her I am terrified of the young fellow's appetite! But we are a great deal together all the same.

I have answered all your points. My best and most delectable of brothers, goodbye.

---

would have happened to her if she didn't have such a good dog?' The messenger who brought Quintus' tragedy *Erigona* to Italy seems to have been attacked on the road. Erigone's dog Maera was proverbially faithful, an Athenian Gelert.

187. Apparently on the Manilius property; see p. 709

188. Cicero had a poor opinion of Diphilus' competence as an architect; cf. p. 710. Philotimus was concerned in work on Quintus' house in Rome (p. 712).

189. The name seems impossible; perhaps 'Scurra', epigraphically attested as a slave-name (='buffoon', 'wag').

INTRODUCTION TO CICERO'S LETTERS TO MARCUS BRUTUS

BORN in 85, M. Junius Brutus was adopted in early life by a maternal uncle, so that his name became for official purposes Quintus (Servilius) Caepio Brutus. But the original style remained in general use among his contemporaries and posterity. His natural father was a nobleman supposedly descended from Rome's first Consul, who held office under the Marians and was killed by Pompey in 78 for his part in an insurrection against the post-Sullan regime. His mother, Servilia, not only belonged to a patrician family with wide aristocratic connections but was half-sister to Marcus Cato and, according to general report, Julius Caesar's mistress. A second marriage and the marriages of three resulting daughters linked her and her son to yet other leading families and individuals. Brutus himself married a daughter of Appius Claudius Pulcher, whose other daughter was the wife of Pompey's elder son (Brutus later divorced her to marry Cato's daughter, the 'Portia' of Shakespeare's *Julius Caesar*). The great account in which he was held by his contemporaries is partly attributable to the extent and brilliance of these family connections.

But Brutus' personal qualities and attainments were far out of the ordinary. An austere intellectual with a deep interest in Greek philosophy, he became as a young man one of the foremost public speakers of the day in the so-called 'Atticist' manner, which aimed at simple elegance in opposition to Ciceronian orotundity. Moreover, he did nothing by halves. 'When he wants something,' said Julius Caesar of Brutus, 'he wants it badly.'

In 58 he accompanied his uncle Cato on a special mission to supervise the annexation of Cyprus to the Roman Empire. In 53 he served as Quaestor under his father-in-law, Appius

Claudius, the governor of Cilicia, and in 49 as Legate to Cicero's successor in the same province, Publius Sestius. The Civil War had now broken out and Brutus passed from Cilicia to Pompey's camp in Greece, where Cicero wrote of him to Atticus as 'zealous in the cause'. But after Pharsalia he was not only pardoned by Caesar but taken into favour, being made governor of Cisalpine Gaul in 46 and City Praetor in 44. Early that year a plot was hatched to assassinate the Dictator, which took effect on 15 March. Brutus was its leader, along with his brother-in-law, C. Cassius Longinus, and a distant kinsman, Decimus Brutus.

The conspirators seem to have planned no further than the act. Mark Antony, the surviving Consul, soon showed a disposition to step into Caesar's shoes. His ascendancy was challenged by Caesar's heir, the eighteen-year-old Octavian, while Brutus and Cassius, the 'Liberators' as they were called, remained helpless spectators until the autumn, when they left for the East. There it was a very different story. The Caesarian commanders in Syria and Egypt, whether from republican sympathies or lack of personal ambition, handed over to Cassius, while Brutus took possession of Greece, defeating and capturing Antony's brother Gaius. By the spring of 43 the 'Liberators' were in control from the Euphrates to the Adriatic. Despite all appeals, they made no effort to come to the rescue of the republican cause in Italy, preferring to wait to be attacked by the new coalition of Antony and Octavian. The end came at Philippi in October 42. Brutus and Cassius perished and the Roman Republic perished with them.

Atticus, who was on friendly terms with Cato and his circle, found himself much drawn to Cato's gifted nephew, and through Atticus an intimacy arose between Brutus and Cicero. It may have ripened when they were together in Pompey's army, and after Cicero's return to Rome in the autumn of 47 we find it fully established. It was publicly signalized *inter alia* by Cicero's dialogue on the history of Roman oratory, to which he gave Brutus' name, and by the dedication of the *Orator*, a work of which he was particularly proud.

Apart from four (or, as I believe, five) letters of recommendation in the collection *ad Familiares* the extant correspondence between Cicero and Marcus Brutus consists of one 'Book' and a portion of another, twenty-six letters in all. They date from March or April to July 43. The first five (= 'Book' II) are known only from an edition printed in 1528, the manuscript which contained them being no longer extant.

The genuineness of the whole collection was impugned in the eighteenth century and long remained in doubt. It is now generally recognized, with the possible exception of Letters 24 (I.16) and 25 (I.16). For Brutus' sake one would be glad to assign to a later forger these repetitious and unjust diatribes, made purportedly from the security of Macedonia against the man who was upholding the Republic in Italy by the only means open to him at the ultimate cost of his life. But proof is lacking.[1]

Watt's Oxford Text of 1958 is again the basis of my translation.[2]

1. The orthodox view, at least until 1971, that the reconciliation between the brothers was genuine and complete cannot be entertained by anyone who has read the contemporary letters to Atticus with attention and without sentimental prejudice.

2. The occasional discrepancies that will be noted between this translation and my edition of the Latin text of these letters with commentary (Cambridge, 1980) are mostly due to second thoughts.

CICERO'S LETTERS TO MARCUS BRUTUS

LETTERS TO M. BRUTUS

I (I or II. I)

CICERO TO M. BRUTUS

Rome, c. 1 April 43

From Cicero to Brutus greetings.

As I write, the ultimate crisis is thought to be upon us. Gloomy letters and messengers are coming in about our friend Decimus Brutus. They do not disturb *me* overmuch, for I cannot possibly lack confidence in our armies and generals, nor do I subscribe to the majority opinion – I do not judge unfavourably of the loyalty of the Consuls, which is under strong suspicion; though in certain respects I could have wished for more wisdom and promptitude. Had that been forthcoming, we should have had public order restored a while ago. You are well aware of the importance of the right moment in political affairs, and what a vast difference it makes whether the same decree or enterprise or course of action be adopted before or after. If only all the strong measures decreed during this turmoil had been carried through the day I proposed them, and not put off from one day to the next or dragged out and procrastinated *after* action upon them had been taken in hand, we should now have no war.

My dear Brutus, I have done for our country all that lies with one who stands where I, by judgement of Senate and People, stand today. I have not only given all that can fairly be demanded of a man – good faith, vigilance, patriotism; for these are what it is everybody's duty to render. But I conceive that something more is required of one whose voice is heard among leading statesmen, namely wisdom. And having presumed to take the helm of state, I should hold myself no less to blame if any counsel I gave the Senate were inexpedient than I should if it were dishonest.

I know you receive full and accurate reports of events both past and current. As coming from myself, I should like you to be well aware that *my* mind is in the fighting line – I am not looking over my shoulder, unless it so happen that the interests of the community make me turn my head; but the minds of the majority are looking back, to you and Cassius. So, Brutus, I would have you adjust yourself to the realization that it will be your duty either to improve our body politic, should the present conflict go well, or to restore it, should we meet with a reverse.

2 (III or II. 3)

M. BRUTUS TO CICERO

Dyrrachium, 1 April 43

From Brutus to Cicero greetings.

I am eagerly waiting for a letter from you written after the news of my doings and of Trebonius' death, not doubting that you will set out your views for me. By a dastardly crime we have lost a fine Roman and have been ousted from a province, which is neither easy to regain nor will the thing be the less shameful and outrageous if it *can* be regained.[1]

Antonius[2] is still with me, but upon my word I am moved by

1. Reading *quam neque reciperari facile est neque ... erit si potest reciperari.*

2. Mark Antony's brother Gaius. Appointed governor of Macedonia, he had been defeated and taken prisoner by Brutus.

his pleas and I am afraid that the fanaticism of certain people may pick him off. I am really troubled. If I knew what course you favoured I should not be worried, for I should be satisfied that it was best. So please let me know your opinion as soon as possible.

Our friend Cassius holds Syria and the Syrian legions. He was called in by Murcus and Marcius and the army itself. I have written to my sister Tertia[3] and my mother to tell them not to make this splendid success of Cassius' public before consulting with you and before you think proper.

I have read your two speeches,[4] the one on the Kalends of January and the one you delivered against Calenus. You won't be waiting for me to praise them.[5] I don't know whether these pieces say more for your spirit or for your genius. I am now willing to let them be called by the proud name of 'Philippics',[6] as you jestingly suggested in one of your letters.

My dear Cicero, I have now two needs: money and reinforcements. The latter you can provide by arranging for a contingent of troops to be sent to me from Italy either by way of a secret understanding with Pansa or through action in the Senate. The former is a necessity, as much for the other armies as for mine, which makes me all the sorrier that we have lost Asia. I hear that Dolabella's oppression of the province makes Trebonius' murder no longer appear the worst of his savageries. However, Antistius Vetus[7] has given me financial help.

Your son Cicero earns my approval by his energy, endur-

3. Wife of Cassius.

4. The Fifth and Seventh Philippics.

5. Reading *non* for *nunc*, which would mean 'Now, no doubt, you expect me to praise them'. Despite *Letters to Atticus* 115 (VI.1).7, Brutus is not likely to have written anything so churlish.

6. After Demosthenes' speeches against Philip of Macedon.

7. C. Antistius Vetus had been in charge of Syria until succeeded by Staius Murcus. Probably late in 44 he (if it is the same man) entered into Brutus' service, handing over the tribute money which he was bringing back to Rome. Cf. Letter 16 (XIX or I.11).

ance, hard work, and unselfish spirit, in fact by every kind of service. Indeed he seems never to forget whose son he is. I cannot make you think more of one whom you so deeply love than you already do, but trust my judgement in assuring yourself that he will have no need to exploit your renown in order to attain his father's honours.

Kalends of April, Dyrrachium.

3 (II or II. 2)

CICERO TO M. BRUTUS

Rome, 11 April 43

From Cicero to Brutus greetings.

From Plancus' letter,[8] of which I think you have been sent a copy, you will have been able to perceive his fine spirit of patriotism as well as the legions, auxiliaries, and resources at his disposal. On the other hand I suppose that letters from your own circle will already have made evident to you the irresponsibility, fickleness, and consistently unpatriotic attitude of your connection Lepidus, who hates his relatives by marriage only one degree less than his brother.[9]

We are anxiously waiting for news from Mutina, where the whole situation is at ultimate crisis-point. All hope lies in relieving Brutus. We are in grave fear for him.

Here I have trouble enough on my hands with that madman Servilius. I put up with him longer than suited my dignity, but I did that for the public sake, not wishing to give traitors a rallying-point – a semi-lunatic, to be sure, but a nobleman; though rally to him they do none the less. Still I thought he had

8. *Letters to his Friends* 371 (x.8).

9. L. Aemilius Paulus, Consul in 50.

better not be estranged from the national cause. Well, my patience with him is at an end. His insolence reached the point that he treated everybody else like slaves. He flared up in an incredible passion over Plancus' matter and battled with me for two days. I quashed him so effectively that I hope he will mend his manners once and for all. Just when this combat was at its height on 9 April a letter was delivered to me in the Senate from our friend Lentulus[10] about Cassius and the legions and Syria. I read it out at once and Servilius, along with several more (there are a number of prominent persons who are thoroughly disloyal), collapsed. But Servilius bitterly resented my gaining my point about Plancus. He is a political monstrosity, but will not last long, take my word.

4 (IV or II. 4)

CICERO TO M. BRUTUS

Rome, 12 April 43

From Cicero to Brutus greetings.

After giving a letter to Scaptius on the morning of 11 April I received that same evening yours dispatched from Dyrrachium on the Kalends of April. So on the morning of the 12th, having been informed by Scaptius that the persons to whom I gave my letter yesterday have not yet left but are leaving directly, I am scribbling these few words in the hubbub of my morning levée.

I am happy about Cassius and congratulate the commonwealth, and myself too in that against Pansa's angry opposition I proposed that Cassius should take military action against Dolabella. Indeed I ventured to maintain that he was already engaged in such action without any decree of ours. I also said

10. The younger Lentulus Spinther. The letter is not extant.

what I thought proper about yourself. The speech[11] will be sent to you, since I see you enjoy my Philippics.

With regard to your question about Antonius, I think he should be held in custody until we know what happens to Brutus. From the letter you have sent me it seems that Dolabella is oppressing Asia and behaving there abominably. Now you have written to several people that Dolabella was refused admission by the Rhodians. If he has approached Rhodes, then I suppose he has left Asia. If that is so, I would advise you to remain where you are, but if he has got possession of Asia I would advise you to pursue him there.[12] I do not think you can do better at this time.

You say you are in want of two necessities, reinforcements and money. It is hard to make any suggestion. No financial resources occur to me as available for your use other than those which the Senate has decreed, namely that you should borrow sums from civic bodies. So far from Pansa assigning you anything from his own army or levies he is not happy that so many volunteers are joining you, because, as I for my part suppose, he thinks that no forces are too large for the issues which are being determined in Italy – but as many suspect, because he does not want even you to be too strong. *I* have no such suspicion.

You say you wrote to your sister Tertia and your mother telling them not to make Cassius' successes public before I thought proper. Evidently you were afraid, and with good reason, that Caesar's party, as it is still called, would be much upset by the news. But the matter was common knowledge before we got your letter. Even your own couriers had brought letters to many of your friends. Accordingly, it was not advisable to suppress it, particularly as that was impossible; and even had it been possible, I should have been in favour of publication rather than concealment.

If my son Marcus has all the qualities with which you credit

11. The Eleventh Phillippic.

12. Reading *a te* for *at*.

him, I am naturally no less glad than I ought to be. And if your affection for him makes you exaggerate, the very fact of your caring for him makes me exceedingly happy.

5 (V or II. 5)

CICERO TO M. BRUTUS

Rome, 19 (?) April 43

From Cicero to Brutus greetings.

I expect you have heard from your own people about your letter which was read out in the Senate on the Ides of April and Antonius'[13] letter which was read at the same time. None of them thinks more of you than I do, but there was no need for everyone to tell you the same tale. There *is* need for me to tell you my views about the nature of this war, how I judge and what I advise.

My general political aims have always been identical with yours, my dear Brutus; my policy in certain matters (not in all) has perhaps been a little more forceful. You know I have always held that the commonwealth should be freed from monarchy, not merely from a monarch. You took a milder view, no doubt to your own eternal credit. But we have realized to our bitter distress, and are realizing to our grave peril, what the better course would have been.[14] In the period we have lately been through your supreme object was peace – which could not be accomplished with words; mine was freedom, for without freedom peace is meaningless. I thought that peace itself could be achieved by war and weapons. Men with the zeal to demand them were not lacking, but we checked their enthusiasm and

13. C. Antonius (see below).
14. i.e. Mark Antony should have been killed along with Caesar.

damped down their ardour. And so matters reached the point that, if some higher power had not inspired Caesar Octavian, we should have lain at the mercy of an abandoned villain, Mark Antony. How desperate a struggle with him is going on at this moment you see. Obviously there would have been none, if Antony's life had not then been spared.

But I leave all this aside. That memorable, almost god-like deed of yours is proof against all criticisms; indeed it can never be adequately praised. Latterly you have appeared in a new and sterner guise. In a short time and by your own efforts you have got an army – forces, legions in sufficient strength. Ah, that was news, that was a letter! The Senate was in transports, the whole community afire. I have never seen anything so universally applauded. News was still awaited about Antonius' remnants – you had despoiled him of the greater part of his horse and foot. That too came out according to our prayers. Your dispatch, read out in the Senate, declares the valour of the soldiers and their commander, and the zealous efforts of your friends, including my son. If your people here had thought fit that a motion be made on the dispatch, and if it had not arrived at a moment of great confusion after Consul Pansa's departure, a thank-offering to the Gods, just and due, would have been decreed.

And then! On the morning of the Ides of April along runs Pilius Celer. What a personage, in heaven's name! So responsible, so consistent, such a fine political record! Two letters he brings, one in your name, the other from Antonius, and delivers them to Tribune Servilius, who hands them to Cornutus. They are read out to the Senate. 'Antonius, Proconsul'! That produced a sensation, as though it had been 'Dolabella, Imperator' – and couriers *had* arrived from Dolabella, but nobody like Pilius with the courage to produce the letter or deliver it to the magistrates. Your letter was read, brief but distinctly mild in tone as regards Antonius. The House was greatly surprised. As for myself, it was not clear to me what I ought to do. If I called this letter a forgery, it might turn out that you had approved it; whereas to acknowledge it as genuine would be bad for your prestige. So that day passed in silence. On the following, after talk had become rife and the sight of Pilius had given strong and general offence, I must admit that I opened the game, with a good deal to say about 'Antonius, Proconsul'. Sestius followed me and supported the cause, pointing out what a dangerous position his son and mine would be in if they had taken up arms against a Proconsul. You know Sestius. He supported the cause. Others spoke as well. Our friend Labeo remarked that your seal was not on the letter, that it was not dated, and that you had not written to your own people as you usually do. He drew the conclusion that the letter was forged, and, if you wish to know, the House agreed with him.

Now, Brutus, it is for you to judge of the whole character of the war. Clearly lenience is to your liking and you think it is the most rewarding policy. Admirable! But the place for clemency is usually found, and ought to be found, in other matters and circumstances. In the present situation what is to be done, my friend? The hopes of needy desperados hang over the temples of the Immortal Gods. What is at issue in this war is our existence; no more, no less. Whom are we sparing? What are we about? Are we concerned for men who, if they win the day, will wipe us out without a trace? For what difference is there between Dolabella and any one of the three Antonii? If we spare any of them, we have been too hard on Dolabella.[15] That this is the sentiment of the Senate and People of Rome comes from the logic of the situation, but also in large measure from my advice and influence. If you do not approve of this attitude, I shall defend your view, but I shall not relinquish my own. Men expect from you neither laxity nor cruelty. It is easy to strike a balance; you need only be strong with the leaders and generous to the rank and file.

I hope you will keep my son at your side as much as possible,

15. Who had been declared a public enemy.

my dear Brutus. He will find no better training in manly excellence than by watching and imitating you.

19 (?) April.

6 (VIII or I. 2a)

CICERO TO M. BRUTUS

Rome, 20 (?) April 43

★ ★ ★ I am delighted that you find the army and the cavalry so loyally disposed towards you. If you get any news of Dolabella, you will inform me, as you say. I am glad that I had the forethought to leave you free to decide about making war on him. That was important for the state, as I recognized at the time, and I now consider that it was important for your prestige.

You say that I ★★★[16] to attack the Antonii and commend the same. I don't doubt that you think so. But I am far from approving the distinction you draw when you say that we should be keener to prevent civil wars thán to wreak vengeance on the defeated. I strongly disagree with you, Brutus. I consider myself as merciful a man as you, but salutary severity is better than the hollow appearance of mercy. If we want to be merciful, we shall never be without a civil war. However, that is your problem. I can say of myself what Plautus' father says in *Song of Sixpence*

> My time is nearly over. You're the party most concerned.[17]

Believe me, Brutus, you and your friends will be overwhelmed if you do not take care. You will not always have a people and a Senate and a leader of the Senate as they are today. You may take this as a Delphic oracle. Nothing can be more true.

20 (?) April.

16. The manuscript reading makes no sense and has not been satisfactorily corrected.

17. *Trinummus*, 319.

7 (IX or I. 3)

CICERO TO M. BRUTUS

Rome, c. 21 April 43

From Cicero to Brutus greetings.

Our affairs are in better shape. I am sure your correspondents have informed you of what has occurred. The Consuls have proved such as I have often described them to you. As for the boy Caesar, his natural worth and manliness is extraordinary. I only pray that I may succeed in guiding and holding him in the fulness of honours and favour as easily as I have done hitherto. That will be more difficult, it is true, but still I do not despair. The young man is persuaded (chiefly through me) that our survival is his work; and certain it is that if he had not turned Antony back from Rome, all would have been lost.

Three or four days before this splendid victory the whole city fell into a panic, and poured out with wives and children to join you; but on 20 April they recovered and would now like you to come over here instead. That day I reaped the richest of rewards for my many days of labour and nights of wakefulness – if there is any reward in true, genuine glory. The whole population of Rome thronged to my house and escorted me up to the Capitol, then set me on the rostra amid tumultuous applause. I am not a vain man, I do not need to be; but the unison of all classes in thanks and congratulations does move me, for to be popular in serving the people's welfare is a fine thing. But I would rather you heard all this from others.

Please keep me very particularly informed about your doings and plans, and take care that your generosity does not look like laxity. It is the feeling of the Senate and People of Rome that no public enemies ever deserved the harshest penalties more than those Romans who have taken up arms against their country in this war. In all my speeches I punish and harry them with the approval of all honest men. Your view on the matter is for you to determine. Mine is that the three brothers are in one and the same boat.

8 (X or I. 3a)

CICERO TO M. BRUTUS

Rome, 27 (?) April 43

From Cicero to M. Brutus greetings.

We have lost two good Consuls – but 'good' is as much as one can say. Hirtius fell in the moment of victory after winning a great battle a few days earlier. Pansa had fled after receiving wounds which were too much for him. Brutus and Caesar are in pursuit of the remnant of the enemy. And all those who have followed Mark Antony's lead have been pronounced public enemies. Most people interpret that decree of the Senate as applying to those whom you have captured or whose surrender you have accepted. For my part I used no harsh language in making a proposal about C. Antonius by name, having made up my mind that the Senate should learn of his case from yourself.

27 (?) April.

9 (XIII or I. 5)

CICERO TO M. BRUTUS

Rome, 5 May 43

From Cicero to Brutus greetings.

In a debate of 27 April on military operations against those who have been declared public enemies, Servilius made a speech mostly about Ventidius, but he also moved that Cassius should take action against Dolabella. I concurred, and proposed in addition that you should take military action against Dolabella if you thought it expedient and in the public interest; but that, if you could not do so with benefit to the commonwealth and did not think it in the public interest, you should keep your army where it now is. The Senate could not pay you a greater compliment than to let you decide for yourself what course you judge most advantageous to the state. My personal feeling is that if Dolabella has a following, a camp, anywhere to make a stand, you should move against him as a matter of loyalty and prestige. We know nothing about our friend Cassius' forces. No letters have arrived from him nor have we any report on which we can firmly rely. I am sure you appreciate how important it is that Dolabella should be crushed, so that he pay for his crime and so that the traitor chiefs in flight from Mutina do not have a rallying point. You may remember from my previous letters that I held this view at an earlier stage, although at that time your camp was our harbour of refuge and your army our vital reserve. Now that our dangers are, as I hope, safely over, we ought to be all the more concerned about crushing Dolabella. But you will give careful thought to all this and come to a wise conclusion. If you see fit, please let me know what you have decided and what you are doing.

I should like our Marcus to be co-opted into your College.[18] I think that candidates at elections to priesthoods can be admitted *in absentia*. It has been done before. C. Marius was elected Augur under the lex Domitia when he was in Cappadocia, and no later law has made this any the less permissible in the future. Also the lex Julia, the most recent law on priesthoods, reads as follows: 'Whosoever shall stand or whose candidature shall be admitted.' That clearly implies that the candidature of one not personally standing is admissible. I have written to him on this subject telling him to abide by your

18. That of Pontiffs.

judgement, as in all matters. And you must decide about Domitius and our young friend Cato.[19] However, even though candidature *in absentia* is allowable, everything is easier for those on the spot. But if you decide that you ought to go to Asia, there will be no chance of fetching our young men back for the elections.

To be sure, I thought everything would go more quickly with Pansa alive. He would have had his new colleague elected at once, and then the elections for the priesthoods would have been held before the praetorian elections. Now I expect a long delay because of the auspices, since so long as we have a single patrician magistrate the auspices cannot revert to the patriciate.[20] It is certainly a very confused situation. I hope you will inform me of your views on the whole matter.

5 May.

10 (XI or I. 4)

M. BRUTUS TO CICERO

Dyrrachium, c. 7 May 43

From Brutus to Cicero greetings.

How delighted I am to learn of the successes of our friend Brutus and the Consuls it is easier for you to imagine than for me to write. I applaud and rejoice at all of it, but especially the fact that Brutus' break-out not only brought safety to himself but also made a major contribution to the victory.

You tell me that the three Antonii are in one and the same boat, and that my view is for me to determine. My only con-

19. Sons of L. Domitius Ahenobarbus and M. Porcius Cato, now serving with Brutus.

20. Thus creating an Interregnum and making possible the holding of consular elections.

clusion is that the Senate or the People of Rome must pass judgement on those citizens who have not died fighting. You will say that my calling men hostile to the state 'citizens' is an impropriety in itself. On the contrary, it is quite proper. What the Senate has not yet decreed, nor the People ordered, I do not take it upon myself to prejudge, I do not make myself the arbiter. This much I maintain: in dealing with a person[21] whose life circumstances did not oblige me to take I have neither despoiled him cruelly nor indulged him laxly, and I have kept him in my power for the duration of the war.

In my judgement it is much more honourable and from a public standpoint allowable to refrain from bearing hard on the unfortunate than to make endless concessions to the powerful which may whet their appetite and arrogance. In which regard, my excellent and gallant friend, whom I love so well and so deservedly both on my own account and on that of the commonwealth, you seem to me to be trusting your hopes too fondly. The moment somebody behaves well you seem to set no bounds to your favours and concessions, as though a mind corrupted by largesse could not possibly be swayed to bad courses. Your heart is too good to take offence at a warning, especially where the common welfare is at stake. But you will do as you think best. I too, when you have informed me ★★★.

II (XII or I. 4a)

M. BRUTUS TO CICERO

Camp, 15 May 43

★★★ Now, Cicero, now is the time to act so that our joy over Antony's collapse does not turn out an illusion and so that the excision of one evil does not always generate a new and worse one. If anything untoward happens now, to our surprise or

21. C. Antonius.

with our tolerance, we shall all be to blame, but you more than any; for the Senate and People of Rome not only allows but desires you to exercise an authority as great as can belong to any one man in a free community. You should live up to that by thinking wisely as well as loyally. Moreover, the only form of wisdom (of which you have enough and to spare) felt to be lacking is restraint in bestowing honours. All else you have in such ample measure that your qualities can be compared with any of the great men of history. This one thing only, which comes from a grateful and generous heart, people criticize: they would like to see your generosity tempered by caution and moderation. The Senate ought not to grant any man a favour which might serve as a precedent or a support to evil-designing persons. Accordingly, I am alarmed about the Consulship. I fear your young friend Caesar may think he has climbed too high through your decrees to come down again if he is made Consul. Antony made use of the apparatus of monarchy left behind by another to make himself a monarch. What do you suppose will be the mentality of one who thinks himself in a position to covet any office of power with the backing, not of a slaughtered tyrant, but of the Senate itself? So I shall applaud your good fortune and foresight when, and only when, I begin to feel assurance that Caesar is going to be satisfied with the extraordinary honours that have come his way. You may ask whether I am going to make you answerable for somebody else's misdoings. Indeed I am, if they could have been foreseen and prevented. I only wish you could see into my heart, how I fear that young man.

After I wrote the above, we heard that you have been elected Consul. The day I see that, I shall begin to envisage a true commonwealth, relying on its own strength. Your son is well and has been sent to Macedonia in advance with a force of cavalry.

Ides of May, from camp.

12 (XIV or I. 6)

M. BRUTUS TO CICERO

Camp in Lower Candavia, 19 May 43

From Brutus to Cicero greetings.

Don't wait for me to thank you. That has long since become inappropriate in our relationship, which has developed into so close a friendship.

Your son is not with me. We shall meet in Macedonia – he has orders to take a squadron of cavalry from Ambracia through Thessaly. I have written to him to meet me at Heraclea. When I see him, since you leave it in our hands, we shall take counsel together about his returning to stand for election or about recommending him for the office.

I very particularly recommend to you Pansa's doctor, Glyco, who is married to our friend Achilleus' sister. We hear that Torquatus[22] suspects him in connection with Pansa's death and that he is being kept in custody like a parricide. That is quite incredible. Pansa's death hit nobody harder. Besides he is a well-conducted, decent fellow, who would not be likely to be driven to crime even by self-interest. I beg you, and very earnestly (for our friend Achilleus is no less disturbed about it than he should be), to get him out of custody and keep him safe. I regard this as a matter of private obligation for me, of equal importance to any other.

As I was writing you these lines, a letter was delivered to me from C. Trebonius' Legate Satrius giving the news that Dolabella has been cut to pieces and put to flight by Tillius and Deiotarus. I am sending you a letter in Greek from a certain Cicereius, sent to Satrius.

Our friend Flavius has chosen you as arbiter in the dispute he

22. Pansa's Quaestor.

has about an inheritance with the township of Dyrrachium. I beg you, Cicero, and so does Flavius, to settle the matter. There is no question but that the town owed money to the person who made Flavius his heir. The townspeople don't deny it, but say that Caesar made them a present of the debt. Don't let a wrong be done to my friend by your friends.[23]

19 May from camp in lower Candavia.

13 (VI or I. I)

CICERO TO M. BRUTUS

Rome, May (?) 43

From Cicero to Brutus greetings.

L. Clodius,[24] Tribune-Designate, has a high regard for me, or rather (to put it with more *empressement*) a great affection. Since I am satisfied of that, I don't doubt that you, knowing me as well as you do, conclude that I have an affection for *him*. Nothing to my way of thinking becomes a human being less than not to respond to a challenge of affection. I think Clodius suspects, and is very sorry to suspect, that something has been passed to you by your people, or rather through ill-wishers of *his*, to set your mind against him. As I think you know, my dear Brutus, it is not my habit to make assertions about another person lightly. That is a dangerous thing to do – people's real sentiments are so often concealed and their dispositions so complex. But Clodius' mind is an open book to me, and my opinion is formed. There are many indications, but they need

23. As to Cicero's relations with the town of Dyrrachium cf. *Letters to his Friends* 7 (XIV.2) and 8 (XIV.I).

24. Not necessarily or even probably identical with Ap. Pulcher's Prefect of Engineers in 51.

not be put into writing. After all, I don't want this to seem like a formal deposition rather than a letter.

He was advanced by Antony, in which favour you had a large share. Accordingly, he would have wished him well, compatibly with *my* welfare. But being, as you know, very far from a fool, he realizes that things have come to the point where both cannot survive, and so he prefers me. As for yourself, he speaks and feels about you in the most friendly way. So if anybody has written or talked to you amiss about him, let me beg you again to trust me, who am in a better position to judge than that somebody-or-other, and have a greater regard for you. Believe that Clodius is a very good friend of yours and as good a citizen as a man of thorough sound sense and excellent worldly position ought to be.

14 (VII or I. 2)

CICERO TO M. BRUTUS

Rome, c. 20 June 43

From Cicero to Brutus greetings.

I had already written and sealed a letter to you when one from you was delivered to me full of news, the most surprising item being that Dolabella has sent five cohorts to the Chersonese. Are his forces so ample that after we were told he was in flight from Asia he is trying to lay hands on Europe? And what did he expect to achieve with five cohorts when you have five legions, excellent cavalry, and large auxiliary forces? I hope those cohorts are now yours, since the bandit has been thus crazy.

I strongly commend your prudence in not moving your army from Apollonia and Dyrrachium before you heard of Antony's rout, Brutus' break-out, and the victory of the

Roman People. You say that thereafter you decided to march your army into the Chersonese and not allow the authority of the Roman People to be flouted by a criminal and a public enemy. That is for your own prestige and the national interest. You further write of a mutiny in the Fourteenth Legion and of C. Antonius' treachery. You will take what I say in good part: I approve of the severity of the soldiers more than of your * * *

15 (XVI or I. 8)

CICERO TO M. BRUTUS

Rome, May or June (?) 43

From Cicero to Brutus greetings.

I have recommended many persons to you, and needs must. For our best men and citizens are most eager for your good opinion and all gallant spirits want to give you enthusiastic service. Nor is there a man who does not believe that my authority and influence counts for a great deal with you. But I recommend to you nobody more earnestly than C. Nasennius, a townsman of Suessa. He was First Centurion of the eighth cohort in the Cretan War[25] under General Metellus. Thereafter he has been busy with his private affairs, but is now moved by party loyalty and your outstanding prestige to wish to take some position of authority by your appointment. I commend him to you, Brutus, as a brave gentleman, a man of worth and (if that is at all relevant) of wealth too. You will greatly oblige me if you handle him so that he can thank me on account of what you do for his benefit.

25. In 68–67.

16 (XIX or I. 11)

M. BRUTUS TO CICERO

Camp, June 43

From Brutus to Cicero greetings.

Antistius Vetus' patriotic spirit is such that I do not doubt he would have shown himself a most ardent champion of our common liberties both against Caesar and against Antony had he been able to meet the occasion. When he encountered Dolabella, who had soldiers and horse, in Greece, he preferred to face any danger from the plots of a totally unscrupulous bandit rather than let it be thought that he had been forced to give money to such an arrant scoundrel or had given it willingly. To me, on the other hand, he voluntarily promised and gave HS2,000,000 out of his own funds and, what is worth much more, put himself in my way and joined me.

I wished to persuade him to remain in his camp as commander-in-chief and defend the commonwealth. He decided that he could not do that since he had dismissed his army. But he gave an assurance that he would take a commission as Legate and return to us if the Consuls were not going to hold praetorian elections. I strongly urged him, being the loyal citizen that he is, not to put off his candidature to a later date. His conduct should have won the gratitude of all who regard this army as in the service of the commonwealth and of yourself above all, who are defending our freedom with so much spirit and glory and will enjoy so great a prestige if our plans are crowned with the success we hope for.

Also, my dear Cicero, I ask you personally as a friend to be kind to Vetus and to desire his advancement. Although nothing can deter him from his purpose, your praise and indulgence can stimulate him to cling more closely and steadfastly to his intention. You will be obliging me greatly.

17 (XXV or I. 17)

M. BRUTUS TO ATTICUS

Camp, June (?) 43

From Brutus to Atticus greetings.

You tell me that Cicero is surprised that I never comment on his proceedings. Since you press me, I will tell you what I think at your insistence. I know that Cicero has always acted with the best intentions. I am as sure of his patriotism as of anything in the world. But in certain respects he has acted – shall I say 'clumsily', of the most worldly-wise of men? Or shall I say 'with a desire to ingratiate' of one who for his country's sake did not hesitate to incur the enmity of Antony in the fulness of his power? I don't know how to put it to you, except simply to say that the boy's ambition and lawlessness have been stimulated rather than checked by Cicero; and that he goes so far in this indulgence as not to refrain from offensive expressions which recoil upon himself in two ways. For he took more than one life, and he must confess himself an assassin before he says what he says against Casca (in Casca's case imitating Bestia in his own). Because we are not bragging every hour about the Ides of March like Cicero with his everlasting Nones of December,[26] is he in any better position to revile a splendid action than Bestia and Clodius when they used to attack his Consulship?

Our friend Cicero in his gown boasts to me that he has taken the brunt of Antony's war. What good is that to me if the price claimed for crushing Antony is to be succession to Antony's place, and if our champion against that evil has emerged in support of another evil, which is likely to be more firmly based and deeply rooted – if we allow it? His present activities make one begin to wonder whether it is despotism he is afraid of or a particular despot, Antony. For my part I don't feel grateful to

26. The Catilinarian conspirators were executed on 5 December 63.

anybody who does not object to slavery as long as his master is not angry with him. Triumph, pay for his troops, encouragement in every decree not to let modesty deter him from coveting the position of the man whose name he has assumed – is that worthy of a Consular, of Cicero?

Since I have not been permitted to hold my tongue, you will have to read what cannot but be disagreeable to you. I know how much pain it has cost me to write these lines. I am not unaware of your political views and how little hope you have of healing the commonwealth even if its freedom is established. I am not criticizing you, Atticus, upon my word. Your age and habits and children[27] make you loth to move, as I saw from the episode of our friend Flavius[28] among other things.

But to get back to Cicero. What difference is there between him and Salvidienus? What more would Salvidienus propose? You may say that he is afraid even now of the remnants of the civil war. So afraid of a war that is as good as over that he sees no cause for alarm in the power of a leader of a victorious army and the rashness of a boy? Or does he do it just because he thinks that the boy's greatness makes it advisable to lay everything at his feet now without waiting to be asked. What a foolish thing is fear! When precaution consists in summoning and inviting the very thing you are afraid of, when you might have been able to avoid it! We dread death and banishment and poverty too much. For Cicero I think they are the ultimate evils. So long as he has people from whom he can get what he wants and who give him attention and flattery he does not object to servitude if only it be dignified – if there is any dignity in the sorriest depth of humiliation.

27. Atticus' daughter was his only child; cf. *Letters to his Friends*, n. 1001.

28. Cornelius Nepos writes that C. Flavius asked Atticus to take the lead in raising a fund for Caesar's assassins by subscription from the Knights. Atticus refused, though he said that his private fortune was at Brutus' disposal (*Life of Atticus*, 8.3f.).

Octavius may call Cicero his father, ask his opinion on everything, flatter him, thank him, but it will be plain to see that the words contradict the realities. It is an outrage to human feeling to regard as a father one who does not even count as a free man. And yet that is his goal and purpose, that is the result which our excellent friend impatiently pursues – for Octavius to be gracious to him! For myself, I no longer allow any value to those arts in which I know Cicero is so well versed. What do they do for him, all his copious writings in defence of national freedom, on dignity, on death, banishment, and poverty? Philippus seems to be much cleverer on these subjects. He has been less ready to make concessions to his stepson[29] than Cicero who makes them to a stranger. So let him stop his boasting which is an aggravation of our distresses. For what is it to us that Antony has been defeated, if his defeat meant that somebody else stepped into his shoes? – though your letter suggests some uncertainty even now.

By all means let Cicero live, since he can live so, as a helpless petitioner, if his age and honours and past achievements don't put him to shame! No slavery will be so comfortable that *I* shall be turned away from waging war against the thing itself, that is to say against monarchy, and extraordinary commands, and despotism, and power which sets itself above the laws – however good a man, as you say, Antony[30] may be, though I have never thought so. But our forbears were not willing that even a parent should be a master.

If my affection for you were not as great as Cicero believes Octavius' regard for himself I should not have written to you in this strain. I am sorry that you are now vexed, fond as you are of all your friends and especially of Cicero. But you may be sure that there has been no falling off in my personal feelings, though my judgement has changed considerably. After all, we

29. L. Marcius Philippus married Octavian's mother Atia after the death of her first husband.

30. So the manuscripts; but Brutus seems to be referring to Octavian.

cannot be expected not to think of things the way we see them.

I wish you had told me what matches are in view for our dear Attica. I could have put down for you something of my own views. Your concern for my Porcia's health is only what I should have expected. Finally, I shall be glad to do as you ask. My sisters make the same request. I shall get to know the man and find out his intentions.

18 (XVIII or I. 10)

CICERO TO M. BRUTUS

Rome, June 43

From Cicero to Brutus greetings.

We have heard nothing from you as yet, not even a rumour to tell us that you have been apprised of the Senate's resolution and are bringing your army to Italy. The public interest urgently demands that you do this, and quickly. For our internal malady grows worse every day, and the enemies within the gates give us as much trouble as those outside. They existed, it is true, from the beginning of the war, but they used to be more easily put down. The Senate was more resolute, animated by my proposals and exhortations. Pansa was there to take a sufficiently strong and stern line with these gentry, his father-in-law[31] especially. As Consul he did not lack spirit from the outset nor loyalty at the end. In the fighting at Mutina Caesar's conduct gave no room for criticism, Hirtius' gave some.[32]

You might say of the fortune of this war

'Unsettled', when our luck is in;
When out, we call it 'fair'.[33]

31. Q. Fufius Calenus, Antony's leading supporter in the Senate.
32. The nature of the criticism is uncertain.
33. Cf. *Letters to Atticus* 73 (IV.1).8.

The national cause was victorious. Antony's forces were cut to pieces and himself driven out. Then Brutus made so many mistakes that the victory somehow slipped through our fingers. Our generals failed to pursue the demoralized, unarmed, wounded enemy, and Lepidus was given time to let us experience in a graver crisis the irresponsibility he has so often demonstrated. Brutus' and Plancus' armies are good but raw, and they have large, very loyal contingents of Gaulish auxiliaries. But Caesar, who has so far been guided by my counsels and is a fine young man in himself, remarkably steady, has been prodded by certain persons with rascally letters and shifty go-betweens into a very confident expectation of the Consulship. As soon as I had an inkling of that, I wrote him letter after letter of warning and taxed those friends of his who seemed to be backing his ambition to their faces, and I did not scruple to expose the origins of these criminal designs in open Senate. The Senate and magistrates behaved as well as I can remember in any context. In the case of an extraordinary office for a powerful individual – or let us say a *very* powerful individual, since power now resides in armed force – it is unheard of that *nobody*, no Tribune nor other magistrate nor private person, should appear as sponsor. But with all this steadiness and courage, the community is anxious. The fact is, Brutus, we are made a mockery by the caprices of the soldiers and the insolence of generals. Everybody demands as much political power as he has force behind him. Reason, moderation, law, tradition, duty count for nothing – likewise the judgement and views of the citizen body and respect for the opinion of those who come after us.

Foreseeing this long beforehand I was making my escape from Italy when the report of your manifestos recalled me. But it was you, Brutus, at Velia, who urged me forward. Grieved though I was to be returning to the city from which you, her liberator, were taking flight – something which had happened to me too in the days gone by in circumstances of similar peril and sadder fortune – I proceeded none the less and returned to

Rome. There, quite unsupported, I shook Antony's position and strengthened the defence against his nefarious arms which Caesar's judgement and prestige had put in our way. If he remains loyal and obeys me, I think we shall have means enough to defend ourselves. But if the advice of miscreants carries more weight with him than mine, or if the frailty of his years proves unequal to the heavy burden of affairs, all hope lies in you.

Therefore, I beg you, hurry here and free with your army the commonwealth of which you are the liberator in virtue of your courage and self-devotion rather than in the actual event. Everyone will rally like one man to your side. Write to Cassius and urge him to do the same. Hope of liberty lies nowhere but in your and his headquarters. To be sure, we have strong armies and generals in the west. For my part, I still think that we can rely on this young man, but so many folk are pushing him the wrong way that I am sometimes afraid of his changing his position.

I have given you a complete picture of the state of the commonwealth, such as it is at the time of dispatching this letter. I hope for better things in the future. If it turns out otherwise (which Heaven forfend!), I shall grieve for the commonwealth, which ought to be everlasting. For myself, how little time remains!

19 (XVII or I. 9)

CICERO TO M. BRUTUS

Rome, June 43

From Cicero to Brutus greetings.

I should do you the same office as you did for me in my

bereavement and write you a letter of consolation if I did not know that you have no need in your grief of the remedies with which you alleviated mine.[34] And I hope you find healing in your own case easier than you found it in mine. It is not like so great a man as you to be unable to do the very thing he recommended to another. The arguments which you assembled and my respect for yourself held me back from undue sorrowing. For when you thought I was taking the blow less bravely than a man should, especially one who was in the habit of consoling others, you wrote and taxed me in terms more severe than you are accustomed to use. And so, esteeming your judgement highly and fearing you were right, I pulled myself together and felt that all I had learned and read and been taught gained added weight from your authority.

At that time I owed nothing except to duty and nature; but now *you* have your obligations to the public and the limelight, as they say. Not only your army but all Romans, one might almost say all nations, have their eyes upon you. It would not be seemly if the man who makes us all braver were himself seen to be broken in spirit. You have indeed suffered a blow (the like of what you have lost was nowhere on earth) and you must grieve in so heavy a calamity. To lack all sense of grief might be more pitiable than grief itself. But moderation in grief, which is expedient for other men, is for you a necessity.

I should write more but that as written to *you* this is already too much. We are waiting for you and your army. Without that it looks as though we shall hardly be sufficiently free, even though everything else goes as we wish. I shall be writing more on the situation in the letter which I intend to give to our friend Vetus and shall then perhaps have more solid news.

34. Brutus' wife Porcia had died.

20 (XV or I. 7)

M. BRUTUS TO CICERO

Camp, May or June 43

From Brutus to Cicero greetings.

How dear L. Bibulus should be to me nobody can judge better than you, who have been through so much struggle and care for our country's sake. His own qualities and our connection ought to make you his friend. So I do not think I need write at length. My good-will ought to weigh with you, provided it be legitimate and in pursuance of a necessary obligation. He has decided to stand for Pansa's vacancy.[35] You cannot do a favour to anyone closer to you than I am, nor can you nominate a worthier candidate than Bibulus.

As for Domitius and Apuleius, it is superfluous for me to write when they are so strongly commended to you by their own persons. But you do have a duty to put your prestige behind Apuleius. However, he shall have a letter to himself to sing his praises. As for Bibulus, don't let him out of your care. He is already a fine fellow and, believe me, he can develop into one on whom the praises of the select few like yourself will be fitly bestowed.

21 (XXI or I. 13)

M. BRUTUS TO CICERO

Camp, 1 July 43

From Brutus to Cicero greetings.

The fears of the rest of the world make me apprehensive

35. In the College of Pontiffs.

about M. Lepidus. If he tears himself away from us (I hope the general suspicion that he will is hasty and unjust), I beg and implore you, Cicero, in the name of our friendship and your good-will towards me, to forget that my sister's children are Lepidus' sons and to regard me as having replaced him as their father. If you grant so much, I am sure there is nothing you will hesitate to do on their behalf. Others may stand on different terms with their kith and kin, but nothing I can do for my sister's children can satisfy my desire or my duty. And what mark of favour can honest men confer upon me (that is, if I am worthy of any such), how am I going to help my mother and my sister and these children, if you and the rest of the Senate will not let their uncle Brutus count against their father Lepidus?

Anxiety and vexation make it impossible for me to write to you at length, nor do I have to. After all, if I need words to rouse and strengthen you in a matter so important and close to my heart, there is no hope of your doing what I ask and what is right. So don't expect a lengthy appeal. Just look at *me*. You ought to grant me this both as a private individual, my very close friend Cicero, and as the great Consular you are, private connections apart. Please write back as soon as you can and let me know your intention.

Kalends of July, from camp.

22 (XX or I. 12)

CICERO TO M. BRUTUS

Rome, July 43

From Cicero to Brutus greetings.

Although I shall be giving a letter to Messalla Corvinus presently, I did not want our friend Vetus to join you without a letter from me.

The commonwealth is in the gravest peril, Brutus, and after our victory we are forced to join battle once more. That has happened because of the criminal folly of M. Lepidus. Many things distress me at this time by reason of the care for the commonwealth which I have taken upon myself, but nothing has distressed me more than my inability to comply with your mother's and your sister's entreaties. As for yourself (which is what matters to me most), I believe I shall have no difficulty in justifying my conduct.

Lepidus' case can in no way be distinguished from Antony's, and is universally judged to be even less defensible than his, in that after the Senate had honoured him with the highest distinctions and only a few days after sending a splendid letter to that body, Lepidus suddenly let in the remnants of the enemy and, not content with that, is waging war energetically by land and sea. What will be its outcome who can say? So when we are asked to extend compassion to his children, not a word is said to suggest that *we* shall not be punished to extremity if the children's father is victorious, which Jupiter forfend!

Not that I do not recognize the harshness of visiting the sins of the fathers upon the children. But the laws have very wisely ordained this in order that parental affection may better dispose the fathers to the commonwealth. Therefore it is Lepidus who is cruel to his children, not those who declare Lepidus a public enemy. If he laid down his arms and was found guilty on charges of breaking the peace, against which he would certainly have no defence, his children would suffer the same penalty – his property being forfeit. Not but what Lepidus, Antony, and the other public enemies are threatening all of us with this very reprisal against which your mother and sister are pleading on behalf of the children, and with many others more cruel.

Accordingly, we pin our best hope at this time on you and your army. It is of great moment to the national cause and to your own glory and prestige that, as I have written before, you return to Italy as soon as possible. The commonwealth sorely needs your strength and your counsel.

Following your letter I have gladly made a friend of Vetus in view of his good-will and outstanding services to you; and I have found him most zealous and loyal to you and to the commonwealth. I hope to see my son Marcus shortly, since I trust that you will quickly come to Italy and he will be with you.

23 (XXII or I. 14)

CICERO TO M. BRUTUS

Rome, 14 July 43

From Cicero to Brutus greetings.

Your short letter – I say 'short', but it was not really a letter at all. Does Brutus write me only three lines in times like these? Better nothing at all. And you think *I* should have written more. Which of your friends ever joined you without a letter from me? And which of my letters lacked weight? If they have not been delivered to you, I think your letters from home have not been reaching you either. You say you will give Marcus a longer letter. Right, but this one too should have been fuller. Now when you wrote to me about Marcus' leaving you I immediately pushed out couriers and a letter to Marcus telling him to rejoin you even if he had already returned to Italy. No other course is more agreeable to me or more honourable to him. To be sure, I had written to him more than once that by dint of a great effort on my part, the elections to priesthoods were put off till next year. I exerted myself to bring that about both for Marcus' sake and for that of Domitius, Cato, Lentulus, Bibulus, and others. I wrote the same to you, but apparently you had not yet heard of it when you dispatched that tiny letter to me.

So I ask you with all urgency, my dear Brutus, not to send my son Marcus away but to bring him back with you. And this latter you should do any day now if you have any thought for the commonwealth which you were bred to serve. For the war is reborn through Lepidus' criminal behaviour, and no small war either. Caesar's army, which used to be excellent, is not only no help but forces us to ask urgently for *your* army. Once the latter touches Italian soil, every Roman who can legitimately be so called will betake himself to your camp. True, we have Brutus in fine combination with Plancus. But you well know how uncertain are the minds of men, tainted with party spirit, and the results of battles. Even if we win, as I hope we shall, the guidance of your counsel and prestige will be greatly needed. So come to our assistance, in God's name, and do so as soon as you can. Be sure that you did your country no greater service on the Ides of March, when you lifted the yoke of servitude from the backs of your fellow-countrymen, than you will do her if you come quickly.

14 July.

24 (XXIII or I. 15)

CICERO TO M. BRUTUS

Rome, July 43

From Cicero to Brutus greetings.

Messalla is with you. However carefully I write, I cannot hope to explain the current proceedings and situation more precisely in a letter than he will expound them with his excellent and comprehensive knowledge, and his ability to present you with all the facts in lucid and well-chosen terms. For I do assure you, Brutus (not that there is any need for me to tell you what you already know, but I cannot pass over such all-round excellence in silence) – I assure you that in uprightness, resolution, concern, and patriotic zeal the like of Messalla does not exist. In him the gift of eloquence, which he possesses in a quite astonishing degree, hardly seems worth commending. And yet his good sense is specially conspicuous in that very sphere, for he has trained himself in the strictest school of oratory with serious judgement and a great deal of technical skill. He is so industrious and indefatigably studious that his pre-eminent natural ability seems a secondary qualification.

But my affection carries me too far. It is not my purpose in this letter to praise Messalla, especially to you, my friend, who know his worth as well as I and who know those very pursuits which I am eulogizing better than I do. My one consolation in the distress I feel at parting with him is that he is going to join you, my *alter ego*, is doing his duty, and seeking no mean laurels. But enough of this.

Now I come rather belatedly to a letter of yours in which, while paying me a number of compliments, you find one fault, namely that I am excessive and, so to speak, prodigal in voting honours. This you criticize; someone else perhaps might tax me with undue harshness in the infliction of punishments – or perhaps you would charge me with both. If so, I am anxious that you should be thoroughly acquainted with my judgement on either point. I will not just quote the saying of Solon, one of the Seven Wise Men and the only one to write a code of law. He said that a state depends on two things, reward and punishment. There is, of course, a due limit in both, as in all other things, a sort of balance in each of the two categories. But it is not my purpose to discuss so wide a theme here. I do, however, think it appropriate to reveal the principle which I have followed in the proposals I have made to the Senate during this war.

You will not have forgotten, Brutus, that after Caesar's death and your memorable Ides of March I said that you and your associates had left one thing undone and that a mighty storm was brewing over the commonwealth. You had driven away a great plague, wiped a great blot from the honour of the Roman people, and won immortal glory for yourselves; but the apparatus of monarchy descended to Lepidus and Antony, one more of a weathercock, the other more of a blackguard, both afraid of peace and hostile to domestic tranquillity. We had no force to pit against their passionate desire for a political upheaval. The community had risen unanimously in defence of freedom, but we appeared too bold, and you and your friends may perhaps have shown greater wisdom in leaving the city you had liberated and in asking nothing of Italy when she proffered you her enthusiastic support. And so, seeing that Rome was in the hands of traitors, that neither you nor Cassius could live there in safety, and that the city was crushed by Antony's armed force, I thought that I too had better go elsewhere. A community crushed by ruffians, with all hope of rendering help cut off, is a hideous spectacle. But my spirit, anchored as ever upon the love of country, could not endure separation from her perils. Halfway to Greece, when the Etesians should have been blowing, the South Wind carried me back to Italy, as though dissuading me from my plan. I saw you at Velia, and was deeply distressed. For you were retiring, Brutus – retiring, since our friends the Stoics say that the Wise Man never flees. On returning to Rome I immediately set myself in opposition to Antony's wickedness and folly. Having stirred him up against me, I embarked upon a policy to free the commonwealth – a truly Brutine policy, since such aspirations run in your family.

The sequel is long and not to be recounted here, since it is about myself. All I will say is that this young man Caesar, thanks to whom (if we choose to admit the truth) we are still alive, drew his inspiration from my counsels. I have given him no honours, Brutus, but what were due and necessary. When we first began to call freedom back, before even D. Brutus' superlative valour had visibly come into action, our only protection was this lad, who had thrust Antony away from our necks. What honour ought we *not* to have voted him? However I at that time paid him a verbal tribute, and that in moderation, and voted him military authority. That no doubt seemed an honour at his age, but it was necessary since he had an army; for what is an army without military authority? Philippus voted him a statue, Servius the right to stand for office in advance of the legal age, a privilege which was later extended by Servilius. Nothing seemed too much at the time.

But for some reason it is easier to find good-will in the hour of danger than gratitude in victory. There came that most joyful day of D. Brutus' liberation, which happened also to be Brutus' birthday. I proposed that Brutus' birthday should be entered in the Calendar beside that day, following the precedent of our ancestors who paid that compliment to a woman, Larentia,[36] at whose altar in Velabrum you Pontiffs offer sacrifice. In trying to confer that on Brutus I wished the Calendar to contain a permanent record of a most welcome victory. That day I realized that gratitude has considerably fewer votes in the Senate than spite. During these same days I showered honours (if you like to put it that way) on the dead, Hirtius and Pansa, even Aquila. Who shall blame me, unless he forgets the bygone danger once the fear is laid aside? Besides the grateful memory of benefit I had another reason, one of advantage to posterity: I wanted memorials of the public hatred for those bloodthirsty rebels to stand for all time. I suspect that another proposal of mine is less to your liking – your friends, excellent persons but lacking political experience, did not like it either – namely that Caesar be granted leave to enter Rome in ovation. For my part (but perhaps I am mistaken, though it is not my way to be particularly pleased with my own performances), I do not think I have made a better proposal in the course of this war. Why that is so I had better not

36. Acca Larentia, a figure of early Roman legend. Various stories are told about her.

reveal, or I might seem more far-sighted than grateful. I have said too much as it is; so let us pass on.

I voted honours to D. Brutus and to L. Plancus. It is a noble mind that is attracted by glory; but the Senate too has shown good sense in using every means, provided it be honourable, to draw this man and that to the aid of the state. But there is Lepidus. Oh yes, we are blamed there – we set up a statue for him in the rostra and then pulled it down. We tried to bring him back from treason by honouring him, but our wisdom was defeated by the folly of a thoroughly irresponsible individual. Not but what the setting up of Lepidus' statue did less harm than the pulling down did good.

That's enough about honours. Let me now say a little about punishment. Your letters have often let me understand that you would like to earn praise by your clemency towards those you have defeated in war. For my part, I look upon anything that comes from you as wise. But to waive the punishment of crime (for that is what is called 'pardoning'), even if it is tolerable in other contexts, I consider to be fatal in this war. Of all the civil wars in our commonwealth that I remember there has not been one in which the prospect of some form of constitution did not exist whichever side won. In this war I should not like to be positive about what constitution we shall have if we win, but there will certainly be none ever again if we lose. Accordingly I proposed stern measures against Antony and against Lepidus too, not so much for vengeance's sake as to deter the criminals among us by terror from attacking our country in the present and to leave an object-lesson for the future, so that none shall be minded to imitate such madness. To be sure this proposal was no more mine than everybody's. One feature seems cruel, the extension of the penalty to innocent children. But that is an ancient rule, found in all communities. Even Themistocles' children lived in poverty. If the same penalty applies to citizens judicially condemned, how could we take a more lenient line with public enemies? And what complaint can anyone have of me who must needs admit that he would have treated me more harshly had he won?

There you have the rationale of my proposals so far as this category of honours and punishments is concerned. Of my speeches and votes on other matters I think you have heard.

But all this is not particularly crucial; what *is* extremely crucial, Brutus, is that you come back to Italy with your army as soon as possible. You are most eagerly awaited. As soon as you touch Italian soil there will be a universal rally to your side. If we win the day, as won it we had most gloriously if Lepidus had not had a craving to destroy everything, including himself and his family, we need your prestige to establish some sort of civic settlement. Whereas if a contest is still to come, our best hope lies in your prestige and the strength of your army. But for heaven's sake hurry! You know how much depends on timing and on speed.

I expect you will hear from your mother and sister about the pains I am taking on behalf of your sister's children. In this I am taking more account of your wishes, which mean a great deal to me, than of my own consistency, as some people see it. But I want to be and seem consistent in my affection for you more than in anything else.

25 (XXIV or I. 16)

M. BRUTUS TO CICERO

July (?) 43

From Brutus to Cicero greetings.

I have read a small part of your letter to Octavius, sent to me by Atticus. Your devoted concern for my welfare gave me no novel pleasure, accustomed as I am (indeed it happens every day) to hear of some loyal and complimentary action or words of yours in support of our public standing. But that same extract from your letter to Octavius in which you write about us gave me all the distress of which my mind is capable. You thank him on public grounds in such a fashion, so imploringly and humbly – I hardly know what to write; I am ashamed of the situation, of what fortune has done to us, but write I must. You commend our welfare to him. Better any death than such welfare! It is a downright declaration that there has been no abolition of despotism, only a change of despot. Read over your words again and then dare to deny that these are the pleadings of a subject to his king. You say that the one thing asked and expected of him is his good wishes for the welfare of those citizens of whom the honest men and the Roman People think well. What if he should refuse? Shall we cease to exist? And indeed it would be better not to exist than to exist on his sufferance. I really do not believe that the Gods have so turned their faces away from the welfare of the Roman People that Octavius has to be begged on behalf of the welfare of any citizen, let alone on behalf of the liberators of the world – it pleases me to be grandiloquent, nor is that out of place in addressing people who do not know in each particular case what fears it is right to entertain and what favours it is right to ask.

Do you admit, Cicero, that Octavius has such power and are you his friend? If you care for me, do you want me to be seen in Rome when in order to make that possible I have to be recommended to the good graces of this boy? Why do you thank him if you think you have to ask him to wish or to suffer us to survive? Are we to consider him as having done us a kindness in preferring that he himself rather than Antony should be the person to whom such requests must be addressed? Is he our champion against the despotism of another or that other's substitute? If the former, does anybody petition him to let the benefactors of our country survive? It is this weakness and despair, for which the blame rests no more with you than with everybody else, that brought Caesar to dream of monarchy, that persuaded Antony after Caesar's death to try to step into the shoes of the man we killed, and that now has raised this boy so high that *you* think the survival of men like ourselves has to be gained by pleading and that we shall be safe through the compassion of an individual (and he scarcely yet a grown man) or not at all. If we remembered that we are Romans, miscreants would not be bolder to become our masters than we to stop them, and Antony would not have been incited by Caesar's monarchy rather than deterred by his death.

As a Consular, one who has put down such atrocious crimes (though I fear that in suppressing them you have only delayed the disaster for a short time), how can you look back on what you have achieved and at the same time give your approval to *this*, or if not approval, a tolerance so submissive and ready as to present the appearance of approval? What private quarrel did you have with Antony? It was surely because he demanded that men's safety should be begged from himself, that we to whom he owed his own liberties should hold civic status by his grace and favour, that he should dispose of the commonwealth as he chose – that was why you thought we should look for weapons with which to prevent his despotism, only, as it seems, in order that after stopping him we should ask someone else to let himself be put in Antony's place. Or was it that rights of ownership over the commonwealth should belong to the commonwealth itself? Perhaps, though, it was not servitude but a particular servile situation that we rejected. And yet we could have had a good master in Antony under whom to put up with our condition. Not only that, we could have enjoyed all the favours and honours we wanted as his partners. What would he have refused to men in whose tolerance he would have seen the best guarantee of his régime? But nothing was worth the surrender of our loyalties and liberties.

This very boy, who is apparently incited by Caesar's name against Caesar's killers – what would he not give, if there were room for bargaining, in return for our support for the power which I suppose will indeed be his, since we want to keep our lives and our money and be called Consulars? Caesar will have perished for nothing (why did we rejoice at his death if we were going to be slaves just the same after he was dead and gone?), if no care is taken. But may the Gods and Goddesses take away everything I have sooner than my determination that nobody shall have more power than the Senate and the laws with my consent. That I did not tolerate in the case of the man I killed, I shall not concede it to his heir, I should not concede it to my own father if he came back to life. Do you believe that a personage without whose permission we can have no place in your community is going to leave the rest their liberties? And how is it possible for your petition to be granted? You ask his good wishes for our welfare. Do you think we are getting welfare if we get our lives? How can we get welfare if we let status and liberty go? Or do you think that to live in Rome is to be a citizen? That is a matter of condition, not of place. I had no citizenship in Caesar's lifetime until after I resolved upon his assassination, nor can I be in exile anywhere so long as I hate to be a slave and suffer indignities more than all other evils. In Greece when tyrants are suppressed their children suffer the same penalty. Here is one who has taken the tyrant's name, and he is being asked to agree to the survival of the avengers and suppressors of despotism. Is not that a relapse into the same old darkness? Should I wish to see a community, or think it worthy of the name, that cannot take freedom when handed on a platter and rammed down its throat, and has more fear of the name of a liquidated monarch borne by a boy than confidence in itself, though it has seen the possessor of unlimited power liquidated by the courage of a few individuals?

No, do not in future commend me to your Caesar, nor yourself either, if you will listen to me. You must set great store by the years that can remain to a man of your age if you are going to humble yourself before that boy on their account.

Have a care, furthermore, lest the admirable line you have taken and are taking against Antony, in which your courage is so highly praised, come to look like fear. For if you see in Octavius one whom you can suitably petition for our welfare, you will appear to have acted not in avoidance of a master but in search of a more friendly one. I fully approve of your praise of his conduct so far. It *is* praiseworthy, provided he entered on it in opposition to someone else's irregular power and not in furtherance of his own. But when you judge that he has the right to be begged not to refuse his good wishes for our welfare, and even yourself accord it to him, you are setting too high a price on his services. You are making him a present of what (thanks to him, as it seems) belongs to the state. Nor has it occurred to you that if Octavius merits any honours because he is making war on Antony, those who have cut out the evil growth of which you are now left with the remnants can never be recompensed by the Roman people as richly as they deserve, even if every imaginable reward be heaped upon them at once.

How much more attention people pay to their fears than to their memories! Antony is alive and fighting, whereas what could and had to be done about Caesar is finished and no one can put back the pieces. And so it is Octavius whose decision about ourselves is awaited by the Roman People, and it is we whose welfare must apparently be asked of a single individual.

For my part, to return to the point I have already made, I am not one to make petitions. I would rather trim to size those who claim the right to receive them. Or else I shall stay far away from a society of serfs, and wherever I can live as a free man there for me shall be Rome. And I shall pity all of you for whom life has a sweetness from which neither years nor honours nor the courage of other men can take away. I shall think myself so happy, if only I always cling steadfastly to this intention, that I shall regard my patriotism as well rewarded. For what is better than to be indifferent to the vicissitudes of life, content with freedom and the memory of deeds well done? But assuredly I shall not submit to the submissive or be defeated by defeatists. I shall try every expedient and never abandon my efforts to draw our society away from thraldom. If deserved good fortune follow the enterprise, we shall all be glad. If not, *I* shall still be glad. My life cannot be better spent than in such actions and thoughts as conduce to the liberation of my fellow-countrymen.

As for yourself, Cicero, I ask and urge you not to grow weary or discouraged, and in forestalling present evils always to be alert for those which, unless measures are taken beforehand, may insinuate themselves into the future. Do not imagine that the free and gallant spirit with which you have championed the state both as Consul and Consular has any value without steadiness and consistency. I must acknowledge that proven merit makes harder demands than merit still unrecognized. Previous good performances are required as due, and if it turns out otherwise we become indignant critics, as though those performances had deceived us. That Cicero should resist Antony is most creditable; but because the Consul that was is felt to guarantee the Consular that is, no one is surprised. But if the same Cicero changes in relation to others the policy he has applied so firmly and nobly in expelling Antony, he will not only rob himself of future laurels but will make his past lose its lustre. No act is great in itself, unless inspired by reasoned judgement. On nobody does the role of patriot and defender of freedom sit more fittingly in virtue of your spirit, your record, and the eager demand of all.

Therefore Octavius is not to be asked to wish us well. Instead, rouse yourself! Believe that the community in which you achieved so much will be free and respected if only the people have leaders to resist the designs of wicked men.

26 (XXVI. or I. 18)

CICERO TO M. BRUTUS

Rome, 27 July 43

From Cicero to Brutus greetings.

I have often urged you by letter to come to the aid of the commonwealth and bring your army over to Italy as soon as possible, and I was under the impression that those close to you were in no doubt on this point. On 25 July that very wise and watchful lady your mother, whose every care begins and ends with you, requested me to visit her. Naturally I did so without delay. On my arrival I found Casca, Labeo, and Scaptius already there. Your mother put the question: What did I think? Should we send for you and did we consider this to be in your best interests, or was it better that you should take your time and hold back? I said in answer what I thought, that it was in the highest degree advantageous to your prestige and reputation that you should lend support to our tottering and almost collapsing commonwealth at the earliest possible moment.

Every imaginable evil chance has dogged us in this war. Victorious armies have refused to pursue a fleeing enemy. An army commander in good standing, eminent in public distinction and private fortune, with a wife and children, related by marriage to you and your brother-in-law, has declared war on the commonwealth. I might add 'in the face of a unanimous Senate and People', were it not that the mischief within the gates remains so strong. As I write I am in great distress because it hardly looks as though I can make good my promises in respect of the young man, boy almost, for whom I went bail to the commonwealth. Responsibility for someone else's mind and sentiment, especially in matters of great importance, is more burdensome and difficult than the pecuniary kind. That can be discharged and the loss of money can be borne. But how is one to discharge a pledge to the state if the person for whom one has made it is quite happy to leave his backer to pay? However, I hope I shall still hold him, though many people are pulling the other way. The natural quality seems to be there, but it is an impressionable age and there are plenty of would-be agents of corruption. They are confident of dazzling his good disposition by dangling in front of him the glitter of a false distinction. So this care is added to my load. I must move every engine at my disposal to hold the young man, or else be judged guilty of indiscretion. And yet, where is the indiscretion? I bound the one on whose behalf I gave the pledge rather than myself. The state has no reason to find fault with that pledge. Its subject proved the steadier in his public actions both from natural disposition and because of my promise.

However, unless I am perhaps mistaken, our knottiest political problem is shortage of money. The honest men become more obdurate every day at the mention of a special levy. The proceeds of the 1%,[37] thanks to the scandalously low returns put in by the wealthy folk, are entirely absorbed in the bounties of the two legions. Yet limitless expenses hang over us both for the armies which are now defending us and for yours. It looks as though our friend Cassius will be able to arrive tolerably well furnished. But these and many other matters I want to discuss with you in person, and that soon.

About your sister's children, my friend, I did not wait for you to write. To be sure the progress of time is leaving the case uncompromised for you to handle, for the war will be protracted. But from the outset, when I could not prophesy the length of the war, I pleaded the children's cause in the Senate, as I think you will have been able to learn from your mother's letters.

37. Income tax, imposed by the Senate.

There shall never be any matter on which I shall not speak and act in accordance with what I take to be your wish and concern, even at the hazard of my life.

27 July.

APPENDIX I

(*i*) *Roman Dates*

UNTIL Julius Caesar reformed the calendar the Roman year consisted of 355 days divided into twelve months, all of which bore the Latin forms of their present names except Quintilis (= July) and Sextilis (= August). Each month had 29 days, except February with 28 and March, May, July, and October with 31. The first, fifth and thirteenth days of each month were called the Kalends (*Kalendae*), Nones (*Nonae*), and Ides (*Idus*) respectively, except that in March, May, July, and October the Nones fell on the seventh and the Ides on the fifteenth. I have kept these names in translation.

The calendar was adjusted by means of 'intercalation'. At the discretion of the College of Pontiffs, usually every other year, an 'intercalary' month of 23 or 22 days was inserted after 24 or 23 February. But in the years immediately before the Civil War the College neglected this procedure, so that by 46 the calendar was well over two months in advance of the sun. Julius Caesar rectified the situation by inserting two 'intercalary' months totalling 67 days between November and December of that year in addition to the traditional one in February. He also gave the months their present numbers of days, thus almost obviating the need for future intercalations, though in 1582 a further discrepancy had to be met by the institution of a Leap-Year.

(*ii*) *Roman Money*

The normal unit of reckoning was the sesterce (HS), though the denarius, equal to 4 sesterces, was the silver coin most generally in use. Differences of price structure make any transposition into modern currency misleading, but very roughly HS25 may be taken as equivalent to the debased pound sterling of 1974. Sometimes sums are expressed in Athenian currency. The drachma was about equal to the denarius, the mina (100 drachmae) to HS400, and the talent

(60 minae) to HS2,400. The Asiatic cistophorus was worth about 4 drachmae.

(*iii*) *Roman Names*

A Roman bore the name of his clan (*gens*), the *nomen* or *nomen gentilicium*, usually ending in *-ius*, preceded by a personal name (*praenomen*) and often followed by a *cognomen*, which might distinguish different families in the same *gens*: e.g., Marcus Tullius Cicero. The *nomen* was always, and the *cognomen* usually, hereditary. Sometimes, as when a family split into branches, an additional *cognomen* was taken: e.g., Publius Licinius Crassus Dives. Other additional *cognomina* were honorific, sometimes taken from a conquered country as Africanus or Numidicus, or adoptive (see below). Women generally had only the one clan-name (e.g., Tullia), which they retained after marriage.

Only a few personal names were in use and they are generally abbreviated as follows: A. = Aulus; Ap(p). = Appius; C. = Gaius; Cn. = Gnaeus; D. = Decimus; L. = Lucius; M. = Marcus; M'. = Manius; N. = Numerius; P. = Publius; Q. = Quintus; Ser. = Servius; Sex. = Sextus; Sp. = Spurius; T. = Titus; Ti. = Tiberius (I omit one or two which do not occur in our text). The use of a *praenomen* by itself in address or reference is generally a sign of close intimacy, whether real or affected, but in the case of a rare or distinctive praenomen, as Appius and Servius, this is not so.

The practice of adoption, of males at any rate, was very common in Rome. According to traditional practice the adopted son took his new father's full name and added his old *nomen gentilicium* with the adjectival termination *-ianus* instead of *-ius:* e.g., C. Octavius, adopted by C. Julius Caesar, became C. Julius Caesar Octavianus. But in Cicero's time the practice had become variable. Sometimes the original name remained in use.

A slave had only one name, and since many slaves came from the East, this was often Greek. If freed, he took his master's *praenomen* and *nomen*, adding his slave-name as a *cognomen*: e.g., Tiro, when freed by M. Tullius Cicero, became M. Tullius Tiro. Occasionally the *praenomen* might be somebody else's. Atticus' slave Dionysius became M. Pomponius Dionysius in compliment to Cicero (instead of Titus).

Much the same applied to Greek or other provincials on gaining Roman citizenship. Such a man retained his former name as a *cognomen* and acquired the *praenomen* and *nomen* of the person to whom he owed the grant: e.g., the philosopher Cratippus became M. Tullius Cratippus after Cicero had got Caesar to give him the citizenship.

APPENDIX II

Consuls, 68–43 B.C.

68 L. Caecilius Metellus
Q. Marcius Rex

67 C. Calpurnius Piso
M'. Acilius Glabrio

66 M'. Aemilius Lepidus
L. Vulcatius Tullus

65 L. Aurelius Cotta
L. Manlius Torquatus

64 L. Julius Caesar
C. Marcius Figulus

63 M. Tullius Cicero
C. Antonius

62 D. Junius Silanus
L. Licinius Murena

61 M. Pupius Piso Frugi
M. Valerius Messalla Niger

60 Q. Caecilius Metellus Celer
L. Afranius

59 C. Julius Caesar
M. Calpurnius Bibulus

58 L. Calpurnius Piso Caesoninus
A. Gabinius

57 P. Cornelius Lentulus Spinther
Q. Caecilius Metellus Nepos

56 Cn. Cornelius Lentulus Marcellinus
L. Marcius Philippus

55 Cn. Pompeius Magnus
M. Licinius Crassus

54 L. Domitius Ahenobarbus
Ap. Claudius Pulcher

53 Cn. Domitius Calvinus
M. Valerius Messalla

52 Cn. Pompeius Magnus (Sole Consul)
. . . .
Q. Caecilius Metellus Pius Scipio

51 Ser. Sulpicius Rufus
M. Claudius Marcellus

50 L. Aemilius Paulus
C. Claudius Marcellus

49 C. Claudius Marcellus
L. Cornelius Lentulus Crus

48 C. Julius Caesar
P. Servilius Isauricus

47 Q. Fufius Calenus
P. Vatinius

46 C. Julius Caesar
M. Aemilius Lepidus

45 C. Julius Caesar (Sole Consul)
. . . .
Q. Fabius Maximus (suffect)
C. Trebonius (suffect)
C. Caninius Rebilus (suffect)

44 C. Julius Caesar
M. Antonius
. . . .
P. Cornelius Dolabella (suffect)

43 C. Vibius Pansa Caetronianus
A. Hirtius

GLOSSARY OF PERSONS

The glossaries cover the whole correspondence, but references are to the *Letters to his Friends*, unless otherwise stated. A number of unimportant names are omitted. 'Nobles' are marked with an asterisk.

ACASTUS: Slave of Cicero's.

ACCIUS: Late second-century writer of Latin tragedies.

ACIDINUS: See MANLIUS.

ACILIUS (M. Acilius Caninus?): Caesarian officer, Proconsul in Sicily 46–45.

M'. ACILIUS Glabrio: Consul in 67.

ADIATORIX: Son of a Galatian Tetrarch under Deiotarus' suzerainty.

AEGYPTA: Freedman, apparently of Cicero's.

L. AELIUS Lamia: Hereditary friend of Cicero's. As a prominent Knight, was banished from Rome by Gabinius in 58 for championing Cicero's cause. Later entered the Senate, becoming Aedile in 45 and probably Praetor in 43.

*L. AELIUS Tubero: Friend and marriage connection of Cicero's and one of Q. Cicero's Legates in Asia. His son prosecuted Q. Ligarius in 45, Cicero defending.

M. AEMILIUS Avianianus: Friend of Cicero's known only from letters of recommendation.

*M'. AEMILIUS Lepidus: Consul in 66. Seems to have died in Italy during the Civil War.

*M. AEMILIUS Lepidus: Consul in 46 and one of Caesar's leading followers. After Caesar's death succeeded him as Chief Pontiff and became governor of Narbonese Gaul and Hither Spain in 44–43. Joined Antony and became Triumvir, Consul again in 42, and governor of Africa in 40–36. Forced by Octavian to retire from public life.

*L. AEMILIUS Paulus: Elder brother of the above and Consul in 50. Allegedly bought by Caesar. Probably neutral in the Civil War, he was proscribed by the Triumvirs but escaped to end his days in Miletus.

*M. AEMILIUS Scaurus: (1) Consul in 115 and Leader of the Senate.

*(2) His son, Praetor in 56. As candidate for the Consulship in 54 was successfully defended by Cicero on a charge of extortion in his province (Sardinia), but found guilty in a second trial for bribery (Cicero still defending) and disappeared into exile.

AESOPUS: See CLODIUS.

L. AFRANIUS (nicknamed 'Aulus' son'): Lieutenant of Pompey, who 'bought' him the Consulship of 60. Later governed Further Spain as Pompey's Legate and fought on his side in the Civil War. Perished in Africa after Caesar's victory in 46.

AFRICANUS: See CORNELIUS Scipio.

AGESILAUS: King of Sparta *c.* 401–360.

AHALA: See SERVILIUS.

C. ALBANIUS: Father-in-law of P. Sestius (manuscripts sometimes, and editors usually, call him Albinius).

ALEDIUS: Friend of Cicero's brother(?)-in-law Publilius in 46–45 and a strong Caesarian.

ALEXANDER: Of Ephesus, called Lychnus ('The Lamp'), perhaps contemporary with Cicero. Among other activities wrote poems on astronomy and geography, the latter named after the three continents.

ALEXIO: (1) Atticus' bailiff (?) in Epirus. (2) Cicero's doctor, who died in 45.

ALEXIS: Favourite slave or freedman of Atticus.

C. ALFIUS Flavus: Praetor (?) in 54.

A. ALLIENUS: Friend of the Ciceros. Praetor in 49 and a supporter of Caesar.

C. AMAFINIUS: Probably the first writer on Epicureanism in Latin, usually thought to have 'flourished' early in the first century.

AMMONIUS (Hammonius): Minister of Ptolemy the Piper and later (if the two are one) of Cleopatra.

T. AMPIUS Balbus: Praetor in 59 and governor of Asia the following year, then transferred to Cilicia. Henchman of Pompey and friend of Cicero, who probably obtained permission for him to return to Italy in 46.

C. ANICIUS: Senator and friend of Cicero.

T. ANICIUS: Agent of Q. Cicero.

M. ANNEIUS: Legate of Cicero in Cilicia.

T. ANNIUS Milo: As Tribune in 57 stoutly championed Cicero's recall and raised armed bands against Clodius. Candidate for the Consulship in 53, was condemned after Clodius' murder in January 52 and retired to Massilia. In 48 returned to Italy to take part in Caelius Rufus' rising and was killed.

ANTEROS: Name of one or more slaves in the Cicero family.

ANTIOCHUS: (1) Of Ascalon, contemporary Greek philosopher. Succeeded Philo as head of the Academy. (2) Literary clerk of Atticus. (3) King of Commagene.

ANTISTHENES: Disciple of Socrates and founder of the Cynic school.

Pacuvius 'ANTISTIUS' Labeo: One of Caesar's assassins, later Legate of M. Brutus, he ordered his slave to kill him after Philippi. His name was probably Pacuvius Labeo (praenomen unknown).

C. ANTISTIUS Reginus: Legate of Caesar in Gaul, apparently in charge of the western coast of Italy in 49 along with the younger Hortensius.

C. ANTISTIUS Vetus: Caesarian officer, in charge of Syria in 44. In 43 an Antistius Vetus figures as a friend of Brutus with republican sympathies. A C. Antistius Vetus was Consul-Suffect in 30 and became owner of Cicero's villa at Puteoli. Whether these are two or one is doubtful.

*C. ANTONIUS: (1) Caesar's colleague in the Consulship of 63, having previously been expelled from the Senate for rapacity and insolvency. Governor of Macedonia in 62–60. Condemned after his return to Rome, went into exile but lived to become Censor (!) in 42. Mark Antony was his nephew. *(2) Brother of Mark Antony. A Caesarian officer in the Civil War, became Praetor in 44. Captured in 43 by Brutus in Greece and later executed.

*L. ANTONIUS: Youngest brother of Mark Antony. Quaestor in 50 to Q. Minucius Thermus in Asia, Tribune in 44, and Consul in 41, when he and Antony's wife Fulvia started an unsuccessful war against Octavian in Italy. His life was spared but probably ended soon afterwards.

M. ANTONIUS: (1) Grandfather of Mark Antony, Consul in 99, and a celebrated orator. *(2) Mark Antony. Caesar's Quaestor in 52 and one of his principal lieutenants in the Civil War. Tribune in 49. Consul with Caesar in 44 and would-be successor to his power, he eventually formed the Triumvirate of 43 along with Octavian and Lepidus. Later quarrelled with Octavian and committed suicide after defeat at Actium (31).

APELLA: Freedman of M. Fabius Gallus (several other persons of this name crop up).

APELLES: The most famous painter of antiquity (late fourth-century).

APOLLODORUS: Of Athens. Second-century writer of a historical chronicle in verse.

APPIUS: See CLAUDIUS.

M. APPULEIUS: Quaestor in 45, Proquaestor in Asia in 44, perhaps Consul in 20.

AQUILA: See PONTIUS.

C. AQUILIUS Gallus: Praetor in 66 and an eminent jurist.

ARCHIAS: See LICINIUS.

ARCHILOCHUS: Seventh-century poet, famous for the virulence of his lampoons.

ARCHIMEDES: Third-century mathematician.

ARIARATHES: Brother of the following, whom in 42 he succeeded as Ariarathes X. Later deposed and probably killed by Antony.

ARIOBARZANES III: Succeeded his murdered father as King of Cappadocia in 52. Killed by Cassius' orders in 42.

ARISTARCHUS: Homeric critic and keeper of the Alexandrian library in the earlier second century.

ARISTIPPUS: Of Cyrene. Pupil of Socrates and author of a hedonistic system of philosophy.

ARISTOPHANES: (1) Fifth–fourth-century Athenian comic dramatist. (2) Grammarian, Aristarchus' predecessor as head of the Alexandrian library.

ARISTOTLE: The great fourth-century philosopher and polymath.

ARISTOXENUS: Pupil of Aristotle, especially noted for his works on music.

ARISTUS: Brother of Antiochus of Ascalon, whom he succeeded as head of the Academy.

C. ARRIUS: Cicero's neighbour at Formiae.

Q. ARRIUS: Henchman of M. Crassus. He seems to have been exiled in 52 and dead by 46.

ARTAVASDES: King of Armenia. Dethroned by Antony in 34 and subsequently executed.

ARTAXERXES I: King of Persia with whom Themistocles took refuge.

ASCLAPO: Doctor who treated Tiro at Patrae in 50–49.

C. ASINIUS Pollio: Born about 76, Praetor in 45, Consul in 40. Soldier, orator, tragic dramatist, and historian. Governor of Further Spain at the time of Caesar's death, he joined Antony in 43 and remained his supporter, but lived on under Augustus until A.D. 5.

C. ATEIUS Capito: As Tribune in 55 an ally of Cato, but after expulsion from the Senate in 50 supported Caesar. A close friend of Cicero.

L. ATEIUS Capito: Senator in 51.

ATHENODORUS: (1) The Bald. Stoic philosopher of Tarsus, brought to Rome by Cato. (2) Son of Sandon. Also a Stoic philosopher, tutor to the future Emperor Augustus.

ATILIUS: Early writer of Latin comedy.

C. ATIUS Paelignus: Pompeian officer.

ATTICA: See CAECILIA.

ATTIUS Dionysius: Friend of Cicero and Cornificius.

P. ATTIUS Varus: Pompeian officer. In 49 irregularly took over the province of Africa, which he had previously governed. Defeated and killed Curio. Probably fell at Munda.

Aulus' son: See AFRANIUS.

*AURELIA Orestilla: Wife of Catiline, 'in whom no respectable person ever found anything to praise except her good looks' (Sallust).

AURELIUS: Apparently acting as agent for M. Tullius Montanus in 44. Perhaps one of the brothers for whom Cicero wrote a recommendatory letter (Letter 59 (XIII. 40)).

*L. AURELIUS Cotta: Consul in 65. A relative of Caesar's mother, he took no part in the Civil War and later seems to have been at Caesar's disposition. After Caesar's murder retired from public life.

*M. AURELIUS Cotta: Governor of Sardinia in 49.

P. AUTRONIUS Paetus: Elected Consul in 66 but deprived of office by a conviction for bribery. Condemned in 62 for complicity with Catiline, he went into exile in Greece.

C. AVIANIUS Evander: Freedman of Aemilius Avianianus and distinguished sculptor.

C. AVIANIUS Flaccus: Corn-merchant of Puteoli, well known to Cicero.

Q. AXIUS: Wealthy Senator. A collection of Cicero's letters to him was extant in antiquity.

BALBUS: See CORNELIUS.

BASILUS: See MINUCIUS.

BASSUS: See CAECILIUS.

BIBULUS: See CALPURNIUS.

BROGITARUS: Galatian, son-in-law of Deiotarus. In return for a bribe Clodius as Tribune had him made Priest of the Great Mother at Pessinus with the title of king.

BRUTUS: See JUNIUS.

BURSA: See MUNATIUS.

CAECILIA Attica: Atticus' daughter, born probably in 51.

*CAECILIA Metella: Wife of the younger P. Lentulus Spinther and perhaps daughter of Clodia ('Ox-Eyes').

Q. CAECILIUS: Atticus' maternal uncle, a Roman Knight. Died in 58 leaving Atticus his heir.

Statius CAECILIUS: Early writer of Latin comedy.

Q. CAECILIUS Bassus: Former Pompeian who raised a mutiny in 46 against Caesar's governor of Syria and took command of his troops.

C. CAECILIUS Cornutus: (1) Tribune in 61 and Praetor in 57, when he supported Cicero's recall. (2) Perhaps son of the foregoing, City Praetor in 43. Committed suicide when Octavian seized Rome.

*L. CAECILIUS Metellus: Tribune in 49.

*Q. CAECILIUS Metellus Celer: As Praetor in 63 cooperated with Cicero against Catiline. Governor of Cisalpine Gaul in 62, Consul in 60. Died in 59. His wife was the notorious Clodia ('Ox-Eyes').

*Q. CAECILIUS Metellus Creticus: Consul in 69. Gained his honorific cognomen by conquering and annexing Crete (68–65).

*Q. CAECILIUS Metellus Nepos: Younger brother of Celer. Served with Pompey in the East. As Tribune in 62 agitated against Cicero and was suspended from office. Consul in 57 and then governor of Hither Spain. Celer and Nepos were P. Clodius' half-brothers.

*Q. CAECILIUS Metellus Numidicus: Consul in 109. In 100 he went into voluntary exile rather than swear an oath to uphold legislation by the demagogue Saturninus, and was brought back the following year.

*Q. CAECILIUS Metellus Pius Scipio: A Scipio Nasica adopted by a Metellus (Numidicus' son), 'vaunting an unmatched pedigree, yet ignorant as well as unworthy of his ancestors, corrupt and debauched in the way of his life' (R. Syme). Became Pompey's father-in-law and colleague in the Consulship of 52. After Pompey's death led the Republican forces in Africa and committed suicide after Thapsus.

A. CAECINA: Friend of Cicero, of noble Etruscan family; noted orator and author among other things of a treatise on divination by lightning.

CAELIUS: A debtor of Faberius.

M. CAELIUS Rufus: Born *c.* 88. Placed by his father under Cicero's patronage and successfully defended by him on a criminal charge in 56. Tribune in 52, Curule Aedile in 50. One of the leading speakers of his time. Previously an opponent of Caesar, he changed sides just before the outbreak of the Civil War and was made Praetor in 48. As such started an agitation in favour of debtors ending in an attempted rising against Caesar in which he and his partner Milo lost their lives.

CAEPIO: See M. JUNIUS Brutus.

CAERELLIA: A friend of Cicero's later years, considerably his senior, with philosophical interests. His letters to her, allegedly of a *risqué* character, were extant in antiquity.

CAESAR: See JULIUS.

L. CAESIUS: Member of Q. Cicero's entourage in Asia, later employed on his building operations near Arpinum.

M. CAESIUS: Aedile of Arpinum in 46.

CALDUS: See COELIUS.

CALENUS: See FUFIUS.

M. CALIDIUS: Distinguished orator. As Praetor in 57 supported Cicero's recall. A Caesarian in the Civil War, he died as governor of Cisalpine Gaul in 47.

CALLISTHENES: Latter-fourth-century historian.

*L. CALPURNIUS Bestia: (1) Tribune in 62 and enemy of Cicero. *(2) Friend of Cicero, defended by him in 56. Some identify the two.

*L. CALPURNIUS Bibulus: Son of the following. Joined his step-father Brutus in 43 but after Philippi served Antony, dying as governor of Syria in 32.

*M. CALPURNIUS Bibulus: As Consul in 59 opposed Caesar's legislation, shutting himself in his house and 'watching the skies'. Governor of Syria in 51–50. Died of overstrain while commanding Pompey's fleet in 48. Married Cato's daughter Porcia, later wife of Brutus.

*C. CALPURNIUS Piso: Consul in 67, then governor of Transalpine and Cisalpine Gaul. Defended by Cicero on a charge brought in this connection in 63.

*L. CALPURNIUS Piso Caesoninus: Consul in 58, when he took a line unfriendly to Cicero. Hence a bitter attack (extant) in 55. As Censor in 50 tried to moderate his colleague Appius Pulcher's harsh measures. Neutral in the Civil War (Caesar was his son-in-law), he opposed Antony in 44 but in 43 tried to promote an understanding.

*C. CALPURNIUS Piso Frugi: Tullia's first husband. Quaestor in 58, he died before Cicero's return from exile.

CALVINUS: See DOMITIUS.

CALVUS: See LICINIUS Macer.

C. CAMILLUS: An expert on business law, friend of Atticus and Cicero.

P. CANIDIUS Crassus: Consul-Suffect in 40. Commanded Antony's land forces at Actium and was executed by Octavian.

L. CANINIUS Gallus: Friend of Cicero, who defended him in 55. As Tribune in 56 he worked for Pompey's appointment to replace Ptolemy the Piper on his throne. Died in 44.

C. CANINIUS Rebilus: Caesarian officer and one-day Consul in 45.

Ti. CANNUTIUS: As Tribune in 43 bitterly hostile to Antony. Escaped proscription, but was later executed by Octavian.

CANUS: See GELLIUS.

CARBO: See PAPIRIUS.

D. CARFULENUS: Able Caesarian officer who, after Caesar's death, opposed Antony as Tribune in 44. Commanded Martian Legion at the battle of Forum Gallorum, in which he was reported killed.

CARNEADES: Second-century philosopher and head of the 'New' Academy.

T. CARRINAS: Caesarian acquaintance of Cicero's in 45. Perhaps the praenomen should be Gaius (C.) to identify him with a Consul-Suffect of 43 who played a considerable role in the Triumviral period.

CASSIUS Barba: Caesarian officer, later supporter of Antony.

*C. CASSIUS Longinus: As Quaestor took charge of Syria after Crassus' death at Carrhae in 53. Gained a success against invading Parthians in 51. As Tribune in 49 joined Pompey. Pardoned and favoured by Caesar, he became Praetor in 44 and one of the leading conspirators against Caesar's life. Subsequently organized forces against the Triumvirs in the East and perished with Brutus at Philippi in 42. Married to Brutus' half-sister, Junia Tertulla.

*L. CASSIUS Longinus: Brother of the above but a Caesarian, Tribune in 44.

*Q. CASSIUS Longinus: Cousin of the foregoing. Formerly a favourite with Pompey, as Tribune in 49 he supported Caesar. His misgovernment of Hither Spain (49–47) provoked mutiny and his attempted assassination. Recalled by Caesar, he died at sea.

C. CASSIUS Parmensis: Quaestor in 43. According to the historian Velleius (who may, however, have confused him with someone else) he was one of Caesar's assassins and the last of them to die (killed at Athens after Actium). Probably the author of elegies mentioned by Horace (*Epistles*, I. 4.3).

M. CASSIUS Scaeva: As a Centurion in 48 his epic courage is recorded by Caesar. It seems to have been matched by his rapacity.

CASTRICIUS: A person with whom Q. Cicero had financial dealings.

CATILINE: See SERGIUS.

CATIUS: Native of Cisalpine Gaul and author of a treatise or treatises on Epicureanism.

CATO: See PORCIUS.

CATULUS: See LUTATIUS.

CELER: See CAECILIUS Metellus and PILIUS.

CENSORINUS: See MARCIUS.

CEPHALIO: Letter-carrier in 49–47.

CHAERIPPUS: Friend, or perhaps freedman or client, of Q. Cicero, probably to be distinguished from a friend of Cornificius mentioned in letters addressed to the latter.

CHRYSIPPUS: (1) Third-century Stoic philosopher. (2) Freedman in charge of Cicero's library. (3) See VETTIUS.

CICERO: See TULLIUS.

L. CINCIUS: Man of business and confidential agent of Atticus.

CINEAS: Minister of King Pyrrhus and author (or rather epitomizer) of a work on strategy.

CINNA: See CORNELIUS.

L. (?) CISPIUS Laevus: Officer (not necessarily Legate) of Plancus in 43.

Ser. CLAUDIUS: Roman knight and scholar, half-brother or cousin to Papirius Paetus. Drew up a list of Plautus' authentic plays.

*C. CLAUDIUS Marcellus: (1) Praetor in 80. *(2) Son of the foregoing. As Consul in 50 in opposition to Caesar, but neutral in the Civil War. Married Caesar's great-niece Octavia. *(3) Cousin of the foregoing and Consul in 49. A naval commander under Pompey in 48, he seems to have died before Pharsalia.

*M. CLAUDIUS Marcellus: Brother of Gaius (no. 3), Consul in 51. A steady though not fanatical opponent of Caesar, he joined Pompey in the war but retired to Mytilene after Pharsalia. Publicly pardoned by Caesar in 46 (hence Cicero's extant speech of gratitude), he was murdered by a friend on his way home.

*Ti. CLAUDIUS Nero: One of Tullia's suitors in 50, he served and held office under Caesar. Praetor in 42, died after various vicissitudes about 35. His wife Livia married Octavian; his son became Octavian's (Augustus') successor, the Emperor Tiberius.

*Ap. CLAUDIUS Pulcher: As Praetor in 57 at enmity with Cicero but later reconciled. Consul in 54, he became Cicero's predecessor as governor of Cilicia. Censor in 50. Supported Pompey in the Civil War, but died before Pharsalia. One of his daughters married Pompey's elder son, another M. Brutus.

*Ap. CLAUDIUS Pulcher (maior): Son of Gaius. Probably served under Caesar in Gaul. After Caesar's death joined Antony, but temporarily regretted it. Later a Triumviral partisan and Consul in 38.

*Ap. CLAUDIUS Pulcher (minor): Younger brother of the above, adopted by his uncle Appius. In 51 figured in the proceedings following C. Pulcher's conviction (this distribution of the two young Appii, due to Mommsen, is generally accepted but not certain).

*C. CLAUDIUS (CLODIUS) Pulcher: Brother of Appius. Legate of Caesar in Gaul, Praetor in 56, then governor of Asia. Condemned for extortion after his return, he may have remained in exile until 43.

CLITARCHUS: Third-century author of a history of Alexander the Great.

*CLODIA (CLAUDIA, 'Ox-Eyes'): Sister to C. Claudius Pulcher (Clodius; above) and wife of Metellus Celer; probably the 'Lesbia' to whom Catullus wrote his love-poems. Perhaps owner of a suburban property which Cicero wanted to buy in 45. The Clodia mentioned in *Letters to Atticus*, 172 (IX.6)3 may have been her sister.

L. CLODIUS: 'Prefect of Engineers' to Ap. Pulcher in 51.

CLODIUS Aesopus: Great tragic actor, well known to Cicero personally. His son (mentioned also by Horace) was a notorious reprobate.

*P. CLODIUS Pulcher: Younger brother of Appius and Gaius. As Tribune in 58 drove Cicero into exile and remained his arch-enemy. From then until his death in an affray with Milo in 52 he was a power in politics through his popularity with the Roman mob and organized street-rowdyism. Often called Publius or Pulchellus ('Little Beauty', 'Pretty-boy') in Cicero's letters.

Sex. CLOELIUS: P. Clodius' chief lieutenant and gang-organizer. Traditionally known as Sex. Clodius after an error in some inferior manuscripts.

CLUATIUS: An architect.

M. CLUVIUS: Wealthy banker of Puteoli from whom Cicero inherited an estate there.

COCCEIUS: Perhaps an agent or surety of Dolabella's, possibly one of the brothers L. and M. Cocceius Nerva, prominent in the Triumviral period (see NERVA).

*C. COELIUS Caldus: Quaestor to Cicero in 50 and left by him in charge of Cilicia.

Q. CONSIDIUS: Wealthy old Senator in 59. Q. Considius Gallus of Letter 431 (XII. 26) may have been a relative, as also the following.

M. CONSIDIUS Nonianus: Praetor perhaps in 52; named by the Senate in 49 as Caesar's successor in Cisalpine Gaul.

C. COPONIUS: Praetor in 49 and Pompeian naval commander in 48.

Q. CORNELIUS: Jurist, teacher of Trebatius Testa.

L. CORNELIUS Balbus: (1) Native of Gades (Cadiz), received Roman citizenship in 72 through L. Cornelius Lentulus Crus. Attached himself to Caesar, becoming his confidential agent and financial adviser, and later to Octavian. Appointed Consul-Suffect in 40, not having held (at least until Caesar's death) any previous magistracy. Present at Atticus' death-bed in 32. (2) Nephew of the foregoing. In Caesar's entourage during the Civil War, he became Quaestor in 44, serving under Pollio in Spain. Rose to Consular rank under Augustus and triumphed in 19.

*L. CORNELIUS Cinna: Consul in 87. Expelled from Rome he reestablished himself by military force and after Marius' death remained at the head of affairs until his own death in 84.

*P. CORNELIUS Dolabella (after adoption Cn. Cornelius Lentulus Dolabella?): Defended by Cicero on two capital charges, he married Tullia in 50, but was divorced in 46. A favoured follower of Caesar (despite demagogic activities as Tribune in 47), whom he succeeded as Consul in 44. After some wavering joined Antony and left for his province of Sytia late in the year. On the way killed C. Trebonius, governor of Asia and one of Caesar's assassins. Soon afterwards committed suicide to avoid capture by Cassius.

C. CORNELIUS Gallus: Distinguished poet, friend of Pollio and Virgil. After high promotion from Augustus his career ended in disgrace and suicide.

*CORNELIUS Lentulus: Son of Dolabella and Tullia, born in January 45; lived only a few months.

*L. CORNELIUS Lentulus: Son of the Flamen, L. Lentulus Niger. Unsuccessfully prosecuted Gabinius in 54.

*L. CORNELIUS Lentulus Crus: Praetor in 58 (friendly to Cicero), Consul in 49. After Pharsalia fled to Egypt, where he was murdered in prison.

*Cn. CORNELIUS Lentulus Marcellinus: Consul in 56. Not heard of thereafter.

*L. CORNELIUS Lentulus Niger: Flamen of Mars. Died in 55.

P. CORNELIUS Lentulus Spinther: (1) As Consul in 57 took a leading part in Cicero's restoration. Governor of Cilicia 56–54. Supported Pompey in the Civil War. Taken prisoner by Caesar at Corfinium and released, he joined Pompey in Greece. Put to death in Africa in 46, perhaps by Caesar's orders. The name Spinther, derived from an actor who resembled him, is used by Cicero only for his son.(2) Son of the foregoing. Falsely claimed to have taken part in Caesar's murder. Went to Asia in 43 as Trebonius' Quaestor, after whose death he was active in support of Brutus and Cassius. Probably put to death after Philippi.

CORNELIUS Nepos: Friend of Atticus and Cicero. Author of a short biography of the former in his book *On Famous Men*.

*P. CORNELIUS Scipio Aemilianus Africanus: Destroyer of Carthage in 146 and leading Roman statesman, idealized by Cicero, who gave him the chief role in his dialogue *On the Republic*.

*Faustus CORNELIUS Sulla: Son of the Dictator, Served with distinction in the East under Pompey, whose daughter he married. Active Republican in the Civil War, killed in Africa.

*P. CORNELIUS Sulla: (1) Nephew of the Dictator. Elected to the Consulship in 66 along with P. Autronius and deprived of office for the same reason, he retired to Naples. Defended in 62 by Cicero in an extant speech on a charge of complicity in Catiline's plot. Prominent after Caesar's victory, he enriched himself by buying confiscated property. Died in 46. *(2) Son of the foregoing. It was probably he rather than his father who held military commands in the Civil War, including that of Caesar's right at Pharsalia.

*L. CORNELIUS Sulla Felix: The Dictator. Held supreme power in Rome from 82 till his abdication in 79. Died in 78.

Q. CORNIFICIUS: (1) Praetor in 67 or 66 and a fellow-candidate with Cicero for the Consulship of 63. (2) Son of the above. Quaestor in 48, he served Caesar in and after the Civil War. Governor of Africa 44–42, until defeated and killed by the neighbouring governor, T. Sextius. A notable orator and poet, friend and correspondent of Cicero.

CORNUTUS: See CAECILUS.

L. COSSINIUS: Like his friend Atticus a Roman Knight and landed proprietor in Epirus, with a role in Varro's dialogue *On Agriculture*.

COTTA: See AURELIUS.

CRASSIPES: See FURIUS.

CRASSUS: See LICINIUS.

CRATERUS: Attica's doctor, a celebrated physician mentioned by Horace and Galen.

CRATIPPUS: Eminent philosopher of the Peripatetic (Aristotelian) school, mentor of young M. Cicero at Athens, Cicero obtained him Roman citizenship from Caesar.

CRISPUS: See MARCIUS.

CULLEO: See TERENTIUS.

CURIO: See SCRIBONIUS.

M'. CURIUS: Roman businessman resident at Patrae, a close friend of Atticus and later of Cicero.

M. CURTIUS: Recommended by Cicero to Caesar for a military Tribunate in 54.

CURTIUS Nicias: A noted scholar. In 45–44 closely attached to Dolabella, who perhaps introduced him to Cicero. Sometimes identified with a despot of Cos, his native island, during Antony's régime.

C. CURTIUS Postumus: A vigorous Caesarian, almost certainly the C. Rabirius Postumus whom Cicero defended in an extant speech in 56.

CYRUS: (1) Founder of the Persian empire. Xenophon's *Education of Cyrus* is a highly idealized account of him. (2) See VETTIUS.

CYTHERIS: See VOLUMNIA.

DAMASIPPUS: Well-known art expert who, as we learn from Horace, went bankrupt and turned Stoic philosopher.

DECIMUS: See JUNIUS.

DEIOTARUS: Tetrarch of part of Galatia, made king by Pompey, whom he supported in the Civil War. Caesar let him keep his throne and acquitted him on a charge of attempted assassination (Cicero's defence is extant). Died about 40 in extreme old age. His son and namesake, also given the royal title by the Senate, probably predeceased him.

DEMETRIUS: (1) A freedman of Pompey (*Letters to Atticus* 86 (IV.11) 1). (2) A freedman, probably of Atticus (*Letters to Atticus* 371 (XIV.17)1). (3) Of Magnesia, a contemporary littérateur, author of a book *On Concord.* (4) A tiresome personage, perhaps identical with No. 1, perhaps an influential freedman of Caesar's (Letters 184–6 (XVI.19, 22, 17)). (5) Caesarian officer in 49 (Letter 149 (VIII.15)). (6) Megas, a Sicilian recommended by Cicero in 46. (7) Of Phalerum, late-fourth-century Athenian orator and statesman.

DEMOCRITUS: Fifth-century philosopher, developed the atomic theory of the universe.

DEMOSTHENES: Great fourth-century Athenian orator and patriot.

DICAEARCHUS: Pupil of Aristotle and like him a polymath, author of works on philosophy, history, literature, etc.

DIODOTUS: (1) Stoic philosopher and Cicero's teacher. Lived in Cicero's house for many years and died leaving him his money. (2) Freedman of Lucullus.

DIOGENES: Greek friend or agent of Caelius Rufus, sent out to Cilicia in 51.

DIONYSIUS: (1) Fourth-century despot of Syracuse. (2) His son and successor. (3) Freedman and librarian of Cicero, pilfered his books and ran away. (4) See ATTIUS, POMPONIUS.

DIPHILUS: (1) An actor. (2) An architect.

DOLABELLA: See CORNELIUS.

*Cn. DOMITIUS Ahenobarbus: Son of the following. Returned to Italy after Pharsalia. Later a partisan of Antony (Shakespeare's Enobarbus), whom he finally deserted. Consul in 32.

*L. DOMITIUS Ahenobarbus: Cato's brother-in-law and bitter opponent of Caesar. Captured at Corfinium in 49 and released, he stood siege in Massilia but fled before the town fell to Caesar's forces. Commanded Pompey's left at Pharsalia and was killed in flight.

*Cn. DOMITIUS Calvinus: Consul in 53. Probably condemned for bribery and restored from exile by Caesar. Held high commands in the war, and a second Consulship and Triumph after Caesar's death.

DRUSUS: See LIVIUS.

DURIS: Historian, 'flourished' *c.* 300.

L. EGNATIUS Rufus: Roman Knight with whom Cicero and his brother had financial dealings.

Q. ENNIUS: Third-second-century Latin poet.

EPAMINONDAS: Theban soldier and statesman, killed in the battle of Mantinea (362).

EPHORUS: Fourth-century historian.

EPICHARMUS: Sixth-century Sicilian writer of comedy.

EPICURUS: Fourth-century philosopher.

ERATOSTHENES: Third-century savant, head of the Alexandrian library and founder of scientific geography.

EROS: Slave (perhaps of Philotimus) or freedman who looked after Cicero's finances in 45–44.

EUPOLIS: Athenian writer of comedy, contemporary with Aristophanes.

EURIPIDES: Athenian writer of tragedy.

EUTRAPELUS: See VOLUMNIUS.

Q. FABERIUS: Caesar's Secretary, served Antony after Caesar's death.

FABIUS: A lover of Clodia's, perhaps identical with Q. Fabius Maximus.

C. FABIUS: Legate of Caesar and friend of Atticus. Seems to have died in 49.

M. FABIUS Gallus: Usually but wrongly called Fadius. Friend of Cicero, author, Epicurean, connoisseur of art.

*Q. FABIUS Maximus: Supporter of Caesar and Consul-Suffect in 45. Died in office.

Q. FABIUS Vergilianus: Legate to Ap. Pulcher in Cilicia. Perhaps the Q. Fabius who brought Pompey a message in 49 (*Letters to Atticus* 161A (VIII.11A)).

L. FADIUS: Aedile of Arpinum in 44.

T. FADIUS: Cicero's Quaestor in 63, Tribune in 57 (supported Cicero's recall), probably Praetor in a later year. Condemned for bribery in 52.

*C. FANNIUS: Anti-triumviral Tribune in 59, probably Praetor later, governor of Asia in 49. Proscribed in 43, he fled to Sex. Pompeius and later to Antony.

*FAUSTA: Sulla's daughter and wife of C. Memmius, later of Milo.

FAUSTUS: See CORNELIUS Sulla.

M. FAVONIUS: Follower of Cato. Fled from Pharsalia with Pompey. Later pardoned by Caesar, but proscribed in 43 and put to death at Philippi.

FIGULUS: See MARCIUS.

FLACCUS: See VALERIUS.

FLAMINIUS Flamma: Debtor mentioned in 45.

C. FLAVIUS: Friend and 'Prefect of Engineers' to M. Brutus. Fell at Philippi.

L. FLAVIUS: As Tribune in 60 acted in Pompey's interest. Praetor in 58. The Caesarian officer of *Letters to Atticus* 190 (x.1).2 may or may not be the same.

FUFIDIUS: The Fufidii were a prominent family in Arpinum.

Q. FUFIUS Calenus: Tribune in 61, Praetor in 59. Served under Caesar in Gaul and the Civil War. Governor of Greece in 48, Consul in 47. After Caesar's death supported Antony in Rome. Disliked by Cicero, who had known and respected his father.

*FULVIA: Wife of P. Crassus, Curio, and Antony.

C. FUNDANIUS: Friend and apparently ex-client of Cicero.

FUNISULANUS: Twice mentioned as carrying a letter from Atticus to Cicero.

T. FURFANUS Postumus: Friend of Cicero and governor of Sicily in 46–45.

*FURIUS Crassipes: Married Tullia about 55, soon afterwards divorced. Quaestor in Bithynia, perhaps in 54.

C. FURNIUS: Friend of Cicero, Tribune in 50. A Caesarian, he served as Munatius Plancus' Legate in 43 and later supported Mark Antony and his brother Lucius. Pardoned and dignified by Octavian, he lived to see his son Consul in 17.

A. GABINIUS: Military lieutenant and political supporter of Pompey. As Consul in 58 backed Clodius against Cicero. As governor of Syria restored Ptolemy the Piper to his throne in 55. Went into exile in 54 after conviction on charges of extortion. Reappears as Caesar's Legate in 48. Died in 47.

GALBA: See SULPICIUS.

M. GALLIUS: Along with his brother prosecuted Calidius in 51. Identifiable with an ex-Praetor and partisan of Antony in 43.

Q. GALLIUS: Brother of the foregoing, both being sons of a former client of Cicero's, Q. Gallius. Probably Praetor in 43, deposed from office by Octavian.

GALLUS: See FABIUS.

L. GAVIUS: Agent of Brutus in Cappadocia 50–49.

GELLIUS Poplicola: Brother of L. Gellius Poplicola, Consul in 72, and a follower of Clodius. F. Münzer wished to identify him with Q. Gellius Canus (or Kanus), a close friend of Atticus, saved by him from proscription in 43. The L. Gellius of Letter 398 (X.17)3 may be his nephew, Consul in 36.

GLABRIO: See ACILIUS.

GNAEUS: See POMPEIUS.

GRAECEIUS: Friend of Cassius and D. Brutus.

HAMMONIUS: See AMMONIUS.

HEGESIAS: Third-century rhetorician, regarded as the creator of the 'Asiatic' style of oratory, one feature of which was a fondness for short, staccato sentences.

HERACLIDES: Of Pontus. Pupil of Plato, author of works on a variety of subjects, mostly in dialogue form.

HERMIA(S): Apparently a slave of Cicero's or of his brother's.

HERODES: An Athenian, probably of high rank, acquainted with Atticus and Cicero.

HERODOTUS: Fifth-century historian.

HESIOD: Early Greek poet.

HILARUS: Four freedmen of this name occur in the Letters.

HIPPARCHUS: Second-century astronomer and geographer.

HIRRUS: See LUCILIUS.

A. HIRTIUS: Caesarian officer, Praetor in 46 and Consul in 43 until his death at Mutina. Man of letters and gourmet. Nine or more books of his correspondence with Cicero were extant in antiquity.

T. HORDEONIUS: Member of a Campanian merchant family and co-heir to the estate of M. Cluvius.

*Q. HORTENSIUS Hortalus: (1) Consul in 69 and before Cicero Rome's leading forensic orator. A devoted friend of Atticus, his relations with Cicero varied. Died in 50. *(2) Son of the foregoing and on bad terms with him. Joined Caesar in the Civil War, who made him Praetor and governor of Macedonia. Joined Brutus in 43. Put to death after Philippi by Antony in reprisal for the execution of his brother Gaius.

HOSTILIUS Saserna: Three brothers of this name, Gaius, Lucius, and Publius, served in Caesar's armies. One of them was with Antony at Mutina.

HYPSAEUS: See PLAUTIUS.

ISOCRATES: Fourth-century Athenian rhetorician.

JUBA: King of Numidia, allied with the Pompeians in the Civil War.

*C. JULIUS Caesar: The Dictator.

*L. JULIUS Caesar: (1) Distant relative of the above. Consul in 64 and Legate in Gaul, he stood neutral in the Civil War. Proscribed in 43, he was saved by his sister, Antony's mother Julia. *(2) Son of the above. After acting as messenger in abortive peace negotiations early in the Civil War he joined Pompey. Killed after Thapsus, perhaps at Caesar's orders.

*C. JULIUS Caesar Octavianus: Caesar's great-nephew and adopted son. Later Triumvir and Emperor Augustus.

*JUNIA: Half-sister of Brutus and wife of Lepidus.

*JUNIA Tertia (or Tertulla): Sister of the above and wife of C. Cassius. Her funeral in A.D.22 is described by Tacitus.

L. JUNIUS Brutus: Rome's first Consul, who drove out the last king, Tarquin the Proud.

*M. JUNIUS Brutus: Sometimes called (Q. Servilius) Caepio (Brutus) after adoption by his uncle Q. Servilius Caepio. On his career see the introductory note on pp. 737 f.

*D. JUNIUS Brutus Albinus: Not closely related to the above. Served under Caesar in Gaul and the Civil War, governor of Transalpine Gaul in 48–46. Regarded by Caesar with special favour and named as Consul for 42 along with L. Plancus, he became a leading conspirator against his life. Later besieged by Antony at Mutina in his province of Cisalpine Gaul, after Antony's defeat and escape he too crossed the Alps to join Plancus. When the latter went over to Antony he fled, but was killed by a Celtic chieftain on Antony's orders.

*D. JUNIUS Silanus: Consul in 62. Married Brutus' mother Servilia by whom he had three daughters (see JUNIA).

*M. JUNIUS Silanus: Officer of Lepidus in 43, who (probably) sent him to Antony at Mutina but later disavowed him. Consul in 25.

*M. JUVENTIUS Laterensis: Praetor in 51. As Lepidus' Legate killed himself when his chief joined Antony.

*JUVENTIUS Talna: Friend of Cicero's, whose son came into consideration as a future husband for Attica. The rascally juryman at Clodius' trial mentioned in *Letters to Atticus* 16 (I.16)6 is no doubt another man.

KANUS: See GELLIUS.

LABEO: See 'ANTISTIUS'.

D. LABERIUS: Roman Knight, author of mimes.

T. LABIENUS: Tribune in 63. Caesar's principal lieutenant in Gaul, but deserted him at the outbreak of the Civil War and fought against him to the end. Killed at Munda.

D. LAELIUS: Family friend and supporter of Pompey. Allowed to return to Italy after Pharsalia.

*C. LAELIUS Sapiens: Consul in 140 and life-long friend of the younger Scipio Africanus.

*LAENAS: Perhaps Popilius Laenas, Senator and friend of Caesar.

LAÏS: Famous Corinthian courtesan.

LAMIA: See AELIUS.

LATERENSIS: See JUVENTIUS.

LENTULUS: See CORNELIUS.

LEONIDES: Athenian, apparently of high position, who kept an eye on M. Cicero junior in 45–44.

LEPIDUS: See AEMILIUS.

LEPTA: See PACONIUS.

LIBO: See SCRIBONIUS.

A. LICINIUS Archias: Poet, author of some surviving epigrams. Cicero successfully defended his title to Roman citizenship in an extant speech (62).

*L. LICINIUS Crassus: Consul in 95 and one of the greatest Roman orators.

*M. LICINIUS Crassus: (1) Consul in 70 and 55. Joined Pompey and Caesar in 60 to form the so-called First Triumvirate. Left for Syria late in 55. Defeated and killed at Carrhae in 53 leading an invasion of Parthia. *(2) Son (probably younger) of the above.

*P. LICINIUS Crassus: Son (probably elder) of the 'Triumvir'. Much attached to Cicero in his early days, he served brilliantly under Caesar in Gaul. Went out to Syria with his father and was killed at Carrhae. In the *Brutus* Cicero seems to blame him for the disaster.

*P. LICINIUS Crassus Dives: See *Cicero's Letters to Atticus*, p. 98, n. 147. He was Praetor in 57.

*L. LICINIUS Lucullus Ponticus: Lieutenant of Sulla and Consul in 74. In 73–66 waged a brilliant series of campaigns against King Mithridates of Pontus, ending ingloriously through disaffection in his army. After supersession by Pompey returned to Rome to live in ease and luxury until his death in 56.

*M. LICINIUS Lucullus: (1) See TERENTIUS. *(2) Son of Ponticus. Died at Philippi, or soon afterwards.

C. LICINIUS Macer Calvus: Son of C. Licinius Macer (see *Cicero's Letters to Atticus*, p. 39, n.15); a distinguished orator and poet.

Q. LIGARIUS: Pompeian, defended in 45 by Cicero before Caesar in an extant speech. Allowed to return to Rome he joined the conspiracy against Caesar.

T. LIGARIUS: Brother of the above. He and another brother perished in the proscriptions of 43.

A. LIGURIUS: Caesarian officer and friend of Cicero's.

L. LIVINEIUS Regulus: Friend of Cicero, at some time Praetor; later exiled.

L. LIVINEIUS Trypho: Freedman of the above.

*M. LIVIUS Drusus Claudianus: Father of Augustus' wife Livia, originally a Claudius Pulcher. Successfully defended by Cicero in 54. Praetor or President of Court in 50. Owner of suburban estate coveted by Cicero in 45. Killed himself in his tent at Philippi.

M. LOLLIUS Palicanus: Tribune in 71. Mob orator and agitator against the post-Sullan régime.

Cn. LUCCEIUS: Member of a locally aristocratic family of Cumae, friend of Cicero and Brutus.

L. LUCCEIUS (son of Quintus): Praetor in 67 and unsuccessful candidate for the Consulship in 60. On amicable terms with Cicero, he remained one of Pompey's most intimate friends until Pharsalia. Pardoned by Caesar, he may have died in the proscriptions of 43. Cicero admired his historical work, which was perhaps never published.

P. LUCCIUS: Friend of Cornificius (wrongly called Lucceius).

C. LUCILIUS: Roman satirist late in the second century.

C. LUCILIUS Hirrus: Great-nephew (probably) of the above and cousin to Pompey. Tribune in 53, he annoyed Cicero by standing against him for the Augurate. Defeated in 51 in his candidature for the Aedileship. Followed Pompey in the Civil War but survived to lend Caesar 6,000 fish for his triumphal banquet in 45 and flee proscription in 43–42. A great landowner and in Cicero's opinion an egregious ass.

LUCIUS: See SAUFEIUS.

Q. LUCRETIUS: Whether certain Lucretii mentioned in the Letters are identical and whether they are to be identified with Q. Lucretius Vespillo, who commanded a Pompeian squadron in the Adriatic and lived to become Consul in 19, is doubtful.

T. LUCRETIUS Carus: One of Rome's greatest poets. His work *On the Nature of Things* is an exposition of Epicurus' physical philosophy.

LUCULLUS: See LICINIUS.

LUPUS: (1) Friend of D. Brutus. (2) See RUTILIUS.

*Q. LUTATIUS Catulus: (1) Colleague of Marius as Consul in 102, killed by his orders in 87. *(2) Son of the foregoing. Consul in 78 and leading conservative figure until his death in 61 or 60.

LYSIPPUS: Fourth-century sculptor.

LYSO: Friend and host of Cicero at Patrae.

P. MAGIUS Cilo: Friend and murderer of M. Marcellus.

MAMURRA: 'Prefect of Engineers' to Caesar and a *nouveau riche*. Savagely lampooned by Catullus.

M'. MANILIUS: (1) Consul in 149, one of Rome's great jurists. *(2) Friend of Trebatius Testa, also a jurist and probably descended from the foregoing.

*MANLIUS Acidinus: Student at Athens in 45, perhaps identical with Horace's friend Torquatus.

*A. MANLIUS Torquatus: Praetor perhaps in 70 and friend of Cicero, who tried through Dolabella to get Caesar's permission for him, as an ex-Pompeian living in Athens, to return to Italy. After Caesar's death an active republican, he was befriended by his old friend Atticus after Philippi.

*L. MANLIUS Torquatus: Of a different branch of the family, Praetor in or before 49. Also friend of Cicero, who made him the Epicurean spokesman in his *De Finibus*, and of Atticus. Perished in Africa in 46. A writer of erotic verse, he is almost certainly the bridegroom in Catullus' Wedding Ode.

*T. (?) MANLIUS Torquatus: Apparently son of Aulus, mentioned in letters to Atticus of 45–44. Probably to be distinguished from Pansa's Quaestor in 43.

MARCELLINUS: See CORNELIUS Lentulus.

MARCELLUS: See CLAUDIUS.

MARCIANUS: See TULLIUS.

*L. MARCIUS Censorinus: Partisan of Caesar, then of Antony. Got possession of Cicero's house on the Palatine after its owner's murder.

C. MARCIUS Crispus: Caesarian officer. Proconsul in Bithynia in 45–44. Brought three legions to help Staius Murcus in Syria against Caecilius Bassus.

*L. MARCIUS (?) Figulus: Commanded Dolabella's fleet in 43.

*L. MARCIUS Philippus: (1) Consul in 91. Censor under Cinna's régime, but joined Sulla when he returned to Italy. *(2) Son of the foregoing. Consul in 56. Husband of Caesar's niece and Cato's father-in-law, he took no part in the Civil War. Counselled caution to his stepson Octavian in 44. A moderating influence in the struggle between the Senate and Antony.

C. MARIUS: Of Arpinum. Great general, seven times Consul, destroyer of invading northern tribes. Driven into exile by Sulla in 88, returned to Rome by force in 87 and killed off numbers of opponents before his own death early the following year.

'C. MARIUS': An impostor, who in 45 claimed to be grandson of the above. Executed by Antony in 44.

M. MARIUS: Friend, correspondent, and perhaps relative of Cicero, resident near Pompeii.

P. MATINIUS: Agent of Brutus in Cilicia in 51–50.

C. MATIUS: Old friend of Cicero's, closely attached to Caesar, whom he accompanied in Gaul without official rank. Cicero calls him by nicknames referring to his baldness.

MAXIMUS: See FABIUS.

MEGABOCCHUS: Friend and contemporary of P. Crassus, he committed suicide at Carrhae.

MEMMIUS: Stepson of P. Sulla, associated with him in a proposed prosecution of Gabinius in 54. Perhaps identical with the following.

C. MEMMIUS (son of Gaius): Tribune in 54.

C. MEMMIUS (son of Lucius): First husband of Sulla's daughter Fausta, who was a ward of L. Lucullus, hence perhaps an enemy of the two Luculli. An erratic political career ended in exile after conviction for bribery in 52. Noted orator and poet, generally supposed to be the friend to whom Lucretius dedicated his poem *On the Nature of Things*.

L. MESCINIUS Rufus: Cicero's Quaestor in Cilicia. Seems to have joined Pompey in the Civil War but was allowed to return to Italy in 46.

MESSALLA: See VALERIUS.

C. MESSIUS: Pro-Ciceronian Tribune in 57 and adherent of Pompey; but in 46 Legate to Caesar in Africa.

METELLUS: See CAECILIUS.

METRODORUS: A doctor, probably a freedman of Cicero's.

MILO: See ANNIUS.

M. MINDIUS: Brother (?) of L. Mescinius Rufus.

L. MINUCIUS Basilus: Legate of Caesar in Gaul and the Civil War and Praetor in 45, joined the conspiracy in 44. Murdered by his slaves the following year. A friend of Cicero, he may or may not be identical with a person or persons here and there referred to as 'Minucius'.

*Q. MINUCIUS Thermus: Governor of Asia in 51–50. A Pompeian in the Civil War and proscribed in 43, he escaped to join Sex. Pompeius and then Antony.

*MUCIA: Pompey's third wife and half-sister to the Metelli, Celer and Nepos.

*Q. MUCIUS Scaevola: (1) The Augur. Consul in 117, died in 87. Cicero knew him well. *(2) Pontifex Maximus. Consul in 95. A great jurist and a model governor of Asia, also well known to Cicero until his murder by the Marians in 82. *(3) Perhaps grandson of the Augur. After Tribunate in 54 served on Ap. Pulcher's staff in Cilicia, but a Caesarian in the Civil War. Author of erotic verse.

L. MUMMIUS Achaicus: Consul in 146 and destroyer of Corinth.

C. MUNATIUS Plancus: See PLOTIUS.

L. MUNATIUS Plancus: Family friend of Cicero. Served under Caesar in Gaul and the Civil War. City Prefect during Caesar's absence in 46–45. As governor of Transalpine Gaul (except the Narbonensis), he finally joined Antony in 43. Consul in 42. Changed sides again before Actium and became Censor in 22.

T. MUNATIUS Plancus Bursa: Brother of the above. Tribune in 52 and follower of Clodius, he was successfully prosecuted by Cicero as a ringleader in the riots following Clodius' death. In exile joined Caesar, who brought him back in 49. Later an active supporter of Antony.

MURCUS: See STAIUS.

MURENA: See TERENTIUS.

Cn. NAEVIUS: Early Roman epic and dramatic poet.

NASICA: See CAECILIUS Metellus Pius Scipio.

L. NASIDIUS: Republican naval commander in 47.

NATTA: See PINARIUS.

NEPOS: See CAECILIUS Metellus and CORNELIUS.

NERO: See CLAUDIUS.

NERVA: Officer under Lepidus, perhaps one of the brothers C. and

M. Cocceius Nerva prominent in the Triumviral period (see also COCCEIUS).

NICIAS: See CURTIUS.

P. NIGIDIUS Figulus: As a Senator assisted Cicero in 63. Praetor in 58. Joined Pompey in the Civil War and died in exile in 45. A prolific writer on various branches of learning, he was chiefly remembered as an astrologer and magician.

L. NINNIUS Quadratus: Member of a distinguished Campanian family. Opposed Clodius as Tribune in 58.

M. NONIUS (Struma?): Probably governor of Macedonia in 50.

M. NONIUS Sufenas: Tribune in 56. Sometimes identified with the above.

OCELLA (L. Livius Ocella?): Friend of Cicero and Atticus, sometime Praetor.

Servius OCELLA: Subject of a Roman scandal in 50.

OCTAVIANUS or OCTAVIUS: See JULIUS.

C. OCTAVIUS: Father of Augustus. Praetor in 61, succeeded C. Antonius as governor of Macedonia. Died in 58.

*M. OCTAVIUS: Caelius Rufus' colleague as Curule Aedile in 50. Active as a Pompeian admiral in the Civil War he probably perished in Africa.

A. OFFILIUS: Jurist, pupil of Ser. Sulpicius. Probably one of Cluvius of Puteoli's heirs in 45.

OPPII: Probably bankers, from Velia in southern Italy.

C. OPPIUS: Roman Knight, friend and agent of Caesar, usually mentioned in conjunction with Cornelius Balbus and like him a friend of Atticus and Cicero.

L. OPPIUS: Subject of several letters of recommendation in 47–46. Was in business at Philomelium and agent of Egnatius Rufus.

ORESTILLA: See AURELIA.

ORODES: King of Parthia 57–37.

OTHO: (1) L. Roscius Otho, Tribune in 67. (2) Co-heir to the estate of one Scapula which included a suburban property coveted by Cicero in 45.

OVIA: In some sort of financial relationship with Cicero in 45 and later co-heir to Cluvius of Puteoli's estate.

PACIAECUS: See VIBIUS.

Q. PACONIUS(?) Lepta: Cicero's 'Prefect of Engineers' in Cilicia.

PACORUS: Son of and eventually co-ruler with Orodes, King of Parthia. Killed in battle in 38.

PAETUS: See PAPIRIUS.

PALICANUS: See LOLLIUS.

PANAETIUS: Eminent second-century Stoic philosopher, friend of the younger Scipio Africanus.

PANSA: See VIBIUS.

*Cn. PAPIRIUS Carbo: Leading Marian, killed by Pompey after surrender in 82.

L. PAPIRIUS Paetus: Wealthy resident of Naples and an old friend of Cicero.

Q. (?) PATISCUS: Apparently a Roman businessman in Asia, then a Caesarian officer, in 43 a Republican Proquaestor taking part in naval operations in the East (if these are identical).

PATRO: Successor of Phaedrus as head of the Epicurean school at Athens, old friend and protégé of Atticus and Cicero.

PAULUS: See AEMILIUS.

Q. PEDIUS: Caesar's nephew or great-nephew. Died in office as Octavian's colleague in the Consulship of 43.

Sex. PEDUCAEUS: (1) Praetor in 77, then governor of Sicily. Cicero served under him as Quaestor. (2) Son of the foregoing and intimate friend of Atticus. References in the Letters, except when explicitly to the father, are probably to the son, whom Cicero sometimes calls simply 'Sextus'.

M. PETREIUS: Sometime Praetor, Legate of C. Antonius in 62, when he commanded the government forces in the final battle against Catiline. Legate to Pompey in Spain 55–49. After the collapse of the Pompeian armies there continued to fight against Caesar and committed suicide in Africa.

PHAEDRUS: Patro's predecessor as head of the Epicurean school. Cicero as a boy heard him lecture in Rome.

PHALARIS: Sixth-century tyrant of Agrigentum in Sicily, notorious for his cruelty.

PHAMEA: Uncle or grandfather of Tigellius. Nothing proves that he was a freedman, as often supposed.

PHANIA(S): Freedman of Ap. Pulcher.

PHARNACES: (1) Son of Mithridates the Great of Pontus and King of Bosporus. Recovered his father's kingdom in 48 and defeated Caesar's lieutenant, Domitius Calvinus. Caesar 'came, saw, and conquered' him the following year. (2) Clerk of Atticus.

PHILIPPUS: See MARCIUS.

PHILISTUS: Fourth-century historian of Sicily.

PHILO: (1) Of Larissa. Antiochus' predecessor as head of the Academic school of philosophy. (2) Freedman of Caelius Rufus, sent out to Cilicia in 51.

PHILOGENES: Freedman of Atticus, employed in financial transactions with Cicero.

PHILOTIMUS: (1) Freedman of Terentia, up till 50 much employed by Cicero in financial business. (2) Clerk of Cicero (it is not always possible to be sure which of the two is meant).

PHILOXENUS: Slave or freedman of Q. Cicero.

PHOCYLIDES: Sixth-century author of versified maxims, which he prefaced: 'This also says Phocylides.'

PILIA: Atticus' wife, married in 56. May have died in 44.

Q. PILIUS Celer: Relative, probably brother, of the above. Supported Caesar in the Civil War and brought letters from M. Brutus and C. Antonius to the Senate in 43. Cicero thought well of him as a speaker.

*L. PINARIUS Natta: Brother-in-law of Clodius, to whom as Pontifex in 58 he gave his services in connection with Cicero's house. The family was immemorially old. Several other Pinarii, probably not of aristocratic origin, crop up in the Letters, not safely to be sorted out.

PINDARUS: Possibly the freedman by whose hand Cassius died after Philippi at his own orders.

PISISTRATUS: Sixth-century 'tyrant' of Athens, type of a 'benevolent despot'.

PISO: See CALPURNIUS and PUPIUS.

PLAETORIUS: The identity of persons of this name occurring in the Letters is doubtful.

Cn. PLANCIUS: Befriended Cicero when Quaestor in Macedonia in 58. Curule Aedile in 54, defended by Cicero on a bribery charge in an extant speech. Last heard of in 45 as a Pompeian awaiting pardon in Corcyra.

PLATO: Fourth-century Athenian philosopher, founder of the Academy.

A. PLAUTIUS: See PLOTIUS.

*P. PLAUTIUS Hypsaeus: Leading adherent and at one time Quaestor of Pompey. Candidate for the Consulship in 53. Pompey let him be condemned on a bribery charge in 52.

PLAUTUS (T. Maccius Plautus): Early writer of Latin comedy.

A. PLOTIUS (or Plautius): City Praetor in 51. Identifiable with a Legate of Pompey in 67, who became Tribune, Curule Aedile, and probably governor of Bithynia in 49–48.

POLA: See SERVIUS Pola.

POLLA: See VALERIA.

POLLEX: Slave of Cicero.

POLLIO: See ASINIUS.

POLYBIUS: Second-century historian.

POLYCLES: Three sculptors of that name are recorded, one in the fourth-century, the other two in the second.

POLYDAMAS: Senior Trojan in the *Iliad*.

A. POMPEIUS Bithynicus: Friend of Cicero, Propraetor in Sicily in 44–42. Accepted Sex. Pompeius as co-governor, who later had him executed.

*Cn. POMPEIUS Magnus: (1) Pompey the Great. *(2) Elder son of the foregoing, killed in Spain after the battle of Munda.

*Sex. POMPEIUS Magnus: Younger son of Pompey the Great. After Caesar's death revived the war in Spain, then came to terms with Lepidus. Eventually gained control of Sicily and was a thorn in Octavian's flesh until defeated in 36. Fled to the East and after further adventures was captured and executed by an officer of Antony's.

*Q. POMPEIUS Rufus: Sulla's grandson, but an associate of P. Clodius, condemned for his part as Tribune in 52 in the riots following Clodius' murder. His prosecutor was Caelius Rufus, who later befriended him when he was living in poverty in Bauli.

Cn. POMPEIUS Theophanes: Of Mytilene, a protégé of Pompey, with whom he had much influence, and author of a history of Pompey's campaigns.

POMPONIA: Sister of Atticus, married to Q. Cicero from about 70 until their divorce in 45 or 44.

T. POMPONIUS Atticus (Q. Caecilius Pomponianus Atticus): Cicero's friend and correspondent.

M. POMPONIUS Dionysius: Learned freedman of Atticus and tutor to the young Ciceros.

C. POMPTINUS: Praetor in 63, then governor of Narbonese Gaul, where he crushed a tribal revolt. Finally granted a Triumph in 54. Legate to Cicero in Cilicia.

PONTIUS: Several persons of this name occur. The following can be distinguished:

L. PONTIUS: Owner of a villa in the Trebula district, where Cicero stayed when travelling between Rome and Brundisium.

PONTIUS Aquila: Tribune in 45 and assassin of Caesar. Legate to D. Brutus in 43. Killed at Mutina.

PONTIUS Titinianus: Son by birth of the Senator Q. Titinius. Joined Caesar at Brundisium in 49.

*PORCIA: (1) Cato's sister, wife of L. Domitius Ahenobarbus. Died in 45. (2) Cato's daughter, married first to M. Bibulus, then to M. Brutus. Died, allegedly by suicide, in 43.

*C. PORCIUS Cato: As Tribune in 56 at first opposed, then supported Pompey (perhaps leagued with Crassus). Tried and acquitted in 54.

*M. PORCIUS Cato: (1) 'Of Utica'. Leader of conservative opposition to the 'First Triumvirate'. Later made common cause with Pompey against Caesar, and after Pompey's death became the life and soul of continuing resistance. Committed suicide at Utica after the republican defeat in 46. Family connections included Servilia (half-sister), her son Brutus, M. Bibulus, L. Domitius, and Hortensius. *(2) Son of the foregoing, who left Cicero and Atticus as his guardians. Killed at Philippi.

POSIDONIUS: Stoic philosopher and polymath, resident in Rhodes.

*POSTUMIA: Wife of Ser. Sulpicius Rufus.

L. (?) POSTUMIUS: Follower of Cato. As his subordinate (Quaestor?) instructed to take over Sicily in 49.

POSTUMUS: See CURTIUS.

PROCILIUS: Perhaps Tribune in 56, under prosecution in 54. May or may not be identical with the author mentioned in *Letters to Atticus* 22 (II.2)2.

PROTOGENES: Fourth-century painter.

PTOLEMY XII: Called 'The Piper', King of Egypt. Driven out by his subjects in 58, restored by Gabinius in 55, died in 51.

PUBLILIA: Cicero's ward and second wife, married towards the end of 46, divorced a few months later.

PUBLILIUS: Relative, probably brother, of the above.

PUBLILIUS Syrus: Contemporary writer of mimes. A collection of maxims taken from his work survives.

PUBLIUS, PULCHELLUS, PULCHER: See CLODIUS.

*M. PUPIUS Piso Frugi: Friend of Cicero's youth, to whom he gave a role in his *De Finibus*. After his Consulship in 61 (severely criticized by Cicero) he disappears.

PYRRHUS: King of Epirus. Campaigned against Rome in 281–275. Wrote a treatise on tactics.

T. QUINTIUS Scapula: Leader of a mutiny against Caesar in Spain.

L. RACILIUS: Tribune in 56.

REBILUS: See CANINIUS.

REGINUS: See ANTISTIUS.

REGULUS: See LIVINEIUS.

RHINT(H)ON: Fourth-century writer of mock-tragedies.

L. ROSCIUS Fabatus: Served with Caesar in Gaul. Praetor in 49 and peace intermediary. Reported dead at the battle of Forum Gallorum.

Q. ROSCIUS Gallus: Rome's greatest comic actor, friend and client of Cicero.

T. (?) RUFRENUS: Officer in Lepidus' army in 43. Apparently Tribune the following year.

RUFUS: See CAELIUS, MESCINIUS, SEMPRONIUS.

*P. RUTILIUS Lupus: Tribune and supporter of Pompey in 56. Praetor in 49. Served under Pompey in Greece in 48.

Cn. SALLUSTIUS: Friend of Cicero and Atticus.

P. SALLUSTIUS: Perhaps brother of the above.

Q. SALVIDIENUS Rufus: Partisan of Octavian. After a distinguished career accused of preparing to desert to Antony and committed suicide in 40.

SALVIUS: (1) Literary slave of Atticus'. (2) Influential freedman of Caesar's.

SASERNA: See HOSTILIUS.

L. SAUFEIUS: Friend of Atticus, who saved his property in the Proscriptions. A devoted Epicurean and prolific writer on the subject.

SCAEVA: See CASSIUS.

SCAEVOLA: See MUCIUS.

M. SCAPTIUS: (1) Agent of Brutus in Cilicia 51–50. (2) Presumably relative of the foregoing, looked after Brutus' interests in Cappadocia.

SCAPULA: (1) Deceased owner of an estate which Cicero wished to buy in 45. (2) See QUINTIUS.

SCAURUS: See AEMILIUS.

SCIPIO: See CAECILIUS and CORNELIUS.

C. SCRIBONIUS Curio: (1) Consul in 76, notable general and orator. Died in 53. *(2) His son, Cicero's friend and correspondent. After some variations appeared as Tribune in 50 in the role of a fervent optimate, but suddenly went over to Caesar, allegedly for a vast bribe. Led expedition to Africa in 49, where he was defeated and killed.

SCROFA: See TREMELLIUS.

M. SEIUS: Roman Knight and man of business, supporter of Caesar. Mentioned by Varro and Pliny the Elder as a noted producer of poultry, etc.

Q. SELICIUS: Friend of Lentulus Spinther, perhaps identical with a wealthy money-lender mentioned in letters to Atticus.

C. SEMPRONIUS Rufus: Acquaintance of Cicero, apparently exiled in 50 and restored by Antony after Caesar's death. Mentioned by Horace as an ex-Praetor and gourmet.

*C. SEMPRONIUS Tuditanus: The father and son (Consul in 129) of that name are the subject of one of Cicero's historical queries.

C. SEPTIMIUS: (1) Secretary to M. Bibulus in 59. (2) Praetor in 57.

SERAPIO: (1) Author of a work on mathematical geography, after Eratosthenes and perhaps before Hipparchus. (2) Owner (?) of a ship in 49.

*L. SERGIUS Catilina: Cicero's rival for the Consulship in 64. Plotted a *coup d'état* in 63, killed in battle the following year.

*SERVILIA: Mother of M. Brutus, half-sister of Cato, allegedly mistress of Caesar, and close friend of Atticus.

*M. SERVILIUS: Tried in connection with C. Claudius Pulcher's conviction in 50. The republican Tribune of 43 who later served as Legate under Cassius and Brutus may be the same.

Q. SERVILIUS: Friend of Ap. Pulcher.

*C. SERVILIUS Ahala: Ancestor of M. Brutus (through his mother and adoptive father), who as Master of the Horse in 439 killed one Sp. Maelius, suspected of plotting to become despot in Rome.

*P. SERVILIUS Isauricus: Earlier an associate of Cato and married to his niece, he joined Caesar in the Civil War and became Consul in 48. Governor of Asia 46–44. Moderate opponent of Antony after Caesar's death, but later reconciled. Consul again in 41.

*P. SERVILIUS Vatia Isauricus: Father of the above. Consul in 79 and Proconsul in Cilicia in 78–74, he gained his triumphal cognomen by operations against the Isaurian mountaineers. Died in extreme old age in 44.

SERVIUS: See SULPICIUS.

SERVIUS Pola: Professional prosecutor.

L. SESTIUS: Probably Quaestor in 44 and later a faithful follower of M. Brutus. None the less became Consul in 23 and recipient of a Horatian Ode.

P. SESTIUS: Father of the above. Quaestor in Macedonia in 62. As Tribune in 57 took a leading part in promoting Cicero's recall. Defended on charges in this connection by Cicero in 56 (speech extant). Later Praetor and Cicero's successor as governor of Cilicia in 49. Went over to Caesar after Pharsalia. Supported Cicero in 43, but kept his life and status in the thirties. A notoriously wearisome speaker.

SEXTILIUS: Four persons of this name may be distinguished in the Letters, identification of any one of them with any other being doubtful. But C. Sextilius Rufus, Quaestor (?) in Cyprus in 49, may be the Sextilius Rufus who commanded Cassius' fleet in 43; and Q. Sextilius, Milo's friend in 57, could be the Pompeian over whose expropriation Cicero waxed indignant in 44.

SEXTUS: See PEDUCAEUS and POMPEIUS.

SICCA: Friend of Cicero's, often mentioned in letters to Atticus and Terentia, perhaps a fellow-Arpinate and Cicero's 'Prefect of Engineers' in 63.

SILANUS: See JUNIUS.

P. SILIUS: Governor of Bithynia in 51–50 and owner of a property which Cicero wished to buy in 45.

SIRO: Epicurean philosopher who lived in Naples and became Virgil's teacher.

P. SITTIUS: Roman Knight, who left Italy for Further Spain and then Mauretania in 64, where, according to our sources, he became a military adventurer. In 57 condemned in absence on an unknown charge. Brought a force to join Caesar in 46 and received a principality in reward. Murdered in 44.

SOCRATES: Plato's teacher and principal speaker in his dialogues.

SOLON: Sixth-century Athenian statesman and law-giver.

SOPHOCLES: Fifth-century Athenian tragic dramatist.

C. SOSIUS: Praetor in 49.

SPARTACUS: Leader of a slave rebellion in 73–71.

SPINTHER: See CORNELIUS Lentulus.

SPURINNA: Haruspex (diviner from entrails). Warned Caesar that his life was in danger before his assassination.

L. STAIUS Murcus: Legate of Caesar's. Proconsul in Syria in 44. Active at sea on behalf of the republicans. After Philippi joined Sex. Pompeius, who eventually put him to death.

STATIUS: Slave, then freedman, of Q. Cicero.

SUFENAS: See NONIUS.

SULLA: See CORNELIUS.

*Ser. SULPICIUS Galba: Legate to C. Pomptinus, then to Caesar in Gaul. Praetor in 54. Supported Caesar in the Civil War and joined the conspiracy in 44. Fought under Pansa at the battle of Forum Gallorum. Probably killed in 43.

*Ser. SULPICIUS Rufus: (1) Friend and contemporary of Cicero's and one of the most famous of Roman jurists. Consul in 51, he worked to avoid the coming clash with Caesar, but in 49 after initial wavering joined Pompey (the common view that he remained neutral is mistaken). After Pharsalia he retired to Samos, but was appointed governor of Achaia by Caesar in

46. Died in 43 on a mission to Antony. *(2) His son. Joined Caesar's army at Brundisium in March 49, but further part in the war is unknown. After Caesar's death a republican and probably a victim of the Proscriptions.

TALNA: See JUVENTIUS.

TARCONDIMOTUS: Ruler (later king) in the Amanus mountains. Died at Actium fighting for Antony.

TERENCE (P. Terentius Afer): Second-century writer of Latin comedy.

TERENTIA: Cicero's wife from about 80 to 46.

TERENTIUS: Several persons with this name cannot be traced outside the passages where they occur.

Q. TERENTIUS Culleo: Tribune in 58 and friend of Pompey. Lepidus' officer Culleo in 43 may have been his son or a younger relative.

P. TERENTIUS Hispo: Friend of Cicero, worked for a tax-farming company (or companies) in Asia and Bithynia.

M. TERENTIUS Varro: Of Reate, the most learned and prolific author of his time. Born in 116. After a distinguished military and political career under Pompey's aegis, he gave up the republican cause after Pharsalia and became head of Caesar's new library. Narrowly escaping proscription in 43 he lived till 27 in tireless literary activity. Of his vast and varied output only a small part, and perhaps the least interesting, survives apart from fragments.

M. TERENTIUS Varro Gibba: See the recommendatory letter, 277 (XIII.10). He was Tribune in 43 and executed at Philippi.

*M. TERENTIUS Varro Lucullus: Brother by birth of L. Lucullus and an almost equally distinguished soldier. Consul in 73, triumphed for victories in the Balkans. Died not long after Lucius.

*A. TERENTIUS Varro Murena: Friend of Cicero and Ap. Pulcher.

TERTIA, TERTULLA: See JUNIA.

TESTA: See TREBATIUS.

THEMISTOCLES: Athenian leader in the Persian War of 481–479. Later exiled and took refuge with the King of Persia.

THEOPHANES: See POMPEIUS.

THEOPHRASTUS: Pupil of Aristotle and prolific writer on philosophy, politics, and natural science.

THEOPOMPUS: (1) Of Chios. Fourth-century historian noted for censoriousness. (2) Of Cnidus. Writer on mythology and friend of Caesar.

THERMUS: See MINUCIUS.

THRASYBULUS: Athenian statesman, who overthrew the oligarchy in 403.

THUCYDIDES: Fifth-century historian of the Peloponnesian War.

THYILLUS: Poet, three of whose epigrams survive in the Greek Anthology.

TIGELLIUS: A Sardinian, favourite of Caesar and later of Octavian.

TIGRANES: King of Armenia 95–*c.* 55.

C. TILLIUS Cimber: One of Caesar's assassins. Later as governor of Bithynia supported Brutus and Cassius. Probably died at Philippi.

TIMAEUS: Fourth–third-century historian.

TIMOLEON: Democratic leader in Sicily in the fourth century.

TIRO: See TULLIUS.

Q. TITINIUS: A wealthy Senator.

P. TITIUS: Tribune in 43 and proposer of the law establishing the Triumvirate. Died in office (other Titii crop up sporadically).

TORQUATUS: See MANLIUS.

TRABEA: Writer of Latin comedy.

TRATORIUS: Friend of Cornificius in 43.

C. TREBATIUS Testa: Of Velia. Friend and correspondent of Cicero, about twenty years his junior, recommended by him to Caesar in 54. Supported Caesar in the Civil War and lived to a ripe old age. Cicero's *Topica* is dedicated to him. Eminent jurist.

L. TREBELLIUS: As Tribune in 47 resisted Dolabella's radical economic programme, thus acquiring the cognomen 'Fides' ('Good Faith', 'Credit'). Officer under Antony in 43.

C. TREBONIUS: Tribune in 55, put through a law extending Caesar's term of command. Legate to Caesar in Gallic and Civil Wars and Praetor in 48. Governor of Further Spain 47–46. Consul-Suffect 45. Joined the conspiracy in 44. Brutally murdered by Dolabella shortly after his arrival in Asia as governor. Friend and correspondent of Cicero.

Cn. TREMELLIUS Scrofa: Praetor in the sixties and governor of Crete in 51–50. A leading character in Varro's dialogue *On Agriculture*.

TRIARIUS: See VALERIUS.

TRYPHO: See LIVINEIUS.

TUBERO: See AELIUS.

TUDITANUS: See SEMPRONIUS.

*TULLIA: Cicero's daughter. Died February 45.

L. TULLIUS: Legate to Cicero in Cilicia.

M. TULLIUS: Cicero's Secretary in Cilicia.

M. TULLIUS Cicero: (1) The orator. *(2) His son.

Q. TULLIUS Cicero: (1) Brother of the orator. (2) His son, Cicero's and Atticus' nephew.

TULLIUS Marcianus: He and the following accompanied young M. Cicero to Athens in 45. They were probably connections or dependants of the family.

L. TULLIUS Montanus: See the foregoing.

M. TULLIUS Tiro: Slave of Cicero, manumitted in 53, a confidential secretary and literary assistant. After Cicero's death devoted himself to propagating his work and memory.

TULLUS: See VULCATIUS.

D. TURULLIUS: Assassin of Caesar, probably Proquaestor to Tillius Cimber in 43. Later joined Antony and was executed by Octavian.

TUTIA: Considered as a possible match for the younger Quintus.

TYRANNIO: Of Amisus, originally called Theophrastus. Settled in Rome about 68 and became rich and well known as a scholar and teacher. Wrote on grammatical and literary subjects. The geographer Strabo was his pupil.

Paula (Polla) VALERIA: Of the Triarius family. Married D. Brutus in 50.

VALERIUS: (1) Called the interpreter. Probably to be distinguished from (2) A friend of Cicero and Trebatius, writer of mimes, possibly identical with the following.

L. VALERIUS: Lawyer friend of Cicero.

P. VALERIUS: (1) Businessman or tax-farmer in Cilicia in 50. (2) Friend at whose villa near Rhegium Cicero stayed in 44.

*C. VALERIUS Flaccus: Son of the following. On staff of Ap. Pulcher in 51. Killed fighting in Pompey's army at Dyrrachium in 48.

*L. VALERIUS Flaccus: Praetor in 63 and governor of Asia. Defended by Cicero in 59 in an extant speech.

*M. VALERIUS Messalla Corvinus: Son of the following. At Athens with young M. Cicero in 45. Distinguished orator and one of the great figures of the Augustan period.

*M. VALERIUS Messalla Niger: As Consul in 61 took an optimate line, but later a supporter of Pompey. Censor in 55–54, apparently died shortly before the Civil War.

*M. VALERIUS Messalla Rufus: Brother-in-law to Sulla and Hortensius' nephew, friend of Atticus and Cicero. Consul in 53, later condemned for electoral malpractice and rehabilitated by Caesar. After Caesar's death lived in scholarly retirement to an advanced age. Wrote on augury.

C. VALERIUS Triarius: Apparently fell on the Pompeian side at Pharsalia. Cicero gave him a role in the *De Finibus*.

P. VALERIUS Triarius: Brother of the above.

VARRO: See TERENTIUS.

P. VATINIUS: Tribune in 59, carried through legislation on Caesar's behalf. Praetor in 55, Consul in 47, governor of Illyricum, triumphed in 42. Cicero attacked him in an extant speech, but in 54 became reconciled under pressure and defended him in court. From then on they remained on good terms.

P. VENTIDIUS Bassus: From humble beginnings rose to a Consulship (Suffect in 43) and Triumph (33). Antony's lieutenant in 43, fought for L. Antonius against Octavian in 40, as Proconsul won important successes against the Parthians.

C. VERGILIUS: Friend of Cicero, but as governor of Sicily refused him admittance in 58. Identifiable with a republican officer in Africa whose life was spared after surrender to Caesar and with a co-heir to the Scapula estate.

C. VESTORIUS: Businessman of Puteoli, friendly with Atticus and Cicero (who was apt to make fun of his lack of culture).

VETTIENUS: Businessman with whom Cicero had transactions in 49–44.

L. VETTIUS: Roman Knight from Picenum, who turned informer

against his Catilinarian associates in 63–62 and was prosecuted and imprisoned for making false charges against Caesar. Revealed or fabricated a plot against Pompey's life in 59. Died mysteriously in prison.

VETTIUS Chrysippus: an architect, freedman of the following.

VETTIUS Cyrus: a well-known architect.

VETUS: See ANTISTIUS.

L. VIBIUS Paciaecus: He and his father were prominent men in Further Spain. Served under Caesar in his final Spanish campaign.

C. VIBIUS Pansa Caetronianus: Son of one of Sulla's victims, served under Caesar in Gaul. Tribune in 51. Governed Bithynia and Cisalpine Gaul under Caesar. Consul in 43, died of wounds received in the battle of Forum Gallorum.

L. VIBULLIUS Rufus: Henchman of Pompey and his 'Prefect of Engineers' in 49.

C. VISELLIUS Varro: Cicero's cousin, son of a notable jurist and himself versed in law.

VOLUMNIA Cytheris: Freedwoman of the following and a well-known actress. Mistress of Mark Antony and allegedly the Lycoris to whom Virgil's friend Cornelius Gallus wrote love poems.

VOLUMNIUS: A Senator, perhaps identical with L. Volumnius Flaccus, bearer of a message from D. Brutus to the Senate in 43.

P. VOLUMNIUS Eutrapelus: Roman Knight and celebrated wit. After Caesar's death an adherent of Antony, probably his 'Prefect of Engineers' in 43–42.

Q. VOLUSIUS: On Cicero's staff in Cilicia.

L. VULCATIUS (or VOLCACIUS) Tullus: (1) Consul in 66. In and after the Civil War his political moderation seems to have turned into subservience to Caesar.*(2) His son, Praetor in 46 and governor of Cilicia (?) in 44. Consul with Octavian in 33.

XENO: (1) Friend and agent of Atticus in Athens. (2) Of Apollonia, commended by Atticus to Cicero in 51.

XENOCRATES: Pupil of Plato and third head of the Academy.

XENOPHON: Fifth–fourth-century Athenian historian.

ZENO: Founder of Stoicism.

GLOSSARY OF PLACES

Some names are omitted as generally familiar or explained in the notes. Italics are used for modern equivalents.

ACHAIA: Southern Greece.
ACTIUM: Promontory on the mainland south of Corfù.
AECULANUM: Town on the Appian Way, east of Beneventum.
AEGINA: Island on the Saronic Gulf, south-west of Athens.
AEMILIAN WAY: Roman road running north-west from Ariminum through Mutina.
AENARIA (*Ischia*): Island off Naples.
AESERNIA: Town in central Italy, about 30 miles east of Arpinum.
AETOLIA: District of Greece, north-west of the Gulf of Corinth.
AFRICA: (1) The continent. (2) The Roman province, part of modern Tunisia.
ALABANDA: Town in Caria.
ALBA: (1) Alba Longa north-east of Rome (Mt Albanus = *Monte Cavi*). (2) Alba Fucens in central Italy near Lake Fucino.
ALLOBROGES: Chief tribe of Narbonese Gaul.
ALSIUM (*Palo*): Town on the coast of Etruria.
ALYZIA: Greek town south of Actium.
AMANUS: Mountain range separating Cilicia from Syria.
AMBRACIA: Town in southern Epirus.
ANAGNIA (*Anagni*): Town about 25 miles west of Arpinum.
ANTANDRUS: Town in Mysia.
ANTILIBANUS: Range of mountains in Syria.
ANTIOCH: Capital of Syria, about 40 miles west of modern Aleppo.
ANTIUM (*Anzio*): Coast town south of Rome, where Cicero owned a house.
APAMEA: Town in Phrygia.
APOLLONIA: Town on the western coast of the province of Macedonia.
APOLLONIS: Town in Asia Minor, north-east of Smyrna.
APPIA: Town in Phrygia.
APPIAN WAY: The great road linking Rome with Brundisium.

GLOSSARY OF PLACES

APPII FORUM: Town on the Appian Way about 40 miles from Rome.

APULIA: District in south-eastern Italy.

AQUINUM (*Aquino*): Town just south of Arpinum.

ARABIA FELIX: The Arabian peninsula.

ARADUS: Island town off the coast of Syria.

ARCADIA: Central district of the Peloponnese.

ARCANUM: Village between Aquinum and Arpinum.

ARGENTEUS (= 'Silver', *Argens*): River in Narbonese Gaul.

ARGENTEUS, PONS (= 'Silverbridge'): Bridge over the above.

ARRETIUM: *Arezzo* in Etruria.

ASIA: (1) The continent. (2) The Roman province, comprising the western part of Asia Minor.

ASTURA: Small island (joined to the mainland) off the coast south of Antium, where Cicero had a villa.

ATELLA: Town in Campania.

ATTICA: Territory of Athens.

AVENTINE: One of the Seven Hills of Rome, south of the Palatine.

BAIAE: Famous resort on the Bay of Naples, near Cumae.

BAREA: Town on the Spanish coast south of New Carthage (*Cartagena*).

BAULI: Seaside resort near Baiae.

BELLOVACI: Gallic tribe.

BENEVENTUM (*Benevento*): Important town on the Appian Way about 30 miles east of Capua.

BITHYNIA: Region in north-western Asia Minor; as a Roman province (Bithynia and Pontus) stretching much further east.

BLAUNDUS: Town in western Asia Minor about 120 miles east of Smyrna.

BOEOTIA: Greek territory north of Attica.

BONONIA: *Bologna*.

BOVILLAE: Ancient Latin town on the Appian Way about 11 miles from Rome.

BRUNDISIUM (*Brindisi*): Adriatic port in the heel of Italy.

BUTHROTUM: Town on the coast of Epirus opposite Corfù. Atticus had an estate near by.

BYLLIS: Town in Illyricum.

CAIETA (*Gaeta*): Port of Formiae.
CALACTE: Town on the northern coast of Sicily.
CALATIA: Campanian town between Capua and Beneventum.
CALES (*Calvi*): Town in northern Campania.
CALPE: Modern Cape of Gibraltar.
CAMERIUM (*Camerino*): Town in the Umbrian Apennines.
CAMPANIA: District south of Latium.
CANDAVIA: District in Illyricum (modern Albania) to the east of Dyrrachium.
CANUSIUM: Apulian town between Arpi and Brundisium.
CAPENA, PORTA: Entrance to Rome from the Appian Way.
CAPENA: Town in Etruria north-east of Veii.
CAPITOL: Highest of the Roman Hills, overlooking the Forum.
CAPPADOCIA: Kingdom in east-central Asia Minor.
CAPUA: Chief town of Campania.
CARIA: Region in south-western Asia Minor.
CARINAE: District of Rome north of the Colosseum.
CARTEIA: Spanish coast town near modern Gibraltar.
CASILINUM: Modern Capua, about three miles west of ancient Capua.
CASSIOPE: Town in the north-east of Corfù.
CASTRUM TRUENTINUM: Coast town about 60 miles south of Ancona.
CASTULO, Pass of: Pass in the Sierra Morena.
CATINA (*Catania*): Town on the eastern coast of Sicily.
CAUNUS: Town in Caria.
CEOS: Aegean island, one of the Cyclades.
CERAMICUS: District of Athens.
CERMALUS: A depression in the Palatine Hill, towards the Tiber.
CHAONIA: District of Epirus.
CHERSONESE: The Gallipoli peninsula.
CHIOS: Large island in the Aegean, not far from Smyrna.
CIBYRA: Town in south-western Asia Minor.
CILICIA: (1) Coastal strip in south-eastern Asia Minor. (2) Roman province comprising the whole southern coast, much of the interior, and the island of Cyprus.
CINGULUM (*Cingoli*): Inland town in Picenum.
CIRCEII: Town on the promontory west of Tarracina.

CISALPINE GAUL: 'Gaul this side of the Alps', i.e., northern Italy between the Alps and the Apennines.

CLATERNA (*Quaderna*): Town in Cisalpine Gaul, on the Aemilian Way between Bononia and Forum Cornelii.

CLITERNUM: Town in central Italy.

COLCHIS: Region bordering the south-eastern coast of the Black Sea.

COLOPHON: Town on the coast of Asia Minor near Ephesus.

COMMAGENE: Kingdom situated west of the Euphrates between Syria and Cappadocia.

COMUM (*Como*): Town on the southern shore of Lake Como, refounded by Julius Caesar (Novum Comum).

CORCYRA (*Corfù*): Island off the coast of Epirus.

CORDUBA: *Cordova*, in southern Spain.

CORFINIUM: Chief town of the Paeligni, east of Lake Fucino.

CORYCUS: Town on the coast of Cilicia.

COSA (*Ansedonia*): Town on the coast of Etruria.

CROMMYACRIS ('Onion Cape'): Headland on the north coast of Cyprus.

CROTON: Town on the east coast of modern Calabria.

CULARO: *Grenoble*.

CUMAE (*Cuma*): Coastal town a few miles west of Naples. Cicero had a villa in its territory.

CYBISTRA: Town in the south-eastern corner of Cappadocia.

CYRRHESTICA: District of Syria, north-east of Antioch.

CYZICUS: Town on the Asiatic coast of the Propontis (*Sea of Marmora*).

DELOS: Aegean island, in the Cyclades.

DERBE: Town in Isauria.

DERTONA (*Tortona*): Town in Liguria.

DIONYSOPOLIS: Town in Phrygia.

DYRRACHIUM (*Durazzo*): Town on the western coast of the Roman province of Macedonia.

ELEUSIS: Town in Attica where the Mysteries were celebrated.

ELIS: Town in the west of the Peloponnese.

EPHESUS: On the western coast of Asia Minor, chief town of the province of Asia.

EPIDAURUS: Town on the eastern coast of the Peloponnese opposite Piraeus.

EPIPHANEA: Town in Cilicia.

EPIRUS: District of north-western Greece opposite Corfù.

EPOREDIA (*Ivrea*): Town in the foot-hills of the Pennine Alps.

EQUUS TUTICUS: Town in central Italy about 20 miles north of Beneventum (also called Equum (or Aequum) Tuticum).

ETRURIA: *Tuscany*.

FABRATERIA (VETUS and NOVA): Towns in Latium.

FALERNUM: District in northern Campania.

FICULEA: Town 5 miles north-east of Rome. Atticus had a villa between there and Nomentum (*La Mentana*).

FIRMUM (*Fermo*): Town near the Adriatic coast between Ancona and Castrum Truentinum.

FORMIAE (*Formia*): Town on the coast of Latium close to the Campanian border. Cicero had a villa near by.

FORUM CORNELIUM (or CORNELII): Town about 20 miles down the Aemilian Way east from Bononia.

FORUM GALLORUM: Village between Mutina and Bononia.

FORUM JULII (*Fréjus*): Town on the coast of Narbonese Gaul.

FORUM VOCONIUM (or VOCONII): Town in Narbonese Gaul between Pons Argenteus and Forum Julii.

FREGELLAE: Latian town destroyed in 125 and replaced by Fabrateria Nova.

FRUSINO (*Frosinone*): Latian town a few miles north-west of Fabrateria Nova.

FUNDI (*Fondi*): Latian town on the Appian Way between Tarracina and Formiae.

GADES: *Cadiz*.

GALATIA: District or kingdom in the east of Asia Minor, north of Cappadocia. The inhabitants were descended from Gaulish invaders.

GETAE: Tribe inhabiting modern Rumania.

HAEDUI: Gallic tribe.

HALAESA: Town in northern Sicily.

HALES (*Alento*): River in south-west Italy on which the town of Velia was situated.

HALICARNASSUS: Town in Caria.

HELLESPONT: The modern Dardanelles.

HERACLEA: (1) Town in Caria. (2) Town on the north coast of the Propontis (*Sea of Marmora*).

HERCULANEUM: Town near Pompeii.

HISPALIS: *Seville*.

HYDRUS (*Otranto*): Port in the heel of Italy south of Brundisium.

HYMETTUS: Mountain near Athens.

HYPAEPA: Town in Asia Minor, north-east of Smyrna.

ICONIUM (*Konya*): Town in Lycaonia.

IGUVIUM (*Gubbio*): Umbrian town on the western slope of the Apennines.

ILIUM: = Troy, near the southern entrance of the Hellespont.

ILLYRICUM: Region bordering the Adriatic from Epirus to the Gulf of Trieste.

INALPINI: Inhabitants of the Alps.

INSUBRES: Tribe of Cisalpine Gaul.

INTERAMNA (*Terni*): Town on the river Nar in Central Italy.

INTIMILII: Tribe of Liguria.

IONIA: Area on the western coast of Asia Minor settled by Ionian Greeks.

ISARA (*Isère*): River, tributary of the Rhône.

ISAURIA: Region south of Lycaonia in southern Asia Minor.

ISSUS: Cilician town on gulf of the same name in the south-eastern corner of the province.

LACEDAEMON: Another name for Sparta.

LANUVIUM: Latian town just off the Appian Way about 20 miles from Rome.

LAODICEA: (1) Town in the south-west of Phrygia. (2) Town in Syria on the coast south of Antioch.

LARINUM (*Larino*): Town in northern Apulia.

LATERIUM: Village between Arpinum and Anagnia where Q. Cicero had a property.

LATIUM: Territory to the south and east of Rome.

LAVERNIUM: Place in the neighbourhood of Formiae.

LESBOS: Large island in the northern Aegean.

LEUCAS: Town on the island of the same name between Actium and Alyzia.

LEUCATA (*Cape Ducato*): South-western extremity of the island of Leucas, south of Actium.
LILYBAEUM (*Marsala*): Town at the western end of Sicily.
LITERNUM (*Tor di Patria*): Coast town just north of Cumae.
LOCRI: Town in the toe of Italy.
LUCA (*Lucca*): Town in north-western Etruria.
LUCERIA (*Lucera*): Apulian town to the west of Arpi.
LUCRINE LAKE (*Lago Lucrino*): Lagoon adjoining the Gulf of Baiae.
LUSITANIA: Region of south-western Spain.
LYCAONIA: Region in central Asia Minor between Phrygia and Cappadocia.
LYCIA: Region on the southern coast of Asia Minor between Caria and Pamphylia.

MAGNESIA BY MT SIPYLUS: Town north-east of Smyrna.
MALEA (*Malia*): Headland at the south-eastern end of the Peloponnese.
MANTINEA: Town in Arcadia, scene of famous battle between Spartans and Thebans.
MARSI: People living near Lake Fucino in central Italy.
MASSILIA: Greek city, now Marseilles.
MEGARA: Town on the Isthmus of Corinth.
MIDAÏUM: Town in Phrygia.
MILETUS: Town on the west coast of Asia Minor, south of Ephesus.
MINTURNAE: Town a few miles south-east of Formiae.
MISENUM: Headland bounding the Bay of Naples to the north.
MOPSUHESTIA (= 'Hearth of Mopsus'): Town in the extreme east of Cilicia.
MULVIAN BRIDGE (*Ponte Molle*): Bridge across the Tiber above Rome.
MYLASA: Chief town of Caria.
MYRINA: Town on the coast north of Smyrna.
MYSIA: Region of north-western Asia Minor.
MYTILENE: Principal town of Lesbos.

NAR (*Nera*): River of central Italy.
NARBO (*Narbonne*): Roman colony in the west of Narbonese Gaul.
NARBONESE GAUL: Old Roman province in southern France.

NARES LUCANAE: Mountain pass in south-west Italy, five miles south-east of modern Acerno.

NARONA: Roman colony in Dalmatia.

NERVII: Tribe of north-eastern Gaul (Belgium).

NESIS (*Nisida*): Island off the coast between Puteoli and Naples.

NICAEA: Town in Bithynia.

NOLA (*Nola*): Inland town of Campania about 20 miles north-east of Capua.

NYSA: Town in Caria.

OLBIA (*Terranova*): Town in Sardinia.

OPUS: Town in Greece.

OSTIA (*Ostia*): Port of Rome.

PAESTUM (*Pesto*): Town on the western coast of Italy, south of Salerno.

PALATINE: Large hill south of the Forum, where according to tradition Rome began. A number of prominent people had houses on it, including Cicero.

PALTOS: Town on the coast of Syria, south of Laodicea.

PAMPHYLIA: Region on the south coast of Asia Minor between Lycia and Cilicia.

PANHORMUS: *Palermo*.

PAPHOS: Town in Cyprus.

PARIUM: Town on the Asiatic side of the Hellespont.

PARMA (*Parma*): Town in northern Italy.

PATRAE (*Patras*): Town on the northern coast of the Peloponnese.

PELLA: Town in Macedonia.

PELLENE: Greek town west of Sicyon.

PERGE or PERGA: Town on the coast of Pamphylia west of Side.

PESSINUS: Town in the west of Galatia.

PETRINUS: Mountain and district near Sinuessa.

PHILOMELIUM: Town in south-east Phrygia.

PHLIUS: Town in the Peloponnese.

PHRYGIA: Region in the middle of western Asia Minor.

PICENUM: Territory bordering the Adriatic south of Ancona.

PINDENISSUM: Town of the 'Free Cilicians' in the Amanus mountains.

PIRAEUS: Port of Athens.

PISAE: *Pisa.*

PISAURUM (*Pesaro*): Town on the coast of the Adriatic south of Ariminum.

PISIDIA: Region in south-west Asia Minor north of Pamphylia.

PLACENTIA (*Piacenza*): Town on the Po in northern Italy.

POLLENTIA (*Polenza*): Inland town in Liguria.

POMPEII: Town on the Bay of Naples where Cicero had a villa.

POMPTINE MARSHES: District adjoining the coast south of Rome.

PONS ARGENTEUS: See ARGENTEUS.

PONTUS: Region in north-eastern Asia Minor.

PORTA CAPENA: See CAPENA.

PRAENESTE (*Palestrina*): Latian town about 20 miles east of Rome.

PUTEOLI (*Pozzuoli*): Town east of Naples on the Bay. Cicero inherited an estate there in 45.

PYRAMUS: River in eastern Cilicia.

QUIRINAL: One of the Seven Hills of Rome.

REATE (*Rieti*): Sabine town south of Interamma.

REGIUM (*Reggio*): Town at the toe of Italy.

REGIUM (LEPIDI, *Reggio Emilia*): Town on the Aemilian Way west of Mutina.

SABINI: People of central Italy, with a reputation for old-fashioned frugality and virtue.

SACRA VIA: Street adjoining the north side of the Forum.

SALAMIS: Town in Cyprus.

SAMAROBRIVA: *Amiens.*

SAMNIUM: Region of central Italy.

SAMOS: Aegean island close to Ephesus.

SATRICUM: Place (village?) near Laterium.

SEGOVIA: Besides modern Segovia in Spain several other towns were so called.

SELEUCIA: City close to the right bank of the Tigris, near the site of ancient Babylon.

SELEUCIA PIERIA: Syrian coastal town west of Antioch.

SICYON: Greek town west of Corinth.

SIDE or SIDA: Harbour town in Pamphylia.

SIDON: Coastal town in Phoenicia (Lebanon).

SIGEUM: Town at the entrance of the Hellespont near ancient Troy.

SINUESSA (*Mondragone*): Town on the coast south of Formiae.

SIPONTUM: Coastal town in Apulia near modern Manfredonia.

SOLONIUM: Area south of the Ostian Way about 12 miles from Rome.

STABIAE: Town on the Bay of Cumae a few miles south of Pompeii.

STATIELLENSES: A Ligurian tribe on the northern slopes of the Apennines. Their chief town, Aquae Statiellae (*Acqui*), lay between Dertona and Pollentia.

SUESSA (*Sessa*): Latian town between Minturnae and Sinuessa.

SUNIUM: Promontory (and 'deme') south of Athens.

SYBOTA: Town on the coast of Epirus opposite a little archipelago of the same name between Corfù and the mainland.

SYNNADA: Town in Phrygia.

TARENTUM (*Taranto*): Town on the south coast of Italy.

TARICHEAE: Town in lower Galilee.

TARRACINA (*Terracina*): Town on the coast of Latium at the southern end of the Pontine Marshes.

TARSUS: Chief town of Cilicia proper.

TAUROMENIUM (*Taormina*): Town on the east coast of Sicily.

TAURUS: Mountain range in south-eastern Asia Minor.

TEANUM (APULUM): Town in the north of Apulia.

TEANUM (SIDICINUM, *Teano*): Inland town in Campania, a few miles south-west of Cales.

TENEDOS: Island south of the Hellespont.

THESPIAE: Town in Boeotia.

THESPROTIA: District in Epirus in which Atticus' estate was situated.

THESSALONICA: *Salonika*.

THESSALY: Region in Greece, south of Macedonia and east of Epirus.

THURII: Town near the Tarentine Gulf at the north-eastern end of the toe of Italy.

THYAMIS: River of Epirus bordering (or flowing through) Atticus' estate.

THYRREUM: Inland town east of Leucas.

TIBUR (*Tivoli*): Town in Latium 18 miles east of Rome.

TRALLES: Town in Caria.

TREBULA: The district of Trebula, near Calatia, bordered the Appian Way about 25 miles from Pompeii.

TRES TABERNAE (= 'Three Cottages'): Station on the Appian Way between Lanuvium and Forum Appii.

TUSCULUM: Latian town near modern Frascati. Cicero spent much time at his villa near by.

TYBA: Town in Cyrrhestica.

TYNDARIS (*Tindaro*): Town on the north coast of Sicily.

ULUBRAE: Small town bordering the Pontine Marshes.

UMBRIA: Region of central Italy east of Etruria.

UTICA: Chief town of the province of Africa.

VADA (*Vado*): Town on the coast of Liguria about 30 miles west of Genoa.

VARDAEI: Illyrian tribe.

VEII: Tuscan town a few miles north of Rome.

VELABRUM: District of Rome south of the Capitol.

VELIA: Town in south-western Italy south of Paestum. Also an area on the Palatine.

VELINE LAKE: Near Interamna.

VENAFRUM (*Venafro*): Town in northern Campania.

VENUSIA (*Venosa*): Town in western Apulia on the Appian Way.

VERCELLAE (*Vercelli*): Town in Cisalpine Gaul.

VESCINUM: District named from the ancient town of Vescia, on the slopes of Mt Massicus including the town of Sinuessa.

VIBO (*Bivona*): Town on the western coast of modern Calabria.

VICETINI: Inhabitants of Vicetia (*Vicenza*) in Venetia.

VIENNE (Latin VIENNA): Town in Narbonese Gaul on the east bank of the Rhône.

VOCONTII: People of Narbonese Gaul between the Rhône and the Alps.

VOLATERRAE (*Volterra*): Town in Etruria.

VOLSCI: Ancient Latin tribe. Arpinum was in their territory.

ZOSTER: Cape in Attica between Piraeus and Sunium.

GLOSSARY OF TERMS

ACADEMY (*Academia*): A hall (*gymnasium*) and park at Athens sacred to the hero Academus, in which Plato established his philosophical school. Hence Plato's school or system of philosophy, which went through various phases after his time. The terminology became confused, but Cicerore cognized the 'Old Academy of Plato and his immediate successors and the 'New' Academy of Arcesilas and Carneades, which maintained the uncertainty of all dogma and to which he himself professed to belong. In his own times this was modified by his teachers Philo of Larissa and Antiochus of Ascalon, the latter of whom claimed to represent the 'Old' Academy with a system akin to Stoicism. Cicero gave the name 'Academy' to a hall which he built on his estate at Tusculum.

AEDILE (*aedilis*): Third in rank of the regular Roman magistracies. Four at this time were elected annually, two Curule and two Plebeian. They were responsible for city administration and the holding of certain public Games. The chief magistrates in some municipalities were also so called.

ASSEMBLY: I sometimes so translate *populus* or *comitia*, as describing the Roman people convened for electoral or legislative purposes. There were several different sorts varying with the convening magistrate and the business to be done.

ATTIC(ISM): One use of the word was in connection with Roman oratory. In Cicero's time a movement principally represented by Calvus and M. Brutus favoured an austere style like that of the Athenian Lysias.

AUGUR: The priestly College of Augurs were official diviners interpreting signs (mostly from the flight and cries of wild birds or the behaviour of the Sacred Chickens) before major acts of public (and sometimes private) business. The College, like that of Pontiffs, was in practice almost a preserve of the nobility, so that for a 'new man' like Cicero membership was a coveted social distinction.

AUSPICES (*auspicia*): Divination from birds or other signs was officially necessary as a preliminary to major acts by magistrates, who were said to 'have auspices', i.e., the power of taking them.

BACCHUS' DAY (*Liberalia*): The festival of Liber Pater, commonly identified with the Greek god Dionysius or Bacchus, and Libera on 17 March. It was the usual day for a coming of age ceremony.

BOARD OF FOUR: Municipalities (not Roman colonies) were commonly governed by four principal magistrates (*quattuorviri*), divided into two pairs (*duoviri*), and a senate of *decuriones*.

BONA DEA: See GOOD GODDESS.

BOY (*puer*): Male slaves of any age were so called, as in later times.

CAMPANIAN LAND (DOMAIN – *ager Campanus*): Fertile land in Campania, originally confiscated by Rome in 211 and leased to small tenants. Caesar as Consul passed a bill (the Campanian Law) to distribute it among Pompey's veterans and the Roman poor.

CAMPUS (MARTIUS): The plain adjoining the Tiber on which assemblies of the Centuries were held, often for elections.

CENSOR: Two magistrates usually elected every five years for a tenure of eighteen months. They revised the roll of citizens, with property assessments, also the rolls of Knights and Senators, removing those deemed guilty of misconduct. They further supervised public contracts, including the lease of revenues to the tax-farmers, and issued decrees as guardians of public morals.

CENTURIES, ASSEMBLY OF (*comitia centuriata*): Form of assembly in which voting took place by 'Centuries', i.e., groups unequally composed so as to give preponderance to birth and wealth. It elected Consuls and Praetors, and voted on legislation proposed by them. The first Century to vote (*centuria praerogativa*) traditionally had a determining effect on the rest.

CENTURION: See LEGION.

COHORT: See LEGION.

COMITIAL DAYS: Days in the Roman calendar on which the popular assemblies (*comitia*) could legally be held. The Senate was normally not allowed to meet on these days.

COMITIUM: An area north of the Forum where assemblies were held.

COMMISSION, FREE or VOTIVE: See LEGATE.

COMPITALIA: See CROSSWAYS' DAY.

CONSUL: Highest of the annual Roman magistrates. Two were elected, usually in July, to take office on the following 1 January.

CONSULAR: An ex-Consul. The Consulars made up a corps of elder statesmen to whom the Senate would normally look for leadership.

CROSSWAYS' DAY (*Compitalia*): Festival in honour of the Lares Compitales (gods of the crossroads) held annually soon after the Saturnalia on a day appointed by the Praetor.

CURIATE LAW (*lex curiata*): A law passed by the Curies (*curiae*), the oldest form of Roman assembly. In Cicero's time it survived only in form, each of the thirty Curies being represented by a lictor, but still had certain legislative functions, notably the passage of laws to confirm the executive authority (*imperium*) of individual magistrates; but the precise nature of these laws is much in doubt.

CURULE CHAIR (*sella curulis*): Ivory chair, or rather stool, of state used by regular 'curule' magistrates, i.e., Consuls, Praetors, and Curule Aediles, and certain others.

DICTATOR: A supreme magistrate with quasi-regal powers appointed to deal with emergencies under the early Republic; his second-in-command, the Master of the Horse, was appointed by himself. The office was revived to legitimize the autocratic régimes of Sulla and of Julius Caesar.

EDICT: A public announcement or manifesto issued by a magistrate. The name applied to the codes issued by City Praetors and provincial governors at the beginning of their terms setting out the legal rules which they intended to follow.

EPICUREANISM: A materialistic school of philosophy named after its founder Epicurus, much in vogue among the Roman intelligentsia in Cicero's time.

EQUESTRIAN ORDER: See KNIGHTS.

ETESIAN WINDS (*etesiae*): Northerly winds which blew every year during the Dog-days.

FASCES: Bundles of rods carried by lictors in front of magistrates as a symbol of authority. Those of victorious generals were wreathed in laurel.

FLAMEN: Priest in charge of the cult of a particular deity. There were fifteen, three (those of Jupiter, Mars, and Quirinus) being superior to the rest.

FORUM: The chief square of Rome, centre of civic life.

FREEDMAN (*libertus*): A 'manumitted' slave.

GAMES (*ludi*): Gladiatorial and other shows, some recurring annually and supervised by magistrates, others put on for an occasion by private individuals. Of the former the Roman Games (*ludi Romani*) were held from 5 to 19 September, the Games of Apollo (*ludi Apollinares*) from 5 to 13 July. 'Greek Games' seem to have consisted of performances of Greek plays in the original language.

GOOD GODDESS (*Bona Dea*): A goddess whose worship was confined to women. Her yearly festival was held in the house of a Consul or Praetor and supervised by his wife.

GOWN (*toga*): Formal civilian dress of a Roman citizen. The gown of boys and curule magistrates (*toga praetexta*) had a purple hem. At sixteen or seventeen on coming of age a boy was given his White (or 'Manly') Gown (*toga pura, toga virilis*).

GREEK GAMES: See GAMES.

GREEKS: In Cicero's time the word was loosely used to include the more or less hellenized inhabitants of Western Asia and Egypt as well as those of Greece proper and the old Greek settlements elsewhere.

HONEST MEN: So I translate Cicero's *boni* ('good men', *les gens de bien*), a semi-political term for people of substance and respectability, supporters of the established order. Their opposites he calls *improbi* ('rascals').

IMPERATOR: Commander of a Roman army. But at this period the title was conferred on Generals by their soldiers after a victory and retained until they relinquished their *imperium*.

IMPERIUM: Literally 'command'; the executive authority appertaining to higher magisterial and promagisterial office.

INTERCALATION: See Appendix I(i).

INTERREGNUM: If through death or otherwise the consular office stood vacant and no patrician magistrates holding *imperium* were in office, an Interrex was appointed from among the patrician members of the Senate to exercise consular functions for five days. He was then replaced by another Interrex, and so on until new Consuls could be elected.

KNIGHTS (*equites*): In effect non-Senators of free birth possessing property over a certain level. They were regarded as forming a class of their own (*ordo equestris*) with special privileges and insignia.

LATIN FESTIVAL (*Feriae Latinae*): Movable annual festival of the Romano-Latin League held on Mt Alba. Its date was determined from year to year by the Consuls.

LECTURE HALL (*gymnasium*): The Greek gymnasium was originally a sports ground containing a *palaestra* (see below). But literature, philosophy, and music were also taught in them.

LEGATE (*legatus*): A provincial governor took several Legates, normally Senators, on his staff as deputies. Caesar in Gaul made them commanders of legions. The duties might, however, be purely nominal. The Senate could also appoint its members to 'free' or 'votive' (i.e., to discharge a vow) *legationes*, thus enabling them to travel abroad with official status. I sometimes translate with 'commission(er)'. The word can also be used for any kind of envoy.

LEGION: Roman army unit with a full complement of 6,000 men divided into ten cohorts. Each legion was officered by six Military Tribunes. Each cohort had six Centurions, the highest in rank being called *primi pili* (Chief Centurion). The ensign of a Legion was an eagle, and each cohort had its standard (*signum*).

LÈSE-MAJESTÉ (*maiestas*): The term *maiestas* covered acts 'in derogation of the majesty of the Roman People', as of magistrates or governors exceeding the bounds of their authority.

LEX CORNELIA (*de provinciis*): Law of Sulla regulating provincial administration.

LEX CURIATA: See above, CURIATE LAW.

LEX GABINIA: A law of 67 or 58 forbidding or restricting loans from Roman citizens to provincials.

LEX JULIA (*de provinciis*): Consular law of Caesar's on provincial administration.

LEX JUNIA-LICINIA: A law of 62 requiring that copies of proposed legislation be deposited in the Treasury.

LEX POMPEIA: Pompey's law against electoral corruption in 52.

LEX ROSCIA: A law of 67 assigning the first fourteen rows in the theatre to the Knights (the Senate sat below in the Orchestra).

LEX SCANTINIA: A law of uncertain date penalizing homosexual acts committed upon persons of free birth.

LIBERALIA: See BACCHUS' DAY.

LICTOR: Official attendant of persons possessing magisterial authority (*imperium*), the number varying with the rank.

LUPERCALIA: Fertility festival on 15 February held in a cave below the Palatine Hill by the Luperci. There were two Colleges of these until 45–44, when Caesar added a third called the *Luperci Iulii*.

MANUMISSION: Process of freeing a slave. This could be done either formally or informally ('between friends'), but in the latter case the master could revoke it at will.

MILE (*mille passus*): The Roman mile was 1,618 yards.

MIME (*mimus*): Type of entertainment with dancing, music, and dialogue which became highly popular in the first century B.C. It was considered more sophisticated and risqué than the Atellan Farce, which it virtually superseded.

MINERVA'S DAY (*Quinquatrus*): Festival of Minerva on 19 March.

NOBILITY: Practically, a noble (*nobilis*) at this period meant a direct descendant of a Consul in the male line. In the early Republic the Roman community was divided into patricians and plebeians, the former holding a virtual monopoly of political power. But after the Consulship was thrown open to plebeians in the fourth century many plebeian families became 'noble', and the remaining patricians were distinguished chiefly by their ineligibility to hold both Consulships in one year and for the plebeian offices of Tribune and Plebeian Aedile.

NOMENCLATOR: A slave whose duty it was to remind his master of the names of clients and acquaintances whom he happened to meet.

OPS: Roman goddess in whose temple on the Capitol Caesar deposited the state treasure.

OPTIMATES: Literally 'those belonging to the best' – the leading conservatives in the Senate and their supporters throughout the community. Sometimes the term is practically equivalent to the 'honest men' (*boni*), though more purely political in its implications.

OVATION: A lesser form of Triumph.

PALAESTRA: A space surrounded by colonnades, found in all *gymnasia*. Literally 'wrestling-school' (Greek).

PATRICIANS: See NOBILITY.

PAYMASTER-TRIBUNES (*tribuni aerarii*): At this time probably a class similar to the Knights but with a lower property qualification. Under the lex Aurelia of 70, juries were composed in equal numbers of Senators, Knights, and Paymaster-Tribunes.

PLEBEIANS: See NOBILITY.

PONTIFF (*pontifex*): These formed a priestly College in general charge of Roman religious institutions (including the Calendar), presided over by the Chief Pontiff (*pontifex maximus*), who was Julius Caesar from 63 until his death.

PRAETOR: Second in rank of the annual magistracies. Eight were elected at this period until Caesar increased the number to twenty. The City Praetor (*praetor urbanus*) was in charge of the administration of justice between Roman citizens, others presided over the standing criminal courts. After his year of office a Praetor normally went to govern a province as Propraetor or Proconsul.

PRAETORIAN COHORT (*cohors praetoria*): A special military unit forming a general's bodyguard.

Prefect: Officer appointed by a magistrate (usually as provincial governor) for military or civil duties. These might be only nominal, the appointment merely conferring official status and privileges. The 'Prefect of Engineers' (*praefectus fabrum*) acted as adjutant to his chief – no longer any connection with engineers.

Proconsul (*pro consule*): 'Acting Consul', one who, not holding the office, exercised consular authority outside Rome by senatorial appointment. Similarly Propraetor (*pro praetore*) and Proquaestor (*pro quaestore*).

Proscription (*proscriptio*): A procedure first employed by Sulla, then by the Triumvirs in 43. Lists of names were published, the persons thus 'proscribed' being declared outlaws and their goods confiscated. Their killers were rewarded, their protectors punished.

Quaestor: The first stage in the regular 'course of offices', election to which carried life-membership of the Senate. Since Sulla's time twenty were elected annually. The two City Quaestors (*quaestores urbani*) had charge of the Treasury and the Quaestors assigned to provincial governors (usually by lot) were largely concerned with finance.

Quartan: A fever recurring every third day; less grave therefore than a tertian, which recurred every other day.

Quirinus' Day (Quirinalia): Festival in honour of Quirinus (the deified Romulus, founder of Rome) on 17 February.

Resolution (*auctoritas*): A decree of the Senate vetoed by a Tribune was sometimes recorded under this name.

Rostra: The speakers' platform in the comitium, so called from the beaks (*rostra*) of captured warships which decorated it.

Saturnalia: Festival of Saturn beginning on 17 December, marked by merrymaking reminiscent of modern Christmas, to which it contributed some elements.

Secretary: I so translate (with a capital letter) Latin *scriba*. The 'scribes' were a corporation of civil servants working in the Treasury and otherwise. City magistrates and provincial governors might be assigned official Secretaries for their personal assistance. Private clerks were called *librarii*.

SENATE: Governing body of the Roman Republic, numbering about 600 (increased to 900 by Caesar) and composed of magistrates and ex-magistrates.

SHEPHERDS' DAY (*Parilia*): Festival of the god and goddess Pales, protectors of flocks and herds, on 21 April.

SOOTHSAYING: For *haruspicina*, an Etruscan system of divination from the entrails of sacrificial animals, from portents, and from lightning. Some of its practitioners (*haruspices*) seem to have been organized as a body of sixty and were consulted officially.

SOPHIST: A professional 'wise man', making money as a teacher and lecturer, often itinerant.

STOICISM: Philosophical school, named from the portico (*stoa*) in which its founder, Zeno of Citium (*c.* 300), taught. Cato was its most prominent Roman adherent in Cicero's time.

SUMPTUARY LAW: A series of laws during the Republic attempted to impose restrictions on luxury spending, especially on food. One was enacted by Julius Caesar in 46.

SUPPLICATION (*supplicatio*): A thanksgiving ceremony decreed by the Senate in honour of a military success, the number of days varying according to the importance of the victory. It was generally regarded as a preliminary to a Triumph.

TABLETS (*codicilli*): Wooden tablets coated with wax and fastened together with thread, used for memoranda and short notes.

TAX-FARMERS (*publicani*): Roman taxes, as on grazing-land in the provinces or excise, were largely farmed out by the Censors to private companies who bid for the right of collection. The capitalists in Rome as well as their local agents were called *publicani*. In political terms *publicani* and Knights often amount to the same thing.

TELLUS: Earth-goddess, whose temple was one of the meeting-places of the Senate.

TESTIMONIAL: Renders *laudatio* (= 'eulogy') in one of its senses. It was customary for defendants to ask prominent persons to offer witness to their good character in court either orally or in writing.

TETRARCH: Literally 'ruler over a fourth part'. In Cicero's time many minor eastern princes were called by this title.

TOGA: See GOWN.

TREASURY (*aerarium*): The Roman state treasury was in the temple of Saturn in the Forum, managed by the City Quaestors with the assistance of Secretaries.

TRIBE (*tribus*): A division, mainly by locality, of the Roman citizen body. The number had risen over the centuries from three to thirty-five (four of them 'urban', the rest 'rustic'). Assemblies voting by tribes (*comitia tributa*) elected magistrates below Praetor and could pass legislation proposed by Tribunes.

TRIBUNE: (1) Of the Plebs. A board of ten, originally appointed to protect plebeians from patrician high-handedness. They had wide constitutional powers, the most important being that any one of them could veto any piece of public business, including laws and senatorial decrees. They could also initiate these. They took office on 10 December. (2) Military: See LEGION. (3) See PAYMASTER-TRIBUNES.

TRIUMPH: Victory celebration by a general on his return to Rome. Permission had to be granted by the Senate.

UNIFORM: Magistrates leaving to take command of armies wore the general's red cloak (*paludamentum*) and were said to set out *paludati*.

VALUATION (*aestimatio*): Process by which a debtor's property could be transferred to his creditor in settlement. Caesar made such transfers compulsory on terms favourable to the debtor.

WEAL: The goddess Salus, who had a temple on the Quirinal Hill near Atticus' house.

MAPS

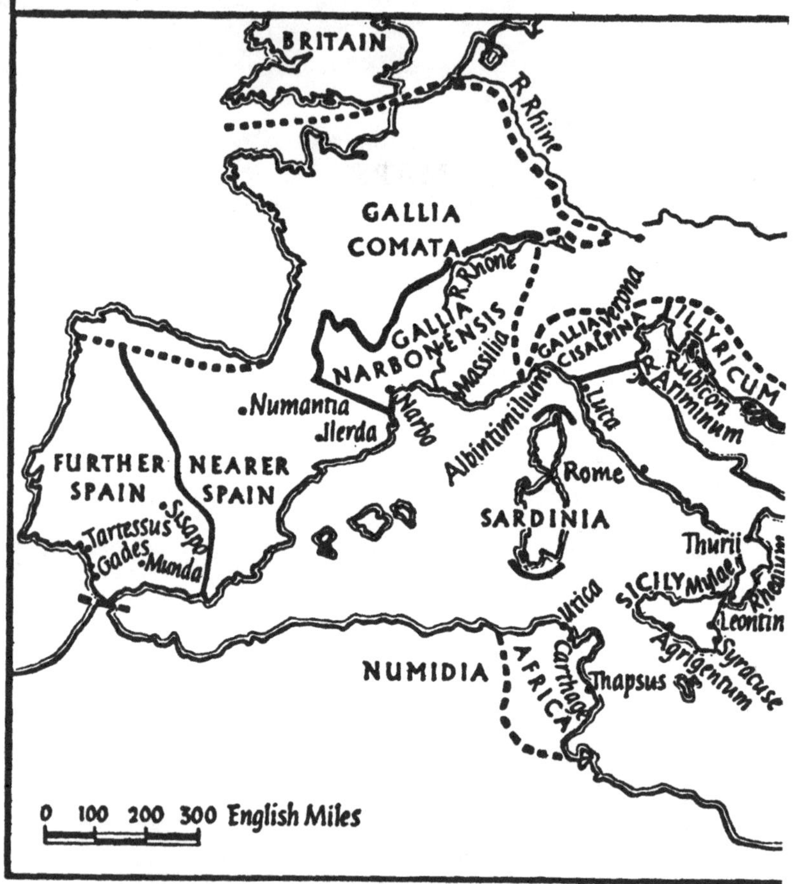
THE ROMAN
BRITAIN
R. Rhine
GALLIA
COMATA
R. Rhone
GALLIA
NARBONENSIS
Massilia
GALLIA
CISALPINA
Verona
ILLYRICUM
R. Rubicon
Ariminum
Numantia
Ilerda
Narbo
Albintimilium
Luca
FURTHER
SPAIN
NEARER
SPAIN
Sucro
Tartessus
Gades
Munda
Rome
SARDINIA
Thurii
SICILY
Mylae
Rhegium
Leontini
Utica
Carthage
Agrigentum
Syracuse
NUMIDIA
AFRICA
Thapsus
0 100 200 300 English Miles

EMPIRE 51 B.C.

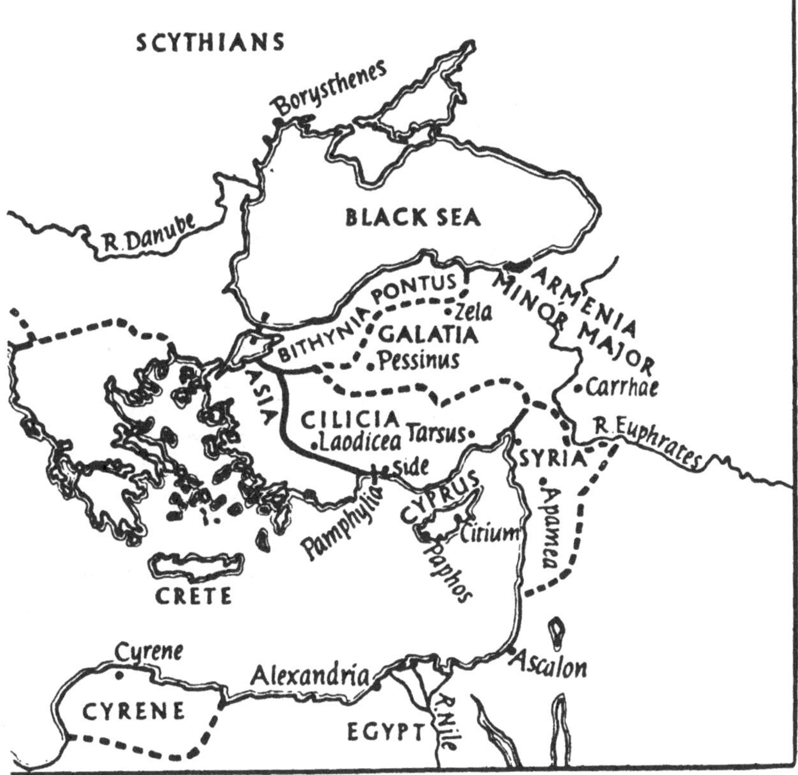
Boundaries of provinces
Boundaries of the empire
SCYTHIANS
Borysthenes
R. Danube
BLACK SEA
PONTUS
Zela
ARMENIA
MINOR
MAJOR
BITHYNIA
GALATIA
Pessinus
ASIA
Carrhae
CILICIA
Laodicea
Tarsus
R. Euphrates
SYRIA
Side
CYPRUS
Pamphylia
Citium
Apamea
Paphos
CRETE
Cyrene
Alexandria
Ascalon
CYRENE
EGYPT
R. Nile

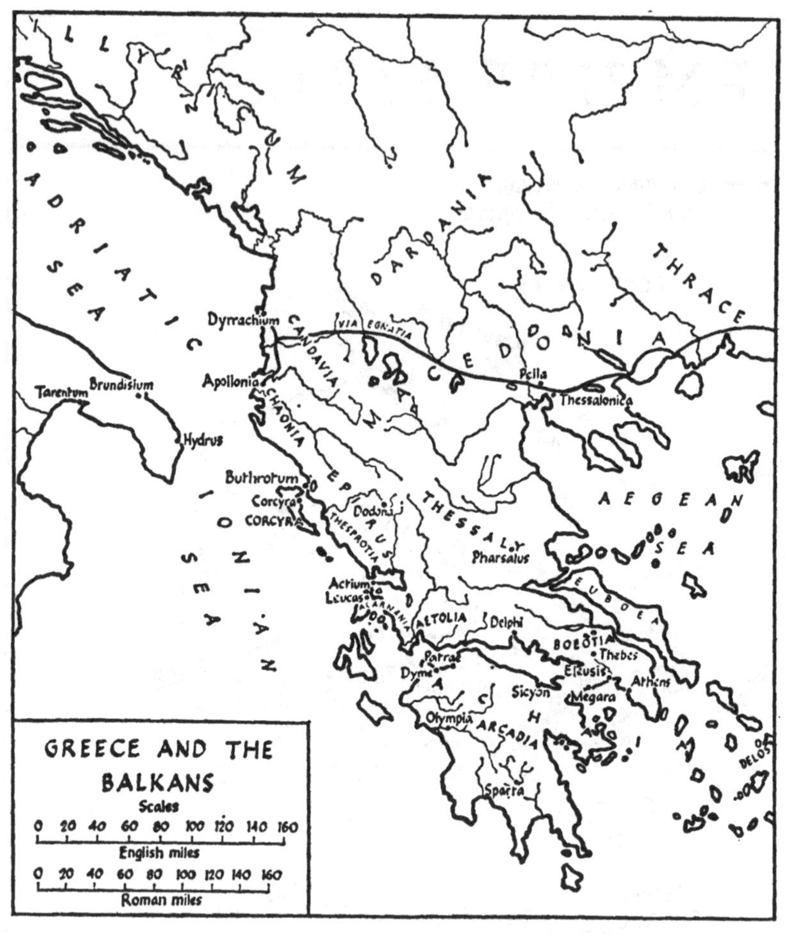
GREECE AND THE BALKANS
Scales
0 20 40 60 80 100 120 140 160
English miles
0 20 40 60 80 100 120 140 160
Roman miles
ILLYRICUM
ADRIATIC SEA
IONIAN SEA
DARDANIA
THRACE
MACEDONIA
VIA EGNATIA
CANDAVIA
CHAONIA
EPIRUS
THESPROTIA
THESSALY
ACARNANIA
AETOLIA
BOEOTIA
EUBOEA
ACHAIA
ARCADIA
AEGEAN SEA
DELOS
Dyrrachium
Apollonia
Brundisium
Tarentum
Hydrus
Buthrotum
Corcyra
CORCYRA
Dodona
Pella
Thessalonica
Pharsalus
Actium
Leucas
Delphi
Thebes
Patrae
Dyme
Eleusis
Athens
Sicyon
Megara
Olympia
Sparta

PONTUS EUXINUS
BITHYNIA ET PONTUS
Halys Fl.
GALATIA
PHRYGIA
ASIA
LYCAONIA
CAPPADOCIA
AEGAEUM MARE
ATHENAE
Piraeus
Ceos
Gyaros
Siros
Delos
Samos
EPHESUS
Nysa
Tralles
Magnesia
Maeander Fl.
LAODICEA
Colossae
Synnada
APAMEA
Philomelium
ICONIUM
PISIDIA
CIBYRA
PAMPHYLIA
Side
LYCIA
RHODOS
TAURUS MONS
Cybistra
Pylae Ciliciae
Pyramus Fl.
CILICIA
TARSUS
Issus
AMANUS MONS
Pindenissum
CYRRHESTICA
ANTIOCHIA
SYRIA
CYPRUS
Salamis
MARE INTERNUM
ASIA MINOR
Scales
0 40 80 120 160
English miles
0 40 80 120 160
Roman miles

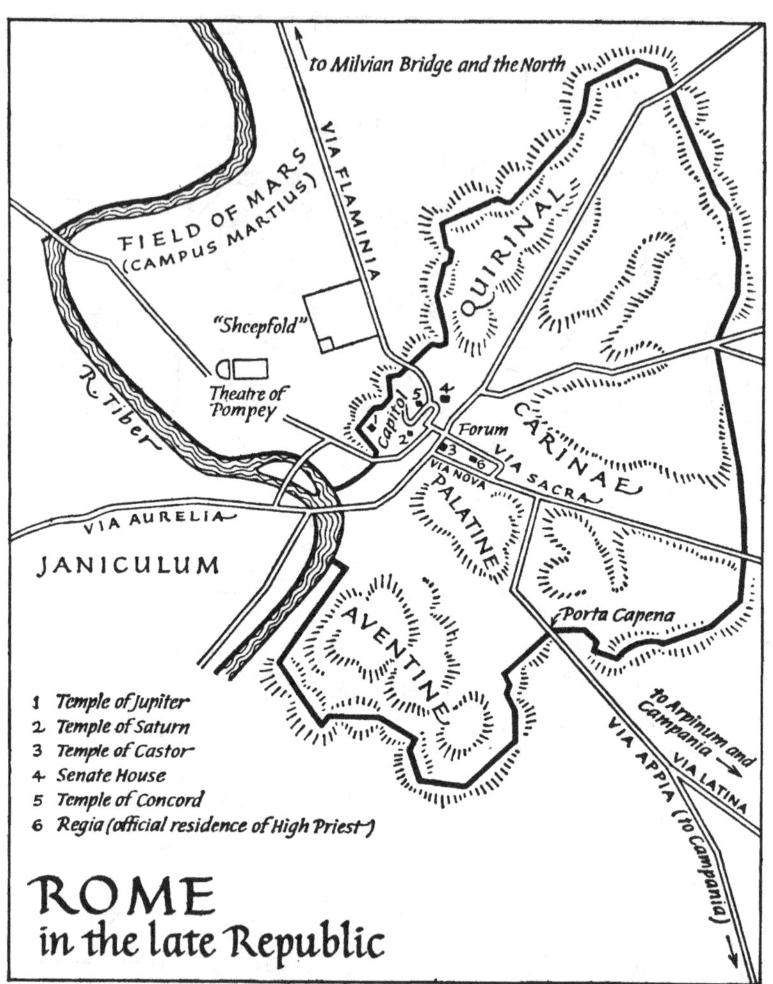
to Milvian Bridge and the North
VIA FLAMINIA
FIELD OF MARS
(CAMPUS MARTIUS)
QUIRINAL
"Sheepfold"
Theatre of Pompey
R. Tiber
Capitol
Forum
CARINAE
VIA NOVA
VIA SACRA
PALATINE
VIA AURELIA
JANICULUM
AVENTINE
Porta Capena
to Arpinum and Campania
VIA LATINA
VIA APPIA (to Campania)
1 Temple of Jupiter
2 Temple of Saturn
3 Temple of Castor
4 Senate House
5 Temple of Concord
6 Regia (official residence of High Priest)
ROME
in the late Republic

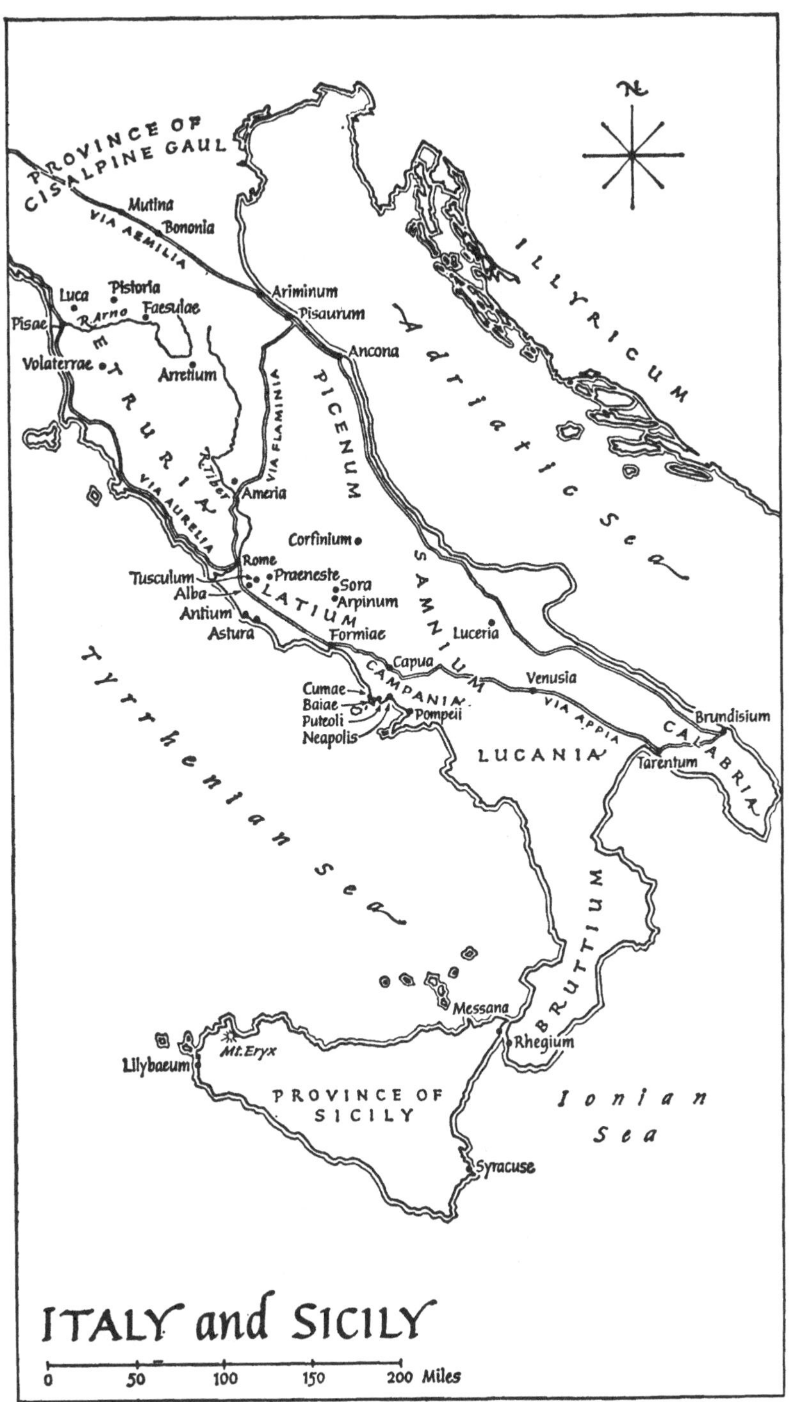
PROVINCE OF CISALPINE GAUL
Mutina
Bononia
VIA AEMILIA
ILLYRICUM
Adriatic Sea
Ariminum
Pisaurum
Ancona
Luca
Pistoria
Faesulae
R. Arno
Pisae
Volaterrae
Arretium
ETRURIA
VIA FLAMINIA
PICENUM
R. Tiber
Ameria
VIA AURELIA
Corfinium
SAMNIUM
Rome
Tusculum
Praeneste
Sora
Alba
Arpinum
LATIUM
Antium
Astura
Formiae
Luceria
Tyrrhenian Sea
Capua
CAMPANIA
Venusia
Cumae
Baiae
Puteoli
Neapolis
Pompeii
VIA APPIA
Brundisium
CALABRIA
LUCANIA
Tarentum
BRUTTIUM
Messana
Rhegium
Mt. Eryx
Lilybaeum
PROVINCE OF SICILY
Ionian Sea
Syracuse
ITALY and SICILY
0
50
100
150
200 Miles

CONCORDANCE

Letters to Friends

Latin	This translation	Latin	This translation
I. 1	12	III. 5	68
I. 2	13	III. 6	69
I. 3	56	III. 7	71
I. 4	14	III. 8	70
I. 5*a*	15	III. 9	72
I. 5*b*	16	III. 10	73
I. 6	17	III. 11	74
I. 7	18	III. 12	75
I. 8	19	III. 13	76
I. 9	20	IV. 1	150
I. 10	21	IV. 2	151
II. 1	45	IV. 3	202
II. 2	46	IV. 4	203
II. 3	47	IV. 5	248
II. 4	48	IV. 6	249
II. 5	49	IV. 7	230
II. 6	50	IV. 8	229
II. 7	107	IV. 9	231
II. 8	80	IV. 10	233
II. 9	85	IV. 11	232
II. 10	86	IV. 12	253
II. 11	90	IV. 13	225
II. 12	95	IV. 14	240
II. 13	93	IV. 15	241
II. 14	89	V. 1	1
II. 15	96	V. 2	2
II. 16	154	V. 3	11
II. 17	117	V. 4	10
II. 18	115	V. 5	5
II. 19	116	V. 6	4
III. 1	64	V. 7	3
III. 2	65	V. 8	25
III. 3	66	V. 9	255
III. 4	67	V. 10*a*.1–2	259

CONCORDANCE

Latin	This translation	Latin	This translation
V. 10*a*.3	256	VII. 1	24
V. 10*b*	258	VII. 2	52
V. 11	257	VII. 3	183
V. 12	22	VII. 4	199
V. 13	201	VII. 5	26
V. 14	251	VII. 6	27
V. 15	252	VII. 7	28
V. 16	187	VII. 8	29
V. 17	23	VII. 9	30
V. 18	51	VII. 10	33
V. 19	152	VII. 11	34
V. 20	128	VII. 12	35
V. 21	182	VII. 13	36
VI. 1	242	VII. 14	38
VI. 2	245	VII. 15	39
VI. 3	243	VII. 16	32
VI. 4	244	VII. 17	31
VI. 5	239	VII. 18	37
VI. 6	234	VII. 19	334
VI. 7	237	VII. 20	333
VI. 8	235	VII. 21	332
VI. 9	236	VII. 22	331
VI. 10.1–3	223	VII. 23	209
VI. 10.4–6	222	VII. 24	260
VI. 11	224	VII. 25	261
VI. 12	226	VII. 26	210
VI. 13	227	VII. 27	148
VI. 14	228	VII. 28	200
VI. 15	322	VII. 29	264
VI. 16	323	VII. 30	265
VI. 17	324	VII. 31	267
VI. 18	218	VII. 32	113
VI. 19	262	VII. 33	192
VI. 20	247	VIII. 1	77
VI. 21	246	VIII. 2	78
VI. 22	221	VIII. 3	79

CONCORDANCE

Latin	This translation
VIII. 4	81
VIII. 5	83
VIII. 6	88
VIII. 7	92
VIII. 8	84
VIII. 9	82
VIII. 10	87
VIII. 11	91
VIII. 12	98
VIII. 13	94
VIII. 14	97
VIII. 15	149
VIII. 16	153
VIII. 17	156
IX. 1	175
IX. 2	177
IX. 3	176
IX. 4	180
IX. 5	179
IX. 6	181
IX. 7	178
IX. 8	254
IX. 9	157
IX. 10	217
IX. 11	250
IX. 12	263
IX. 13	311
IX. 14	326
IX. 15	196
IX. 16	190
IX. 17	195
IX. 18	191
IX. 19	194
IX. 20	193
IX. 21	188
IX. 22	189
IX. 23	198
IX. 24	362
IX. 25	114
IX. 26	197
X. 1	340
X. 2	341
X. 3	355
X. 4	358
X. 5	359
X. 6	370
X. 7	372
X. 8	371
X. 9	379
X. 10	375
X. 11	382
X. 12	377
X. 13	389
X. 14	384
X. 15	390
X. 16	404
X. 17	398
X. 18	395
X. 19	393
X. 20	407
X. 21	391
X. 21*a*	392
X. 22	423
X. 23	414
X. 24	428
X. 25	403
X. 26	424
X. 27	369
X. 28	364
X. 29	426
X. 30	378
X. 31	368

CONCORDANCE

Latin	*This translation*	*Latin*	*This translation*
X. 32	415	XI. 29	335
X. 33	409	XII. 1	327
X. 34	396	XII. 2	344
X. 34*a*	400	XII. 3	345
X. 35	408	XII. 4	363
XI. 1	325	XII. 5	365
XI. 2	329	XII. 6	376
XI. 3	336	XII. 7	367
XI. 4	342	XII. 8	416
XI. 5	353	XII. 9	421
XI. 6	343	XII. 10	425
XI. 6*a*	356	XII. 11	366
XI. 7	354	XII. 12	387
XI. 8	360	XII. 13	419
XI. 9	380	XII. 14	405
XI. 10	385	XII. 15	406
XI. 11	386	XII. 16	328
XI. 12	394	XII. 17	204
XI. 13	388	XII. 18	205
XI. 13*a*	418	XII. 19	206
XI. 13*b*	381	XII. 20	339
XI. 14	413	XII. 21	429
XI. 15	422	XII. 22	346
XI. 16	434	XII. 22*a*	357
XI. 17	435	XII. 23	347
XI. 18	397	XII. 24	361
XI. 19	399	XII. 24.3	430
XI. 20	401	XII. 25	373
XI. 21	411	XII. 25*a*	383
XI. 22	427	XII. 26	431
XI. 23	402	XII. 27	432
XI. 24	412	XII. 28	374
XI. 25	420	XII. 29	433
XI. 26	410	XII. 30	417
XI. 27	348	XIII. 1	63
XI. 28	349	XIII. 2	314

CONCORDANCE

Latin	*This translation*	*Latin*	*This translation*
XIII. 3	315	XIII. 37	308
XIII. 4	318	XIII. 38	309
XIII. 5	319	XIII. 39	310
XIII. 6	57	XIII. 40	59
XIII. 6*a*	58	XIII. 41	54
XIII. 7	320	XIII. 42	53
XIII. 8	321	XIII. 43	268
XIII. 9	139	XIII. 44	270
XIII. 10	277	XIII. 45	271
XIII. 11	278	XIII. 46	272
XIII. 12	279	XIII. 47	274
XIII. 13	280	XIII. 48	142
XIII. 14	281	XIII. 49	313
XIII. 15	317	XIII. 50	266
XIII. 16	316	XIII. 51	61
XIII. 17	283	XIII. 52	312
XIII. 18	284	XIII. 53	130
XIII. 19	285	XIII. 54	132
XIII. 20	286	XIII. 55	129
XIII. 21	287	XIII. 56	131
XIII. 22	288	XIII. 57	133
XIII. 23	289	XIII. 58	140
XIII. 24	290	XIII. 59	141
XIII. 25	291	XIII. 60	55
XIII. 26	292	XIII. 61	135
XIII. 27	293	XIII. 62	136
XIII. 28	294	XIII. 63	137
XIII. 28*a*	295	XIII. 64	138
XIII. 29	282	XIII. 65	134
XIII. 30	301	XIII. 66	238
XIII. 31	302	XIII. 67	296
XIII. 32	303	XIII. 68	211
XIII. 33	304	XIII. 69	297
XIII. 34	305	XIII. 70	298
XIII. 35	306	XIII. 71	299
XIII. 36	307	XIII. 72	300

CONCORDANCE

Latin	This translation	Latin	This translation
XIII. 73	273	XV. 6	112
XIII. 74	269	XV. 7	99
XIII. 75	60	XV. 8	100
XIII. 76	62	XV. 9	101
XIII. 77	212	XV. 10	108
XIII. 78	275	XV. 11	118
XIII. 79	276	XV. 12	102
XIV. 1	8	XV. 13	109
XIV. 2	7	XV. 14	106
XIV. 3	9	XV. 15	174
XIV. 4	6	XV. 16	215
XIV. 5	119	XV. 17	214
XIV. 6	158	XV. 18	213
XIV. 7	155	XV. 19	216
XIV. 8	164	XV. 20	208
XIV. 9	161	XV. 21	207
XIV. 10	168	XVI. 1	120
XIV. 11	166	XVI. 2	121
XIV. 12	159	XVI. 3	122
XIV. 13	169	XVI. 4	123
XIV. 14	145	XVI. 5	124
XIV. 15	167	XVI. 6	125
XIV. 16	163	XVI. 7	126
XIV. 17	162	XVI. 8	147
XIV. 18	144	XVI. 9	127
XIV. 19	160	XVI. 10	43
XIV. 20	173	XVI. 11	143
XIV. 21	165	XVI. 12	146
XIV. 22	172	XVI. 13	40
XIV. 23	171	XVI. 14	41
XIV. 24	170	XVI. 15	42
XV. 1	104	XVI. 16	44
XV. 2	105	XVI. 17	186
XV. 3	103	XVI. 18	219
XV. 4	110	XVI. 19	184
XV. 5	111	XVI. 20	220

CONCORDANCE

Latin	This translation	Latin	This translation
XVI. 21	337	XVI. 25	338
XVI. 22	185	XVI. 26	351
XVI. 23	330	XVI. 27	352
XVI. 24	350		

CONCORDANCE

Letters to Quintus

Latin	*This translation*	*Latin*	*This translation*
I. 1	1	II. 11 (10)	15
I. 2	2	II. 12 (11)	16
I. 3	3	II. 13 (12)	17
I. 4	4	II. 14 (13)	18
II. 1	5	II. 15 (14)	19
II. 2	6	II. 16 (15)	20
II. 3	7	III. 1	21
II. 4 (4.1–2)	8	III. 2	22
II. 5 (4.3–7)	9	III. 3	23
II. 6 (5)	10	III. 4	24
II. 7 (6)	11	III. 5 (5–7)	25
II. 8 (7)	12	III. 6 (8)	26
II. 9 (8)	13	III. 7 (9)	27
II. 10 (9)	14		

Letters to Marcus Brutus

I.1	13	I.11	16
I.2	14	I.12	22
I.2a	6	I.13	21
I.3	7	I.14	23
I.3a	8	I.15	24
I.4	10	I.16	25
I.4a	11	I.17	17
I.5	9	I.18	26
I.6	12	II.1	1
I.7	20	II.2	3
I.8	15	II.3	2
I.9	19	II.4	4
I.10	18	II.5	5

Printed in the USA/Agawam, MA
December 14, 2021

786184.117